DEVELOPING MICROSOFT

ASP.NET
SERVER CONTROLS
AND COMPONENTS

Nikhil Kothari
Vandana Datye

PUBLISHED BY
Microsoft Press
A Division of Microsoft Corporation
One Microsoft Way
Redmond, Washington 98052-6399

Library of Congress Cataloging-in-Publication Data
Kothari, Nikhil, 1976-
    Developing Microsoft ASP.NET Server Controls and Components / Nikhil Kothari, Vandana K. Datye.
        p. cm.
        Includes index.
    ISBN 0-7356-1582-9
        1. Internet programming. 2. Active server pages. 3. Web servers. 4. Microsoft .NET. I.
Datye, Vandana, 1955- II. Title.

QA76.625 .K68 2002
005.2'76--dc21

2002072724

Printed and bound in the United States of America.

1 2 3 4 5 6 7 8 9   QWE   7 6 5 4 3 2

Distributed in Canada by H.B. Fenn and Company Ltd.

A CIP catalogue record for this book is available from the British Library.

Microsoft Press books are available through booksellers and distributors worldwide. For further information about international editions, contact your local Microsoft Corporation office or contact Microsoft Press International directly at fax (425) 936-7329. Visit our Web site at www.microsoft.com/mspress. Send comments to *mspinput@microsoft.com*.

ActiveX, JScript, Microsoft, Microsoft Press, Visual C#, Visual J#, Visual Basic, Visual Studio, and Windows are either registered trademarks or trademarks of Microsoft Corporation in the United States and/or other countries. Other product and company names mentioned herein may be the trademarks of their respective owners.

The example companies, organizations, products, domain names, e-mail addresses, logos, people, places, and events depicted herein are fictitious. No association with any real company, organization, product, domain name, e-mail address, logo, person, place, or event is intended or should be inferred.

Acquisitions Editor: Anne Hamilton
Project Editor: Kathleen Atkins
Technical Editor: Marc Young

Body Part No. X08-73259

Contents at a Glance

Table of Contents

Part II   Server Controls—First Steps

4   User Controls: From Page to Control   59

5   Developing a Simple Custom Control   87

Foreword

The ASP.NET project began in December of 1997, shortly after the release of IIS 4.0. At the time, we had just completed a grueling ship cycle that included a major update of both IIS and ASP, and most of the IIS team was spending some quiet time recuperating from our recent product release. The month immediately following any major software release is often a good time for reflection, and several of us on the IIS/ASP team used the relative calm after shipping IIS 4.0 to look back, discuss, and debate the merits of the product we had just built.

ASP at the time was only 12 months old and was quickly becoming the most popular way to build dynamic Web pages. From an ease-of-use perspective, ASP made a giant leap over anything before it. Developers no longer needed to write complicated ISAPI extensions or awkward CGI programs. Instead, they could author HTML pages and gradually weave dynamic server script functionality into them.

But as we spent time that month looking at the types of applications customers were actually building with ASP, we quickly discovered that while ASP was clearly better than previous server programming products a lot of improvement opportunity remained.

In particular, we found that almost all nontrivial ASP pages quickly evolved into a confusing mixture of HTML and intermingled server code. Instead of being able to consolidate page logic code into a separate section of a page (or even into a separate file), developers were forced by the ASP model to embed chunks of logic and functionality in multiple sections all over the page. One customer we spoke with described his frustration with the pages he had built by describing them (not too affectionately) as spaghetti code.

Compounding the lack of structure within an ASP page was the fact that common page tasks—such as data presentation, input validation, and round-trip form field state management—all required explicit coding by the developer. There was no *declarative* way to enable these features in a page—you always needed to write code.

Last but not least, ASP lacked good tool support. Specifically, the unstructured intermingling of HTML and code meant that it was impossible to build WYSIWYG page designers, and the lack of declarative functionality support made it hard to encapsulate and automate common tasks with a development tool.

As we progressed in our investigation and conversations with customers, we slowly concluded that we needed to fundamentally reconsider the way developers built dynamic Web applications—we needed to address all of the issues I just mentioned as well as more common requests and complaints we had in other areas about ASP (lack of Web farm session state support, poor component deployment story, inflexible security model, and so on). In the spring of 1998, three of us from the old IIS team formed a new team to build this product, which is of course now known as ASP.NET.

Key among the innovations in ASP.NET is the ASP.NET page and server control framework. Specifically designed to address the issues with classic ASP, it provides an easy and powerful model for developers to declaratively build rich Web pages that are capable of targeting any client browser or device.

What makes the ASP.NET page framework so powerful is that the set of supported server controls is not fixed to just those built into the core product. Instead, the rich extensibility model of ASP.NET allows developers an almost unlimited number of opportunities to innovate and improve upon the core platform, producing a rich ecosystem of components and collaborative offerings that enables ASP.NET to grow richer and richer over time.

This book provides an excellent roadmap that teaches developers how to unlock the full potential of ASP.NET by leveraging and building rich server controls. The book begins with a detailed look at the ASP.NET page programming model and architecture and then expertly walks through the nuts and bolts of building real-world ASP.NET server controls. It is a must have for all serious ASP.NET component developers.

Scott Guthrie
Product Unit Manager
ASP.NET Product Team
Redmond, Washington

Acknowledgments

We would like to thank various people from Microsoft who helped make this book a reality.

Our technical reviewers played a big role in shaping the contents of this book. Mike Pope reviewed nearly every chapter and provided detailed feedback, prompting us to rewrite various sections and add new content to improve clarity. David Ebbo reviewed selected chapters and shared his expertise in the ASP.NET page framework. Andrew Lin, Polita Huff, and Kavita Kamani reviewed various chapters, flagged errors, and pointed out inconsistencies. Brad Abrams shared his experience in designing .NET class libraries and reviewed the chapter on component programming.

We are grateful to the team at Microsoft Press for their help in publishing this book. David Clark, our initial contact, Anne Hamilton, program manager, and Thomas Pohlmann, managing editor, took care of administrative matters. Kathleen Atkins, project editor, edited each chapter and kept us on schedule despite our protests. Marc Young, technical editor, went out of his way to track technical issues. Michelle Goodman, copy editor, was the relentless language and style cop. Thanks also go to Paula Gorelick, desktop publisher, and Joel Panchot, graphic artist.

Nikhil Kothari's Acknowledgments

It has been extremely exciting and satisfying to write this book and to be able to describe in detail the Web Forms architecture and its extensibility, the area of ASP.NET that I have worked on for the past few years. I would like to thank David Ebbo, Dmitry Robsman, and other ASP.NET team members with whom I worked closely during these years and have had many interesting and enlightening technical discussions. I would like to thank the team for bearing with me while I prioritized my writing work over my other responsibilities. I would also like to thank three other people at Microsoft: B. Ashok, Chris Anderson, and Steve Millet because of the influence they've had in shaping my career over the years by providing me with challenges and responsibilities that met my interests.

I would like to thank Vandana for choosing to be a part of this book. Without her help, it's quite possible this book would have simply remained a thought. I must also thank her along with Mike Pope and the editors at Microsoft Press for reviewing my writing and showing me ways of improving it. Writing this book has been an interesting learning experience, to say the least.

Finally, I would like to send out a special thanks to my parents, Suman and Usha Kothari, for doing everything they did over the years to make it possible for me to have the opportunities that I have today.

Vandana Datye's Acknowledgments

It has been a pleasure to write this book with Nikhil and to learn from him many details about the architecture and implementation of server controls. I also developed a better understanding of various aspects of ASP.NET through discussions with others on the ASP.NET team, whom I would like to thank for their help: David Ebbo, Scott Guthrie, Susan Warren, Bradley Millington, David Gutierrez, and Anthony Moore. I would also like to thank Seth Manheim and Lisa Supinski of the .NET Framework user education team for enabling me to access several resources I needed while working on this book.

Jim Langer, distinguished physicist and physics professor, emphasized the importance of patterns to me years ago when I was his graduate student. That training proved especially valuable when I made the transition from physics to software.

I am greatly indebted to Drs. Jarrell and Angell for helping me fight advanced cancer and subsequently to Dr. Goff for helping me stay in remission these past seven years.

Finally, special thanks to my husband, Satish Thatte, and my daughter, Arita, for their patience and understanding while I was working on this book. I could always count on Satish's support. Arita didn't complain when I reneged on nearly all my promises to do things with her during these past eight months.

Introduction

ASP.NET enables the creation of Web sites and XML Web services and is a core element of the .NET Framework, Microsoft's new application development platform. Based on an extensible component-based architecture, ASP.NET provides an approach to building dynamic Web applications that is radically simpler yet more powerful than its predecessor, Active Server Pages. ASP.NET contains a page and control framework that is used by developers to create the user interface (UI) of their Web applications. This framework is often referred to as *Web Forms*. Server controls (also known as *Web Forms controls*) are the essence of the Web Forms programming model. Server controls simplify the page development experience. These controls provide a mechanism for reuse and encapsulation and are well-suited for use in a rapid application development (RAD) visual designer. Furthermore, the server control architecture is extensible and opens the door to a large and vibrant community of component developers who can add to the set of built-in ASP.NET server controls by implementing new and exciting custom controls.

This book is a comprehensive guide to authoring ASP.NET server controls. It contains architectural guidelines, detailed task-based information, and a large number of code samples that range from simple illustrative examples to advanced case studies. The sample code provided in the book follows the same standards and techniques that were used by the ASP.NET development team in implementing the standard ASP.NET server controls. In addition to control development, this book shows how to implement advanced design-time features that provide powerful RAD capabilities to server controls in a visual designer such as Microsoft Visual Studio .NET. Furthermore, the book examines XML Web services and the HTTP runtime and shows you how to incorporate these technologies into server controls. You will find this book useful whether you are a new control developer or an experienced one and whether you are developing controls for your own use or for commercial deployment.

We wrote this book in response to numerous requests and questions appearing on external and Microsoft internal discussion lists regarding in-depth information about implementing server controls. One of us, Nikhil Kothari, is a developer on the ASP.NET team who has designed and developed the Web Forms control framework and the standard ASP.NET server controls. The other, Vandana Datye, is a freelance programmer and writer who has been writing about server controls on MSDN since the early versions of the .NET Framework. We believe that server controls offer a compelling component solution that will grow in popularity as earlier component technologies such as COM and ActiveX did and that will make ASP.NET even more widespread in use. Our goal in writing this book was to provide a definitive resource for server control developers that contains hands-on and in-depth coverage of control authoring topics. We also wanted to provide an architectural overview of server controls that would enable advanced ASP.NET page developers to further their understanding of the page programming model. We hope you find this book informative and enjoyable.

Prerequisites

This book does not assume any previous background in authoring ASP.NET server controls. However, we do expect that you are familiar with creating ASP.NET pages and have used at least some of the built-in ASP.NET server controls. We assume that you have some exposure to the .NET Framework and are familiar with object-oriented programming. Finally, we expect that you are reasonably proficient in C# or in Microsoft Visual Basic .NET. The samples in the book are coded in C#; however, the .NET Framework enables you to access all the necessary APIs from Visual Basic .NET and from any other programming language that targets the common language runtime. If differences between the C# and Visual Basic .NET implementations exist, we call those out in the book.

Structure of the Book

This book is organized into five parts. The chapters in the first three parts build upon each other and are intended to be read sequentially.

Part I, "Overview," provides an overview of ASP.NET and describes the relationship of ASP.NET to the rest of the .NET Framework. This part also examines the Web Forms programming model and offers an overview of the essential constructs in programming components and controls using the .NET Framework.

Part II, "Server Controls—First Steps," provides an introduction to the two models that ASP.NET provides for implementing server controls. This section of the book demonstrates declaratively authored user controls and programmatically authored custom controls and provides guidelines for choosing between the two control authoring models.

Part III, "Server Controls—Nuts and Bolts," examines the architecture of ASP.NET server controls and provides in-depth coverage of the essential control authoring tasks. This part illustrates core ASP.NET concepts, including properties, state management, events, postback data processing, and rendering. It shows how to develop composite and templated controls, controls with client-side behavior, validator controls, and data-bound controls. This portion of the book also demonstrates how to incorporate design-time functionality so that controls provide a rich experience in a visual designer such as Visual Studio .NET. It concludes with a discussion of localization and licensing.

Part IV, "Server Components," describes XML Web services and HTTP handlers. It provides a quick overview of creating and deploying Web services and an in-depth explanation of building custom HTTP handlers. It also shows how to incorporate these technologies into server controls.

Part V, "Server Control Case Studies," contains examples of real-world controls that are similar to the standard set of ASP.NET server controls that ship with the .NET Framework. The sample controls in this part of the book bring together the concepts described in earlier chapters and provide an implementation of a set of professional-quality controls.

In addition, this book has three appendices. Appendix A, "Metadata Attributes," describes the metadata attribute classes that are commonly used by control developers when implementing server controls. Appendix B, "Object Model for Common Classes," lists the base classes for server controls and other classes that provide functionality that is commonly utilized by server controls. Appendix C, "Microsoft ASP.NET Web Matrix," introduces the Web development tool provided by the ASP.NET team and describes its relevance to control developers.

Sample Files

The complete code for the samples described in this book can be downloaded as a .zip archive from the book's Web site (*http://www.microsoft.com/mspress/books/5728.asp*). The archive contains a ReadMe file that describes the organization of the samples and provides directions for installing them for use with Visual Studio .NET as well as with the standalone .NET Framework SDK.

The archive holds the following contents:

- A ServerControls directory that builds into the MSPress.ServerControls.dll assembly. This assembly contains the samples from Part III of the book.

- A ServerComponents directory that builds into the MSPress.ServerComponents.dll assembly. This assembly contains the samples from Part IV of the book.

- A WebControls directory that builds into the MSPress.WebControls.dll assembly. This assembly contains the samples from Part V of the book.

- A BookWeb directory containing an ASP.NET Web application that contains sample pages that exercise the server controls implemented in the book.

- An EventsSample directory that builds into the EventsSample.exe assembly. This assembly contains code to demonstrate implementing events, as described in Chapter 3, "Component Programming Overview."

- A Tools directory that contains two tools: AddXmlMapping.vbs, which is described in Chapter 19, "HTTP Handlers," and EncLicGen.exe, which is described in Chapter 17, "Localization, Licensing, and Other Miscellany."

The archive contains a Visual Studio .NET solution file and corresponding project files that you can use to compile the samples with. In addition, the archive contains a set of batch files that you can use to build the samples by using the .NET Framework SDK alone.

Software Needed to Run the Samples

You will need the .NET Framework SDK on your local machine to compile the sample controls and use them in the sample ASP.NET pages provided in this book. The .NET Framework SDK includes ASP.NET and all the tools you will need to use the samples we have provided. The .NET Framework SDK is free and can be downloaded from *http://www.microsoft.com/fwlink/?linkid=77*.

ASP.NET requires one of the following operating systems: Microsoft Windows 2000, Windows XP Professional, or Windows .NET Server. In addition, ASP.NET Web applications run within the Internet Information Services (IIS) Web server.

If you want to use the solution file and related project files we have provided along with the samples, you will need Visual Studio .NET. You can find more information about Visual Studio .NET at *http://msdn.microsoft.com/vstudio*.

If you plan to use the .NET Framework SDK alone, we recommend that you download ASP.NET Web Matrix from *http://www.asp.net/webmatrix*. Web Matrix is a free ASP.NET Web development tool with a WYSIWYG design-time environment. This tool will enable you to open the sample pages in a design-time environment. Web Matrix also comes with a development Web server you can use instead of IIS if you want to run the samples pages on Microsoft Windows XP Home Edition.

Creating an IIS Virtual Directory

As mentioned earlier, the ReadMe file accompanying this book's sample files provides the instructions to install the samples for this book. However, you might also want to create your own ASP.NET Web application so that you can develop .aspx pages to test any controls that you implement. If you are using the standalone .NET Framework SDK, you will have to create an IIS virtual root, which maps the physical directory containing your Web application to an IIS virtual directory. (If you are using Visual Studio .NET, you do not need to do this because the ASP.NET Web application wizard creates a virtual root for you.)

We will assume that you have created a directory (such as C:\MySample-Web) that will contain pages and other elements of your ASP.NET Web application. We will also assume that you have installed IIS and the .NET Framework SDK on your computer. The following list shows how to create an IIS virtual directory that maps to the physical directory of your Web application:

1. If you are using Windows XP, from the Start menu select Control Panel, then select Performance And Maintenance, Administrative Tools, and finally Internet Information Services. If you are using Windows 2000, from the Start menu select Applications, then select Administrative Tools, and finally Internet Services Manager.

2. Expand the local computer node and then the Web Sites node.

3. Right-click the Default Web Sites node to bring up a drop-down menu. Select New | Virtual Directory from the menu choices. This will launch the Virtual Directory Creation Wizard, which will walk you through the steps for creating a virtual directory.

4. In the Virtual Directory Alias page, enter a name such as **MySampleWeb** in the Alias text box. You can enter any name you want for your Web application, as long as it does not conflict with an existing IIS virtual directory. Click Next to access the next page of the wizard.

5. In the Web Site Content Directory page, enter the path to the physical directory for your Web application in the Directory text box—for example, enter **C:\MySampleWeb**. You can also enter the path by browsing to the directory for your Web application. Click Next.

6. In the Access Permissions page, you can accept the defaults or modify the permissions as needed. Click Next.

7. Click Finish on the final page of the wizard to complete the creation of the virtual directory.

If you named your Web application MySampleWeb and it contains a page named MyPage.aspx, you can test whether the IIS virtual directory was successfully created by entering *http://localhost/MySampleWeb/MyPage.aspx* in the address bar of your Web browser.

You should also create a bin subdirectory to place assemblies that your Web application requires, such as the assembly that contains your controls. To create the bin directory of your application, you must create a directory named bin within the root of your Web application—for example, C:\MySampleWeb\bin. Chapter 5, "Developing a Simple Custom Control," describes the purpose of the bin directory in more detail.

Tools for Control Authoring and Related Tasks

This book refers to various tools that are used for building controls, creating resources, viewing assemblies, and performing other tasks. Most of these tools ship with the .NET Framework SDK. If you are using a development environment such as Visual Studio .NET, you will generally not use the SDK tools directly because the development environment integrates them into its own feature set.

Tools in the .NET Framework SDK

The following list describes the tools from the .NET Framework SDK that are commonly utilized by control developers. These tools are described in detail in the .NET Framework SDK documentation.

- **Al.exe**   The Assembly Linker allows you to embed resources into satellite assemblies or link resources to an assembly.

- **Csc.exe**   The C# compiler allows you to build managed assemblies from C# source code.

- **DbgClr.exe**   The Microsoft CLR Debugger allows you to debug managed applications and components by using a graphical user interface.

- **GacUtil.exe**   The Global Assembly Cache (GAC) utility allows you to add assemblies to the GAC and to view and manage the contents of the GAC.

- **IlDasm.exe**   The Microsoft Intermediate Language (MSIL) Disassembler allows you to view the MSIL contained within an assembly as generated by a compiler.

- **ResGen.exe**   The Resource File Generator allows you to convert .txt or .resx text files into binary .resources files that can be embedded as resources within assemblies.

- **Sn.exe**   The Strong Name tool allows you to generate test key pairs for signing assemblies.

- **Vbc.exe**   The Visual Basic .NET compiler allows you to build managed assemblies from Visual Basic .NET source code.

- **Wsdl.exe**   The Web Services Description Language (WSDL) tool allows you to generate proxy classes for accessing XML Web services from your applications and components.

FxCop Tool for Checking Compliance with Design Guidelines

The FxCop tool is provided by the .NET Framework team for checking whether the classes in your assemblies comply with the design guidelines of the .NET Framework so that they appear as a natural extension of the .NET Framework. This tool does not ship with the .NET Framework SDK but can be downloaded from the GotDotNet Web site (*http://www.gotdotnet.com/team/libraries*). FxCop is still under development. The .NET Framework team continues to update it regularly with improvements and additional features. As a result, FxCop might report a certain number of spurious messages. In general, the tool goes a long way in identifying potential issues with your assemblies. Furthermore, you can customize FxCop with your own set of rules.

The design guidelines used by the .NET Framework team are available as a white paper on MSDN titled "Design Guidelines for Class Library Developers." The white paper is periodically updated by the .NET Framework team. The latest version of the document is available as part of the sample files associated with this book. Future updates to this document will be provided on MSDN and on the GotDotNet Web site.

Other Resources

The ASP.NET Web site (*http://www.asp.net*) provides a number of discussion forums where the ASP.NET community comes together to ask questions, find answers, and support their peers. The ASP.NET team, as well as the authors of this book, participate and interact directly with the community to help answer questions and to receive feedback to incorporate into future versions of ASP.NET. These forums can be found at *http://www.asp.net/forums*. The list of forums includes those targeted at Web Forms in general as well as other advanced ASP.NET topics. A forum named Building Controls is dedicated to control developers.

The ASP.NET Web site also contains a control gallery at *http://www.asp.net/ controlgallery*, where you can browse for controls by category. In addition, you can make your own controls available to other ASP.NET developers for searching and browsing.

Support

Every effort has been made to ensure the accuracy of this book. Microsoft Press provides corrections for books through the World Wide Web at the following address:

http://www.microsoft.com/mspress/support/

To connect directly to the Microsoft Press Knowledge Base and enter a query regarding a question or an issue that you may have, go to

http://www.microsoft.com/mspress/support/search.asp

If you have comments, questions, or ideas regarding this book, please send them to Microsoft Press using either of the following methods:

Postal Mail:

Microsoft Press
Attn: *Developing Microsoft ASP.NET Server Controls and Components* Editor
One Microsoft Way
Redmond, WA 98052-6399

E-Mail:

MSPINPUT@MICROSOFT.COM

Please note that product support is not offered through the above mail addresses. For support information regarding Visual Studio or the .NET Framework, visit the Microsoft Product Standard Support Web site at

http://support.microsoft.com

Part I

Overview

Part I of the book provides an overview of ASP.NET, Microsoft's new Web application development technology, and describes the relationship of ASP.NET to the rest of the Microsoft .NET Framework. This part also examines the Web Forms programming model and offers an overview of the essential constructs in programming .NET components and controls.

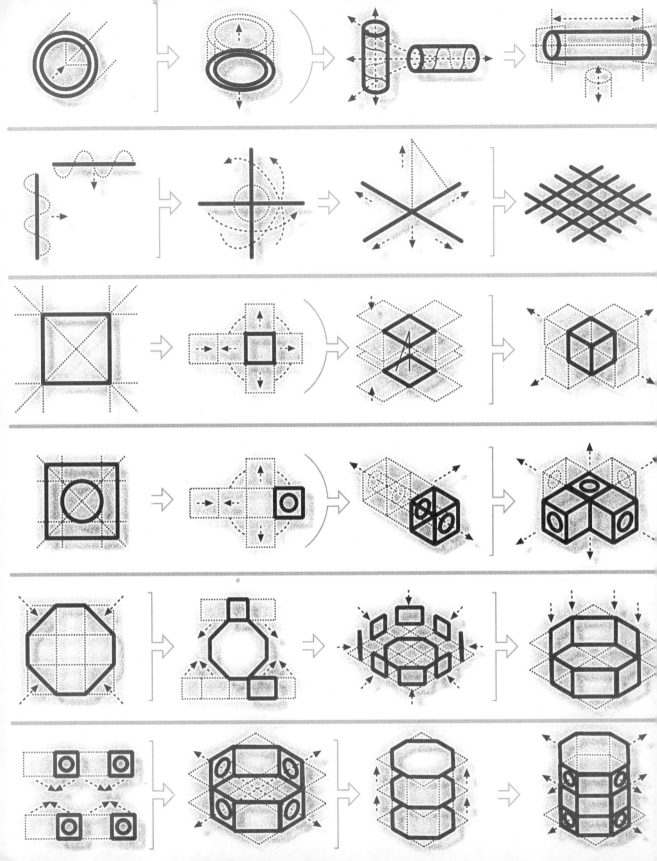

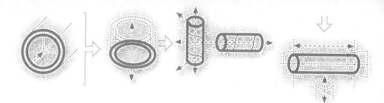

1

ASP.NET Overview

ASP.NET is a core piece of the .NET Framework, Microsoft's new platform for application development, and is the successor to the highly popular Active Server Pages technology. ASP.NET is a complete and extensible Web application development framework that introduces a new programming model for creating rich, dynamic Web sites, Web applications, and XML Web services. This new programming model distinguishes itself from its predecessors by its component-based architecture and development paradigm. In this chapter, we will provide an overview of ASP.NET and the .NET Framework from a component developer's perspective.

The .NET Framework

ASP.NET inherits its programming model from the .NET Framework. This new application development platform brings together the best object-oriented features from languages such as C++ and Java, along with the ease and simplicity of development associated with languages such as Microsoft Visual Basic. The .NET Framework features a run-time execution environment and a rich class library built on top of that.

Figure 1-1 shows the pieces of the .NET Framework and how they build on each other.

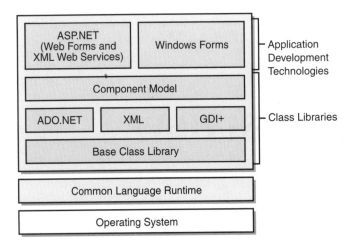

Figure 1-1   A logical view of the .NET Framework

The Common Language Runtime

The common language runtime (CLR) forms the foundation of the .NET Framework by providing a run-time execution environment. Applications and components developed to run in this environment are referred to as *managed* applications and components. They are referred to as *managed* because the CLR manages the execution of code in these applications and components and provides a number of services that simplify their development and deployment.

The CLR takes care of a number of low-level plumbing details. One of the most important features in the CLR is its automatic memory management and garbage collection functionality. This feature allows you to focus on implementing your component's behavior by making it almost unnecessary for you to worry about memory management– and memory allocation–related programming errors. This feature also enables components to easily interact with one another because they all share a common memory management scheme.

The CLR allows you to express the functionality of your component with a well-designed, simple, and intuitive API or object model via constructs such as properties, methods, and events that you can declaratively describe by using metadata attributes. These concepts are discussed in detail in Chapter 3, "Component Programming Overview."

Another important feature of the CLR is that once you have implemented your component, the CLR automatically makes it available for use in one or more applications without any extra registration requirements. The assembly containing the component can be versioned and deployed in a side-by-side manner. In other words, the CLR enables multiple versions of your component to coexist. This allows you to develop and deploy future versions of your component without inadvertently breaking any existing applications that rely on the exact behavior of the current version of your component.

Finally, the CLR provides true language interoperability. Your component can be developed, consumed, and inherited from in any .NET programming language, such as C#, Visual Basic .NET, Microsoft JScript .NET, and Microsoft Visual J#. This enables you to develop your component in the language you prefer, without arbitrarily imposing your language choice on your component's consumers.

The .NET Framework Class Library

The .NET Framework class library builds on top of the CLR (as shown in Figure 1-1) and provides a rich hierarchy of classes covering a wide variety of application and component development scenarios in a consistent and intuitive manner. This class library truly makes component-based programming a reality by providing a common substrate and API that can be shared by all components and applications. This extensive class library can be divided into multiple parts, as Figure 1-1 shows. Each logical part is associated with a set of related namespaces used to create a logical and hierarchical grouping of classes in a class library based on their common purpose, functionality, or targeted technology.

The Base Class Library (BCL) encompasses a number of commonly used namespaces, such as *System*, *System.Collections*, and *System.Diagnostics*. It provides basic functionality that is useful in all applications and components, including the basic primitive types (*Int32*, *String*, and *Boolean*) and commonly used data structures (such as *Array*, *Stack*, and *Hashtable*). The BCL also contains features such as network connectivity, protocol implementations, file and stream I/O classes, multithreading, text processing, regular expressions, globalization support, and reflection. Various higher-level class libraries are built on top of this foundation.

The ADO.NET layer in Figure 1-1 represents the data access functionality built into the .NET Framework as part of the *System.Data* namespace and its subnamespaces. ADO.NET provides the ability to operate on disconnected or offline caches of relational data. The data access layer also enables access to a variety of database engines. In particular, it provides very high-performance connectivity to Microsoft SQL Server.

The XML layer in Figure 1-1 is a counterpart of the ADO.NET layer and includes the classes in the *System.Xml* namespace and its subnamespaces. This XML layer enables efficient access to XML data, both structured and unstructured. In addition, it provides an implementation of various industry standards, such as Extensible Stylesheet Language Transformations (XSLT), XML Path Language (XPath), and XML schemas. This layer also gives you the ability to serialize objects to and from XML format.

The GDI+ layer in Figure 1-1 represents the object-oriented drawing and painting functionality provided by the *System.Drawing* namespace and its subnamespaces. The graphics capabilities of GDI+ include rendering primitive objects, vector art, and typography (formatted text). Furthermore, GDI+ enables the use and creation of image files in various formats, including JPEG, GIF, BMP, and TIFF.

The component model layer consists of classes in the *System.Component-Model* and *System.ComponentModel.Design* namespaces. It provides the architecture that turns classes into components that can be designed, customized, serialized, and deserialized in a design-time tool such as Microsoft Visual Studio .NET. In addition, this layer enables different application development technologies to share similar component creation and usage techniques as well as design-time features.

The topmost layers in Figure 1-1 represent the application development technologies. The .NET Framework enables the development of graphical Win32 client applications and server applications. Windows Forms, which is implemented in the *System.Windows.Forms* namespace, enables the development of applications targeting the Win32 platform. ASP.NET and Web Forms, implemented in the *System.Web* namespace and its subnamespaces, enable the development of Web applications and XML Web services.

The next section lets you take a deeper look at ASP.NET, the portion of the .NET Framework that this book directly addresses.

A Quick Tour of ASP.NET

ASP.NET, which is implemented in the *System.Web* namespace and its various subnamespaces, collectively represents the features used in developing both Web applications and XML Web services. As a component developer in the

ASP.NET space, you'll be using classes from these namespaces in your component implementation. Table 1-1 lists these namespaces and their associated functionality.

Table 1-1   ASP.NET Namespaces

Namespace	Functionality
System.Web	Contains classes such as *HttpContext*, *HttpRequest*, and *HttpResponse*, which are used to implement the HTTP runtime, its basic request processing architecture, and the commonly used intrinsic objects. It also contains other interface definitions (such as *IHttpModule* and *IHttpHandler*) that define the extensible architecture of ASP.NET request processing logic.
System.Web.UI, *System.Web.UI.HtmlControls,* *System.Web.UI.WebControls*	Collectively form the page framework, the control architecture, and the standard ASP.NET controls. As a single unit, these namespaces implement the feature commonly referred to as *Web Forms*. Chapter 2, "Page Programming Model," discusses the page framework in greater detail. Part II and Part III of this book, "Server Controls—First Steps" and "Server Controls—Nuts and Bolts," cover the technical details of extending this page framework.
System.Web.Services	Provides the functionality used in the implementation, description, and discovery of XML Web services developed in the form of .asmx files. Chapter 18, "XML Web Services," discusses how to incorporate XML Web services into controls.
System.Web.Caching	Provides the implementation of an in-memory caching system that holds cached data based on custom dependency and expiration rules. This namespace can be used to optimize the performance and responsiveness of Web applications. The caching system is also used by the output caching functionality of user controls, as described in Chapter 4, "User Controls: From Page to Control."
System.Web.SessionState	Provides an implementation of the Session state object. Session state is scoped to a single user session, and its data can be held either in memory or in a database using SQL Server across multiple requests.
System.Web.Security	Provides the implementation of various authentication mechanisms commonly used by Web applications, such as forms-based authentication, Microsoft Windows authentication, and Microsoft Passport authentication.
System.Web.Mail	A utility namespace in ASP.NET that enables the incorporation of email delivery functionality using Simple Mail Transfer Protocol (SMTP).

HTTP Runtime—Request Processing in an ASP.NET Application

As mentioned at the beginning of this chapter, ASP.NET is a complete Web application development platform. It is complete in the sense that it contains all the pieces and layers necessary to handle incoming requests and to create an output response in a Web application or XML Web service. The ASP.NET runtime can be hosted in a custom application outside the Internet Information Services (IIS) Web server. However, both the diagram and the description that follow are based on the most common ASP.NET usage scenario: ASP.NET hosted in IIS.

Figure 1-2 illustrates a single incoming request into an ASP.NET Web application and the associated response that is generated by the components that participate in the request-processing life cycle.

At its core, the HTTP runtime handles an incoming Web request from a client application such as a Web browser, routes the request through the appropriate components in the application that process it, and then generates a response that is returned to the client application issuing the request.

An incoming HTTP Web request is first received by the IIS Web server, which hands this request to the ASP.NET ISAPI based on the extensions that ASP.NET is registered to handle. Some of the common file extensions handled by ASP.NET include .aspx, .asmx, and .ashx. The ASP.NET HTTP runtime serves as a bridge between IIS and the managed Web application.

The ASP.NET HTTP runtime initializes a number of objects to process the request. The HTTP runtime first creates an instance of the *HttpContext* object, which contains information about the request that is currently being processed, and it then makes that context object available to all other components involved in the processing logic. This context object flows through the linear processing chain shown in Figure 1-2, in which each object can add other data or objects as context information.

The *HttpContext* instance provides access to the request object, which is an instance of the *HttpRequest* class, and to the response object, which is an instance of the *HttpResponse* class. The request object represents the data being sent to the Web server by the requesting application and contains information such as the requested URL, any posted data, and HTTP headers. The response object contains the output content (such as the HTML stream) being sent back to the requesting application from the Web server. It allows the components involved in processing the request to generate content into the output stream and to add information about the type of the content, such as its MIME type. The *HttpContext* object also provides access to various services that are available for the duration of the request processing. These services include application and session state, the ASP.NET cache, and information about the user identity.

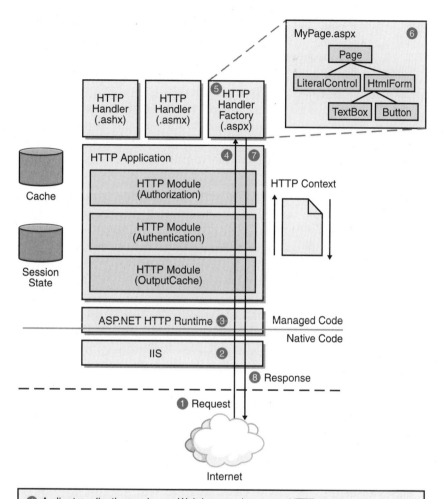

Figure 1-2   Request processing inside an ASP.NET Web application

1. A client application such as a Web browser issues an HTTP request.
2. IIS receives the request and hands it off for processing to the ASP.NET ISAPI.
3. The HTTP runtime in ASP.NET resolves the request to determine the appropriate HTTP handler or HTTP handler factory it will invoke. It also composes a *pipeline*, or sequence, of HTTP modules to process the request.
4. The HTTP modules perform preprocessing of the request, which includes steps such as cache lookup and authorization.
5. The HTTP handler or HTTP handler factory is invoked, which then does the real work associated with the request.
6. In the case of .aspx page requests, the page instantiates a control tree and renders the tree to form the response. The control tree corresponds to the user interface defined in the .aspx page.
7. The HTTP modules perform postprocessing of the request.
8. The resulting response is sent back to the Web client.

The HTTP runtime assembles a processing pipeline composed of components referred to as *HTTP modules* to perform request preprocessing actions (such as cache lookup and authorization) and postprocessing actions (such as updating the cache). These components implement the *IHttpModule* interface. Each module in the pipeline handles various global application-level and request-specific events to perform its logic. These events include application start and end notifications, request start and end notifications, and various hooks into the life cycle of a request, such as authentication and authorization. Each module can also raise its own set of events that an application developer can handle.

The HTTP runtime also selects a single *HTTP handler* or *HTTP handler factory* that will be invoked to perform the actual processing of the incoming request, based on the request URL. An *HTTP handler* is a component that implements the *IHttpHandler* interface, while an *HTTP handler factory* is a component that implements the *IHttpHandlerFactory* interface. ASP.NET provides a number of built-in HTTP handler implementations to handle file extensions such as .aspx, .asmx, and .ashx. A handler uses the *HttpContext* object to gather information about the request and to write out the resulting response. ASP.NET does not impose arbitrary limitations on the implementation of an HTTP handler. A handler can use any of the information it is handed—such as the request URL, request headers, and posted data—and it can generate any form of output, either textual or binary.

One of the most commonly used HTTP handlers is the page handler. Each .aspx page in a Web application is an HTTP handler that handles incoming requests for that particular page. The implementation of this HTTP handler instantiates a hierarchy of server objects and user interface components named *server controls* that derive directly or indirectly from the *System.Web.UI.Control* class corresponding to the declarative content present in the .aspx file, and assembles them into a control tree. The control tree has its own life cycle. Essentially, the control tree inside each page handler processes a request and forms the response by rendering itself into some form of markup (typically HTML) that forms the response content. Chapter 2 provides a more detailed overview of how a page processes a request.

Extending ASP.NET

As we mentioned earlier in the chapter, ASP.NET is an extensible Web application development platform. The extensibility of ASP.NET—a feature in and of itself—results from the modular design and componentized architecture of

ASP.NET. As a component developer, you can create components that fit into different levels of ASP.NET to customize various aspects of the request/response cycle. These custom components take the form of custom controls or new HTTP handlers and HTTP modules.

The primary focus of the book is to explain the control architecture and to enable you to develop custom controls for use in the ASP.NET page framework. Controls form the building blocks that are used to create the user interface of all ASP.NET Web applications. They provide a run-time programming model and a design-time experience that are used by the page developer and the page designer. They contain the functionality to render themselves as part of the response generated by the page when it is requested. Server controls represent the most widely used components in an ASP.NET Web application. You can create new controls and extend or combine existing controls to implement and encapsulate new behavior, functionality, and user interface elements. Part II of the book provides an overview of control authoring, and Part III provides an in-depth look at control development.

ASP.NET allows you to develop and register custom HTTP handlers and HTTP handler factories to process new file extensions, substitute a built-in HTTP handler, and customize the processing of specific URLs. Chapter 19 describes the details of implementing and registering custom HTTP handlers.

Finally, ASP.NET allows you to develop and register custom HTTP modules to participate in its pipeline architecture and perform preprocessing and postprocessing of all incoming requests. As a component developer, you can develop custom modules that add extra processing for each request, substitute one of the built-in modules, or generate content and content headers into the response stream.

Summary

ASP.NET, along with the rest of the .NET Framework, creates an exciting new platform for both Web application developers and component developers. The .NET Framework provides a modern, consistent, and intuitive class library as the foundation for building components and component-based applications. Furthermore, ASP.NET provides a powerful Web application development framework that features well-designed architecture for extending and customizing its built-in capabilities with custom controls and components.

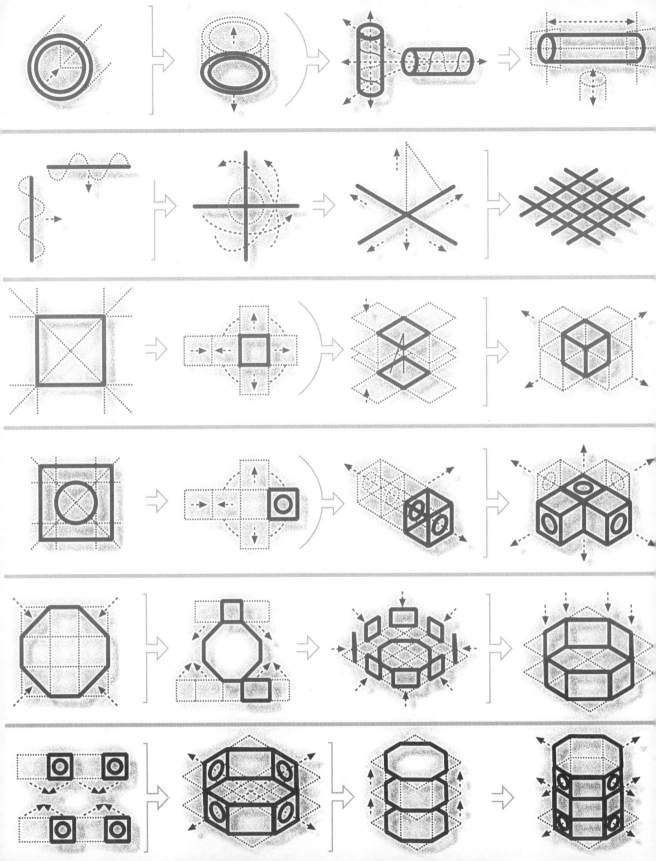

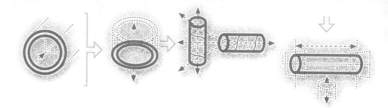

2

Page Programming Model

ASP.NET provides a new programming model for creating the user interface of a Web application. This programming model makes it possible to create programmable Web pages that have a clean separation of code and presentation. If you have used Active Server Pages, the previous generation of the Microsoft Web programming technology, you will find that ASP.NET is significantly richer and easier to use. Web Forms, the user interface technology in ASP.NET, provides an object-oriented approach for developing server applications. It provides the benefits of abstraction, a rich object model, compilation, encapsulation, modular design, and object reuse.

Server controls are the fundamental building blocks of Web Forms pages. This chapter lays the foundation for the rest of this book by providing an overview of the page programming model and the role of server controls in this technology.

A Sample Page

We expect that you have some experience developing ASP.NET pages, but for completeness, we will begin with a very simple page that shows the typical contents of an .aspx file and the HTML that it generates. Listing 2-1 presents the code needed to create this page.

```
<%@ Page language="c#" %>
<html>
  <head>
    <title>Sample Page</title>
    <script runat="server">
    public void button1_OnClick(object sender, EventArgs e) {
      label1.Text = "Hello " + textBox1.Text + "!";
    }
    </script>
  </head>
  <body>
    <form runat="server">
      Enter your name:
      <asp:TextBox runat="server" id="textBox1"/>
      <asp:Button runat="server" id="button1" Text="OK"
          OnClick="button1_OnClick"/>
      <hr>
      <asp:Label runat="server" id="label1"/>
    </form>
  </body>
</html>
```

Listing 2-1   A very simple .aspx file

When a user requests this page, fills in some text, and then submits the page to the server, the page executes on the server and produces HTML content similar to that shown in Listing 2-2.

```
<html>
  <head>
    <title>Sample Page</title>
  </head>
  <body>
    <form name="_ctl0" method="post" action="MyPage.aspx" id="_ctl0">
<input type="hidden" name="__VIEWSTATE" value="dDwtMTM3NjQ2NjY2NTt0PDt
sPGk8MT47PjtsPHQ8O2w8aTw1Pjs+O2w8dDxwPHA8bDxUZXh00z47bDxIZWxsbyBXb3JsZ
Ds+Pjs+Ozs+Oz4+O2w+" />
```

Listing 2-2   HTML content generated by the sample page

Listing 2-2   *(continued)*

```
    Enter your name:
    <input name="textBox1" type="text" value="World" id="textBox1" />
    <input type="submit" name="button1" value="OK" id="button1" />
    <hr>
    <span id="label1">Hello World!</span>
  </form>
 </body>
</html>
```

In general, an ASP.NET page consists of static text and markup text (such as HTML elements), with server controls interspersed. Server controls are represented by tags with a *runat="server"* attribute. On the other hand, literal text and tags without this special attribute are treated as static text. The sample page shown in Listing 2-1 has a few basic server controls. For example, it contains the *<asp:TextBox>* tag, which represents the standard ASP.NET *TextBox* Web control. On the server, the *TextBox* control renders itself as the *<input type="text">* HTML element, as shown in the generated HTML content in Listing 2-2.

Server Controls

Server controls are components used in ASP.NET pages to define the user interface of a Web application. Server controls are the essential element of the Web Forms programming model. They form the basis of a modern, component-based, intuitive forms package that simplifies the development of Web user interfaces, similar to the way that the Microsoft Visual Basic forms package simplified Windows programming. At a high level, server controls provide abstractions of an underlying Web application and presentation technology. For example, the Web controls that ship as part of ASP.NET are abstractions of the HTML and HTTP technologies used in the creation of browser-based applications. These controls are described as abstractions because they do not directly represent HTML elements; instead, they offer a more abstract object model for creating those elements.

The Web Forms programming model greatly simplifies application development for page developers and designers and is characterized by the server control features and capabilities that follow.

■ Server controls create an intuitive and simpler programming model for the page developer by hiding the inconsistencies and complexities of the underlying technology. For example, the *Button* Web control maps directly to the *<input type="submit">* HTML tag and hides the inconsistencies of the *type* attribute of the *<input>* tag. The *TextBox* Web control is slightly more sophisticated and maps to one of the multiple text entry tags provided by HTML: *<input type="text">*, *<input type="password">*, and *<textarea>*. At the other end of the spectrum, controls such as *Calendar* and *DataGrid* provide new functionality that is not inherently available in HTML, such as date selection and data binding.

■ They hide the differences between various browsers and viewing devices, as well as the various browser versions that a Web application might need to target. The ability of server controls to render content as appropriate to the target browser enables the page developer to write a single application that can target multiple viewing platforms at run time. Server controls contain the logic to provide the best possible experience by examining the capabilities of the requesting browser or device.

■ They function as true components, providing the same benefits that you might expect from working with components in other types of applications. Server controls provide a rich server-side programming model. They expose their functionality through properties and methods. They also provide an event-based programming model, which allows page developers to implement application logic in response to user interaction. The object model exposed by server controls is strongly typed—unlike that of DHTML, which is loosely typed. Not only does being strongly typed lead to better server control performance, it also reduces programming errors.

■ They manage their state across postbacks and round-trips. A scalable Web application is *stateless*—in other words, the application doesn't maintain data and state on the server corresponding to each user accessing the application. Server controls use a feature of the ASP.NET page framework known as *view state* to manage their state across individual Web requests. This feature allows controls to provide a stateful programming model that creates the illusion of continuity while preserving the scalability of a stateless application.

■ They contain logic to handle postback data associated with a Web request and to enable the page developer to process user input and handle user actions in their server-side code. The page developer is freed from understanding the details of postback and can instead focus on the object model of the controls—in other words, the controls' properties and events.

■ They provide a compelling data-binding model. Most Web applications are dynamic and feature content based on a variety of data sources. Data-bound server controls—those server controls associated with a data source—greatly simplify the creation of dynamic pages. ASP.NET features an efficient data-binding model that provides the page developer with complete control over the data-binding process and over data access. The data-binding model features a simple and generic data source model that provides the page developer with a wide choice of objects that can be used as data sources.

■ They provide page developers with multiple mechanisms to customize their rendering. Server controls can provide style properties as a means to customize their formatting. They can also provide template properties for customization of their content and layout. Server controls use both these mechanisms to provide a *lookless* user interface, which is an interface that does not provide a single preestablished look but instead can blend seamlessly into the rest of the application's user interface.

■ They are configurable on a machine level (via the machine.config file) or on a Web application level (via the web.config file). Server controls can support configurable defaults for their properties, which enables page developers to control or change their behavior uniformly across pages without having to change or recompile the application itself.

■ They provide a rapid application development (RAD) user experience in a visual design-time environment such as Microsoft Visual Studio .NET. This enables page developers and designers to visually compose their pages and customize the appearance of the server controls in a WYSIWYG fashion.

In Part III of this book, "Server Controls—Nuts and Bolts," we will provide detailed explanations of these features and characteristics. We'll also show you how to incorporate them into your own custom controls to provide an intuitive user model that is consistent with the standard ASP.NET server controls.

ASP.NET Server Control Hierarchy

The ASP.NET server control classes are implemented in the *System.Web.UI, System.Web.UI.HtmlControls,* and *System.Web.UI.WebControls* namespaces in the *System.Web* assembly. Figure 2-1 provides a high-level view of these namespaces.

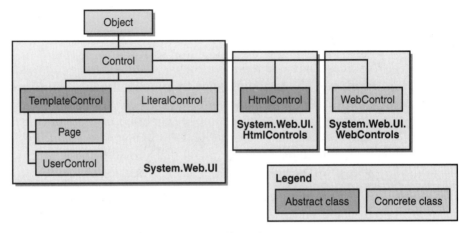

Figure 2-1   The ASP.NET server control hierarchy

All server controls derive directly or indirectly from the *System.Web.UI.Control* class. The *Page* and *UserControl* classes represent .aspx and .ascx files, respectively, while the *LiteralControl* class represents a contiguous range of static content present in these files.

In the *System.Web.UI.HtmlControls* namespace, the *HtmlControl* class provides a base class for all HTML controls. These controls represent plain HTML tags with a *runat="server"* attribute and provide an HTML-centric object model.

In the *System.Web.UI.WebControls* namespace, the *WebControl* class provides a base class for most Web controls and for custom controls that render themselves as HTML elements. These controls provide an object model that is strongly typed, simpler, more intuitive, and more consistent than the HTML controls.

In addition to the standard HTML-based controls, ASP.NET provides support for authoring mobile Web applications targeted at small devices such as cell phones via a suite of mobile controls in the *System.Web.UI.MobileControls* namespace.

ASP.NET Web Controls

The controls in the *System.Web.UI.WebControls* namespace are referred to as the *Web controls*. Most of the controls in this namespace derive directly or indirectly from the *WebControl* base class. This suite includes controls that render as the basic HTML form elements, such as buttons and text boxes used for collecting user input, as well as other common HTML elements, such as anchors, images, and tables. It includes a set of validation controls that can be associated with the input controls to perform both client-side and server-side validation. The suite also contains data-bound controls, such as *DataGrid* and *Repeater*, used to generate dynamic pages based on a data source. The class hierarchy presented in Figure 2-2 shows the complete set of controls.

Why Write Server Controls?

Although the standard ASP.NET server controls address the most common application scenarios, they are by no means exhaustive. In fact, many scenarios are not directly addressed by these controls. For example, the standard ASP.NET server controls do not address image maps, chart-generation capabilities, or the creation of masked-edit data entry forms. However, ASP.NET does provide an extensible control architecture that allows you to develop custom controls that can behave in the same way as the standard ones at both run time and design time. There are several reasons and scenarios for which you might develop server controls:

■   To encapsulate application logic in the form of reusable and intuitive abstractions that can then be used in multiple Web applications. In this sense, server controls can provide a toolbox of common user interface components and behaviors.

■   To create commercial component libraries similar to the ActiveX controls in Microsoft Visual Basic and the tag libraries in Java Server Pages (JSP). It is expected that the third-party component industry will make the ASP.NET platform even more compelling, just as Win32 ActiveX components popularized Visual Basic. Developing custom controls that target this space is a compelling market opportunity because Web Forms is the primary programming model for Web application development in the .NET platform.

■   To provide a clean mechanism for dividing work across a large team. For example, in corporations, developers on the team can put together controls for use by page designers who design and implement the application user interface.

■   To enable Internet service providers (ISPs) that host ASP.NET Web sites to add substantial value to their service by offering a gallery of custom server controls. This richer functionality can enable an ISP's members to create more powerful and interactive Web sites, thereby enabling the ISP to distinguish itself from other competing service providers.

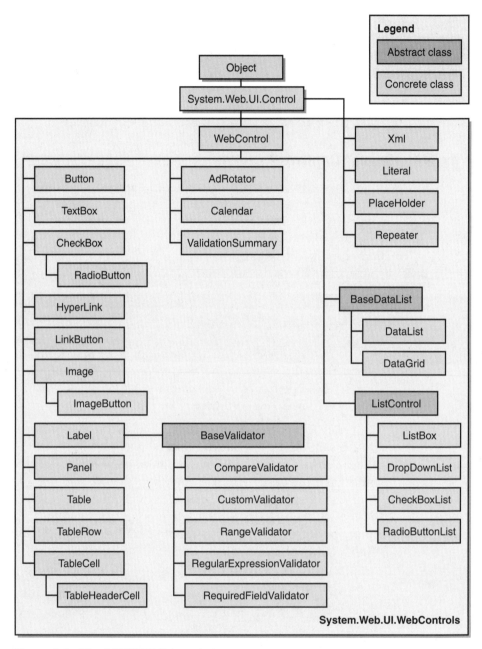

Figure 2-2   The ASP.NET Web controls

An example of an add-on library of controls built using the control architecture in ASP.NET is the Microsoft Internet Explorer Web controls library. This library includes the DHTML-based *TreeView* and *TabStrip* controls, among others. All these controls are available for download on MSDN.

From Text to Controls

Page developers and designers create ASP.NET pages in a declarative text format (as you can see in Listing 2-1) by using either a visual designer such as Visual Studio .NET or a simple source editor. A typical .aspx page contains static text, static markup tags (such as HTML elements), server controls, and optional server-side code represented by script tags with the *runat="server"* attribute.

At run time, the page framework parses the text in the .aspx file and creates instances of server control classes that correspond to each tag that has a *runat="server"* attribute. In addition to creating specific server controls, the page framework creates a special control, *LiteralControl*, to represent each span of contiguous static text and markup present in the page. The instantiated controls are assembled into a control tree. For example, the control tree corresponding to the page you saw in the Listing 2-1 is shown in Figure 2-3.

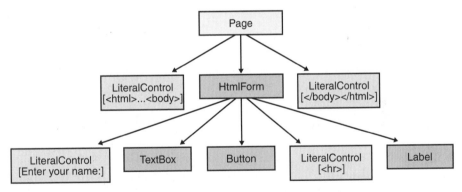

Figure 2-3 The control tree created as a result of parsing the page shown in Listing 2-1

The control tree is a hierarchical arrangement of controls. The *Page* class, which derives indirectly from the *System.Web.UI.Control* class (shown in Figure 2-1), represents the .aspx file and is the root of the tree. Its children represent

the contents of the .aspx file. Each control (other than the *Page* instance) has a reference to its parent in the hierarchy. At the same time, each control can act as a parent for other controls. The page framework allows the page developer and custom controls to perform standard operations on this control tree, such as adding and removing child controls and retrieving controls by either their identifier or their position in the tree.

Page processing is very closely tied to the control tree that results from the parsing process. The page framework processes each control in each processing phase it goes through, such as the initialization and rendering phases. The page framework processes the controls in a preordered fashion—in other words, the parent is processed first, followed by its children. This processing scheme ensures that controls are processed in the order in which they appear in the .aspx file.

Code Model

ASP.NET pages consist of two parts: the definition of the user interface using static text and server controls, and the implementation of the user interface behavior and the Web application logic in the form of server-side code.

ASP.NET provides a new code model that enables both page developers and development tools to cleanly and easily separate code from presentation. This feature is a significant improvement over Active Server Pages, which required code to be interspersed with the static content of the page. The ASP.NET code model enables easier division of labor among a team of developers and designers, and it increases the readability and maintainability of both code and content. This new code model is commonly used in one of two forms. The first form involves simply embedding code in a *runat="server"* script block within the .aspx file itself, as you saw in Listing 2-1. This form is sometimes referred to as *inline code*. The second form involves implementing a class deriving from *Page*, saving the code in a separate file, and associating it with the .aspx file via the *Page* directive. This form is generally referred to as *code-behind*.

In this book, we will use the inline code model for most examples, primarily because it is easier to illustrate concepts with and it is easier to develop by using only the standard tools available with the .NET Framework SDK. The second approach—implementing code in a separate file—is the model favored by Visual Studio .NET because it enables editing of the code using the standard Visual Studio .NET code editor. The two models are functionally equivalent and produce the same output at run time. But, for our purposes, what's most important is that the custom controls function identically in both models.

The code model in ASP.NET is also language agnostic, as is the programming model associated with any other application built using the .NET Framework. You can use any .NET programming language—such as C#, Visual Basic .NET, Microsoft Visual J#, and Microsoft JScript .NET—to implement the behavior and logic of the page. You specify the code language of the page using the *Language* attribute of the *Page* directive. If you are using the inline code model, a single application might have pages implemented in multiple languages, which work together seamlessly. Each page can use only a single language. However, in the code-behind model used by Visual Studio .NET, all the code-behind class files are precompiled into a single assembly at design time and therefore must be implemented in the same language.

Page Execution Model

The page execution model in ASP.NET ties together all aspects of the page programming model. Chapter 1, "ASP.NET Overview," provided the outline for request processing inside an ASP.NET Web application. This section takes a deeper look at how a page handles an incoming request to generate an output response.

Figure 2-4 illustrates two incoming requests for the same page and shows how the page framework processes these two requests.

As described in Chapter 1, the incoming request is handled by Internet Information Services (IIS), which hands the request to the HTTP runtime in ASP.NET for processing. The page execution model begins with the page HTTP handler factory, which is registered with the HTTP runtime to handle requests for all .aspx files. The page handler factory is responsible for creating an instance of a *Page* object, which is an HTTP handler that will eventually process the request to produce the response output.

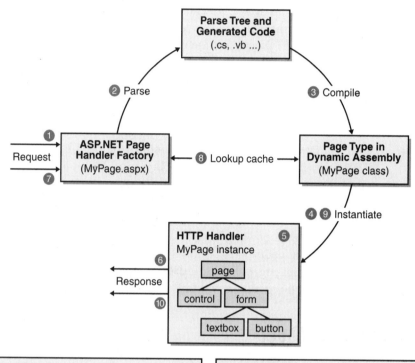

Figure 2-4   How a page handles requests

First Request

1 A Web client issues an HTTP request, which is handled by the HTTP runtime and is routed to the page HTTP handler factory for processing.

2 The page HTTP handler factory parses the .aspx file being requested and dynamically generates code representing the parse tree.

3 The generated code is compiled, and the resulting class (derived from *Page*) is stored in the ASP.NET cache.

4 An instance of the dynamically generated class is created and is used to handle the incoming request in the form of an HTTP handler.

5 The instantiated page is executed and the generated control tree is processed. The individual controls produce the appropriate HTML output.

6 The resulting response is sent back to the Web client issuing the Web request.

Second Request

7 A Web client (either the same one as before or a different one) issues an HTTP request for the same page.

8 The page HTTP handler factory successfully looks up the type stored in the ASP.NET cache during the previous request.

9 A new instance of the previously cached *Page* class is created and is used as the HTTP handler for this incoming request, as in steps 4 and 5.

10 The resulting response is sent back to the Web client issuing this second Web request.

The page handler factory first attempts to look for a previously compiled page class in the ASP.NET cache associated with the .aspx file being requested. When this lookup fails, as it does during the first request, the handler factory reads in the file and parses it to create a *parse tree*. A parse tree is similar to a control tree. But instead of containing controls, a parse tree contains instances of objects known as *control builders*. Control builders contain information about controls that is gathered during the parsing process. The parse tree is then converted into code in the language associated with the page via the *Language* attribute of the *Page* directive. The page handler factory then invokes the appropriate compiler—for example, the C# compiler, csc.exe—to dynamically compile a class deriving from *Page*. The page handler factory also places the newly created page class into the ASP.NET cache and associates the cache entry with a file dependency. The file dependency monitors changes made to the .aspx file and ensures that any change automatically invalidates the cache entry, which causes the modified file to be reparsed the next time it is requested.

The page handler factory instantiates the dynamically compiled page class and allows the newly created instance to process the incoming request. An important aspect of the page programming model is that the pages execute as fully compiled code. This provides significantly better performance than interpreted code (such as code contained in Active Server Pages). The page executes the code generated from the parse tree, which creates and processes the control tree contained in the original .aspx file. The control tree has its own life cycle involving initialization, loading, rendering, and disposing. This life cycle is described in Chapter 9, "Control Life Cycle, Events, and Postback." In its final processing phase, the page renders itself to produce the response content. At the end of its processing cycle, the page is completely disposed of. Thus, the page framework does not maintain any state or page instances across requests. This enables the development of stateless and scalable Web applications.

During any subsequent request, the same page HTTP handler factory can use the previously compiled and cached page class and continue with its normal processing logic by again instantiating a new page instance to handle the new incoming request. This allows the handler factory to skip all the work of opening, reading, and parsing the file; generating code; and invoking the compiler. This single-parse-and-compile aspect of the page execution model greatly improves the performance and responsiveness of the Web application.

Viewing the Generated Code

You can view the code for the class that the page parser generates to transform the .aspx file into a control tree by turning on page debugging. In debug mode, the class file containing the generated code is preserved. However, this file is deeply nested in a temporary folder. The following steps provide a quick alternative to viewing the generated source code:

1.   Enable debugging by setting the *Debug* attribute of the *Page* directive to *true* in the .aspx file:

     ```
     <%@ Page Debug="true" %>
     ```

2.   Introduce a syntax error (such as an unbalanced parenthesis or a missing semicolon statement terminator) in your code inside a server-side script block in your page, and save the file.

3.   Request the page in your Web browser. The server will return an error message that contains various links at the bottom of the page.

4.   Click the Show Complete Compilation Source link. This displays the autogenerated code for your page.

You don't necessarily need to study and understand the generated code to use ASP.NET or develop server controls. However, you might find it useful to examine the code to understand the creation of the control tree. It can be useful to view the parser-generated source code for the page when debugging your application or controls.

ASP.NET Pages in a Visual Designer

The declarative syntax of ASP.NET pages greatly simplifies the development of Web applications and complements the efficient execution model. In addition, server controls have rich design-time support in visual designers such as Visual Studio .NET, which further simplifies the design and authoring of ASP.NET pages.

Visual Studio .NET features a rich design-time environment that allows the page developer to start using ASP.NET quickly and brings together other aspects of Web application development, such as data access and site management.

Figures 2-5 and 2-6 illustrate various features of the Visual Studio .NET integrated development environment (IDE) that come into play in designing the user interface of .aspx pages and developing the code-behind files associated with pages.

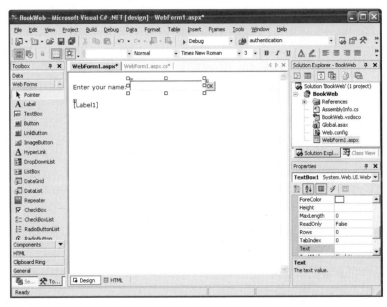

Figure 2-5   The Visual Studio .NET IDE with the Web Forms designer in Design view

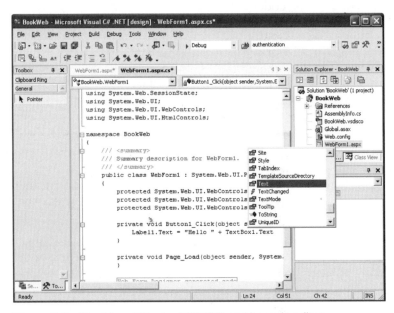

Figure 2-6   The Visual Studio .NET IDE and its code editor

Figure 2-5 shows the Visual Studio .NET Web Forms designer in Design view. In this view, the designer allows WYSIWYG editing of HTML content. It also creates instances of server controls as users add them to the page so that the controls participate in the design-time rendering of the page. The toolbox in the IDE provides a palette consisting of the standard ASP.NET controls and, optionally, any custom controls you develop for use while designing pages. The property browser presents the object model of the selected control and allows the page developer to customize its appearance and behavior by setting the control's properties. The designer also allows the page developer to associate event handlers with events raised by the server controls.

Figure 2-6 shows the code editor inside the Visual Studio .NET IDE. The code editor allows the page developer to implement code to handle events raised by server controls and other pieces of logic that make up the Web application. The source editor includes many features designed to enhance developer productivity, including IntelliSense functionality such as statement completion, auto-formatting, and syntax checking.

Summary

Server controls play a crucial role in the ASP.NET page framework and are responsible for the programming model referred to as Web Forms—a radically simple, high-performance Web user interface development technology. Part II of this book, "Server Controls—First Steps," provides an overview of control authoring. Part III delves deeper into the control architecture and the technical aspects of writing controls and provides detailed explanations that are illustrated with sample controls. And Part V of this book, "Server Control Case Studies," presents several real-world controls, along with their complete source code.

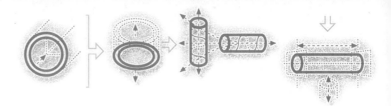

3

Component Programming Overview

Components are the building blocks of software applications. A component encapsulates state and execution logic and can be reused in different applications. Components make applications modular, easier to develop, and easier to maintain. The .NET Framework class library contains a large number of components that you can readily use in your applications. In addition, the .NET Framework enables you to write components that can interact seamlessly with other .NET components. In this book, we will develop several kinds of .NET components, including ASP.NET server controls, XML Web services, and HTTP handlers.

In this chapter, we will discuss the main characteristics of .NET components and describe the common constructs that you will encounter when developing your own components: properties, methods, events, and metadata attributes. Unless you are already proficient in using these constructs in managed code, we encourage you to read this chapter to familiarize yourself with the design patterns for these constructs. However, if this chapter feels as though it contains a lot of terminology and guidelines, you can browse through it and return to this chapter for a more detailed look at these programming constructs after you start using them.

The components that you develop should be consistent with the components in the .NET Framework, especially if you plan to distribute them in the form of a class library. The white paper on MSDN entitled ".NET Framework Design Guidelines—Writing Class Libraries for the .NET Framework," contains the recommendations of the .NET Framework team. You can also use a tool named FxCop to check your components for compliance with the .NET Framework design guidelines. The Introduction of this book contains a brief description of FxCop and provides the location from which you can download this tool.

Managed Component Overview

If you have developed COM or ActiveX components, you will find managed components significantly easier to develop. Managed components execute on top of the common language runtime (CLR) and automatically benefit from CLR features such as language interoperability, automatic memory management, and code access security. In addition, managed components have a simpler deployment model and are easier to version. Because the CLR provides low-level plumbing for managed components, you can focus on designing and implementing the real functionality of your components.

Authoring a managed component is no different from writing a class in a programming language that targets the CLR. Unlike COM components written in C++, you do not have to do any additional work to convert a class into a component.

When developing managed components, you need to be aware of a few basic programming constructs and follow a few simple guidelines. The following list contains a high-level summary of the guidelines that you should follow when designing and implementing a component.

- Author your component in a programming language that targets the CLR, such as C# or Microsoft Visual Basic .NET.

- Expose an object model that consists of properties, methods, and events. You do not have to expose all these constructs, but the public and protected members of a component should correspond to these constructs. In addition, you can describe your component's members through metadata attributes. We'll describe these programming constructs in more detail later in this chapter.

■ Expose members that are compliant with the common language specification (CLS) to ensure that your component is usable from other programming languages that target the CLR. The CLS is a subset of programming features that are common to all languages targeting the CLR.

■ Make sure that your component conforms to .NET Framework design guidelines. These guidelines include naming conventions and implementation patterns. By conforming to the design guidelines, you will ensure that your component interoperates seamlessly with classes in the .NET Framework and provides a similar developer experience.

■ To get the full benefit of the designer architecture in the .NET Framework, implement the *IComponent* interface or derive from a class such as *System.ComponentModel.Component* that implements this interface. We'll discuss design-time functionality in detail in Chapter 15, "Design-Time Functionality."

■ Deploy your managed component as part of a class library in an assembly (managed library). We'll discuss deployment in Chapter 17, "Localization, Licensing, and Other Miscellany."

Next we'll look at the main constructs in component programming—properties, methods, events, and metadata attributes.

Properties

Properties encapsulate the state of a component and are the essence of rapid application development (RAD). They allow users to customize components in a design-time environment. The property construct has been supported in Visual Basic for several editions but is not offered by object-oriented programming languages such as C++ and Java. (Properties in JavaBeans are supported indirectly by adherence to a naming convention for accessor methods.) The .NET Framework brings the ease of RAD programming to the object-oriented world by supporting properties as a first-class object-oriented programming construct.

We'll look at the property construct first. Then we'll look at naming guidelines for properties and the advantages of exposing properties.

The Property Construct

Properties are like smart fields that are accessed using fieldlike syntax but implemented using accessor methods. The following example illustrates a simple property construct that defines a *Name* public property in the *Person* class:

```
public class Person {
    ⋮
    // The private field below is not part of the property
    // construct but contains data that holds the value of
    // the Name property.
    private string _name;

    public string Name {
        get {
            return _name;
        }
        set {
            _name = value;
        }
    }
    ⋮
}
```

The boldface elements—*get*, *set*, and *value*—are keywords in the C# property syntax. The compiler transforms the code in the *get* and *set* blocks into methods that are called *property accessors*. The *get* accessor—also called the *getter*—retrieves the value of the property, while the *set* accessor—also called the *setter*—assigns a value to the property. The *value* identifier denotes the implicit parameter that is passed into the setter.

C# does not have a keyword named *property*. However, Visual Basic .NET does use the *Property* keyword as shown in the following example, which shows the keywords in Visual Basic .NET property syntax in boldface:

```
Private String _name

Public Property Name() As String
    Get
        Return _name
    End Get
    Set (ByVal value As String)
        _name = value
    End Set
End Property
```

In contrast with C#, *value* in Visual Basic .NET is not a keyword in property syntax.

Although the *get* and *set* accessors are equivalent to methods, they cannot be invoked as methods in C# and Visual Basic .NET but are indirectly accessed by code that assigns or retrieves a property.

The syntax for *setting* a property is the same as that for setting a field. When you are setting a property, the assigned value must match the declared type of the property:

```
Person aPerson = new Person();
aPerson.Name = "John"; //Type of Name is string.
```

The property construct allows you to abstract the storage and implementation of a property from the clients of your component. In our example, a private field holds the data for the *Name* property. While the backing data for a property is often a private field, the data could reside elsewhere—for example, on disk or in a database—or it could be generated dynamically, as in a property that returns the system time.

A property can define both the *get* and *set* accessors or just a single accessor. A property with only a *get* accessor is a read-only property, while a property with only a *set* accessor is a write-only property. Although the CLR allows write-only properties, the design guidelines for the .NET Framework discourage them. If your component needs a write-only property, you should implement a method instead of a property to provide the equivalent functionality.

A property can have any access level allowed by the runtime, including public, private, protected, or internal. In C# and Visual Basic .NET, the access level of a property applies to both accessors; it is not possible to have a different access level for each accessor.

Although the *get* and *set* accessors are not directly accessible as methods, they are semantically equivalent to methods. Furthermore, they can perform any program logic, be overridden, and throw exceptions. In the next two sections, we'll show you how to override a property and perform value checking in a property accessor.

Virtual Properties

You generally provide *virtual* (overridable) properties to allow derived classes to narrow the range of permissible values, alter associated metadata, or perform additional logic when the value of the property changes.

To make a property overridable, you must mark it with the *virtual* keyword in C#—and the *Overridable* keyword in Visual Basic .NET—in the class in which the property is first declared. Here's a C# example:

```
public class AnyInteger {
    private int _number;
```

```
    public virtual int Number {
        get {
            return _number;
        }
        set {
            _number = value;
        }
    }
    ⋮
}
```

Here's a Visual Basic .NET example:

```
Public Class AnyInteger
    Private _number As Integer

    Public Overridable Property Number() As Integer
        Get
            Return _number
        End Get
        Set (ByVal value As Integer)
            _number = value
        End Set
    End Property
    ⋮
End Class 'AnyInteger
```

Overriding a property is similar to overriding a method. To override a property in a derived class, mark the property with the *override* keyword in C# and the *Overrides* keyword in Visual Basic .NET. Here's a C# example:

```
public class NonNegativeInteger : AnyInteger {
    public override int Number {
        get {
            return base.Number;
        }
        set {
            if (value < 0) {
                throw new ArgumentOutOfRangeException(
                    "The number cannot be less than 0.");
            }
            base.Number = value;
        }
    }
    ⋮
}
```

And here's a Visual Basic .NET example:

```
Public Class NonNegativeInteger
    Inherits AnyInteger

    Public Overrides Property Number() As Integer
        Get
            Return MyBase.Number
        End Get
        Set (ByVal value As Integer)
            If value < 0 Then
                Throw New ArgumentOutOfRangeException( _
                "The number cannot be less than 0.")
            End If
            MyBase.Number = value
        End Set
    End Property
    ⋮
End Class 'PositiveInteger
```

If both property accessors are defined in the base class, you must override both accessors when overriding a property. If you want to override the logic in only one of the accessors, you can let the other accessor delegate to the base class, as the getter for the *Number* property does in the previous example.

Although *virtual* properties make it easier to extend your component, you should keep a few considerations in mind when you define virtual properties. A *virtual* property cannot be sealed (made nonoverridable) in a derived class. *Virtual* properties also have implications for versioning. Once you define a *virtual* property, you must mark the property as *virtual* in later versions of your component; otherwise, you could break existing derived classes.

Properties and Validation

Property accessors can perform error checking (validation) in addition to getting or setting a property. If a property value is not acceptable, an accessor should throw an exception. In the previous example, we saw a property whose setter throws an *ArgumentOutOfRangeException* exception when the value assigned to the property is not a positive integer.

A well-designed component should perform argument validation in its property setters. When a setter throws an exception, it flags an erroneous property assignment as soon as it is made. This helps identify the location in user code where the error occurred. If your setter accepts erroneous values, there could be undesirable side effects during program execution when the erroneous value of the property adversely affects the behavior of your component. If a property does not throw exceptions, it is much harder for the user of your component to debug and track the cause of the unexpected behavior.

The .NET Framework class library provides a number of exception types, such as *ArgumentException*, *ArgumentNullException*, and *ArgumentOutOfRangeException*. You should use the most appropriate exception type, along with meaningful error messages.

Naming Guidelines for Properties

To ensure that your naming scheme for properties conforms to that of the .NET Framework, follow these naming guidelines:

- Use a noun or a noun phrase as a property name—for example, *Count*, *Font*, or *Size*.

- Use Pascal casing. In other words, capitalize the first letter of the property name and the first letter of each subsequent word in the name—for example, *MinimumLevel* and *ViewState*.

Advantages of Properties

It is standard object-oriented practice to encapsulate your component's data. Therefore, it should come as no surprise that we recommend that you should not expose fields from your components but instead expose properties. Properties offer many benefits over fields:

- **Data hiding**   The storage and implementation of properties, unlike that of fields, is invisible to the user.

- **Validation**   The setter can perform logic to check whether the assigned value satisfies any constraints that are required by your program logic. This also enables better error tracking. You cannot implement validation when using a field.

- **Overriding**   Properties can be overriden, thus allowing a derived class to alter the property implementation of the base class.

- **Versioning**   Because the implementation of a property is hidden from the user, you can modify the implementation in future versions without breaking compatibility—that is, without requiring any changes to user code.

- **Designer support**   When a user selects a component on the design surface of a visual designer, the component's properties are displayed in the property browser, but its fields are not. We'll look at design-time support in Chapter 15.

- **Data binding**   The data-binding architecture in ASP.NET and Windows Forms supports binding to properties but not to fields. We'll discuss data binding in Chapter 16, "Data-Bound Controls."

In general, because of just-in-time (JIT) optimizations, properties are no less performant than fields—as long as the accessors get or set an underlying field without adding a significant amount of new logic.

In this section, we covered general concepts related to the property construct in the .NET Framework. In Chapter 7, "Simple Properties and View State," and Chapter 10, "Complex Properties and State Management," we'll discuss details specific to properties in ASP.NET controls. We'll also show you how to implement different types of properties, such as primitive, reference, and collection properties.

In general, you should implement properties to represent state (data). However, in some situations, you should implement methods instead of properties, as we'll describe in the next section.

Methods

Not much is significantly different between methods in the managed world and methods in the unmanaged world. The most notable points are the following:

- Determining when you should implement a method instead of a property

- Naming conventions for method names and method parameter names

Implementing Methods Instead of Properties

In general, methods represent actions and properties represent data. However, in some situations, it is not appropriate to implement properties. Because property accessors are equivalent to methods, you should instead implement methods in those situations. Here are some examples:

- If a property accessor has observable side effects, implement a method instead of a property.

- If the implementation of a property is considerably more expensive than that of a field, implement a method instead. When you expose a property, you suggest to users that making frequent calls to it is acceptable. When you implement a method, you suggest to users that they should save and reuse a returned value if they repeatedly need it.

■ If some properties require a user to set them in a predefined order, implement those properties as methods. In general, you should design your components so that properties can be set in any order.

■ If you need a write-only property, implement a method instead.

Examples of these cases and additional ones appear in the white paper ".NET Framework Design Guidelines—Writing Class Libraries for the .NET Framework," on MSDN.

Naming Guidelines for Methods and Method Parameters

To ensure that your naming scheme for methods conforms to that of the .NET Framework, follow these guidelines:

■ Use method names that consist of verbs or verb phrases that indicate the task accomplished—for example, *Add*, *Dispose*, and *Verify*.

■ Use Pascal casing for method names—for example, *CreateChildControls* and *SaveViewState*.

You should also follow the .NET Framework naming guidelines for parameter names. It is imperative to follow the guidelines for method parameter names because parameters are displayed in the designer when visual design tools provide context-sensitive IntelliSense and class-browsing functionality. These are the guidelines:

■ Use descriptive parameter names. They should be descriptive enough so that, in most scenarios, the parameter name and type are sufficient to determine the parameter's meaning. Descriptive parameter names provide valuable information to the user.

■ Use camel casing for parameter names. This means using lowercase for the first word in the parameter name and capitalizing the first letter of each subsequent word in the name—for example, *level*, *minimumLevel*, and *maxHits*.

■ Use a name based on the parameter meaning rather than its type. For example, if a parameter is of type integer, a name such as *count* is much more informative than a name such as *int*.

■ Do not prefix parameter names with Hungarian notation.

Events

An event is a message or notification sent by a class to signal the occurrence of an action or a change in its state. The occurrence or change in state could be initiated by a user interface action, such as when a user clicks a button, or caused by some other program logic, such as when a method finishes reading records from a database. The class that raises the event (sends the notification) is called the *event source* or *sender*, and the class that receives the event is called the *event sink* or *receiver*. Event-based architecture uses the publish-subscribe model in which the source (or publisher) of an event allows its users (or subscribers) to specify logic that is executed when the event occurs.

In general, the event source does not know its subscribers ahead of time and does not know the logic that its subscribers would want to implement. Event-based programming thus requires an intermediary mechanism that connects the source and the receiver. In programming terms, event architecture needs some sort of callback mechanism. In C++, callbacks are implemented using function pointers; in Java, they are implemented using interfaces. The .NET Framework provides a new construct—called a *delegate*—to provide the functionality of a callback.

Delegates combine the best of the earlier paradigms. A delegate has the granularity of a function pointer and the type safety of an interface. In effect, a delegate is equivalent to a type-safe function pointer. And that is not all. A delegate also holds a linked list of other delegates, which is very useful for multicasting events (sending an event to multiple subscribers). Let's take at look at the delegate construct next and then examine how delegates are used in the event architecture of the .NET Framework.

Delegates

A delegate in the .NET Framework is a class that can hold a reference to a static or instance method of a class. The signature of the method must match the signature of the delegate. To understand this, let's begin with a declaration of a delegate class. The following line of code contains the declaration of a delegate named *MyDelegate* that can refer (bind) to only those methods that have a void return type and take one argument of type integer:

```
public delegate void MyDelegate(int number);
```

Before we see how to bind a delegate to a method, let's look at the delegate declaration more closely. A delegate declaration is similar to a method declaration, with the addition of the *delegate* keyword. However, a delegate is not a method—it is a class with its own methods and other members. You do not provide the implementation for a delegate class; the delegate declaration causes the compiler to generate a class that derives from *System.MulticastDelegate*. For example, using our earlier declaration, the compiler generates a *MyDelegate* class that derives from *System.MulticastDelegate*. If you want to see the compiler-generated class, you can use the ILDASM disassembler tool that ships with the .NET Framework SDK. The tool is briefly described in the Introduction of this book.

System.MulticastDelegate is the base class for delegates in the .NET Framework. *MulticastDelegate* derives from the *System.Delegate* class. Delegate types in the .NET Framework class library do not derive directly from *Delegate*—they derive from *MulticastDelegate*, which inherits from *Delegate* the functionality to bind a delegate to a method. *MulticastDelegate* also contains a linked list of delegates—called the *invocation list*—from which it can add or and remove delegates. When an instance of *MulticastDelegate* is invoked, it sequentially invokes the delegates in its invocation list.

You should not define a delegate by deriving from *MulticastDelegate* yourself. Only language compilers and the runtime are intended to generate types that derive from *MulticastDelegate*. To define a delegate in C# or Visual Basic, specify the *delegate* keyword and provide a class name and signature, as shown in our definition of *MyDelegate*.

To see delegates in action, let's look at an example. In the code, we'll define a delegate, a class that exposes a property of the delegate type, and a class that binds the delegate to a method. Let's look at the code first and then discuss what the sample does. The delegate-related code is boldface in Listing 3-1:

```
using System;

namespace MSPress.DelegateSample {

    public delegate void PrintCallback(int number);

    public class Printer {

        private PrintCallback _print;

        public PrintCallback PrintCallback {
            get {
                return _print;
            }
```

Listing 3-1   A delegate used as a callback   *(continued)*

Listing 3-1 *(continued)*

```
        set {
            _print = value;
        }
    }
}

public class Driver {
    private void PrintInteger(int number) {
        Console.WriteLine(
            "From PrintInteger: The number is {0}.", number);
    }

    static void Main(string[] args) {
        Driver driver = new Driver();
        Printer printer = new Printer();
        printer.PrintCallback = new PrintCallback(driver.PrintInteger);
        printer.PrintCallback(10);
        printer.PrintCallback(100);
        Console.WriteLine("Press Enter to exit...");
        Console.ReadLine();
    }
}
```

If you compile and execute the sample, the output should look like this:

```
From PrintInteger: The number is 10.
From PrintInteger: The number is 100.
Press Enter to exit...
```

Here's what the sample does: It defines a delegate named *PrintCallback* that has a return type *void* and accepts a single parameter of type *integer*. The *Printer* class has a delegate property, *PrintCallback*, of type *PrintCallback*. The *Driver* class defines a *PrintInteger* method that has the same signature as *Print-Callback*. In its *Main* method, the *Driver* class binds the *PrintCallback* delegate of its *Printer* instance to its *PrintInteger* method. Now, whenever the *PrintCall-back* delegate is invoked, the method it binds to—*PrintInteger*—is executed.

We would like to make one minor point about the delegate constructor. If you look at the constructor of the *System.MulticastDelegate* class, you will see that it takes two parameters. But we have supplied only one parameter in our delegate constructor: *new PrintCallback(driver.PrintInteger)*. The reason for this difference is that the other parameter is implicit and points to the object that contains the callback method. The C# and Visual Basic .NET compilers use the implicit parameter and the supplied parameter to create the two-parameter con-structor the runtime needs. The two-parameter constructor is intended for com-pilers and other tools. You should always use the one-parameter constructor in your code, as we showed in the sample. If the method you are binding to is a static method (instead of an instance method), use the class name instead of the class instance name in the constructor. For example, if the *PrintInteger* method were a static method, you would instantiate the delegate as *new PrintCallback(Driver.PrintInteger)*.

That completes our quick tour of delegates. Delegates have more features than we have covered, but the background we've provided should be adequate for using them in event programming.

Event Delegates

Now that you have seen how delegates work, it is easy to understand how they are used in event programming. In essence, a class that wants to raise an event (send notifications) has a delegate member. A class that wants to receive the event provides a method that performs some logic in response to the event (an event-handler method). The receiver—or some other class—then binds the event handler to a delegate and adds that delegate to the invocation list of the event source. To raise an event, the event source invokes its delegate, which in turn invokes the delegates in its invocation list. Those delegates in turn invoke the handlers they are bound to, thus completing the event sequence. The .NET Framework event model is elegant, powerful, and easy to implement. We'll soon translate this high-level overview into concrete implementation details, but first let's take a look at event delegates, which are at the core of this event model.

Event delegates in the .NET Framework follow a certain convention for their signature and their naming scheme. This convention is relied upon by visual design tools and provides a consistent pattern for client code. To understand the convention, let's look at a commonly accessed event delegate in the .NET Framework, *System.EventHandler*:

```
public delegate void EventHandler(object sender, EventArgs e);
```

The signature of an event delegate in the .NET Framework is analogous to that of the *EventHandler* delegate. These are the specifics of the signature convention:

- The return type of an event delegate is *void*.

- An event delegate takes two arguments. The first argument—of type *Object*—represents the sender of the event. The second argument represents data for the event and is an instance of a class that derives from *System.EventArgs*.

To interoperate with the .NET Framework and for your component to work in a visual designer, you must follow the signature convention for any event delegates that you define. Notice that the signature convention is not limiting; you can include any data that you want to provide for your event in the event data class.

Classes that hold event data go hand in hand with event delegates. The base class *EventArgs* does not hold any event data. Its corresponding event delegate, *EventHandler*, is used for events that do not have associated data, such as the *Click* event of the *System.Web.UI.WebControls.Button* server control. An example of a class that holds event data is *System.Web.UI.ImageClickEventArgs*, which holds x and y coordinates for the *Click* event of the *System.Web.UI.Web-Controls.ImageButton* server control. Its associated event delegate is *System.Web.UI.ImageClickEventHandler*. Many namespaces in the .NET Framework contain event data classes and event delegates.

You should follow the .NET Framework convention for naming event data classes and event delegates. Event data classes are given the name of the event, appended by the suffix *EventArgs*, such as *MonthChangedEventArgs*. Event delegates are given names that consist of the event name, appended by the suffix *EventHandler*, such as *MonthChangedEventHandler*. Event delegates are named event handlers because they bind to methods that handle events.

Wiring Events

For completeness, we'll briefly describe the syntax for attaching an event handler to an event. (In this book, we'll focus on showing you how to raise events from your components and assume that you are familiar with handling events in ASP.NET pages or in other .NET applications.)

The process of associating an event handler with an event (adding a delegate to the invocation list) is called *event wiring*, while that of removing an event handler from an event (removing a delegate from the invocation list) is called *event unwiring*. In C#, the syntax for wiring and unwiring an event handler to an event looks like this:

```
button.Click += new EventHandler(this.Button_Clicked);
button.Click -= new EventHandler(this.Button_Clicked);
```

In the preceding code fragment, *button* is an instance of the *Button* control and is created in a class that has a *Button_Clicked* method that handles the button's *Click* event.

In Visual Basic .NET, event wiring and unwiring syntax looks like this:

```
AddHandler button.Click, AddressOf Me.Button_Clicked
RemoveHandler button.Click, AddressOf Me.Button_Clicked
```

The declarative syntax of ASP.NET pages hides much of the event architecture from the page developer. However, the underlying event mechanism in

ASP.NET is no different from the rest of the .NET Framework. We'll discuss events in ASP.NET server controls in detail in Chapter 9, "Control Life Cycle, Events, and Postback."

Raising an Event

In this section, we'll walk you through the .NET Framework design pattern for raising an event from your class. In the next section, we'll show a complete sample that demonstrates these steps. The sample files contain the sample in C# and in Visual Basic .NET.

To implement an event in your class, you need a class for event data, an event delegate, a delegate member in your class that holds the invocation list, and a method that sends the event notification. The actual implementation of an event is relatively straightforward—the major effort is in understanding how the pieces fit together. Here's a high-level overview of the steps that you have to perform. We'll elaborate on these steps in the next section.

1. If your class does not have any associated event data, use the *Event-Args* class for event data. Or you can use another preexisting event data class if it matches your event. If a suitable event data class does not exist, define a class to hold event data. This class must derive from *System.EventArgs* and, by convention, its name should be the name of the event appended by *EventArgs*—such as *AdCreatedEvent-Args*, *CommandEventArgs*, or *MonthChangedEventArgs*. The following code fragment declares an event data class:

   ```
   public class LowChargeEventArgs : EventArgs {...}
   ```

2. If your event does not have associated data and you used *EventArgs* in step 1, use *System.EventHandler* as your event delegate. Or you can use another preexisting delegate if it matches your event. If a suitable event delegate does not exist, define an event delegate whose second argument has the type of the event data class from step 1. By convention, the name of the event delegate is the name of the event appended by *EventHandler*—such as *AdCreatedEvent-Handler*, *CommandEventHandler*, or *MonthChangedEventHandler*. The following code defines an event delegate:

   ```
   public delegate void LowChargeEventHandler(object sender,
       LowChargeEventArgs e);
   ```

3. In your class, define an event member using the *event* keyword. Give the event member the name of your event. The type of this member is the event delegate you used in step 2. Here's an example:

```
public event LowChargeEventHandler LowCharge;
```

The event member holds the list of delegates that subscribe to the event. When this member is invoked, it dispatches the event by invoking the delegates.

4.   In your class, define a virtual (overridable) method that invokes the event delegate—after checking whether any event listeners exist. The name of this method contains the event name prefixed by *On*. Here's an example:

```
protected virtual void OnLowCharge(LowChargeEventArgs e) {
    if (LowCharge != null) {
        LowCharge(this, e);
    }
}
```

The purpose of the *On<EventName>* method is to allow classes that derive from your class to handle the event without attaching an event handler to themselves.

Note that the first two steps in the list describe classes that generally exist outside your class (defined by you, or in the .NET Framework or third party class library), while the next two steps are implemented in your class. Here's the skeleton of a class that implements the *LowCharge* event we just described:

```
public class Battery {
    ⋮
    public event LowChargeEventHandler LowCharge;
    protected virtual void OnLowCharge(LowChargeEventArgs e) {
        if (LowCharge != null) {
            LowCharge(this, e);
        }
    }
}
```

As you can see, you have to write very little code to implement an event. When the C# or Visual Basic .NET compiler sees a member marked with the *event* keyword, it automatically generates the three members shown in the following code. (You can see these members by using the ILDASM tool described in the Introduction of this book.)

■   A private field of the same type as the event delegate, such as the following:

```
private LowChargeEventHandler LowCharge = null;
```

- A method that adds delegates to the event delegate, such as the following:

```
// The access level of this method is the same as that of
// the event member.
public void Add_LowCharge(LowChargeEventHandler handler) {
    LowCharge =
        (LowChargeEventHandler)Delegate.Combine(LowCharge, handler);
}
```

- A method that removes delegates from the event delegate, such as the following:

```
// The access level of this method is the same as that of
// the event member.
public void Remove_LowCharge(LowChargeEventHandler handler) {
    LowCharge =
        (LowChargeEventHandler)Delegate.Remove(LowCharge, handler);
}
```

The two methods generated by the compiler are event accessors that enable a user to attach or remove event handlers to or from your event. The access level of the compiler-generated methods is the same as the access level of the event member. However, even when the compiler-generated methods are public, they are not directly accessible from client code in C# and Visual Basic .NET. A user must wire and unwire handlers using the += and −= syntax in C# and the *AddHandler* and *RemoveHandler* syntax in Visual Basic .NET, as we showed earlier.

When a class raises a large number of events, it might not be efficient to allocate one delegate field per event, especially when only a few of the events are commonly handled. This is because each delegate field contributes memory overhead to the class instance, regardless of whether any event handlers are wired to the associated event. For such situations, the .NET Framework provides a utility class, *System.ComponentModel.EventHandlerList*, which provides a more optimal storage mechanism for event delegates. In Chapter 9, we will describe how to use this utility class to implement step 3 in the numbered list at the beginning of this section.

Event Sample

In this sample, we'll put together the steps we described in the preceding discussion. We'll define a *Battery* class that raises two events—*LowCharge* and *Depleted*. Later we'll complete the sample with a *LapTop* class that contains a *Battery* instance and provides event-handling methods that are wired to the *Battery* instance.

Here are the event-related features of the *Battery* class:

■   The *Battery* class defines event members named *LowCharge* and *Depleted*.

■   The *LowCharge* event uses the *LowChargeEventArgs* class for event data and the *LowChargeEventHandler* class as the event delegate. The *LowChargeEventArgs* and *LowChargeEventHandler* classes are also defined in the sample. The event data in *LowChargeEventArgs* represents the charge level of the battery.

■   The *Depleted* event does not carry any data and uses the *EventArgs* class for event data and the *EventHandler* class as the event delegate.

■   The *Battery* class defines the *OnLowCharge* and *OnDepleted* methods, which raise the *LowCharge* and *Depleted* events.

The *Battery* class raises both its events in the set accessor of its *CurrentLevel* property by invoking the *OnLowCharge* and the *OnDepleted* methods.

Listings 3-2, 3-3, and 3-4 show the complete code for the sample. The event-related constructs are boldface in the code listings.

```
using System;
using System.ComponentModel;

namespace MSPress.EventSample {
    // Class that holds data for the LowCharge event.
    public class LowChargeEventArgs : EventArgs {

        private double _level;
        public LowChargeEventArgs (double batteryLevel) {
            _level = batteryLevel;
        }

        public double Level {
            get {
                return _level;
            }
        }
    }
}
```

Listing 3-2   LowChargeEventArgs.cs

```
namespace MSPress.EventSample {
    // Delegate for the LowCharge event.
    public delegate void LowChargeEventHandler(object sender,
        LowChargeEventArgs e);
}
```

Listing 3-3   LowChargeEventHandler.cs

```
using System;
using System.ComponentModel;

namespace MSPress.EventSample {

    // Class that raises events.
    public class Battery {

        private const double DepletedLevel = 0.05;
        private double _currentLevel;
        private double _minimumLevel;

        // Event members.
        public event LowChargeEventHandler LowCharge;
        public event EventHandler Depleted;

        public Battery() : this(1.0, 0.15) { }

        public Battery(double currentLevel, double minimumLevel) {
            _currentLevel = currentLevel;
            _minimumLevel = minimumLevel;
        }

        public double CurrentLevel {
            get {
                return _currentLevel;
            }
            set {
                if (value < 0.0 || value > 1.0) {
                    throw new ArgumentOutOfRangeException("value",
                        value,
                        "CurrentLevel must be between 0.0 and 1.0.");
                }

                _currentLevel = value;
                if (_currentLevel > DepletedLevel &&
                    _currentLevel < MinimumLevel) {
                    LowChargeEventArgs e =
```

Listing 3-4   Battery.cs

Listing 3-4   *(continued)*

```
                        new LowChargeEventArgs(_currentLevel);
            OnLowCharge(e);
        }
        else if (_currentLevel > 0.0 &&
            _currentLevel <= DepletedLevel) {
            OnDepleted(EventArgs.Empty);
        }
    }
}


public double MinimumLevel {
    get {
        return _minimumLevel;
    }
    set {
        if (value <= DepletedLevel || value > 0.5) {
            throw new ArgumentOutOfRangeException("value",
                value, String.Format("MinimumLevel must be " +
                "greater than {0:F2} and less than 0.5.",
                DepletedLevel));                          }
        _minimumLevel = value;
    }
}


// Raises the LowCharge event.
protected virtual void OnLowCharge(LowChargeEventArgs e) {
    if (LowCharge != null) {
        LowCharge(this, e);
    }
}


// Raises the Depleted event.
protected virtual void OnDepleted (EventArgs e) {
    if (Depleted != null) {
        Depleted(this, e);
    }
}
    }
}
```

The following example performs a simulation that drains the battery in a laptop. The battery raises events in response to changes in its charge level. Those events are handled by the laptop. The example defines a class named *LapTop*, which contains a *Battery* instance and defines handlers that perform logic in response to the events raised by the *Battery* class. *LapTop* wires its event handlers to the events of its *Battery* instance using event delegates.

Notice that the *Battery* class (shown in Listing 3-4) does not implement any logic to handle its *LowCharge* or *Depleted* events. The logic to handle those events is supplied by the *LapTop* class in its event handlers: *Battery_LowCharge* and *Battery_Depleted*. The event handlers and the event wiring code are boldface in the *LapTop* source code, shown in Listing 3-5.

```
using System;
using System.ComponentModel;
using System.Threading;

namespace MSPress.EventSample {
    public class LapTop {

        private Battery _battery;

        public LapTop() {
            _battery = new Battery();
            _battery.LowCharge +=
                new LowChargeEventHandler(this.Battery_LowCharge);
            _battery.Depleted +=
                new EventHandler(this.Battery_Depleted);
        }

        private void Battery_LowCharge(object sender,
            LowChargeEventArgs e) {
            Console.WriteLine(
                "Battery is low, {0:F2} percent charged.",
                e.Level * 100.0);
            Console.WriteLine("Save your work!!");
        }

        private void Battery_Depleted (object sender, EventArgs e) {
            Console.WriteLine("Battery is out of juice!!!");
            Console.WriteLine("Powering down in 30 seconds...");
        }

        public void Start() {
            do {
                double newLevel = _battery.CurrentLevel - 0.05;
                if (newLevel < 0.0)
                    _battery.CurrentLevel = 0.0;
                else
                    _battery.CurrentLevel = newLevel;
                Thread.Sleep(50);
            } while(_battery.CurrentLevel > 0.0);
        }
```

Listing 3-5 LapTop.cs

Listing 3-5   *(continued)*

```
        public static void Main() {
            LapTop lapTop = new LapTop();
            lapTop.Start();
            Console.WriteLine("Press Enter to exit...");
            Console.ReadLine();
        }
    }
}
```

To build the sample, execute the following command from the directory containing the sample code:

```
csc /out:EventSample.exe /r:System.dll Battery.cs LapTop.cs
    LowChargeEventArgs.cs LowChargeEventHandler.cs
```

When you run EventSample.exe, you should see output similar to the following listing:

```
Battery is low, 15.00 percent charged.
Save your work!!
Battery is low, 10.00 percent charged.
Save your work!!
Battery is out of juice!!!
Powering down in 30 seconds...
Press Enter to exit...
```

For this sample, we intentionally chose a scenario that does not involve ASP.NET controls or, for that matter, any user interface classes because we wanted to emphasize that the main elements of the .NET Framework event pattern are the same across the .NET Framework. In Chapter 9, where we describe events in ASP.NET server controls, you'll see that the underlying event pattern in server controls is the same as in the sample described here.

Metadata Attributes

The .NET Framework attribute construct allows you to supply metadata for your component and its members. The information contained in the metadata attribute is queried using reflection by the runtime or by design-time tools.

Let's look at the syntax for the attribute construct. In the following example, the decoration (shown in square brackets in C#, and in angle brackets in Visual Basic .NET) is an instance of the attribute class *System.Component-Model.BrowsableAttribute. BrowsableAttribute* is a design-time metadata attribute that tells the designer whether or not to display a property in the property browser.

Here's the C# example:

```
[Browsable(false)]
public int Hits {...}
```

Here's a Visual Basic .NET example:

```
<Browsable(false)> Public Hits As Integer
```

By convention, attribute class names end with the *Attribute* suffix, such as *BrowsableAttribute*, *DefaultValueAttribute*, *DesignerAttribute*, and *ParseChildren-Attribute*. In C# and Visual Basic .NET, the *Attribute* suffix is implied and can be omitted from the name of the attribute class when applying an attribute. For example, *Browsable*(false) is equivalent to *BrowsableAttribute*(false).

When programming server controls, you will work with the set of attribute classes that are listed in Appendix A, "Metadata Attributes." Server controls are marked with both design-time and run-time attributes. Run-time attributes (such as *ParseChildrenAttribute*) are essential for the functioning of an ASP.NET control during a request/response cycle, while design-time attributes (such as *BrowsableAttribute* and *DesignerAttribute*) enhance the design-time appearance and behavior of a control in a visual design tool. We will explain specific attributes in greater detail in context wherever they are applied.

Applying Attributes

Attributes in server controls are applied at the class level as well as to properties, methods, and events. Attributes can also be applied to an assembly. In Chapter 5, we'll show you how to apply the *System.Web.UI.TagPrefixAttribute* attribute to an assembly that contains server controls.

Class-Level Attributes

The following example applies a class-level design-time attribute named *DesignerAttribute* to the *MyControl* class. The *DesignerAttribute*, which we will describe in Chapter 15, enables you to associate classes called *designers* with your components. Designer classes govern the design-time appearance of your control.

Here's the C# version:

```
// Attribute that associates the designer class
// MSPress.ServerControls.Design.MyControlDesigner
// with MyControl.
[Designer(typeof(MSPress.ServerControls.Design.MyControlDesigner))]
public class MyControl : WebControl { //... }
```

And here's the Visual Basic .NET version:

```
' Attribute that associates the designer class
' MSPress.ServerControls.Design.MyControlDesigner
' with MyControl.
<Designer(GetType(MSPress.ServerControls.Design.MyControlDesigner))> _
Public Class MyControl
    Inherits WebControl
    ' ...
End Class
```

Property-Level and Event-Level Attributes

Here's a C# example that shows how to apply an attribute to a property:

```
// To apply CategoryAttribute to the MyBorderColor
// property, place it before the declaration
// of the MyBorderColor property.
[Category("Appearance")]
public Color MyBorderColor {...}
```

And here's a Visual Basic .NET example:

```
' To apply CategoryAttribute to the MyBorderColor
' property, place it before the property declaration.
<Category("Appearance")> Public MyBorderColor As Color
```

Attributes can be applied to event members in much the same way that they are to property members.

Here's a C# example that shows how to apply an attribute to an event:

```
// To apply DescriptionAttribute to the Click event,
// place it before the event declaration.
[Description("The Click event of the button")]
public event EventHandler Click;
```

And here's a Visual Basic .NET example:

```
' To apply DescriptionAttribute to the Click event,
' place it before the event declaration.
<Description("The Click event of the button")> Public Event Click
```

We will discuss design-time attributes in general in Chapter 15 and design-time attributes applied specifically to properties in Chapter 7 and Chapter 10.

Designable Components

The .NET Framework provides special support for components that are used in a visual designer. In this section, we'll provide a high-level overview of designable components in the .NET Framework.

In the .NET Framework, a *designable component* is a class that directly or indirectly derives from *System.ComponentModel.Component* or implements the *System.ComponentModel.IComponent* interface. The most significant features of a designable component are as follows:

- Design-time support

- Control over external resources

A designable component can be added to the toolbox of a designer such as Microsoft Visual Studio .NET. It can then be dragged and dropped onto a design surface, and, when selected, its properties will be automatically displayed in the property browser. This kind of designer support is not available to a class that does not derive from *Component* or implement the *IComponent* interface.

In Chapter 5, "Developing a Simple Custom Control," we will show you how to add a custom control to the toolbox in Visual Studio .NET. If you try to add a class that does not implement *IComponent*, the user interface to customize the toolbox will inform you that your assembly does not contain components that it can add to the toolbox.

Now let's examine how designable components control external resources. The *IComponent* interface derives from the *System.IDisposable* interface, which contains the *Dispose* method that gives a component a chance to free external resources or references that it holds. Although managed objects are automatically garbage collected, *IDisposable* allows a class to perform cleanup in a more deterministic manner. This cleanup is required when a class contains references to unmanaged resources that must be explicitly freed, such as database connections. We'll describe how to implement the *Dispose* method when we look at examples of components that need to free unmanaged resources.

Controls

In the .NET Framework, a *control* is a designable component that renders a user interface or facilitates the rendering of visual elements. The .NET Framework defines two base control classes:

- The base class for ASP.NET server controls is *System.Web.UI.Control*. This class implements the *IComponent* interface and renders markup text that is used by a client's browser or viewing device to render visual elements.

■   The base class for client-side Windows Forms controls is *System.Windows.Forms.Control*. This class derives from *System.ComponentModel.Component*, which implements the *IComponent* interface. *System.Windows.Forms.Control* is capable of drawing using GDI+).

Because this book is about server controls, we will not describe client-side Windows Forms controls in any detail. However, when we describe design-time support in Chapter 15, we will briefly look at a few Windows Forms controls because the designer for ASP.NET Web Forms uses Windows Forms controls for features that involve a design-time user interface.

Summary

In this chapter, we looked at the basic constructs that you'll use when implementing managed components—properties, events, methods, and metadata attributes. In the following chapters, you'll see these constructs used repeatedly as we develop server controls and components.

If you are developing a class library for distribution, we hope you read and follow the recommendations of the white paper ".NET Framework Design Guidelines—Writing Class Libraries for the .NET Framework." You can use the FxCop tool to check your components for compliance with the .NET Framework.

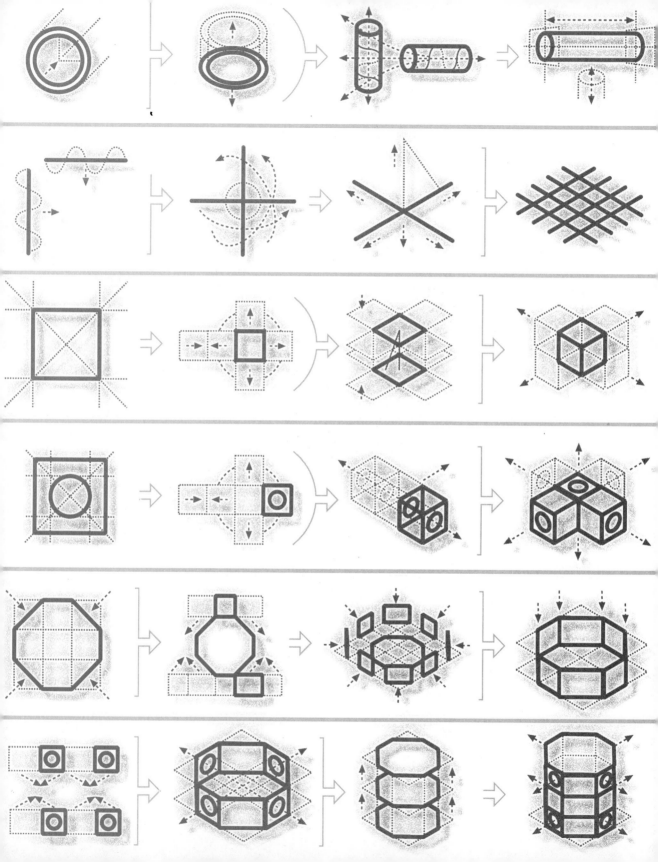

Part II

Server Controls— First Steps

Part II provides an introduction to the two models that ASP.NET provides for implementing server controls. It demonstrates declaratively authored user controls and programmatically authored compiled controls, and provides guidelines for choosing between the two control authoring models.

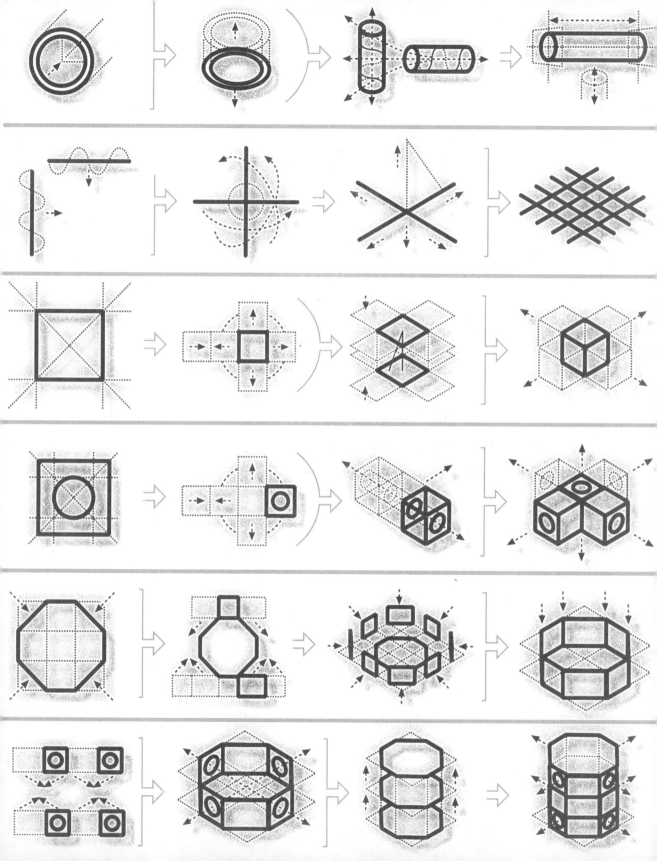

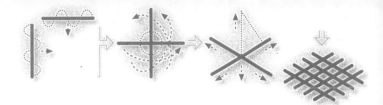

4

User Controls: From Page to Control

In this chapter, we will describe the user control model, show how to author a user control, and discuss the features of user controls. In Chapter 5, "Developing a Simple Custom Control," we will introduce the custom control model, and in Chapter 6, "Custom Controls vs. User Controls," we'll compare the two models to help you decide which one to use when developing your own ASP.NET server controls.

A user control is a server control that you author in the same WYSIWYG and declarative style as an ASP.NET page and save as a text file with an .ascx extension. You do not have to precompile a user control. When a user control is used in an .aspx page, the page parser dynamically generates a class from the

.ascx file and compiles it into an assembly (managed library). This combination of page-style authoring and no-compile deployment makes it easy to develop a user control.

User controls enable you to save common user interface (UI) portions of a page—such as headers, footers, and navigation bars—and to reuse them across an application. User controls also enable you to partition pages into smaller units, which simplifies the task of developing and maintaining pages.

User controls are a significantly better solution for UI reuse than *server-side includes*, the main reuse mechanism available in traditional Active Server Pages programming. A server-side include merely inserts inline text from an included file and is similar to file concatenation. A user control, on the other hand, is a class with its own object model that a page developer can program against. A user control has an added benefit: its programming language can differ from that of the containing page. This means user controls written in different programming languages can be used on a single page. A server-side include, on the other hand, must be written in the same language as the including page. (The user control model in Microsoft Visual Studio .NET is slightly different. A user control in Visual Studio .NET must be developed in the same language as its containing page and project.)

Converting a Page to a User Control

It is easiest to understand the user control model by converting a portion of an existing ASP.NET page into a user control. We'll start with a page that provides a simple user interface for entering data. We'll convert the portion of the user interface that contains a *TextBox* with an associated *RequiredFieldValidator* into a user control. Listing 4-1 shows in boldface the portion that we want to move into a reusable user control.

```
<%@ Page language="c#"%>
<html>
  <head>
    <script runat="server">
      private void okButton_Click(object sender, EventArgs e) {
          infoLabel.Text = "You entered '" + entryTextBox.Text + "'.";
      }
    </script>
  </head>
  <body>
    <form id="MyPage" method="post" runat="server">
      <p />
```

Listing 4-1   MyPage.aspx

```
        This page demonstrates a simple user interface consisting
        of a TextBox and a RequiredFieldValidator, which will be
        encapsulated into a user control.
        <p />
        Enter a value:
        <p />
        <asp:TextBox id="entryTextBox" runat="server" />
         
        <asp:RequiredFieldValidator id="RequiredFieldValidator1"
          runat="server" ErrorMessage="(required)"
          ControlToValidate="entryTextBox"
          ToolTip="You must enter a value." />
         
        <p />
        <asp:Button id="okButton" runat="server"
          Text="OK" Width="75px" OnClick="okButton_Click" />
        <p />
        <asp:Label id="infoLabel" runat="server" />
        <p />
      </form>
  </body>
</html>
```

Listing 4-2 shows the source code for the user control. If you save this listing as a text file with an .ascx extension in an ASP.NET Web application, you create a user control. If you installed the code from the sample files, you will find this control in the BookWeb Web application at the location Chapter4\UserControls\RequiredTextField.ascx.

```
<%@ Control Language="c#" ClassName="RequiredTextField" %>
<script runat="server">
  public string Text {
      get {
          return entryTextBox.Text;
      }
      set {
          entryTextBox.Text = value;
      }
  }
</script>
<asp:TextBox id="entryTextBox" runat="server" />
 
<asp:RequiredFieldValidator id="RequiredFieldValidator1"
  runat="server" ErrorMessage="(required)"
  ControlToValidate="entryTextBox"
  ToolTip="You must enter a value." />
 
```

Listing 4-2   RequiredTextField.ascx

To create our user control, we created a text file with a *Control* directive at the top and copied the boldface lines in Listing 4-1 into it. In addition, we exposed a property, *Text*, which allows our users to access the *Text* property of the contained *TextBox* control. Properties enable page code to interact with (program against) your control.

The *Control* directive at the top of the file specifies the programming language for the user control and provides a class name for the control. The *Control* directive is analogous to the *Page* directive at the top of an .aspx file. The "ASP.NET Page Syntax" topic in the .NET Framework SDK documentation contains a complete list of directives and attributes used with user controls.

A user control can contain any valid page syntax, including templates, data-binding syntax, and event handlers. However, a user control should not contain enclosing tags such as *<html>*, *<body>*, or *<form>* because these tags are provided by the containing page.

A file with an .ascx extension cannot be served to a Web client. If you enter *http://localhost/BookWeb/Chapter4/UserControls/RequiredTextField.ascx* in your browser's address bar, you will get a server error message that states, "This type of page is not served." A file with an .ascx extension can be used only from another page or user control.

Accessing a User Control from a Page

Before you can use a user control declaratively in a page, you must register the user control with the page by including a *Register* directive at the top of the page, as shown in the following example:

```
<%@ Register TagPrefix="mspuc" TagName="RequiredTextField"
  Src="RequiredTextField.ascx" %>
```

The *TagPrefix* attribute supplies a tag prefix for the user control (which is similar to the *asp* tag prefix for Web controls that ship with the .NET Framework SDK), the *TagName* attribute supplies a tag name, and the *Src* attribute specifies the path to the user control. You can specify any value (other than *asp*) for the *TagPrefix* attribute and any value for the *TagName* attribute. The *TagPrefix:TagName* combination creates a tag that the parser associates with the user control specified in the *Src* attribute. This combination must be unique for each user control registered with the page. For example, once you have registered the control with the page, the parser loads RequiredTextField.ascx when it sees the following declaration on the page:

```
<mspuc:RequiredTextField runat="server"/>
```

The value of the *Src* attribute must be specified as a virtual path within your Web application (/BookWeb/Chapter4/UserControls/RequiredTextField.ascx or ~/Chapter4/UserControls/RequiredTextField.ascx or RequiredTextField.ascx). It cannot be specified as an absolute URL (*http://localhost/BookWeb/Chapter4/UserControls/RequiredTextField.ascx*) or as a physical path (<path to Book-Web>)\Chapter4\UserControls\RequiredTextField.ascx).

Note that a user control can be used within another user control. If you want to access a user control from another user control, you have to register the inner (nested) user control with the containing user control.

The page in Listing 4-3 uses the *RequiredTextField* user control that we defined in Listing 4-2.

```
<%@ Page language="c#" %>
<%@ Register TagPrefix="mspuc" TagName="RequiredTextField"
  Src="UserControls/RequiredTextField.ascx"%>
<html>
  <head>
    <script runat="server">
    protected void okButton_Click(object sender, EventArgs e) {
        infoLabel.Text = "You entered '" +
            RequiredTextField1.Text + "'.";
    }
    </script>
  </head>
  <body>
    <form id="MyPage" method="post" runat="server">
      <p />
      This page uses the RequiredTextField user control.
      <p />
      Enter a value:
      <p />
      <mspuc:RequiredTextField id="RequiredTextField1"
        runat="server" />
      <p />
      <asp:Button id="okButton" runat="server"
        Text="OK" Width="75px" OnClick="okButton_Click" />
      <p />
      <asp:Label id="infoLabel" runat="server" />
      <p />
    </form>
  </body>
</html>
```

Listing 4-3   RequiredTextFieldTest.aspx

If you access this page in your browser, you will see that the page behaves the same way as MyPage.aspx. However, some of the UI in RequiredTextField-Test.aspx is encapsulated in the reusable control *RequiredTextField*.

Reusable User Controls: The *SiteHeader* and *SiteFooter* Examples

User controls are often used to provide header and footer functionality on pages. Listing 4-4 shows a simple header user control that we use on all our pages.

```
<%@ Control Language="c#" ClassName="SiteHeader"%>
<script runat="server">
  public string Heading {
      get {
          return headingLabel.Text;
      }
      set {
          headingLabel.Text = value;
      }
  }

  public string SubHeading {
      get {
          return subHeadingLabel.Text;
      }
      set {
          subHeadingLabel.Text = value;
      }
  }
</script>
<asp:Panel id="headerPanel" runat="server" Width="100%">
  <p>
    <asp:Label id="headingLabel" runat="server" Font-Names="Verdana"
      Font-Size="14pt" Font-Bold="True" />
    <br>
    <asp:Label id="subHeadingLabel" runat="server"
      Font-Names="Trebuchet MS" Font-Size="12pt" Font-Bold="True"
      Font-Italic="True" />
    <hr>
  </p>
</asp:Panel>
```

Listing 4-4   SiteHeader.ascx

The *SiteHeader* user control exposes the *Heading* and *SubHeading* properties to enable a user to provide a heading and a subheading for the page.

We also use on our pages a footer control that displays static text, as shown in Listing 4-5.

```
<%@ Control Language="c#" ClassName="SiteFooter"%>
<asp:Panel id="headerPanel" runat="server" Width="100%">
  <p>
    <br>
    <hr>
    <asp:Label id="subHeadingLabel" runat="server" Font-Size="8pt"
      Font-Names="Verdana">
      <b>Developing ASP.NET Server Controls and Components</b>
      <br>
      By Nikhil Kothari and Vandana Datye
      <br>
      Copyright (c) 2002, Microsoft Press.
    </asp:Label>
  </p>
</asp:Panel>
```

Listing 4-5   SiteFooter.ascx

The page shown in Listing 4-6 uses the *SiteHeader* and *SiteFooter* controls and sets the *Heading* and *SubHeading* properties on the *SiteHeader* user control.

```
<%@ Page language="c#" %>
<%@ Register TagPrefix="mspuc" TagName="SiteHeader"
  Src="~/UserControls/SiteHeader.ascx" %>
<%@ Register TagPrefix="mspuc" TagName="SiteFooter"
  Src="~/UserControls/SiteFooter.ascx" %>
<html>
  <head>
    <link href="../Default.css" type="text/css" rel="stylesheet" />
  </head>
  <body>
    <form id="SiteHeaderTest" method="post" runat="server">
      <mspuc:SiteHeader id="SiteHeader1" runat="server" Heading="Chapter 4"
        SubHeading="SiteHeader and SiteFooter Test Page" />
      <br>
      This page demonstrates the SiteHeader and SiteFooter
      user controls.
      <br>
      These user controls are used throughout the BookWeb application
      for a consistent look and feel.
      <br>
```

Listing 4-6   SiteHeaderFooterTest.aspx   *(continued)*

Listing 4-6 *(continued)*

```
      <mspuc:SiteFooter id="SiteFooter1" runat="server"
        Heading="Chapter 4"
        SubHeading="SiteHeader and SiteFooter Test Page" />
    </form>
  </body>
</html>
```

We used the ~ syntax in Listing 4-6 to specify values for relative URLs in the *Src* attribute *(Src="~/UserControls/SiteHeader.ascx")*. This syntax can be used only within an ASP.NET Web application and denotes a Web application–relative URL—that is, a URL relative to the virtual root of your Web application. For example, the virtual root for our Web application is */BookWeb*, and the Web application–relative URLs in Listing 4-6 resolve to */BookWeb/UserControls/Site-Header.ascx* and */BookWeb/UserControls/SiteHeader.ascx*.

We have used the *SiteHeader* and *SiteFooter* controls—as well as a simple style sheet—on all our pages. When listing pages throughout the rest of this book, however, we will not show these user controls, the corresponding *Register* directives, or the style sheet. These elements are present in the .aspx pages in the sample files.

Figure 4-1 shows the SiteHeaderFooterTest.aspx page viewed in a browser.

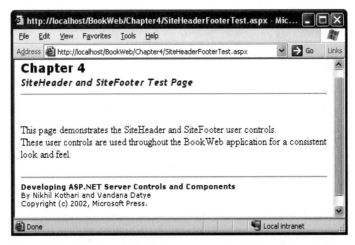

Figure 4-1 SiteHeaderFooterTest.aspx viewed in a browser

The User Control Model

Processing a user control is similar to processing a page, which we described in Chapter 2, "Page Programming Model." A user control consists of a declarative .ascx file and an optional code-behind file (which we will soon describe). The transformation of the source files into a server control works like this: When a page with a user control is requested, the page parser parses the .ascx file specified in the *Src* attribute and generates a class that derives from *System.Web.UI.UserControl*. The parser dynamically compiles the class into an assembly, thus defining a new type that corresponds to the user control. (In the case of a user control that uses the Visual Studio .NET code-behind model, the page parser generates a class that derives from a *UserControl*-derived code-behind class, as you will soon see.) If the .ascx page contains a *Control* directive that provides a *ClassName* attribute, the value supplied for the *ClassName* attribute becomes the name of the parser-generated class. Thus, in the example discussed in the "Converting a Page to a User Control" section, the parser will generate a class named *RequiredTextField* because we specified *ClassName="RequiredTextField"* in the *Control* directive.

While the *ClassName* attribute is optional, you should always use it to provide a name for the strong (exact) type of your user control. The type name is needed to cast a control from a base type to its exact type. For example, if a user invokes the *FindControl* method (that returns an object of type *Control*) to get your control, the user code must downcast the returned object to the exact type of your user control to access your control's object model. Here is an example:

```
RequiredTextField textField =
    (RequiredTextField)Page.FindControl(requiredTextField1);
// The next line would not be possible without
// casting the returned control to RequiredTextField
// because the Control class does not expose a Text property.
string text = textField.Text;
```

If you do not specify a *ClassName* attribute, the parser provides a default name for the autogenerated class. The parser-supplied name of the autogenerated class generally consists of the suffix *_ascx* appended to the filename—for example, *RequiredTextField_ascx*. However, the parser is not guaranteed to abide by this naming pattern, and a user could encounter an error when using the assumed default type name. Hence, we recommend that you always specify the *ClassName* attribute.

When processing a user control, the page framework performs two additional steps that are not needed for a custom (compiled) control:

1.   It parses the declarative syntax to generate the source code for a managed class that derives from *System.Web.UI.UserControl.*

2.   It dynamically compiles the autogenerated class into an assembly.

These steps are executed only once—the first time a page containing the user control is requested—and they do not result in any additional overhead on subsequent requests.

Viewing the Class Generated by the Parser from an .ascx File

If you would like to see the class that is autogenerated by the page parser from an .ascx file, perform the following steps:

1.   Add a debug attribute at the top of the page that contains the user control (*<%@ Page debug="true" %>*).

2.   Introduce a syntax error (such as an unbalanced parenthesis or a missing colon statement terminator) in a server-side script block in your user control, and save the file.

3.   Request a page that contains the user control in your browser. The server will return an error message with links at the bottom of the page.

4.   Click the Show Complete Compilation Source link to display the autogenerated code for your control.

User Controls in Visual Studio .NET

Visual Studio .NET uses the code-behind model for user controls, which is similar to the code-behind model for pages that we described in Chapter 2. In this model, the declarative syntax is contained in an .ascx file, while the server-side code exists in a separate file in a class (called the *code-behind class*) that derives from *System.Web.UI.UserControl.* The Web Forms Designer generates the code-behind class and precompiles all of the Web application's page and user control code-behind classes into an assembly. The designer creates the assembly in the Web application's bin directory.

If you develop a user control similar to *RequiredTextField* (shown in Listing 4-2) using the Web User Control template in Visual Studio .NET, the code for a designer-generated code-behind class will be similar to that shown in Listing 4-7.

```
namespace BookWeb.Chapter4.UserControls
{
    using System;
    using System.Data;
    using System.Drawing;
    using System.Web;
    using System.Web.UI.WebControls;
    using System.Web.UI.HtmlControls;

    /// <summary>
    ///     The code-behind class for MyVSUserControl.ascx.
    /// </summary>
    public abstract class MyVSUserControl : System.Web.UI.UserControl
    {
        protected TextBox entryTextBox;
        protected RequiredFieldValidator requiredFieldValidator1;

        public string Text
        {
            get
            {
                return entryTextBox.Text;
            }
            set
            {
                entryTextBox.Text = value;
            }
        }

        private void Page_Load(object sender, System.EventArgs e)
        {
            // Put user code to initialize the page here.
        }

        #region Web Form Designer generated code
        override protected void OnInit(EventArgs e)
        {
            //
            // CODEGEN: This call is required by the ASP.NET
            // Web Form Designer.
            //
```

Listing 4-7   MyVSUserControl.ascx.cs   *(continued)*

Listing 4-7 *(continued)*

```
            InitializeComponent();
            base.OnInit(e);
        }


        ///     Required method for designer support; do not modify
        ///     the contents of this method with the code editor.
        /// </summary>
        private void InitializeComponent()
        {
            this.Load += new System.EventHandler(this.Page_Load);
        }
        #endregion
    }
}
```

The declarative portion of the control is in an .ascx file, shown in Listing 4-8.

```
<%@ Control Language="c#" AutoEventWireup="false"
   ClassName="VSRequiredTextField" Codebehind="MyVSUserControl.ascx.cs"
   Inherits="BookWeb.Chapter4.UserControls.MyVSUserControl" %>
<asp:TextBox id="entryTextBox" runat="server" />
 
<asp:RequiredFieldValidator id="requiredFieldValidator1" runat="server"
   ErrorMessage="(required)" ControlToValidate="entryTextBox"
   ToolTip="You must enter a value." />
 
```

Listing 4-8   MyVSUserControl.ascx

The *Control* directive in the code-behind case is slightly different from that in the embedded script case. The *Inherits* attribute specifies the name of the code-behind class, and the *Codebehind* attribute specifies the location of the code-behind file.

Although the code-behind class is precompiled by the designer, the user control still must go through the process of dynamic code generation and compilation. The *real* user control is the class that is autogenerated by the page parser by deriving from the code-behind class and adding code to correspond to the declarative syntax in the .ascx file.

If you use the code-behind model for your pages, you should also use it for your user controls. If you mix the two models, you might encounter errors. For example, you cannot programmatically access members of a user control that has an embedded script block from the code-behind class of the containing .aspx page. Such access is possible, however, if you define a code-behind class for the user control.

Listings 4-9 and 4-10 show the declarative and code-behind files for a designer-generated page that uses *MyVSUserControl*. This page is similar in behavior to the RequiredTextFieldTest.aspx page in Listing 4-3.

```
<%@ Page language="c#" Codebehind="MyVSUserControlTest.aspx.cs"
  AutoEventWireup="false" Inherits="BookWeb.Chapter4.MyVSUserTest" %>
<%@ Register TagPrefix="ucl" TagName="MyVSUser"
  Src="UserControls/MyVSUserControl.ascx" %>
<!DOCTYPE HTML PUBLIC "-//W3C//DTD HTML 4.0 Transitional//EN" >
<HTML>
  <HEAD>
    <title>MyVSUserTest</title>
    <meta name="GENERATOR" Content="Microsoft Visual Studio 7.0">
    <meta name="CODE_LANGUAGE" Content="C#">
    <meta name="vs_defaultClientScript" content="JavaScript">
    <meta name="vs_targetSchema"
      content="http://schemas.microsoft.com/intellisense/ie5">
  </HEAD>
  <body>
    <form id="MyVSUserTest" method="post" runat="server">
      <p>
        This page uses the MyVSUserControl user control.
      </p>
      <p>
        Enter a value:
      </p>
      <ucl:MyVSUser id="MyVSUser1" runat="server"></ucl:MyVSUser>
      <p>
        <asp:Button id="okButton" runat="server" Text="OK"
          Width="75px"></asp:Button>
      </p>
      <p>
        <asp:Label id="infoLabel" runat="server"></asp:Label>
      </p>
    </form>
  </body>
</HTML>
```

Listing 4-9   MyVSUserControlTest.aspx

```
using System;
using System.Collections;
using System.ComponentModel;
using System.Data;
using System.Drawing;
using System.Web;
using System.Web.SessionState;
```

Listing 4-10   MyVSUserControlTest.aspx.cs   *(continued)*

Listing 4-10   *(continued)*

```csharp
using System.Web.UI;
using System.Web.UI.WebControls;
using System.Web.UI.HtmlControls;

namespace BookWeb.Chapter4
{
    /// <summary>
    /// Summary description for MyVSUserControlTest.
    /// </summary>
    public class MyVSUserTest : System.Web.UI.Page
    {
        protected System.Web.UI.WebControls.Button okButton;
        protected System.Web.UI.WebControls.Label infoLabel;
        protected BookWeb.Chapter4.UserControls.MyVSUserControl
            MyVSUser1;

        private void Page_Load(object sender, System.EventArgs e)
        {
            // Put user code to initialize the page here.
        }

        #region Web Form Designer generated code
        override protected void OnInit(EventArgs e)
        {
            //
            // CODEGEN: This call is required by the ASP.NET
            // Web Form Designer.
            //
            InitializeComponent();
            base.OnInit(e);
        }

        /// <summary>
        /// Required method for designer support; do not modify
        /// the contents of this method with the code editor.
        /// </summary>
        private void InitializeComponent()
        {
            this.okButton.Click += new
                System.EventHandler(this.okButton_Click);
            this.Load += new System.EventHandler(this.Page_Load);

        }
        #endregion
```

```
        private void okButton_Click(object sender, System.EventArgs e)
        {
            infoLabel.Text = "You entered '" + MyVSUser1.Text + "'.";
        }
    }
}
```

The main item to note in this example is that if you need to access the user control in the code-behind class of your page—for example, in an event handler—you must declare a public or protected field in the code-behind class of the page that corresponds to the user control instance on the page. The designer will not generate this field for you. The name of the field must match the *ID* assigned to the user control in the .aspx page. The code that declares and accesses this field is boldface in Listing 4-10.

Deploying a User Control

Because a user control is dynamically generated and compiled, the page framework requires that the path to a user control be specified in one of three ways: relative to the page that uses (consumes) the user control (RequiredText-Field.ascx), relative to the Web application root (~/Chapter4/UserControls /RequiredTextField.ascx), or as an absolute virtual path that lies within the current Web application (/BookWeb/Chapter4/UserControls/RequiredText-Field.ascx). This requirement means that the files for a user control must reside in the directory (or subdirectory) of the consuming Web application. A user control can be developed as a part of any Web application, but to be used in another Web application, the .ascx file and other associated files—such as the code-behind file and images, if any exist—must be physically copied to the directory of the consuming Web application.

In Visual Studio .NET, all the code-behind pages for user controls and for pages in a Web application are compiled into a single assembly. This imposes the additional requirement that all the code-behind pages be written in the same programming language.

An Application-Specific User Control: The *CruiseSelector* Example

Our next user control sample, *CruiseSelector*, is an application-specific user control that is not generic like the *SiteHeader* and *RequiredTextField* user controls we developed earlier in the chapter. Application-specific user controls are useful because they allow pages to be partitioned into smaller units of functionality.

CruiseSelector uses declarative data-binding page syntax and handles events raised by its constituent controls, demonstrating that user controls can use templates and data-binding syntax, perform event handling, and use other page-programming elements in much the same fashion as pages do. *CruiseSelector* contains a *DataList* control and a *Label* control. The *DataList* displays a list of ASP.NET dinner cruises. When the user selects a cruise and submits the page, the *DataList* raises an *ItemCommand* event on the server, which *CruiseSelector* handles by displaying the cruise selection and disabling the *DataList* control.

Listing 4-11 contains the source code for *CruiseSelector*.

```
<%@ Control Language="c#" ClassName="CruiseSelector" %>
<script runat="server">
  private void LoadDataSource() {
      ArrayList list = new ArrayList();
      list.Add("Programming ASP.NET Pages");
      list.Add("ASP.NET Tips and Tricks");
      list.Add("ASP.NET Web Services");
      list.Add("Authoring Server Controls 101");
      list.Add("Professional Server Controls");
      myList.DataSource = list;
  }

  void Page_Load(object sender, EventArgs e) {
      if (!IsPostBack) {
          label1.Text =
              "Last chance to sign up for an ASP.NET dinner cruise!!";
          LoadDataSource();
          myList.DataBind();
      }
  }

  // The handler for the ItemCommand event of the DataList.
  private void MyList_ItemCommand(object source,
      DataListCommandEventArgs e)
  {
      Label l = (Label)e.Item.FindControl("label");
      string s = "You are registered for the "
                  + "<b>" + l.Text
                  + "</b> dinner cruise.";
      label1.Text = s;
      myList.Enabled = false;
  }
</script>
<p />
<asp:Label id="label1" Font-Name="Verdana" Font-Size="12pt"
  runat="server" />
```

Listing 4-11 CruiseSelector.ascx

```
<p />
<asp:DataList runat="server" id="myList" Font-Name="Verdana"
  Font-Size="16pt" BorderColor="Gray" BorderWidth="1px"
  CellSpacing="0" CellPadding="2" GridLines="Both"
  onItemCommand="MyList_ItemCommand">
  <HeaderStyle ForeColor="Black" BackColor="LightBlue"
    HorizontalAlign="Center" />
  <ItemStyle ForeColor="Black" BackColor="#EEEEEE"
    HorizontalAlign="Right" />
  <AlternatingItemStyle BackColor="#DCDCDC" />
  <SelectedItemStyle ForeColor="White" BackColor="#000084" />
  <HeaderTemplate>
    <asp:Label id="headerLabel" runat="server"
      Text="ASP.NET Dinner Cruises" />
  </HeaderTemplate>
  <ItemTemplate>
    <asp:Label id="label" runat="server"
      Text='<%# Container.DataItem %>'/>
      
    <asp:Button button="button" runat="server" id="selectButton"
      CommandName="Select" Text="Select" ForeColor="Blue" />
  </ItemTemplate>
</asp:DataList>
</p>
```

A user control can handle the events raised by its child controls, as *Cruise-Selector* does, and it can also bubble those events up to its parent control. We will describe event bubbling in Chapter 12, "Composite Controls." In addition to handling or bubbling events raised by its child controls, a user control can also raise events of its own, as any other server control would. We'll discuss events in server controls in Chapter 9, "Control Life Cycle, Events, and Postback."

The ASP.NET page in Listing 4-12 uses the *CruiseSelector* user control. Note that the page does very little work; most of the work is done by the user control.

```
<%@ Page Language="C#" %>
<%@ Register TagPrefix="mspuc" Tagname="CruiseSelector"
  Src="UserControls/CruiseSelector.ascx" %>
  <body>
    <form runat="server">
      <p/>
      <asp:Label Text="Welcome to .NET Cruise Registration"
        runat="server" Font-Name="Verdana" Font-Size="20pt"
        BorderColor="Gray" BorderWidth="2px" ForeColor="Black"
        BackColor="LightGray" HorizontalAlign="Center" />
      <mspuc:CruiseSelector id="selector" runat="server" />
```

Listing 4-12   CruiseSelectorTest.aspx   *(continued)*

Listing 4-12 *(continued)*

```
    <p/>
  </form>
 </body>
</html>
```

Figures 4-2 and 4-3 show CruiseSelectorTest.aspx as viewed from a Web browser on first request and on postback.

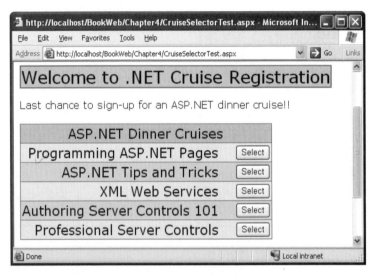

Figure 4-2 CruiseSelectorTest.aspx viewed in a browser on first request

Figure 4-3 CruiseSelectorTest.aspx viewed in a browser on postback

Relative URLs in User Controls

If your user control contains child controls that have URL properties, you might want to expose some of those properties from your control directly. To do this correctly, you have to be aware of a few subtleties of URL resolution in a user control. By default, a relative URL passed into a user control is resolved with respect to the directory containing the user control. This URL resolution can be confusing to page developers who expect relative URLs that they pass into the control to be resolved with respect to the containing page. To provide a more intuitive model for page developers, we recommend that you invoke the *Page.ResolveUrl* method to resolve a URL that is passed into your user control before passing it on to a child control. This process is best understood with an example.

To demonstrate this technique, we'll create a user control (*LinkGlyph* shown in Figure 4-4) that displays an image next to a hyperlink. *LinkGlyph* contains two child controls, an *Image* control and a *HyperLink* control. The *Image* control is an internal resource of *LinkGlyph*, and *LinkGlyph* itself sets the *ImageUrl* property of its *Image* control. On the other hand, *LinkGlyph* exposes the *NavigateUrl* property of its *HyperLink* control as a top-level property to be set by its users. Notice in Listing 4-13 that *LinkGlyph* resolves the URL that is passed into it before passing it on to its *HyperLink* child control.

```
<%@ Control Language="C#" ClassName="LinkGlyph" %>
<script runat="server">
  private string _navigateUrl;

  public string NavigateUrl {
      get {
          if (_navigateUrl == null) {
              return String.Empty;
          }
          return _navigateUrl;
      }
      set {
          _navigateUrl = value;
          link.NavigateUrl = Page.ResolveUrl(NavigateUrl);
      }
  }

  public string Text {
      get {
          return link.Text;
      }
```

Listing 4-13   LinkGlyph.ascx   *(continued)*

Listing 4-13 *(continued)*

```
    set {
        link.Text = value;
    }
  }
</script>
<asp:Image id="image" ImageUrl="Image.gif" runat="server" />
<asp:HyperLink id="link" runat="server" />
<p/>
```

The ASP.NET page in Listing 4-14 uses *LinkGlyph* and sets its *NavigateUrl* property by specifying a page-relative URL. Figure 4-4 shows LinkGlyph-Test.aspx accessed in a browser.

```
<%@ Page Language="C#" %>
<%@ Register TagPrefix="mspuc" TagName="LinkGlyph"
  Src="UserControls/LinkGlyph.ascx" %>
<html>
  <body>
    <form runat="server">
      <p>
        <mspuc:LinkGlyph id="linkglyph"
          NavigateUrl="CruiseSelectorTest.aspx"
          Text="Click To Register For an ASP.NET Cruise"
          runat="server" />
      </p>
    </form>
  </body>
</html>
```

Listing 4-14 LinkGlyphTest.aspx

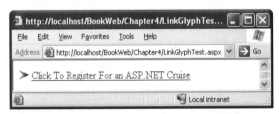

Figure 4-4 LinkGlyphTest.aspx viewed in a browser

Request LinkGlyphTest.aspx in a browser, and examine the client-side HTML. You will see that the two relative URLs in the user control are resolved this way:

```
<img id="linkglyph_image"
  src="/BookWeb/Chapter4/UserControls/Image.gif" border="0" />
<a id="linkglyph_link"
  href="/BookWeb/Chapter4/CruiseSelectorTest.aspx">
  Click To Register For an ASP.NET Cruise
</a>
```

The relative URL for the image was specified in LinkGlyph.ascx as *Image.gif*, and the relative URL for the hyperlink was specified in LinkGlyphTest.aspx as *CruiseSelectorTest.aspx*. The virtual root for our application is */BookWeb*. Link-Glyph.ascx is in */BookWeb/Chapter4/UserControls*, and the containing page LinkGlyphTest.aspx is in */BookWeb/Chapter4*. Notice that the internally set *ImageUrl* property of the *Image* control is resolved relative to LinkGlyph.ascx as */BookWeb/Chapter4/UserControls/Image.gif*, while the externally set *Navigate-Url* of the *Hyperlink* control is resolved relative to LinkGlyphTest.aspx as */Book-Web/Chapter4/CruiseSelectorTest.aspx*. If the user control did not invoke *Page.ResolveUrl* to resolve the externally set *NavigateUrl*, the relative URL set from the page would be resolved as */BookWeb/Chapter4/UserControls/Cruise-SelectorTest.aspx*, leading to a broken link.

If your user control is nested inside another user control, however, the technique we have recommended will not work if the containing user control passes in a URL that is relative to itself. In that case, it is best to pass in an absolute URL or a Web application–relative URL into the nested user control.

> **Warning**   Finally, we'd like to add a warning about using URLs in HTML content—in other words, tags that do not have *runat="server"*. You should never use relative URLs in HTML content in a user control. This is because HTML is rendered without change by the user control. A relative URL in HTML will not be resolved by the control but will eventually be resolved with respect to the page on which the user control appears. A relative URL in the user control's HTML thus is meaningless, because a user control can be reused on different ASP.NET pages.

Programmatically Instantiating a User Control

Because the type for a user control is dynamically generated, a user control can-not be created programmatically using the *new* syntax for instantiating a class. To create a user control programmatically, you must invoke the *LoadControl* method of the containing page. The *LoadControl* method takes the relative path to a user control source file and returns an object of type *Control*, which you can cast to the strong type of the user control. The page shown in Listing 4-15 programmatically creates the user control *LinkGlyph* and casts it to its strong type. The *Reference* directive specifies the relative path to the .ascx file for the user control. The page uses the *PlaceHolder* control to mark a location in the page for rendering the dynamically added user control.

```
<%@ Page Language="C#" %>
<%@ Reference Control="UserControls/LinkGlyph.ascx" %>
<html>
  <head>
    <script runat="server">
      protected override void OnLoad(EventArgs e) {
          LinkGlyph demo = (LinkGlyph)
              Page.LoadControl("UserControls/LinkGlyph.ascx");
          demo.NavigateUrl = "CruiseSelectorTest.aspx";
          demo.Text = "Click Me";
          holder.Controls.Add(demo);
      }
    </script>
  </head>
  <body>
    <form id="form" runat="server">
      <p>
        <asp:PlaceHolder id="holder" runat="server" />
      </p>
    </form>
  </body>
</html>
```

Listing 4-15   LoadControlTest.aspx

When a page creates a user control programmatically, it does not need to register a tag prefix or tag name for the user control if it does not have any declarative instances of that user control. In that case, a page should have the *Reference* directive instead of the *Register* directive, as shown in Listing 4-15.

Caching a User Control

Like ASP.NET pages, user controls can be cached to improve performance. Caching a user control involves saving and reusing the output of the control. We will briefly discuss the options that ASP.NET provides for user control caching—also called *fragment caching*—and provide one complete sample. We'll point you to the IBuySpy Web sites (see the following sidebar) and to the .NET Framework SDK documentation for other samples.

The IBuySpy ASP.NET Demonstration Sites

The IBuySpy Web sites demonstrate how to utilize user controls in the design and layout of ASP.NET Web applications. There are two IBuySpy Web applications: a store (*http://www.ibuyspystore.com*) and a portal (*http://www.ibuyspyportal.com*). We strongly recommend that you visit the sites and look at the source code for user controls. The documentation page for the store (*http://www.ibuyspystore.com/docs/docs.htm*) contains links to the source code for user controls used in the IBuySpy store. The documentation page for the portal (*http://www.ibuyspyportal.com/docs/docs.htm*) contains links to the source code for user controls used in the IBuySpy portal.

To enable caching of your user control, apply the *OutputCache* directive at the top of your control's .ascx file. There are four variations of the *Output-Cache* directive:

- Specify the cache duration using the *Duration* attribute:

```
<%@ OutputCache Duration="1200" VaryByParam="None" %>
```

   The *Duration* attribute specifies the period (in seconds) for which the control will be cached. In this version of caching, the *VaryByParam* attribute is not used but must be included and set to *None*. A cache entry is created corresponding to each instance of the user control and reused for the specified period. Use this version to cache a control that does not depend on input parameters. For an example, see the source code for the *PopularItems* user control in the IBuySpy store documentation (*http://www.ibuyspystore.com/docs/docs.htm*).

- Specify the *Duration* and *VaryByParam* attributes:

```
<%@ OutputCache Duration="100" VaryByParam="category" %>
```

The *VaryByParam* attribute specifies GET query string parameters or form POST parameters. A new cache entry is created for each new name/value pair in the parameter list of the *VaryByParam* attribute. To specify multiple parameters, separate them by semicolons (for example, *VaryByParam="category; selectionID")*. If *VaryBy-Param="*"* is specified, all the parameters for the request are used to govern caching. Use this version of caching if the output of your user control depends on GET or POST parameters for the containing page—for instance, if your user control displays a database entry based on a user request. For an example, see the source for the *Menu* user control in the IBuySpy store documentation (*http://www.ibuyspystore.com/docs/docs.htm*).

■   Specify the *Duration* and *VaryByControl* attributes:

```
<%@ OutputCache Duration="150" VaryByControl="list1;radio1" %>
```

The *VaryByControl* attribute specifies the *ID*s of one or more child controls that correspond to form controls contained within the user control. A new cache entry is created for each new combination of inputs to the specified controls. Use this type of caching if your user control contains form controls such as *DropDownList*, *RadioButton*, and *TextBox* and you want to govern caching behavior by the values of these controls. In the next subsection, we'll show an example of caching using the *VaryByControl* attribute.

■   Specify the *Duration* and the *VaryByCustom* attributes:

```
<%@ OutputCache Duration="60" VaryByParam="None"
  VaryByCustom="CustomString" %>
```

The *VaryByCustom* attribute specifies a string that is used to govern caching. In this version of caching, the *VaryByParam* attribute is not used but must be included and set to *None*. The *Vary-ByCustom* attribute works the same way in a user control as it does in a page. For an example of page caching with this attribute, see "Caching Versions of a Page, Based on Custom Strings" in the .NET Framework SDK documentation.

When you use the *VaryByCustom* attribute, you have to override the *GetVaryByCustomString* method in the Global.asax file for your application. You can implement logic within the *GetVaryByCustomString* method so that its return value is dependent on the custom string. Here is a simple user control that is cached using the *VaryByCustom* attribute:

```
<%@ Control Language="c#" ClassName="VaryByCustomUser" %>
<%@ OutputCache Duration=20 VaryByParam="none"
  VaryByCustom="myCustomString" %>

<%= DateTime.Now %>
```

Here is how you could override the *GetVaryByCustomString* method in the Global.asax file. The example does not do anything useful; it merely illustrates the concept:

```
<%@ Language=c# debug=true %>

<script runat="server">
  public override string GetVaryByCustomString(HttpContext context,
      string custom) {

      switch (custom) {
      case "myCustomString":
          return Request.QueryString["foo"];
      // Other cases for other custom strings
      }
      return null;
  }
</script>
```

VaryByControl Example

The user control shown in Listing 4-16, *CachedUserControl*, uses the *VaryByControl* attribute to govern caching. *CachedUserControl* creates cache entries based on the selected item in its *DropDownList* control. To demonstrate caching behavior, we have added a timestamp in *CachedUserControl* to indicate when the code for the user control is executed.

```
<%@ Control Language="C#" ClassName="CachedUserControl" %>
<%@ OutputCache Duration="60" VaryByControl="language" %>
<script runat="server">
  public void Page_Load(object sender, EventArgs e) {
      label1.Text="The selected language is " +
          language.SelectedItem.Text + ".";
      timeLabel.Text = DateTime.Now.TimeOfDay.ToString();
  }
</script>
<p/>
Timestamp on user control:
<asp:label id="timeLabel" runat="server" />
<p/>
```

Listing 4-16   CachedUserControl.ascx   *(continued)*

Listing 4-16 *(continued)*

```
Select a programming language.
<p/>
<asp:DropDownList width="100" id="language" runat="server">
  <asp:ListItem>C#</asp:ListItem>
  <asp:ListItem>Visual Basic .NET</asp:ListItem>
  <asp:ListItem>JScript .NET</asp:ListItem>
</asp:DropDownList>
<p/>
<asp:label id="label1" runat="server" />
<p/>
```

The page shown in Listing 4-17 uses *CachedUserControl*. The page has a timestamp that indicates when it's executed.

```
<%@ Page language="C#" %>
<%@ Register TagPrefix="mspuc" TagName="CachedUserControl"
  Src="UserControls/CachedUserControl.ascx" %>
<html>
  <head>
    <script runat="server">
      void Page_Load(object sender, EventArgs e) {
          timeLabel.Text = "Timestamp on page: " +
              DateTime.Now.TimeOfDay.ToString();
      }
    </script>
  </head>
  <body>
    <form runat="server">
      <asp:Label id="timeLabel" runat="server" />
      <p />
      The following user control is cached using the
      VaryByControl attribute.
      <mspuc:CachedUserControl id="user" runat="server" />
      <asp:Button Font-Bold="true" Text="Submit"
        runat="server" id="Button1" />
      <p />
    </form>
  </body>
</html>
```

Listing 4-17 CachedUserControlTest.aspx

For a demonstration of user control caching, access the page CachedUser-ControlTest.aspx in your browser. Notice that the timestamp on the page changes with each request. However, during the cache process, the timestamp on the user control changes only if you change the selection in the *DropDownList*.

How User Control Caching Works

When the page parser encounters a declarative instance of a user control with an *OutputCache* directive, it creates an instance of the *StaticPartialCaching-Control* class and adds it in the logical position of the user control in the control tree. (We described the control tree in Chapter 2.) If a user control with an *Out-putCache* directive is dynamically added to a page, the parser creates an instance of the *PartialCachingControl* class instead. A *StaticPartialCaching-Control* (or *PartialCachingControl*) object is capable of adding entries to and retrieving them from the ASP.NET *Cache* object. If the *StaticPartialCaching-Control* (or *PartialCachingControl*) object does not find a cache entry for a given combination of inputs, it dynamically creates an instance of the user control and adds the user control instance to its own control tree, executes the code for the user control, and adds a corresponding entry to the cache.

If a user control has an *OutputCache* directive applied, you must check for the user control's existence (for example, *myUserID != null*) before accessing it programmatically from a containing page. This step is necessary because when a cache entry exists, an instance of the user control is not created, and you could get a null reference exception when you access the user control.

Summary

In this chapter, we looked at the user control model for authoring server controls. We showed you how to author a user control and looked at how an .ascx text file is dynamically parsed and compiled into an assembly. We also examined how user controls can be cached to improve performance.

In Chapter 5, we will introduce you to the custom control model, and in Chapter 6, we'll provide guidelines to help you choose between the two ASP.NET models for creating your own controls.

User controls are equivalent to composite controls, which we'll describe in Chapter 12. Nearly all control-authoring concepts that we will describe in later chapters apply to user controls too. Other than in Chapter 6, we will not discuss user controls again in this book unless there are special considerations that apply to them.

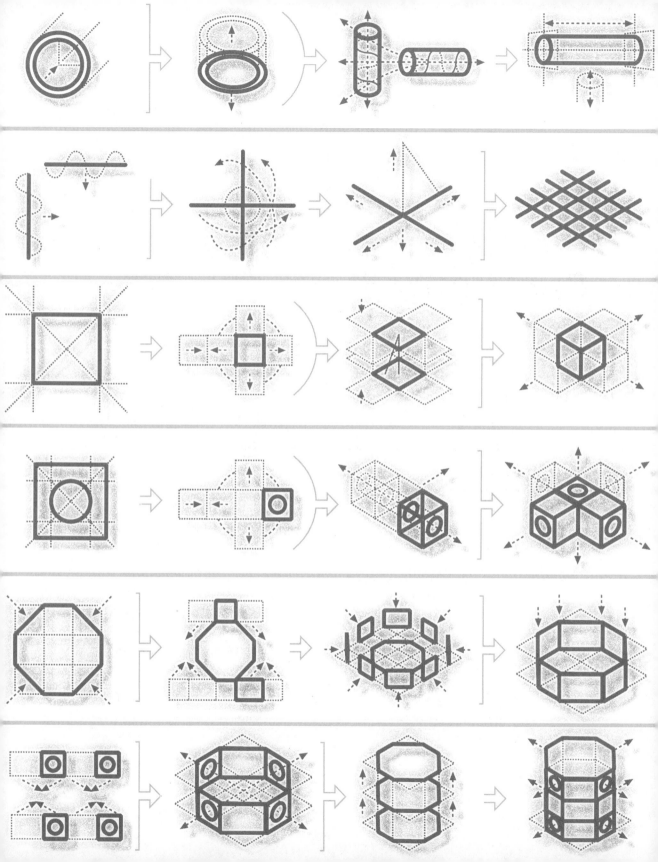

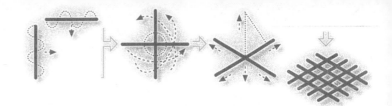

5

Developing a Simple Custom Control

In Chapter 4, "User Controls: From Page to Control," we described declaratively authored user controls that are deployed as text files (.ascx and optional code-behind files). In this chapter, we will describe controls that are authored in code and deployed in the form of compiled class libraries. To differentiate between the two control authoring models, we will use the term *custom control* when referring to a control that is authored as a managed class and compiled before deployment.

You can develop custom controls by using any code editor and the .NET Framework SDK. In this chapter, we will describe the essential steps for authoring a custom control and show you how to enable design-time features that give your control a professional look and feel when it is used in a designer such as Visual Studio .NET. We will also show you how to compile a custom control using command-line tools that ship with the .NET Framework SDK. In addition, we'll describe how to debug a server control using command-line tools and using Visual Studio .NET. Because this chapter focuses on programming, we will not get into the details of authoring a server control in Visual Studio .NET. You can see those details in the topic "Walkthrough: Creating a Web Custom Control" in the .NET Framework SDK or MSDN documentation.

Server Control Overview

An ASP.NET server control is a component that executes program logic on the server, provides a programmable object model, and renders markup text (such as HTML, XML, and WML) to a Web browser client or other viewing device. A server control is a fundamental building block of an ASP.NET Web application. Although a significant amount of plumbing is needed to enable a class to interact with the ASP.NET page framework and to participate in an HTTP request/ response scenario, ASP.NET frees you from low-level details by providing a base class (*System.Web.UI.Control*) that implements the necessary plumbing. To author a server control, you must define a class that directly or indirectly derives from *System.Web.UI.Control*. All ASP.NET controls that ship with the .NET Framework SDK derive from *Control* or from one of its derived classes.

Figure 5-1 shows the hierarchy of the base classes for server controls. The full class hierarchy containing all the server controls in ASP.NET is shown in Chapter 2, "Page Programming Model."

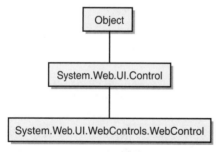

Figure 5-1   Hierarchy of the base classes for server controls

The Control class provides the basic functionality for participating in the page framework. In particular, it provides the functionality that allows a server control to be placed within the control tree that represents an .aspx page. The *Control* class also implements the *System.ComponentModel.IComponent* interface, which makes it a designable component. A designable component can be added to the toolbox of a visual designer, can be dragged onto a design surface, can display its properties in a property browser, and can provide other kinds of design-time support.

The *WebControl* class adds functionality to the base *Control* class for rendering HTML content. *WebControl* provides support for styles through properties such as *Font*, *Height*, *Width*, *BackColor*, and *ForeColor*. Later in this chapter, in the "Choosing the Base Class for Your Control" section, we will provide scenario-based guidelines to help you determine the base control class from which you should derive your control.

A Trivial Server Control Example

To demonstrate the mechanics of implementing a control, we'll start by creating a very simple server control that merely renders a text string to the client. Our control derives from the base *Control* class to participate in the HTTP request/response processing provided by the page framework and overrides the inherited *Render* method to write to the output text stream. Listing 5-1 shows the code for our control.

```
using System;
using System.Web.UI;

namespace MSPress.ServerControls {
    public class SimpleControl : Control {
        protected override void Render(HtmlTextWriter writer) {
            writer.Write("I don't do anything useful, ");
            writer.Write("but at least I'm a control...");
        }
    }
}
```

Listing 5-1   SimpleControl.cs

Note   If you are using Visual Studio .NET, start a new Microsoft Visual C# Control Library project, delete the designer-generated code in WebCustomControl1.cs, and replace it with the code we provide for the control.

System.Web.UI.HtmlTextWriter is a utility class that encapsulates the functionality of writing HTML to a text stream. In Chapter 8, "Rendering," we will show you how to use the methods of the *HtmlTextWriter* class to simplify HTML rendering. For now, *SimpleControl* simply passes text into the *Write* method of the *HtmlTextWriter* instance. The *Write* method outputs the specified text to the HTTP response stream and is equivalent to the *Response.Write* method in traditional Active Server Pages programming. Do not directly invoke *Page.Response.Write* from your controls because doing so breaks the encapsulation provided by the page framework. Instead, override one of the rendering methods provided by the *Control* or *WebControl* class to write to the response stream. We'll explain the rendering process in greater detail in Chapter 8.

The *using* declarations enable you to access types by shorter names instead of their fully qualified class names. Thus, *Control* is equivalent to *System.Web.UI.Control*. The *using* declarations do not add any overhead, and they make your code more readable. You must declare your control in a namespace so that page developers can use your control declaratively on pages, as you will soon see.

The *Render* method, which *SimpleControl* overrides, corresponds to the Render phase in a control's life cycle. A control writes text to the underlying HTTP response stream during this phase.

Compiling and Deploying a Server Control

For a custom control to be usable on a page, the control must be compiled into an assembly and made accessible to the ASP.NET runtime. If you are not familiar with the concept of assembly, think of it as a dynamic-link library (DLL) implemented in managed code.

In this book's sample files, we have provided batch files for building from the command line and provided a Visual Studio .NET solution file (BookCodeCS.sln for C#) for opening the project in Visual Studio .NET. We will discuss the command-line procedure in this section, and we'll show how to use a custom control in Visual Studio .NET in the section "Custom Controls in Visual Studio .NET."

The batch files in the book's sample files contain commands that will compile all the control samples in this book. If you want to get a feel for building a server control assembly, follow the instructions in the next paragraph. However, before executing the commands, copy the source files for the control samples in this chapter to a directory other than the one in which you installed the source code so that you don't overwrite the installed files.

To compile the control shown in Listing 5-1, navigate to the directory that contains the source file for *SimpleControl* (for example, C:\MyBookCodeCS\MyServerControls) and execute the following command:

```
csc /t:library /out:MSPress.ServerControls.dll /r:System.dll
    /r:System.Web.dll SimpleControl.cs
```

The csc command invokes the C# compiler. The /t option tells the compiler that the target assembly is a library. The /out option provides the name of the output file. The /r option provides the names of the assemblies whose metadata is referenced by the classes being compiled. At this point, we need to reference only two assemblies: *System* and *System.Web*. When you execute the compiler command, it will generate a library assembly named MSPress.Server-Controls in the file MSPress.ServerControls.dll.

Each ASP.NET application has a special location from which it can access private assemblies. (We'll explain what *private* means shortly.) That location is the bin directory immediately under the virtual root representing an Internet Information Services (IIS) Web application. If your Web application's virtual root is named BookWeb and maps to a path such as C:\BookWebDir, the directory C:\BookWebDir\bin should hold assemblies referenced by pages in the BookWeb Web directory. Binaries that are needed by pages in subdirectories must also be placed in the bin directory directly under the virtual root. For example, the bin directory for pages in C:\BookWebDir\Chapter5 is also C:\BookWebDir\bin. If you ran the setup program included with the book's sample files, the BookWeb Web application and its bin directory are already created for you.

If you want to follow the instructions in this chapter to understand the mechanics of the process, create an IIS virtual root different from the BookWeb application that was created for you when you installed the samples. If you have not created an IIS virtual root before, see the Introduction of this book for instructions. It is important that you create a new Web application (such as MyBookWeb) so that you don't overwrite the pages and binaries that are part of the BookWeb application. You must also create a directory named bin under the virtual root.

Next copy the MSPress.ServerControls.dll file that you created earlier to the bin directory of your Web application. Here's an example:

```
copy MSPress.ServerControls.dll <path to the root of your Web application>\bin
```

The assembly that you created and copied into the application's bin directory is known as a private assembly because only pages in your Web application can reference it. In Chapter 17, we will show you how to create an assembly that can be deployed in the global assembly cache (GAC) and thus shared by multiple applications.

Our first custom control is now ready to be used by any page in your Web application. We'll show you next how to use *SimpleControl* on a page.

Using a Custom Control on a Page

Using a custom control on a page is similar to using a server control that ships with the SDK, with one difference. The page developer must register a tag prefix (analogous to the *asp* tag prefix used for standard ASP.NET controls) for your control by using a *Register* directive at the top of the page, as shown in the following example:

```
<%@ Register TagPrefix="msp" Namespace="MSPress.ServerControls"
  Assembly="MSPress.ServerControls" %>
```

The *TagPrefix* attribute creates an alias that maps to a custom control's namespace and assembly. A page developer can specify any name for the tag prefix (other than *asp*) as long as it does not conflict with the name of another tag prefix specified on the page. The *Namespace* attribute specifies the namespace in which the custom control is declared. The *Assembly* attribute specifies the assembly into which the control is compiled. Do not use the .dll file extension when specifying the assembly attribute because the file extension is not part of the assembly name. Listing 5-2 shows you a page that uses our first custom control.

```
<%@ Page Language="C#" %>
<%@ Register TagPrefix="msp" NameSpace="MSPress.ServerControls"
  Assembly="MSPress.ServerControls" %>
<html>
  <body>
    <br>
    Here is the output from our first custom control.
    <br>
    <msp:SimpleControl id="simple1" runat="server" />
    <br>
  </body>
</html>
```

Listing 5-2   SimpleControlTest.aspx

We mentioned earlier that you must declare your control in a namespace. You can now see why that is needed. A namespace allows a control to be used declaratively on a page because the tag prefix in the *Register* directive maps to the namespace in which the control is declared.

To test the page, save it with an .aspx extension, copy it to your Web application, and open it in your browser. If you ran the setup program included with the book's sample files, you will find SimpleControlTest.aspx in the Chapter5 directory of your BookWeb application. Enter the following URL in your browser's address bar:

```
http://localhost/BookWeb/Chapter5/SimpleControlTest.aspx
```

Figure 5-2 shows how the output should look.

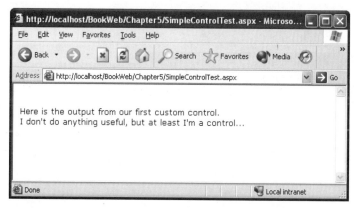

Figure 5-2   SimpleControlTest.aspx page that tests *SimpleControl*, viewed in a browser

Exposing a Property: The *PrimeGenerator* Control Example

Now that we have seen the main steps for authoring and deploying a server control, we'll write a control that exposes a property and does some useful work. Our next sample, *PrimeGenerator*, is a simple server control that computes and displays prime numbers less than or equal to a given number. The main task of our control is to render the computed primes to the client.

A user of our control should be able to specify an upper limit for the primes' computation. For this purpose, we will expose a property named *Number* from our control. Properties are accessed similarly to the way fields are, but they are implemented as accessor methods, effectively acting as "smart" fields. (We described the property construct in Chapter 3, "Component Programming Overview.")

Listing 5-3 provides the complete code for the *PrimeGenerator* control. *PrimeGenerator* derives from *Control*, exposes the *Number* property, and overrides the *Render* method to output the result of the computation of primes.

```
using System;
using System.Web.UI;

namespace MSPress.ServerControls {
    public class PrimeGenerator : Control {
        private int _number;
        public int Number {
            get {return _number;}
            set {_number = value;}
        }
        protected override void Render(HtmlTextWriter writer) {
            // Sieve is a class that computes primes.
            // We will define this class later.
            int[] primes = Sieve.GetPrimes(Number);
            // Notice that we write successive strings to the
            // output stream instead of concatenating them into
            // longer strings before writing. This is more efficient
            // than string concatenation.
            writer.Write("Primes less than or equal to: ");
            writer.Write(Number);
            writer.Write("<br>");
            for (int i = 0; i < primes.Length; i++){
                writer.Write(primes[i]);
                writer.Write(" ");
            }
            writer.Write("<br>");
        }
    }
}
```

Listing 5-3 PrimeGenerator.cs

All that remains to do is implement a utility class that contains the logic for computing primes. The implementation of this class is not important for control authoring; we have included it here for completeness.

Sieve of Eratosthenes

The sieve of Eratosthenes (circa 275–195 B.C.) is an elegant algorithm for computing primes smaller than a given number. The algorithm proceeds like this: Given a set of positive integers from 2 to N, start with the number 2 and cross out all its multiples. Repeat with each successive number that is not crossed out—and thus must be a prime because it has no factors smaller than itself. When you are finished, you will be left with only prime numbers less than or equal to N. Notice that when you get to a prime number i, you have to consider only its multiples with integers j >= i. (This is because multiples with integers j < i have already been considered.) The algorithm terminates when you reach a prime greater than the square root of N.

We expose the prime computation functionality from an independent class named *Sieve* because that functionality does not belong in a control. Listing 5-4 shows the code for the *Sieve* class.

```
using System;
using System.Collections;

namespace MSPress.ServerControls {
    // Sieve is a utility class that uses the sieve of Eratosthenes
    // algorithm to compute primes less than or equal to
    // a given positive integer.
    internal sealed class Sieve {
        private Sieve() { }
        public static int[] GetPrimes(int n) {
            // Use an array of n+1 bits to correspond to
            // the numbers from 0 to n. Initially, set all the bits
            // to true. The goal of the computation is to cycle through
            // the bit array using the sieve of Eratosthenes algorithm
            // and to set the bits corresponding to nonprimes to false.
            // The remaining true bits represent primes.
            BitArray flags = new BitArray(n+1, true);
            for (int i=2; i <= (int)Math.Sqrt(n); i++){
                if (flags[i]){
                    for (int j = i; j*i <= n; j++) {
                        flags[i*j]= false;
                    }
                }
```

Listing 5-4   Sieve.cs

Listing 5-4 *(continued)*

```
        }
    }

    // Count the number of primes <= n.
    int count = 0;
    for (int i=2; i <= n; i++) {
        if (flags[i]) count++;
    }

    // Create an int array to store the primes.
    int[] primes = new int[count];

    // Check bit flags and populate primes
    // array with numbers corresponding to
    // true bits.
    for (int i=2, j = 0; j < count; i++) {
        if (flags[i]) primes[j++] = i;
    }
    return primes;
    }
  }
}
```

Deriving from *WebControl*

If we derive our custom control from *WebControl* instead of from *Control*, our control inherits many additional properties, such as *Font*, *Height*, *Width*, and other style-related properties that enable a page developer to customize the visual appearance of the control. When deriving from *WebControl*, keep the following stipulations in mind:

- Include a reference to the *System.Web.UI.WebControls* namespace.

- Do not directly write to the output stream by overriding the *Render* method because the *Render* method of *WebControl* implements logic to render the outer tag with style information. Instead, override *RenderContents* if you want to provide content to render within the control's tags. We will explain this in more detail in Chapter 8.

- Override the *TagKey* property or the *TagName* property (in the case of a nonstandard HTML tag) inherited from *WebControl* if you want to render a tag that is different from *<span>*. By default, *WebControl* renders an HTML *<span>* tag. In our example, we will not override either of these properties.

Listing 5-5 highlights the changes to our control when it derives from *Web-Control*.

```
using System;
using System.Web.UI;
using System.Web.UI.WebControls;

namespace MSPress.ServerControls {
    public class StyledPrimeGenerator : WebControl {
        private int _number;
        public int Number{
            get {return _number;}
            set {_number = value;}
        }

        protected override void RenderContents(HtmlTextWriter writer) {
            // Note that the implementation of the RenderContents
            // method is identical to the implementation of Render in
            // PrimeGenerator.
            int[] primes = Sieve.GetPrimes(Number);
            writer.Write("Primes less than or equal to: ");
            writer.Write(Number);
            writer.Write("<br>");
            for (int i=0; i<primes.Length; i++){
                writer.Write(primes[i]);
                writer.Write(" ");
            }
            writer.Write("<br>");
        }
    }
}
```

Listing 5-5   StyledPrimeGenerator.cs

Test Page for the *PrimeGenerator* Control

The page shown in Listing 5-6 tests the *PrimeGenerator* and *StyledPrimeGenerator* controls. Note that *StyledPrimeGenerator* inherits properties such as *Height*, *Width*, *ForeColor*, and *BackColor* for free because it derives from *Web-Control*.

```
<%@ Page Language="C#" %>
<%@ Register TagPrefix="msp" NameSpace="MSPress.ServerControls"
  Assembly="MSPress.ServerControls" %>
<html>
  <head>
      <script runat="server">
        void ButtonClicked(object sender, EventArgs e) {
            primegen1.Number = Int32.Parse(num1.Text);
            primegen2.Number = Int32.Parse(num2.Text);
            sprimegen1.Number = Int32.Parse(num3.Text);
        }
      </script>
  </head>
  <body>
    <form runat="server">
      <br>
      <br>
      <msp:PrimeGenerator Number="15" id="primegen1" runat="server" />
      <br>
      <msp:PrimeGenerator Number="100" id="primegen2" runat="server" />
      <br>
      <msp:StyledPrimeGenerator Number="51" id="sprimegen1"
        Width="500" Font-Name="Verdana" Font-Size="14pt"
        BackColor="#EEEEEE" ForeColor="Black" runat="server" />
      <br>
      Enter 3 positive integers:
      <asp:TextBox id="num1" width="50" text="0" runat="server" />
      <asp:TextBox id="num2" width="50" text="0" runat="server" />
      <asp:TextBox id="num3" width="50" text="0" runat="server" />
      <br>
      <asp:Button text="Submit" id="submit"
        onclick="ButtonClicked" runat="server" />
      <br>
    </form>
  </body>
</html>
```

Listing 5-6   PrimeGeneratorTest.aspx

When you access PrimeGeneratorTest.aspx, the output in your browser should be similar to that shown in Figure 5-3. The third output block is rendered by *StyledPrimeGenerator*, which is visually distinct because of values assigned to some of its style properties.

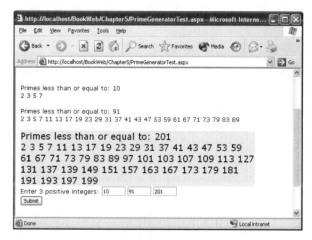

Figure 5-3   The PrimeGeneratorTest.aspx page that tests the *PrimeGenerator* and *StyledPrimeGenerator* controls, viewed in a browser

Choosing the Base Class for Your Control

These guidelines will help you determine the base class from which to derive your control:

- Derive from *System.Web.UI.Control* if your control renders nonvisual elements or renders to a non-HTML client. The *<meta>* and *<xml>* tags are examples of nonvisual rendering.

- Derive from *System.Web.UI.WebControls.WebControl* if you want to render HTML that generates a visual interface on the client.

- Derive from an existing control—such as *Label*, *Button*, and *Text-Box*—when you want to extend or modify the functionality of that control. You can derive from any control in the *System.Web.UI.Web-Controls* namespace or from a custom control. However, do not derive from controls in the *System.Web.UI.HtmlControls* namespace. Controls that derive directly or indirectly from *HtmlControl* are not allowed in the Visual Studio .NET designer because they break the HTML control model. HTML controls are intended to appear without a tag prefix in declarative page syntax (such as *<Button runat="server" />*). However, all custom controls—including those deriving from *HtmlControl* or its descendants—require a tag prefix when used declaratively on a page.

The object models for the *Control* and *WebControl* base classes are described in Appendix B, "Object Model for Key Classes."

Applying Design-Time Attributes

Although the *PrimeGenerator* control works as expected on an .aspx page, you will find that if you use it in a visual designer such as Visual Studio. NET (which we'll demonstrate in the next section), it lacks some standard features that are expected at design time. For example, you might expect the *Number* property to be automatically highlighted when a page developer clicks the control on the design surface. To get this and other design-time features, you have to provide metadata that the designer uses to improve the design-time experience. The .NET Framework enables metadata to be supplied for a class and its members through a feature known as *attributes*. (We described metadata attributes in Chapter 3.) We have marked *PrimeGenerator* with design-time attributes (in square brackets) in the following code:

```
using System;
using System.ComponentModel;
using System.Web.UI;

namespace MSPress.ServerControls {
    [
    DefaultProperty("Number"),
    ToolboxData("<{0}:PrimeGenerator Number=\"15\" runat=\"server\">" +
        "</{0}:PrimeGenerator>")
    ]
    public class PrimeGenerator : Control {
        ⋮
        public int Number{
            ⋮
        }
        protected override void Render(HtmlTextWriter writer) {
            ⋮
        }
    }
}
```

DefaultPropertyAttribute specifies the default property for the control, and *ToolboxDataAttribute* specifies the tag that is written to the page when the control is dragged from the toolbox onto the design surface. *ToolboxDataAttribute* is optional; if this attribute is not applied, the designer generates a standard tag to the page.

We will discuss design-time attributes in more detail in Chapter 15, "Design-Time Functionality." Appendix A, "Metadata Attributes," provides information about the syntax and usage of attributes commonly applied to controls. In this chapter, we'll describe only one attribute—*TagPrefixAttribute*—in more detail because it is especially important at design time.

Applying *TagPrefixAttribute*

TagPrefixAttribute is an assembly-level attribute that provides a tag prefix that a designer uses for a control when it is dragged from the toolbox onto the design surface. If this attribute is not applied, the designer generates a default tag prefix such as *"cc1"* on the page. Because *TagPrefixAttribute* is an assembly-level attribute, it is not applied directly to any particular control; instead, it is declared in a separate file that is compiled into the same assembly as the control.

The *TagPrefixAttribute* attribute is already applied to the sample controls in the book's sample files. If you are re-creating the controls in this chapter to walk through the steps for compilation and deployment, you can apply this attribute as described next.

To apply *TagPrefixAttribute* in Visual Studio .NET, edit the Assembly-Info.cs file in your project to include the following lines of code and rebuild your control project:

```
using System.Web.UI;
[assembly:TagPrefix("MSPress.ServerControls", "msp")]
```

The tag prefix just shown associates the *msp* tag prefix with the namespace *MSPress.ServerControls* so that the tag prefix is generated when a user drags and drops your controls from the toolbox onto a page.

If you are building from the command line, create a file named Assembly-Info.cs and place it in the directory that contains the source files for your controls (for example, C:\MyBookCodeCs\MyServerControls). This file does not necessarily have to be named AssemblyInfo.cs, but for consistency with Visual Studio .NET projects, we recommend that you give it this name.

Add the following code to AssemblyInfo.cs, and save the file:

```
// AssemblyInfo.cs
using System.Reflection;
using System.Runtime.CompilerServices;
using System.Web.UI;
//
// General information about an assembly is controlled
// through assembly-level attributes.
// The TagPrefixAttribute associates a tag prefix with a
// namespace. If you have multiple control namespaces in a single
```

(continued)

```
// assembly, you will need a TagPrefixAttribute corresponding
// to each namespace.
[assembly:TagPrefix("MSPress.ServerControls", "msp")]
```

Recompile the code for your controls and for AssemblyInfo.cs into an assembly using the same command that you used earlier:

```
csc /t:library /out:MSPress.ServerControls.dll /r:System.dll
    /r:System.Web.dll SimpleControl.cs PrimeGenerator.cs
    StyledPrimeGenerator.cs AssemblyInfo.cs
```

See the instructions outlined earlier in the chapter in the section "Compiling and Deploying a Server Control" to make sure that you do not overwrite the assembly generated by the batch file you downloaded with the book's sample files.

The *Register* directive with the tag prefix specified in the *TagPrefixAttribute* is generated only when the control is dragged and dropped onto a page in the designer. If you author pages in a text editor outside the designer, you must manually add the *Register* directive. The next section shows how the *TagPrefixAttribute* is used by a visual designer such as Visual Studio .NET.

Custom Controls in Visual Studio .NET

In this section, we'll show you how to use a custom control in Visual Studio .NET and how you can associate a custom icon with your control.

Adding a Custom Control to the Toolbox

To add *PrimeGenerator* (or any other custom component) to the Toolbox, perform the following steps:

1. Open an .aspx page in Design view, and make the Web Forms tab active in the Toolbox.

2. From the Tools menu, click Customize Toolbox.

3. In the Customize Toolbox dialog box, click the .NET Framework Components tab.

4. Click the Browse button on the lower right below the components list.

5. Navigate to the directory that contains the assembly into which your controls are compiled, and click the name of that assembly (for example, C:\MyBookCodeCS\MyServerControls\MSPress.Server-Controls.dll).

6. You will see that our three controls (*PrimeGenerator*, *SimpleControl*, and *StyledPrimeGenerator*) now appear, along with the other .NET Framework components. Make sure that the boxes next to the control names are checked, as shown in Figure 5-4.

7. Click OK to close the dialog box. You'll see that our three controls now appear in the Toolbox under the Web Forms tab.

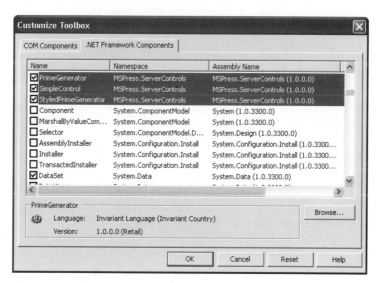

Figure 5-4   User interface for customizing the Toolbox

Using Custom Controls from the Toolbox

To use our custom controls on a page, perform the following steps:

1. Create a new ASP.NET Web application project. (When you create a Web application, Visual Studio .NET automatically creates an IIS virtual root for you.)

2. Double-click the WebForm1.aspx file in Solution Explorer so that the page opens in Design view.

3. Click the Web Forms tab of the Toolbox and you will see that the *SimpleControl*, *PrimeGenerator*, and *StyledPrimeGenerator* controls are now included in the Toolbox.

4. Drag *PrimeGenerator* and *StyledPrimeGenerator* onto the page. When you drag a custom control onto the design surface, Visual Studio .NET copies the assembly that contains the control to your Web

application's bin directory. For example, if your Web application is named MyBookWeb, you will find that MyBookWeb\bin now contains MSPress.ServerControls.dll.

Set some of the style properties of *StyledPrimeGenerator* in the property browser. In HTML view, you should see page syntax similar to that shown in Listing 5-7. Note that the designer automatically generates the tag prefix *msp* corresponding to the namespace *MSPress.ServerControls*, as we specified in the *TagPrefixAttribute*. If our assembly did not have a *TagPrefixAttribute*, the designer would generate a default tag prefix such as *cc1*.

```
<%@ Register TagPrefix="msp" Namespace="MSPress.ServerControls"
  Assembly="MSPress.ServerControls" %>
<%@ Page language="c#" Codebehind="WebForm1.aspx.cs"
  AutoEventWireup="false" Inherits="BookWeb.Chapter5.WebForm1" %>
<!DOCTYPE HTML PUBLIC "-//W3C//DTD HTML 4.0 Transitional//EN" >
<HTML>
  <HEAD>
    <title>WebForm1</title>
    <meta name="GENERATOR" Content="Microsoft Visual Studio 7.0">
    <meta name="CODE_LANGUAGE" Content="C#">
    <meta name="vs_defaultClientScript" content="JavaScript">
    <meta name="vs_targetSchema"
      content="http://schemas.microsoft.com/intellisense/ie5">
  </HEAD>
  <body>
    <form id="WebForm1" method="post" runat="server">
      <msp:PrimeGenerator id="PrimeGenerator1" runat="server"
        Number="91">
      </msp:PrimeGenerator>
      <p>
        <msp:StyledPrimeGenerator id="StyledPrimeGenerator1"
          runat="server" Number="329" BackColor="Gainsboro"
          Font-Size="Medium" Font-Names="Verdana" Width="300px">
        </msp:StyledPrimeGenerator>
      </p>
    </form>
  </body>
</HTML>
```

Listing 5-7 Designer-generated HTML for a page that uses *PrimeGenerator* and *StyledPrimeGenerator*

Figure 5-5 shows the page in Design view in the Visual Studio .NET environment.

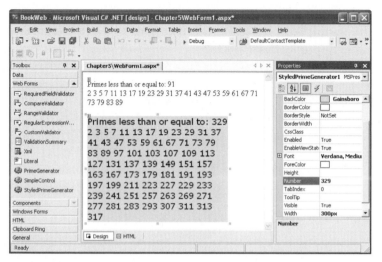

Figure 5-5   A page that uses *PrimeGenerator* and *StyledPrimeGenerator* in Design view in Visual Studio .NET

Notice that unlike *PrimeGenerator*, *StyledPrimeGenerator* has style properties that it inherits from its base class, *WebControl*. In this example, we have set the *ForeColor*, *BackColor*, *BorderColor*, and *BorderStyle* properties of the *StyledPrimeGenerator* instance.

Customizing the Toolbox Icon 16×16 bitmap.

Our custom controls appear with default icons (images of gears) in the Toolbox. You can provide a different icon for your control by embedding a bitmap file in the control's assembly. The bitmap file must contain a 16-by-16 bitmap and must be embedded as a managed resource in the same namespace as the control with which it is associated. The bitmap must be named the same way as its associated control class—for example, *PrimeGenerator.bmp*. By convention, the lower-left pixel of the bitmap determines its transparent color.

To embed a bitmap into an assembly as a managed resource from the command line, add the bitmap to the directory containing the source files for your control and compile using the /res option:

```
csc /res:PrimeGenerator.bmp,MSPress.ServerControls.PrimeGenerator.bmp
    /t:library /out:MSPress.ServerControls.dll /r:System.dll
    /r:System.Web.dll *.cs
```

To embed a bitmap using Visual Studio .NET, add the bitmap to your project and click the bitmap in Solution Explorer. Set the build action to Embedded Resource in the property browser, and rebuild your project.

To see the custom icon in the Toolbox, delete the previous version of your control from the Toolbox, rebuild your control so that the bitmap is embedded in the assembly, and add the control to the Toolbox as before. To delete a control from the Toolbox, you can right-click the control and select the Delete option.

In our example, the visual appearance of our custom controls at design time is the same as the run-time appearance. However, if we want our controls to be displayed differently at design time, we can do so by associating special classes known as *designers* with our controls. We will describe designers in Chapter 15.

Debugging a Server Control

To debug a server control, you must attach a debugger to an application that uses the server control because server controls are compiled into libraries, while a debugger can be attached only to an executable.

You can debug a server control using the debugging capabilities of the Visual Studio .NET IDE, or, if you have the .NET Framework SDK alone, you can use the graphical debugger DbgClr or the command-line debugger, CorDbg.

To debug a control in Visual Studio .NET, perform the following steps:

1.   Create a solution that contains these projects: a class library that contains the control you want to debug and a Web application that contains a Web Forms page that uses your control. Make sure that you have enabled debugging by specifying the *Debug="true"* attribute in the *Page* directive at the top of the page.

2.   Set breakpoints in the source code for your control and build the solution.

3.   In Solution Explorer, right-click the page that uses your control and click Set As Start Page.

4.   From the Debug menu, click Start (or press F5 on the keyboard) to start debugging.

   The debugger will stop at the first breakpoint in the code for your control. From there on, you can perform normal debugging operations such as stepping into code and inspecting variables.

The graphical debugger that ships with the .NET Framework SDK, DbgClr, provides the same debugging capabilities as Visual Studio .NET. However, you must manually perform the steps to compile your controls library, to load your Web application and to attach the debugger to the Web application.

To debug a server control using the DbgClr graphical debugger, perform the following steps:

1. Compile your control using the /debug option. This generates the assembly (.dll) and the program database (.pdb) file that contains debugging information.

2. Create a Web application and copy the .dll and .pdb files to your Web application's bin directory.

3. Create an ASP.NET page that uses the control you want to debug and place it within your Web application. (This step is not needed if your Web application already contains a page or pages that use your control.) Make sure that you have enabled debugging on the page by specifying the *Debug="true"* attribute in the *Page* directive at the top of the page.

4. Start the debugger by opening the FrameworkSDK\GuiDebug directory in Windows Explorer and double-clicking DbgClr.exe.

    From the File menu click Open to browse to the file that contains the source code for the control you want to debug, and open that file.

5. Set breakpoints in the source code of your control.

6. From the Debug menu click Debug Processes. This will launch the Processes dialog box, which displays running processes to which you can attach the debugger.

7. Click aspnet_wp.exe to select the ASP.NET worker process and click the Attach button on the right to attach the debugger to it. In Windows .NET Server, you should attach to the IIS worker process, w3wp.exe, which replaces the ASP.NET worker process.

8. Click the Close button in the upper right corner of the Processes dialog box to close the dialog box.

9. Open a browser window and request a page that uses your control.

    The debugger will stop at the first breakpoint in the code for your control. From there on you can perform normal debugging operations.

Summary

In this chapter, we walked through the process of writing, compiling, using, and debugging a custom control. We examined the *Control* and *WebControl* base classes and looked at design-time metadata attributes that modify the appearance and behavior of a control in a visual designer. We looked at custom controls in Visual Studio .NET and saw that a custom control can be added to the toolbox of a design environment and used on a design surface just as a standard ASP.NET control. In Part III of this book, "Server Controls—Nuts and Bolts," we'll get into the details of control authoring, design-time programming, and deployment so that you can author and distribute professional quality server controls similar to the standard ASP.NET controls.

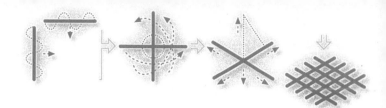

6

Custom Controls vs. User Controls

In Chapter 4, "User Controls: From Page to Control," and Chapter 5, "Developing a Simple Custom Control," we introduced the two models that ASP.NET provides for creating your own controls—the user control model and the custom control model. These two models are geared for different scenarios. In general, the user control model is well suited for authoring in-house, application-specific controls, while the custom (or compiled) control model is better suited for authoring generic and redistributable controls. In this brief chapter, we will compare the two models and provide some basic guidelines to help you decide which alternative is more suited to your particular needs.

Deployment

Deployment is the most important factor to consider when choosing between the two control-authoring models.

The custom control model is designed for authoring redistributable components in the form of an assembly (compiled class library) that can be used by a number of applications. The assembly containing the controls can be used by a single application at a time when placed in the application's private bin directory, or it can be shared across multiple applications when placed into the *global assembly cache*, commonly referred to as the *GAC*. The assembly can be deployed and used in its compiled binary form without the associated source code.

The user control model is designed for single-application scenarios. As we described in Chapter 4, a user control is dynamically compiled at run time when a page that uses it is first requested. As a result, a user control must be deployed in source form, and the .ascx file (and its associated code-behind, if any exists) must be copied into every application that requires the user control. These requirements have the side effect of increasing maintenance costs because changes made to one copy must be manually replicated in all applications in which the user control is deployed. Note that this is a limitation of the current version; future versions of ASP.NET might enable you to statically compile declarative .ascx files into the equivalent of custom controls.

Authoring

The technique for authoring a custom control is quite different from the one that is used for authoring a user control.

Custom controls are authored by writing a managed class that derives directly or indirectly from *System.Web.UI.Control* in a .NET programming language. There is no designer support for authoring custom controls. Custom controls provide an effective way to extend an existing control with new or modified functionality.

At run time, the dynamically compiled user control class also indirectly derives from *System.Web.UI.Control*. However, user controls are authored declaratively in the form of .ascx files, which is very similar to the way ASP.NET pages are designed and developed. A designer such as Microsoft Visual Studio .NET supports drag-and-drop layout for authoring user controls, just as it does for authoring ASP.NET pages. The authoring experience for user controls, which includes visual layout and declarative persistence, is thus simpler and much more suited to rapid application development (RAD). The user control model should be especially useful to page developers who are looking for a quick and easy way to create server controls.

> **Note**   If you need to extend or modify the functionality of an existing control, create a custom control that derives from the existing control. Do not place an instance of the control inside a user control to add functionality and behavior to it because the user control approach does not retain or enable programming against the existing control's object model. You should develop a user control only when you want to provide new functionality by combining more than one existing control.

Content and Layout

Custom controls and user controls offer different capabilities for content and layout because of their differing authoring mechanisms. A control's content includes any static text as well as any child controls it contains or renders within itself. A control's layout provides the structure within which its content is rendered.

Custom controls are very well suited to dynamic content presented in a programmatically generated layout. For example, scenarios such as a data-bound table control with dynamic rows, a tree control with dynamic nodes, or a tab control with dynamic tabs are best implemented as custom controls. In these scenarios, the content and layout are typically dependent on property values and logical conditions based on those values. Custom controls are usually designed for reuse across applications and almost never have any static hard-coded text. Instead, any textual content in their rendering is customizable via string properties.

Because the layout of a user control is declared at authoring time within the .ascx file, user controls are a much better choice when you want relatively static content with a fixed layout. A perfect example of user controls with relatively static content are user controls utilized as headers and footers in pages within a site or application (such as the *SiteHeader* and *SiteFooter* user controls used in the sample pages within the BookWeb application) to implement a consistent and easily modifiable look. A user control can offer a small degree of customizability through properties such as *Text* or *URL* (as the *LinkGlyph* sample in Chapter 4 demonstrates). A user control that implements dynamic layout cannot fully utilize the declarative model and layout capabilities that are available at authoring time, even though these are the essence of the user control model. An application-specific user control is well suited for containing static textual content—a common scenario when you need to factor out a reusable snippet of application-specific HTML content.

Design-Time Behavior

Currently, Visual Studio .NET offers significantly different design-time capabilities for custom controls and user controls.

Visual Studio .NET supports a wide range of RAD design-time capabilities for a custom control. Design-time behavior can range from simple customization of design-time display to enhanced property editing in the property grid to template editing and data binding. Custom controls can also be assigned a customized icon and can be placed on the toolbox of the design-time environment. In addition, custom controls can be associated with custom designers that provide the same RAD experience on a design surface as the standard set of ASP.NET controls. We will describe these custom designers in Chapter 15, "Design-Time Functionality."

User controls have minimal design-time support in the current version of Visual Studio .NET. The design surface provides all user controls with a simple default design-time appearance similar to that of a placeholder block. A user control does not offer its properties in the property grid and cannot be placed on the toolbox.

Performance

Although custom controls and user controls follow different authoring models and have different characteristics, both derive indirectly from the same base class, *System.Web.UI.Control*. A user control's implementation is declarative; however, it is parsed as a control and compiled into an assembly the first time it is used by a page. Thereafter, a user control behaves like any other compiled (or custom) control. As a result, there is no significant performance difference between the two models. Therefore, you should choose between the two models based on factors other than performance, such as deployment, authoring, and design-time support.

Summary

This chapter compared custom controls and user controls based on their characteristics. Table 6-1 provides recommendations for some of the common server control development scenarios.

Table 6-1   Recommendations for Server Control Development Scenarios

Scenario	Recommendation	Deciding Requirement
Commercial or redistributable package of controls—for example, standard ASP.NET controls	Custom controls	Must be able to deploy precompiled binaries.
Data-bound controls—for example, the *DataGrid* control	Custom controls	Need to generate content and layout dynamically based on the data source. The ability to use static content functionality of .ascx does not help. In addition, data-bound controls generally need to provide design-time functionality that is not available to user controls.
Templated controls—for example, the *DataList* control	Custom controls	Need the ability to specify the content for the control as a template in the page containing the control. The ability to use static content functionality of .ascx does not help in this scenario. Template editing features require an associated designer that isn't available to user controls.
Extended controls—for example, a hypothetical *HoverImage* control that derives from the standard *Image* control	Custom controls	Need to add new functionality to an existing control or to modify its behavior while preserving the object model of the inherited control class.
Reusable HTML snippets—for example, the *SiteHeader* and *Site-Footer* user controls described in Chapter 4	User controls	Need to reuse HTML snippets. These snippets are usually application specific and primarily contain static content or markup.
Composite controls—for example, the *RequiredTextField* user control described in Chapter 4	User controls	Need to create a new control by compositing (combining) a predetermined set of controls in a fixed layout. Composite controls are very easily authored using the RAD authoring support available for .ascx files.
Fragment caching—for example, the *CachedUserControl* sample from Chapter 4	User controls	Need to cache fragments of a page. A user control offers a convenient declarative mechanism for caching by using the *OutputCache* directive.

This chapter should serve as a guide that helps you choose between the two control-authoring models provided by ASP.NET. At a high level, custom controls are suited for the creation of general purpose, redistributable, and oftentimes commercial class libraries, while user controls are suited for the creation of reusable user interfaces scoped to a single application or project.

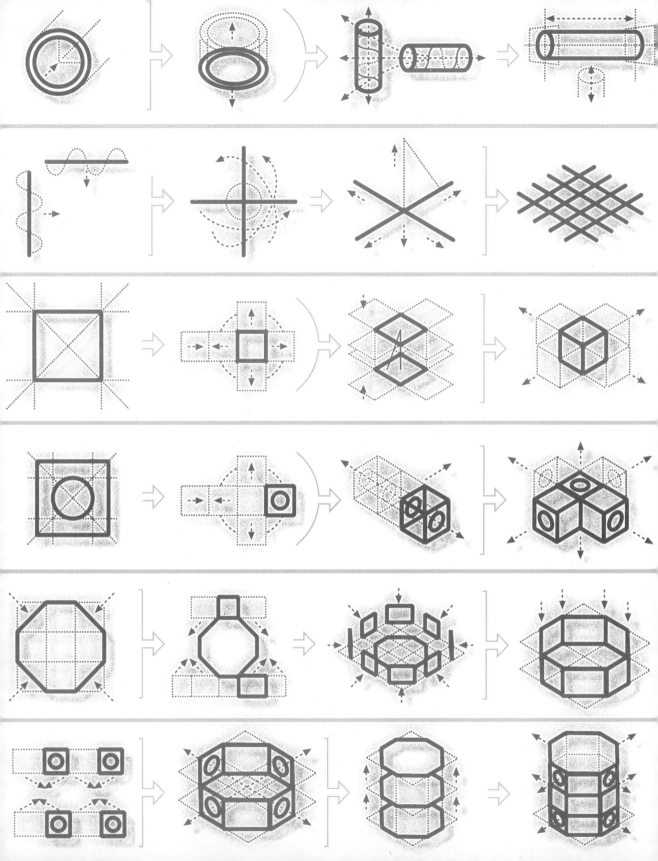

Part III

Server Controls—Nuts and Bolts

This part examines the architecture of ASP.NET server controls and provides in-depth coverage of the essential control authoring tasks. It illustrates core concepts including properties, state management, events, postback data processing, and rendering. It shows how to develop composite and templated controls, controls with client-side behavior, validator controls, and data-bound controls. It demonstrates how to incorporate design-time functionality so that controls provide a rich experience in a visual designer such as Visual Studio .NET. It concludes with a discussion of localization and licensing.

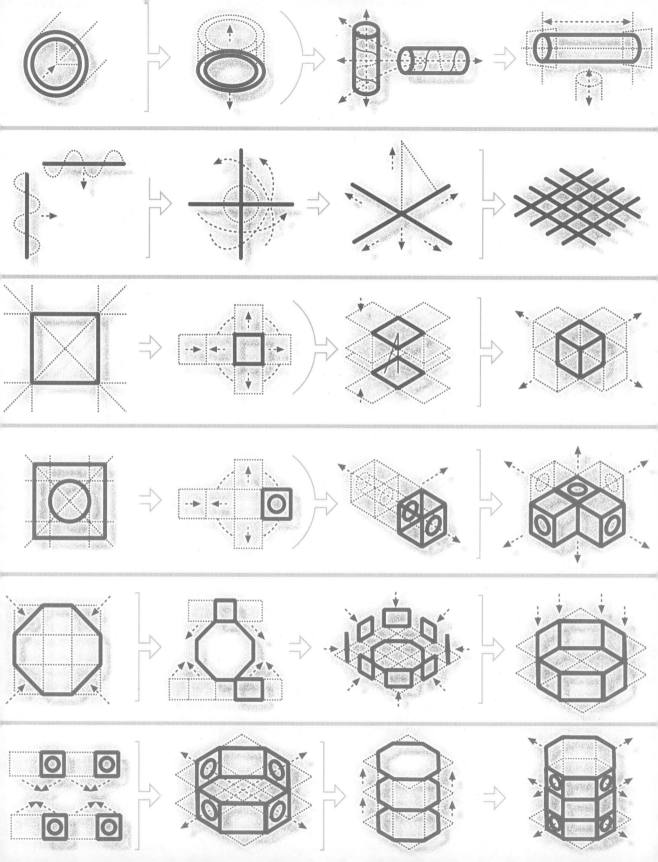

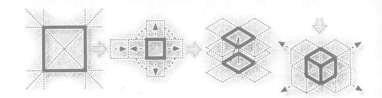

7

Simple Properties and View State

In Chapter 3, "Component Programming Overview," we described the syntax of the property construct and discussed why you should expose properties instead of fields from your components. In this chapter, we'll get into details that are specific to properties in server controls. We'll describe how to maintain state for simple properties across round-trips. We'll also describe how declarative syntax is enabled for simple properties in an .aspx page and show you how simple properties are supported in a designer. In addition, we'll examine the basic set of properties you inherit when you derive from *Control* or *WebControl*.

It is important to clarify what we mean by *simple properties* and how they differ from *complex properties*. Simple properties are properties whose values can be easily converted into a textual (string) representation. These include primitive types such as *Int32*, *Boolean*, and *DateTime* as well as other commonly used types such as *String* and enumerations. On the other hand, complex properties represent types that are not easily expressed as single strings. These include nonprimitive value types, reference types other than *String*, and collection types. We'll describe complex properties in Chapter 10, "Complex Properties and State Management."

View State and State Management

Web applications are built on top of HTTP, which is a stateless protocol. A page and its child controls are created upon each request and disposed of at the end of the request, as we described in Chapter 2, "Page Programming Model." However, it is often necessary to maintain information beyond the duration of a single Web request. The mechanisms that were available in traditional Active Server Pages programming for state management—such as the *Session* object on the server and cookies on the client—are still available in ASP.NET. However, Session state is not scalable, and cookies cannot be depended upon for all applications. ASP.NET offers a new mechanism known as *view state* that enables a page and its controls to maintain state across a round-trip from the server to the client and back. View state offers a simple and convenient technique to create the illusion of a stateful and continually executing page on top of an inherently stateless environment. In essence, the default view state mechanism involves the persistence of state information through a hidden variable on a page, as we'll see in the next section of the chapter.

The simplest way to use the view state mechanism is through the *View-State* property that your control inherits from the *Control* class. The *ViewState* property is of type *System.Web.UI.StateBag*—a dictionary of key/value pairs in which you can store values of your control's properties. To get a feel for using the *ViewState* (dictionary) property, let's develop a control that uses *ViewState* for storing properties.

Using *ViewState* as the Property Store— The *ViewStateDemoLabel* Example

The ViewStateDemoLabel control that we'll develop defines two properties, *Text* and *TextInViewState*. We'll store *Text* in a private field and *TextInViewState* in the *ViewState* dictionary. The code for the control is shown in Listing 7-1.

```
using System;
using System.ComponentModel;
using System.Web.UI;
using System.Web.UI.WebControls;

namespace MSPress.ServerControls {
    public class ViewStateDemoLabel : WebControl {
        private string _text;
```

Listing 7-1   ViewStateDemoLabel.cs

```
public string Text {
    get {
        return (_text == null) ? String.Empty : _text;
    }
    set {
        _text = value;
    }
}

public string TextInViewState {
    get {
        object o = ViewState["TextInViewState"];
        return (o == null)? String.Empty : (string)o;
    }
    set{
        ViewState["TextInViewState"] = value;
    }
}

protected override void RenderContents(HtmlTextWriter writer) {
    writer.Write("Text = ");
    writer.Write(Text);
    writer.Write("<br>");
    writer.Write("TextInViewState = ");
    writer.Write(TextInViewState);
}
}
}
```

When the page framework reloads a control after postback, it automatically restores any properties that store their values in *ViewState* to their state at the end of processing the previous request. You do not have to do any additional work in your control to restore the state of those properties. When a property is stored in the *ViewState* dictionary, *ViewState* tracks the property after the control is initialized and saves its value in the control's serializable view state only if the property is modified after initialization. This process minimizes the size of the data that is round-tripped. We'll describe the initialization and tracking phases in more detail in Chapter 9.

Using *ViewState* as its property storage, a custom control can easily perform basic state management without implementing custom state management logic. If the property is not present in the *ViewState* dictionary, the property getter must return the default value associated with the property.

The keys used to store properties in *ViewState* are strings that typically represent the names of properties. We'll list the types of values you can store in *ViewState* later in this section.

Listing 7-2 shows a page that uses the *ViewStateDemoLabel* control. The page has two *TextBox* controls, two *Button* controls (Submit and Reload), and an instance of the *ViewStateDemoLabel* control.

```
<%@ Page Language="C#" %>
<%@ Register TagPrefix="msp" Namespace="MSPress.ServerControls"
  Assembly="MSPress.ServerControls" %>
<html>
  <head>
    <script runat="server">
      void button1_Click(object sender, EventArgs e) {
          demolabel1.Text = textbox1.Text;
          demolabel1.TextInViewState = textbox2.Text;
      }
    </script>
  </head>
  <body>
    <form runat="server">
      <br>
      Enter your first name: <asp:TextBox id="textbox1"
        runat="server" />
      <br>
      Enter your last name:  <asp:TextBox id="textbox2"
        runat="server" />
      <br><br>
      <asp:Button text="Submit" onClick="button1_Click"
        id="button1" Runat="server" />
      <asp:Button Text="Reload" Runat="server" id="Button2" />
      <br><br>
      Here is the output from the ViewStateDemoLabel:
      <br>
      <msp:ViewStateDemoLabel id="demolabel1" runat="server"
        Font-Names="Verdana" Font-Size="Medium" />
      <br>
    </form>
  </body>
</html>
```

Listing 7-2   ViewStateDemoLabelTest.aspx

The Submit button has an associated event handler that populates the two properties of the *ViewStateDemoLabel* instance with user input from the text boxes, thus changing the initial state of the *ViewStateDemoLabel* instance. The Reload button causes the page to be submitted without changing the state of the *ViewStateDemoLabel* instance. When the Reload button is clicked, the

ViewStateDemoLabel control is loaded with the state that was saved after processing the previous request.

Figure 7-1 shows the page in a browser after a user has entered text in the text boxes and clicked the Submit button.

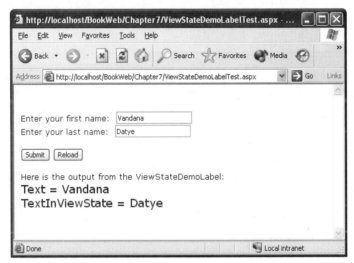

Figure 7-1   ViewStateDemoLabelTest.aspx viewed in the browser after entering values in the text boxes and clicking the Submit button

Figure 7-2 shows the page in a browser after the user reloads it by clicking the Reload button.

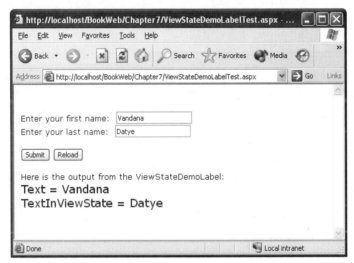

Figure 7-2   ViewStateDemoLabelTest.aspx viewed in the browser after clicking the Reload button

Notice that in Figure 7-2, only one of the properties of the *ViewStateDemo-Label* instance is displayed: the *TextInViewState* property that saves its value in *ViewState*. Because the *Text* property of *ViewStateDemoLabel* uses a private field as its property store, the value of the *Text* property is not saved across a round-trip. On postback, the page framework re-creates the page and its control tree and restores state using the serialized state. Thus, the *TextInViewState* property returns the value that was saved in view state after processing the previous request and that was round-tripped, while the *Text* property returns its default value (an empty string).

To see the hidden variable that contains the serialized state, view the HTML source in your browser corresponding to Figure 7-1 or 7-2. You will see a hidden element on the HTML page named __VIEWSTATE, as shown here:

```
<input type="hidden" name="__VIEWSTATE"
  value="dDwxMTc3NDI5NDg1O3Q802w8aTwyPjs+02w8dDw7bDxpPDExPjs+02w8dDxw
PHA8bDxUZXh0SW5WaWV3U3RhdGU7PjtsPERhdHl1Oz4+0z470z47Pj47Pj47Pg==" />
```

The hidden __VIEWSTATE field holds the base-64 encoded string that contains the serialized view state for the page and all its controls.

To see the size of the view state for the page and for each control, add the *Trace* attribute to the *Page* directive in your .aspx Page—for example, *<%@ Page Language="C#" Trace ="true" %>*. The page rendered in your browser will contain a detailed description of the view state size.

More About View State

Let's take a more detailed look at the view state mechanism. In this chapter (and elsewhere in this book), we'll use *ViewState* to denote the property *Control.ViewState* and the term *view state* to denote the overall mechanism in ASP.NET for maintaining state across a round-trip by serializing it into a string representation.

How View State Works

At the end of processing a Web request, the page framework collects the state from all the controls in the control tree and creates a single object graph. The *ViewState* dictionary of each control is one part of its saved state. We'll examine the other pieces of the saved state in Chapter 10. The page framework serializes the entire object graph into a single string representation, which it then sends to the client as a hidden variable by default. The hidden variable is round-tripped to the server upon postback. (A page developer can change the default persistence mechanism by overriding the *LoadPageStateFromPersistenceMedium* and *SavePageStateToPersistenceMedium* methods of the *Page* class to persist the serialized state elsewhere, instead of round-tripping the state as a hidden field.)

When the browser posts the page back to the server, the page framework reads back the hidden variable and deserializes it to repopulate the saved state into the respective controls in the control tree. As part of this reloading, the *View-State* dictionary is automatically repopulated with the values that existed in it at the end of the previous request. Any state that a control saved in its *ViewState* dictionary is thus automatically restored.

Hidden variables have been traditionally used for maintaining state in Web programming. The difference between the traditional use of hidden variables and the view state technique is that the page framework does the work of serializing and deserializing state. In simple controls, all you have to do as a control author is use *ViewState* for storing your property values. When developing complex controls, you will often have to use a combination of *ViewState* and custom state management (by implementing *IStateManager*), as we'll describe in Chapter 10.

Enabling View State

The *Control* class exposes a Boolean property named *EnableViewState* that allows the user of a control to specify whether the view state for that control and its children should be serialized by page framework at the end of a request. The default value of *EnableViewState* is *true*. If *EnableViewState* is *false* on a control, the view state of the control itself and that of its child controls (if any exist) are not serialized. A page developer can decide which controls to serialize by selectively setting *EnableViewState* to *true* or *false* on the controls in the page.

You should not modify the value of your control's *EnableViewState* property to disable persistence of view state. This property is meant to provide page developers with a mechanism to optimize their use of view state. If needed, within your control you can modify the *EnableViewState* property of any child controls that your control might create and contain.

Types You Can Store in View State

The view state of a control can store a variety of types. However, it is optimized in terms of speed and serialization size for a certain set of commonly used types. The types that the view state serialization mechanism natively supports are *Int32*, *Boolean*, *String*, *Unit*, and *Color*. In addition, the view state is optimized for *Array*, *ArrayList* and *Hashtable* objects that contain the types listed earlier. When a type does not fall within this set of optimized types, the value is converted to and from a string by using its associated type converter. *Type converters* are classes that perform type conversions, including string-to-value and value-to-string conversions. We'll describe type converters in Chapter 10. If a type converter is not found, the page framework serializes the value by using the binary serialization functionality provided by the .NET Framework, which is significantly more expensive. When you use view state in your control, you should try to restrict yourself to the optimized types. Alternatively, you can implement an efficient conversion algorithm in a type converter and associate it with the type.

View State and Performance

It is important to make judicious use of view state because it can create a performance overhead. Any data in the view state that is modified after a control is initialized is serialized by the page framework and sent to the client over the network by default. It is then sent back to the server when the user posts the form. The size of the view state also determines the amount of processing time required for the serialization and deserialization of the view state. You should not save computed values in view state. If there are several properties that depend on common data, you can optimize performance by persisting only one copy of the common data into the view state.

View State and Security

The page framework round-trips the serialized string representation of the view state as clear text with standard base-64 encoding. By default, the page framework also sends a digest of the view state string, which allows the page to check on postback if the view state was tampered with during the round-trip. Thus, a hacker can read but not alter the content of the hidden variable that stores the view state. To make view state more secure, a page developer can choose to encrypt the view state for the page so that it cannot be read during the round-trip.

Note that page security is entirely in the hands of the page developer. As a server control author, you have no control over how a page developer implements security on a page that consumes your control. Therefore, you should not make any assumptions about the security mechanism of the containing page when implementing your control. You should never save any information (such as passwords, connection strings, and file paths) in view state that could compromise the security of an application. You should instead use private member variables to store such information and require the page developer to set those property values on each request.

Using *Session* and *Application* Objects

At times, your control might need to reuse data across a user session or even across an application. The following are overall guidelines for using the intrinsic *Session* and *Application* objects that ASP.NET provides:

■ Use view state to store data that your control needs to restore its state after postback.

■ Use the *System.Web.SessionState.HttpSessionState* object, available to your control as *Page.Session*, to store data that is needed across a user's browser session. You can store sensitive information in *Page.Session* because this object exists only on the server. The *Session* object is created for each user session; you do not have to be concerned with thread safety when using the *Session* object. However, note that a page developer is allowed to turn off the Session state feature for a particular Web application.

■ Use the *System.Web.HttpApplicationState* object, available to your control as *Page.Application*, to store data that is needed across an entire application. This object exists only on the server. The *Page.Application* object is not thread-safe because multiple users could access a page at the same time. You are responsible for thread safety when using the *Page.Application* object.

At the end of this chapter, we'll look at the *PageTracker* control, which uses all three mechanisms for maintaining its state.

Declarative Persistence of Simple Properties

The ASP.NET *parser* supports a declarative model for setting properties on controls as attributes on the control's tag. This declarative model works with custom controls just as it does with standard ASP.NET controls and greatly simplifies the customization of controls by a page developer. As with standard controls, property values in a custom control can also be set programmatically (in code) in the containing page.

The following example recapitulates the declarative syntax for setting a property as an attribute on the control's tag:

```
<asp:TextBox id="textBox1" Text="Enter your name" ForeColor="Black"
   runat="server" />
```

The page parser converts the property value to and from its textual format by using an instance of a type converter class. A type converter class derives from *System.ComponentModel.TypeConverter* and is capable of converting from a string representation to the given type as well as from the given type to a string representation. Commonly used types such as *Int32*, *Boolean*, and enumeration types have corresponding type converters implemented in the .NET

Framework (*System.ComponentModel.Int32Converter*, *System.Component-Model.BooleanConverter*, and *System.ComponentModel.EnumConverter*, respectively). Therefore, when you define a property whose type corresponds to a common built-in type, you do not have to do anything special to enable declarative syntax for that property. Note that type conversion is performed on the page for declarative syntax only. When the property is set in code, the assigned value must match the type of the property, as shown in the following code fragment:

```
TextBox1.ForeColor = Color.Black;
```

To enable declarative persistence when you define a property of a custom type, you must implement a custom type converter that provides the logic to convert the property from its textual representation to its declared type. For example, ASP.NET defines a type converter (*System.Web.UI.WebControls.Web-ColorConverter*) that performs string-to-value conversions for the *System.Draw-ing.Color* type properties of *WebControl*, such as *ForeColor* and *BackColor*. In the previous example, the *ForeColor* property on a *TextBox* instance is assigned declaratively by using a color name (*ForeColor="Black"*). The page parser uses the *WebColorConverter* to convert the text string that specifies the color (as a name or as #RRGGBB notation) into a *Color* object and assigns it to the *Fore-Color* or *BackColor* property. In Chapter 10, we'll look at an example of implementing a type converter and associating it with a property.

At the end of this chapter, we'll implement simple properties of several different types (*Int32*, *String*, and enumeration) in the *PageTracker* sample control.

Declarative Syntax for Enumeration Properties

In declarative syntax, you set an enumerated property by specifying the enumeration value without using the type name of the enumeration. In the following example, we set the *TextMode* property of a *System.Web.UI.WebControls.TextBox* control to a value from the *System.Web.UI.WebControls.TextBox-Mode* enumeration:

```
<asp:TextBox id="textBox1" TextMode="MultiLine" runat="server" />
```

The page parser resolves *MultiLine* as *TextBoxMode.MultiLine* by inferring the enumeration type from the property type. However, when you set an enumerated property in code, you must use the standard enumeration syntax, as shown in the following code fragment:

```
textBox1.TextMode = TextBoxMode.MultiLine;
```

When you expose enumeration properties from your control, you do not have to do any additional work in terms of parsing or persisting to enable the declarative enumeration syntax. The *System.ComponentModel.EnumConverter* type converter that the .NET Framework automatically associates with all enumeration types provides this functionality. In addition, the *EnumConverter* provides special editing support in the designer, which enables the property browser to display the enumeration values as choices in a drop-down list.

Properties Inherited from *Control* and *WebControl*

In this section, we'll walk you through the properties that your control inherits from the base control classes.

Control Properties

The *System.Web.UI.Control* class defines properties that are essential for a server control to participate in the ASP.NET page framework. Table 7-1 lists the important public properties that every server control inherits from *Control*.

Table 7-1   Public Properties of the *Control* Class

Public Property	Type	Description
ClientID	*String*	A unique identifier assigned to a control by the ASP.NET page framework and rendered as the HTML *id* attribute. We'll describe *ClientID* when we look at client-side scripting in Chapter 13, "Client-Side Behavior."
Controls	*ControlCollection*	The collection of a control's child controls in the control tree. We'll describe the *Controls* property in Chapter 12.
EnableViewState	*Boolean*	Specifies whether a control's state is persisted in view state across round-trips. We described *EnableViewState* earlier in this chapter in the section "Enabling View State."
ID	*String*	A user-supplied identifier for a control that is used to access the control. The page framework uses the ID value and the location of the control in the control tree to generate the *ClientID* and *UniqueID* properties.

(continued)

Table 7-1   Public Properties of the *Control* Class   *(continued)*

Public Property	Type	Description
NamingContainer	*Control*	The nearest control, upward in the control hierarchy, that implements the *System.Web.UI.INaming-Container* interface. We will describe *NamingContainer* in Chapter 12.
Page	*Page*	The page that contains the control.
Parent	*Control*	The control's parent control in the control tree. (Control *A* is a parent of control *B* if *B* belongs to *A.Controls*.) We'll describe *Parent* in Chapter 12.
UniqueID	*String*	The hierarchically qualified unique identifier assigned to a control by the page framework. We'll describe *UniqueID* in Chapter 12.
Visible	*Boolean*	Specifies whether the control should be rendered into the response stream when the page is rendered.

Table 7-2 describes the important protected properties that your control inherits from the *Control* class.

Table 7-2   Protected Properties of the *Control* Class

Protected Property	Type	Description
Context	*HttpContext*	Provides access to the *System.Web.HttpContext* object for the current Web request. The *Context* property allows a control to access other HTTP intrinsic objects, such as *Application*, *Session*, *Request*, and *Response*.
ViewState	*StateBag*	A dictionary of state information that is serialized and round-tripped across postbacks.

Appendix B, "Object Model for Key Classes," lists the complete object model for the *Control* class and provides an exhaustive list of all its properties.

WebControl Properties

You should derive your control from the *System.Web.UI.WebControls.WebControl* base class if you want to generate visible HTML elements. *WebControl* derives from *Control* and adds properties that enable a page developer to customize the appearance and behavior of the HTML element that is rendered by your control. These properties include strongly typed style properties such as *Font*, *ForeColor*, *BackColor*, and *Width*.

Table 7-3 lists the important public properties of *WebControl*.

Table 7-3 Public Properties Defined by the *WebControl* Class

Public Property	Type	Description
AccessKey	*String*	The keyboard shortcut key used to set focus on the rendered HTML element.
Attributes	*AttributeCollection*	A collection of custom name/value pairs rendered as attributes on the HTML element rendered by the control. We'll describe this property in Chapter 10.
BackColor	*Color*	The background color of the HTML element rendered by the control.
BorderColor	*Color*	The color of the border around the HTML element rendered by the control.
BorderStyle	*BorderStyle*	The border style of the HTML element rendered by the control, such as solid, double, or dotted.
BorderWidth	*Unit*	The thickness of the border around the HTML element rendered by the control.
ControlStyle	*Style*	The strongly typed style of the control that encapsulates all its appearance-related functionality. We'll describe *ControlStyle* in Chapter 11, "Styles in Controls." The type of *ControlStyle* is a class that derives from *System.Web.UI.WebControls.Style*, which exposes properties such as *Font*, *Width*, *BackColor*, and *ForeColor*.
CssClass	*String*	The CSS class rendered by the control on the client. Page developers can use this property to associate the rendered element with style attributes declared in a style sheet.
Enabled	*Boolean*	Specifies whether the HTML element rendered by a Web server control is enabled. Typically, an HTML element that is not enabled is dimmed in the Web browser and cannot receive input focus.
Font	*FontInfo*	The font used to display the text within the HTML element rendered by the control.
ForeColor	*Color*	The foreground color of the text within the HTML element rendered by the control.
Height	*Unit*	The height of the HTML element rendered by the control.
ToolTip	*String*	The text shown in the ToolTip that is displayed when the cursor is situated over the HTML element rendered by the control.
Width	*Unit*	The width of the HTML element rendered by the control.

Table 7-4 lists the protected properties that your control inherits when you derive from *WebControl*.

Table 7-4   Protected Properties of the *WebControl* Class

Protected Property	Type	Description
TagKey	*HtmlTextWriterTag*	Override this property to render a standard HTML tag that is included in the *System.Web.UI.HtmlTextWriterTag* enumeration instead of the default *<span>* tag that *WebControl* renders.
TagName	*String*	Override this property to render a nonstandard HTML tag (one that is not included in the *System.Web.UI.HtmlText-WriterTag* enumeration) instead of the default *<span>* tag.

Appendix B lists the complete object model for the WebControl class and provides an exhaustive list of all its properties.

Design-Time Attributes for Properties

In the section "Metadata Attributes" in Chapter 3, we provided an overview of metadata attributes in the .NET Framework. In the *PageTracker* example in the next section of this chapter, you will see several metadata attributes in action. We'll apply design-time attributes to properties of the *PageTracker* control to inform the designer how to display and serialize properties at design time.

You should apply a core set of design-time attributes to properties to enhance the design-time behavior of your control. Table 7-5 lists design-time metadata attributes that are commonly applied to properties. A complete list of design-time attributes is provided in Appendix A, "Metadata Attributes." Note that design-time attributes are applied only to public properties because properties that are not public are never visible in the designer.

Table 7-5   Design-Time Metadata Attributes for Properties

Attribute	Description
BindableAttribute	Specifies whether it is meaningful to bind data to the property. We'll discuss data binding in Chapter 16, "Data-Bound Controls."
BrowsableAttribute	Specifies whether the property should be displayed in the property browser. By default, a public property is always displayed in the property browser. Apply this attribute as *Browsable(false)* only if you do not want a property to be displayed. You should generally mark read-only properties as *Browsable(false)*.

(continued)

Table 7-5   Design-Time Metadata Attributes for Properties   *(continued)*

Attribute	Description
CategoryAttribute	Specifies the category that a property should be grouped by in the property browser. When the page developer selects the category filter, this attribute makes it possible to organize properties in logical groupings, such as Appearance, Behavior, Data, and Layout.
DefaultValueAttribute	Specifies a default value for the property, which is used by the designer to assign a value to the property. The value that you pass into this attribute should be the same as the default value returned by the property.
DescriptionAttribute	Provides a brief description of the property that is displayed at the bottom of the property browser when the page developer selects the property.
DesignerSerialization-VisibilityAttribute	Specifies whether and how a property should be serialized in code. For example, you should mark a read-only property as *DesignerSerializationVisibility(DesignerSerializationVisibility.Hidden)* so that the property is excluded from the designer's serialization mechanism. You will see an example of this attribute in the *PageTracker* example in the next section. We'll discuss this attribute in more detail in Chapter 10.

Multiple Meanings of Attribute

In this book, we use the term *attribute* to mean three different things:

- Metadata attributes that are used in managed code, such as *Browsable(false)*

- Attributes within a control's tag that are used for setting a control's properties in ASP.NET declarative page syntax—for example, *<asp:TextBox* **Text="Some Text"** *runat="server"/>*

- HTML attributes in an HTML element that is rendered to the client

In general, the meaning of the term *attribute* is clear from the context. But where there is ambiguity, we'll qualify *attribute* as a .NET metadata attribute, an attribute in a control's tag, or an HTML attribute rendered by a control.

Overriding an Attribute

You can override the attributes that your control inherits from its base class. To modify existing attributes on a property, you have to override the property and reapply attributes to it. For example, the *BackColor* property that a control inherits from *WebControl* is displayed in the property browser by default. If you do not want this property to be displayed in the property browser, you can override the *BrowsableAttribute* as shown in the following example:

```
[Browsable(false)]
public override Color BackColor {
    get {
        return base.BackColor;
    }
    set {
        base.BackColor = value;
    }
}
```

Putting It Together—The *PageTracker* Example

We'll now develop a control (*PageTracker*) that brings together the different ideas we've introduced in this chapter. The *PageTracker* control tracks the number of hits a page receives per application or per session and computes the round-trip time for a page. *PageTracker* exposes simple properties of several different types: *PageTrackingMode* (a custom enumeration type that we will define) and three built-in types: *Int32*, *String,* and *TimeSpan*. *PageTracker* uses three different mechanisms for state management (*ViewState*, *Session*, and *Application*) and applies design-time attributes for designer support. We'll show the code for *PageTracker* first and then describe the details.

Listing 7-3 contains the code for the *PageTrackingMode* enumeration that is used by *PageTracker*.

```
using System;

namespace MSPress.ServerControls {
    public enum PageTrackingMode {
        ByApplication,
        BySession,
        ByTripTime
    }
}
```

Listing 7-3 PageTrackingMode.cs

Listing 7-4 contains the code for the *PageTracker* control.

```
using System;
using System.ComponentModel;
using System.Web.UI;
using System.Web.UI.WebControls;

namespace MSPress.ServerControls {

    [
    DefaultProperty("TrackingMode"),
    ]
    public class PageTracker : WebControl {

        private TimeSpan _tripTime;

        [
        Category("Appearance"),
        DefaultValue("{0}"),
        Description("The formatting string used to display the " +
            "value being tracked.")
        ]
        public virtual string FormatString {
            get {
                string s = (string)ViewState["FormatString"];
                return ((s == null) ? "{0}" : s);
            }
            set {
                ViewState["FormatString"] = value;
            }
        }

        [
        Browsable(false),
        DesignerSerializationVisibility(
            DesignerSerializationVisibility.Hidden)
        ]
        public int Hits {
            get {
                PageTrackingMode mode = TrackingMode;
                object o = null;
                if (mode == PageTrackingMode.ByApplication) {
                    o = Page.Application[HitsKey];
                }
                else if (mode == PageTrackingMode.BySession) {
                    o = Page.Session[HitsKey];
                }
```

Listing 7-4   PageTracker.cs   *(continued)*

Listing 7-4   *(continued)*

```
            else {
                throw new NotSupportedException("Hits is only " +
                    "supported when TrackingMode is " +
                    "PageTrackingMode.ByApplication or " +
                    "PageTrackingMode.BySession");
            }
            return ((o == null) ? 0 : (int)o);
        }
    }


    [
    Category("Behavior"),
    DefaultValue(PageTrackingMode.ByApplication),
    Description("The type of tracking to perform.")
    ]
    public virtual PageTrackingMode TrackingMode {
        get {
            object mode = ViewState["TrackingMode"];
            return ((mode == null) ?
                PageTrackingMode.ByApplication :
                (PageTrackingMode)mode);
        }
        set {
            if (value < PageTrackingMode.ByApplication ||
                value > PageTrackingMode.ByTripTime) {
                throw new ArgumentOutOfRangeException("value");
            }
            ViewState["TrackingMode"] = value;

            // Perform cleanup of the old storage.
            // We have to check that the Page is not null
            // because the control could be initialized
            // before it is added to the control tree.
            // Note that the Application and Session
            // objects are not available in the designer.
            switch (TrackingMode) {
                case PageTrackingMode.ByApplication:
                    if (Page != null && Page.Application != null) {
                        Page.Application.Remove(HitsKey);
                    }
                    break;
                case PageTrackingMode.BySession:
                    if (Page != null && Page.Session != null) {
                        Page.Session.Remove(HitsKey);
                    }
                    break;
```

```
                case PageTrackingMode.ByTripTime:
                    ViewState.Remove("TimeStamp");
                    break;
            }
        }
    }

    [
    Browsable(false),
    DesignerSerializationVisibility(
        DesignerSerializationVisibility.Hidden)
    ]
    public TimeSpan TripTime {
        get {
            if (TrackingMode != PageTrackingMode.ByTripTime) {
                throw new NotSupportedException("TripTime is " +
                    "only supported when TrackingMode is " +
                    "PageTrackingMode.ByTripTime");
            }
            return _tripTime;
        }
    }

    protected override HtmlTextWriterTag TagKey {
        get {
            return HtmlTextWriterTag.Div;
        }
    }

    private string HitsKey {
        get {
            // Create a unique HitsKey for the page for keying
            // in hits per page in the Application and Session
            // objects.
            return Page.GetType().FullName;
        }
    }

    protected override void OnLoad(EventArgs e) {
        base.OnLoad(e);
        switch (TrackingMode) {
            case PageTrackingMode.ByApplication:
                // Update the page hits in the Application
                // object. This operation needs a lock because
                // multiple users could access a page at the same
                // time.
```

(continued)

Listing 7-4   *(continued)*

```
                    lock(Page.GetType()){
                        Page.Application[HitsKey] = Hits + 1;
                    }
                    break;
                case PageTrackingMode.BySession:
                    Page.Session[HitsKey] = Hits + 1;
                    break;
                case PageTrackingMode.ByTripTime:
                    // Get the timestamp for the previous request
                    // from ViewState and compute the difference
                    // between the previous
                    // and current timestamp.
                    object timeStamp = ViewState["TimeStamp"];
                    DateTime requestTime = Context.Timestamp;
                    if (timeStamp == null) {
                        _tripTime = TimeSpan.Zero;
                        this.Visible = false;
                    }
                    else {
                        this.Visible = true;
                        _tripTime =
                            (requestTime - (DateTime)timeStamp);
                    }
                    ViewState["TimeStamp"] = requestTime;
                    break;
            }
        }

        protected override void RenderContents(HtmlTextWriter writer) {
            switch (TrackingMode) {
                case PageTrackingMode.ByApplication:
                case PageTrackingMode.BySession:
                    writer.Write(FormatString, Hits);
                    break;
                case PageTrackingMode.ByTripTime:
                    writer.Write(FormatString, TripTime.TotalSeconds);
                    break;
            }
        }
    }
}
```

The *PageTracker* control performs the following tasks:

■   Exposes properties of various types. The *FormatString* property is of type *String*, the *Hits* property is of type *Int32*, the *TrackingMode* property is an enumeration type (*PageTrackingMode* enumeration, defined in Listing 7-3), and the *TripTime* property is of type *TimeSpan*.

■   Exposes read/write properties (*FormatString* and *TrackingMode*) as well as read-only properties (*Hits* and *TripTime*).

■   Exposes virtual, or overridable, properties (*FormatString* and *TrackingMode*) as well as nonvirtual properties (*Hits* and *TripTime*).

■   Implements public properties (*FormatString*, *TrackingMode*, *Hits*, and *TripTime*) as well as a private property (*HitsKey*). The public properties have metadata that specifies how they appear within the property browser and whether they are serialized in the designer. The private property, however, does not require this metadata.

■   Maintains the state of its *FormatString* and *TrackingMode* properties across round-trips by using *ViewState* and indirectly uses *ViewState* to compute its *TripTime* property by round-tripping an old timestamp.

■   Maintains the state of its *Hits* property by using the *Session* object or the *Application* object (based on the tracking mode). *PageTracker* uses a lock when writing hits to the *Application* object because multiple threads could request the same page at the same time.

■   Updates the state of its *Hits* and *TripTime* properties in its *OnLoad* method. This method corresponds to the Load phase in a control's life cycle, which we'll discuss in Chapter 9, "Control Life Cycle, Events, and Postback." In brief, the Load phase occurs after page initialization during the initial request and subsequent to postback processing after a round-trip.

■   Applies the *BrowsableAttribute* and *DesignerSerializationVisibilityAttribute* attributes to its read-only properties (*Hits* and *TripTime*) so that these properties are not displayed in the property browser or serialized by the designer.

■   Overrides the *TagKey* property it inherits from *WebControl* in order to generate an HTML *<div>* tag instead of the default *<span>* that is generated by *WebControl*.

Figure 7-3 shows the properties of *PageTracker* in the property browser of Microsoft Visual Studio .NET, sorted by category. Among the properties displayed, we defined *FormatString* and *TrackingMode*, while *PageTracker* inherited the other properties from *WebControl*. The *Hits* and *TripTime* read-only properties are not displayed because we marked those properties as *Browsable(false)*. The *HitsKey* property does not appear either because it is private. The property browser never displays properties that are not public. Notice that the *TrackingMode* property displays a drop-down list that shows the values of the *PageTrackingMode* enumeration. We did not do any extra work to provide this functionality; the .NET Framework enables it by automatically associating an *EnumConverter* with an enumeration. The descriptive string at the bottom of the property browser displays the text in the *DescriptionAttribute* that we applied to the *TrackingMode* property.

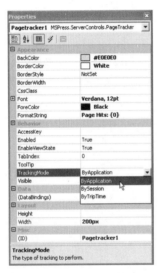

Figure 7-3   The PageTracker properties displayed in Visual Studio .NET

Page That Uses the *PageTracker* Control

The ASP.NET page shown in Listing 7-5 has four instances of the *PageTracker* control. The first three instances correspond to the three tracking options specified in the *PageTrackingMode* enumeration. In the last instance of *PageTracker*, view state is disabled by setting *EnableViewState="false"*. As with enumerated properties in standard ASP.NET controls, the *TrackingMode* property is set declaratively by specifying the value of the *PageTrackingMode* enumeration without the qualifying *PageTrackingMode* type name.

```
<%@ Page Language="C#" %>
<%@ Register TagPrefix="msp" Namespace="MSPress.ServerControls"
  Assembly="MSPress.ServerControls" %>
<html>
  <body>
    <form runat="server">
      <br>
      <asp:Button Text="Submit" Runat="server" id="Button1" />
      <br><br>
      <msp:PageTracker id="Pagetracker1" TrackingMode="ByApplication"
        FormatString="Page Hits: {0}" Width="200px"
        Font-Name="Verdana" Font-Size="14pt" ForeColor="Black"
        BackColor="#E0E0E0" runat="server" BorderStyle="None"
        BorderColor="White" />
      <br>
      <msp:PageTracker id="Pagetracker2" TrackingMode="BySession"
        FormatString="Session Hits: {0}" Width="200px"
        Font-Name="Verdana" Font-Size="14pt" ForeColor="Black"
        BackColor="#E0E0E0" runat="server" />
      <br>
      <msp:PageTracker id="Pagetracker3" TrackingMode="ByTripTime"
        FormatString="Round-Trip Time: {0:F2} seconds"
        Width="350px" Font-Name="Verdana" Font-Size="14pt"
        ForeColor="Black" BackColor="#E0E0E0" runat="server" />
      <br>
      <msp:PageTracker id="Pagetracker4" EnableViewState="false"
        TrackingMode="ByTripTime" Width="300px" Font-Name="Verdana"
        Font-Size="14pt" ForeColor="Black" BackColor="#E0E0E0"
        runat="server" />
      <br>
      <br>
    </form>
  </body>
</html>
```

Listing 7-5   PageTrackerTest.aspx

Open PageTrackerTest.aspx in your browser. Press the Submit button several times. Then close the browser window and open another browser window. Access PageTrackerTest.aspx again, and submit the page several times. The output in your browser should be similar to that shown in Figure 7-4. Note that the last instance of *PageTracker* is not displayed because when view state is disabled, the *TripTime* value cannot be computed. In that case, *PageTracker* sets its *Visible* property to *false* so that the control is not rendered.

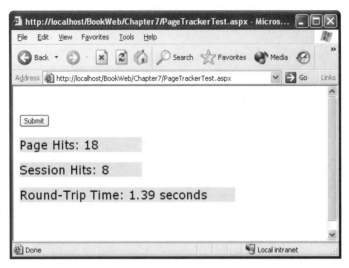

Figure 7-4 PageTrackerTest.aspx accessed in a browser

Summary

In this chapter, we described how to implement simple properties and how to use the *ViewState* dictionary property to maintain state across round-trips. We examined the properties that your control inherits from *Control* and from *Web-Control* and looked at common design-time attributes. In Chapter 10, we'll describe how to implement complex properties whose types correspond to collections and other reference types.

8

Rendering

In user interface programming, the term *rendering* generally refers to the process of drawing or painting on a screen. However, in the case of server controls, rendering refers to the process of writing markup text (such as HTML, XML, and WML) to the HTTP response stream. The server sends the generated markup text to the requesting client, such as a Web browser, where it is finally transformed into its visual representation.

You have already seen some examples of rendering a control in Chapter 5, "Developing a Simple Custom Control," and Chapter 7, "Simple Properties and View State." In Chapter 5, we implemented rendering in the *PrimeGenerator* and *StyledPrimeGenerator* controls, and in Chapter 7, in the *PageTracker* control. In this chapter, we'll take a more detailed look at the rendering functionality that is available to a control. We'll examine the rendering methods provided by the base control classes, describe the *HtmlTextWriter* class that encapsulates the HTTP response stream, and look at the various utility classes that ASP.NET provides for rendering. We'll also examine the ASP.NET mechanism that enables server controls to automatically render markup text that matches the capabilities of the requesting browser. Server controls can automatically generate HTML 4.0 for uplevel Web browsers and HTML 3.2 for downlevel browsers.

Note that a control can render textual content only. You can render other response types such as images by implementing custom HTTP handlers, which are described in Chapter 19, "HTTP Handlers." An HTTP handler can generate any content type permitted by the HTTP protocol.

If you are migrating to ASP.NET from traditional Active Server Pages programming and are accustomed to invoking *Response.Write* to render page output, we must caution you against invoking *Page.Response.Write* from your control. Although this method will write to the HTTP response stream, the rendered content might appear before or after the page renders its control tree. The rendered content will not appear in the location where a page developer expects it to appear, based on the position of your control in the page hierarchy. In addition, when you invoke *Page.Response.Write* from a control, you break the encapsulation provided by the page framework. Therefore, to implement rendering functionality in your control, you should override one of the rendering methods provided by the base *Control* and *WebControl* classes, as we'll describe in this chapter.

Base Classes and Rendering

CONTROL OR WEBCONTROL

To implement rendering functionality in your control, you have to override the rendering methods of the *Control* class or the *WebControl* class. The work that you must do depends on the base class from which your control derives. In Chapter 5, we briefly discussed how to choose the base control class from which to derive your control. Now we'll take a closer look at how rendering determines that choice.

If you want to implement a control that renders markup other than HTML (such as XML or WML) or renders a nonvisual HTML element, you should derive from the *Control* class. You should also derive from *Control* if your control merely renders literal HTML without offering your users the ability to alter the appearance of the rendered elements. To explain these guidelines, let's look at examples of controls that derive from *Control*. The *System.Web.UI.WebControls* namespace contains four controls that derive from *Control*—*Literal*, *PlaceHolder*, *Repeater*, and *Xml*. The *Xml* control renders XML markup, and the *Literal* control renders literal text specified by a page developer. The text rendered by *Literal* could contain HTML markup, but the *Literal* control itself does not expose any properties that enable its users to modify the appearance of the rendered content. Similarly, the *Repeater* and *PlaceHolder* controls do not render visual HTML elements or expose properties related to appearance.

If you want to implement a control that renders a visual HTML element—that is, HTML associated with a visual representation in a Web browser—you should derive your control from the *WebControl* class. The *WebControl* class has built-in functionality for rendering styles that enable a user to specify the appearance of the rendered element. All the controls in the *System.Web.UI.Web-Controls* namespace (barring the four controls discussed in the previous paragraph) derive directly or indirectly from *WebControl*. These include simple controls (such as *Button* and *TextBox*) that represent HTML form elements, as well as complex controls (such as *Calendar*, *DataList*, and *DataGrid*).

Rendering Methods of the *Control* Class

The base *Control* class defines three methods for *rendering*, which Table 8-1 shows. All three methods take an instance of the *HtmlTextWriter* class as their only parameter. This object encapsulates the HTTP response stream into which the control will render its output. We'll examine the *HtmlTextWriter* class later in this chapter, in the section "*HtmlTextWriter* and Related Enumerations."

Table 8-1 The Rendering Methods of the *Control* Class

Method	Description
protected virtual void Render(HtmlTextWriter writer)	Enables a control to render itself by writing markup text. You should override this method to render content when your control derives directly from the *Control* class.
protected virtual void RenderChildren(HtmlTextWriter writer)	Renders a control's children into the stream represented by the *HtmlTextWriter* object. By default, children are rendered in the order in which they are added to the *Controls* collection of a control. Override this method only if you want to replace the default logic. For example, you might override this method if you want to intersperse text between child controls.
public void RenderControl(HtmlTextWriter writer)	Renders a control. *Render* is protected, while *RenderControl* is public and allows a class that consumes (uses) the control to render it. For example, when a page renders its control tree, *RenderControl* is invoked on each child control. A control's designer also invokes *RenderControl* to render the control on a visual design surface. As a control developer, you will invoke the *RenderControl* method when you want to render a child control. Under the hood, *RenderControl* invokes *Render* when a control's *Visible* property is *true*.

Page Rendering

As we described in Chapter 2, " Page Programming Model," a page is an HTTP handler, which has the ultimate responsibility of writing to the response stream. However, a page is also a control (the *Page* class derives indirectly from *Control*) and has the same rendering capabilities as other controls. This makes it possible for a page to render itself and its children by using the rendering methods described in Table 8-1 in a recursive manner.

Every page has a control tree that represents the child controls contained in the page, as we described in Chapter 2. The page represents the root of the control tree. To render the control tree, a page creates an instance of an *HtmlTextWriter* class, which encapsulates the response stream, and then passes the *HtmlTextWriter* object to its *RenderControl* method. The *RenderControl* method checks whether the *Visible* property of a control is *true*. If it is, *RenderControl* invokes the *Render* method. The default implementation of the *Render* method invokes the *RenderChildren* method, which *by default* invokes the *RenderControl* method on each child control. This leads to a recursive rendering of the control tree. Each control in the tree is rendered unless its *Visible* property is assigned a value of *false*. If a control's *Visible* property is *false*, that control and its children are excluded from the rendering logic. The public *RenderControl* method is needed in addition to the *Render* method because *Render* is protected.

The page-rendering logic is best understood by examining the call to *RenderControl* in the *Page* class and the implementation of the *RenderControl*, *Render*, and *RenderChildren* methods of the *Control* class.

The invocation of the *RenderControl* method in the *Page* class is as follows:

```
RenderControl(new HtmlTextWriter(Response.Output));
```

The *Control* class implements the *RenderControl*, *Render,* and *RenderChildren* methods as follows:

```
public void RenderControl(HtmlTextWriter writer) {
    if (Visible) {
        Render(writer);
    }
}

protected virtual void Render(HtmlTextWriter writer) {
    RenderChildren(writer);
}

protected virtual void RenderChildren(HtmlTextWriter writer) {
    foreach (Control c in Controls) {
        c.RenderControl(writer);
    }
}
```

As the code shows, the rendering methods of the *Control* class set up the rendering architecture but do not write any characters to the output stream. Content gets written to the stream because the controls in the page's control tree are derived classes (such as *Button*, *Label*, and *TextBox*) that override the *Render* method (or the rendering methods of the *WebControl* class) to write content such as tags and text.

If you override the *Render* method or the *RenderChildren* method, you should invoke the corresponding method of the base class to ensure that the children of your control are recursively rendered (unless you specifically do not want to use the default logic to render child controls). The order of invocation is important, and you must invoke the base class's method exactly where you want children to be rendered.

Overriding Render—The *MetaTag* Control Example

As an example of a control that generates a nonvisual HTML element, we'll derive from *Control* to create a *MetaTag* control that renders as a *<meta>* tag in the *<head>* section of an HTML page. Listing 8-1 contains the code for the *MetaTag* control.

```
using System;
using System.ComponentModel;
using System.Web.UI;

namespace MSPress.ServerControls {
    [
    DefaultProperty("Name")
    ]
    public class MetaTag : Control {
        [
        Category("Behavior"),
        DefaultValue(""),
        Description("The name of the meta tag")
        ]
        public string Name {
            get {
                string s = (string)ViewState["Name"];
                return (s == null) ? String.Empty : s;
            }
            set {
                ViewState["Name"] = value;
            }
```

Listing 8-1   MetaTag.cs

Listing 8-1 *(continued)*

```
        }

        [
        Category("Default"),
        DefaultValue(""),
        Description("The data or value associated with the meta tag")
        ]
        public string Content {
            get {
                string s = (string)ViewState["Content"];
                return (s == null) ? String.Empty : s;
            }
            set {
                ViewState["Content"] = value;
            }
        }

        // This ensures that there are no child controls.
        protected override ControlCollection CreateControlCollection() {
            return new EmptyControlCollection(this);
        }

        protected override void Render(HtmlTextWriter writer) {
            string name = Name;
            if (name.Length == 0) {
                throw new InvalidProgramException("The Name property" +
                    " of the MetaTag control must be set.");
            }
            writer.AddAttribute(HtmlTextWriterAttribute.Name, name);
            writer.AddAttribute("content", Content);
            writer.RenderBeginTag(HtmlTextWriterTag.Meta);
            writer.RenderEndTag();
        }
    }
}
```

When you derive from the *Control* class, you override the *Render* method to write markup text to the response stream. In Chapter 5, when overriding the *Render* method in the *PrimeGenerator* example (shown in Listing 5-3), we directly wrote HTML markup using the *Write* method of the *HtmlTextWriter* object. In the *MetaTag* example, we do not directly write HTML but instead use the tag-rendering methods of the *HtmlTextWriter* object. We also use the *HtmlTextWriterAttribute* and *HtmlTextWriterTag* enumerations in conjunction with the tag-rendering functionality. The *HtmlTextWriter* class and its related enumerations simplify formatting, help to reduce errors, and make your code more readable.

Note that we didn't invoke the *Render* method of the base class or the *RenderChildren* method because the *MetaTag* control does not have any child controls in its *Controls* collection. (We overrode the *CreateControlCollection* method to return an instance of the *EmptyControlCollection* class, which ensures that the *Controls* collection is empty by disallowing a user from adding child controls to our control.)

Multiple Calls to *HtmlTextWriter* vs. String Concatenation

When you write text into an *HtmlTextWriter* object, it is more efficient to make multiple calls to the *Write* method of that object than to concatenate strings before writing them. String concatenation consumes time and memory (because strings are immutable) and is unnecessary when writing to a stream. This is an important efficiency consideration that new control authors often overlook. The *PrimeGenerator* control in Chapter 5 (shown in Listing 5-3) demonstrates successive calls that write to the output stream.

At times, it is necessary to combine strings—for example, when you want to build up an attribute value. In those cases, use string concatenation if the number of operations is small; otherwise, use the *System.Text.StringBuilder* class, which provides an optimized implementation of string concatenation. However, you should not use *StringBuilder* to build a string to pass into the *Write* method, because the underlying response stream already provides that functionality when you make multiple calls to *Write*.

Listing 8-2 shows a page that uses the *MetaTag* control.

```
<%@ Page Language="C#" %>
<%@ Register TagPrefix="msp" Namespace="MSPress.ServerControls" Assem-
bly="MSPress.ServerControls" %>
<html>
  <head>
    <msp:MetaTag name="author"
      content="Nikhil Kothari and Vandana Datye"
      runat="server" id="metaTag1" />
  </head>
  <body>
    <br>
```

Listing 8-2   MetaTagTest.aspx

Listing 8-2 *(continued)*

```
   This page uses the MetaTag control in its head section.
   Select View Source in your Web browser to view the control
   rendered as a &lt;meta&gt; tag.
   <br>
  </body>
</html>
```

If you access MetaTagTest.aspx in your browser and view the HTML source for the rendered page, you will see the *<meta>* tag rendered by the *MetaTag* control in the *<head>* section of the rendered HTML content:

```
<head>
  <meta name="author" content="Nikhil Kothari and Vandana Datye" />
</head>
```

HtmlTextWriter and Related Enumerations

In Table 8-1, you saw that each rendering method of the *Control* class takes a *System.Web.UI.HtmlTextWriter* object as a parameter. *HtmlTextWriter* derives from *System.IO.TextWriter*, which provides the capability of writing text to an output stream. *HtmlTextWriter* adds to the functionality of the base class by providing methods that simplify the writing and formatting of HTML tags and attributes. In the *MetaTag* control (Listing 8-1), we invoked some of the methods of *HtmlTextWriter* (such as *AddAttribute*, *RenderBeginTag*, and *RenderEndTag*) to render HTML tags and attributes on the tags. Later in this chapter, we'll look at another example, *LoginUI* (Listing 8-5), which utilizes the *AddStyleAttribute* method of *HtmlTextWriter* to render CSS style attributes.

Various methods of *HtmlTextWriter* take as their arguments the values of the following three enumerations—*HtmlTextWriterTag*, *HtmlTextWriterAttribute*, and *HtmlTextWriterStyle*. These enumerations list common HTML 4.0 tag names, attributes, and CSS style attributes. Many methods of *HtmlTextWriter* are overloaded; you can pass in either a string or an enumerated value as an argument. If you use the enumerations, you gain a number of benefits. Most important is the automatic downlevel rendering of HTML tags by using the HTML 3.2 subset, as we'll describe at the end of this chapter, in the section "Downlevel Rendering." When you use an enumerated value such as *HtmlTextWriterTag.Meta* instead of using the string *"meta"*, you gain the benefit of type checking, which eliminates errors that could result from an incorrect string value. In addition, when you use the enumerations, you get IntelliSense support in Microsoft Visual Studio .NET, which displays the enumeration values in the code editor. Let's look at the enumerations next.

HtmlTextWriterTag Enumeration

The *HtmlTextWriterTag* enumeration contains values such as *Button*, *Div*, *Input*, and *Span* that map to standard HTML 4.0 tags with the same names. For example, *HtmlTextWriterTag.Button* maps to the *<button>* HTML tag. For a complete list of values, see the *HtmlTextWriterTag* enumeration in the *System.Web.UI* namespace. We use the *HtmlTextWriterTag* enumeration in the *MetaTag* (Listing 8-1) and the *LoginUI* (Listing 8-5) examples in this chapter.

HtmlTextWriterAttribute Enumeration

The *HtmlTextWriterAttribute* enumeration contains values such as *Background*, *Border*, *Height*, *Href*, and *Id* that map to standard HTML 4.0 attributes with the same names. For example, *HtmlTextWriterAttribute.Background* maps to the *background* attribute on the *<body>* tag. For a complete list of values, see the *HtmlTextWriterAttribute* enumeration in the *System.Web.UI* namespace. We use the *HtmlTextWriterAttribute* enumeration in this chapter's *MetaTag* (Listing 8-1) and *LoginUI* (Listing 8-5) examples.

HtmlTextWriterStyle Enumeration

The *HtmlTextWriterStyle* enumeration contains values such as *Background-Color*, *BorderStyle*, *Color*, *FontFamily*, and *Width* that map to standard HTML 4.0 CSS style attributes such as *background-color*, *border-style*, *color*, *font-family*, and *width*. For a complete list of values, see the *HtmlTextWriterStyle* enumeration in the *System.Web.UI* namespace. We use the *HtmlTextWriterStyle* enumeration in the *LoginUI* (Listing 8-5) example in this chapter.

Rendering Methods of *WebControl*

If your control renders a visual HTML element, you should derive from the *WebControl* class. We'll use the term *Web control* to denote a class that derives from *WebControl*. The *WebControl* class provides methods that allow you to modify the tag rendered by a Web control, add attributes to the rendered tag, and write content (sometimes referred to as *inner HTML*) within the rendered tags. Table 8-2 lists the methods of *WebControl* that provide rendering functionality. Like the rendering methods of *Control* that we described in Table 8-1, these methods take only one argument—an instance of the *HtmlTextWriter* class.

Table 8-2   The Rendering Methods of the *WebControl* Class

Method	Description
protected virtual void AddAttributesToRender(HtmlTextWriter writer)	Enables a Web control to specify name/value pairs, which are rendered as attributes on the tag of the HTML element. When overriding *AddAttributesToRender*, you must invoke the corresponding method of the base class; otherwise, your control will lose important functionality. The base *WebControl* class renders many of the control's properties as HTML attributes in its implementation of this method. For example, *WebControl* renders its *ClientID* property as the *id* HTML attribute. *WebControl* also renders any style properties that are set on your control as CSS values in an HTML *style* attribute. We'll provide an example of overriding the *AddAttributesToRender* method in the *HoverLabel* sample in the next section.
public virtual void RenderBeginTag(HtmlTextWriter writer)	Enables a Web control to write a begin tag to the output stream. You should override this method when you want to provide a different implementation for the begin tag—for example, when you want to generate multiple begin tags, such as *<table><tr><td>*. If your control generates a single tag and you want to override the default *<span>* tag that *WebControl* generates, you should override either the *TagKey* property or the *TagName* property that we described in Chapter 7 (in Table 7-4), instead of overriding *RenderBeginTag*.
protected virtual void RenderContents(HtmlTextWriter writer)	Enables a Web control to render content within the control's tags. By default, this method renders the tree of child controls. Override this method if you want to write text (inner HTML) or other content within your control's tags. Be sure to invoke the corresponding method of the base class if you want to use the default logic to render your child controls. We'll provide an example of overriding this method in the *HoverLabel* sample in the next section.
public virtual void RenderEndTag(HtmlTextWriter writer)	Enables a Web control to write an end tag to the output stream. You need to override this method only to provide a matching end tag for the tag created by the *RenderBeginTag* method (if you overrode that method in your control). For example, if you render multiple begin tags (*<table><tr><td>*) in *RenderBeginTag*, you must render the end tags *</table></tr></td>* in *RenderEndTag*.

To implement rendering in a class that derives from *WebControl*, you should override one or more of the methods listed in Table 8-2 instead of overriding the *Render* method as you would if your control derived from *Control*. Overriding a method other than *Render* is important because the base *WebControl* class provides tag-rendering capabilities that you will lose if you override *Render* in your Web control. The best way to understand this is by examining the implementation of some of the rendering methods in *WebControl*. *WebControl* implements *Render* as shown in the following code:

```
protected override void Render(HtmlTextWriter writer) {
    RenderBeginTag(writer);
    RenderContents(writer);
    RenderEndTag(writer);
}
```

WebControl implements *RenderBeginTag* as follows:

```
public virtual void RenderBeginTag(HtmlTextWriter writer) {
    AddAttributesToRender(writer);
    HtmlTextWriterTag tagKey = TagKey;
    if (tagKey != HtmlTextWriterTag.Unknown) {
        writer.RenderBeginTag(tagKey);
    }
    else {
        writer.RenderBeginTag(this.TagName);
    }
}
```

Finally, *WebControl* implements *RenderContents* as follows:

```
protected virtual void RenderContents(HtmlTextWriter writer) {
    // This invokes the Render method of the Control class,
    // which in turn invokes RenderChildren to render
    // child controls.
    base.Render(writer);
}
```

When you want to render content within your Web control's tags, you should override the *RenderContents* method, as we'll show in the *HoverLabel* example in the next section. With some Web controls, it is necessary to override the *Render* method, as we'll demonstrate in Chapter 12.

Rendering a Web Control—The *HoverLabel* Example

We'll now develop a simple control, *HoverLabel*, shown in Figure 8-1, which derives from *WebControl* and binds JavaScript event handlers (for example, *onmouseover="handler script"*) on the rendered HTML tag. The example demonstrates a common technique that you can use to add basic client-side behavior to your server control. We'll look at more complex client-side behavior in Chapter 13, "Client-Side Behavior."

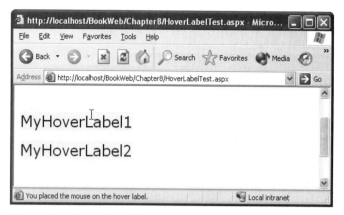

Figure 8-1   HoverLabelTest.aspx viewed in a browser

The *HoverLabel* example in Listing 8-3 overrides the *AddAttributesToRender* method to render the *onmouseover* and *onmouseup* DHTML attributes with JavaScript event handlers as values on the HTML tag. *HoverLabel* also overrides the *RenderContents* method to render text (inner HTML) within HTML tags. In addition, *HoverLabel* overrides the *TagKey* property to generate a *<div>* tag to demonstrate how to override the default *<span>* tag generated by *WebControl*.

```
using System;
using System.ComponentModel;
using System.Web.UI;
using System.Web.UI.WebControls;

namespace MSPress.ServerControls {
    [
    DefaultProperty("Text")
    ]
    public class HoverLabel : WebControl {

        [
        Bindable(true),
        Category("Appearance"),
        DefaultValue(""),
        Description("The text rendered in the label."),
        ]
        public virtual string Text {
            get {
                string s = (string)ViewState["Text"];
                return ((s == null) ? String.Empty : s);
```

Listing 8-3   HoverLabel.cs

```
        }
        set {
            ViewState["Text"] = value;
        }
    }


    [
    Bindable(true),
    Category("Appearance"),
    DefaultValue(""),
    Description("The text to display in the status bar."),
    ]
    public virtual string StatusBarText {
        get {
            string s = (string)ViewState["StatusBarText"];
            return((s == null) ? String.Empty : s);
        }
        set {
            ViewState["StatusBarText"] = value;
        }
    }


    protected override HtmlTextWriterTag TagKey {
        get {
            return HtmlTextWriterTag.Div;
        }
    }


    // This ensures that there are no child controls.
    protected override ControlCollection CreateControlCollection() {
        return new EmptyControlCollection(this);
    }


    protected override
        void AddAttributesToRender(HtmlTextWriter writer) {
        // Invoke the method of the base class to render
        // style and other attributes that WebControl renders.
        base.AddAttributesToRender(writer);
        writer.AddAttribute("onmouseover",
            "this.style.textDecoration = 'underline'; status = '" +
            StatusBarText + "';");

        // The third parameter of the AddAttribute method is a
        // Boolean variable that specifies whether the value of
        // the attribute should be HTML encoded. By default,
        // attributes that are not listed in the
        // HtmlTextWriterAttribute enumeration (unknown attributes)
        // are HTML encoded. onmouseout is unknown but does not
```

(continued)

Listing 8-3   *(continued)*

```
            // require HTML encoding because its value does not contain
            // user-specified text.We did not specify the third
            // parameter when adding the onmouseover attribute because
            // we used the default value (true). The onmouseover
            // attribute contains the StatusBarText property, which
            // should be encoded because it is a user-entered string
            // that could contain characters such as a quotation mark
            // or an ampersand.
            writer.AddAttribute("onmouseout",
                "this.style.textDecoration = 'none'; status = '';",
                false);
        }

        protected override void RenderContents(HtmlTextWriter writer) {
            writer.Write(Text);
            // We do not invoke the RenderContents method of the base
            // class because there are no children to render.
        }
    }
}
```

Note that *HoverLabel* derives from *WebControl* instead of deriving from *Label* because we want to demonstrate how to render text within a Web control's tags. If you want to develop a label that has client-side behavior, you should derive from *Label* so that you can reuse its functionality. *Label* already exposes a *Text* property and renders it within the control's tags.

Listing 8-4 contains a page that uses the *HoverLabel* control.

```
<%@ Page Language="C#" %>
<%@ Register TagPrefix="msp" Namespace="MSPress.ServerControls"
  Assembly="MSPress.ServerControls" %>
<html>
  <body>
    <form runat="server">
      <br>
      <msp:HoverLabel id="HoverLabel1" runat="server"
        StatusBarText="You placed the mouse on the hover label."
        Text="MyHoverLabel1" BackColor="WhiteSmoke" Font-Size="18pt"
        BorderColor="Silver" Width="150px" />
      <br>
      <msp:HoverLabel id="Hoverlabel2" runat="server"
        StatusBarText="You placed the mouse on the hover label."
        Text="MyHoverLabel2" BackColor="WhiteSmoke"
        Font-Size="18pt" BorderColor="Silver" Width="150px" />
```

Listing 8-4   HoverLabel.cs

```
    <br>
   </form>
  </body>
</html>
```

In Figure 8-1, HoverLabelTest.aspx is viewed in a browser. The underlined text style in the first instance of *HoverLabel* and the message in the status bar are caused by the *onmouseover* and *onmouseout* client-side event handlers specified on the HTML tag rendered by *HoverLabel*.

If you look at the HTML source for the page, you will see content rendered by each *HoverLabel* instance that is similar to the HTML listed after this paragraph. The boldface attributes in the example are the result of overriding the *AddAttributesToRender* method in *HoverLabel*. The other attributes come from properties that *HoverLabel* inherits from *WebControl* and are rendered by *WebControl*'s implementation of *AddAttributesToRender*. These attributes are rendered because we invoked the base class's *AddAttributesToRender* method when overriding *AddAttributesToRender*. The text within the HTML element's tags corresponds to the *Text* property of *HoverLabel*, which we wrote out in the *RenderContents* method.

```
<div id="HoverLabel1" onmouseover="this.style.textDecoration =
  'underline'; status = 'You placed the mouse on the hover label.';"
  onmouseout="this.style.textDecoration = 'none'; status = '';"
  style="background-color:WhiteSmoke;border-color:Silver;
  font-size:18pt;width:150px;">
  MyHoverLabel1
</div>
```

Exercising *HtmlTextWriter*—The *LoginUI* Example

We'll now develop the *LoginUI* control, which uses the methods of the *Html-TextWriter* class to render a user interface that enables a user to log into a Web site. Unlike the earlier samples in this chapter, *LoginUI* exercises the style-rendering capabilities of *HtmlTextWriter*. *LoginUI* renders two HTML text boxes (one for name information, and one for password information) and a button to submit the form, as shown in Figure 8-2. *LoginUI* renders these elements as cells in an HTML table. At this stage, *LoginUI* merely renders a user interface; it does not have the ability to process data or handle events. We will implement that functionality in Chapter 9, "Control Life Cycle, Events, and Postback."

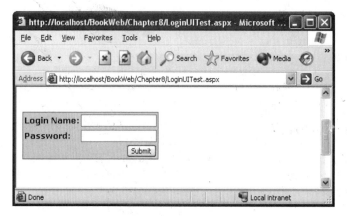

Figure 8-2   LoginUITest.aspx viewed in a browser. The page demonstrates the UI rendered by the LoginUI control.

To demonstrate the functionality of the *HtmlTextWriter* class, the *LoginUI* control derives from *Control* and exposes many style-related properties, such as *BackColor*, *BorderStyle*, and *FontFamily*. Note, however, that *LoginUI* is an "artificial" control that we've developed purely to exercise the methods of *HtmlTextWriter*. If your control needs style-related functionality, you should derive from *WebControl*, which exposes strongly typed style properties.

At this point, it might appear that we are doing a lot of extra work to render a user interface that could be rendered as a few lines of raw HTML. However, if you want to create reusable controls, you should use strongly typed styles and the tag-rendering capabilities of *HtmlTextWriter*. Also bear in mind that the *LoginUI* control is unnecessarily long because we created it for demonstration purposes without reusing the functionality of the *WebControl* class. Listing 8-5 contains the code for the *LoginUI* control.

```
using System;
using System.ComponentModel;
using System.Drawing;
using System.Globalization;
using System.Web.UI;
using System.Web.UI.WebControls;

namespace MSPress.ServerControls {

    public class LoginUI : Control {

        [
        Bindable(true),
```

Listing 8-5   LoginUI.cs

```
Category("Appearance"),
DefaultValue(typeof(Color), ""),
Description("The background color"),
// The WebColorConverter is a type converter
// that allows a string specifying an HTML color
// to be converted to a System.Drawing.Color type.
TypeConverter(typeof(WebColorConverter))
]
public Color BackColor {
    get {
        object o = ViewState["BackColor"];
        return (o == null) ? Color.Empty : (Color)o;
    }
    set {
        ViewState["BackColor"] = value;
    }
}


[
Bindable(true),
Category("Appearance"),
DefaultValue(typeof(Color), ""),
Description("The border color"),
TypeConverter(typeof(WebColorConverter))
]
public Color BorderColor {
    get {
        object o = ViewState["BorderColor"];
        return ((o == null) ? Color.Empty : (Color)o);
    }
    set {
        ViewState["BorderColor"] = value;
    }
}


[
Bindable(true),
Category("Appearance"),
DefaultValue(BorderStyle.NotSet),
Description("The border style")
]
public BorderStyle BorderStyle {
    get {
        object o = ViewState["BorderStyle"];
        return (o == null) ? BorderStyle.None : (BorderStyle)o;
    }
    set {
```

(continued)

Listing 8-5 *(continued)*

```
            ViewState["BorderStyle"] = value;
        }
    }

    [
    Bindable(true),
    Category("Appearance"),
    DefaultValue(typeof(Unit), ""),
    Description("The border width")
    ]
    public Unit BorderWidth {
        get {
            object o = ViewState["BorderWidth"];
            return (o == null) ? Unit.Empty : (Unit)o;
        }
        set {
            if (value.Value < 0)
                throw new ArgumentOutOfRangeException("value");
            ViewState["BorderWidth"] = value;
        }
    }

    [
    Bindable(true),
    Category("Appearance"),
    DefaultValue(""),
    Description("The text to display on the button")
    ]
    public string ButtonText {
        get {
            string s = (string)ViewState["ButtonText"];
            return (s == null) ? String.Empty : s;
        }
        set {
            ViewState["ButtonText"] = value;
        }
    }

    [
    Bindable(true),
    Category("Appearance"),
    DefaultValue(""),
    Description("The font")
    ]
    public string FontFamily {
        get {
```

```
                string s = (string)ViewState["FontFamily"];
                return (s == null) ? String.Empty : s;
            }
        set {
            ViewState["FontFamily"] = value;
        }
    }


    [
    Bindable(true),
    Category("Appearance"),
    DefaultValue(typeof(FontUnit), ""),
    Description("The size of the font")
    ]
    public FontUnit FontSize {
        get {
            object o = ViewState["FontSize"];
            return (o == null) ? FontUnit.Empty : (FontUnit)o;
        }
        set {
            ViewState["FontSize"] = value;
        }
    }


    [
    Bindable(true),
    Category("Appearance"),
    DefaultValue(false),
    Description("The weight of the font")
    ]
    public bool FontBold {
        get {
            object o = ViewState["FontBold"];
            return (o == null) ? false : (bool)o;
        }
        set {
            ViewState["FontBold"] = value;
        }
    }


    [
    Bindable(true),
    Category("Appearance"),
    DefaultValue(""),
    Description("The label for the Name textbox")
    ]
    public string NameLabel {
```

(continued)

Listing 8-5 *(continued)*

```
        get {
            string s = (string)ViewState["NameLabel"];
            return (s == null) ? String.Empty : s;
        }
        set {
            ViewState["NameLabel"] = value;
        }
    }


    [
    Bindable(true),
    Category("Appearance"),
    DefaultValue(""),
    Description("The label for the Password textbox")
    ]
    public string PasswordLabel {
        get {
            string s = (string)ViewState["PasswordLabel"];
            return (s == null) ? String.Empty : s;
        }
        set {
            ViewState["PasswordLabel"] = value;
        }
    }


    // The id attribute to render on the HTML button tag.
    // The id attribute enables client-side script to access
    // an HTML element and must be unique for every
    // HTML element on the page.
    // We use the server control's ClientID property
    // as the HTML "id" because it is guaranteed to
    // be unique and does not have any invalid characters.
    // The UniqueID uses the invalid ":" character
    // as a separator, as we'll explain in Chapter 12.
    [
    Browsable(false),
    DesignerSerializationVisibility(
        DesignerSerializationVisibility.Hidden)
    ]
    public string ButtonID {
        get {
            return this.ClientID + "_Button";
        }
    }


    // The name attribute to render on the HTML button tag.
    // The name attribute is required on every HTML form
```

```
// element and is used by the client to post name/value
// pairs to the server when the user submits the form.
// On the server, the name is used by the
// page framework to process postback data and must be
// unique for each control on the page.
// To enable the page framework to handle postback events,
// the name attribute of an HTML element that causes postback
// (such as an HTML button) must equal the UniqueID
// of the control.
[
Browsable(false),
DesignerSerializationVisibility(
    DesignerSerializationVisibility.Hidden)
]
public string ButtonName {
    get {
        return this.UniqueID + ":Button";
    }
}


// The id attribute to render on the HTML TextBox
// for the password. We'll base this on the
// ClientID to guarantee a unique id.
[
Browsable(false),
DesignerSerializationVisibility(
    DesignerSerializationVisibility.Hidden)
]
public string PasswordInputID {
    get {
        return this.ClientID + "_Password";
    }
}


// The name attribute to render on the HTML TextBox
// for the password. We'll base this on the
// UniqueID to guarantee a unique name.
[
Browsable(false),
DesignerSerializationVisibility(
    DesignerSerializationVisibility.Hidden)
]
public string PasswordInputName {
    get {
        return this.UniqueID + ":Password";
    }
}
```

(continued)

Listing 8-5   *(continued)*

```
// The id attribute to render on the HTML TextBox
// for the user name. We'll base this on the
// ClientID to guarantee a unique id.
[
Browsable(false),
DesignerSerializationVisibility(
    DesignerSerializationVisibility.Hidden)
]
public string UserNameInputID {
    get {
        return this.ClientID + "_UserName";
    }
}


// The name attribute to render on the HTML TextBox
// for the user name. We'll base this on the
// UniqueID to guarantee a unique name.
[
Browsable(false),
DesignerSerializationVisibility(
    DesignerSerializationVisibility.Hidden)
]
public string UserNameInputName {
    get {
        return this.UniqueID + ":UserName";
    }
}


protected override void Render(HtmlTextWriter writer) {
    writer.AddAttribute(HtmlTextWriterAttribute.Cellspacing,
        "1");

    // You must pass in each style attribute by making a
    // separate call to AddStyleAttribute.
    // The HtmlTextWriter combines all the style
    // attributes into a single semicolon-delimited list,
    // which it assigns to the style HTML attribute
    // on the HTML tag.
    if (!BackColor.IsEmpty) {
        // The ColorTranformer.ToHtml method converts a
        // System.Drawing.Color object to a string that
        // represents the color in HTML.
        writer.AddStyleAttribute(
            HtmlTextWriterStyle.BackgroundColor,
            ColorTranslator.ToHtml(BackColor));
    }
```

```
        if (!BorderColor.IsEmpty) {
            writer.AddStyleAttribute(
                HtmlTextWriterStyle.BorderColor,
                ColorTranslator.ToHtml(BorderColor));
        }
        if ((BorderStyle != BorderStyle.None) &&
            (BorderStyle != BorderStyle.NotSet)) {
            writer.AddStyleAttribute(
                HtmlTextWriterStyle.BorderStyle,
                BorderStyle.ToString());
        }
        if (!BorderWidth.IsEmpty) {
            writer.AddStyleAttribute(
                HtmlTextWriterStyle.BorderWidth,
                BorderWidth.ToString(CultureInfo.InvariantCulture));
        }
        if (FontFamily != String.Empty) {
            writer.AddStyleAttribute(
                HtmlTextWriterStyle.FontFamily, FontFamily);
        }
        if (!FontSize.IsEmpty) {
            writer.AddStyleAttribute(HtmlTextWriterStyle.FontSize,
                FontSize.ToString(CultureInfo.InvariantCulture));
        }
        if (FontBold == true) {
            writer.AddStyleAttribute(
                HtmlTextWriterStyle.FontWeight, "Bold");
        }
        // Render an id on the outer tag.
        writer.AddAttribute(HtmlTextWriterAttribute.Id,
            this.ClientID);
        writer.RenderBeginTag(HtmlTextWriterTag.Table);

        writer.RenderBeginTag(HtmlTextWriterTag.Tr);
        writer.RenderBeginTag(HtmlTextWriterTag.Td);
        if (NameLabel != String.Empty){
            writer.Write(NameLabel);
        }
        writer.RenderEndTag();  // Td
        writer.RenderBeginTag(HtmlTextWriterTag.Td);
        writer.AddAttribute(HtmlTextWriterAttribute.Type, "Text");
        writer.AddAttribute(HtmlTextWriterAttribute.Name,
            UserNameInputName);
        writer.AddAttribute(HtmlTextWriterAttribute.Id,
            UserNameInputID);
        writer.AddAttribute(HtmlTextWriterAttribute.Value,
            String.Empty);
```

(continued)

Listing 8-5 *(continued)*

```
        writer.RenderBeginTag(HtmlTextWriterTag.Input);
        // Each call to RenderBeginTag must have a matching
        // call to RenderEndTag.
        writer.RenderEndTag();  // Input
        writer.RenderEndTag();  // Td
        writer.RenderEndTag();  // Tr

        writer.RenderBeginTag(HtmlTextWriterTag.Tr);
        writer.RenderBeginTag(HtmlTextWriterTag.Td);
        if (PasswordLabel != String.Empty){
            writer.Write(PasswordLabel);
        }
        writer.RenderEndTag();  // Td
        writer.RenderBeginTag(HtmlTextWriterTag.Td);
        writer.AddAttribute(HtmlTextWriterAttribute.Type,
            "Password");
        writer.AddAttribute(HtmlTextWriterAttribute.Name,
            PasswordInputName);
        writer.AddAttribute(HtmlTextWriterAttribute.Id,
            PasswordInputID);
        writer.AddAttribute(HtmlTextWriterAttribute.Value,
            String.Empty);
        writer.RenderBeginTag(HtmlTextWriterTag.Input);
        writer.RenderEndTag();  // Input
        writer.RenderEndTag();  // Td
        writer.RenderEndTag();  // Tr

        writer.RenderBeginTag(HtmlTextWriterTag.Tr);
        writer.AddAttribute(HtmlTextWriterAttribute.Colspan, "2");
        writer.AddAttribute(HtmlTextWriterAttribute.Align,
            "right");
        writer.RenderBeginTag(HtmlTextWriterTag.Td);
        writer.AddAttribute(HtmlTextWriterAttribute.Type,
            "Submit");
        writer.AddAttribute(HtmlTextWriterAttribute.Name,
            ButtonName);
        writer.AddAttribute(HtmlTextWriterAttribute.Id, ButtonID);
        writer.AddAttribute(HtmlTextWriterAttribute.Value,
            ButtonText);
        writer.RenderBeginTag(HtmlTextWriterTag.Input);
        writer.RenderEndTag();  // Input
        writer.RenderEndTag();  // Td
        writer.RenderEndTag();  // Tr

        writer.RenderEndTag();  // Table
    }
  }
}
```

The *LoginUI* control invokes the *AddAttribute*, *AddStyleAttribute*, *Render-BeginTag*, and *RenderEndTag* methods of the *HtmlTextWriter* instance to build up the output to be added to the response stream. You must provide all the attributes and style attributes of a tag before invoking the *RenderBeginTag* method because the *HtmlTextWriter* object needs the attribute information before it can start writing a tag. You must pass in each style attribute by making a separate call to *AddStyleAttribute*. The *HtmlTextWriter* combines all the style attributes into a single semicolon-delimited list, which it assigns to the style HTML attribute on the HTML tag *(style="background-color:Gainsboro;border-color:Gray;border-style:Solid;border-width:1px;font-family:Verdana;font-size:10pt;font-weight:Bold;")*. Note that every *RenderBeginTag* method call must have a matching *RenderEndTag* call. This also applies to tags that do not have corresponding closing tags in HTML, such as the *<input>* tag.

Notice that *LoginUI* renders *name* and *id* attributes for each HTML form element that it generates (the two text boxes and the button). The *id* attribute is useful to access the element in client-side script and must be unique for each element to which it is assigned. We've created unique *id* attributes based on the *ClientID* property, which the page framework provides specifically for this purpose. It is good practice to render an *id* attribute for every HTML element that can have client-side behavior. *WebControl* renders the *ClientID* property as the value of the HTML *id* attribute by default.

If your control renders form input elements, you must render a unique *name* attribute on each form element to enable that element to participate in postback data processing. The browser uses the *name* attribute to post name/value pairs to the server when the user submits the form. On the server, the ASP.NET page framework uses the *name* attribute to route events and data to the control after postback. The standard ASP.NET form controls assign the *UniqueID* of the control to the *name* attribute. Because we have multiple form elements, we have created unique names for each element based on the *UniqueID* of the control.

As we mentioned earlier, *LoginUI* does not have postback data-processing or event-handling capabilities. However, we've added *name* attributes to the form elements of *LoginUI* because we'll derive from this control in Chapter 9 to develop a control that implements postback data-processing and event-handling functionality.

Listing 8-6 shows a page that uses the *LoginUI* control and sets its properties.

```
<%@ Page Language="C#" %><%@ Register TagPrefix="msp"
Namespace="MSPress.ServerControls"
  Assembly="MSPress.ServerControls" %>
<html>
  <body>
    <form runat="server">
      <br>
      <msp:LoginUI id="LoginUI1" runat="server" ButtonText="Submit"
        NameLabel="Login Name:" PasswordLabel="Password:"
        BackColor="Gainsboro" BorderColor="Gray"
        BorderStyle="Solid" BorderWidth="1px"
        FontFamily="Verdana"
        FontSize="10pt" FontBold="True" />
      <br>
      <br>
    </form>
  </body>
</html>
```

Listing 8-6   LoginUI.cs

If you view the source for the page shown in Figure 8-2, you will see that the HTML rendered by the *LoginUI* instance is similar to the following HTML:

```
<table cellspacing="1" id="LoginUI1" style="background-color:Gainsboro;
  border-color:Gray;border-style:Solid;border-width:1px;font-family:
  Verdana;font-size:10pt;font-weight:Bold;">
  <tr>
    <td>Login Name:
    </td>
    <td>
      <input type="Text" name="LoginUI1:UserName"
        id="LoginUI1_UserName" value="" />
    </td>
  </tr>
  <tr>
    <td>Password:
    </td>
    <td>
      <input type="Password" name="LoginUI1:Password"
        id="LoginUI1_Password" value="" />
    </td>
  </tr>
  <tr>
    <td colspan="2" align="right"><input type="Submit"
      name="LoginUI1:Button" id="LoginUI1_Button" value="Submit" />
    </td>
  </tr>
</table>
```

Notice that the style properties that we set on the control are rendered on the opening *<table>* tag as a semicolon-delimited list, which is the value of the style HTML attribute. We did not write this HTML syntax. The *HtmlTextWriter* object generated it for us because, in the *Render* method of the *LoginUI* control, we called the *AddAttribute* method to supply *style* attributes before rendering the tag. All the attributes that you provide by using the *AddAttribute* and *AddStyleAttribute* methods before invoking a *RenderTag* method are rendered on the corresponding tag.

Downlevel Rendering

It is possible that some browsers that do not support HTML 4.0 will access a page that uses your control. As a control author, you do not have to do much work to support this scenario. The page framework provides a mechanism that automatically takes responsibility for rendering the appropriate content to various types of browsers and to various versions of the same browser.

There are two versions of the *HtmlTextWriter* class: *HtmlTextWriter*, which renders HTML 4.0, and *Html32TextWriter*, which derives from *HtmlText-Writer* and renders HTML 3.2. *HtmlTextWriter* is extensible, meaning that it can be customized to target a specific browser. The following list describes some of the significant conversions and approximations performed by *Html32TextWriter* to convert tags, attributes, and CSS style attributes into their most appropriate downlevel HTML 3.2 equivalent:

■   Renders the *font-family*, *font-size*, and *color* CSS attributes as attributes on a *<font>* tag instead of rendering a *style* attribute on the element's tag.

■   Renders the *font-weight* CSS attribute as opening and closing *<b>* tags around content.

■   Renders the *font-style* CSS attribute as opening and closing *<i>* tags around content.

■   Renders the *text-decoration* CSS attribute as opening and closing *<u>* or *<strike>* tags.

■   Propagates the font information specified on a table into the table cell and renders it as a *<font>* tag around the content (because specifying *<font>* around the table itself has no effect on its content).

■   Renders a *<div>* as an equivalent table.

- Renders the *border-color* CSS attribute as a *bordercolor* attribute for an enclosing table.

- Renders the *background-color* CSS attribute as a *bgcolor* attribute for a *<table>* or *<td>*.

A Web application specifies the *HtmlTextWriter* to be used for a given browser via the *tagwriter* attribute in the *browserCaps* section of the web.config or machine.config configuration file. As a control author, you are not responsible for the settings in the configuration file. The following example shows the *clientTarget* section and a part of the *browserCaps* section of the machine.config file that installs with the .NET Framework:

```
<configuration>
  <system.web>
    <clientTarget>
      <add alias="ie5"
        userAgent="Mozilla/4.0 (compatible; MSIE 5.5; Windows NT 4.0)"/>
      <add alias="ie4"
        userAgent="Mozilla/4.0 (compatible; MSIE 4.0; Windows NT 4.0)"/>
      <add alias="uplevel"
        userAgent="Mozilla/4.0 (compatible; MSIE 4.0; Windows NT 4.0)"/>
      <add alias="downlevel" userAgent="Unknown"/>
    </clientTarget>
    <browserCaps>
      <result type="System.Web.HttpBrowserCapabilities"/>
      <use var="HTTP_USER_AGENT"/>
      browser=Unknown
      version=0.0
      majorversion=0
      minorversion=0
      frames=false
      tables=false
      cookies=false
      backgroundsounds=false
      vbscript=false
      javascript=false
      javaapplets=false
      activexcontrols=false
      win16=false
      win32=false
      beta=false
      ak=false
      sk=false
      aol=false
```

```
        crawler=false
        cdf=false
        gold=false
        authenticodeupdate=false
        tagwriter=System.Web.UI.Html132TextWriter
        ecmascriptversion=0.0
        msdomversion=0.0
        w3cdomversion=0.0
        platform=Unknown
        clrVersion=0.0
        css1=false
        css2=false
        xml=false
    ...
      </browserCaps>
    </system.web>
</configuration>
```

When a page receives a Web request, it detects the browser type by using the HTTP_USER_AGENT server variable and creates the *HtmlTextWriter* specified in the web.config file for that browser type. The correct *HtmlTextWriter* object is thus automatically passed into the rendering methods of your control. However, your control benefits from the automatic tag conversion capability provided by the *HtmlTextWriter* object only if it uses the *HtmlTextWriterTag* enumeration to render tags. If you render tags as strings, they are rendered by the *HtmlTextWriter* instance without any additional processing and your control cannot utilize the uplevel/downlevel-rendering architecture that is built into the page framework.

A page developer can also specify the target browser via the *ClientTarget* attribute in the *Page* directive. This attribute overrides automatic browser detection and results in creating the *HtmlTextWriter* that maps to the browser specified by the attribute value.

To test the downlevel or HTML 3.2 rendering capabilities of *LoginUI*, replace the *Page* directive at the top of LoginUITest.aspx (shown in Listing 8-6) with the following *Page* directive to force a downlevel rendering:

```
<%@ Page Language="C#" ClientTarget="downlevel" %>
```

Access the page in your browser. If you view the source for the page, you should see HTML rendered by *LoginUI* that is similar to this:

```
<table cellspacing="1" id="LoginUI1" bgcolor="Gainsboro">
  <tr>
    <td>
      <font face="Verdana" size="2">
      <b>Login Name:</b>
```

(continued)

```
      </font>
    </td>
    <td>
      <font face="Verdana" size="2">
      <b><input type="Text" name="LoginUI1:UserName"
        id="LoginUI1_UserName" value="" /></b>
      </font>
    </td>
  </tr>
  <tr>
    <td>
      <font face="Verdana" size="2">
      <b>Password:</b>
      </font>
    </td>
    <td>
      <font face="Verdana" size="2">
      <b><input type="Password" name="LoginUI1:Password"
        id="LoginUI1_Password" value="" /></b>
      </font>
    </td>
  </tr>
  <tr>
    <td colspan="2" align="right">
      <font face="Verdana" size="2">
      <b>
      <input type="Submit" name="LoginUI1"
        id="LoginUI1" value="Submit" />
      </b>
      </font>
    </td>
  </tr>
</table>
```

Notice that a *style* attribute is no longer generated on the *<table>* tag because HTML 3.2 browsers do not support CSS styles. Notice also that the *<font>* and *<b>* tags are propagated into the content within the table cells. We did not do any extra work in the implementation of the *LoginUI* control to enable downlevel rendering. The *LoginUI* control benefits from the automatic downlevel-rendering capability of *Html32TextWriter* because we invoked the rendering methods of *HtmlTextWriter* to write attributes, styles, and tags and because we used enumerations instead of strings when specifying tag names. If we had rendered the user interface by using raw HTML, *LoginUI* would not be able to automatically generate HTML 3.2.

Summary

In this chapter, we looked at the functionality that is available to your control for rendering markup text. We examined the rendering methods of the *Control* and *WebControl* classes, and we examined the *HtmlTextWriter* class that is responsible for rendering markup text to the HTTP response stream. We discussed when to derive from *Control* and when to derive from *WebControl* and showed how to override the rendering methods of these classes. We also showed how to utilize the methods of *HtmlTextWriter* to render HTML tags, attributes, and style attributes. In addition, we looked at how the page framework automatically generates HTML 4.0 or HTML 3.2, depending on the capabilities of the user's Web browser.

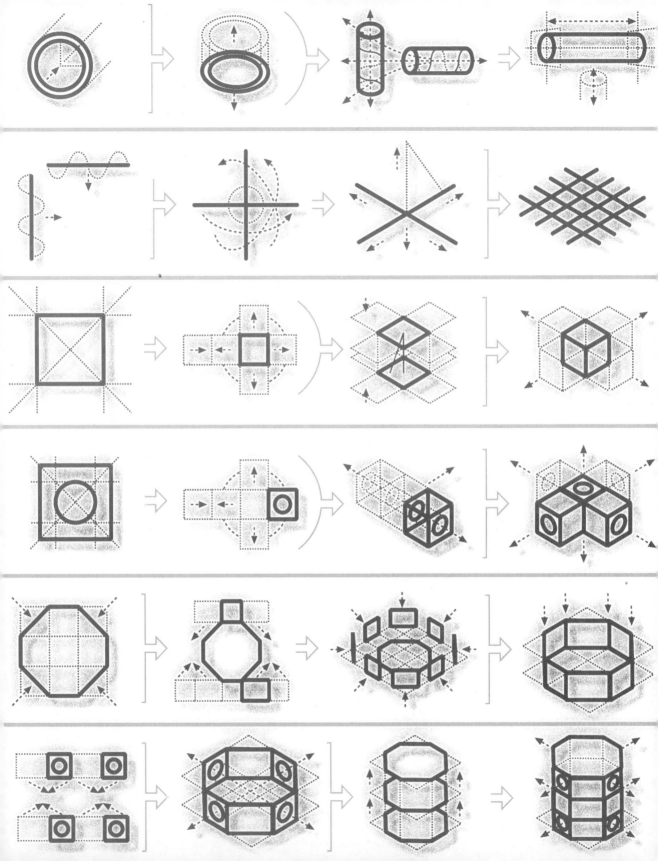

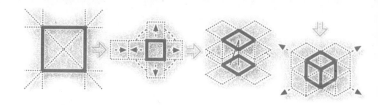

9

Control Life Cycle, Events, and Postback

In Chapter 2, "Page Programming Model," we described how ASP.NET re-creates a page and its control tree upon each request. In this chapter, we'll begin where Chapter 2 left off. We'll look at the *life cycle* of a control—that is, we'll examine what a control does at various stages of processing an HTTP request. The control life cycle is the most important architectural concept that you need to understand as a control developer. Your control's life cycle dictates when your control can save and restore its state, interact with the page and other controls, perform its main processing logic, and render markup to the output stream.

In this chapter, we'll also look at the events that your control inherits from the *Control* class and show how you can raise additional events from your control. Furthermore, we'll describe the ASP.NET architecture that enables a control to respond to postback events and process posted form data, and we'll show how you can incorporate that functionality in your control.

Control Life Cycle

When a browser makes requests to an ASP.NET page, communication takes place over the stateless HTTP protocol. However, the page framework creates an illusion of stateful execution that enables a page to provide a user experience similar to that of a continuously executing desktop process. To create the illusion of continuity, on each subsequent request after the initial request, the page effectively begins execution where it left off at the end of the previous request. The page saves its state at the end of processing a request and, upon postback, uses the saved state to restore its state before processing the new request. This process of saving and restoring state is the most important aspect of the life cycle of a page and its controls.

The page framework divides request processing into several distinct, logical phases so that it can re-create and save the page and its control tree in a predictable manner. Once the page framework restores the control tree, controls can execute and interact as though in a continuously executing process.

As a control developer, you must understand a control's life cycle so that you know which logic to implement in the various phases. However, if you are new to control development, you do not have to understand the full complexity of the control life cycle before you begin implementing useful controls. To get started, you merely need an overview of the various phases in a control's life cycle, as Figure 9-1 depicts.

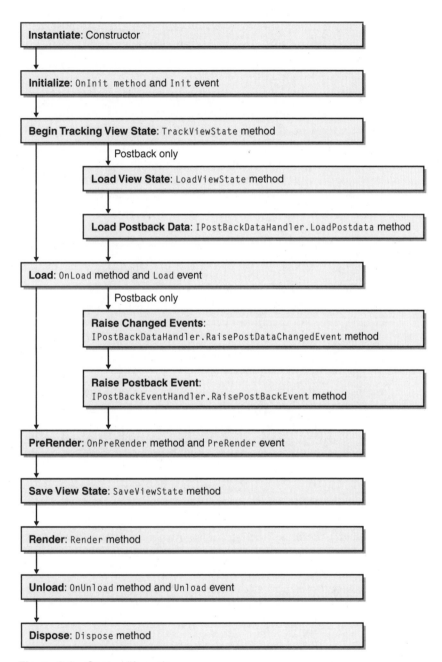

Figure 9-1 Control life cycle

The methods that begin with *On* (such as *OnInit*) are part of your control's event infrastructure and raise the corresponding event (such as *Init*). Some of the phases are implemented as events so that a page developer can respond to them by attaching event handlers.

Here's an overview of what happens in each phase and what you need to implement in your control. If you are new to control authoring, the phases that you must understand to get started are Instantiate, Initialize, Load, PreRender, and Render. You can skim the descriptions of the other phases for now and return to them when you create more advanced controls.

- ■ **Instantiate** The control is instantiated by the page or by another control by invoking its constructor. The phases that are listed after this stage occur only if the control is added to the control tree, as you'll see in the LifeCycleDemoTest.aspx demonstration in Listing 9-2.

- ■ **Initialize** In this phase, the page and all the controls in its control tree invoke their *OnInit* method by default (which raises the *Init* event). Prior to executing its life cycle phases, the page builds its initial control tree based on the declarative syntax of the .aspx page. Consequently, control properties specified in declarative page syntax are assigned before the Initialize phase. A page developer can provide additional logic to initialize the page by implementing the *Page_Init* method, which the page framework wires up to the *Init* event of the page. You can provide initialization logic for your control by overriding your control's *OnInit* method. At this point in its life cycle, your control can safely access child controls that are present in its *Controls* collection, but it cannot access its parent or any other control (such as the page) higher in the control hierarchy.

- ■ **Begin Tracking View State** This phase occurs at the end of the Initialize phase. In this phase, the page automatically invokes the *TrackViewState* method of your control. The *TrackViewState* method ensures that, after this phase, changes made to properties that use the *ViewState* dictionary are persisted in your control's view state. We introduced the view state concept in Chapter 7, "Simple Properties and View State," and will examine it in more detail in Chapter 10, "Complex Properties and State Management." The page framework invokes *TrackViewState* after initialization for efficiency. Initial values are always reloaded by the page framework when it reconstructs the control tree on postback, and it is inefficient to save those values in your control's view state. For the most part, the implementation of

TrackViewState provided by the base *Control* class is adequate. You have to override *TrackViewState* only if your control defines complex properties, as we'll describe in Chapter 10.

- **Load View State (postback only)**   This phase occurs on postback and not during the initial request. In this phase, your control must restore its state to where it was at the end of processing the previous request. The page framework automatically restores the *ViewState* dictionary in this phase. If your control does not maintain state or it uses the *ViewState* dictionary for storing all its state information (as we described in Chapter 7), you do not have to implement logic for this phase. However, if your control requires custom state management, you must override the *LoadViewState* method to implement custom state restoration, as we'll describe in Chapter 10.

- **Load Postback Data (postback only, optional)**   This phase occurs on postback only if your control participates in postback data processing by implementing the *IPostBackDataHandler* interface. An example is the *TextBox* control. In this stage, a control must update its state from posted form data by implementing the *Load-PostData* method of the *IPostBackDataHandler* interface. We'll look at two examples of postback data processing, *SimpleTextBox* and *Login*, later in this chapter.

- **Load**   By the beginning of this phase, all the controls in the control tree are initialized and restored to the state they had at the end of the previous cycle. In addition, postback controls have been populated with posted form data. At this point in the life cycle (but not earlier), your control can safely access other controls in the page. In this phase, you should implement logic that is common to each request by overriding the *OnLoad* method. You saw an example of overriding the *OnLoad* method in the *PageTracker* example in Chapter 7 and will see this method implemented in other examples in subsequent chapters. If you need to implement logic that is executed only during the initial request for the page, you should check the *IsPostBack* property of the page (*if (Page.IsPostBack == false) {...}*) when implementing that logic. The page and all the controls in its control tree raise their *Load* event during this phase by default.

- **Raise Changed Events (postback only, optional)**   This phase occurs on postback only if your control participates in postback data processing by implementing the *IPostBackDataHandler* interface. During this stage, a control raises events (such as the *TextChanged* event of the *TextBox* control) to signal that its state changed as a result of postback. To participate in this phase, your control must implement the *RaisePostDataChangedEvent* method of the *IPostBackDataHandler* interface. We'll look at two examples of raising changed events later in this chapter, when we examine the *SimpleTextBox* and *Login* controls.

- **Raise Postback Event (postback only, optional)** This phase occurs on postback only if your control participates in postback event processing by implementing the *IPostBackEventHandler* interface. In this phase, you can implement logic to map a client event into a server-side event by implementing the *RaisePostBackEvent* method of the *IPostBackEventHandler* interface. An example is the *Button* control, which raises a *Click* event on the server to enable the page developer to handle the client-side postback event. Later in this chapter, we'll look at several controls that contain examples of postback events (*SimpleButton, PostbackButtons,* and *Login*) and show you how to raise events during this phase.

- **PreRender** In this phase, you should implement any work that your control needs to do before it is rendered, by overriding the *OnPreRender* method. We'll see an example of overriding the *OnPreRender* method later in this chapter when we examine the *Login* control. The page and all the controls in its control tree raise their *PreRender* event during this phase.

- **Save View State** If your control does not maintain state or it uses the *ViewState* dictionary for storing all its state information, you do not have to implement any additional logic during this phase. The page framework automatically saves the *ViewState* dictionary during this phase. If your control requires custom state management, you must override the *SaveViewState* method to implement custom state restoration, as you will see in Chapter 10. This method is called only for controls whose *EnableViewState* property (and recursively, that of its parent) is set to *true*. Any changes made to your control after this phase will not be persisted in your control's view state.

- **Render** In this method, your control writes markup text to the output stream by overriding the *Render* method of *Control* or one of the rendering methods of the *WebControl* class. We described rendering in depth in Chapter 8, "Rendering."

- **Unload**   A page performs cleanup in this phase by implementing the *Page_Unload* method. As a control developer, you should instead override the *Dispose* method to perform cleanup. The page and all the controls in its control tree raise their *Unload* event during this phase by default.

- **Dispose**   In this phase, you should override the *Dispose* method to free any resources that your control holds.

We'll now examine the mechanics of the page execution cycle. As we described in Chapter 2, a page is an HTTP handler and is responsible for processing an HTTP request to an .aspx file. When it starts processing a request, the page creates its control tree. It then sequentially executes the phases shown in Figure 9-1 by recursively invoking the methods appropriate to each phase on the control tree. Note that a page is a control (derives from *Control*) and, like any other control, inherits the methods and events shown in Figure 9-1. Because several of the methods listed in Figure 9-1 are protected, you might wonder how a page can invoke them on its child controls. This invocation is possible because every control inherits—from the *Control* class—some internal (assembly-accessible) framework methods that recursively invoke the protected methods.

> **Note**   The execution sequence that we just described applies to controls that are created declaratively on the page. But what if a control is created in an event handler and dynamically added to the control tree? In that case, the control plays catch-up. As soon as it is added to the control tree, it starts to execute its phases until it reaches the current phase of the page. At that point, it follows along with the page.

To demonstrate the execution sequence, we'll create the simple *LifeCycle-Demo* control shown in Listing 9-1. *LifeCycleDemo* uses the tracing feature of ASP.NET to write a simple message from each execution phase by overriding the relevant methods (such as *OnInit* and *OnLoad*).

```
using System;
using System.Web.UI;

namespace MSPress.ServerControls {

    public class LifeCycleDemo : Control {

        public LifeCycleDemo() {
        }

        protected override void OnInit(EventArgs e) {
            base.OnInit(e);
            Page.Trace.Write(this.ID, "In Init...");
        }

        protected override void TrackViewState() {
            base.TrackViewState();
            Page.Trace.Write(this.ID, "In TrackViewState...");
        }

        protected override void LoadViewState(object savedstate) {
            base.LoadViewState(savedstate);
            Page.Trace.Write(this.ID, "In LoadViewState...");
        }

        protected override void OnLoad(EventArgs e) {
            base.OnLoad(e);
            Page.Trace.Write(this.ID, "In Load...");
        }

        protected override object SaveViewState() {
            Page.Trace.Write(this.ID, "In SaveViewState...");
            return base.SaveViewState();
        }

        protected override void OnPreRender(EventArgs e) {
            base.OnPreRender(e);
            Page.Trace.Write(this.ID, "In PreRender...");
        }

        protected override void Render(HtmlTextWriter writer) {
            Page.Trace.Write(this.ID, "In Render...");
        }
```

Listing 9-1 LifeCycleDemo.cs

```
        public override void Dispose() {
            base.Dispose();
        }
    }
}
```

Listing 9-2 shows a page that uses the *LifeCycleDemo* control. The page has three instances of the *LifeCycleDemo* control—one created declaratively and two created dynamically in its *button1_Click* event handler. The page adds one of the dynamically created instances of *LifeCycleDemo* to its control tree, but not the other. You'll see that the execution phases occur only in the instance that is added to the control tree. Tracing is enabled on the page by setting *trace="true"* in the *Page* directive. Figures 9-2 and 9-3 show the trace log for the page on initial request and after postback.

```
<%@ Page Language="C#" Trace="true"%>
<%@ Register TagPrefix="msp" Namespace="MSPress.ServerControls"
  Assembly="MSPress.ServerControls" %>
<html>
  <head>
    <script runat="server" >
      void button1_Click(object sender, EventArgs e) {
          LifeCycleDemo dynamic1 = new LifeCycleDemo();
          dynamic1.ID = "dynamic1";
          this.Controls.Add(dynamic1);

          // The next instance of LifeCycleDemo is not added to the
          // control tree of the page.
          LifeCycleDemo dynamic2 = new LifeCycleDemo();
          dynamic2.ID = "dynamic2";
      }
    </script>
  </head>
  <body>
    <form runat="server">
      <asp:Button id="button1" OnClick="button1_Click" Text="Submit"
        runat="server" />
      <br
      <msp:LifeCycleDemo runat="server" id="declarative1" />
    </form>
  </body>
</html>
```

Listing 9-2   LifeCycleDemoTest.aspx

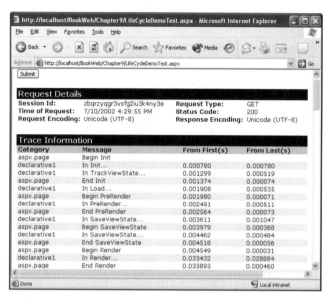

Figure 9-2 A section of the trace log from LifeCycleDemoTest.aspx on first request. The messages corresponding to aspx.page in the Category column are written by the page. The other messages are written by the declarative instance of *LifeCycleDemo*.

On first request, you can see the execution sequence of the declarative instance of *LifeCycleDemo* with *ID="declarative1"* in the trace log. On postback, another instance of *LifeCycleDemo* with *ID="dynamic1"* is created in the Raise Postback Event phase, as shown in Figure 9-3. This instance plays catch-up, and three of its execution phases occur in succession after it is created and added to the control tree. Note that the instance of *LifeCycleDemo* with *ID="dynamic2"* that is created in the *button1_Click* event handler (shown in Listing 9-2) does not execute its phases after instantiation because the page did not add the control to the control tree. A control cannot participate in request processing unless it is added to the control tree. When a control is created declaratively on a page, the page parser adds it to the control tree. If you create a control dynamically, you are responsible for adding it to the control tree yourself.

Figure 9-2 contains two calls to the *SaveViewState* method of the *declarative1* control instance. The first call is an artifact of tracing and does not occur in normal execution. When tracing is enabled, the page makes the additional call to estimate the size of the view state.

Although tracing helps you to understand processing of the page and its controls, you should not include trace statements in production-quality code. Trace output is not rendered when tracing is disabled on the page; nonetheless, the trace statements execute and add an unnecessary overhead.

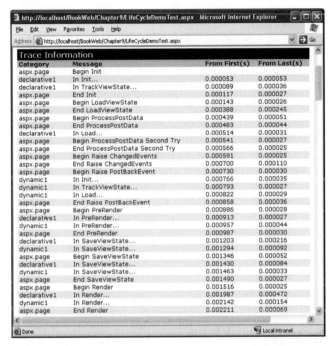

Figure 9-3   A section of the trace log from LifeCycleDemoTest.aspx on postback. This log shows the additional phases that occur in a postback scenario. It also contains messages from a second (dynamically added) instance of *LifeCycleDemo*.

Events in Server Controls

Every server control inherits five events from the base *Control* class. The following four events correspond to phases in a control's life cycle that we described in the previous section:

- Init
- Load
- PreRender
- Unload

In addition, the *Control* class exposes another event: *DataBinding*. A control raises the *DataBinding* event whenever the page developer's code calls the control's *DataBind* method. We'll describe the *DataBinding* event in Chapter 16, "Data-Bound Controls."

Events in server controls follow the standard event pattern that we described in Chapter 3, "Component Programming Overview." Each event has an associated virtual method named *On<EventName>* that invokes the delegates that are attached to the event. If you want to respond to an event in your control, you should override the corresponding *On<EventName>* method instead of attaching a delegate. When you override an *On<EventName>* method, you must invoke the corresponding method of the base class so that delegates registered with the event are invoked.

In addition to the events your control inherits from the *Control* class, you can raise other events from your control. The page framework is based on an event-driven programming model, which enables a page developer to attach handlers that execute in response to events raised by controls. When you expose events from your control, you enable a page developer to respond to actions of your control or to changes in the state of your control. For example, the *TextBox* control raises a *TextChanged* event when its *Text* property changes after a round-trip, and the *DataGrid* control raises an *ItemCreated* event for each row (or item) it creates.

Like the events exposed by standard ASP.NET controls, the events that you expose from your control are amenable to design tools. The designer displays all the events of the selected control in the property grid, and a page developer can double-click an event to attach an event handler. You should apply *DefaultEventAttribute* (analogous to the *DefaultPropertyAttribute*) to your control so that a page developer can also double-click a control to attach an event handler to its default event. You will see this attribute applied in the examples shown later in this chapter.

Declarative Syntax for Event Wiring

ASP.NET pages provide a declarative syntax for wiring server-side event handlers on the control's tag:

```
<asp:Button id="button1" OnClick="button1_Click" Text="Submit"
  runat="server" />
```

This syntax provides an intuitive model for page developers because it is similar to the syntax for binding a client-side event handler on an HTML tag (*onmouseover="client-side script function name"*).

When the page parser parses the .aspx file (as we described in "From Text to Controls" in Chapter 2), it transforms the declarative syntax into code that binds an event handler to an event via an event delegate instance:

```
button1.Click += new EventHandler(this.button1_Click);
```

Another point—which will be of more interest to page developers than to control developers—is that pages and user controls automatically bind methods named *Page_Init*, *Page_Load*, *Page_PreRender*, and *Page_Unload* to the corresponding intrinsic events (*Init*, *Load*, *PreRender*, and *UnLoad*).

Postback Architecture

A postback is an HTTP POST request (or an HTTP GET request with data in the URL query string) that occurs when a user submits a form. A control that renders a form element needs to respond to postback, capture form data, update its state, and implement other logic on postback. For the most part, you will not have to implement postback processing in your own controls because ASP.NET provides form controls such as *Button*, *TextBox*, and *DropDownList* that implement postback processing for the standard HTML form elements. You can easily reuse the existing ASP.NET form controls via class composition, as we will show in Chapter 12, "Composite Controls." However, in some scenarios, when performance requirements do not permit the cost of object creation that is concomitant with class composition, you might have to implement postback processing in your own control. This section provides an overview of the postback processing architecture of the page framework; the rest of this chapter shows how to implement that architecture. Although the remainder of this chapter will be useful background information for control authoring, you might want to browse through it on your first reading and return to it when you need to implement postback processing in your controls.

ASP.NET provides a simple and intuitive architecture that enables controls to perform tasks related to postback by implementing one or both of two interfaces—*IPostBackEventHandler* and *IPostBackDataHandler*.

The *IPostBackEventHandler* interface enables a control to raise an event that signals that postback has occurred. In effect, this interface enables a control to map the client-side form submit event to a server-side event, which allows page developers to handle the client-side event by attaching event handlers to the server-side event. For example, the *Button* control raises a *Click* event on the server when a form is submitted. Note that a postback event, which occurs when a user submits a form, is the only client-side event that is transmitted to the server. All other client-side events—such as key press or mouse hover events—can be handled on the client only, as we'll discuss in Chapter 13, "Client-Side Behavior." A control that implements *IPostBackEventHandler* participates in the Raise Postback Event phase shown in Figure 9-1.

The *IPostBackDataHandler* interface enables a control to retrieve posted form data, update its state accordingly, and raise events on the server to signal changes in its state. For example, the *TextBox* control updates its state with text entered by the user and raises a *TextChanged* event when its state changes. A control that implements the *IPostBackDataHandler* interface participates in the Load Postback Data and Raise Changed Events phases shown in Figure 9-1.

> **Note**   If your control merely needs to examine posted form data without participating in the relevant postback processing phases, it can do so via the *Context* property of its containing page (*Page.Context.Request.Form* or *Page.Context.Request.QueryString*). You have to implement *IPostBackEventHandler* and/or *IPostBackDataHandler* only when your control needs to participate in the appropriate processing phase.

In the remainder of the chapter, we'll examine how to implement *IPost-BackEventHandler* and follow with a discussion on implementing *IPostBack-DataHandler*. Finally, we'll develop a *Login* control that implements both of these interfaces.

Mapping a Postback Event to a Server Event— The *IPostBackEventHandler* Interface

We'll now examine the event architecture that enables a server control to map a client-side event into a corresponding server-side event. To develop a control that raises events in response to postback, you must implement the *System.Web.UI.IPostBackEventHandler* interface, which contains one method:

```
public interface IPostBackEventHandler {
    void RaisePostBackEvent(string eventArgument);
}
```

The argument that the page passes into this method is useful if your control renders multiple HTML elements that cause postback events. In this section, we will look at controls that render a single postback element. We'll show an example that uses this argument in "Rendering Multiple Elements That Use Client Script for Postback—The *NavButtons* Example."

Upon postback, the page searches its control tree for a control whose *UniqueID* matches the name of the element that caused postback. (Later in this section, we'll show you how your control can cause the *UniqueID* to appear in the posted form data.) If the page finds a matching control and that control implements *IPostBackEventHandler*, the page invokes the control's *RaisePost-BackEvent* method. If your control cannot render its *UniqueID* as the name attribute of a form element—which means that its *UniqueID* does not appear in the posted form data— there is an alternate way to ensure that your control is invoked by the page during the Raise Postback Event phase. To do this, your control must invoke the *RegisterRequiresPostBack* method of the containing page, as we'll show in the *Login* example at the end of this chapter.

The *RaisePostBackEvent* method is where you implement the logic that your control should perform on postback. In general, a control will raise one or more server-side events in the *RaisePostBackEvent* method. For example, the *Button* control raises the *Click* event from its *RaisePostBackEvent* method. To make the discussion concrete, we'll now develop a *SimpleButton* control that is similar to the ASP.NET *Button* control.

Implementing *IPostBackEventHandler*—The *SimpleButton* Example

The *SimpleButton* control implements the *IPostBackEventHandler* interface and raises a server-side *Click* event in response to postback. In Chapter 3, we described the event architecture in the .NET Framework and provided an example that walks through the steps of exposing an event from a class. Implementing an event in a server control is no different from implementing an event in any other managed class. The implementation of the *Click* event in *SimpleButton* follows the standard event pattern that we described in Chapter 3—an event member named *Click* and an *OnClick* method that raises the event. If you have not implemented .NET events, you should look at the section "Raising an Event" in Chapter 3 because, throughout the rest of the book, we assume that you are familiar with the basics of raising an event from a class.

Listing 9-3 contains the code for the *SimpleButton* control. The highlighted code provides the functionality to map a postback event into a server event. We'll discuss the example after the code listing.

```
using System;
using System.ComponentModel;
using System.Web.UI;
using System.Web.UI.WebControls;

namespace MSPress.ServerControls {
    [// The DefaultEventAttribute allows a page
     // developer to attach a handler to the default
     // event by double-clicking on the control.
```

Listing 9-3 SimpleButton.cs   *(continued)*

Listing 9-3   *(continued)*

```
    DefaultEvent("Click"),
    DefaultProperty("Text")]
public class SimpleButton: WebControl, IPostBackEventHandler {

    [Bindable(true),
     Category("Behavior"),
     DefaultValue(""),
     Description("The text to display on the button")]
    public virtual string Text {
        get {
            string s = (string)ViewState["Text"];
            return((s == null) ? String.Empty : s);
        }
        set {
            ViewState["Text"] = value;
        }
    }

    protected override HtmlTextWriterTag TagKey {
        get {
            return HtmlTextWriterTag.Input;
        }
    }

    [Category("Action"),Description("Raised when the button is clicked")]
    public event EventHandler Click;

    protected override void AddAttributesToRender(HtmlTextWriter writer)
    {
        base.AddAttributesToRender(writer);
        writer.AddAttribute(HtmlTextWriterAttribute.Name, this.UniqueID);
        writer.AddAttribute(HtmlTextWriterAttribute.Type, "Submit");
        writer.AddAttribute(HtmlTextWriterAttribute.Value, this.Text);

    }


    // Method of IPostBackEventHandler that raises postback events.
    void IPostBackEventHandler.RaisePostBackEvent(string eventArgument){

        OnClick(EventArgs.Empty);
    }
```

```
        // Invokes delegate registered with the Click event.
        protected virtual void OnClick(EventArgs e) {
            if (Click != null) {
                Click(this, e);
            }
        }


        protected override void Render(HtmlTextWriter writer) {
            // Make sure this control is nested in a form.
            if (Page != null) {
                Page.VerifyRenderingInServerForm(this);
            }
            base.Render(writer);
        }
    }
}
```

SimpleButton demonstrates the following tasks, which are essential for implementing postback event functionality:

■   Implements *IPostBackEventHandler*.

■   Raises the *Click* event in the *RaisePostBackEvent* method by invoking the *OnClick* method. In effect, this maps the client-side submit event to a server-side *Click* event.

■   Renders an HTML *name* attribute whose value is the *UniqueID* of the control. The *UniqueID* of the control is assigned to it by the page and is guaranteed by the page framework to be unique on the page. The page generates the *UniqueID* based on the control's user-assigned (or autogenerated by the page) *ID* property. By assigning the value of the *UniqueID* to the *name* attribute, you ensure that your control renders an element whose name is unique in the form post data and that the page can route the postback event to your control.

In addition, *SimpleButton* invokes—from its *Render* method—the *Verify-RenderingInServerForm* method of the page to ensure the page developer uses the control in a server-side form *(<form runat="server"> </form>)*. The *Verify-RenderingInServerForm* method causes the page to throw an exception if the page developer does not place the control within server-side form tags. The page framework requires that form controls must be nested within a server-side form to ensure that the name/value pairs for the rendered HTML elements are part of the form data posted by the browser. In general, if your control renders a form input element, you should include the call to *VerifyRenderingInServerForm*.

SimpleButton also demonstrates a feature that is not specific to ASP.NET but is a feature of the C# programming language—*explicit interface method implementation*, also known as *private interface method implementation*. Explicit interface method implementation in effect allows you to implement a method of an interface without adding the method to the public object model of your class. This is in contrast to standard interface implementation, which requires that interface methods must have public access in a class that implements the interface. An explicitly implemented interface method is not really private—it can be accessed from outside the class. However, the class that implements this interface method must be cast into the interface type before the method can be invoked. Thus, if *simpleButton1* is an instance of *SimpleButton*, *(IPostBackEventHandler)simpleButton1.RaisePostBackEvent(eventArgument)* is allowed, but *simpleButton1.RaisePostBackEvent(eventArgument)* is not.

To explicitly implement an interface method, you must qualify the name of the method with the name of the interface. In addition, you cannot provide any modifiers, such as *private*, *protected*, or *virtual*. Here's an example of explicit interface method implementation from the *SimpleButton* control:

```
void IPostBackEventHandler.RaisePostBackEvent(string eventArgument){
    OnClick(EventArgs.Empty);
}
```

Listing 9-4 contains a page that uses the *SimpleButton* control and attaches an event handler to its *Click* event. Figures 9-4 and 9-5 show the page viewed in a browser before and after postback.

```
<%@ Page Language="C#" %>
<%@ Register TagPrefix="msp" Namespace="MSPress.ServerControls"
  Assembly="MSPress.ServerControls" %>
<html>
  <head>
    <script runat="server" >
      void simpleButton1_Click(object sender, EventArgs e) {
          label1.Text = "You clicked the button.";
      }
    </script>
  </head>
  <body>
    <form runat="server">
      <br>
      Click the button to raise its server-side Click event.
      <br>
      <msp:SimpleButton Text="Submit" Runat="server"
```

Listing 9-4   SimpleButtonTest.aspx

```
      OnClick="simpleButton1_Click" id="simpleButton1" />
    <br>
    <asp:Label Font-Size="10pt" Font-Bold="true" id="label1"
      runat="server" />
  </form>
 </body>
</html>
```

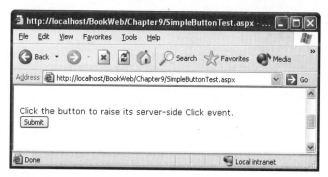

Figure 9-4   SimpleButtonTest.aspx viewed in a browser on initial request

Figure 9-5   SimpleButtonTest.aspx viewed in a browser after postback

Optimizing Event Implementation

We'll now digress from the main topic to show you a more efficient way to implement events in server controls. In Chapter 3, we mentioned that if a class raises many events, it is not efficient to implement them by declaring an event member for each event as we did in *SimpleButton*. Let's examine why and look at a more optimal implementation.

> **Note**   The optimized event implementation relies on the event property construct, which is not available in Microsoft Visual Basic .NET.

There are two reasons why it is not efficient to declare an event member for each event. First, when you declare an event member such as *public event EventHandler Click*, the compiler generates a private field of type delegate for that event, such as *private EventHandler Click*. In Chapter 3, we looked at that field using the ILDASM disassembler tool. The delegate field is created for each event declared by the class, irrespective of whether any event handlers are attached to the event in user code. This is an inefficient use of memory, especially if your control raises a large number of events.

Second, the compiler-generated *add* and *remove* methods are marked as *synchronized* for thread safety, which means they acquire a lock every time a user adds or removes a delegate from the event. Locks add unnecessary overhead because page developers rarely use multithreading on a single page.

We'll now examine a more efficient event implementation pattern in the .NET Framework that uses the *System.ComponentModel.EventHandlerList* class, which is a linked list optimized for the storage and retrieval of delegates. Let's see how the base *Control* class implements events by using the optimized event pattern. The *Control* class defines a property named *Events* of type *EventHandlerList*:

```
private EventHandlerList _events;
protected EventHandlerList Events {
    get {
        if (_events == null) {
            _events = new EventHandlerList();
        }
        return _events;
    }
}
```

The *Control* class defines a key for each event, which it uses to store and retrieve event delegates in the *EventHandler*. The following code shows the key for the *Init* event:

```
protected static readonly object EventInit = new object();
```

The key is static (shared across all instances of the control) and thus is created only once for each event.

Instead of using event fields, the *Control* class uses the event property construct to define events. The C# event property construct is illustrated in the following code, which shows the declaration of the *Init* event in the *Control* class:

```
public event EventHandler Init {
    add {
        Events.AddHandler(EventInit, value);
    }
    remove {
        Events.RemoveHandler(EventInit, value);
    }
}
```

— Like properties

Whenever user code adds or removes a delegate from an event, the control instance adds or removes the delegate from the *EventHandler* list by using the key for that event (such as *EventInit*). Under the hood, the *EventHandler* instance performs one of the following tasks when its *AddHandler* method is invoked:

■ If there is no delegate corresponding to the key, the *EventHandler* instance adds the delegate as a new list element.

■ If a delegate already exists in the list corresponding to the key, *EventHandler* uses the *Combine* method of the *Delegate* class to add the new delegate to the existing delegate.

The *RemoveHandler* method of the instance works in a similar way, except that it invokes the *Remove* method of the *Delegate* class to remove a delegate from an existing delegate. If there is no delegate in the list corresponding to the key, the *RemoveHandler* method does nothing.

Unlike the event field construct that we used in *SimpleButton*, the event property construct never creates a delegate field for each event. Memory is allocated for event keys (which are static and created only once for each event that the class defines) and for the *EventHandlerList*. As we mentioned earlier, another important benefit is that the *add* and *remove* methods of *EventHandlerList* are not automatically marked as synchronized and therefore do not acquire locks when adding or removing delegates. Event properties implemented by using *EventHandlerList* do involve lookup but, on the whole, lead to better performance than event fields because they use less memory and do not have the synchronization overhead.

One final detail in the event property construct is the implementation of the *On <EventName>* method that raises an event. When you use an event property, you must retrieve the delegate from the *EventHandlerList* and cast it to the type of your event delegate before invoking the attached handlers:

```
protected virtual void OnInit(EventArgs e) {
    EventHandler initHandler = (EventHandler)Events[EventInit];
    if (initHandler != null) {
        initHandler(this, e);
    }
}
```

If you author your controls in C#, you should use the optimized event pattern as the samples throughout the rest of this book do.

Generating Client-Side Script for Postback

We'll now return to our discussion of postback and show how to implement a control that causes postback via client-side script. Only two HTML elements, *<input type="button">* and *<input type="image">*, are intrinsically capable of posting a form back to the server. However, other form elements (such as a link or a text box) can be made to cause postback by submitting the form via a client-side event handler. The page framework makes it easy for you to implement such postback functionality in a form control. To see how this works, we'll create a *SimpleLinkButton* control (similar to the ASP.NET *LinkButton*) that renders a hyperlink that, when clicked, posts the form back to the server.

Listing 9-5 shows the code for the *SimpleLinkButton* control. *SimpleLinkButton* renders a hyperlink instead of a button, but the code is similar to that of the *SimpleButton* control shown in Listing 9-3. As with the *SimpleButton* control, *SimpleLinkButton* implements *IPostBackEventHandler* and raises a *Click* event on the server in response to a client-side submit event. The main difference between the two controls is that *SimpleLinkButton* generates client-side script to cause postback. The code that provides this functionality is highlighted in Listing 9-5. Let's look at the code first and then discuss what it does. You will also see that *SimpleLinkButton* uses the optimized event property construct that we described in the previous section.

```csharp
using System;
using System.ComponentModel;
using System.Web.UI;
using System.Web.UI.WebControls;

namespace MSPress.ServerControls {
    [DefaultEvent("Click"),
     DefaultProperty("Text")]
    public class SimpleLinkButton: WebControl, IPostBackEventHandler {

        private static readonly object EventClick = new object();

        [Bindable(true),
         Category("Behavior"),
         DefaultValue(""),
         Description("The text to display on the link")]
        public virtual string Text {
            get {
                string s = (string)ViewState["Text"];
                return((s == null) ? String.Empty : s);
            }
            set {
                ViewState["Text"] = value;
            }
        }

        protected override HtmlTextWriterTag TagKey {
            get {
                return HtmlTextWriterTag.A;
            }
        }

        [Category("Action"),Description("Raised when the
          hyperlink is clicked")]
        public event EventHandler Click {
            add {
                Events.AddHandler(EventClick, value);
            }
            remove {
                Events.RemoveHandler(EventClick, value);
            }
        }
```

Listing 9-5 SimpleLinkButton.cs   *(continued)*

Listing 9-5 *(continued)*

```
// Method of IPostBackEventHandler that raises postback events.
void IPostBackEventHandler.RaisePostBackEvent(
    string eventArgument) {
    OnClick(EventArgs.Empty);
}

protected override void AddAttributesToRender(
    HtmlTextWriter writer) {
    base.AddAttributesToRender(writer);
    writer.AddAttribute(HtmlTextWriterAttribute.Href,
        Page.GetPostBackClientHyperlink(this, String.Empty));
}

// Retrieves the delegate for the Click event and
// invokes the handlers registered with the delegate.
protected virtual void OnClick(EventArgs e) {
    EventHandler clickHandler =
        (EventHandler)Events[EventClick];
    if (clickHandler != null) {
        clickHandler(this, e);
    }
}

protected override void Render(HtmlTextWriter writer) {
    // Make sure this control is nested in a form.
    if (Page != null) {
        Page.VerifyRenderingInServerForm(this);
    }
    base.Render(writer);
}

protected override void RenderContents(HtmlTextWriter writer) {
    writer.Write(Text);
}
    }
}
```

The key feature of the *SimpleLinkButton* control is the call to the *GetPost-BackClientHyperlink* method of its containing page. This method of the *Page* class generates client-side script that causes postback from the hyperlink. The more general method that generates client-side script is *GetPostBackEventReference*. We'll describe *GetPostBackEventReference* later in this section. To see what the *GetPostBackClientHyperlink* method does, use the *SimpleLinkButton* control on a page and view the page in a browser. Listing 9-6 provides a sample page.

```
<%@ Page Language="C#" %>
<%@ Register TagPrefix="msp" Namespace="MSPress.ServerControls"
  Assembly="MSPress.ServerControls" %>
<html>
  <head>
    <script runat="server" >
      void simpleLinkButton1_Click(object sender, EventArgs e) {
          label1.Text = "You clicked the button.";
      }
    </script>
  </head>
  <body>
    <form runat="server">
      Click the link to raise its server-side Click event.
      <br>
      <msp:SimpleLinkButton Text="Click Me" runat="server"
        OnClick="simpleLinkButton1_Click" id="simpleLinkButton1" />
      <br>
      <asp:Label Font-Size="10pt" Font-Bold="true" id="label1"
        runat="server" />
    </form>
  </body>
</html>
```

Listing 9-6   SimpleLinkButtonTest.aspx

If you view the source for the page, you will see HTML such as the following, which is generated by *SimpleLinkButton*:

```
<a id="simpleLinkButton1"
  href="javascript:__doPostBack('simpleLinkButton1','')">Click Me</a>
```

At the bottom of the page, you will see two hidden fields and a script block containing a JavaScript function that causes postback:

```
<input type="hidden" name="__EVENTTARGET" value="" />
<input type="hidden" name="__EVENTARGUMENT" value="" />
<script language="javascript">
<!--
  function __doPostBack(eventTarget, eventArgument) {
      var theform = document._ctl0;
      theform.__EVENTTARGET.value = eventTarget;
      theform.__EVENTARGUMENT.value = eventArgument;
      theform.submit();
  }
// -->
</script>
```

Let's examine how these elements are rendered. If you look at the *Add-AttributesToRender* method in *SimpleLinkButton* (shown in Listing 9-5), you will see the following call:

```
writer.AddAttribute(HtmlTextWriterAttribute.Href,
    Page.GetPostBackClientHyperlink(this, String.Empty));
```

The *GetPostBackClientHyperlink* method does two things. First, *GetPostBackClientHyperlink* returns the string *"javascript:__doPostBack('simpleLinkButton1','')"* that contains a call to the *__doPostBack* JavaScript function generated by the page framework. You can assign this string to the *href* attribute of the HTML *<a>* tag. The values that *GetPostBackClientHyperlink* passes in as the parameters of the *__doPostBack* event handler are: the *UniqueID* of the control and an optional string argument that is used when your control renders multiple postback elements. We did not use the second argument in *SimpleLinkButton*, because it renders only one HTML element. We will use it in the next section in the *NavButtons* control, which renders multiple elements that cause postback.

Second, *GetPostBackClientHyperlink* tells the page to render two hidden fields (*__EVENTTARGET* and *__EVENTARGUMENT*) and a JavaScript function that causes postback (*__doPostBack*). The page makes sure that the hidden elements and the script function are rendered only once on the page, even if it contains multiple controls that cause postback.

When the user clicks the hyperlink in the browser, the JavaScript function *__doPostBack* is invoked. On the client, this function assigns the *UniqueID* of the control to the value of the *__EVENTTARGET* hidden field, assigns the event argument (if any) to the *__EVENTARGUMENT* hidden field, and posts the form. On the server, the page reads the *__EVENTTARGET* variable in the form post data and invokes the *RaisePostBackEvent* method of the control whose *UniqueID* matches the value of the *__EVENTTARGET* variable. In addition, the page passes the value of the *__EVENTARGUMENT* variable in the form post data as the argument to the *RaisePostBackEvent* method.

When your control renders script for postback, you do not have to render the *UniqueID* of your control as the *name* attribute on the HTML tag because the *__EVENTTARGET* hidden field contains the *UniqueID* of your control. This is different from the *SimpleButton* control (shown in Listing 9-3), which does not use client-side script for postback and renders the *UniqueID* as the *name* attribute on the HTML tag.

Under the hood, *GetPostBackClientHyperlink* invokes a more general method that generates client-side script: *GetPostBackEventReference*. *GetPostBackClientHyperlink* prepends the string *"javascript:"* to the string returned by *GetPostBackEventReference*. This prefix is needed to invoke the event handler on the client when a user clicks the hyperlink. When you render a form element other than a hyperlink, invoke the method *GetPostBackEventReference* and assign the returned string to an HTML attribute (such as *onchange* or *onclick*) on the tag of the HTML element that your control renders. The process of script generation and hidden variables is identical to that described earlier for *GetPostBackClientHyperlink*. Next we'll provide an example of a control that uses *GetPostBackEventReference*.

Rendering Multiple Elements That Use Client Script for Postback— The *NavButtons* Example

We'll now create a *NavButtons* control that renders Previous/Next navigational buttons that cause postback. *NavButtons* renders client-side script that writes a value corresponding to the button clicked by the user into the *__EVENT-ARGUMENT* hidden field, which we described in the previous section. The page passes this argument into the *RaisePostBackEvent* method of the control, and the control can use the argument to determine which element caused postback and accordingly raise the appropriate event. Listing 9-7 contains the code for the *NavButtons* control.

```
using System;
using System.ComponentModel;
using System.Web.UI;
using System.Web.UI.WebControls;

namespace MSPress.ServerControls {
    [DefaultEvent("ClickNext"),
     DefaultProperty("NextText")]
    public class NavButtons: WebControl, IPostBackEventHandler {

        private static readonly object EventClickNext = new object();
        private static readonly object EventClickPrevious =
            new object();

        [Bindable(true),
         Category("Behavior"),
         DefaultValue(""),
         Description("The text to display on the Next button")]
        public virtual string NextText {
            get {
                string s = (string)ViewState["NextText"];
```

Listing 9-7   NavButtons.cs   *(continued)*

Listing 9-7 *(continued)*

```
            return((s == null) ? String.Empty : s);
        }
        set {
            ViewState["NextText"] = value;
        }
    }

    [Bindable(true),
     Category("Behavior"),
     DefaultValue(""),
     Description("The text to display on the Previous button")]
    public virtual string PreviousText {
        get {
            string s = (string)ViewState["PreviousText"];
            return((s == null) ? String.Empty : s);
        }
        set {
            ViewState["PreviousText"] = value;
        }
    }

    [Category("Action"),
     Description("Raised when the Next button is clicked")]
    public event EventHandler ClickNext {
        add {
            Events.AddHandler(EventClickNext, value);
        }
        remove {
            Events.RemoveHandler(EventClickNext, value);
        }
    }

    [Category("Action"),
     Description("Raised when the Previous button is clicked")]
    public event EventHandler ClickPrevious {
        add {
            Events.AddHandler(EventClickPrevious, value);
        }
        remove {
            Events.RemoveHandler(EventClickPrevious, value);
        }
    }

    // Invokes delegates registered with the ClickNext event.
    protected virtual void OnClickNext (EventArgs e) {
        EventHandler clickNextHandler =
            (EventHandler)Events[EventClickNext];
```

```
        if (clickNextHandler != null) {
            clickNextHandler(this, e);
        }
    }


    // Invokes delegates registered with the ClickPrevious event.
    protected virtual void OnClickPrevious (EventArgs e) {
        EventHandler clickPreviousHandler =
            (EventHandler)Events[EventClickPrevious];
        if (clickPreviousHandler != null) {
            clickPreviousHandler(this, e);
        }
    }


    // Method of IPostBackEventHandler that raises postback events.
    void IPostBackEventHandler.RaisePostBackEvent(
        string eventArgument) {
        if (eventArgument == "Previous")
            OnClickPrevious(EventArgs.Empty);
        else if (eventArgument == "Next")
            OnClickNext(EventArgs.Empty);
    }


    protected override void Render(HtmlTextWriter writer) {
        // Make sure this control is in a form tag with
        // runat=server.
        if (Page != null) {
            Page.VerifyRenderingInServerForm(this);
        }
        base.Render(writer);
    }


    protected override void RenderContents(HtmlTextWriter writer) {
        writer.AddAttribute(HtmlTextWriterAttribute.Onclick,
            Page.GetPostBackEventReference(this, "Previous"));
        writer.AddAttribute("language", "javascript");
        writer.RenderBeginTag(HtmlTextWriterTag.Button);
        writer.Write(this.PreviousText);
        writer.RenderEndTag();

        writer.AddAttribute(HtmlTextWriterAttribute.Onclick,
            Page.GetPostBackEventReference(this, "Next"));
        writer.AddAttribute("language", "javascript");
        writer.RenderBeginTag(HtmlTextWriterTag.Button);
        writer.Write(this.NextText);
        writer.RenderEndTag();
    }
}
}
```

Listing 9-8 shows a page that uses the *NavButtons* control, and Figure 9-6 shows the page viewed in a browser.

```
<%@ Page Language="C#" %>
<%@ Register TagPrefix="msp" Namespace="MSPress.ServerControls"
  Assembly="MSPress.ServerControls" %>
<html>
  <head>
    <script runat="server" >
      void navButtons1_ClickPrevious(object sender, EventArgs e) {
          label1.Text = "You clicked the Previous button.";
      }
      void navButtons1_ClickNext(object sender, EventArgs e) {
          label1.Text = "You clicked the Next button.";
      }
    </script>
  </head>
  <body>
    <form runat="server">
      <br>
      Click a button:
      <br>
      <msp:NavButtons NextText="Next" PreviousText="Previous"
        runat="server" OnClickPrevious="navButtons1_ClickPrevious"
        OnClickNext="navButtons1_ClickNext" id="navButtons1" />
      <br>
      <asp:Label Font-Size="10pt" Font-Bold="true" id="label1"
        runat="server" />
    </form>
  </body>
</html>
```

Listing 9-8 NavButtonsTest.aspx

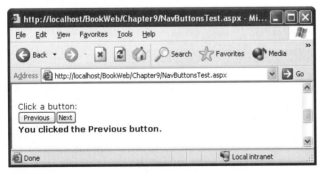

Figure 9-6 NavButtonsTest.aspx viewed in a browser. The event that is raised on the server depends on the button that is clicked.

IPostBackDataHandler and Postback Data

We'll now look at the postback data processing architecture that enables a control to retrieve form data submitted by a user, update its state, and raise events in response to changes in its state. To participate in postback data processing, a control must implement the *IPostBackDataHandler* interface and render elements whose HTML *name* attributes have unique values on the page. The *IPostBackDataHandler* interface has the following two methods:

```
public interface IPostBackDataHandler {
    bool LoadPostData(string postDataKey,
        NameValueCollection postCollection);
    void RaisePostDataChangedEvent();
}
```

In the Load Postback Data phase, which occurs before the Load phase (as shown in Figure 9-1), a page looks at each name in the name/value form post collection and searches the control tree for a control with a *UniqueID* that matches that name. If the page finds such a control and that control implements *IPostBackDataHandler*, the page invokes *LoadPostData* on that control. If your control does not render the value of its *UniqueID* as the *name* attribute of a form element, as an alternative, it can participate in the Load Postback Data phase by invoking the *RegisterRequiresPostBack* method of the containing page in the control's *PreRender* method. Later in this chapter, we'll show a *Login* control example that uses this alternate technique.

The *LoadPostData* method has two arguments: a string that contains the name of the postback element, and a *System.Collections.Specialized.NameValueCollection* instance that contains the name/value collection of posted form data. Your control can use the postback data to update its state. If the state of your control changes on postback and you want to raise events to signal that change, you must return *true* from the *LoadPostData* method.

In the Raise Changed Events phase described in Figure 9-1, the page invokes the *RaisePostDataChangedEvent* method of each control that implements *IPostBackDataHandler* and returned *true* when the page called the *LoadPostData* method on the control. The *RaisePostDataChangedEvent* method is so named because a control that wants to raise events to signal changes in its state must do so here. For example, the *TextBox* control raises a *TextChanged* event in this phase, and the *DropDownList* control raises a *SelectedIndexChanged* event.

The Raise Changed Events phase occurs after the Load phase when the entire control tree has been loaded. The page framework splits postback data processing into two phases—Load Postback Data and Raise Changed Events—so that all the controls in the control tree have a chance to update their state before raising changed events.

If your control renders multiple form elements, you can generate unique names for them based on the *UniqueID* of your control, such as *UniqueID* + *":tag1"* and *UniqueID* + *":tag2"*. In Chapter 8, we developed the *LoginUI* control, which generates multiple form elements that have unique names.

Now let's look at an implementation of postback data processing in the *SimpleTextBox* example, which is similar to the ASP.NET *TextBox* control.

Processing Postback Data—The *SimpleTextBox* Example

The *SimpleTextBox* control shown in Listing 9-9 renders an HTML text box and implements the *IPostBackDataHandler* interface. On postback, *SimpleTextBox* updates its *Text* property by using the posted value of the text box in the form post data and raises a *TextChanged* event if the *Text* property has changed on postback. The implementation of postback data processing is highlighted in the code listing.

```
using System;
using System.ComponentModel;
using System.Collections.Specialized;
using System.Web.UI;
using System.Web.UI.WebControls;

namespace MSPress.ServerControls {
    [DefaultEvent("TextChanged"),
     DefaultProperty("Text")]
    public class SimpleTextBox: WebControl, IPostBackDataHandler {

        private static readonly object EventTextChanged = new object();

        [Bindable(true),
         Category("Behavior"),
         DefaultValue(""),
         Description("The text in the TextBox")]
        public virtual string Text {
            get {
                string s = (string)ViewState["Text"];
                return((s == null) ? String.Empty : s);
            }
            set {
                ViewState["Text"] = value;
            }
        }
    }
```

Listing 9-9 SimpleTextBox.cs

```
protected override HtmlTextWriterTag TagKey {
    get {
        return HtmlTextWriterTag.Input;
    }
}

[Category("Action"),
 Description("Raised when the text in the text box is changed")]
public event EventHandler TextChanged {
    add {
        Events.AddHandler(EventTextChanged, value);
    }
    remove {
        Events.RemoveHandler(EventTextChanged, value);
    }
}

bool IPostBackDataHandler.LoadPostData(string postDataKey,
    NameValueCollection values) {
    String presentValue = Text;
    String postedValue = values[this.UniqueID];
    if (!presentValue.Equals(postedValue)) {
        Text = postedValue;
        return true;
    }
    return false;
}

void IPostBackDataHandler.RaisePostDataChangedEvent() {
    OnTextChanged(EventArgs.Empty);
}

protected virtual void OnTextChanged(EventArgs e) {
    EventHandler textChangedHandler =
        (EventHandler)Events[EventTextChanged];
    if (textChangedHandler != null) {
        textChangedHandler(this, e);
    }
}

protected override void AddAttributesToRender(
    HtmlTextWriter writer) {
    base.AddAttributesToRender(writer);
    writer.AddAttribute(HtmlTextWriterAttribute.Name,
        this.UniqueID);
    writer.AddAttribute(HtmlTextWriterAttribute.Type, "Text");
    writer.AddAttribute(HtmlTextWriterAttribute.Value,
        this.Text);
}
```

(continued)

Listing 9-9 *(continued)*

```
        protected override void Render(HtmlTextWriter writer) {
            // Make sure this control is in a server form.
            if (Page != null) {
                Page.VerifyRenderingInServerForm(this);
            }
            base.Render(writer);
        }
    }
}
```

Listing 9-10 contains a page that uses the *SimpleTextBox* control and attaches an event handler to its *TextChanged* event. As with other form controls, the *SimpleTextBox* control must be declared within server-side form tags. Figures 9-7 and 9-8 show the page viewed in a browser upon the first request and after submitting the form.

```
<%@ Page Language="C#" %>
<%@ Register TagPrefix="msp" Namespace="MSPress.ServerControls"
  Assembly="MSPress.ServerControls" %>
<html>
  <head>
    <script runat="server" >
      void simpleTextBox1_TextChanged(object sender, EventArgs e) {
          label1.Text = "The text in the text box changed after " +
              "postback. Its new value is: " + simpleTextBox1.Text;
      }
    </script>
  </head>
  <body>
    <form runat="server">
      <br>
      <asp:Button Text="Submit" Runat="server" />
      <br>
      Enter some text:
      <msp:SimpleTextBox Font-Size="10pt" Font-Bold="true"
        runat="server" OnTextChanged="simpleTextBox1_TextChanged"
        id="simpleTextBox1" />
      <br>
      <asp:Label Font-Size="10pt" id="label1" runat="server"
        EnableViewState="false"/>
    </form>
  </body>
</html>
```

Listing 9-10 SimpleTextBoxTest.aspx

Figure 9-7   SimpleTextBoxTest.aspx viewed in a browser on first request

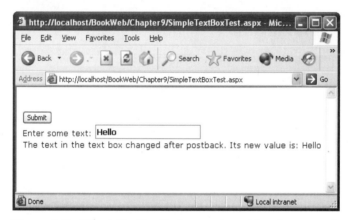

Figure 9-8   SimpleTextBoxTest.aspx viewed in a browser after text is entered and the form is posted

If you resubmit the page without changing the text, you will see that the *TextChanged* event is not raised by the *SimpleTextBox* control on postback. We set *EnableViewState="false"* on the *Label* control in the page so that the *Label* instance does not persist its text across round-trips and displays a message only when the text in the text box changes.

Putting It Together—The *Login* Example

We'll now develop a *Login* control that implements postback event handling and data processing functionality to allow a user to log into a Web site.

In Chapter 8, we developed a *LoginUI* control that renders two HTML text boxes and a button and provides unique names for those elements. We'll now derive from that control and add event-handling and data-processing functionality to it. Note that *LoginUI* derives from *Control* to demonstrate rendering only; we are reusing *LoginUI* only because it has most of the functionality we need. In general, if you want to implement a control such as *Login*, you should derive from *WebControl* and use *WebControl*'s built-in style properties.

Listing 9-11 contains the code for *Login*. The highlighted code is responsible for ensuring that, on postback, the page calls *Login* in the postback data-processing and event phases. We'll discuss the sample after the code listing.

```
using System;
using System.Collections.Specialized;
using System.ComponentModel;
using System.Web.UI;

namespace MSPress.ServerControls {
    [DefaultEvent("Logon")]
    public class Login : LoginUI, IPostBackDataHandler, IPostBackEventHandler
    {
        private static readonly object EventLogon = new object();
        private string _password;
        private string _userName;

        [Browsable(false),
         DesignerSerializationVisibility(
            DesignerSerializationVisibility.Hidden)]
        public string UserName {
            get {
                return ((_userName == null) ? String.Empty : _userName);
            }
        }

        [Browsable(false),
         DesignerSerializationVisibility(
            DesignerSerializationVisibility.Hidden)]
        public string Password {
            get {
                return ((_password == null) ? String.Empty : _password);
            }
        }
```

Listing 9-11   Login.cs

```
[Category("Action"),
 Description("Raised when the button is clicked to log in")]
public event EventHandler Logon {
    add {
        Events.AddHandler(EventLogon, value);
    }
    remove {
        Events.RemoveHandler(EventLogon, value);
    }
}

bool IPostBackDataHandler.LoadPostData(string postDataKey,
    NameValueCollection values) {
    // UserInputName is defined in LoginUI.
    _userName = values[UserNameInputName ];

    // PasswordInputName is defined in LoginUI.
    _password = values[PasswordInputName];

    // Check whether the button was clicked on the
    // client. If it was, tell the page to
    // invoke IPostBackEventHandler.RaisePostBackEvent.
    // ButtonName is defined in LoginUI.
    string buttonValue = values[ButtonName];
    bool buttonClicked =
        (buttonValue != null) && (buttonValue.Length != 0);
    if (buttonClicked) Page.RegisterRequiresRaiseEvent(this);

    // Return false because we do not want to raise a
    // changed event.
    return false;
}

void IPostBackDataHandler.RaisePostDataChangedEvent() {
}

void IPostBackEventHandler.RaisePostBackEvent(
    string eventArgument) {
    OnLogon(EventArgs.Empty);
}

protected virtual void OnLogon(EventArgs e) {
    EventHandler logonHandler =
        (EventHandler)Events[EventLogon];
```

(continued)

Listing 9-11   *(continued)*

```
            if (logonHandler != null) {
                logonHandler(this, e);
            }
        }

        protected override void OnPreRender(EventArgs e) {
            base.OnPreRender(e);
            Page.RegisterRequiresPostBack(this);
        }

        protected override void Render(HtmlTextWriter writer) {
            // Ensures that this control is nested in a server form.
            if (Page != null) {
                Page.VerifyRenderingInServerForm(this);
            }
            base.Render(writer);
        }
    }
}
```

The *Login* control accomplishes the following:

■ Handles a postback event and processes postback data by implementing both the *IPostBackEventHandler* and *IPostBackDataHandler* interfaces.

■ Exposes *UserName* and *Password* properties. However, it does not use the *ViewState* dictionary as the backing store for these properties because it is unnecessary to round-trip the properties. Note that a password value should never be round-tripped in a control's view state because it could compromise security.

■ Populates the *UserName* and *Password* properties with form data in the *LoadPostData* method. *Login* returns *false* from this method because it does not want to raise any changed events.

■ Defines a *Logon* postback event and raises the event from its *RaisePostBackEvent* method.

■ Invokes the *RegisterRequiresPostBack* method of its page in *OnPreRender* to ensure that the page calls the control during postback processing, even though its *UniqueID* does not exist in the posted names in the form's name/value collection. (If you look at the code for the base *LoginUI* control in Chapter 8, you will see that the *name* attributes it renders for the three elements are *UniqueID* + ":UserName"*, *UniqueID* + ":Password"*, and *UniqueID* + ":Button"*.)

■   Invokes the *RegisterRequiresRaiseEvent* of its containing page in *LoadPostData* to inform the page that, in addition to processing postback data, *Login* raises a postback event. *Login* makes this call only if the user has clicked the HTML button it renders. Your control needs the call to *RegisterRequiresRaiseEvent* when it implements both *IPostBackDataHandler* and *IPostBackEventHandler*. Otherwise, the page will not invoke the *RaisePostBackEvent* method of your control in the Raise Postback Event phase.

Listing 9-12 contains a page that uses the *Login* control and handles its *Logon* event to validate the user. Figures 9-9 and 9-10 show the page viewed in a browser before and after the form is submitted.

```
<%@ Page Language="C#" %>
<%@ Register TagPrefix="msp" Namespace="MSPress.ServerControls"
  Assembly="MSPress.ServerControls" %>
<html>
  <head>
    <script runat="server">
      void login1_Logon(object sender, EventArgs e) {
          if (ValidateUser()) {
              login1.Visible = false;
              label1.Text = "Hello " + login1.UserName +
                  ", you are logged in.";
          }
          else {
              label1.Text = "Login failed." +
              "Enter your user name and password.";
          }
      }

      bool ValidateUser() {
          // Perform logic to authenticate user. We'll
          // simply return true for this demo.
          return true;
      }
    </script>
  </head>
  <body>
    <form runat="server">
      <br>
      <msp:Login id="login1" runat="server" ButtonText="Submit"
        NameLabel="Login Name:" PasswordLabel="Password:"
        BackColor="Gainsboro" BorderColor="Gray" BorderStyle="Solid"
```

Listing 9-12   LoginTest.aspx   *(continued)*

Listing 9-12 *(continued)*

```
        BorderWidth="1px" FontFamily="Verdana" FontSize="10"
        FontBold="True" onLogon="login1_Logon" />
    <br>
    <asp:Label id="label1" runat="server" />
  </form>
  </body>
</html>
```

Figure 9-9   LoginTest.aspx viewed in a browser on first request

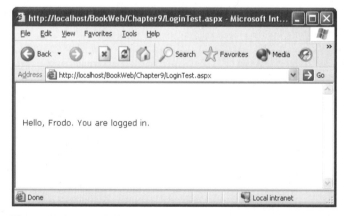

Figure 9-10   LoginTest.aspx viewed in a browser after data is entered
and form is submitted

Exposing Other Semantic Events—The *HitTracker* Example

So far, all the events that we implemented in controls are related to postback. However, your control can also expose events that are not related to postback.

The *HitTracker* control that we'll now develop tracks page hits and raises an event related to the number of hits. Figure 9-11 shows this control.

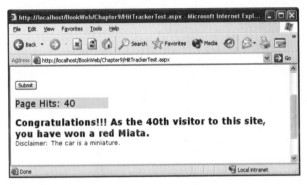

Figure 9-11   HitTrackerTest.aspx viewed in a browser after an *Announce-Hits* event is raised on the server

To reuse existing code, we'll derive *HitTracker* from the *PageTracker* control we developed in Chapter 7. We'll override the *TrackingMode* property so that *HitTracker* always tracks the total hits per page. We'll also expose a *Multiple* property and an *AnnounceHits* event. *HitTracker* raises the *AnnounceHits* event when the number of hits is divisible by the value of the *Multiple* property. For example, if a page developer assigns 100 to *Multiple*, *HitTracker* raises the *AnnounceHits* event when the number of hits is 100, 200, and so on. Listing 9-13 contains the code for *HitTracker*.

```
using System;
using System.ComponentModel;
using System.Web.UI;
using System.Web.UI.WebControls;

namespace MSPress.ServerControls {
    [DefaultEvent("AnnounceHits"),
     DefaultProperty("Multiple")]
    public class HitTracker : PageTracker {

        private readonly object EventAnnounceHits = new object();
```

Listing 9-13   HitTracker.cs   *(continued)*

Listing 9-13 *(continued)*

```
[Bindable(true),
 DefaultValue("100")]
public int Multiple {
    get {
        object o = ViewState["Multiple"];
        return (o == null) ? 100 : (int)o;
    }
    set {
        if (value < 1)
            throw new ArgumentOutOfRangeException(
                "Multiple cannot be less than 1");
        ViewState["Multiple"] = value;
    }
}


[
Browsable(false),
DesignerSerializationVisibility(
    DesignerSerializationVisibility.Hidden),
EditorBrowsable(EditorBrowsableState.Never)
]
public override PageTrackingMode TrackingMode {
    get {
        return PageTrackingMode.ByApplication;
    }
    set {
        if (value != PageTrackingMode.ByApplication ) {
            throw new ArgumentException("TrackingMode must " +
                "equal PageTrackingMode.ByApplication.");
        }
        base.ViewState["TrackingMode"] = value;
    }
}


[Category("Default"),
 Description("Raised when Hits is divisible by Multiple.")]
public event EventHandler AnnounceHits {
    add {
        Events.AddHandler(EventAnnounceHits, value);
    }
    remove {
        Events.RemoveHandler(EventAnnounceHits, value);
    }
}
```

```
    protected virtual void OnAnnounceHits(EventArgs e) {
        EventHandler announceHitsHandler =
            (EventHandler)Events[EventAnnounceHits];
        if (announceHitsHandler != null) {
            announceHitsHandler(this, e);
        }
    }

    protected override void OnLoad(EventArgs e) {
        base.OnLoad(e);
        if (Hits % Multiple == 0)
            OnAnnounceHits(EventArgs.Empty);
    }
  }
}
```

Unlike postback events, which a control raises in the Raise Changed Events phase or the Raise Postback Event phase, you can raise an event that is not related to postback from any logical place in your control's code. In *Hit-Tracker*, we raise the *AnnounceHits* event in the *OnLoad* method because the base class, *PageTracker*, sets the *Hits* property in *OnLoad*. *HitTracker* does not implement *IPostBackDataHandler* or *IPostBackEventHandler* because it does not participate in postback processing. In general, if you implement *IPostBack-DataHandler* or *IPostBackEventHandler*, you might want to raise nonpostback events along with related postback events.

Listing 9-14 contains a page that uses the *HitTracker* control and attaches an event handler to its *AnnounceHits* event to announce prizes to visitors to the site. Figure 9-11 shows the page viewed in a browser.

```
<%@ Page Language="C#" %>
<%@ Register TagPrefix="msp" Namespace="MSPress.ServerControls"
  Assembly="MSPress.ServerControls" %>
<html>
  <head>
    <script runat="server" >
      void hitTracker1_AnnounceHits(object sender, EventArgs e) {
          label1.Text = String.Format("Congratulations!!! As the " +
              "{0}th visitor to this site, you have won a red Miata.",
              hitTracker1.Hits);
          label2.Text = "Disclaimer: The car is a miniature.";
      }
    </script>
  </head>
```

Listing 9-14   HitTrackerTest.aspx   *(continued)*

Listing 9-14   *(continued)*

```
<body>
  <form runat="server">
    <br>
    <asp:Button Text="Submit" Runat="server" id="Button1" />
    <br><br>
    <msp:HitTracker id="hitTracker1" FormatString="Page Hits: {0}"
      Width="200px" Font-Name="Verdana"
      Font-Size="14pt" ForeColor="Black"
      BackColor="#E0E0E0" runat="server"
      BorderStyle="None" BorderColor="White"
      Multiple="20"
      OnAnnounceHits="hitTracker1_AnnounceHits" />
    <br>
    <asp:Label Font-Size="14pt" Font-Bold="true" id="label1"
      runat="server" EnableViewState="False" />
    <br>
    <asp:Label id="label2" runat="server" EnableViewState="False" />
  </form>
</body>
</html>
```

Summary

In this chapter, we looked at the life cycle of a control and described the logic that a control developer should implement in the various execution phases. We also examined server-side events and showed how you can incorporate post-back data and event-processing functionality in your control by implementing the *IPostBackDataHandler* and the *IPostBackEventHandler* interfaces.

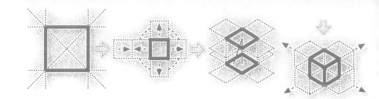

10

Complex Properties and State Management

In Chapter 7, "Simple Properties and View State," we looked at simple properties—that is, properties of primitive types and strings. We examined how the page framework automatically supports declarative page syntax (declarative persistence) for simple properties. We showed how to apply attributes that enable design-time support for properties in a visual design environment. And we showed how you can easily implement state management by storing simple properties in your control's *ViewState* dictionary.

In this chapter, we will examine *complex properties*—that is, properties whose types do not have a simple string representation. These types include nonatomic value types, reference types other than *String,* and collection types. When you expose complex properties from your control, you have to do additional work to support declarative persistence and state management. We'll show how to implement those features by walking through examples of controls that expose complex properties. We'll begin by describing the pieces that enable declarative persistence and show how to implement them. We'll then look at state management and show how you can implement custom state management for a complex property. Finally, we'll examine collection properties and implement an *ImageMap* control that demonstrates custom types, state management, and collection properties. Custom state management for properties is a more advanced aspect of control authoring. If you do not need this functionality, feel free to skim the sections that describe custom state management.

The *ImageMap* control that we'll implement toward the end of this chapter provides a strongly typed abstraction over the HTML *<map>* element, an image which contains regions that are activated when a user clicks them. ASP.NET does not provide a built-in map control. The HTML *<map>* element is described in the HTML 4.0 specification at: *http://www.w3.org/TR/REC-html40/struct/objects.html#h-13.6.*

Subproperties

In earlier chapters, we showed how to implement simple properties whose types are primitive types, strings, and enumerations. In those cases, you do not have to do any extra work to enable a page developer to specify the property values on the control's tag (declarative persistence). However, with complex properties, you have to do additional work to enable declarative persistence.

Complex properties typically have *subproperties,* that is, properties exposed by the type of the complex property. For example, the *WebControl* class exposes a *Font* property whose type is the *System.Web.UI.WebControls.FontInfo* class, which in turn exposes properties such as *Bold*, *Name*, and *Size*. The properties of *FontInfo* are subproperties of the *Font* property.

Two related entities work together to enable declarative persistence of complex properties:

- Metadata attributes related to serialization

- Type converter classes that perform conversions to and from the given type to the *String* type and to other types

In this section, we'll look at the metadata attributes that enable different forms of declarative persistence for complex properties. In the next section, we'll look at type converter classes.

Subproperties Persisted on a Control's Tag

To persist a subproperty on a control's tag, a page developer specifies the subproperty by using a hyphen between the property name and the subproperty name. The following example specifies the *Name* and *Size* subproperties of the *Font* property on the *TextBox* control's tag:

```
<asp:TextBox id="textBox1" Font-Name="Verdana" Font-Size="12pt"
  runat="server" />
```

The page parser automatically handles the hyphenated subproperty syntax, provided there is a type converter associated with the type of the subproperty. (We will show how to associate a type converter with a property in the next section.) However, to enable the designer to generate the hyphenated subproperty syntax, you must apply certain design-time metadata attributes to the property and to its subproperties. The *Font* property in the following code fragment shows the design-time metadata attributes that you must apply to a complex property.

```
public class WebControl : Control {
    [
    DesignerSerializationVisibility(
        DesignerSerializationVisibility.Content),
    NotifyParentProperty(true)
    ]
    public FontInfo Font { ... }
    ⋮
}
```

The *DesignerSerializationVisibility(DesignerSerializationVisibility.Content)* attribute tells the design-time serializer to step into the subproperties and serialize their values. The designer persists properties on the control's tag and generates the hyphenated syntax for each subproperty. The *NotifyParentProperty(true)* attribute causes change notifications from subproperties in the property browser to bubble up the object model and generate change notifications on the control whose subproperties are changed so that the control gets marked as dirty in the designer. This procedure is essential for the correct persistence in HTML of properties that a page developer modifies in the designer.

You must also apply the *NotifyParentProperty(true)* attribute to the properties of the type of the complex property. The following example shows this attribute applied to the *Name* and *Size* properties of the *FontInfo* class. These properties are subproperties of the *Font* property of *WebControl*.

```
[
TypeConverter(typeof(ExpandableObjectConverter))
]
public sealed class FontInfo {
    [
    NotifyParentProperty(true),
    ]
    public string Name { ... }

    [
    NotifyParentProperty(true)
    ]
    public FontUnit Size { ... }
    ⋮
}
```

For completeness, the example shows the *System.Component-Model.ExpandableObjectConverter* type converter associated with the *FontInfo* type via the *TypeConverterAttribute* described in the next section. The *ExpandableObjectConverter* tells the property browser to provide the expand/collapse UI that allows a page developer to edit subproperties. By default, the subproperties of the *Font* property are collapsed in the property browser. When a page developer clicks the *Font* property, the *ExpandableObjectConverter* causes the property browser to display a hierarchical list that shows the subproperties.

Inner Property Persistence

By default, subproperties are persisted on a control's tag using the hyphenated syntax. However, you can enable a different persistence format for complex properties, which consists of nesting them within your control's tags on a page. This is known as *inner property persistence*. The following example shows inner property persistence for the *HeaderStyle* property of the *DataGrid* control, where *ForeColor* is a subproperty of *HeaderStyle* property:

```
<asp:DataGrid runat="server">
  <HeaderStyle ForeColor="Red"/>
</asp:DataGrid>
```

To enable inner property persistence, you must mark your control with the *ParseChildren(true)* attribute, which tells the page parser to parse the content within the control's tags as properties. In addition, you must apply the design-time *PersistChildren(false)* attribute, which tells the designer to persist the inner content as properties, not as child controls. (The *ParseChildrenAttribute* and the *PersistChildrenAttribute* attributes use opposing conventions for the semantics of their argument.) *WebControl* already has these attributes applied, as shown in the following code. Therefore you do not have to reapply these attributes when your control derives from *WebControl*.

```
[
ParseChildren(true),
PersistChildren(false)
]
public class WebControl : Control, ... { ... }
```

Furthermore, you must mark the property with the design-time metadata attributes shown in the following example:

```
[
DesignerSerializationVisibility(
    DesignerSerializationVisibility.Content),
NotifyParentProperty(true),
PersistenceMode(PersistenceMode.InnerProperty)
]
public virtual TableItemStyle HeaderStyle { ... }
```

We described the first two attributes earlier in this section. The last attribute, *PersistenceMode(PersistenceMode.InnerProperty)*, tells the designer to persist the property as an inner property. By default, a designer persists sub-properties on the control's tag by using the hyphenated syntax. The default persistence mode does not require the *PersistenceModeAttribute* applied to a property, as you saw earlier with the *Font* property.

The page framework supports an additional form of inner property persistence: *inner default property persistence*, which is generally used for persisting a collection property of a control. The following example shows inner default property syntax for the *Items* property of a *ListBox* control. Each element within the control's tags is an element of the *Items* collection property:

```
<asp:ListBox id=ListBox1 Width="100px" runat="server">
  <asp:ListItem>Item 1</asp:ListItem>
  <asp:ListItem>Item 2</asp:ListItem>
  <asp:ListItem>Item 3</asp:ListItem>
</asp:ListBox>
```

When a control has an inner default property, content within the control's tags can correspond only to that property. The page parser will not permit any other properties within the control's tags. This explains why the property is called an inner *default* property. Note that the name of the inner default property (*Items* in the preceding example) is not specified within the control's tags.

To enable inner default property persistence, you must mark your control with the following variation of the *ParseChildrenAttribute*, where the second argument of the attribute is the name of the inner default property:

```
[
ParseChildren(true, "<DefaultPropertyName>")
]
public class MyControl : WebControl { ... }
```

Furthermore, to persist an inner default property correctly in the designer, you must mark the property as *PersistenceMode(PersistenceMode.InnerDefault-Property)*. For example, the *Items* property of the ASP.NET *ListControl* is marked this way:

```
[
PersistenceMode(PersistenceMode.InnerDefaultProperty)
]
public virtual ListItemCollection Items { ... }
```

In the next section, we will develop a *MapDemo* control that exposes two properties that have subproperties. Toward the end of this chapter, we will develop an *ImageMap* control that exposes a collection property persisted as an inner default property.

Properties and Type Converters

The metadata attributes that we described in the previous section represent one piece of the architecture that enables declarative property persistence. The other piece consists of type converter classes that perform conversions to and from the given type to the *String* type and to other types. When a property is specified declaratively, as *Width="100px"* is, the page parser invokes an instance of a type converter class to convert the string value to the declared type of the property. For example, when parsing *Width="100px"*, the parser invokes the *System.Web.UI.WebControls.UnitConverter* to convert the string *"100px"* to the *System.Web.UI.WebControls.Unit* type, which can be assigned to the *Width* property.

A *type converter* is a class that derives from the *System.Component-Model.TypeConverter* class, which provides methods that perform conversions to and from other types to the given type. In the previous paragraph, we showed an example of how the page parser uses type converters. The page framework also uses type converters to perform view state serialization. And visual designers use type converters to display properties in the property browser and to perform design-time serialization.

Primitive types and many other types in the .NET Framework class library have type converters associated with them. For example, the *Boolean, Char, Enum,* and *Int32* types have corresponding *BooleanConverter, CharConverter, EnumConverter,* and *Int32Converter* classes associated with them.

To associate a type converter with a type, you apply the *TypeConverter-Attribute* to the type. The following code fragment associates the *System.Web.UI. WebControls.UnitConverter* with the *System.Web.UI.WebControls.Unit* type:

```
[
TypeConverter(typeof(UnitConverter))
]
public struct Unit { ... }
```

When a type converter is associated with a type, it is automatically available to properties of that type. If you want to associate a different type converter with a property of that type, you can override the property and specify another type converter via the *TypeConverterAttribute.* The following example shows how the *WebControl* class implements the *BackColor* property to associate a different type converter from the default *ColorConverter* associated with the *Color* type:

```
[
TypeConverterAttribute(typeof(WebColorConverter))
]
public virtual Color BackColor { ... }
```

When the type of a property does not have a type converter associated with it, you can associate a type converter with the property by applying *Type-ConverterAttribute* to the property. If you define custom types for properties, you must also implement type converters and associate them with the types. We'll next show how to implement a type converter class.

Implementing a Type Converter

Let's define a few custom types and their associated type converters. We will use these types in the *MapDemo* example later in this section. The *MapDemo* control is a simple abstraction over the HTML *<map>* element that allows a page developer to specify circular and rectangular regions that are activated when the user clicks within an image. The custom types that we will define represent geometrical entities such as a point, circle, or rectangle. Figure 10-1 shows the custom types displayed in the property browser.

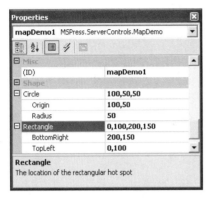

Figure 10-1   The *Circle* and *Rectangle* properties of the *MapDemo* control displayed in the property browser

The *MapDemo* control exposes *Circle* and *Rectangle* properties whose types are the *MapCircle* and *MapRectangle* custom types:

```
public class MapDemo : Image, IPostBackEventHandler {
    public MapCircle Circle { ... }
    public MapRectangle Rectangle { ... }
}
```

The properties of the *MapCircle* and *MapRectangle* classes are subproperties of the *Circle* and *Rectangle* properties of the *MapDemo* class:

```
public class MapCircle {
    public MapPoint Origin { ... }
    public int Radius { ... }
}
public class MapRectangle {
    public MapPoint TopLeft { ... }
    public MapPoint BottomRight { ... }
}
```

Here's how a type converter comes into the picture. The *MapCircle* and *MapRectangle* custom types define properties of another custom type: *MapPoint*. When the *MapDemo* control is used declaratively on a page—as shown in the following example—the page parser uses a type converter to convert the specified string values of the subproperties into the corresponding *MapPoint* types:

```
<msp:MapDemo runat="server" Circle-Origin="100,50" Circle-Radius="50">
  <Rectangle TopLeft="0,100" BottomRight="200,150"></Rectangle>
</msp:MapDemo>
```

In addition, the property browser uses type converters to enable editing of these properties, and the designer uses them to serialize these properties.

Now let's look at the implementation of *MapPoint* and its associated type converter.

MapPoint and *MapPointConverter*

Listing 10-1 contains the code for the *MapPoint* class. The type converter associated with the *MapPoint* type is shown in Listing 10-2.

```
using System;
using System.ComponentModel;
using System.Globalization;

namespace MSPress.ServerControls {
    [
    TypeConverter(typeof(MapPointConverter))
    ]
    public class MapPoint {

        private int _x;
        private int _y;

        public MapPoint() : this(0, 0) {
        }

        public MapPoint(int x, int y) {
            _x = x;
            _y = y;
        }

        public bool IsEmpty {
            get {
                return (_x == 0 && _y == 0);
            }
        }

        public int X {
            get {
                return _x;
            }
            set {
                _x = value;
            }
        }
    }
```

Listing 10-1   MapPoint.cs   *(continued)*

Listing 10-1   *(continued)*

```csharp
        public int Y {
            get {
                return _y;
            }
            set {
                _y = value;
            }
        }

        public override bool Equals(object obj) {
            MapPoint other = obj as MapPoint;

            if (other != null) {
                return (other.X == X) && (other.Y == Y);
            }
            return false;
        }

        public override int GetHashCode() {
            return _x.GetHashCode() ^ _y.GetHashCode();
        }

        public override string ToString() {
            return ToString(CultureInfo.CurrentCulture);
        }

        public virtual string ToString(CultureInfo culture) {
            return TypeDescriptor.GetConverter(
                typeof(MapPoint)).ConvertToString(null, culture, this);
        }
    }
}
```

The *MapPointConverter* class in Listing 10-2 shows the essential aspects of implementing a type converter that is needed for a read-write property.

```csharp
using System;
using System.ComponentModel;
using System.ComponentModel.Design.Serialization;
using System.Globalization;
using System.Reflection;
```

Listing 10-2   MapPointConverter.cs

```
namespace MSPress.ServerControls {

    public class MapPointConverter : TypeConverter {

        public override bool CanConvertFrom(
            ITypeDescriptorContext context, Type sourceType) {
            if (sourceType == typeof(string)) {
                return true;
            }
            return base.CanConvertFrom(context, sourceType);
        }

        public override bool CanConvertTo(
            ITypeDescriptorContext context, Type destinationType) {
            if ((destinationType == typeof(string)) ||
                (destinationType == typeof(InstanceDescriptor))) {
                return true;
            }
            return base.CanConvertTo(context, destinationType);
        }

        public override object ConvertFrom(
            ITypeDescriptorContext context, CultureInfo culture,
            object value) {
            if (value == null) {
                return new MapPoint();
            }

            if (value is string) {
                string s = (string)value;
                if (s.Length == 0) {
                    return new MapPoint();
                }

                string[] parts =
                    s.Split(culture.TextInfo.ListSeparator[0]);

                if (parts.Length != 2) {
                    throw new ArgumentException("Invalid MapPoint",
                        "value");
                }

                TypeConverter intConverter =
                    TypeDescriptor.GetConverter(typeof(Int32));
                return new MapPoint(
                    (int)intConverter.ConvertFromString(
```

(continued)

Listing 10-2 *(continued)*

```
                context, culture, parts[0]),
            (int)intConverter.ConvertFromString(
                context, culture, parts[1]));
    }

    return base.ConvertFrom(context, culture, value);
}

public override object ConvertTo(
    ITypeDescriptorContext context, CultureInfo culture,
    object value, Type destinationType) {
    if (value != null) {
        if (!(value is MapPoint)) {
            throw new ArgumentException("Invalid MapPoint",
                "value");
        }
    }

    if (destinationType == typeof(string)) {
        if (value == null) {
            return String.Empty;
        }

        MapPoint point = (MapPoint)value;

        TypeConverter intConverter =
            TypeDescriptor.GetConverter(typeof(Int32));
        return String.Join(culture.TextInfo.ListSeparator,
            new string[] {
                intConverter.ConvertToString(context, culture,
                    point.X),
                intConverter.ConvertToString(context, culture,
                    point.Y)
            });
    }
    else if (destinationType == typeof(InstanceDescriptor)) {
        if (value == null) {
            return null;
        }

        MemberInfo mi = null;
        object[] args = null;

        MapPoint point = (MapPoint)value;
```

```
            if (point.IsEmpty) {
                mi = typeof(MapPoint).GetConstructor(new Type[0]);
            }
            else {
                Type intType = typeof(int);
                mi = typeof(MapPoint).GetConstructor(
                    new Type[] { intType, intType });
                args = new object[] { point.X, point.Y };
            }

            if (mi != null) {
                return new InstanceDescriptor(mi, args);
            }
            else {
                return null;
            }
        }

        return base.ConvertTo(context, culture, value,
            destinationType);
    }
}
```

MapPointConverter performs string-to-value conversions and generates an abstract representation of a constructor that creates an instance of the *MapPoint* type. It implements the following logic:

- Derives from *System.ComponentModel.TypeConverter*.

- Overrides the *CanConvertFrom* method of the base class to specify that it can convert from a *String* type to a *MapPoint* type.

- Overrides the *CanConvertTo* method of the base class to specify that it can convert a *MapPoint* type to a *String* type as well as to a *System.ComponentModel.Design.Serialization.InstanceDescriptor* type. The conversion to an *InstanceDescriptor* is required when a property is read-write and the parser needs to generate code that creates an instance of the type.

- Overrides the *ConvertFrom* method of the base class to take a *String* value, parses the value, and creates and returns a *MapPoint* instance.

■ Overrides the *ConvertTo* method of the base class to take a *MapPoint* instance and, based on the destination type requested, returns either a *String* object or an *InstanceDescriptor* object. The *InstanceDescriptor* object provides information about the constructor used to create the *MapPoint* instance passed into the *ConvertTo* method. This information is used by the parser to generate code that creates an instance of the *MapPoint* type.

Type Converters for the *MapCircle* and *MapRectangle* Types

Before looking at the *MapCircle* and *MapRectangle* types, we will define an abstract *MapShape* base class that expresses the common characteristics of a shape. We will also define a *MapShapeConverter* class, which derives from *ExpandableObjectConverter* and enables hierarchical UI for subproperties in the property browser. We will associate the *MapShapeConverter* with the *MapShape* base class via a type converter attribute. Listing 10-3 contains the code for the *MapShape* class.

```
using System;
using System.ComponentModel;
using System.Globalization;

namespace MSPress.ServerControls {
    public abstract class MapShapeConverter:
        ExpandableObjectConverter { }

    [TypeConverter(typeof(MapShapeConverter))]
    public abstract class MapShape {

        [Browsable(false),
         DesignerSerializationVisibility(
            DesignerSerializationVisibility.Hidden)]
        public abstract bool IsEmpty {
            get;
        }

        [Browsable(false),
         DesignerSerializationVisibility(
            DesignerSerializationVisibility.Hidden)]
        public abstract string MapCoordinates {
            get;
        }
```

Listing 10-3 MapShape.cs

```
[Browsable(false),
 DesignerSerializationVisibility(
     DesignerSerializationVisibility.Hidden)]
protected abstract MapShapeName MapShapeName {
    get;
}

[Browsable(false),
 DesignerSerializationVisibility(
     DesignerSerializationVisibility.Hidden)]
public string ShapeName {
    get {
        return MapShapeName.ToString().ToLower(
            CultureInfo.InvariantCulture);
    }
}

public abstract void LoadFromString(string value);

public abstract string SaveToString();

public override string ToString() {
    return ToString(CultureInfo.InvariantCulture);
}

public virtual string ToString(CultureInfo culture) {
    return TypeDescriptor.GetConverter(
        GetType()).ConvertToString(null, culture, this);
}
    }
}
```

Listing 10-4 shows the *MapShapeName* enumeration, which contains the shape names allowed by the HTML map specification: circle, rectangle, and polygon.

```
using System;
namespace MSPress.ServerControls {
    public enum MapShapeName {
        Circle,
        Rectangle,
        Polygon
    }
}
```

Listing 10-4   MapShapeName.cs

The *MapCircle* and *MapRectangle* classes derive from the *MapShape* class. You'll find the complete code for the *MapCircle* and *MapRectangle* classes in this book's sample files. We have not defined a *MapPolygon* type, but you can extend the samples in this chapter by defining and using this type. The code fragments in Listing 10-5 show the definition of properties in the *MapCircle* and *MapRectangle* classes:

```
[
TypeConverter(typeof(MapCircleConverter))
]
public class MapCircle : MapShape {
    [
    DefaultValue(typeof(MapPoint), ""),
    NotifyParentProperty(true)
    ]
    public MapPoint Origin {
        get {
            return _origin;
        }
        set {
            if (value == null) {
                throw new ArgumentNullException("value");
            }
            _origin = value;
        }
    }


    [
    DefaultValue(0),
    NotifyParentProperty(true)
    ]
    public int Radius {
        get {
            return _radius;
        }
        set {
            if (value < 0) {
                throw new ArgumentOutOfRangeException("value");
            }
            _radius = value;
        }
    }
    ⋮
}
```

Listing 10-5 Property definitions in the *MapCircle* and *MapRectangle* classes

```
[
TypeConverter(typeof(MapRectangleConverter))
]
public class MapRectangle : MapShape {
    [
    DefaultValue(typeof(MapPoint), ""),
    NotifyParentProperty(true)
    ]
    public MapPoint BottomRight {
        get {
            return _bottomRight ;
        }
        set {
            if (value == null) {
                throw new ArgumentNullException("value");
            }
            _bottomRight = value;
        }
    }


    [
    DefaultValue(typeof(MapPoint), ""),
    NotifyParentProperty(true)
    ]
    public MapPoint TopLeft {
        get {
            return _topLeft;
        }
        set {
            if (value == null) {
                throw new ArgumentNullException("value");
            }
            _topLeft = value;
        }
    }
    ⋮
}
```

We'll now examine the type converters for the *MapCircle* and *MapRectangle* types. When a server control defines properties of these types (and any other complex type), they should be defined as read-only properties because of state management, as we'll explain in the next section. When a property is read-only, a page parser does not require a type converter for the type of the property. However, a designer needs a type converter for a complex property that will be displayed in the property browser. The *MapDemo* control, which we'll look at shortly, illustrates this point. *MapDemo* contains the *Circle* property and the

Rectangle property, whose respective types are *MapCircle* and *MapRectangle*. These properties are read-only, and property syntax such as *Circle="100,50,50"* is not allowed. Therefore, the page parser never has to convert from string representations to instances of the *MapCircle* or *MapRectangle* types. However, the designer needs type converters for these types because it uses them to display the string representations of the properties in the property browser. Figure 10-1 shows how the *Circle* and *Rectangle* properties of the *MapDemo* control are displayed in the property browser in Microsoft Visual Studio .NET.

Listing 10-6 contains the code for the *MapCircleConverter* class. The implementation of *MapRectangleConverter* is similar to that of *MapCircleConverter* and is provided in the book's sample files. The type converter implementation in these cases is simpler than that of *MapPointConverter* because *MapCircleConverter* and *MapRectangleConverter* do not have to convert to an *InstanceDescriptor*. As we described earlier in the *MapPointConverter* example, an *InstanceDescriptor* is needed only if the type converter is used to generate code that creates an instance of the type, which is not needed for a read-only property.

```
using System;
using System.ComponentModel;
using System.ComponentModel.Design.Serialization;
using System.Globalization;
using System.Reflection;

namespace MSPress.ServerControls {

    public class MapCircleConverter : MapShapeConverter {

        public override bool CanConvertFrom(
            ITypeDescriptorContext context, Type sourceType) {
            if (sourceType == typeof(string)) {
                return true;
            }
            return base.CanConvertFrom(context, sourceType);
        }

        public override bool CanConvertTo(
            ITypeDescriptorContext context, Type destinationType) {
            if (destinationType == typeof(string)) {
                return true;
            }
            return base.CanConvertTo(context, destinationType);
        }
```

Listing 10-6   MapCircleConverter.cs

```
public override object ConvertFrom(
    ITypeDescriptorContext context, CultureInfo culture,
    object value) {
    if (value == null) {
        return new MapCircle();
    }

    if (value is string) {
        string s = (string)value;
        if (s.Length == 0) {
            return new MapCircle();
        }

        string[] parts =
            s.Split(culture.TextInfo.ListSeparator[0]);

        if (parts.Length != 3) {
            throw new ArgumentException("Invalid MapCircle",
                "value");
        }

        TypeConverter intConverter =
            TypeDescriptor.GetConverter(typeof(Int32));
        return new MapCircle(
            new MapPoint(
                (int)intConverter.ConvertFromString(
                    context, culture, parts[0]),
                (int)intConverter.ConvertFromString(context,
                    culture, parts[1])),
                (int)intConverter.ConvertFromString(context,
                    culture, parts[2]));
    }

    return base.ConvertFrom(context, culture, value);
}

public override object ConvertTo(
    ITypeDescriptorContext context, CultureInfo culture,
    object value, Type destinationType) {
    if (value != null) {
        if (!(value is MapCircle)) {
            throw new ArgumentException("Invalid MapCircle",
                "value");
        }
    }
```

(continued)

Listing 10-6   *(continued)*

```
            if (destinationType == typeof(string)) {
                if (value == null) {
                    return String.Empty;
                }

                MapCircle circle = (MapCircle)value;
                if (circle.IsEmpty) {
                    return String.Empty;
                }

                TypeConverter intConverter =
                    TypeDescriptor.GetConverter(typeof(Int32));
                return String.Join(culture.TextInfo.ListSeparator,
                    new string[] {
                        intConverter.ConvertToString(context, culture,
                            circle.Origin.X),
                        intConverter.ConvertToString(context, culture,
                            circle.Origin.Y),
                        intConverter.ConvertToString(context, culture,
                            circle.Radius)
                    });
            }

            return base.ConvertTo(context, culture, value,
                destinationType);
        }
    }
}
```

Putting It Together—The *MapDemo* Example

We'll now use the *MapPoint*, *MapCircle*, and *MapRectangle* custom types and their associated type converters to implement a *MapDemo* control. The *Map-Demo* control allows a page developer to create a circular region and a rectangular region (hot spots) in an image that cause postback to the server when a user clicks inside them. *MapDemo* is a trimmed-down version of the *ImageMap* control that we will implement later in this chapter. Figure 10-2 shows a page that uses the *MapDemo* control.

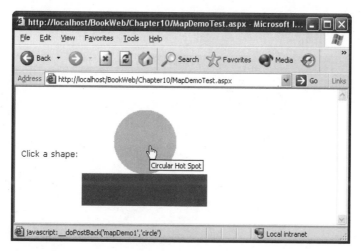

Figure 10-2   MapDemoTest.aspx viewed in a browser. The rendered
image has an associated HTML map with two hot spots.

The *MapDemo* control, shown in Listing 10-7, derives from the ASP.NET
Image control and adds to it the functionality to render an image map.

```
using System;
using System.ComponentModel;
using System.Web.UI;
using System.Web.UI.WebControls;

namespace MSPress.ServerControls {
    [
    DefaultEvent("MapClick"),
    DefaultProperty("Rectangle")
    ]
    public class MapDemo : Image, IPostBackEventHandler {

        private static readonly object EventMapClick = new object();

        private const string MapCircleArg = "circle";
        private const string MapRectangleArg = "rectangle";

        private MapCircle _circle;
        private MapRectangle _rectangle;
        private bool _hasHotSpots;
```

Listing 10-7   MapDemo.cs   *(continued)*

Listing 10-7   *(continued)*

```
[
Category("Shape"),
DefaultValue(typeof(MapCircle), ""),
Description("The location of the circular hot spot"),
DesignerSerializationVisibility(
    DesignerSerializationVisibility.Content),
NotifyParentProperty(true)
]
public MapCircle Circle {
    get {
        if (_circle == null) {
            _circle = new MapCircle();
        }
        return _circle;
    }
}


[
Category("Shape"),
DefaultValue(""),
Description("The location of the rectangular hot spot"),
DesignerSerializationVisibility(
    DesignerSerializationVisibility.Content),
PersistenceMode(PersistenceMode.InnerProperty),
NotifyParentProperty(true)
]
public MapRectangle Rectangle {
    get {
        if (_rectangle == null) {
            _rectangle = new MapRectangle();
        }
        return _rectangle;
    }
}


[
Category("Action"),
Description("Raised when a hot spot is clicked")
]
public event MapClickEventHandler MapClick {
    add {
        Events.AddHandler(EventMapClick, value);
    }
    remove {
        Events.RemoveHandler(EventMapClick, value);
    }
}
```

```
protected override void AddAttributesToRender(
   HtmlTextWriter writer) {
   base.AddAttributesToRender(writer);

   if (_hasHotSpots) {
      writer.AddAttribute("UseMap", "#ImageMap" + ClientID,
         false);
   }
}


protected virtual void OnMapClick(MapClickEventArgs e) {
   MapClickEventHandler mapClickHandler =
      (MapClickEventHandler)Events[EventMapClick];
   if (mapClickHandler != null) {
      mapClickHandler(this, e);
   }
}


protected override void Render(HtmlTextWriter writer) {
   if ((((_circle != null) && (_circle.IsEmpty == false)) ||
      ((_rectangle != null) &&
      (_rectangle.IsEmpty == false))) {
      _hasHotSpots = true;
   }

   base.Render(writer);

   if (_hasHotSpots) {
      writer.AddAttribute(HtmlTextWriterAttribute.Name,
         "ImageMap" + ClientID);
      writer.RenderBeginTag(HtmlTextWriterTag.Map);

      if ((_circle != null) && (_circle.IsEmpty == false)) {
         writer.AddAttribute("shape", _circle.ShapeName,
            false);
         writer.AddAttribute("coords",
            _circle.MapCoordinates);
         writer.AddAttribute(HtmlTextWriterAttribute.Href,
            Page.GetPostBackClientHyperlink(this,
               MapCircleArg));
         writer.AddAttribute(HtmlTextWriterAttribute.Title,
            "Circular Hotspot", false);
         writer.RenderBeginTag("area");
         writer.RenderEndTag();
      }
```

(continued)

Listing 10-7 *(continued)*

```
            if ((_rectangle != null) &&
                (_rectangle.IsEmpty == false)) {
                writer.AddAttribute("shape", _rectangle.ShapeName,
                    false);
                writer.AddAttribute("coords",
                    _rectangle.MapCoordinates, false);
                writer.AddAttribute(HtmlTextWriterAttribute.Href,
                    Page.GetPostBackClientHyperlink(this,
                        MapRectangleArg));
                writer.AddAttribute(HtmlTextWriterAttribute.Title,
                    "Rectangular Hotspot", false);
                writer.RenderBeginTag("area");
                writer.RenderEndTag();
            }

            writer.RenderEndTag();  // Map
        }
    }

    #region Custom State Management Implementation
    protected override void LoadViewState(object savedState) {
        base.LoadViewState(savedState);
        string s = null;

        s = (string)ViewState["Circle"];
        if (s != null) {
            Circle.LoadFromString(s);
        }

        s = (string)ViewState["Rectangle"];
        if (s != null) {
            Rectangle.LoadFromString(s);
        }
    }

    protected override object SaveViewState() {
        string currentState = null;
        string initialState = null;

        if (_circle != null) {
            currentState = _circle.SaveToString();
            initialState = (string)ViewState["Circle"];
            if (currentState.Equals(initialState) == false) {
                ViewState["Circle"] = currentState;
            }
        }
```

```
            if (_rectangle != null) {
                currentState = _rectangle.SaveToString();
                initialState = (string)ViewState["Rectangle"];
                if (currentState.Equals(initialState) == false) {
                    ViewState["Rectangle"] = currentState;
                }
            }

            return base.SaveViewState();
        }

        protected override void TrackViewState() {
            if (_circle != null) {
                ViewState["Circle"] = _circle.SaveToString();
            }

            if (_rectangle != null) {
                ViewState["Rectangle"] = _rectangle.SaveToString();
            }

            base.TrackViewState();
        }
        #endregion Custom State Management Implementation

        #region Implementation of IPostBackEventHandler
        void IPostBackEventHandler.RaisePostBackEvent(
            string eventArg) {
            string s = string.Empty;
            if (eventArg != null) {
                if (eventArg.Equals(MapCircleArg))
                    s = MapCircleArg;
                else if (eventArg.Equals(MapRectangleArg))
                    s = MapRectangleArg;
            }
            OnMapClick(new MapClickEventArgs(s));
        }
        #endregion Implementation of IPostBackEventHandler
    }
}
```

Listings 10-8 and 10-9 contain the code for the *MapClickEventArgs* and *MapClickEventHandler* classes associated with the *MapClick* event.

```
using System;
namespace MSPress.ServerControls {
    public class MapClickEventArgs : EventArgs {
        private string _action;
        public MapClickEventArgs(string action) {
            _action = action;
        }
        public string Action {
            get {
                return _action;
            }
        }
    }
}
```

Listing 10-8   MapClickEventArgs.cs

```
using System;
namespace MSPress.ServerControls {
    public delegate void MapClickEventHandler(object sender,
        MapClickEventArgs e);
}
```

Listing 10-9   MapClickEventHandler.cs

MapDemo illustrates the following points:

■ **Design-time attributes for complex properties** *MapDemo* defines the *Circle* and *Rectangle* properties of the custom types *Map-Circle* and *MapRectangle*. The *DesignerSerializationVisibility(Content)* attribute on these properties tells the designer that their content (subproperties) should be serialized. To illustrate various forms of persistence for complex properties, *MapDemo* enables persistence of the *Circle* property on the control's tag and enables persistence of the *Rectangle* property as an inner property. The *Persistence-Mode(PersistenceMode.InnerProperty)* attribute on the *Rectangle* property tells the designer that this property should be persisted as an inner property. The *Circle* property is not marked with the *Persis-tenceModeAttribute*; therefore, the designer persists it on the control's tag, which is the default persistence mode.

In general, you should pick a single model of persistence and use that model consistently. The *NotifyParentProperty(true)* attributes on the *Circle* and *Rectangle* properties cause changes in their subproperties to be persisted into the page. Note that design-time attributes are not used by the page parser. If you use the *Map-Demo* control in a page that is created without the help of a visual designer, you will be able to specify each of the *Circle* and *Rectangle* properties on the tag or as an inner property. Persistence on the control's tag is always allowed by the page parser, and inner persistence is possible because *MapDemo* derives from *WebControl*, which is marked as *ParseChildren(true)*.

■ **Complex properties should be read-only**   The *Circle* and *Rect-angle* properties of *MapDemo* are read-only. In general, complex properties that require state management should be defined as read-only properties. This allows a control to have complete responsibility for creating and handing out an instance of the type that represents the property and for managing the state of the property.

■ **State management**   *MapDemo* implements state management by overriding the *TrackViewState*, *SaveViewState*, and *LoadViewState* methods it inherits from the *Control* class. When overriding these methods, the order of invocation of the methods of the base class is important.

In *TrackViewState*, *MapDemo* saves a string representation of the *Circle* and *Rectangle* properties in its *ViewState* dictionary before invoking the *TrackViewState* method of the base class. This ensures that the initial values are not marked dirty.

In *SaveViewState*, *MapDemo* compares the current values of the string representations of the *Circle* and *Rectangle* properties with those initially saved in *ViewState*. If the values differ, *MapDemo* stores the new values in *ViewState*. Because property tracking is on during this phase, the values saved in *ViewState* are automatically marked dirty. *MapDemo* next invokes the *SaveViewState* method of the base class.

In *LoadViewState*, *MapDemo* first invokes the *LoadViewState* method of the base class so that the *ViewState* dictionary is restored after postback. *MapDemo* then checks whether there are values in *ViewState* corresponding to the *Circle* and *Rectangle* properties. If *MapDemo* finds saved values, it uses them to load state into these properties.

■ **Rendering**   *MapDemo* overrides the *AddAttributesToRender* method of the base class to render the *usemap* attribute on the HTML *<img>* tag rendered by the base *Image* control. *MapDemo* overrides the *Render* method to render data for the HTML *<map>* element after it invokes the *Render* method of the base class to render the image.

■ **Implementing *IPostBackEventHandler*** *MapDemo* renders client-side script to cause postback (as shown by the *NavButtons* control in Chapter 9, "Control Life Cycle, Events, and Postback") when a
user clicks a hot spot (image map region) in the browser. *MapDemo*
implements *IPostBackEventHandler* to capture the postback event
caused by clicking a hot spot and maps it to a server-side *MapClick*
event. Lisings 10-8 and 10-9 contain the code for the event data and
event delegate classes associated with the *MapClick* event: *Map-
ClickEventArgs* and *MapClickEventHandler*.

Listing 10-10 shows the MapDemoTest.aspx page that uses the *MapDemo*
control. The *Circle* property is persisted on the control's tag by using the
hyphenated syntax for subproperties, and the *Rectangle* property is persisted as
an inner property. Figure 10-2 shows the page accessed in a browser.

```
<%@ Page Language="C#" %>
<%@ Register TagPrefix="msp" Namespace="MSPress.ServerControls"
  Assembly="MSPress.ServerControls" %>
<html>
  <head>
      <script runat="server">
        void mapDemo1_MapClick(object sender, MapClickEventArgs e) {
            label1.Text =
                string.Format("You clicked the {0}.", e.Action);
        }
      </script>
  </head>
  <body>
    <form runat="server">
      <br>
      Click a shape:
      <msp:MapDemo ImageUrl="Shapes.gif" ImageAlign="Middle"
        runat="server" OnMapClick="mapDemo1_MapClick" id="mapDemo1"
        Circle-Origin="100,50" Circle-Radius="50">
        <Rectangle BottomRight="200,150" TopLeft="0,100"></Rectangle>
      </msp:MapDemo>
      <asp:Label Font-Size="10 pt" Font-Bold="true" id="label1"
        runat="server" />
    </form>
  </body>
</html>
```

Listing 10-10   MapDemoTest.aspx

If you view the source for the page rendered in your browser, you will see the *<map>* element in the HTML rendered by the *MapDemo* instance:

```
<img id="mapDemo1" src="/BookWeb/Chapter10/Shapes.gif"
  align="Middle" border="0" UseMap="#ImageMapmapDemo1" />
<map name="ImageMapmapDemo1">
  <area shape="circle" coords="100,50,50"
    href="javascript:__doPostBack('mapDemo1','circle')"
    title="Circular Hot Spot">
  </area>
  <area shape="rectangle" coords="0,100,200,150"
    href="javascript:__doPostBack('mapDemo1','rectangle')"
    title="Rectangular Hot Spot">
  </area>
</map>
```

State Management, *IStateManager*, and the *ViewState* Dictionary

We'll now take a closer look at view state management, starting where we left off in Chapter 7. View state is the ASP.NET state management mechanism that the page framework uses to serialize the state that needs to be restored after each round-trip to the client. In this section, we'll examine how the page serializes and restores its view state, how custom types can participate in state management, and how the *ViewState* property performs default state management for a control.

How a Page Serializes and Restores Its View State

We described a control's life cycle in Chapter 9. In the Save View State phase, a page recursively invokes the *SaveViewState* method on each control in its control tree. In turn, each control returns an object that contains the information it needs to restore its state on a postback request. The page then creates an object graph that represents its own state information, which includes the objects returned by its child controls as well as other objects that contain information about the control tree. This object graph constitutes the view state of the page. In its Render phase, the page serializes its view state to a string representation by utilizing an instance of the *System.Web.UI.LosFormatter* class, a utility class that performs serialization that is optimized for a number of commonly used types. The serialized view state string is round-tripped to the client in the *__VIEWSTATE* hidden field by default, as we showed in Chapter 7.

In its *LoadViewState* method, a page creates a *LosFormatter* object to dese-rialize the string representation of the view state back into an object graph. The page then performs the inverse of the operations it performed in *SaveViewState*. It recursively invokes the *LoadViewState* method of each child control by hand-ing to it the object that represents the saved state for that control. Each control must perform logic to restore its own state in its *LoadViewState* method.

The *LosFormatter* class is optimized to perform serialization of integers, Booleans, and strings as well as for *Array, ArrayList,* and *Hashtable* objects that contain these types. In addition, this class can serialize other primitive types, any other types that have associated type converters, and *Array, ArrayList*, and *Hashtable* objects that contain those types. *LosFormatter* uses type converters to convert values to and from strings. *LosFormatter* can also serialize types that are marked with the *Serializable* attribute or that implement the *ISerializable* inter-face by using binary serialization. However, serialization for those types is much slower than serialization for types that have type converters defined.

Finally, *LosFormatter* can optimally serialize two utility classes: *Pair* and *Triplet*. These classes are used by controls to group objects to add to the view state, as we will show later in this chapter. Any objects that your control saves in its *ViewState* dictionary or returns from its *SaveViewState* method must belong to the set of types that is serializable by the *LosFormatter* class. If your control saves state by using types that are not serializable by *LosFormatter*, your control might compile, but it will cause a run-time exception. In addition, you need to choose types that can be serialized in an optimal fashion to improve the performance of your control and of the pages in which it is used.

The default implementation of the *Control* class delegates state manage-ment to its *ViewState* dictionary. However, when your control defines complex properties, it is generally not possible to use the *ViewState* dictionary to manage the state of those properties. Custom types that represent complex properties can participate in state management by implementing the *IStateManager* inter-face, which we will examine next.

The *IStateManager* Interface

The page framework provides the *System.Web.UI.IStateManager* interface to allow types other than controls to participate in the view state management. This interface is defined as follows:

```
public interface IStateManager {
    bool IsTrackingViewState { get; }
    void LoadViewState(object state);
    object SaveViewState();
    void TrackViewState();
}
```

The *Control* class performs state management by using the same members that are in the *IStateManager* contract, although *Control* does not implement *IStateManager*.

The *TrackViewState* method marks the end of the initialization phase, after which any modifications to properties must be tracked by the *IStateManager* implementation. The *IsTrackingViewState* property indicates that property-change tracking has started. The *SaveViewState* method returns an object that represents the combined state of all the properties that were modified after initialization. The *LoadViewState* method restores properties by using the object that was returned by *SaveViewState*. We'll make this discussion concrete in the next section, where we implement the *IStateManager* interface in a custom type.

We'll now look at the *ViewState* property that provides the default mechanism for state management in the *Control* class.

The *ViewState* Property and Default State Management

The *ViewState* property is a complex property that performs its own state management. To use the *ViewState* property as the storage mechanism for other properties in your control, you do not need to understand custom state management. However, we'll examine the *ViewState* property because it provides insight into the default state management mechanism of the *Control* class and enables you to mimic this mechanism when you implement state management in a custom type. In the next section, we'll define a *HotSpot* custom type that defines its own *ViewState* property to provide state management.

The type of the *ViewState* property is the *System.Web.UI.StateBag* class, which is a dictionary that participates in state management by implementing the *IStateManager* interface. The *StateBag* holds key/value pairs in which the keys are strings and the values are objects. When an object is added to a *StateBag* instance, *StateBag* automatically stores an additional bit with the object, which it uses to flag modifications to the stored object. More accurately, each item in a *StateBag* is a *StateItem* object that holds the actual property value and an associated Boolean flag that indicates whether the property is *dirty*, or modified after initialization.

The *StateBag* class implements the *IStateManager* interface as follows:

■ In its *TrackViewState* method, the class sets the private field that it uses for its *IsTrackingViewState* property to *true*. This indicates whether property change tracking has been turned on. When *IsTrackingViewState* is *true*, the *StateBag* class marks a *StateItem* as dirty when it is added to the *StateBag* or when its value is modified.

■ In its *SaveViewState* method, the *StateBag* class cycles through its contents and creates and returns two *ArrayLists* that respectively contain the keys and values of the items that are marked dirty.

■ In its *LoadViewState* method, *StateBag* performs the inverse of the operations it performed in *SaveViewState*. It uses the *ArrayLists* of keys and values to load the saved state into the appropriate *StateItems*. (It is the responsibility of the user of a *StateBag* object to pass into *LoadViewState* the same object that the *StateBag* returned in *SaveViewState*.)

We'll now examine how the *Control* class implements default state management by delegating to its *ViewState* property. In Chapter 7, Chapter 8, and Chapter 9, you saw several examples of controls that use the *ViewState* property to maintain the state of simple properties. The following code fragments show the definition of the *ViewState* property and the implementation of the *TrackViewState*, *SaveViewState*, and *LoadViewState* methods in the *Control* class:

```
private StateBag _viewState;
protected virtual StateBag ViewState {
    get {
        if (_viewState != null) {
            return _viewState;
        }
        _viewState = new StateBag(ViewStateIgnoresCase);
        if (IsTrackingViewState)
            _viewState.TrackViewState();
        return _viewState;
    }
}
protected virtual void TrackViewState() {
    if (_viewState != null) {
        _viewState.TrackViewState();
    }
}

protected virtual object SaveViewState() {
    if (_viewState != null) {
        return _viewState.SaveViewState();
    }
    return null;
}

protected virtual void LoadViewState(object savedState) {
    if (savedState != null) {
        ViewState.LoadViewState(savedState);
    }
}
```

When you save properties in *ViewState*, their state is automatically maintained for you. You can also store any other data in *ViewState* that your control needs across round-trips. As we mentioned in Chapter 7, you should store only those properties or data that need to maintain state in *ViewState*. Any types you save in *ViewState* must be serializable by *LosFormatter*. State tracking starts in *TrackViewState*, which is invoked after the Initialize phase. Items in *ViewState* added or modified before tracking begins are not marked dirty and thus are not saved in the serialized view state which is round-tripped to the client. This is important for efficiency. If you want to perform any initialization in your control, you should do so in your control's constructor or by overriding the *OnInit* method so that initial values are not serialized by the page framework. Note that a property stored in *ViewState* is marked dirty if it is assigned to after the Initialize phase, even if its value does not change. For example, if the *Text* property of a *Label* instance is initialized as *label1.Text="sometext"*, a subsequent property set of *label1.Text="sometext"* will cause the property to be marked dirty, although the value of the property did not change.

Next we'll look at custom state management for custom types that cannot be saved in *ViewState*.

Implementing *IStateManager* in a Custom Type

In this section, we'll define a *HotSpot* class that takes responsibility for managing its own state by implementing the *IStateManager* interface. The *HotSpot* class will serve as the base class for types that correspond to circular and rectangular hot spot regions in an image map. In the *ImageMap* example in the next section, we will use the *HotSpot* type to define a collection of hot spots in an image map.

Listing 10-11 contains the code for the abstract *HotSpot* class. Later in this section, you'll see concrete classes that derive from *HotSpot*, including *CircleHotSpot* and *RectangleHotSpot*.

```
using System;
using System.Collections;
using System.ComponentModel;
using System.Web.UI;

namespace MSPress.ServerControls {

    [
    TypeConverter(typeof(ExpandableObjectConverter))
    ]
```

Listing 10-11   HotSpot.cs   *(continued)*

Listing 10-11   *(continued)*

```
public abstract class HotSpot : IStateManager {

    private bool _isTrackingViewState;
    private StateBag _viewState;

    protected HotSpot() : this(String.Empty, String.Empty) {
    }

    protected HotSpot(string action, string toolTip) {
        this.Action = action;
        this.ToolTip = toolTip;
    }

    [
    Category("Behavior"),
    DefaultValue(""),
    Description(
        "URL for navigation or argument for postback event"),
    NotifyParentProperty(true),
    ]
    public String Action {
        get {
            string action = (string)(ViewState["Action"]);
            return (action == null)? String.Empty : action;
        }
        set {
            ViewState["Action"] = value;
        }
    }

    [
    Browsable(false),
    DesignerSerializationVisibility(
        DesignerSerializationVisibility.Hidden)
    ]
    public abstract MapShape Shape {
        get;
    }

    [
    Category("Behavior"),
    DefaultValue(""),
    Description("Tool tip to display over the hot spot"),
    NotifyParentProperty(true)
    ]
    public String ToolTip {
```

```
        get {
            string tip = (string)ViewState["ToolTip"];
            return (tip == null)? String.Empty : tip;
        }
        set {
            ViewState["ToolTip"] = value;
        }
    }

    protected abstract bool ShapeCreated {
        get;
    }


    [
    Browsable(false),
    DesignerSerializationVisibility(
        DesignerSerializationVisibility.Hidden)
    ]
    protected StateBag ViewState {
        get {
            if (_viewState == null) {
                _viewState = new StateBag(false);
                if (_isTrackingViewState) {
                    ((IStateManager)_viewState).TrackViewState();
                }
            }
            return _viewState;
        }
    }

    internal void SetDirty() {
        if (_viewState != null) {
            ICollection Keys = _viewState.Keys;
            foreach (string key in Keys) {
                _viewState.SetItemDirty(key, true);
            }
        }
    }

    public override string ToString() {
        return GetType().Name;
    }

    #region IStatemanager implementation
    bool IStateManager.IsTrackingViewState {
```

(continued)

Listing 10-11   *(continued)*

```
            get {
                return _isTrackingViewState;
            }
        }

        void  IStateManager.LoadViewState(object savedState) {
            if (savedState != null) {
                ((IStateManager)ViewState).LoadViewState(savedState);

                string savedShape = (string)ViewState["Shape"];
                if (savedShape != null) {
                    Shape.LoadFromString(savedShape);
                }
            }
        }

        object IStateManager.SaveViewState() {
            if (ShapeCreated) {
                string currentShape = Shape.SaveToString();
                string initialShape = (string)ViewState["Shape"];
                if (currentShape.Equals(initialShape) == false) {
                    ViewState["Shape"] = currentShape;
                }
            }

            if (_viewState != null) {
                return ((IStateManager)_viewState).SaveViewState();
            }
            return null;
        }

        void  IStateManager.TrackViewState() {
            if (ShapeCreated) {
                ViewState["Shape"] = Shape.SaveToString();
            }

            _isTrackingViewState = true;

            if (_viewState != null) {
                ((IStateManager)_viewState).TrackViewState();
            }
        }
        #endregion
    }
}
```

HotSpot defines three public properties:

- **Action**   Contains a URL if the hot spot causes navigation and contains a postback argument if the hot spot causes postback.

- **ToolTip**   Allows a page developer to specify a tool tip for the hot spot.

- **Shape**   An abstract property that is overridden by a derived class to return a *Shape* type such as the *MapCircle* or *MapRectangle* types we defined earlier in the chapter, in "Properties and Type Converters."

The most interesting feature of *HotSpot* is its state management. *HotSpot* defines a protected *ViewState* property of type *StateBag* and delegates state management to it. This is analogous to the default implementation of state management in the *Control* class and is a convenient technique for implementing state management if you implement a custom type that has several properties. Note, however, that *HotSpot* is not a *Control*; it does not derive from *Control* or share any other characteristics of the *Control* class.

HotSpot implements its simple properties (such as *Action* and *ToolTip*) as read-write properties and stores them directly in its *ViewState* dictionary. *HotSpot* implements its complex *Shape* property as a read-only property and performs state management for *Shape* in its implementation of the *IStateManager* interface.

In the *TrackViewState* method, *HotSpot* saves the string representation of the *Shape* property in its *ViewState* dictionary and then invokes *TrackViewState* on its *ViewState* property. The order of these operations is important and ensures that the initial state of the *Shape* property is not marked dirty in *ViewState*.

In the *SaveViewState* method, *HotSpot* checks whether the value of its *Shape* property differs from the initial state stored in *ViewState*. If the value does differ, *HotSpot* stores the new state in *ViewState*, which *ViewState* now marks as dirty. *HotSpot* next invokes *SaveViewState* on its *ViewState* property.

In the *LoadViewState* method, *HotSpot* first invokes the *LoadViewState* method on its *ViewState* property to load state into *ViewState*. *HotSpot* then looks up the value of its *Shape* property in *ViewState*, and if it finds any saved state, *HotSpot* uses that saved state to load the state of the *Shape* property.

Listing 10-12 shows the code for the *CircleHotSpot* class. The code for the *RectangleHotSpot* class is similar and is provided in the book's sample files.

```
using System;
using System.ComponentModel;
using System.Web.UI;

namespace MSPress.ServerControls {

    public class CircleHotSpot : HotSpot {

        private MapCircle _circle;

        public CircleHotSpot() :
            this(0, 0, 0, String.Empty, String.Empty) {
        }

        public CircleHotSpot(int x, int y, int radius, string action,
            string toolTip) : base(action, toolTip) {
            if ((x != 0) || (y != 0) || (radius != 0)) {
                Origin = new MapPoint(x, y);
                Radius = radius;
            }
        }

        [
        Category("Shape"),
        DefaultValue(typeof(MapPoint), ""),
        Description("The origin of the circular hot spot"),
        NotifyParentProperty(true)
        ]
        public MapPoint Origin {
            get {
                return ((MapCircle)Shape).Origin;
            }
            set {
                if (value == null) {
                    throw new ArgumentNullException("value");
                }
                ((MapCircle)Shape).Origin = value;
            }
        }

        [
        Category("Shape"),
        DefaultValue(0),
        Description("The radius of the circular hot spot"),
        NotifyParentProperty(true)
        ]
```

Listing 10-12   CircleHotSpot.cs

```
public int Radius {
    get {
        return ((MapCircle)Shape).Radius;
    }
    set {
        if (value < 0) {
            throw new ArgumentOutOfRangeException("value");
        }
        ((MapCircle)Shape).Radius = value;
    }
}

public override MapShape Shape {
    get {
        if (_circle == null) {
            _circle = new MapCircle();
        }
        return _circle;
    }
}

protected override bool ShapeCreated {
    get {
        return (_circle != null);
    }
}
```

Collection Properties—The *ImageMap* Example

We'll now implement an *ImageMap* control that has a *HotSpots* collection property that contains the *CircleHotSpot* and *RectangleHotSpot* custom types we defined in the previous section. The *HotSpots* property allows a page developer to specify an arbitrary number of circular and rectangular areas in an image, which *ImageMap* renders as regions of an HTML image map. The *ImageMap* control has two modes: *navigation*, in which each hot spot causes navigation to its specified URL, and *postback*, in which each hot spot causes postback to the page. Figure 10-3 shows the *ImageMap* control used in navigation mode. When the user's cursor rests in a map region (hot spot), the browser displays a tool tip over the hot spot and shows the URL for the hot spot in the status bar. When the user clicks a hot spot, the browser navigates to the specified URL.

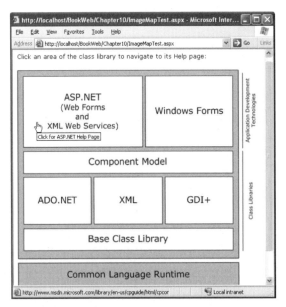

Figure 10-3   The ImageMapTest.aspx page viewed in a browser. The image is an HTML map generated by an *ImageMap* control instance used in navigation mode.

Listing 10-13 shows the ImageMapTest.aspx page. The page demonstrates inner default property persistence, whereby the content nested within the *ImageMap* control's tags corresponds to items of the *HotSpots* inner default property. Although rectangular areas are the most intuitive map regions for the image shown in Figure 10-3, we have added a few circular hot spots in the page to demonstrate that the *HotSpots* property can contain both *CircleHotSpot* and *RectangleHotSpot* objects. If you want to see the view state information for the control tree, turn on page tracing by adding the *Trace="true"* attribute to the *Page* directive. You will see that there is no view state for the *ImageMap* instance in the ImageMapTest.aspx page. However, if you change any properties of *ImageMap* after initialization—for example, in the *Page_Load* event handler—you will see view state for the control displayed in the trace output for the control tree.

```
<%@ Page Language="C#" %>
<%@ Register TagPrefix="msp" Namespace="MSPress.ServerControls"
  Assembly="MSPress.ServerControls" %>
<html>
  <body>
```

Listing 10-13   ImageMapTest.aspx

```
<form runat="server">
  <p>
    Click an area of the class library to navigate to its Help page:
  </p>
  <p>
    <msp:ImageMap ImageUrl="ClassLibrary.jpg" Mode="Navigation"
      ImageAlign="Middle" Runat="server" id="imageMap1">
      <msp:RectangleHotSpot ToolTip="Click for ASP.NET Help Page"
        BottomRight="270,159"
        Action="http://www.msdn.microsoft.com/library/en-us/cpguide
        /html/cpconcreatingaspwebapplications.asp?frame=true"
        TopLeft="11,14">
      </msp:RectangleHotSpot>
      <msp:RectangleHotSpot
        ToolTip="Click for Windows Forms Help Page"
        BottomRight="464,158" Action="http://www.msdn.microsoft.com
        /library/en-us/vbcon/html/
        vboriCreatingStandaloneAppsVB.asp?frame=true"
        TopLeft="278,15">
      </msp:RectangleHotSpot>
      <msp:RectangleHotSpot
        ToolTip="Click for Component Model Help Page"
        BottomRight="464,212"
        Action="http://www.msdn.microsoft.com/library/en-us/cpguide
        /html/cpconcomponentprogrammingessentials.asp?frame=true"
        TopLeft="13,169">
      </msp:RectangleHotSpot>
      <msp:CircleHotSpot ToolTip="Click for ADO.NET Help Page"
        Radius="50" Origin="87,269"
        Action="http://www.msdn.microsoft.com/library/en-us/cpguide
        /html/cpconaccessingdatawithadonet.asp?frame=true">
      </msp:CircleHotSpot>
      <msp:CircleHotSpot ToolTip="Click for XML Help Page"
        Radius="50" Origin="237,269"
        Action="http://www.msdn.microsoft.com/library/en-us/cpguide
        /html/cpconemployingxmlinnetframework.asp?frame=true">
      </msp:CircleHotSpot>
      <msp:CircleHotSpot ToolTip="Click for GDI+ Help Page"
        Radius="50" Origin="388,269"
        Action="http://www.msdn.microsoft.com/library/en-us/cpguide
        /html/cpcondrawingeditingimages.asp?frame=true">
      </msp:CircleHotSpot>
      <msp:RectangleHotSpot
        ToolTip="Click for Common Language Runtime Help Page"
        BottomRight="477,452"
        Action="http://www.msdn.microsoft.com/library/en-us/cpguide
        /html/cpconthecommonlanguageruntime.asp?frame=true"
```

(continued)

Listing 10-13 *(continued)*

```
            TopLeft="1,401">
          </msp:RectangleHotSpot>
        </msp:ImageMap>
      </p>
    </form>
  </body>
</html>
```

Before we show the code for the *ImageMap* class, we'll demonstrate a design-time feature of collection properties. In the property browser, a collection property is displayed in the same manner as the *HotSpots* property shown in Figure 10-4.

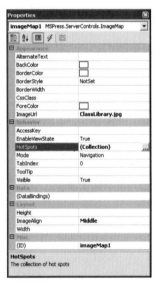

Figure 10-4   Properties of the *ImageMap* instance, as displayed in the Visual Studio property browser. Collection properties are always displayed the same way as the *HotSpots* property.

When the page developer clicks the ellipsis shown beside the *HotSpots* collection property in Figure 10-4, the property browser will provide a collection editor UI such as that shown in Figure 10-5. To enable support for collection editing, you have to associate a collection editor with a collection. (We will describe collection editors in greater detail in Chapter 15, "Design-Time Functionality.") A *collection editor* provides a user interface that allows a page developer to easily add or remove collection items, edit a collection item, and move an item up or down in the list.

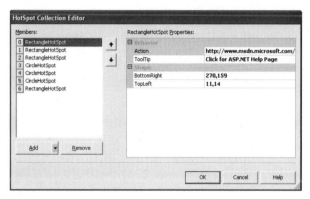

Figure 10-5 Collection editor for the *HotSpots* property of the *ImageMap* control

Listing 10-14 contains the code for the *ImageMap* control, which is similar to the *MapDemo* control we described in Listing 10-7. The most significant feature of *ImageMap* is that it defines a *HotSpots* collection property and implements custom state management related to this property.

```
using System;
using System.ComponentModel;
using System.Web.UI;
using System.Web.UI.WebControls;

namespace MSPress.ServerControls {
    [
    DefaultEvent("MapClick"),
    DefaultProperty("HotSpots"),
    ParseChildren(true, "HotSpots")
    ]
    public class ImageMap : Image, IPostBackEventHandler {

        private static readonly object EventMapClick = new object();
        private bool _hasHotSpots;
        private HotSpotCollection _hotSpots;


        [
        Category("Behavior"),
        Description("The collection of hot spots"),
        DesignerSerializationVisibility(
            DesignerSerializationVisibility.Content),
        NotifyParentProperty(true),
```

Listing 10-14   ImageMap.cs   *(continued)*

Listing 10-14 *(continued)*

```
        PersistenceMode(PersistenceMode.InnerDefaultProperty)
        ]
        public HotSpotCollection HotSpots {
            get {
                if (_hotSpots == null) {
                    _hotSpots = new HotSpotCollection();
                    if (IsTrackingViewState) {
                        ((IStateManager)_hotSpots).TrackViewState();
                    }
                }
                return _hotSpots;
            }
        }


        [
        Category("Behavior"),
        DefaultValue(ImageMapMode.Navigation),
        Description("Specifies whether the image map causes postback" +
            " or navigation."),
        ]
        public ImageMapMode Mode {
            get {
                object obj = ViewState["Mode"];
                return (obj == null) ?
                    ImageMapMode.Navigation : (ImageMapMode)obj;
            }
            set {
                if (value < ImageMapMode.Navigation ||
                    value > ImageMapMode.Postback) {
                    throw new ArgumentOutOfRangeException("value");
                }
                ViewState["Mode"] = value;
            }
        }


        [
        Category("Action"),
        Description("Raised when a hotspot is clicked")
        ]
        public event MapClickEventHandler MapClick {
            add {
                Events.AddHandler(EventMapClick, value);
            }
            remove {
                Events.RemoveHandler(EventMapClick, value);
            }
        }
```

```
protected override void AddAttributesToRender(
    HtmlTextWriter writer) {
    base.AddAttributesToRender(writer);

    if (_hasHotSpots) {
        writer.AddAttribute("UseMap", "#ImageMap" + ClientID,
            false);
    }
}

protected virtual void OnMapClick(MapClickEventArgs e) {
    MapClickEventHandler mapClickHandler =
        (MapClickEventHandler)Events[EventMapClick];
    if (mapClickHandler != null) {
        mapClickHandler(this, e);
    }
}

protected override void Render(HtmlTextWriter writer) {
    _hasHotSpots =
        ((_hotSpots != null) && (_hotSpots.Count > 0));

    base.Render(writer);

    if (_hasHotSpots) {
        writer.AddAttribute(HtmlTextWriterAttribute.Name,
            "ImageMap" + ClientID);
        writer.RenderBeginTag(HtmlTextWriterTag.Map);

        ImageMapMode mode = Mode;
        int hotSpotIndex = 0;
        foreach (HotSpot item in _hotSpots) {
            writer.AddAttribute("shape", item.Shape.ShapeName,
                false);
            writer.AddAttribute("coords",
                item.Shape.MapCoordinates);
            if (mode == ImageMapMode.Postback) {
                writer.AddAttribute(
                    HtmlTextWriterAttribute.Href,
                    Page.GetPostBackClientHyperlink(this,
                        hotSpotIndex.ToString()));
            }
            else {
                writer.AddAttribute(
                    HtmlTextWriterAttribute.Href, item.Action);
            }
```

(continued)

Listing 10-14 *(continued)*

```
                writer.AddAttribute(HtmlTextWriterAttribute.Title,
                    item.ToolTip, false);
                writer.RenderBeginTag("area");
                writer.RenderEndTag();

                ++hotSpotIndex;
            }
            writer.RenderEndTag();  // Map
        }
    }

    #region Custom State Management Implementation
    protected override void LoadViewState(object savedState) {
        object baseState = null;
        object[] myState = null;

        if (savedState != null) {
            myState = (object[])savedState;
            if (myState.Length != 2) {
                throw new ArgumentException("Invalid view state");
            }

            baseState = myState[0];
        }

        base.LoadViewState(baseState);

        if ((myState != null) && (myState[1] != null)) {
            ((IStateManager)HotSpots).LoadViewState(myState[1]);
        }
    }

    protected override object SaveViewState() {
        object baseState = base.SaveViewState();
        object hotSpotsState = null;

        if ((_hotSpots != null) && (_hotSpots.Count > 0)) {
            hotSpotsState =
                ((IStateManager)_hotSpots).SaveViewState();
        }

        if ((baseState != null) || (hotSpotsState != null)) {
            object[] savedState = new object[2];
            savedState[0] = baseState;
            savedState[1] = hotSpotsState;
```

```
                return savedState;
            }

            return null;
        }

        protected override void TrackViewState() {
            base.TrackViewState();
            if (_hotSpots != null) {
                ((IStateManager)_hotSpots).TrackViewState();
            }
        }
        #endregion Custom State Management Implementation

        #region Implementation of IPostBackEventHandler
        void IPostBackEventHandler.RaisePostBackEvent(
            string eventArg) {
            if (eventArg != null) {
                int hotSpotIndex = Int32.Parse(eventArg);
                string action = _hotSpots[hotSpotIndex].Action;

                OnMapClick(new MapClickEventArgs(action));
            }
        }
        #endregion Implementation of IPostBackEventHandler
    }
}
```

Listing 10-15 shows the *ImageMapMode* enumeration.

```
using System;

namespace MSPress.ServerControls {
    public enum ImageMapMode {
        Navigation,
        Postback
    }
}
```

Listing 10-15   ImageMapMode.cs

There are several points to note regarding the *ImageMap* control:

■   *ImageMap* is marked with the *ParseChildren(true, "HotSpots")* attribute, which tells the page parser that *HotSpots* is the inner default property for the control.

- The *HotSpots* property is marked with the *PersistenceMode(PersistenceMode.InnerDefaultProperty)* attribute, which tells the designer to persist the *HotSpots* property as the inner default property for the control. This causes the designer to persist the items of the *HotSpots* collection within the control's tags.

- *ImageMap* defines a *Mode* property that allows a page developer to specify whether the hot spots cause navigation or postback. The type of the *Mode* property is the *ImageMapMode* enumeration, which is shown in Listing 10-15.

- *ImageMap* performs custom state management by overriding the *TrackViewState*, *SaveViewState*, and *LoadViewState* methods of the base class. The *HotSpotCollection* class performs its own state management, as we will soon describe. In each of its state management methods, *ImageMap* first invokes the relevant method of the base class and then invokes the corresponding method of its *HotSpots* property. The view state of the *ImageMap* control has two parts: the view state of the base class, and the view state of the *HotSpots* collection. Note that the *SaveViewState* method could return a *Pair* object because the view state has two parts. However, this method returns an array of objects to demonstrate a technique that you can use in a more general scenario.

- *ImageMap* cycles through the *HotSpots* collection to render each hot spot. If *ImageMap* is used in navigation mode, it renders the navigation URL for each *HotSpot* object. If *ImageMap* is used in postback mode, it renders JavaScript that causes postback for each hot spot.

- *ImageMap* implements *IPostBackEventHandler* to provide server-side event functionality (as described in Chapter 9) when it is used in postback mode. In this mode, *ImageMap* maps the postback event to the server-side *MapClick* event, to which a page developer can attach an event handler.

Implementing State Management in a Collection Type—The *HotSpotCollection* Example

We'll now look at the implementation of the *HotSpotCollection* class, which is the type of the *HotSpots* property of the *ImageMap* control. *HotSpotCollection* is a list (it implements *IList*) and participates in state management by implementing *IStateManager*.

The complete code for the *HotSpotCollection* class appears in the book's sample files; Listing 10-16 shows the code that is relevant for state management.

HotSpotCollection contains a private *ArrayList* field (named *_hotSpots*), which provides the core list functionality of the class. *HotSpotCollection* exposes an indexer property that accesses the private *_hotSpots* field and implements *IList* methods that are mindful of state management when they add or remove from the underlying *ArrayList*. For example, the *Add* and *Insert* methods of *HotSpot-Collection* allow *CircleHotSpot* and *RectangleHotSpot* objects to be added, but not other types that derive from *HotSpot*. This helps to reduce the size of the view state, as we explain after Listing 10-16. The *EditorAttribute* applied to the *HotSpotCollection* class enables the collection editor UI shown in Figure 10-5.

```
using System;
using System.Collections;
using System.ComponentModel;
using System.Drawing.Design;
using System.Web.UI;

namespace MSPress.ServerControls {

    [
    Editor(typeof(
        MSPress.ServerControls.Design.HotSpotCollectionEditor),
        typeof(UITypeEditor))
    ]
    public sealed class HotSpotCollection : IList, IStateManager {

        private ArrayList _hotSpots;
        private bool _isTrackingViewState;
        private bool _saveAll;

        internal HotSpotCollection() {
            _hotSpots = new ArrayList();
        }

        public HotSpot this[int index] {
            get {
                return (HotSpot)_hotSpots[index];
            }
        }

        public int Add(HotSpot item) {
            if (item == null) {
                throw new ArgumentNullException("item");
            }
```

Listing 10-16 Code related to state management in the *HotSpotCollection* class

(continued)

Listing 10-16 *(continued)*

```
        if (!((item is CircleHotSpot) ||
            (item is RectangleHotSpot))) {
            throw new ArgumentException("Item must be a " +
                "CircleHotSpot or a RectangleHotSpot.");
        }

        _hotSpots.Add(item);
        if (_isTrackingViewState) {
            ((IStateManager)item).TrackViewState();
            item.SetDirty();
        }

        return _hotSpots.Count - 1;
    }

    public void Clear() {
        _hotSpots.Clear();
        if (_isTrackingViewState) {
            _saveAll = true;
        }
    }

    public void Insert(int index, HotSpot item) {
        if (item == null) {
            throw new ArgumentNullException("item");
        }
        if (!((item is CircleHotSpot) ||
            (item is RectangleHotSpot))) {
            throw new ArgumentException("Item must be a " +
                "CircleHotSpot or a RectangleHotSpot.");
        }

        _hotSpots.Insert(index, item);
        if (_isTrackingViewState) {
            ((IStateManager)item).TrackViewState();
            _saveAll = true;
        }
    }

    public void RemoveAt(int index) {
        _hotSpots.RemoveAt(index);
        if (_isTrackingViewState) {
            _saveAll = true;
        }
    }
```

```
#region IStateManager Implementation
bool IStateManager.IsTrackingViewState {
    get {
        return _isTrackingViewState;
    }
}

void IStateManager.LoadViewState(object savedState) {
    if (savedState == null) {
        return;
    }

    if (savedState is Pair) {
        // All items were saved.
        // Create new HotSpots collection using view state.
        _saveAll = true;
        Pair p = (Pair)savedState;
        ArrayList types = (ArrayList) p.First;
        ArrayList states = (ArrayList) p.Second;
        int count = types.Count;

        _hotSpots = new ArrayList(count);
        for (int i = 0; i < count; i++) {
            HotSpot hotSpot = null;
            if (((char)types[i]).Equals('c')) {
                hotSpot = new CircleHotSpot();
            }
            else {
                hotSpot = new RectangleHotSpot();
            }
            Add(hotSpot);
            ((IStateManager)hotSpot).LoadViewState(states[i]);
        }
    }
    else {
        // Load modified items.
        Triplet t = (Triplet) savedState;
        ArrayList indices = (ArrayList)t.First;
        ArrayList types = (ArrayList)t.Second;
        ArrayList states = (ArrayList)t.Third;

        for (int i = 0 ;  i < indices.Count; i++) {
            int index = (int)indices[i];
            if (index < this.Count) {
                ((IStateManager)
                    _hotSpots[index]).LoadViewState(states[i]);
            }
```

(continued)

Listing 10-16 *(continued)*

```
                else {
                    HotSpot hotSpot = null;
                    if (((char)types[i]).Equals('c')) {
                        hotSpot = new CircleHotSpot();
                    }
                    else {
                        hotSpot = new RectangleHotSpot();
                    }
                    Add(hotSpot);
                    ((IStateManager)
                        hotSpot).LoadViewState(states[i]);
                }
            }
        }
    }

    void IStateManager.TrackViewState() {
        _isTrackingViewState = true;
        foreach (HotSpot hotSpot in _hotSpots) {
            ((IStateManager)hotSpot).TrackViewState();
        }
    }

    object IStateManager.SaveViewState() {
        if (_saveAll == true) {
            // Save all items.
            ArrayList types = new ArrayList(Count);
            ArrayList states = new ArrayList(Count);
            for (int i = 0; i < Count; i++) {
                HotSpot hotSpot = (HotSpot)_hotSpots[i];
                hotSpot.SetDirty();
                if (hotSpot is CircleHotSpot) {
                    types.Add('c');
                }
                else {
                    types.Add('r');
                }
                states.Add(
                    ((IStateManager)hotSpot).SaveViewState());
            }
            if (types.Count > 0) {
                return new Pair(types, states);
            }
            else {
                return null;
            }
        }
```

```
        else {
            // Save only the dirty items.
            ArrayList indices = new ArrayList();
            ArrayList types = new ArrayList();
            ArrayList states = new ArrayList();

            for (int i = 0; i < Count; i++) {
                HotSpot hotSpot = (HotSpot)_hotSpots[i];
                object state =
                    ((IStateManager)hotSpot).SaveViewState();
                if (state != null) {
                    states.Add(state);
                    indices.Add(i);
                    if (hotSpot is CircleHotSpot) {
                        types.Add('c');
                    }
                    else {
                        types.Add('r');
                    }
                }
            }

            if (indices.Count > 0) {
                return new Triplet(indices, types, states);
            }

            return null;
        }
    }
    #endregion IStateManager Implementation
}
// The implementation of ICollection and IEnumerable
// and of several methods of IList is not shown.
}
```

Let's examine the methods of *HotSpotCollection* that add, remove, and insert items and are involved in state management.

The *Add* method checks whether state tracking is turned on. If state tracking is on, the method turns on tracking for the added item by invoking its *Track-ViewState* method. The *CircleHotSpot* and *RectangleHotSpot* items that are added to the collection implement *IStateManager*. In addition, if tracking is on, the *Add* method invokes the *SetDirty* method on the added item, which causes the entire state of the added *HotSpot* to be persisted in the view state of *HotSpotCollection*. This is necessary because when an item is added after initialization of the *HotSpotCollection*, the item's initial state is not present in the collection's initial state.

The *Insert* and *RemoveAt* methods perform their main task and then check whether state tracking is turned on. If this tracking is on, the methods set the private Boolean *_saveAll* field to *true*. This tells the *SaveViewState* method to save all items in the view state, not just the modified items. When items are inserted or removed in a list, the initial order is lost and the list cannot be re-created by using changes alone. In this case, it is necessary to persist the entire list in view state and use it to re-create the list on postback. The *Clear* method also sets *_saveAll* to *true*. In that case, a null object is saved in view state to re-create an empty list on postback.

Now we'll examine how *HotSpotCollection* implements *IStateManager*.

In the *TrackViewState* method, *HotSpotCollection* sets its own *_isTrackingViewState* field to *true* and invokes *TrackViewState* on each *HotSpot* in its *_hotSpots* list.

The *SaveViewState* implementation has two branches based on the value of *_saveAll* field.

If *_saveAll* is *true*, *SaveViewState* saves the state of all the items in the list. *SaveViewState* creates two *ArrayLists*: the first holds type information for the *HotSpots*, and the second holds the states of the *HotSpots*. As we described earlier, the list must be re-created entirely from the saved state when *_saveAll* is *true*. Therefore, *SaveViewState* invokes *SetDirty* on each *HotSpot* so that the entire state of the *HotSpot* is persisted in view state. *SaveViewState* next cycles through the *_hotSpots* list and adds the type and the state of each *HotSpot* to the two *ArrayLists* it created earlier. *SaveViewState* obtains the view state for each *HotSpot* by invoking *SaveViewState* on that *HotSpot* object. Finally, *SaveViewState* returns a *Pair* object that holds the two *ArrayLists*. The returned object constitutes the view state of the *HotSpotCollection*.

If *_saveAll* is *false*, *SaveViewState* saves only the changed items in the list. It creates three *ArrayLists*: the first holds indexes of the changed items, the second holds type information for the *HotSpots*, and the third holds the states of the *HotSpots*. The method cycles through its *_hotSpots* list and invokes *SaveViewState* on each *HotSpot*. If the returned state is non-null, *SaveViewState* adds the index of the *HotSpot*, its type, and its state to the corresponding *ArrayList*. Finally, *SaveViewState* returns a *Triplet* object that holds the three *ArrayLists*. (A *System.Web.UI.Triplet* class is merely an ordered set of three objects.) The returned *Triplet* object constitutes the view state of the *HotSpotCollection*.

The *LoadViewState* method performs the inverse logic of the *SaveViewState* method. *LoadViewState* has two branches based on the type of the object handed to it.

If the saved state is a *Pair*, *LoadViewState* discards the initial state of *HotSpotCollection* and re-creates the *_hotSpots* list by using the saved state.

LoadViewState creates a new, empty *_hotSpots* list. It then creates each *HotSpot* based on the saved type information and loads the corresponding saved state into the *HotSpot*. Next *LoadViewState* adds the *HotSpot* to the *_hotSpots* list.

If the saved state is a *Triplet*, *LoadViewState* restores state for the items that were changed after initialization—that is, the items whose indexes appear in the first *ArrayList* in the *Triplet*. Items whose indexes are greater than the initial *Count* of the *HotSpotCollection* did not exist during initialization and must be created entirely from the saved state. In that case, *LoadViewState* creates a *HotSpot* by using type information in the second *ArrayList*, loads state into it from the third *ArrayList*, and adds it to the *_hotSpots* field.

Because view state tracking is on when *LoadViewState* is invoked by the *ImageMap* control on its *HotSpotCollection*, any items in *HotSpotCollection* that are added or modified in the *LoadViewState* method are automatically tracked. This causes the items to be repersisted in view state when *SaveViewState* is subsequently invoked.

Now let's examine why the *HotSpotCollection* must restrict its items to specific *HotSpot*s, such as *CircleHotSpot* and *RectangleHotSpot*. The *SaveViewState* method must save in view state information that specifies the type of *HotSpot* to be created on postback. To keep the view state small, we store this information as a single character ('c' or 'r'). If *HotSpotCollection* allowed any type that derived from *HotSpot*, we would have to save much more information—in other words, we'd have to save the assembly-qualified name of the type—so that the type could be re-created by using reflection on postback. This would lead to significant view state overhead.

If you want to implement a more general *ImageMap* control that also allows the polygonal shapes permitted by the HTML map specification, you can define a new *PolygonHotSpot* that derives from *HotSpot* and has a *Shape* property that is a *MapPolygon* type that derives from the *MapShape* class in Listing 10-3. Then you can modify the implementation of *HotSpotCollection* to allow a *PolygonHotSpot* type as a member and save information about that type by using a single character, such as 'p'.

Expando Attributes—The *IAttributeAccessor* Interface

If the page developer declaratively specifies attributes on a Web control's tag that do not correspond to public properties of that control, the page parser adds those attributes as custom name/value pairs to the *Attributes* collection property of the control. This functionality is enabled because *WebControl* implements the *System.Web.UI.IAttributeAccessor* interface.

The *Attributes* property of *WebControl* allows the control's user to add custom HTML attributes that the control does not expose as properties. *Web-Control* renders its *Attributes* collection in the form of HTML attributes without any processing on the server. Such user-added attributes are also referred to as *expando attributes*. Any control that derives from *WebControl* automatically provides support for expando attributes. This functionality is especially useful for tying in client-side script functionality, as shown in the following example, where the page has a *TextBox* control with two user-supplied attributes (*onmouseover* and *onmouseout*) that do not correspond to properties of the *TextBox* control:

```
<%@ Page Language="C#" %>
<html>
<head>
  <style>
    .beige { background-color:beige }
  </style>
  <script language="JavaScript">
    function OnMouseOver(element) { ... }
    function OnMouseOut(element) { ... }
  </script>
</head>
<body>
  <form runat="server">
   <asp:TextBox runat="server" CssClass="beige"
     onmouseover="OnMouseOver(this)" onmouseout="OnMouseOut(this)"/>
  </form>
</body>
</html>
```

On the client, the markup rendered by the *TextBox* instance is similar to the following HTML:

```
<input name="_ctl0" type="text" class="beige"
  onmouseover="OnMouseOver(this)" onmouseout="OnMouseOut(this)" />
```

If a user tries to add expando attributes to a control that does not implement the *IAttributeAccessor* interface, the parser will throw an exception. The *Control* class does not implement the *IAttributeAccessor* interface because expando attributes are not meaningful in all server controls. If you want to support expando attributes in a custom control that derives from *Control*, you must implement the *IAttributeAccessor* and define an *Attributes* property. The following code shows how *WebControl* implements these members:

```
public class WebControl : Control, IAttributeAccessor {
    private StateBag _attrState;
    private AttributeCollection _attrColl;
```

```
[
Browsable(false),
DesignerSerializationVisibility(
    DesignerSerializationVisibility.Hidden)
]
public AttributeCollection Attributes {
    get {
        if (_attrColl == null) {
            if (_attrState == null) {
                _attrState = new StateBag(true);
                if (IsTrackingViewState)
                    _attrState.TrackViewState();
            }
            _attrColl = new AttributeCollection(attrState);
        }
        return _attrColl;
    }
}


[
Browsable(false),
DesignerSerializationVisibility(
    DesignerSerializationVisibility.Hidden)
]
public bool HasAttributes {
    get {
        return (_attrState != null) && (_attrState.Count > 0);
    }
}

string IAttributeAccessor.GetAttribute(string name) {
    return ((HasAttributes != null) ?
        (string)_attrState[name] : null);
}

void IAttributeAccessor.SetAttribute(string name, string value) {
    Attributes[name] = value;
}
}
```

The *AttributeCollection* type of the *Attributes* property has its own *State-Bag* and manages its own state by implementing *IStateManager*. To support expando attributes in a custom control that derives from *Control*, you can use the preceding implementation as a starting point. You can then perform custom state management in your control by using the pattern we showed earlier in the chapter for the *ImageMap* control, which has a collection property that manages its own state.

Summary

In this chapter, we looked at complex properties and showed how to enable declarative persistence and design-time support for such properties. We also examined the view state mechanism in detail and showed how to implement state management in a custom type. To illustrate the implementation of complex properties, we developed an *ImageMap* control that uses many custom types and exposes a collection property that performs its own state management. The *ImageMap* control can also be a useful addition to the Web Forms toolbox because the set of standard ASP.NET controls does not contain a control that provides map functionality.

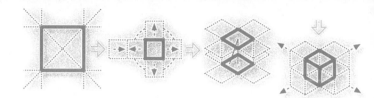

11

Styles in Controls

The *WebControl* class exposes style properties such as *ForeColor*, *BackColor*, and *Font* that govern the visual appearance of the HTML element rendered by a Web control. These properties provide an object-oriented abstraction of appearance-related HTML and cascading style sheet (CSS) attributes. As we described in Chapter 8, "Rendering," if your control renders visual HTML elements, you should derive from the *WebControl* class so that your control inherits basic style properties and the style architecture that enables you to modify or add style properties.

In this chapter, we'll examine the style properties of the *WebControl* class and the methods that *WebControl* provides for working with styles. We'll look at the *Style* class that is responsible for providing style functionality to *WebControl*. And we'll show how you can override or add to the style properties of *WebControl*.

Styles Overview

There are several benefits to exposing style properties from a control vs. merely rendering styles as HTML and CSS attributes. Style properties can be programmed against and have IntelliSense support when a Web control is used in a code editor. In addition, strongly typed style properties provide the benefit of compile-time type checking. For example, *WebControl* defines the *ForeColor*, *Font*, and *Width* properties by using the *Color*, *FontInfo*, and *Unit* types respectively, instead of using the generic *String* type. If a page developer makes an error when specifying the *ForeColor*—such as specifying "Briwn" instead of "Brown"—the parser will be unable to convert the specified string to the *Color* type and will generate an error message.

We will now examine the architecture that supports style functionality in a Web control. You do not need to understand this architecture if the basic style functionality that your control inherits from *WebControl* is adequate for your purposes. However, if you need to modify or extend the inherited style functionality, you should go through the background we provide in this section.

The style functionality of the *WebControl* class is encapsulated in its *ControlStyle* property. Style properties are really subproperties of the *Control-Style* property. *WebControl* exposes these properties as top-level properties, as shown in the following code fragment, which contains the definition of the *Back-Color* property of *WebControl*:

```
public virtual Color BackColor {
    get {
        if (ControlStyleCreated == false) {
            return Color.Empty;
        }
        return ControlStyle.BackColor;
    }
    set {
        ControlStyle.BackColor = value;
    }
}
```

The type of the *ControlStyle* property is the *System.Web.UI.WebControls.Style* class, which implements style properties and has built-in capabilities for state management and rendering. The object model of the *Style* class is shown in Appendix B, "Object Model for Common Classes." *WebControl* implements all its style properties, as well as the state management and rendering of these properties, by delegating to its *ControlStyle* property.

The following code fragment shows the definition of the *ControlStyle* property in *WebControl*:

```
private Style _controlStyle;
public Style ControlStyle {
    get {
```

```
        if (_controlStyle == null) {
            _controlStyle = CreateControlStyle();
            if (IsTrackingViewState) {
                ((IStateManager)_controlStyle).TrackViewState();
            }
        }
        return _controlStyle;
    }
}
```

The *ControlStyle* property is read-only and is created when it is first accessed. The accessor of this property checks the *_controlStyle* field, and if this field is null, the accessor invokes the protected virtual *CreateControlStyle* method to create a *Style* instance.

The *ControlStyleCreated* property indicates whether the *WebControl* class's style has been created:

```
public bool ControlStyleCreated {
    get {
        return (_controlStyle != null);
    }
}
```

WebControl implements the *CreateControlStyle* method as follows:

```
protected virtual Style CreateControlStyle() {
    return new Style(ViewState);
}
```

The default implementation of the *CreateControlStyle* method returns a *Style* object. A derived control can override this method to create and return a custom style that derives from the *Style* class, as we will show in the *MyPanel* example in the "Implementing a Custom Typed Style—The *MyPanelStyle* Example" section later in this chapter.

Classes that derive from the *Style* class are known as *typed styles*. The *Style* class can be extended by a control developer to create a custom typed style that overrides or adds to the properties of the *Style* class. A Web control can use a custom typed style as the type of the *ControlStyle* property. For example, the *ControlStyle* property of the *Table* control is of the *TableStyle* type, which extends *Style* to add properties such as *CellPadding*, *CellSpacing*, and *GridLines*. Later in this chapter, we'll show how you can create and use your own custom typed style. In the future, ASP.NET will support server-side style sheets consisting of typed styles. Looking ahead, you should consider creating typed styles that encapsulate appearance-related properties of your controls.

WebControl exposes the *Styles* collection property that accepts CSS attributes as name/value pairs. This allows a page developer to add styles that the control does not expose as style properties. We recommend that you do not use the *Styles* property because it does not offer the benefits of the strongly typed style properties that we described earlier. If your control needs additional style properties, you should define and use a custom typed style that implements those properties, as we will show in the *MyPanel* and the *MyPanelStyle* examples later in this chapter. *WebControl* also exposes a *CssClass* property that allows a page developer to specify a CSS class name as a string argument.

WebControl defines the following three methods for working with its *ControlStyle* property:

- **CreateControlStyle** Creates the *ControlStyle*, as shown earlier in this section. A custom control can override this method to modify the default values for style properties or to create a new typed style for its *ControlStyle property*. We'll show examples of this later in the chapter.

- **ApplyStyle** Copies style properties that are set in the style passed into the method to the control's own *ControlStyle*.

- **MergeStyle** Copies style properties from the style passed into the method to the control's own *ControlStyle*, copying those properties that are set in the specified style but not in *ControlStyle*.

Next we'll examine how *WebControl* delegates the rendering of styles to its *ControlStyle* property. In its *AddAttributesToRender* method, *WebControl* invokes the *AddAttributesToRender* method of its *ControlStyle* property:

```
protected virtual void AddAttributesToRender(HtmlTextWriter writer) {
    :
    if (ControlStyleCreated && !ControlStyle.IsEmpty) {
        // Let the style add attributes.
        ControlStyle.AddAttributesToRender(writer, this);
    }
    :
}
```

As we described earlier, the style properties of *WebControl* are really sub-properties of the *ControlStyle* property. The *AddAttributesToRender* method of the *ControlStyle* property implements logic to render these properties as HTML attributes or as CSS attributes (as appropriate) on the control's tag. In Chapter 8, we showed you how to use the attribute rendering methods of the *HtmlText-Writer* class. Later in this chapter, in the *MyPanelStyle* example, we'll show you how to override the *AddAttributesToRender* method of the *Style* class.

The final aspect of the style functionality of *WebControl* is the state management of styles. We'll now examine how *WebControl* delegates style-related state management to its *ControlStyle* property. The *Style* type of the *ControlStyle* property implements *IStateManager* and performs its own state management. From its *TrackViewState*, *SaveViewState*, and *LoadViewState* methods, *WebControl* invokes the corresponding methods of its *ControlStyle* property. In addition, when a control creates its *ControlStyle*, the control starts state tracking on the newly created *Style* object if the control is tracking state. You can see this functionality in the code fragment at the beginning of this section, which shows the definition of the *ControlStyle* property.

To implement state management, the *Style* class uses a *ViewState* property of type *StateBag*, just as the *Control* class uses for default state management. The *Style* class has two constructors: one takes a single parameter of the *State-Bag* type, and the other does not take any parameters. When creating the control's style in *CreateControlStyle*, *WebControl* uses the one-parameter constructor and passes its own *ViewState* into the constructor, as we showed in the code for *CreateControlStyle* earlier in this section. This allows the *Style* object to use the same *StateBag* as the control that owns the style, which leads to a significant performance improvement. We'll show another example of using the one-parameter constructor in the *MyPanelStyle* example later in this chapter. In Chapter 12, "Composite Controls," we will use the no-parameter constructor of *Style* to create styles for child controls, which manage their state using their own *StateBag* instance.

Overriding Style Properties—The *Spreadsheet* Example

Overriding style properties is similar to overriding other properties. The main point to keep in mind is that changes that you make to property values must be propagated into the *ControlStyle* property of your control.

We'll demonstrate how to override style properties by implementing a *Spreadsheet* control that derives from the ASP.NET *Table* control. *Spreadsheet* overrides the *CellSpacing* and *GridLines* properties so that the *CellSpacing* is always *0* and the *GridLines* are rendered by default. This renders a table that resembles a spreadsheet with collapsed cell borders, as shown in Figure 11-1.

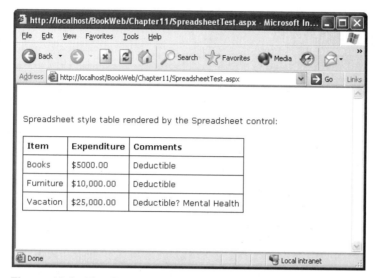

Figure 11-1   The SpreadsheetTest.aspx page that uses the *Spreadsheet* control

Listing 11-1 contains the code for the *Spreadsheet* control.

```
using System;
using System.ComponentModel;
using System.Web.UI;
using System.Web.UI.WebControls;

namespace MSPress.ServerControls {
    public class Spreadsheet : Table {
        public Spreadsheet() {
            base.CellSpacing = 0;
            base.GridLines = GridLines.Both;
        }

        [
        Bindable(false),
        Browsable(false),
        DefaultValue(0),
        DesignerSerializationVisibility(
            DesignerSerializationVisibility.Hidden),
        EditorBrowsable(EditorBrowsableState.Never)
        ]
        public override int CellSpacing {
```

Listing 11-1   Spreadsheet.cs

```
        get {
            return base.CellSpacing;
        }
        set {
            throw new NotSupportedException(
                "Cannot set CellSpacing");
        }
    }


    [
    DefaultValue(GridLines.Both)
    ]
    public override GridLines GridLines {
        get {
            return base.GridLines;
        }
        set {
            base.GridLines = value;
        }
    }
}
}
```

The *Spreadsheet* control demonstrates how to override style properties by performing the following tasks:

■   In its constructor, *Spreadsheet* assigns the value *0* to the *CellSpacing* property of the base class. This propagates the value into the *ControlStyle* property. *Spreadsheet* does not return a constant value from the *CellSpacing get* accessor for reasons that we explain after this bulleted list. *Spreadsheet* throws an exception from the *CellSpacing set* accessor to inform a user that this property cannot be assigned to. In addition, *Spreadsheet* applies design-time attributes to the *Cell-Spacing* property that tell the designer that the property is not browsable and that it should be hidden from the designer's serialization mechanism.

■   Overrides the *GridLines* property and reapplies the *DefaultValue-Attribute* to specify the new default value, *GridLines.Both*. In addition, in its constructor, *Spreadsheet* assigns the new default value to the *GridLines* property of the base class. This propagates the new default value into the *ControlStyle* property.

By setting the *CellSpacing* and *GridLines* properties of the base class in its constructor, *Spreadsheet* propagates the new values into the *ControlStyle* property, which is responsible for state management and for the rendering of style properties. If you do not propagate changes into *ControlStyle*, the over-ridden style property will not render as expected.

Listing 11-2 contains a page that uses the *Spreadsheet* control.

```
<%@ Page Language="C#" %>
<%@ Register TagPrefix="msp" Namespace="MSPress.ServerControls"
  Assembly="MSPress.ServerControls" %>
<html>
  <body>
    <form runat="server">
      <p>Spreadsheet style table rendered by the Spreadsheet control:
      </p>
      <p>
        <msp:Spreadsheet id="spreadSheet1" runat="server"
          BorderWidth="1" BorderColor="Black" CellPadding="6">
          <asp:TableRow>
            <asp:TableCell Font-Bold="True" Text="Item">
            </asp:TableCell>
            <asp:TableCell Font-Bold="True"
              Text="Expenditure"></asp:TableCell>
            <asp:TableCell Font-Bold="True" Text="Comments">
            </asp:TableCell>
          </asp:TableRow>
          <asp:TableRow>
            <asp:TableCell Text="Books"></asp:TableCell>
            <asp:TableCell Text="$5000.00"></asp:TableCell>
            <asp:TableCell Text="Deductible"></asp:TableCell>
          </asp:TableRow>
          <asp:TableRow>
            <asp:TableCell Text="Furniture"></asp:TableCell>
            <asp:TableCell Text="$10,000.00"></asp:TableCell>
            <asp:TableCell Text="Deductible"></asp:TableCell>
          </asp:TableRow>
          <asp:TableRow>
            <asp:TableCell Text="Vacation"></asp:TableCell>
            <asp:TableCell Text="$25,000.00"></asp:TableCell>
            <asp:TableCell Text="Deductible? Mental Health">
            </asp:TableCell>
          </asp:TableRow>
        </msp:Spreadsheet>
      </p>
    </form>
  </body>
</html>
```

Listing 11-2   SpreadsheetTest.aspx

Implementing a Custom Typed Style— The *MyPanelStyle* Example

We'll now demonstrate how to implement and use a custom typed style by creating a *MyPanel* control and its associated typed style, *MyPanelStyle*. The *MyPanel* control is similar to the ASP.NET *Panel* control, which allows a page developer to add controls to its *Controls* collection by nesting them within the control's tags. In a visual designer, you can do this by dragging controls onto the *Panel*'s design surface.

The ASP.NET *Panel* control does not have an associated *PanelStyle* and does not follow the recommended pattern of encapsulating style-related behavior in a typed style. Instead, *Panel* defines its style properties just as it defines other nonstyle properties. We'll demonstrate the technique that you should follow to add style properties by implementing a *MyPanelStyle* typed style and delegating the style functionality of the *MyPanel* control to it. In terms of functionality, *MyPanel* is identical to the *Panel* control and exposes the three style properties in the following list. Note that these properties are actually properties of the *MyPanelStyle* typed style.

- **BackImageUrl**   Specifies the URL for a background image.

- **HorizontalAlign**   Specifies the horizontal alignment for the added controls.

- **Wrap**   Specifies whether to enable wrapping for the added content.

We'll first show how the *MyPanel* control uses the *MyPanelStyle* typed style, and then we'll describe *MyPanelStyle*. Listing 11-3 shows the code for the *MyPanel* control.

```
using System;
using System.ComponentModel;
using System.ComponentModel.Design;
using System.Drawing.Design;
using System.Web.UI;
using System.Web.UI.Design;
using System.Web.UI.WebControls;

namespace MSPress.ServerControls {
```

Listing 11-3   MyPanel.cs   *(continued)*

Listing 11-3 *(continued)*

```
[
Designer(typeof(MSPress.ServerControls.Design.MyPanelDesigner)
ParseChildren(false),
PersistChildren(true)
]
public class MyPanel : WebControl {

    public MyPanel() : base(HtmlTextWriterTag.Div) {
    }

    [
    Bindable(true),
    Category("Appearance"),
    DefaultValue(""),
    Editor(typeof(ImageUrlEditor), typeof(UITypeEditor)),
    Description("The URL for the background image")
    ]
    public virtual string BackImageUrl {
        get {
            if (ControlStyleCreated) {
                return ((MyPanelStyle)ControlStyle).BackImageUrl;
            }
            return String.Empty;
        }
        set {
            ((MyPanelStyle)ControlStyle).BackImageUrl = value;
        }
    }

    [
    Bindable(true),
    Category("Layout"),
    DefaultValue(HorizontalAlign.NotSet),
    Description("The Horizontal Alignment")
    ]
    public virtual HorizontalAlign HorizontalAlign {
        get {
            if (ControlStyleCreated) {
                return
                    ((MyPanelStyle)ControlStyle).HorizontalAlign;
            }
            return HorizontalAlign.NotSet;
        }
```

```
            set {
                ((MyPanelStyle)ControlStyle).HorizontalAlign = value;
            }
        }


        [
        Bindable(true),
        Category("Layout"),
        DefaultValue(true),
        Description(
            "Specifies whether content wraps within the panel")
        ]
        public virtual bool Wrap {
            get {
                if (ControlStyleCreated) {
                    return ((MyPanelStyle)ControlStyle).Wrap;
                }
                return true;
            }
            set {
                ((MyPanelStyle)ControlStyle).Wrap = value;
            }
        }

        protected override Style CreateControlStyle() {
            return new MyPanelStyle(ViewState);
        }
    }
}
```

The *MyPanel* control overrides the *CreateControlStyle* method to return an instance of the *MyPanelStyle* style. This indirectly causes the returned *MyPanelStyle* instance to be assigned to the *ControlStyle* property. As we described in the "Styles Overview" section, the *ControlStyle* property is read-only and is indirectly set when its accessor invokes the *CreateControlStyle* method. Notice that *CreateControlStyle* passes the *MyPanel* control's *ViewState* into the constructor of *MyPanelStyle*. When you create a new style for your control in *CreateControlStyle*, you must pass your control's *ViewState* into the *Style* constructor so that the style object uses the same *StateBag* as your control. If you are overriding existing style properties, you should not create a new *Style* instance, as we saw in the *Spreadsheet* example in the previous section.

MyPanel also defines new style properties by exposing properties of *MyPanelStyle* as its own top-level properties. As we described in the previous paragraph, the type of the *ControlStyle* property is *MyPanelStyle*.

MyPanel also has a designer that is associated with it via the *DesignerAttribute*. The code for the designer is included with the book's sample files. Designers are explained in Chapter 15, "Design-Time Functionality."

We'll now implement the *MyPanelStyle* class that we used in the *MyPanel* control. These are the key steps in implementing a typed style:

1. Create a class that derives from *System.Web.UI.WebControls.Style*. The object model of the *Style* class is listed in Appendix B.

2. Define properties that your style will offer to a control. Store the properties in your style's *ViewState* dictionary.

3. Override the *CopyFrom* and *MergeWith* methods to copy from or merge the properties you defined with the properties of a given style.

4. Override the *Reset* method to remove the properties you added to *ViewState*.

5. Override the *AddAttributesToRender* method to generate HTML and CSS attributes as part of the rendering process.

Listing 11-4 contains the code for the *MyPanelStyle* typed style.

```
using System;
using System.ComponentModel;
using System.Web.UI;
using System.Web.UI.WebControls;

namespace MSPress.ServerControls {

    public class MyPanelStyle : Style {

        internal const int PROP_BACKIMAGEURL = 1;
        internal const int PROP_HORIZONTALALIGN = 2;
        internal const int PROP_WRAP = 3;

        public MyPanelStyle() {
        }

        public MyPanelStyle(StateBag bag) : base(bag) {
        }
```

Listing 11-4   MyPanelStyle.cs

```
[
Bindable(true),
Category("Appearance"),
DefaultValue(""),
Description("The background image of the Panel"),
NotifyParentProperty(true)
]
public virtual string BackImageUrl {
    get {
        if (IsSet(PROP_BACKIMAGEURL)) {
            return (string)ViewState["BackImageUrl"];
        }
        return String.Empty;
    }
    set {
        ViewState["BackImageUrl"] = value;
    }
}


[
Bindable(true),
Category("Layout"),
DefaultValue(HorizontalAlign.NotSet),
Description("The horizontal alignment of the Panel's contents"),
NotifyParentProperty(true)
]
public virtual HorizontalAlign HorizontalAlign {
    get {
        if (IsSet(PROP_HORIZONTALALIGN)) {
            return
                (HorizontalAlign)ViewState["HorizontalAlign"];
        }
        return HorizontalAlign.NotSet;
    }
    set {
        if (value < HorizontalAlign.NotSet ||
            value > HorizontalAlign.Justify) {
            throw new ArgumentOutOfRangeException("value");
        }
        ViewState["HorizontalAlign"] = value;
    }
}

protected new internal bool IsEmpty {
```

(continued)

Listing 11-4   *(continued)*

```
        get {
            return base.IsEmpty &&
                !IsSet(PROP_BACKIMAGEURL) &&
                !IsSet(PROP_HORIZONTALALIGN) &&
                !IsSet(PROP_WRAP);
        }
    }


    [
    Bindable(true),
    Category("Layout"),
    DefaultValue(true),
    Description("Whether the Panel's contents can wrap around"),
    NotifyParentProperty(true)
    ]
    public virtual bool Wrap {
        get {
            if (IsSet(PROP_WRAP)) {
                return (bool)ViewState["Wrap"];
            }
            return true;
        }
        set {
            ViewState["Wrap"] = value;
        }
    }

    public override void AddAttributesToRender(
        HtmlTextWriter writer, WebControl owner) {
        base.AddAttributesToRender(writer, owner);

        if (IsSet(PROP_BACKIMAGEURL)) {
            string s = BackImageUrl;
            if (s.Length > 0) {
                if (owner != null) {
                    s = owner.ResolveUrl(s);
                }
                writer.AddStyleAttribute(
                    HtmlTextWriterStyle.BackgroundImage,
                    "url(" + s + ")");
            }
        }
```

```
        if (IsSet(PROP_HORIZONTALALIGN)) {
            HorizontalAlign hAlign = HorizontalAlign;
            if (hAlign != HorizontalAlign.NotSet) {
                TypeConverter hac =
                    TypeDescriptor.GetConverter(
                        typeof(HorizontalAlign));
                writer.AddAttribute(HtmlTextWriterAttribute.Align,
                    hac.ConvertToInvariantString(hAlign));
            }
        }

        if (IsSet(PROP_WRAP)) {
            bool wrap = Wrap;
            if (!Wrap)
                writer.AddAttribute(HtmlTextWriterAttribute.Nowrap,
                    "nowrap");
        }
    }

    public override void CopyFrom(Style s) {
        if (s != null) {
            base.CopyFrom(s);

            if (s is MyPanelStyle) {
                MyPanelStyle mps = (MyPanelStyle)s;

                if (!mps.IsEmpty) {
                    if (mps.IsSet(PROP_BACKIMAGEURL))
                        this.BackImageUrl = mps.BackImageUrl;
                    if (mps.IsSet(PROP_HORIZONTALALIGN))
                        this.HorizontalAlign = mps.HorizontalAlign;
                    if (mps.IsSet(PROP_WRAP))
                        this.Wrap = mps.Wrap;
                }
            }
        }
    }

    internal bool IsSet(int propNumber) {
        string key = null;
        switch (propNumber) {
            case PROP_BACKIMAGEURL:
                key = "BackImageUrl";
                break;
            case PROP_HORIZONTALALIGN:
                key = "HorizontalAlign";
                break;
```

Listing 11-4 *(continued)*

```
            case PROP_WRAP:
                key = "Wrap";
                break;
        }              if (key != null) {
            return ViewState[key] != null;
        }
        return false;
    }

    public override void MergeWith(Style s) {
        if (s != null) {
            if (IsEmpty) {
                // Merging with an empty style is equivalent to copying,
                // which is more efficient.
                CopyFrom(s);
                return;
            }

            base.MergeWith(s);

            if (s is MyPanelStyle) {
                MyPanelStyle mps = (MyPanelStyle)s;

                if (!mps.IsEmpty) {
                    if (mps.IsSet(PROP_BACKIMAGEURL) &&
                        !this.IsSet(PROP_BACKIMAGEURL))
                        this.BackImageUrl = mps.BackImageUrl;
                    if (mps.IsSet(PROP_HORIZONTALALIGN) &&
                        !this.IsSet(PROP_HORIZONTALALIGN))
                        this.HorizontalAlign = mps.HorizontalAlign;
                    if (mps.IsSet(PROP_WRAP) &&
                        !this.IsSet(PROP_WRAP))
                        this.Wrap = mps.Wrap;
                }
            }
        }
    }

    public override void Reset() {
        base.Reset();
        if (IsEmpty) {
            return;
        }              if (IsSet(PROP_BACKIMAGEURL))
            ViewState.Remove("BackImageUrl");
        if (IsSet(PROP_HORIZONTALALIGN))
            ViewState.Remove("HorizontalAlign");
```

```
        if (IsSet(PROP_WRAP))
            ViewState.Remove("Wrap");
    }
  }
}
```

The *MyPanelStyle* typed style performs the following tasks:

■ Derives from the *Style* class and defines three new properties, *BackImageUrl*, *HorizontalAlign*, and *Wrap*. These properties support the corresponding style properties in *MyPanel*. Notice that these properties are implemented by using the *ViewState* dictionary of the *Style* class.

■ Overrides the *AddAttributesToRender* method to render its properties as HTML attributes and CSS attributes. *MyPanelStyle* calls the method of the base class and then performs its own logic. The implementation of this method is almost identical to the implementation of the *AddAttributesToRender* method in a Web control, which we described in Chapter 8. However, there is a difference between the signature of this method in a typed style and the signature of this method in a Web control. The *AddAttributesToRender* method of *Style* takes two arguments, while the corresponding method of *Web-Control* takes one argument. The second argument passed into the *AddAttributesToRender* method in *Style* is non-null when the style is used as the *ControlStyle* of a Web control; this second argument represents the control that owns the *Style* object.

■ Overrides the *CopyFrom* and *MergeWith* methods to copy or merge a given *MyPanelStyle* with itself. The *CopyFrom* method replaces existing property values with those properties that have been set in the *Style* instance that is passed into the method. The *MergeWith* method preserves the values of properties that are already set and copies other properties that are set in the *Style* instance that is passed into the method. Both of these methods invoke the corresponding methods of the base class and then perform their own logic.

■ Overrides the *Reset* method to remove the properties it added to *ViewState*. This method invokes the corresponding method of the base class and then performs its own logic.

Summary

In this chapter, we looked at how *WebControl* implements styles and examined the *Style* class, which encapsulates style functionality. In addition, we showed how to override style properties and how to extend the style functionality of *WebControl* by implementing and using custom typed styles.

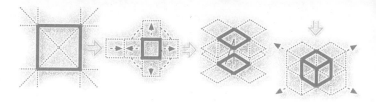

12

Composite Controls

Composite controls contain other controls and reuse their functionality via class composition. A composite control delegates responsibility to its child controls while defining its own object model, which is independent of the controls it contains. Composite controls are equivalent to user controls, which we described in Chapter 4, "User Controls: From Page to Control." However, user controls are deployed as text files, while composite controls are precompiled and deployed in binary assembly files, as other custom controls are. In Chapter 6, "Custom Controls vs. User Controls," we provided guidelines to help you choose between user controls and custom controls.

In this chapter, we will look at the basic implementation pattern of composite controls as well as related features such as event bubbling and styles. We will also examine *templated controls,* an important subset of composite controls. A templated control allows page developers to specify some or all of its user interface via declarative page syntax contained in one or more templates. Templated controls therefore have dynamic content and layout and offer significant customization capabilities to page developers.

Composite Controls—Key Concepts

A composite control contains two or more existing controls and reuses the implementation provided by the child controls to enable rendering, postback handling, and other functionality. Composition simplifies control development because it allows you to delegate many tasks to child controls. For example, when your control contains the standard *TextBox* control that can process postback data, you do not have to implement the *IPostBackDataHandler* interface. In a similar vein, you could use the existing *Button* control to capture form postback instead of implementing the *IPostBackEventHandler* interface.

You can derive your composite control from the *Control* class or from the *WebControl* class. There are two key tasks that you must perform when implementing a composite control:

■ Override the *CreateChildControls* method to instantiate child controls, initialize them, and add them to the control tree. Do not perform this logic in the constructor or in the *OnInit* method.

■ Implement the *System.Web.UI.INamingContainer* interface, which creates a new naming scope under your control.

Let's examine the reasons for these implementation details. You must create your child controls in the *CreateChildControls* method—instead of creating them in a specific phase such as Instantiate or Initialize—so that the children can be created on demand when needed in your control's life cycle. This is especially important when you create a composite control whose child controls handle postback data.

To ensure that child controls are created before code tries to access them, the *Control* class defines the protected *EnsureChildControls* method. This method checks whether the child controls have been created and invokes the *CreateChildControls* method to create child controls only if they have not been created. Any code in your control's implementation that needs to access a child control must first invoke the *EnsureChildControls* method. For example, the default implementation of the *FindControl* method, which the page uses to locate a child control, first invokes the *EnsureChildControls* method. Note that if child controls have not been created in your control's life cycle prior to the PreRender phase, they are created on demand at this point. This is because the default implementation of the *PreRender* method invokes the *EnsureChildControls* method of all controls whose *Visible* property is *true*.

Let's now examine why you must implement the *INamingContainer* interface. *INamingContainer* is a marker interface that does not have any methods but causes the page to create a new naming scope under your control. When you implement this interface, any child controls that your control contains are guaranteed to have identifiers (represented by the *UniqueID* property) that are truly unique on the page. For example, if a page developer placed two instances of your composite control on a page, the child controls within the first instance would have different unique identifiers from those within the second instance, even though both sets of child controls have the same *ID* property values. This is especially important if the page needs to find a control to route postback data or route a postback event to it. We will describe the *UniqueID* property in more detail at the end of the next section.

Composition vs. Rendering

Composition simplifies control development by allowing you to reuse the functionality of existing controls. However, composition does carry a performance overhead. Composite controls incur the additional cost of child control instantiation. They also increase the size of the control tree and the size of the view state. If performance is of paramount importance to you, you can develop a fully *rendered* control that directly renders HTML to generate the user interface and implements its own postback functionality.

The sample files for this chapter contain examples that demonstrate the differences between the implementation of composite controls and that of rendered controls. The *CompositeLogin* example that we will implement in the next section delegates its functionality to child controls. The *RenderedLogin* control in the sample files is similar in functionality to *CompositeLogin* but does not contain child controls. The two controls offer nearly equivalent functionality; however, *CompositeLogin* also provides validation. *RenderedLogin* does not offer validation because it is considerably more complex to implement validation without using child validator controls.

RenderedLogin is similar to the *Login* control we implemented in Chapter 9, "Control Life Cycle, Events, and Postback." Because *Login* has properties that demonstrate concepts extraneous to composition, we have provided *RenderedLogin* as a cleaner parallel to *CompositeLogin*.

Implementing a Composite Control—The *CompositeLogin* Example

We'll now implement a composite control (*CompositeLogin*) that generates a UI that enables a user to enter a name and a password to log on to a Web site. *CompositeLogin* is similar in functionality to the *Login* control we implemented in Chapter 9. The *Login* control rendered HTML to generate the UI, implemented *IPostBackDataHandler* to process postback data, and implemented *IPostBackEventHandler* to raise events. *CompositeLogin* implements its functionality by delegating to its child controls—a pair of *TextBox* controls that correspond to the name and password fields, and a *Button* control to submit the form. *CompositeLogin* also contains two *RequiredFieldValidator* controls that are associated with the name and password fields.

Figure 12-1 shows the UI rendered by the *CompositeLogin* control. The asterisks next to the empty text boxes and the tool tip are rendered by the *RequiredFieldValidator* controls associated with the name and password fields. The page, shown later in this section, also has a *ValidationSummary* control, which renders a summary of the error messages at the bottom of the page.

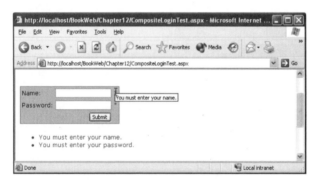

Figure 12-1 The CompositeLoginTest.aspx page viewed in a browser. The page illustrates the UI generated by the *CompositeLogin* control.

Listing 12-1 contains the code for the *CompositeLogin* control. *CompositeLogin* exposes properties of its child controls as top-level properties and bubbles the *Command* event of its *Button* control as a top-level event.

```
using System;
using System.ComponentModel;
using System.ComponentModel.Design;
using System.Web.UI;
using System.Web.UI.WebControls;
```

Listing 12-1 CompositeLogin.cs

```
namespace MSPress.ServerControls {

    [
    DefaultEvent("Logon"),
    DefaultProperty("Name"),
    Designer(typeof(
        MSPress.ServerControls.Design.CompositeControlDesigner))
    ]
    public class CompositeLogin : WebControl, INamingContainer {

        private Button _button;
        private TextBox _nameTextBox;
        private Label _nameLabel;
        private TextBox _passwordTextBox;
        private Label _passwordLabel;
        private RequiredFieldValidator _nameValidator;
        private RequiredFieldValidator _passwordValidator;

        private static readonly object EventLogon = new object();

        #region Overriden properties
        public override ControlCollection Controls {
            get {
                EnsureChildControls();
                return base.Controls;
            }
        }
        #endregion Overriden properties

        #region Properties delegated to child controls
        [
        Bindable(true),
        Category("Appearance"),
        DefaultValue(""),
        Description("The text to display on the Button")
        ]
        public string ButtonText {
            get {
                EnsureChildControls();
                return _button.Text;
            }
            set {
                EnsureChildControls();
                _button.Text = value;
            }
        }
```

(continued)

Listing 12-1   *(continued)*

```
[
Bindable(true),
Category("Default"),
DefaultValue(""),
Description("The user name")
]
public string Name {
    get {
        EnsureChildControls();
        return _nameTextBox.Text;
    }
    set {
        EnsureChildControls();
        _nameTextBox.Text = value;
    }
}


[
Bindable(true),
Category("Appearance"),
DefaultValue(""),
Description(
    "Error message of the validator used for the Name")
]
public string NameErrorMessage {
    get {
        EnsureChildControls();
        return _nameValidator.ErrorMessage;
    }
    set {
        EnsureChildControls();
        _nameValidator.ErrorMessage = value;
        _nameValidator.ToolTip = value;
    }
}


[
Bindable(true),
Category("Apperance"),
DefaultValue(""),
Description("The text for the name Label")
]
public string NameLabel {
    get {
        EnsureChildControls();
        return _nameLabel.Text;
    }
```

```
        set {
            EnsureChildControls();
            _nameLabel.Text = value;

        }
    }


    [
    Browsable(false),
    DesignerSerializationVisibility(
        DesignerSerializationVisibility.Hidden)
    ]
    public string Password {
        get {
            EnsureChildControls();
            return _passwordTextBox.Text;
        }
    }


    [
    Bindable(true),
    Category("Appearance"),
    DefaultValue(""),
    Description(
        "Error message of the validator used for the Password")
    ]
    public string PasswordErrorMessage {
        get {
            EnsureChildControls();
            return _passwordValidator.ErrorMessage;
        }
        set {
            EnsureChildControls();
            _passwordValidator.ErrorMessage = value;
            _passwordValidator.ToolTip = value;
        }
    }


    [
    Bindable(true),
    Category("Appearance"),
    DefaultValue(""),
    Description("The text for the password Label")
    ]
```

(continued)

Listing 12-1   *(continued)*

```
public string PasswordLabel {
    get {
        EnsureChildControls();
        return _passwordLabel.Text;
    }
    set {
        EnsureChildControls();
        _passwordLabel.Text = value;

    }
}
#endregion Properties delegated to child controls

#region Events
[
Category("Action"),
Description("Raised when the user clicks the login button")
]
public event EventHandler Logon {
    add {
        Events.AddHandler(EventLogon, value);
    }
    remove {
        Events.RemoveHandler(EventLogon, value);
    }
}

protected virtual void OnLogon(EventArgs e) {
    EventHandler logonHandler =
        (EventHandler)Events[EventLogon];
    if (logonHandler != null) {
        logonHandler(this, e);
    }
}
#endregion

#region Event bubbling
// The use of event bubbling in this scenario is somewhat contrived;
// we have implemented it mainly for demonstration purposes.
// In this case you could instead
// raise the Logon event from an event handler wired to the
// Click event or to the Command event of the Button control.
protected override
    bool OnBubbleEvent(object source, EventArgs e) {
    bool handled = false;
```

```
        if (e is CommandEventArgs) {
            CommandEventArgs ce = (CommandEventArgs)e;
            if (ce.CommandName == "Logon") {
                OnLogon(EventArgs.Empty);
                handled = true;
            }
        }
    }
    return handled;
}
#endregion Event bubbling

#region Overriden methods
protected override void CreateChildControls() {
    Controls.Clear();

    _nameLabel = new Label();

    _nameTextBox = new TextBox();
    _nameTextBox.ID = "nameTextBox";

    _nameValidator = new RequiredFieldValidator();
    _nameValidator.ID = "validator1";
    _nameValidator.ControlToValidate = _nameTextBox.ID;
    _nameValidator.Text = "*";
    _nameValidator.Display = ValidatorDisplay.Static;

    _passwordLabel = new Label();

    _passwordTextBox = new TextBox();
    _passwordTextBox.TextMode = TextBoxMode.Password;
    _passwordTextBox.ID = "passwordTextBox";

    _passwordValidator = new RequiredFieldValidator();
    _passwordValidator.ID = "validator2";
    _passwordValidator.ControlToValidate = _passwordTextBox.ID;
    _passwordValidator.Text = "*";
    _passwordValidator.Display = ValidatorDisplay.Static;

    _button = new Button();
    _button.ID = "button1";
    _button.CommandName = "Logon";

    this.Controls.Add(_nameLabel);
    this.Controls.Add(_nameTextBox);
    this.Controls.Add(_nameValidator);
    this.Controls.Add(_passwordLabel);
```

(continued)

Listing 12-1   *(continued)*

```
        this.Controls.Add(_passwordTextBox);
        this.Controls.Add(_passwordValidator);
        this.Controls.Add(_button);
}

protected override void Render(HtmlTextWriter writer) {
    AddAttributesToRender(writer);

    writer.AddAttribute(HtmlTextWriterAttribute.Cellpadding,
        "1", false);
    writer.RenderBeginTag(HtmlTextWriterTag.Table);

    writer.RenderBeginTag(HtmlTextWriterTag.Tr);
    writer.RenderBeginTag(HtmlTextWriterTag.Td);
    _nameLabel.RenderControl(writer);
    writer.RenderEndTag();  // Td
    writer.RenderBeginTag(HtmlTextWriterTag.Td);
    _nameTextBox.RenderControl(writer);
    writer.RenderEndTag();  // Td
    writer.RenderBeginTag(HtmlTextWriterTag.Td);
    _nameValidator.RenderControl(writer);
    writer.RenderEndTag();  // Td
    writer.RenderEndTag();  // Tr

    writer.RenderBeginTag(HtmlTextWriterTag.Tr);
    writer.RenderBeginTag(HtmlTextWriterTag.Td);
    _passwordLabel.RenderControl(writer);
    writer.RenderEndTag();  // Td
    writer.RenderBeginTag(HtmlTextWriterTag.Td);
    _passwordTextBox.RenderControl(writer);
    writer.RenderEndTag();  // Td
    writer.RenderBeginTag(HtmlTextWriterTag.Td);
    _passwordValidator.RenderControl(writer);
    writer.RenderEndTag();  // Td
    writer.RenderEndTag();  // Tr

    writer.RenderBeginTag(HtmlTextWriterTag.Tr);
    writer.AddAttribute(HtmlTextWriterAttribute.Colspan, "2");
    writer.AddAttribute(HtmlTextWriterAttribute.Align,
        "right");
    writer.RenderBeginTag(HtmlTextWriterTag.Td);
    _button.RenderControl(writer);
    writer.RenderEndTag();  // Td
    writer.RenderBeginTag(HtmlTextWriterTag.Td);
    writer.Write(" ");
    writer.RenderEndTag();  // Td
    writer.RenderEndTag();  // Tr
```

```
            writer.RenderEndTag();  // Table
        }
        #endregion Overriden methods
    }
}
```

CompositeLogin performs the following tasks, which are common to composite controls:

■ Implements *INamingContainer* to provide a new naming scope for its child controls. This causes the page to assign unique identifiers to the child controls. On postback, the page uses the unique identifiers to find the child controls and route form data and the postback event to the children. In addition, because the parent control provides a new naming scope, each validator control can find the sibling it is associated with by simply using the *ID* property (instead of the *UniqueID* property) of the sibling.

■ Derives from *WebControl* so that it inherits the common set of style properties, which allows a page developer to customize the visual appearance of the control.

■ Overrides the accessor of the *Controls* property to invoke the *EnsureChildControls* method before returning the *Controls* collection of the base class. This ensures that child controls are created before any code tries to access them.

■ Exposes properties that are implemented by delegating to the properties of child controls. *CompositeLogin* first invokes *EnsureChildControls* in the property accessors of the delegated properties to make sure that child controls are created before it accesses them.

■ Instantiates, initializes, and adds child controls to its *Controls* collection by overriding the *CreateChildControls* method. If you want to attach event handlers to the events of child controls, you should do so in *CreateChildControls*. For optimization, *CompositeLogin* initializes each child control (sets properties) before adding the control to the *Controls* collection. Note that if the parent control is tracking changes to property values, the child control starts tracking changes to its property values as soon as it is added to the control tree, as we explained in Chapter 9. When you perform initialization before adding a control to the control tree, any property values you assign are considered initial values, which are not persisted into view state.

- Clears its *Controls* collection before performing any other logic in *CreateChildControls*. This action ensures that multiple copies of child controls are not added to the *Controls* collection when your control—or a control that derives from your control—invokes the protected *CreateChildControls* method.

- Handles the *Command* event that is bubbled by its contained *Button* control and exposes it as a top-level *Logon* event. We'll explain the event bubbling architecture in the "Event Bubbling" section later in this chapter.

- Renders its child controls within a table by rendering an outer *<table>* tag and HTML for creating rows and cells (*<tr>* and *<td>* tags). *CompositeLogin* invokes the *AddAttributesToRender* method before rendering the *<table>* tag so that the top-level style properties are automatically rendered as attributes on the *<table>* tag. *Composite-Login* does not invoke the *RenderContents* method because it does not want to utilize the default rendering of the control tree. Instead, the control renders its child controls by invoking *RenderControl* on each child control within table cells (*<td>* tags). In general, as shown in Listing 12-1, you should directly render HTML for formatting and layout in the Render phase, instead of creating and adding *Literal-Control* instances that contain the required formatting markup in *CreateChildControls*. When you create *LiteralControls*, such as *new LiteralControl("<td>")* for formatting, you incur the additional expense of control creation and increase the size of the control tree. Furthermore, you violate the semantics of the control tree when you add to it controls that represent static text and are used only for formatting and layout.

- Exposes properties (instead of using hard-coded strings in its code) to enable the page developer to provide text for the contained name and password labels and the login button. A reusable control should not render hard-coded strings or fixed strings in the user interface.

Base Class for Composite Controls

You might find it useful to define a *CompositeControl* base class from which to derive all your composite controls. The base class should implement *INamingContainer* and override the *Controls* collection:

```
using System;
using System.ComponentModel;
using System.ComponentModel.Design;
using System.Web.UI;
using System.Web.UI.WebControls;

[
Designer(typeof(CompositeControlDesigner))
]
public abstract class CompositeControl : WebControl, INamingContainer {
    public override ControlCollection Controls {
        get {
            EnsureChildControls();
            return base.Controls;
        }
    }
}
```

In addition, you should define a designer for composite controls and associate it with your composite controls via the *DesignerAttribute*. The code for the designer is included in the samples files and described in Chapter 15, "Design-Time Functionality."

Ideally, these base classes should be included in the ASP.NET Framework to serve as a guide to composite control implementers. However, they are not provided in the present version. They might be available in a future version of the .NET Framework as part of the class library.

Listing 12-2 contains the CompositeLoginTest.aspx page that uses the *CompositeLogin* control. You saw the page viewed in a browser in Figure 12-1.

```
<%@ Page Language="C#" %>
<%@ Register TagPrefix="msp" Namespace="MSPress.ServerControls"
  Assembly="MSPress.ServerControls" %>
```

Listing 12-2   CompositeLoginTest.aspx   *(continued)*

Listing 12-2   *(continued)*

```
<html>
  <head>
    <script runat="server">
    void compositeLogin1_Logon(object sender, EventArgs e)
    {
        if (AuthenticateUser()) {
            compositeLogin1.Visible = false;
            label1.Text = "Hello, " + compositeLogin1.Name +
                ". You are logged in.";
        }
        else {
            label1.Text = "Login failed." +
                "Enter your user name and password.";
        }
    }

    bool AuthenticateUser() {
        // Perform logic to authenticate user. We'll
        // simply return true for this demo.
        return true;
    }
    </script>
  </head>
  <body>
    <form runat="server">
      <msp:CompositeLogin id="compositeLogin1" runat="server"
        OnLogon="compositeLogin1_Logon" ButtonText="Submit"
        NameLabel="Name: " PasswordLabel="Password: "
        BackColor="Silver" BorderColor="Gray" BorderWidth="1px"
        NameErrorMessage="You must enter your name."
        PasswordErrorMessage="You must enter your password."/>
      <br>
      <asp:Label id="label1" runat="server" />
      <asp:ValidationSummary runat="server" id="ValidationSummary1" />
    </form>
  </body>
</html>
```

Listing 12-3 shows the HTML rendered by the *CompositeLogin* control in the CompositeLoginTest.aspx page. The HTML rendered by the control includes the tags used to create the HTML table layout. The HTML within the *<td>* tags is rendered by the child controls that *CompositeLogin* contains.

```
<table id="compositeLogin1" cellpadding="1"
  style="background-color:Silver;border-color:Gray;border-width:1px;
order-style:solid;">
  <tr>
    <td><span>Name: </span></td>
    <td><input name="compositeLogin1:nameTextBox" type="text"
      id="compositeLogin1_nameTextBox" /></td>
    <td><span id="compositeLogin1_validator1"
      title="You must enter your name."
      controltovalidate="compositeLogin1_nameTextBox"
      errormessage="You must enter your name."
      evaluationfunction="RequiredFieldValidatorEvaluateIsValid"
      initialvalue="" style="color:Red;visibility:hidden;">*</span>
    </td>
  </tr>
  <tr>
    <td><span>Password: </span></td>
    <td><input name="compositeLogin1:passwordTextBox" type="password"
      id="compositeLogin1_passwordTextBox" /></td>
    <td><span id="compositeLogin1_validator2"
      title="You must enter your password."
      controltovalidate="compositeLogin1_passwordTextBox"
      errormessage="You must enter your password."
      evaluationfunction="RequiredFieldValidatorEvaluateIsValid"
      initialvalue="" style="color:Red;visibility:hidden;">*</span>
    </td>
  </tr>
  <tr>
    <td colspan="2" align="right"><input type="submit"
      name="compositeLogin1:button1" value="Submit"
      onclick="if (typeof(Page_ClientValidate) == 'function')
Page_ClientValidate(); "
      language="javascript" id="compositeLogin1_button1" /></td>
    <td> 
    </td>
  </tr>
</table>
```

Listing 12-3   HTML rendered by the *CompositeLogin* control within the
                  CompositeLoginTest.aspx page

The *name* and *id* attributes in the HTML tag rendered by a control correspond to the *UniqueID* and *ClientID* property values assigned to the control by
the page. When a composite control implements *INamingContainer*, the page
generates *UniqueID*s for each child control by concatenating the *UniqueID* of
the *NamingContainer* to the *ID* of the child by using the colon character as a

separator. For example, the value of the *UniqueID* property of the first *TextBox* instance is *"compositeLogin1:nameTextBox"*. The *NamingContainer* provides a new naming scope so that the *UniqueID* of the child control does not conflict with that of another control on the page. The *UniqueID* thus represents a hierarchically qualified unique identifier that specifies the exact location of a control within the control tree.

The *ClientID* is also unique on the page and is the client script–friendly version of the *UniqueID*. For example, the value of the *ClientID* property of the first *TextBox* instance in CompositeLoginTest.aspx is *"compositeLogin1_nameTextBox"*. The *ClientID* uses the underscore as the separator character because the colon character is not allowed in variable names that are accessed in JavaScript. To ensure that the *ClientID* does not contain the colon character, the page framework does not allow the colon as a valid character in the string assigned to the *ID* property of a control. If you use the colon character in the string that is assigned to the *ID* property of a control, you will find that the page parser returns an error message.

The page framework uses the colon character as the separator character for generating the *UniqueID* because it cannot be used inside a valid *ID* property. This enables the *FindControl* method to use the colon character to recursively split the *UniqueID* string, navigate the control tree, and locate a control.

APIs Related to Composite Controls

As a handy reference, this section will list the various members that the *Control* class exposes for working with child controls. Unless otherwise noted, you do not have to override the implementation provided by the base class:

■ The public *Controls* property of type *ControlCollection* represents the child controls. You can utilize the methods of *ControlCollection*, such as *Add*, *Remove*, and *Clear*, to work with the *Controls* collection. You must override the accessor of the *Controls* property, as we showed in the *CompositeLogin* control in the previous section, to ensure that child controls are created before any code tries to access them.

■ The public *NamingContainer* property returns the first control upward in the control hierarchy that implements the *INamingContainer* interface. A composite control that implements *INamingContainer* is the *naming container* of its child controls.

- The protected *CreateChildControls* method is where you perform the logic related to creating child controls, as we described earlier in this chapter.

- The protected *EnsureChildControls* method checks the *ChildControlsCreated* property. If the value of that property is *false*, *EnsureChildControls* invokes the *CreateChildControls* method. You should always invoke *EnsureChildControls* before accessing a child control to ensure that child controls have been created.

- The public *FindControl* method takes in a string that represents the *ID* or the *UniqueID* of a control and recursively searches the control tree to locate the control. *FindControl* invokes *EnsureChildControls* before it starts searching. The automatically generated *UniqueID* of a control provides the exact location of a control in the control tree, as we showed at the end of the previous section. If the search is successful, *FindControl* returns the control; otherwise, the method returns null.

- The protected *ChildControlsCreated* property indicates whether the *CreateChildControls* method was invoked. *EnsureChildControls* checks this property before invoking the *CreateChildControls* method.

- The public *HasControls* method returns a *Boolean* value that indicates whether the *Controls* collection contains controls.

- The protected *CreateControlCollection* method is invoked by the getter of the *Controls* property when the *Controls* collection is null. The default implementation of *CreateControlCollection* creates and returns an instance of the *ControlCollection* class.

In addition, *Control* provides two members that are used for state management of child controls:

- The protected *HasChildViewState* property indicates whether the control has view state corresponding to child controls.

- The protected *ClearChildViewState* method clears any view state corresponding to child controls. This method is used when a composite control needs to rebuild a new control hierarchy upon postback that does not correspond to the earlier control hierarchy it created.

View State and Child Controls

To implement a composite control, you do not need to know how the view state mechanism works in child controls. However, if you are curious about view state in composite controls, this section will provide a behind-the-scenes look. In Chapter 9, we described the phases in a control's life cycle where it performs state management, and in Chapter 10, "Complex Properties and State Management," we showed how you can implement custom state management. In this section, we will not repeat the background information we provided earlier. Instead, we will focus on how state management is applied to child controls.

The *Control* class has built-in functionality to track, save, and restore the state of its child controls. In the Begin Tracking View State phase, *Control* sequentially invokes the *TrackViewState* method on the controls in its *Controls* collection to start tracking state in the child controls. In addition, if a child control is added to the *Controls* collection after the parent has started tracking state, the child control's *TrackViewState* method is invoked as soon as it is added to the control tree.

In the Save View State phase, *Control* first invokes its *SaveViewState* method. By default, this method invokes *SaveViewState* on its *ViewState* dictionary and saves the returned object as the first part of a control's view state. *Control* next invokes *SaveViewState* on each child control in the control tree. If the state that a child returns is non-null, *Control* saves the index of the child control and the corresponding view state in two *ArrayLists*, which correspond to two additional parts of the view state. The first *ArrayList* holds the indices (in the *Controls* collection) of child controls that have non-null state to serialize, and the second *ArrayList* holds the saved states of those children. Finally, at the end of the Save View State phase, *Control* returns its three-part view state.

In the Load View State phase, *Control* performs the inverse of the operations it performed in the Save View State phase. The state that the page hands to *Control* in the Load View State phase is the same state that the control saved at the end of the previous request. *Control* loads the first part of the saved state by invoking its *LoadViewState* method, which in turn loads the saved state into its *ViewState* dictionary. *Control* then accesses its *Controls* collection to load the remaining state into child controls. The remaining state consists of the *ArrayLists* that represent the indices and saved states of child controls. *Control* uses the indices and the states to load state into each child control that saved its state at the end of the previous request. This completes the state restoration in a control and in its child controls. If child controls have not been created in the Load View State phase, *Control* stores the state of its child controls for later use. *Control* then loads state into the child controls when they are created and added to the control tree. Note that view state tracking starts before the Load View State phase. Therefore, any properties that a control restores by using view state automatically are marked dirty and therefore are resaved in view state during the Save View State phase. On postback, these properties are reloaded during the Load View State phase. The view state mechanism thus perpetuates itself over subsequent requests.

The steps that we just described for each state management phase are recursively executed within the control tree. The view state of a control thus represents the collective view state of the entire control hierarchy under that control.

Notice that *Control* uses the index of a child control in the *Controls* collection to identify the saved view state of a child control. *Control* does not use the type or the *ID* of the child control. This leads to better performance because it reduces the size of the view state. However, this implies that the view state mechanism can work only if the control tree is re-created on postback in exactly the same order in which it was saved at the end of the previous request. You can maintain that order—for the controls you create in *CreateChildControls*—by overriding the *Controls* property. We showed how in the *CompositeLogin* example earlier in the chapter:

```
public override ControlCollection Controls {
    get {
        EnsureChildControls();
        return base.Controls;
    }
}
```

This code causes the child controls that you created in *CreateChildControls* to be added to the control tree before other controls (if any) are added by user code. The child controls you created in *CreateChildControls* are thus re-created on postback in the same order in which they were saved. This allows the page framework to restore their state by using view state.

Event Bubbling

The page framework provides an event bubbling architecture that allows a control to bubble an event up the control hierarchy. A bubbled event can be handled at the location where it is raised or at another, more convenient location higher up in the control tree. A composite control can use this feature to expose events bubbled by its child controls as top-level events. For example, the *DataList* control exposes the *Command* event of a *Button* control contained in its *ItemTemplate* as a top-level *ItemCommand* event. While *command events*

(events whose event data class derives from *CommandEventArgs*) are the only events that are bubbled by the built-in ASP.NET controls, you can implement other events that initiate bubbling, as we will show at the end of this section.

Event bubbling is enabled by the *OnBubbleEvent* and *RaiseBubbleEvent* methods, which are defined in the *Control* class like this:

```
protected virtual bool OnBubbleEvent(object source, EventArgs args) {
    return false;
}

protected void RaiseBubbleEvent(object source, EventArgs args) {
    Control currentTarget = _parent;
    while (currentTarget != null) {
        if (currentTarget.OnBubbleEvent(source, args)) {
            return;
        }
        currentTarget = currentTarget.Parent;
    }
}
```

By default, an event that initiates bubbling is automatically bubbled up through the control hierarchy, as you can see from the definition of the *Raise-BubbleEvent* method and the default implementation of *OnBubbleEvent*.

To handle a bubbled event, you override the *OnBubbleEvent* method. A composite control often contains more than one child control that bubbles an event. An event can also be bubbled from farther down in the control hierarchy (from a child of a child). You can use the arguments passed into the *OnBubbleEvent* method to determine which events to handle. After you have handled the event, return *true* from the *OnBubbleEvent* method if you want to stop the event from bubbling further.

One way to handle a bubbled event is to raise a new event in response to the bubbled event. This enables a page developer to handle a bubbled event as a top-level event of your control. To expose a bubbled event as a top-level event from your control, define an event in your control and raise that event from the *OnBubbleEvent* method. The following fragment shows how the *CompositeLogin* control captures the *Command* event of the *Button* child control and raises its own *Logon* event:

```
protected override bool OnBubbleEvent(object source, EventArgs e) {
    bool handled = false;
    if (e is CommandEventArgs) {
        CommandEventArgs ce = (CommandEventArgs)e;
```

```
        if (ce.CommandName == "Logon") {
            OnLogon(EventArgs.Empty);
            handled = true;
        }
    }
    return handled;
}
```

Although we provided this example as a simple case of event bubbling, it is somewhat contrived because it is not essential to use event bubbling to raise the *Logon* event. You could instead attach an event handler to the *Click* event of the *Button* control and raise the *Logon* event from the handler, as we show in the *StyledCompositeLogin* control in the sample files. Bubbling is more useful when your control does not have a direct reference to the control that raises the event. We will show a more realistic example of event bubbling when we examine the *ListView* control in Chapter 20, "Data-Bound Templated Controls."

Finally, let's take a look at how you can implement an event that initiates bubbling. Define your event as always, but invoke the *RaiseBubbleEvent* method from the *On<EventName>* method that raises your event. The following example shows how the *OnCommand* method that raises the *Command* event of the *Button* control initiates the bubbling of this event:

```
protected virtual void OnCommand(CommandEventArgs e) {
    CommandEventHandler handler =
        (CommandEventHandler)Events[EventCommand];
    if (handler != null) {
        handler(this, e);
    }

    // Bubble the Command event up the control hierarchy.
    RaiseBubbleEvent(this, e);
}
```

Styles in Composite Controls—The *StyledCompositeLogin* Example

To enable the page developer to customize the appearance of child controls, you can expose styles and apply them to child controls. Top-level styles for child controls enable the page developer to easily access and modify the style properties of a child control. When you do not provide styles, the page developer has to use the error-prone technique of indexing the *Controls* collection to access child controls and then modifying their styles.

One way to enable page developers to access the style properties of child controls is to implement multiple delegated properties such as *ButtonForeColor*,

ButtonBackColor, LabelForeColor, and *LabelBackColor* for each child control. However, this approach does not scale as the number of child controls increases because each child Web control defines numerous style properties. The recommended technique, which we will demonstrate in this section, is to implement properties of type *Style* that correspond to each child control (or each type of child control), such as *ButtonStyle* and *LabelStyle*. These top-level style properties are equivalent to the *ControlStyle* property of your control.

We will now implement a *StyledCompositeLogin* control, which is similar to the *CompositeLogin* control we developed earlier in the chapter but exposes styles for child controls. In the designer, the style properties are associated with an expand/collapse UI in the property browser, which allows the page developer to set individual style properties, as Figure 12-2 shows.

Figure 12-2   Styles of *StyledCompositeLogin* displayed in the property browser of Microsoft Visual Studio .NET

Listing 12-4 shows the code for the *StyledCompositeLogin* control that contains the style implementation. The code that is not shown was described in the *CompositeLogin* sample earlier in the chapter and is included in the sample files. *StyledCompositeLogin* exposes the *ButtonStyle, LabelStyle*, and *TextBox-Style* properties; applies these styles to its child controls; and performs state management for the style properties. Because styles are complex properties, they require custom state management, as we described in Chapter 10, "Complex Properties and State Management" and Chapter 11, "Styles in Controls."

```csharp
using System;
using System.ComponentModel;
using System.ComponentModel.Design;
using System.Web.UI;
using System.Web.UI.WebControls;

namespace MSPress.ServerControls {

    [
    DefaultEvent("Logon"),
    DefaultProperty("Name"),
    Designer(typeof(
        MSPress.ServerControls.Design.CompositeControlDesigner))
    ]
    public class StyledCompositeLogin : WebControl, INamingContainer {

        #region Composite control implementation
        :
        #endregion Composite control implementation

        private Style _buttonStyle;
        private Style _labelStyle;
        private Style _textBoxStyle;

        #region Styles for child controls
        [
        Category("Style"),
        Description("The style to be applied to the button"),
        DesignerSerializationVisibility(
            DesignerSerializationVisibility.Content),
        NotifyParentProperty(true),
        PersistenceMode(PersistenceMode.InnerProperty),
        ]
        public virtual Style ButtonStyle {
            get {
                if (_buttonStyle == null) {
                    _buttonStyle = new Style();
                    if (IsTrackingViewState)
                        ((IStateManager)_buttonStyle).TrackViewState();
                }
                return _buttonStyle;
            }
        }
```

Listing 12-4   StyledCompositeLogin.cs   *(continued)*

Listing 12-4 *(continued)*

```
[
Category("Style"),
Description("The style to be applied to a label"),
DesignerSerializationVisibility(
    DesignerSerializationVisibility.Content),
NotifyParentProperty(true),
PersistenceMode(PersistenceMode.InnerProperty),
]
public virtual Style LabelStyle {
    get {
        if (_labelStyle == null) {
            _labelStyle = new Style();
            if (IsTrackingViewState)
                ((IStateManager)_labelStyle).TrackViewState();
        }
        return _labelStyle;
    }
}


[
Category("Style"),
Description("The style to be applied to a text box"),
DesignerSerializationVisibility(
    DesignerSerializationVisibility.Content),
NotifyParentProperty(true),
PersistenceMode(PersistenceMode.InnerProperty),
]
public virtual Style TextBoxStyle {
    get {
        if (_textBoxStyle == null) {
            _textBoxStyle = new Style();
            if (IsTrackingViewState)
                ((IStateManager)_textBoxStyle).TrackViewState();
        }
        return _textBoxStyle;
    }
}
#endregion

protected override void Render(HtmlTextWriter writer) {
    AddAttributesToRender(writer);

    writer.AddAttribute(HtmlTextWriterAttribute.Cellpadding,
        "1", false);
    writer.RenderBeginTag(HtmlTextWriterTag.Table);
```

```
        // Child controls are always created by this time.
        // Therefore, we do not have to check for their
        // existence before accessing them.
        // We apply styles to the child controls in the Render method
        // so that style property changes are not persisted in the
        // view state of the child controls.
        if (_buttonStyle != null) {
            _button.ApplyStyle(ButtonStyle);
        }
        if (_textBoxStyle != null) {
            _nameTextBox.ApplyStyle(TextBoxStyle);
            _passwordTextBox.ApplyStyle(TextBoxStyle);
        }
        if (_labelStyle != null) {
            _nameLabel.ApplyStyle(LabelStyle);
            _passwordLabel.ApplyStyle(LabelStyle);
        }
        // Render child controls within table cells.
        :
        writer.RenderEndTag();  // Table
}


#region Custom state management for styles of child controls
protected override void LoadViewState(object savedState) {
    if (savedState == null) {
        // Always invoke LoadViewState on the base class,
        // even if there is no saved state, because the base
        // class might have implemented some logic that needs
        // to be executed even if there is no state to restore.
        base.LoadViewState(null);
        return;
    }

    if (savedState != null) {
        object[] myState = (object[])savedState;
        if (myState.Length != 4) {
            throw new ArgumentException("Invalid view state");
        }

        base.LoadViewState(myState[0]);
```

(continued)

Listing 12-4 *(continued)*

```
        if (myState[1] != null)
            ((IStateManager)ButtonStyle).LoadViewState(
                myState[1]);                    if (myState[2] != null)
            ((IStateManager)LabelStyle).LoadViewState(
                myState[2]);
        if (myState[3] != null)
            ((IStateManager)TextBoxStyle).LoadViewState(
                myState[3]);
    }
}

protected override object SaveViewState() {
    // Customized state management to save the state of styles.
    object[] myState = new object[4];

    myState[0] = base.SaveViewState();
    myState[1] = (_buttonStyle != null) ?
        ((IStateManager)_buttonStyle).SaveViewState() : null;
    myState[2] = (_labelStyle != null) ?
        ((IStateManager)_labelStyle).SaveViewState() : null;
    myState[3] = (_textBoxStyle != null) ?
        ((IStateManager)_textBoxStyle).SaveViewState() : null;

    for (int i = 0; i < 4; i++) {
        if (myState[i] != null) {
            return myState;
        }
    }

    // If there is no saved state, it is more performant to
    // return null than to return an array of null values.
    return null;
}

protected override void TrackViewState() {
    // Customized state management to track the state
    // of styles.
    base.TrackViewState();

    if (_buttonStyle != null)
        ((IStateManager)_buttonStyle).TrackViewState();
    if (_labelStyle != null)
        ((IStateManager)_labelStyle).TrackViewState();
```

```
        if (_textBoxStyle != null)
            ((IStateManager)_textBoxStyle).TrackViewState();
    }
    #endregion Custom state management for styles of child controls
  }
}
```

The definition of the *ButtonStyle*, *LabelStyle*, and *TextBoxStyle* properties shows that when creating a style that is associated with a child control you must use the parameterless constructor of *Style*. You should not pass the control's *ViewState* into the constructor of the *Style* class because a control shares its *ViewState* only with its own *ControlStyle* property, as we described in Chapter 11. Style properties of child controls use their own internal *ViewState* instance, which is independent of the parent control's *ViewState*.

StyledCompositeLogin applies styles to child controls at the beginning of the Render phase via calls to the *ApplyStyle* method. When styles are applied to child controls in the Render phase, the resulting property changes do not contribute to the view state of the child controls. (Remember, the Render phase occurs after the Save View State phase.) Because the parent composite control performs state management for styles, as we will describe next, you should not duplicate state information for styles in the view state of the child controls.

Styles are complex properties and require custom state management, as we described in Chapter 10. The code at the end of the *StyledCompositeLogin* example shows you how to implement state management for the styles of child controls. *Style* implements *IStateManager* and manages its own state, as we described in Chapter 11. You essentially delegate state management to each style instance that you create. In the *TrackViewState* method of your control, you must invoke *TrackViewState* on each typed style that you define. In *SaveViewState*, you must collect the state from each typed style and return an array of those states in addition to the state that your base class saves. In *LoadViewState*, you should load the first part of the saved state into the base class and the remaining state into the typed styles of the child controls.

Listing 12-5 shows a fragment from the StyledCompositeLoginTest.aspx page that uses the *StyledCompositeLogin* control. Notice that child style properties are persisted as inner (nested) properties.

```
<msp:StyledCompositeLogin id="styledCompositeLogin1" runat="server"
  OnLogon="styledCompositeLogin1_Logon" ButtonText="Submit"
  NameLabel="Name: " PasswordLabel="Password: " BackColor="Silver"
  BorderColor="Gray" BorderWidth="1px"
  NameErrorMessage="You must enter your name."
  PasswordErrorMessage="You must enter your password.">
  <LabelStyle Font-Size="Smaller"
    Font-Names="Verdana" Font-Bold="True"/>
  <ButtonStyle BorderStyle="Outset" Font-Size="Smaller"
    Font-Names="Verdana" BorderWidth="2px"
    ForeColor="Black" BorderColor="Gray"
    BackColor="#E0E0E0" />
  <TextBoxStyle Font-Names="Arial"/>
</msp:StyledCompositeLogin>
```

Listing 12-5 Fragment from the StyledCompositeLoginTest.aspx page
that shows nested style properties

Templated Controls Overview

A templated control enables page developers to specify some or all of the UI it renders via *templates*. Templates are fragments of page syntax that can include server controls along with static HTML and other literal text. Templated controls offer significant customization capabilities and are often referred to as *lookless controls* because they do not render a predetermined user interface.

It is important to understand the difference between styles and templates—two distinct mechanisms that a control offers to page developers for customizing the UI it renders. Styles allow page developers to customize the visual appearance of the rendered UI, while templates allow page developers to customize the content of the rendered UI. For example, styles allow a page developer to modify the *BackColor* or *ForeColor* of text that a control might render. On the other hand, a template allows a page developer to tell the control which element to render: a check box, a table, or some other content.

We will assume that you are familiar with the standard ASP.NET templated controls, such as *Repeater* and *DataList*, and will focus on showing you how to implement a templated control. The main functionality of a templated control is expressed via one or more properties of the *System.Web.UI.ITemplate* type. (We will describe the *ITemplate* interface later in this section.) The user typically specifies a template property by using declarative syntax, as shown in the following example, which specifies the *ItemTemplate* property for the *DataList* control:

```
<asp:DataList runat="server">
  <ItemTemplate>
    <asp:Label id="label" runat="server"
      Text='<%# Container.DataItem %>'/>
      
    <asp:Button button="button" runat="server"
      id="selectButton" CommandName="Select"
      Text="Select" ForeColor="Blue" />
  </ItemTemplate>
</asp:DataList>
```

The page parser parses the text within the template tags and generates a parse tree that represents the content of the template, just as it would when parsing an entire page. The parser uses the parse tree (which consists of *System.Web.UI.ControlBuilder* objects) to create an instance of an *ITemplate* type. The *ITemplate* instance is capable of creating within a given container control the control hierarchy that represents the content of the template. Here is the definition of the *ITemplate* interface:

```
public interface ITemplate {
    // Iteratively populates a provided control
    // with a subhierarchy of child controls
    // represented by the template.
    void InstantiateIn(Control container);
}
```

The parser assigns the *ITemplate* instance to the corresponding *ITemplate* property of your control. Your control can call the *InstantiateIn* method of the template one or more times when building its control hierarchy. Each time its *InstantiateIn* method is invoked, the template creates a copy of the control tree that is represented by the template's content. You can define a template in code by implementing the *ITemplate* interface manually, as we will describe at the end of the next section.

Templates are often used in the context of data-bound controls. This chapter focuses on core concepts related to implementing controls that use templates; Chapter 20 provides a sample of a data-bound control that uses templates.

Implementing a Templated Control—The *ContactInfo* Example

We'll now demonstrate how to implement a templated control by implementing the *ContactInfo* control. *ContactInfo* resembles a Web business card and provides a customizable UI through a template property that can be used to provide contact information. If the page developer does not define a template, the control generates a default UI. Figure 12-3 shows a page that uses the *ContactInfo* control.

Figure 12-3   The ContactInfoTest.aspx page that shows the UI rendered
by using a template in the *ContactInfo* control

Listing 12-6 contains the ContactInfoTest.aspx page that uses the *ContactInfo* control. The first instance of the control contains a template that is specified within the *<ContactTemplate>* tags. The second instance uses the default template that is provided by the control itself.

```
<%@ Page Language="C#" %>
<%@ Register TagPrefix="msp" Namespace="MSPress.ServerControls"
  Assembly="MSPress.ServerControls" %>
<html>
  <head>
    <script runat="server">
      void Page_Load(object sender, EventArgs e) {
          contactInfo1.DataBind();
          contactInfo2.DataBind();
      }
    </script>
  </head>
  <body>
    <form runat="server">
      This UI is created by the ContactInfo control using a
      template specified on the page:
```

Listing 12-6   ContactInfoTest.aspx

```
    <p>
        <msp:ContactInfo id="contactInfo1" runat="server"
        Caption="Net Geek" Info="NetGeek@DevCepts.com"
        BorderWidth="2px" BorderColor="Gainsboro">
        <ContactTemplate>
          <table>
            <tr>
              <td>
                <img src="Logo.gif" align="middle" />
                 
                <asp:Label Text="<%# Container.Caption %>"
                  runat="server" id="Label1"
                  Font-Names="Verdana" Font-Size="12"/>
              </td>
            </tr>
            <tr>
              <td>
                <asp:HyperLink runat="server"
                  Text="<%# Container.Info %>"
                  NavigateUrl='<%# String.Format("mailto:{0}",
Container.Info) %>' />
              </td>
            </tr>
          </table>
        </ContactTemplate>
      </msp:ContactInfo>
    </p>
    This UI is created by the ContactInfo control using its
    default template:
    <p>
        <msp:ContactInfo id="contactInfo2" runat="server"
        Caption="Net Geek" Info="NetGeek@DevCepts.com" />
    </p>
  </form>
  </body>
</html>
```

Listing 12-7 contains the code for the *ContactInfo* control. *ContactInfo* exposes two properties, *Caption* and *Info*, which allow a user to specify a name and associated contact information. The main items of interest in the *Contact-Info* control are the *ContactTemplate* property and the implementation of the *CreateChildControls* method. The designer associated with the *ContactInfo* control via the *DesignerAttribute* metadata attribute is described in Chapter 15.

```
using System;
using System.ComponentModel;
using System.Web.UI;
using System.Web.UI.WebControls;

namespace MSPress.ServerControls {
    [
    DefaultProperty("Caption"),
    Designer(
        typeof(MSPress.ServerControls.Design.ContactInfoDesigner))
    ]
    public class ContactInfo : WebControl, INamingContainer {

        private ITemplate _contactTemplate;
        private ContactPanel _contactPanel;

        [
        Bindable(true),
        Category("Behavior"),
        DefaultValue(""),
        Description("The caption for contact information")
        ]
        public virtual string Caption {
            get {
                String caption = (string)ViewState["Caption"];
                return ((caption == null)? String.Empty : caption);
            }
            set {
                ViewState["Caption"] = value;
            }
        }

        [
        Browsable(false),
        DesignerSerializationVisibility(
            DesignerSerializationVisibility.Hidden)
        ]
        public ContactPanel ContactPanel {
            get {
                EnsureChildControls();
                return _contactPanel;
            }
        }
```

Listing 12-7   ContactInfo.cs

```
[
Browsable(false),
DefaultValue(null),
Description("The template property"),
PersistenceMode(PersistenceMode.InnerProperty),
TemplateContainer(typeof(ContactPanel))
]
public virtual ITemplate ContactTemplate {
    get {
        return _contactTemplate;
    }
    set {
        _contactTemplate = value;
    }
}


public override ControlCollection Controls {
    get {
        EnsureChildControls();
        return base.Controls;
    }
}


[
Bindable(true),
Category("Behavior"),
DefaultValue(""),
Description("The contact information")
]
public virtual string Info {
    get {
        String info = (string)ViewState["Info"];
        return ((info == null)? String.Empty : info);
    }
    set {
        ViewState["Info"] = value;
    }
}
protected override void CreateChildControls () {
    Controls.Clear();

    _contactPanel = new ContactPanel(Caption, Info);
```

(continued)

Listing 12-7   *(continued)*

```
        ITemplate template = ContactTemplate;
        if (template == null) {
            template = new DefaultContactTemplate();
        }

        template.InstantiateIn(_contactPanel);
        Controls.Add(_contactPanel);
    }

    public override void DataBind() {
        CreateChildControls();
        ChildControlsCreated = true;
        base.DataBind();
    }

    #region Implementation of the DefaultContactTemplate class
    :
    #endregion
    }
}
```

As with any other composite control, *ContactInfo* implements the *INamingContainer* interface and overrides the accessor of the *Controls* property to invoke the *EnsureChildControls* method.

The *ContactTemplate* property demonstrates the following main characteristics of an *ITemplate* property. It is

■   Implemented as a read-write property. The template value is held in a member variable.

■   Marked with the *TemplateContainerAttribute* metadata attribute. The argument of this attribute specifies the type of the control, which is the naming container for the child controls in the template. The page parser uses the type specified in the *TemplateContainerAttribute* to infer the exact type of the *Container* identifier when parsing data-binding syntax such as *<%# Container.Info %>* within the template content. When the control instance passed into the *InstantiateIn* method of the *ITemplate* property implements the *INamingContainer* interface, you specify its type in the *TemplateContainerAttribute*. When the control passed into *InstantiateIn* does not implement the *INamingContainer* interface, in the *TemplateContainerAttribute* you specify the type of the first naming container upward in the control hierarchy.

- Marked with the *PersistenceModeAttribute* metadata attribute. The argument passed into this attribute (*PersistenceMode.InnerProperty*) indicates that the designer should persist the template as an inner property within the control's tag in the .aspx file.

- Marked with the *BrowsableAttribute* metadata attribute. The argument passed into this attribute (*false*) indicates that the property browser should not display an *ITemplate* property. *ITemplate* properties are edited on the design surface directly rather than in the property browser.

If your control exposes more than one *ITemplate* property, you might define additional containers for the templates.

In Chapter 15, "Design-Time Functionality," we'll show you how to implement an associated designer for a templated control that enables editing of its *ITemplate* properties. A visual designer allows the page developer to edit the contents of a template property by dragging controls in a WYSIWYG fashion onto the design surface.

ContactInfo demonstrates the following steps, which you must perform in the *CreateChildControls* method:

1. Create an instance of the container class for the template property (*ContactPanel* in our example). The container class typically implements *INamingContainer* and provides a new naming scope for *IDs* of controls defined within the template.

2. Pass the template container instance into the *InstantiateIn* method of the template property (*ContactTemplate* in our example). As we described in the previous section, the *InstantiateIn* method adds the child controls represented by the template to the container instance.

3. Add the template container instance to the *Controls* collection of your control.

In a data-bound templated control, you must repeat these steps to create multiple instances of the template in different container instances, as we will demonstrate in Chapter 20.

ContactInfo has the following additional features:

- Does not implement rendering logic because the default implementation of the *RenderContents* method in the *Control* class renders the child controls.

■   Exposes the template container instance as a (read-only) *Contact-Panel* property. This enables a page developer to invoke *FindControl* on the container and locate child controls in the template. The *ContactPanel* property is analogous to each *RepeaterItem* within the *Items* collection of the *Repeater* or to each *DataListItem* within the *Items* collection of the *DataList* control.

■   Provides a default template by implementing an *ITemplate* type (*DefaultContactTemplate*). If the *ContactTemplate* property has not been set by the page developer, *ContactInfo* uses the *DefaultContactTemplate* type as the default *ITemplate* implementation. We'll describe the *DefaultContactTemplate* class later in this section.

Because *ContactInfo* derives from *WebControl*, it does not need the *ParseChildren(true)* metadata attribute; this attribute is already applied to the *WebControl* class. However, if you implement a templated control that derives from *Control*, you must apply the *ParseChildren(true)* metadata attribute to tell the parser to interpret nested content as properties rather than as child controls. We will describe control parsing in more detail in the next section. You must also apply the related design-time *PersistChildren(false)* attribute when your templated control derives from *Control*.

Listing 12-8 shows the code for the *ContactPanel* class that acts as the container for the *ContactTemplate* property. The *ToolboxItem(false)* metadata attribute applied to *ContactPanel* is a design-time attribute that tells the designer not to display this control in the toolbox. When a page developer customizes the toolbox to add components from an assembly, by default the designer lists every class in that assembly that derives from *Component*. We do not want to display *ContactPanel* in the toolbox because it is a helper control used internally by the *ContactInfo* control.

```
using System;
using System.ComponentModel;
using System.Web.UI;
using System.Web.UI.WebControls;


namespace MSPress.ServerControls {

    [ToolboxItem(false)]
    public class ContactPanel : Panel, INamingContainer {
        private string _caption;
        private string _info;
```

Listing 12-8   ContactPanel.cs

```
        internal ContactPanel(string caption, string info) {
            _caption = caption;
            _info = info;
        }

        public string Caption {
            get {
                return _caption;
            }
        }
        public string Info {
            get {
                return _info;
            }
        }
    }
}
```

The template container must derive from *Control*; you can derive from any control that will serve as an appropriate container. For example, the *RepeaterItem* in the *Repeater* control derives from *Control*, and the *DataListItem* in the *DataList* control derives from *WebControl*. For variety, we derive the template container from the *Panel* class. While we have not defined a style for the container, you can create a style for the template container and expose it as a top-level style from your parent control, that is, the control that exposes template properties.

If you repeatedly instantiate the template in your control, your template container should implement the *INamingContainer* interface so that the child controls represented by the template are created within a new naming scope. In our example, *ContactPanel* does not need to implement *INamingContainer* because it is not repeatedly instantiated. However, we have implemented this interface as a reminder that you must implement it in the more common case of a templated data-bound control.

If you want to support data binding within the template, your template container should expose one or more properties that represent data to bind to. For example, in the *Repeater* control, the *RepeaterItem* exposes a *DataItem* property that the page developer binds to the property of a control specified within the template. To illustrate this feature, we have exposed the *Caption* and *Info* properties from the *ContactPanel* template container, which allow the template content to contain data-binding expressions such as *Container.Caption* and *Container.Info*.

Listing 12-9 contains the code for the *DefaultContactTemplate* class, which serves as the default template when the *ContactTemplate* property has not been assigned a template by the page developer. We implemented *DefaultContact-Template* as a private inner class in the *ContactInfo* control because it is not meaningful outside the *ContactInfo* control. A default template is not essential; you can render the default UI by other means. We have provided a default template in this example mainly to illustrate how to implement the *ITemplate* interface and thus to create dynamic templates.

```
private sealed class DefaultContactTemplate : ITemplate {

    void ITemplate.InstantiateIn(Control container) {
        Label captionLabel = new Label();
        captionLabel.DataBinding +=
            new EventHandler(CaptionLabel_DataBinding);

        LiteralControl linebreak = new LiteralControl("<br>");

        Label infoLabel = new Label();
        infoLabel.DataBinding +=
            new EventHandler(InfoLabel_DataBinding);

        container.Controls.Add(captionLabel);
        container.Controls.Add(lt);
        container.Controls.Add(infoLabel);
    }

    private static void CaptionLabel_DataBinding(object sender,
        EventArgs e) {
        Control targetControl = (Control)sender;
        ContactPanel container =
            (ContactPanel)(targetControl.NamingContainer);

        ((Label)targetControl).Text = container.Caption;
    }

    private static void InfoLabel_DataBinding(object sender,
        EventArgs e) {
        Control targetControl = (Control)sender;
        ContactPanel container =
            (ContactPanel)(targetControl.NamingContainer);

        ((Label)targetControl).Text = container.Info;
    }
}
```

Listing 12-9   The default template for the *ContactInfo* control, implemented as a private inner class

The *DefaultContactTemplate* class implements the *ITemplate* interface, which has only one method, *InstantiateIn*, which we described in the previous section. In this method, *DefaultContactTemplate* creates two *Label* controls that are separated by a *LiteralControl* that represents a line break. The class then adds the two *Label* controls to the *Controls* collection of the control that is passed into the *InstantiateIn* method.

If you want data-binding functionality in a dynamic template, you must provide event handlers that you wire up to the *DataBinding* events of child controls defined in the template. In the event handlers, you assign values to properties of the child controls by using data (values of properties) present on the controls' *NamingContainer*. For example, in the event handlers that we have defined, we assign the values of the *Caption* and *Info* properties of the *ContactPanel* instance to the *Text* properties of the *Label* controls.

Controls can repeatedly instantiate a template (in different container instances), as they do in common data-binding scenarios. Therefore, a template should not contain any control instances as member variables because these would be overwritten with new values each time the template is instantiated. To emphasize that our template does not have any control instances, we have declared the event handlers by using the *static* modifier.

Control Parsing and Control Builders

We'll now take a brief look at how the page parser parses a declarative instance of a control and how you can override the default parsing logic.

> **Note**   The information provided in this section is not specific to composite controls but is general background information. It is relevant to any control that allows nested content within its tags.

In Chapter 10, you saw how you can specify parsing logic for your control by marking your control with the *ParseChildrenAttribute* metadata attribute. Specifying *ParseChildren(true)* tells the parser to interpret content within the control's tags as properties. Alternatively, specifying *ParseChildren(true, "<PropertyName>")* tells the parser that content nested within the control's tags corresponds to the property name passed into the attribute. In many Web controls, the *ParseChildrenAttribute* metadata attribute provides adequate parsing functionality. However, if your control needs specialized parsing logic, it is useful to understand the more general parsing functionality and the extensibility features that allow you to modify the existing functionality.

The page parser uses classes referred to as *control builders* to parse any content that exists between the tags of a server control. A control builder is an instance of the *System.Web.UI.ControlBuilder* class (or of a class that derives from *ControlBuilder*). The parser builds a parse tree once it has parsed the content of an .aspx page. This parse tree is similar to the control tree; however, it is a tree comprised of control builder instances rather than control instances. This parse tree is then converted into code that is compiled based on the dynamic compilation model described in Chapter 2, "Page Programming Model."

Based on the metadata provided in the *ParseChildrenAttrribute* metadata attribute, the parser divides controls into two broad parsing categories:

- Controls marked with the *ParseChildren(true)* metadata attribute. In this case, the parser interprets nested content as properties of the control and uses a set of internal control builders to parse the nested properties, including subproperties, templates, and collection properties.

- Controls not marked with the *ParseChildren(true)* metadata attribute. In this case, the parser uses the *ControlBuilder* associated with your control to interpret the content within your control's begin and end tags. Every control has the base *ControlBuilder* class associated with it by default. The default *ControlBuilder* implementation allows server controls to contain objects, other server controls, and static text (in the form of *LiteralControls*). These parsed objects are added to your control via the *AddParsedSubObject* method of your control. By default, the *AddParsedSubObject* method expects server controls and adds these parsed controls into your control's *Controls* collection as child controls.

Controls that derive from *Control* (which does not have the *ParseChildrenAttribute* metadata attribute applied), controls that derive from *WebControl* but are marked with the *ParseChildren(false)* metadata attribute, and other controls marked with the *ParseChildren(true)* metadata attribute, are all parsed as described in the second bullet. The rest of this section is devoted to controls in this parsing category—that is, controls whose nested content does not correspond to properties.

To modify the default parsing logic of a control whose nested content does not correspond to properties, you can implement a class that derives from the *ControlBuilder* class and override its methods. You can then associate that control builder with your control by applying the *ControlBuilderAttribute* metadata attribute to your control. In addition, you can override the *AddParsed-SubObject* method in your control to make it do something other than adding the parsed objects to your control tree. Note that any logic you implement in a *ControlBuilder* is executed once at parse time before code generation, whereas any logic you implement in *AddParsedSubObject* is executed upon every request. It is therefore much more efficient to perform all parsing logic in the *ControlBuilder*. For example, the built-in control builders for handling properties perform type conversions from strings into strongly typed objects at parse time rather than performing this conversion upon every request.

We will now implement an *InnerTextLabel* control that has an associated custom control builder that trims white spaces inside the control's tags and decodes HTML specified within the control's tags. *InnerTextLabel* also overrides the *AddParsedSubObject* method to parse the text within its control's tags. Listing 12-10 contains the code for the control as well as the code for the *InnerText-LabelBuilder* control builder associated with the control.

```
using System;
using System.ComponentModel;
using System.Web;
using System.Web.UI;
using System.Web.UI.WebControls;

namespace MSPress.ServerControls {

    public class InnerTextLabelControlBuilder : ControlBuilder {
        public override bool AllowWhitespaceLiterals() {
            return false;
        }

        // A ControlBuilder allows you to check errors
        // at parse time, which is more efficient than
        // performing checks at run time in a control's
        // AddParsedSubObject method.
        // In this sample, the AppendSubBuilder is commented
        // to demonstrate the AddParsedSubObject method of the
        // InnerTextLabel control. If you uncomment the
        // following code, a page that nests objects within the
        // tags of an InnerTextLabel will cause
        // parse errors rather than runtime exceptions.
```

Listing 12-10   InnerTextLabel.cs   *(continued)*

Listing 12-10 *(continued)*

```
    //
    // public override
    //     void AppendSubBuilder(ControlBuilder subBuilder) {
    //     throw new Exception(
    //         "An InnerTextLabel control cannot contain objects.");
    // }

    public override bool HtmlDecodeLiterals() {
        return true;
    }
}


[
ControlBuilder(typeof(InnerTextLabelControlBuilder)),
DefaultProperty("Text"),
ParseChildren(false)
]
public class InnerTextLabel : WebControl {
    protected override HtmlTextWriterTag TagKey {
        get {
            return HtmlTextWriterTag.Label;
        }
    }


    [
    Bindable(true),
    Category("Appearance"),
    DefaultValue(""),
    Description("The text property"),
    PersistenceMode(
        PersistenceMode.EncodedInnerDefaultProperty)
    ]
    public string Text {
        get {
            string s = (string)ViewState["Text"];
            return (s == null)? String.Empty : s;
        }
        set{
            ViewState["Text"] = value;
        }
    }

    protected override void AddParsedSubObject(object obj) {
        if (obj is LiteralControl) {
            Text = ((LiteralControl)obj).Text;
        }
```

```
        else {
            // Instead of performing the following
            // check at run time, it is more efficient
            // to perform it at parse time,
            // in the control's ControlBuilder,
            // as shown in InnerTextLabelControlBuilder.
            throw new ArgumentException(
                "The inner content must contain static text ");
        }
    }

    protected override void RenderContents(HtmlTextWriter writer) {
        writer.Write(HttpUtility.HtmlEncode(Text));
    }
    }
}
```

The *InnerTextLabelControlBuilder* overrides the *AllowWhitespaceLiterals* method to trim the white spaces in content within the control's begin and end tags. *InnerTextLabelControlBuilder* also overrides the *HtmlDecodeLiterals* to remove HTML encoding in text entered by the page developer between the control's tags. In addition, *InnerTextLabelControlBuilder* shows how you can override the *AppendSubBuilderMethod* to perform checks at parse time, which are more efficient than run-time checks, since the code in the control builder executes only once, when the page is parsed.

The *InnerTextLabel* control is marked with the *ParseChildren(false)* metadata attribute so that the parser interprets content within its tags as a control. *InnerTextLabel* overrides the *AddParsedSubObject* method to allow only literal text between its tags. The control assigns the value of the *Text* property of the parsed *LiteralControl* passed into it by the control builder to its own *Text* property. Finally, *InnerTextLabel* renders the HTML-encoded value of its *Text* property.

The *InnerTextLabel* allows a page developer to specify its *Text* property within the control's tags, as shown in Listing 12-11. Without the special parsing logic we have implemented, simple properties such as the *Text* property can be persisted only on the control's tag.

```
<%@ Page Language="C#" %>

<%@ Register TagPrefix="msp" NameSpace="MSPress.ServerControls"
  Assembly="MSPress.ServerControls" %>
<html>
  <body>
    <msp:InnerTextLabel id="innerTextLabel1" runat="server"
      Font-Size="Medium" Font-Names="Verdana">
    Text property persisted as inner text.
    </msp:InnerTextLabel>
  </body>
</html>
```

Listing 12-11   InnerTextLabelTest.aspx

Here are a few scenarios that require a custom *ControlBuilder*:

■   Overriding the *AllowWhitespaceLiterals* and *HtmlDecodeLiterals* methods and customizing the handling of literal text within a control's begin and end tags, as shown in the *InnerTextLabelControlBuilder* example in Listing 12-10.

■   Overriding the *GetChildControlType* and customizing the mapping of tag names to types. The default *ControlBuilder* implementation maps every tag that contains the *runat="server"* attribute to its associated class based on the tag's prefix and name. Your custom control builder can map tags to types even if the tag does not contain the *runat="server"* attribute or a tag prefix. This allows types to be declared by using a more terse declarative syntax. To enable this scenario, a control builder must override the *GetChildControlType* method whose arguments represent the complete tag and a dictionary of name/value pairs corresponding to the attributes of the tag.

■   Providing a different parsing logic from that implemented by the ASP.NET parser. For example, the *Xml* control in ASP.NET uses a control builder that gets the content within the control's tags and invokes the XML parser to parse that content. A control builder indicates that it is interested in the content within a control's tag by overriding the *NeedsTagInnerText* to return *true*. The parser then calls the control builder's *SetTagInnerText* to hand it the string of text containing the contents of the control.

The use of control builders is not limited to controls. You can associate a control builder with any class that is used declaratively within your control's tags. For example, the *ListItem* class in ASP.NET is associated with a *ControlBuilder* similar to the *InnerTextLabelControlBuilder* (shown in Listing 12-10) to allow a page developer to specify the text of a *ListItem* within the *<asp:ListItem>* tag.

> **Note**   Debugging a control builder is tricky because a control builder executes during page parsing, which occurs only when the page containing the control is first requested. If you want the control builder to execute again, you must make some change in the page to cause it to be reparsed.
>
> To debug a control builder, request a page that does not use the control whose control builder you want to debug and attach the debugger. Next make a first request to a page that contains the control whose control builder you want to debug. The debugger will stop at the first breakpoint in the control builder, and you can perform the usual debugging operations. (We described how to debug a control in Chapter 5, "Developing a Simple Custom Control.")

Summary

In this chapter, we examined control composition, a powerful technique that enables you to simplify control development through control reuse. We provided examples that demonstrated the basic implementation pattern of composite controls and features such as event bubbling and styles. We described templated controls, which allow page developers to customize their UI or rendered content through *ITemplate* properties. In addition, we briefly examined control parsing and showed you how to override the default parsing logic associated with your control by implementing a custom *ControlBuilder* and associating it with your control.

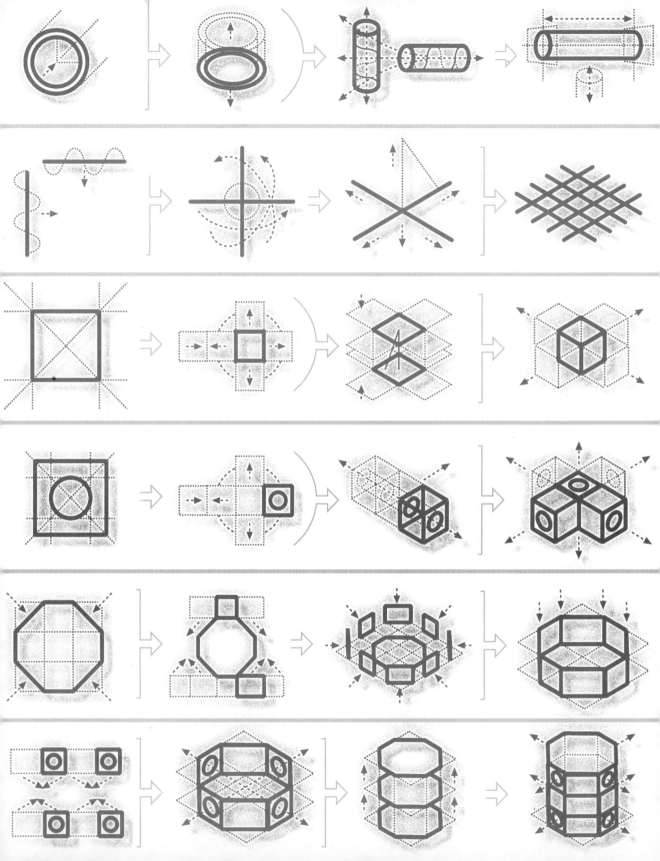

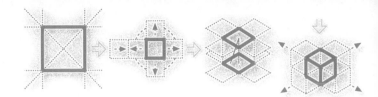

13

Client-Side Behavior

Server-side processing has always been a core functionality of Web applications. In addition, client-side functionality—or application logic that executes on the user's machine—is becoming an increasingly important feature of Web applications. Client-side features in a Web application are typically implemented in scripting languages such as JavaScript (also known as ECMAScript) and use the DHTML functionality offered by the latest versions of Web browsers. Client-side functionality enables a Web application to create an interactive user interface and to reduce the number of postbacks made to the server. This functionality also enables a Web application to reduce the work that needs to be done on the server.

At the same time, Web applications need to degrade gracefully and remain functional when they are accessed from Web browsers that do not provide the required level of client-scripting support. This requirement poses a substantial challenge to Web application developers and increases the complexity of their task. In addition to encapsulating server-side logic, server controls can encapsulate logic that takes advantage of available client functionality as well as logic that allows Web applications to degrade gracefully into purely server-side applications. This encapsulation of client-side behavior into server controls allows the code in the overall Web application to remain readable and maintainable. The most important benefit of this encapsulation is that server controls allow page developers to focus on the logic of their Web applications, rather than on targeting their applications for multiple Web browsers.

The validation controls in ASP.NET are an example of server controls that provide the functionality to validate form input on the client and reduce round-trips to the server. At the same time, the validation controls fall back on server-side validation when their client-side functionality is inactive. In this chapter, we will first introduce the concepts involved in incorporating client-side functionality into a server control's feature set. We will then implement an *HtmlEditor* server control that illustrates these concepts.

Browser Capabilities and Client-Side Behavior

Server controls that contain client-side behavior should degrade gracefully into a more limited mode (usually into a server side–only mode) that preserves the core functionality of the control. This characteristic of server controls enables the page developer to write a single page that works across various browsers without having to write additional switching logic.

A server control should discover the capabilities of the requesting browser to determine whether the control can use its client-side functionality. ASP.NET encapsulates information about the requesting Web browser in an instance of the *System.Web.HttpBrowserCapabilities* object that can be retrieved by accessing the *Browser* property of the current *HttpRequest* object. This property is initialized by the ASP.NET runtime using the *HTTP_USER_AGENT* request header value sent by the Web browser to the server when the browser makes a request. As the name suggests, an *HttpBrowserCapabilities* object exposes properties that enable a server control to inspect the capabilities of the requesting browser and to determine when to activate its client-side functionality. Some especially useful properties of this object are *MajorVersion*, *MinorVersion*, *MSDomVersion*, and *EcmaScriptVersion*, which respectively indicate the version of the browser, its Document Object Model (DOM), and the version of ECMAScript available in the browser. A server control should inspect the properties of this object to render the appropriate content. A control can then support varied levels of client-side behavior based on the level of features available in the requesting Web browser.

In addition, a server control should offer the page developer a mechanism to turn off its client script features completely, regardless of the capabilities of the requesting browser. This functionality is typically implemented by providing a property such as *EnableClientScript* on the control, as the *HtmlEditor* control you'll see later in this chapter demonstrates.

Client Script–Related API

We will now examine the APIs in the page framework that provide the basic functionality needed to incorporate client-side behavior in your server controls.

Each control has a *ClientID* property that is generated by the page framework and is guaranteed to be unique across all controls within the page. The default implementation of *WebControl* renders the *ClientID* as the HTML *id* attribute on the primary tag rendered by the server control. *ClientID* is a script-friendly version of the *UniqueID* property and can be used in client script to programmatically access the HTML element rendered by the control.

The *Page* class provides a number of other methods to emit client-side script. A control should invoke these methods on its containing page in the PreRender phase by overriding the *OnPreRender* method, as shown in the *HtmlEditor* example later in the chapter. It is important to call these methods at the right time in the control life cycle. Calling these methods during the PreRender phase allows every control to inform the page about any client-side script that the page should render on the control's behalf. Subsequently in the Render phase, the page renders all the client-side script that it collected as a result of these methods. You should not call these methods from your control's *Render* method because the page has already completed a portion of its rendering before your control is called to render itself.

Table 13-1 lists the methods of the *Page* class that allow your control to generate client-script and include this script in the page's rendering.

Table 13-1   Methods Exposed by Page to Enable Client-Script Rendering

Method	Description
RegisterClient-ScriptBlock	*void RegisterClientScriptBlock(string key, string script)*
	Allows you to emit the specified script block at the top of the page. Every script block is associated with a key. Every instance of your control on the page should use the same key. This allows the page to render the registered script a single time, even though it may be registered several times. The script is rendered before the control and therefore enables the control to refer to script methods implemented in the script block in event handlers for client-side events. The script block can contain embedded code or can be a reference to an external script file.
IsClientScript-BlockRegistered	*bool IsClientScriptBlockRegistered(string key)*
	Checks whether the specified script block has been registered. Strictly speaking, you do not need to call this method because registering the same script block multiple times is allowed, as described in the explanation of the *RegisterClient-ScriptBlock* method. However, you might find it useful to check whether the script block has been registered if generating the script block for registration purposes is expensive and time-consuming.

(continued)

Table 13-1   Methods Exposed by Page to Enable Client-Script Rendering *(continued)*

Method	Description
RegisterStartup-Script	*void RegisterStartupScript(string key, string script)*
	Shares the same semantics as the *RegisterClientScriptBlock* method. However, instead of rendering the script at the top of the page, this method renders the specified script block at the bottom of the page. This allows controls to generate script that needs to refer to the tags that the control renders into the page, which requires the tags to precede the script in the generated HTML. This method is especially useful for emitting inline script that executes as the document loads.
IsStartupScript-Registered	*bool IsStartupScriptRegistered(string key)*
	Shares the same semantics as the *IsClientScriptBlockRegistered* method.
RegisterArray-Declaration	*void RegisterArrayDeclaration(string arrayName, string arrayValue)*
	Allows your control to emit a value within the specified array. A page creates a single array variable in client script with the name given in *arrayName* which contains all the values registered with the same *arrayName*. This allows all instances of your control to add entries into a single array or list of values that can then be easily processed by client script that your control also generates.
RegisterHidden-Field	*void RegisterHiddenField(string hiddenFieldName, string initialValue)*
	Allows your control to render a hidden field that can be accessed by using client-side script to submit values back to the server when the page is submitted. Chapter 9, "Control Life Cycle, Events, and Postback," explains the details of handling postback data.
RegisterOn-SubmitStatement	*void RegisterOnSubmitStatement(string key, string script)*
	Registers the specified script statement to be executed when the page is submitted and allows your control's client-side behavior to participate in the submission process. The statement is executed as part of the *onsubmit* event of the *<form>* tag that is raised before the page is submitted to the server. The script statement is executed only once, even if it is registered multiple times (with the same key).

As you will see later in this chapter, the *HtmlEditor* sample control uses the *RegisterClientScriptBlock*, *RegisterStartupScript*, and *RegisterArrayDeclaration* methods in its implementation.

Using Client Script and DHTML

The client script and DHTML features of Web browsers allow controls to implement varying levels of client-side behavior. Web browsers such as Microsoft Internet Explorer provide a DOM that allows access to each tag in the page as an element. An element has properties, events, and methods that can be programmed against by using client-side script. Client script can be provided on a tag as the value of an attribute, embedded in the page within a *<script>* block, or placed in a separate file and included by using the *src* attribute of the *<script>* tag.

The simplest form of client-side behavior is to render simple script statements that are executed in response to events raised by various tag elements. The *HoverLabel* control we implemented in Chapter 8, "Rendering," rendered simple script statements to be executed in response to the *onmouseover* and *onmouseout* events.

When a control supports more complex client-side behavior, it typically packages its script into a set of script files and uses them as a script library by including references to the files with the *<script src="">* syntax. In addition, the control can emit some script into the actual page that ties in the functionality of the referenced script files. The ASP.NET validation controls follow this model for implementing their client-side behavior.

Finally, a control might emit custom tags or elements into the page and provide the implementation of those tags as element behaviors in .htc files. Internet Explorer 5.5 and later versions support the ability to implement custom tags or elements that provide their own object model. This approach allows a server control to create a client-side programming model if needed. The Internet Explorer Web controls library uses this model in its implementation of controls such as *TreeView* and *TabStrip*.

Deploying Client Files

The recommended approach for incorporating client-side behavior into your controls is to create a script library or a set of files that are referenced by the HTML that your control renders, rather than rendering the client script your control needs directly into the page. There are a number of benefits associated with this approach:

■ Because your controls emit only references to script files, this technique reduces the size of the rendered pages.

■ Web browsers can cache your script files for use across various pages. This improves the overall performance of a Web application.

■ You can support multiple instances of the same control within the same page more easily. Each instance uses the same script reference, as opposed to rendering slight variations (based on the *ID* of the control) of the same script functionality into the page.

■ Packaging the script outside the code for your control allows you to maintain and modify the script much more easily, without having to recompile your control.

ASP.NET provides a shared location that is a common directory and virtual root to be used for all client files. This shared location allows the client files to be reused across multiple applications. It also allows page developers to use controls without having to copy the client files associated with them into every application they use a control in. This capability is particularly important for controls that are installed into the global assembly cache (GAC) for use across multiple applications. Because the GAC supports side-by-side installation of multiple versions of your control, this shared location is associated with a deployment scheme that enables multiple versions of your client script files to coexist.

For example, the validation controls in ASP.NET deploy their client file, WebUIValidation.js, in this shared location. On a machine that has Internet Information Services (IIS) installed at c:\inetpub\wwwroot, WebUIValidation.js is installed as the following:

```
c:\inetpub\wwwroot\aspnet_client\system_web\1_0_3705_0\
WebUIValidation.js
```

WebUIValidation.js is referenced by using a root-relative URL:

```
/aspnet_client/system_web/1_0_3705_0/WebUIValidation.js
```

When the .NET Framework is installed, the "aspnet_client" directory is created and registered as the IIS virtual root "aspnet_client." ASP.NET also creates the "system_web" and "1_0_3705_0" subdirectories, which correspond to the *System.Web* assembly whose version number is 1.0.3705.0.

If you provide an installation program along with your control, it should create a folder with the same name as your control's assembly. This isolates your client files from other controls installed on the same machine. Your control's installation program should also create a subfolder based on your assembly's version. This allows a number of versions of your control to coexist. Your control is then free to implement any directory structure underneath the version folder. We'll show you how to create references to these files from your control in the next section, where we examine the *HtmlEditor* control. If you do not provide an installation program, you should provide alternate instructions for the page developer to create the necessary directory structure manually.

The files that you can include in this library of client files are not limited to script files. You can also package any other files that your control might need, such as image files and style sheets.

Putting It Together—The *HtmlEditor* Example

In this section, we'll put together the pieces of implementing client-side features that we described earlier in the chapter and create an HTML editor server control. The *HtmlEditor* control enables the user to enter formatted text as an HTML fragment and edit the HTML source in a WYSIWYG fashion. *HtmlEditor* could be useful in applications that involve online content editing, Web-based page authoring, guestbook entries, and so on.

The control uses client script and DHTML behaviors that are available in Internet Explorer 5.5 and later to implement its editing user interface (UI) as a custom HTML tag or element (*<h:HtmlArea>*). *HtmlEditor* also uses the HTML editing feature built into Internet Explorer that is available by setting the *contentEditable* attribute of an element to *true*. When these client features are not available, the *HtmlEditor* control generates a standard HTML *<textarea>* that can be used to enter the HTML source manually.

Figure 13-1 illustrates the HTML editing UI generated by the *HtmlEditor* control.

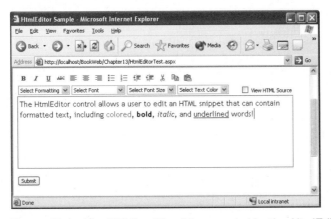

Figure 13-1   The HTML editing UI generated by the *HtmlEditor* control allows the entry of formatted text.

Listing 13-1 lists the sample page used to test the *HtmlEditor* control. In particular, this code demonstrates how the page does not have to provide any logic to incorporate client-side behavior.

```
<%@ Page language="c#" %>
<%@ Register TagPrefix="msp" Assembly="MSPress.ServerControls"
  Namespace="MSPress.ServerControls" %><html>
  <script runat="server">
  protected void Button1_Click(object sender, EventArgs e) {
      if (HtmlEditor1.Text.Equals(String.Empty) == false) {
          Label1.Visible = true;
          Label1.Text = HtmlEditor1.Text;
          HtmlEditor1.Visible = false;
          Button1.Visible = false;
      }
  }
  </script>
  <head>
    <title>HtmlEditor Sample</title>
  </head>
  <body>
    <form id="HtmlEditorTest" method="post" runat="server">
      <p>
        <msp:HtmlEditor id="HtmlEditor1" runat="server"
          Width="75%" Height="200px" Text="Edit the HTML..."/>
        <asp:Label id="Label1" runat="server" Visible="false" />
        <br />
        <br />
        <asp:Button id="Button1" runat="server" Text="Submit"
          OnClick="Button1_Click"/>
      </p>
    </form>
  </body>
</html>
```

Listing 13-1   HtmlEditorTest.aspx

The emphasized HTML in Listing 13-2 shows the HTML rendered by the *HtmlEditor* control.

```
<html>
  ⋮
<body>
  <form name="HtmlEditorTest" method="post"
    action="HtmlEditorTest.aspx" id="HtmlEditorTest">
```

Listing 13-2   The HTML rendered by the sample page

```
  <script language="JavaScript"
    src="/aspnet_client/mspress_servercontrols/1_0_0_0/HtmlArea.js">
    </script>
  <?xml:namespace prefix="h"/>
  <?import namespace="h"
    implementation=
      "/aspnet_client/mspress_servercontrols/1_0_0_0/HtmlArea.htc"/>
⋮
  <textarea id="HtmlEditor1" name="HtmlEditor1" style="display:none;">
Edit the HTML...</textarea>
  <h:HtmlArea id="HtmlEditor1HtmlArea"
    onHtmlChanged=
      "ha_OnHtmlChanged(this, document.all['HtmlEditor1'])"
    style="height:200px;width:75%;">
  </h:HtmlArea>
⋮
  <script language="JavaScript">
  <!--
    var HtmlAreaList =  new Array('HtmlEditor1');
  // -->
  </script>
  <script language="JavaScript">ha_InitializeElements()</script>
  </form>
</body>
</html>
```

Listing 13-3 contains the code for the *HtmlEditor* control.

```csharp
using System;
using System.ComponentModel;
using System.ComponentModel.Design;
using System.Collections;
using System.Collections.Specialized;
using System.Reflection;
using System.Web;
using System.Web.UI;
using System.Web.UI.WebControls;

namespace MSPress.ServerControls {

    // HtmlEditor provides a rich HTML editor on Internet Explorer 5.5
    // and later that allows WYSIWYG HTML editing and entry.
    // On other browsers, the control renders as a TextArea, requiring
    // users to enter HTML source manually.
    public class HtmlEditor : TextBox {
        private static string ClientFilesUrlPrefix;
```

Listing 13-3   HtmlEditor.cs   *(continued)*

Listing 13-3 *(continued)*

```
    private bool _renderClientScript;

    public HtmlEditor() {
        base.TextMode = TextBoxMode.MultiLine;
    }
    [
    Category("Behavior"),
    DefaultValue(true),
    Description(
        "Whether to enable the client script-based HTML editor.")
    ]
    public bool EnableClientScript {
        get {
            object b = ViewState["EnableClientScript"];
            return (b == null) ? true : (bool)b;
        }
        set {
            ViewState["EnableClientScript"] = value;
        }
    }


    [
    Browsable(false),
    DefaultValue(TextBoxMode.MultiLine),
    EditorBrowsable(EditorBrowsableState.Never)
    ]
    public override TextBoxMode TextMode {
        get {
            return base.TextMode;
        }
        set {
            if (value != TextBoxMode.MultiLine) {
                throw new ArgumentOutOfRangeException("value");
            }
            base.TextMode = value;
        }
    }

    private void DetermineRenderClientScript() {
        // In a client script-enabled control, always determine
        // whether to render the client script-based functionality.
        // The decision should be based on both browser
        // capabilities and on the page developer's choice.
```

```
        _renderClientScript = false;
    if ((Page != null) && (Page.Request != null)) {
        // The page developer can decide to turn off script
        // completely.
        if (EnableClientScript) {
            // The next set of checks involves looking at the
            // capabilities of the browser making the request.

            HttpBrowserCapabilities browserCaps =
                Page.Request.Browser;
            bool hasEcmaScript =
                (browserCaps.EcmaScriptVersion.CompareTo(
                    new Version(1, 2)) >= 0);
            bool hasDOM = (browserCaps.MSDomVersion.Major >= 4);
            bool hasBehaviors =
                (browserCaps.MajorVersion > 5) ||
                ((browserCaps.MajorVersion == 5) &&
                (browserCaps.MinorVersion >= .5));

            _renderClientScript =
                hasEcmaScript && hasDOM && hasBehaviors;
        }
    }
}

private string GetClientFileUrl(string fileName) {
    if (ClientFilesUrlPrefix == null) {
        // Use the config setting to determine where the client
        // files are located. Client files are located in the
        // aspnet_client v-root and then distributed into
        // subfolders by assembly name and assembly version.
        string location = null;
        if (Context != null) {
            IDictionary configData =
                (IDictionary)Context.GetConfig(
                    "system.web/webControls");
            if (configData != null) {
                location =
                    (string)configData["clientScriptsLocation"];
            }
        }

        if (location == null) {
            location = String.Empty;
        }
```

(continued)

Listing 13-3   *(continued)*

```
        else if (location.IndexOf("{0}") >= 0) {
            AssemblyName assemblyName =
                this.GetType().Assembly.GetName();

            string assembly =
                assemblyName.Name.Replace('.', '_').ToLower();
    string version =
                assemblyName.Version.ToString().Replace(
                    '.', '_');

            location =
                String.Format(location, assembly, version);
        }

        ClientFilesUrlPrefix = location;
    }
    return ClientFilesUrlPrefix + fileName;
}

private string GetClientIncludes() {
    return String.Format(
        "<script language=\"JavaScript\" src=\"{0}\">" +
        "</script>\r\n" +
        "<?xml:namespace prefix=\"h\"/>\r\n" +
        "<?import namespace=\"h\" implementation=\"{1}\"/>",
        GetClientFileUrl("HtmlArea.js"),
        GetClientFileUrl("HtmlArea.htc"));
}

protected override void OnPreRender(EventArgs e) {
    base.OnPreRender(e);

    DetermineRenderClientScript();
    if (_renderClientScript) {
        string scriptKey = typeof(HtmlEditor).FullName;
        Page.RegisterClientScriptBlock(scriptKey,
            GetClientIncludes());

        Page.RegisterArrayDeclaration("HtmlAreaList",
            "'" + ClientID + "'");
        Page.RegisterStartupScript(scriptKey,
            "<script language=\"JavaScript\">" +
            "ha_InitializeElements()" + "</script>");
    }
}
```

```
protected override void Render(HtmlTextWriter writer) {
    if (_renderClientScript == false) {
        // Use the default TextBox rendering.
        base.Render(writer);
    }
    else {
        writer.RenderBeginTag(HtmlTextWriterTag.Span);

        writer.AddAttribute(HtmlTextWriterAttribute.Id,
            ClientID);
        writer.AddAttribute(HtmlTextWriterAttribute.Name,
            UniqueID);
        writer.AddStyleAttribute("display", "none");
        writer.RenderBeginTag(HtmlTextWriterTag.Textarea);
        writer.Write(Text);
        writer.RenderEndTag();

        writer.WriteLine();

        if (ControlStyleCreated) {
            ControlStyle.AddAttributesToRender(writer, this);
        }

        writer.AddAttribute(HtmlTextWriterAttribute.Id,
            ClientID + "HtmlArea");
        writer.AddAttribute("onHtmlChanged",
            "ha_OnHtmlChanged(this, document.all['" +
            ClientID + "'])",
            false);
        writer.RenderBeginTag("h:HtmlArea");
        writer.RenderEndTag();

        writer.RenderEndTag();  // Span
    }
}
```

HtmlEditor is similar to a multiline *TextBox* that allows the entry of HTML-formatted text. Therefore, *HtmlEditor* derives from the standard ASP.NET *TextBox* control. By doing so, *HtmlEditor* inherits all the postback-handling and event-raising logic of *TextBox*. The control limits its inherited *TextMode* property to the *TextBoxMode.MultiLine* value, and simply adds the client-side behavior needed to create a WYSIWYG editing UI. When the requesting browser does not provide the right level of client-side functionality, *HtmlEditor* simply degrades to an ordinary *TextBox* (or *<textarea>*).

The *HtmlEditor* implementation shown in Listing 13-3 illustrates the following aspects of incorporating client-side functionality, which are generally applicable to all controls with client-side behavior:

■   Provides an *EnableClientScript* property whose default value is *true*. This property allows the page developer to completely turn off the client-side functionality for a specific control instance by disabling the logic it contains to automatically detect the capabilities of the Web browser client.

■   Includes a method named *DetermineRenderClientScript* to encapsulate the logic the control uses to discover the capabilities of the requesting browser and determine whether it should activate its client-side behavior. This method starts by assuming that it should not activate its client-side behavior and decides to do otherwise only when all its requirements are met. The method first checks whether the user has explicitly turned off client-side behavior by setting the *EnableClientScript* property to *false*. If the user has not turned off this behavior, the method retrieves the *HttpBrowserCapabilities* object and checks for the availability of ECMAScript 1.2 or later, Internet Explorer 5.5 or later, and the DHTML 4.0 DOM, all of which are needed to successfully use the control's editor UI implementation.

■   Overrides the *OnPreRender* method to call the *DetermineRenderClientScript* method. In a control's life cycle, *OnPreRender* is called after any user code that might change property values has executed, but before *Render*, where the control needs to know whether its client-side behavior has been activated. If the control's client-side behavior is enabled, the control needs to render script blocks within the page. The control does not render these script blocks itself because it needs to render them only once, even if the page contains multiple instances of the *HtmlEditor* control. Instead, the control calls the *RegisterClientScriptBlock*, *RegisterStartupScript*, and *RegisterArrayDeclaration* methods of its containing *Page* instance, and the page renders them as part of its own rendering logic.

■   Renders a reference to the script file, HtmlArea.js, by using a *<script>* tag. The control also renders the definition of the *<h:HtmlArea>* custom tag based on the behavior implemented in HtmlArea.htc by using the *<?xml:namespace>* and *<?import>* tags. As mentioned earlier, this reference and definition need to be rendered just once per given page, regardless of whether the page contains multiple instances of the server control. Furthermore, both the reference and the definition need to be rendered before any of the HTML is rendered by the control. Thus, the control uses the *RegisterClientScriptBlock* method of its containing *Page* instance. *HtmlEditor* uses its type name as the key value used to identify the script block so that the key will be constant across all instances of the control. You'll see these script files in a moment, when we look at the next set of code listings.

■ Contains a method named *GetClientFileUrl* that builds the URL used to refer to a client file. In an ideal world, this method would have been implemented by the *Page* class in ASP.NET, but because it isn't, we've provided the implementation in this sample control. In essence, the implementation retrieves the URL to the shared location created by ASP.NET that contains all client files from the machine-wide configuration setting. The implementation then proceeds to include the assembly name and version into the URL in accordance with the recommended scheme for deploying client files, which we described in the previous section, "Deploying Client Files." Finally, the implementation appends the path of the specific client file that needs to be referred to and returns the resulting URL. The resulting URL is a root-relative URL that can be referred to by any application running on the server. For example, the URL generated for HtmlArea.js is */asp-net_client/mspress_servercontrols/1_0_0_0/HtmlArea.js*.

■ In its *Render* method override, *HtmlEditor* checks its *_renderClientScript* field, which indicates whether its client-side behavior was activated during the PreRender phase. When its client-side behavior is disabled, the control simply delegates to the *Render* method of its base class, the *TextBox* control. When client-side behavior is enabled, *HtmlEditor* does not use any rendering functionality from its base class. The control first renders an invisible *<textarea>* tag. This tag contains the initial text within the *HtmlEditor* and it is used by client script to include the modified text as part of the data posted back to the server. The *HtmlEditor* simply reuses the postback data-handling logic built into its base class. This is possible because the *name* attribute of the hidden *<textarea>* is set to the *UniqueID* of the control, just as the base class would have done. The data contained in the hidden *<textarea>* is loaded by the *TextBox* into the control's *Text* property. Next, *HtmlEditor* renders a custom tag, *<h:HtmlArea>*, which contains the editing UI of the control. All the control's appearance-related properties are rendered on this custom tag. Notice that the *Render* method uses the *ClientID* property to render the *id* attribute and the identifier used in client event-handler script statements. *HtmlEditor* generates client script to track changes made to the HTML in the *<h:HtmlArea>* tag and update the value of the hidden *<textarea>* tag accordingly.

This book does not focus on client-side scripting. However, the client-side files used to implement the client-side behavior of the *HtmlEditor* control are provided in Listings 13-4 and 13-5 for completeness. Notice in Listing 13-4 that HtmlArea.js contains the methods called by the script that was rendered on the attributes and that was emitted via the *RegisterStartupScript* method. Also notice that the script references the array created by calls to *RegisterArrayDeclaration*.

```
function ha_OnHtmlChanged(htmlAreaElement, textAreaElement) {
    textAreaElement.value = htmlAreaElement.html;
}


function ha_InitializeElements() {
    for (i = 0; i < HtmlAreaList.length; i++) {
        var htmlAreaElementID = HtmlAreaList[i] + "HtmlArea";
        var textAreaElementID = HtmlAreaList[i];
        document.all[htmlAreaElementID].html =
            document.all[textAreaElementID].value;
    }
}
```

Listing 13-4 HtmlArea.js

```
<html>
<head>
  <public:component tagName="HtmlArea">
    <public:defaults viewLinkContent />
    <public:defaults viewInheritStyle="false" />
    <public:property name="html" get="get_html" put="set_html" />
    <public:event id="htmlChangedEvent" name="onHtmlChanged" />
    <public:attach event="onContentReady" onevent="OnContentReady()" />
  </public:component>
  <style>
    label, textarea, select { font-family: tahoma; font-size: 8pt; }
    img.ToolBarButton { cursor: hand; height: 22px; width: 23px; }
  </style>
  <script language="JavaScript">
    function get_html() {
        if (viewHtmlCheckBox.checked == true) {
            return editorTextArea.value;
        }
```

Listing 13-5 HtmlArea.htc

```
        else {
            return editorDiv.innerHTML;
        }
    }

    function set_html(data) {
        if (viewHtmlCheckBox.checked == true) {
            editorTextArea.value = data;
        }
        else {
            editorDiv.innerHTML = data;
        }
    }

    function DoEditorAction(actionString) {
        if (viewHtmlCheckBox.checked == true) {
            alert("Enable HTML editing by unchecking the 'View HTML
Source' checkbox.");
            return;
        }

        if (actionString == 'createlink') {
            alert('[' + editorDiv.createTextRange().text + ']');
            if (document.body.createTextRange().text == "") {
                return;
            }
        }
        document.execCommand(actionString);
        editorDiv.focus();
    }

    function DoEditorActionWithData(actionString, actionData) {
        if (viewHtmlCheckBox.checked == true) {
            alert("Enable HTML editing by unchecking the 'View HTML
Source' checkbox.");
            return;
        }       document.execCommand(actionString, false, actionData);
        editorDiv.focus();
    }

    function OnBlurEditorDiv(divElement) {
        htmlChangedEvent.fire();
    }

    function OnBlurEditorTextArea(textAreaElement) {
        htmlChangedEvent.fire();
    }
```

(continued)

Listing 13-5 *(continued)*

```
function OnContentReady() {
    var url = document.URL + "/../";
    for (i = 0; i < 14; i++) {
        var srcFile = document.all['i' + i].srcFile;
        document.all['i' + i].src = url + srcFile;
    }
}


function OnClickShowHtmlCheckBox(checkBoxElement) {
    if (viewHtmlCheckBox.checked == true) {
        editorTextArea.value = editorDiv.innerHTML;

        editorDiv.style.display = 'none';
        editorTextArea.style.display = '';
        editorTextArea.focus();
    }
    else {
        editorDiv.innerHTML = editorTextArea.value;

        editorTextArea.style.display = 'none';
        editorDiv.style.display = '';
        editorDiv.focus();
    }
}
    function OnClickToolBarButton(actionString) {
    DoEditorAction(actionString);
}

function OnSelectedIndexChangedFontColorList(listElement) {
    DoEditorActionWithData('foreColor',
        listElement[listElement.selectedIndex].value);
    listElement.selectedIndex = 0;
}
function OnSelectedIndexChangedFontFaceList(listElement) {
    DoEditorActionWithData('fontName',
        listElement[listElement.selectedIndex].value);
    listElement.selectedIndex = 0;
}

function OnSelectedIndexChangedFontSizeList(listElement) {
    DoEditorActionWithData('fontSize',
        listElement[listElement.selectedIndex].value);
    listElement.selectedIndex = 0;
}
```

```
        function OnSelectedIndexChangedFormattingList(listElement) {
            if (listElement.selectedIndex == 1) {
                DoEditorActionWithData('formatBlock', 'Normal');
                DoEditorAction('removeFormat');
            }
            else {
                DoEditorActionWithData('formatBlock',
                    listElement[listElement.selectedIndex].value);
            }
            listElement.selectedIndex = 0;
        }
    </script>
</head>
<body unselectable="on">
  <table height="100%" cellspacing="0" cellpadding="0" width="100%"
    border="0">
    <tr style="HEIGHT: 22px">
      :
      <!-- HTML to generate the ToolBar UI snipped out -->
      <textarea id="editorTextArea"
        onblur="OnBlurEditorTextArea(this)"
        style="display: none; width:100%; height:100%">
      </textarea>
      <div id="editorDiv" onblur="OnBlurEditorDiv(this)"
        style="width: 100%; height: 100%; border: solid 1px
highlight; padding: 4px;"
          contentEditable="true"></div>
      </td>
    </tr>
  </table>
</body>
</html>
```

Listing 13-5 contains the definition of the *<h:HtmlArea>* custom tag and the JavaScript implementation used to create it. One way to think of custom tags implemented by using DHTML behaviors is to view them as the equivalent of user controls for client-side programming.

The *HtmlEditor* sample represents a very basic HTML editing control, and the implementation can be extended in several ways. One useful feature would be to allow the page developer to indicate whether the HTML entered by the user can contain script. This is especially important from a security perspective because enabling script entry would allow an unscrupulous user to enter potentially malicious scripts and this might be undesirable based on the intent of the application. Another useful addition to the control's features would be the ability to specify the actions and options available on its editing toolbars.

Summary

Server controls can enable Web applications to easily access and use the capabilities of Web browsers and to optimize their user experience without the added complexity of client-side programming. Server controls offer a mechanism for encapsulating client-side behavior and making it available for use across an application. The *HtmlEditor* control we implemented in this chapter enables the entry of formatted text and works best on Internet Explorer 5.5 and later. However, this control preserves its core functionality on other browsers, without requiring any additional logic from the page developer. The *HtmlEditor* control also illustrates the general implementation pattern that applies to all server controls that incorporate client-side behavior into their feature set.

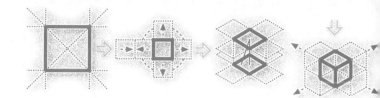

14

Validator Controls

Almost all Web applications share a common functionality: allowing users to input data and then gathering and processing that data on the server. Web applications use form-based input fields such as text boxes, check boxes, and buttons as the primary mechanism to allow users to enter data. Data entry and data validation go hand in hand. It is essential to validate all user input before it is processed and stored on the server. Validation of user input typically has been a tedious aspect of Web application development. ASP.NET simplifies validation in Web applications immensely by providing a set of validation controls that implement commonly used validation rules on the server and on the client without requiring any application code. In addition, ASP.NET defines an extensible validation architecture for component developers to use in their controls.

As a component developer, you can develop your own validator controls to implement new validation rules. In this chapter, we will first describe the validation feature of Web Forms and then implement a new validator control named *StringValidator* that complements the built-in set of validators.

Validation Architecture—*IValidator*, *BaseValidator*, and *CustomValidator*

Validation in ASP.NET involves two categories of controls: *validators* and *validation targets*. Validators are the controls that perform validation, and validation targets are the controls that expose properties that need to be validated. The page developer makes the association between a validator and a validation target.

Validation targets are usually input controls—in other words, controls that render as form elements that allow data entry. Any control that contains a *ValidationPropertyAttribute* in its metadata can be a validation target. In general, these controls provide access to the user's entry via a single property. To support validation, the control identifies this property for validation by using the *ValidationPropertyAttribute* metadata attribute. For example, the *Text* property of a *TextBox* is marked as the property that needs to be validated using this attribute. We will look at an example of a validation target in Chapter 21, "DHTML-Based Server Controls."

A validator control implements a specific validation rule. Each validator control instance can be associated with a single validation target instance. Validators also have an associated error message that is rendered when the user data is invalid. The page developer can associate multiple validators with a single validation target. This allows multiple validation checks to be performed on a single value. Having multiple validators bound to the same validation target also allows page developers to use a different error message for each validation rule that fails.

By definition, any class that implements the *System.Web.UI.IValidator* interface qualifies as a validator in the ASP.NET validation framework. The *IValidator* interface is defined as follows:

```
public interface IValidator {
    string ErrorMessage { get; set; }
    bool IsValid { get; set; }
    void Validate();
}
```

The intent behind defining this interface was that component developers could implement custom validators by implementing *IValidator*. However, in version 1.0 of ASP.NET, this is not possible. The implementation of the validation framework is distributed across the *Page* class; the *BaseValidator* class (which is the base class for all the built-in validators); and controls that trigger validation, such as *Button* and *LinkButton*. The interdependencies of these components do not allow arbitrary *IValidator* implementations. However, it is still possible to create custom validation controls by deriving from *BaseValidator* instead.

BaseValidator is an abstract base class that derives from the *Label* class. *BaseValidator* implements the *IValidator* interface. In addition, this base class performs several tasks that are common to all validators:

■ Exposes the *ControlToValidate* property, which allows page developers to associate validators with validation targets. Exposes the *GetControlValidationValue* method to extract the value from the associated control that needs to be validated.

■ Defines the *EvaluateIsValid* abstract method that you must override in your validator to implement your validation logic.

■ Registers itself with the *Validators* collection of the *Page* in its *OnInit* method so that a validator can participate in the validation framework.

■ Generates script to implement the client-side validation functionality if the client supports scripting. Exposes the *RenderUplevel* property, which is set to *true* when it determines that the browser making the request contains the features needed to implement client-side validation.

■ Automatically renders the validator when its *IsValid* property is *false*—in other words, when the associated validation target contains an invalid entry.

In short, *BaseValidator* provides the plumbing needed to participate in the validation feature of Web Forms and simplifies the implementation of custom validators.

ASP.NET also provides a built-in validator named *CustomValidator*. The name of this validator suggests that it could be a base class for custom validators. However, *CustomValidator* is actually a validator control that page developers can use to add custom validation logic. This control exposes a *ServerValidate* server-side event and a *ClientValidationFunction* property to allow the page developer to supply server-side and client-side validation logic. *CustomValidator* does not provide a reuse mechanism for control developers. Furthermore, it does not get invoked to perform its validation when the value to be validated is empty. Therefore, we recommend that you derive new validators from *BaseValidator* instead of extending *CustomValidator*. The *StringValidator* example that we will examine later in this chapter is consistent with this recommendation and derives from *BaseValidator*.

The Validation Framework

The validation framework in ASP.NET provides a set of standard validator controls and a simple model for page developers to incorporate validation into their Web applications.

Validator Controls Provided by ASP.NET

ASP.NET provides a set of validator controls in the *System.Web.UI.WebControls* namespace. Table 14-1 lists this set of validator controls along with the validation rules they encapsulate.

Table 14-1   Built-In Validators in ASP.NET

Validator	Validation Rule
RequiredFieldValidator	Ensures that the user enters a non-empty value.
RangeValidator	Ensures that the user's entry lies within a specific range of values.
CompareValidator	Ensures the validity of the user's entry by comparing it to a reference value. The reference value can be either a constant value or the value of another validation target. The comparison can be one of several operators, such as equality, greater than, and so on. In addition, the validator can check that the entered value matches a specified data type.
RegularExpressionValidator	Ensures that the user's entry matches the specified regular expression pattern.
CustomValidator	Allows the page developer to supply custom validation logic to perform validation of the user's entry.

The built-in set of validator controls provides an implementation of some of the commonly used validation rules. However, this set is by no means exhaustive. The extensibility of the validation framework allows you to create new validator controls that encapsulate additional validation rules.

Using Validation in a Page

The validation framework is geared toward simplicity. The page developer does not need to implement any validation logic to use the validation framework. Instead, he or she simply needs to add one or more validator controls to the page and associate them with validation targets declaratively in the .aspx file. Once the page developer has included validator controls on his or her page, he or she can examine the *IsValid* property that is exposed by the *Page* class. The page aggregates the valid or invalid state of all the validators it contains in this property. This allows the page developer to check the value of a single property in order to skip the processing of data if any value is invalid.

How the Page Performs Validation

The *Page* class contains a *Validators* collection that contains references to all the validators that exist on the page. Each validator control registers itself with its page by overriding its *OnInit* method and adding itself to the *Validators* collection. The *Page* class also exposes a *Validate* method that in turn invokes the *Validate* method of each registered validator. If the validator is visible and enabled, it executes its validation logic to update the value of its own *IsValid* property. The validator does so by retrieving the user entry to be validated from the validation target and checking the value against a set of validation rules.

A page developer can invoke the *Validate* method of the page to trigger validation. However, it is rare to see an explicit call to *Validate*. Rather, various controls that cause postback—the *Button*, *LinkButton*, and *ImageButton* controls—invoke the *Validate* method on behalf of the page developer. Each of these controls contains a Boolean *CausesValidation* property, which is set to *true* by default. When this property is *true*, these controls automatically trigger validation by invoking the *Validate* method of the page before raising their *Click* event. Thus, these controls ensure that the *IsValid* property of the *Page* is updated before any event handler is invoked. The logic in an event handler can inspect this page property to determine whether to process the user's data or to allow the user to fix any errors before resubmitting the page.

> **Note**   In ASP.NET, various controls other than buttons can cause the page to be submitted and raise change events. For example, the *Text-Box* control submits the page when its *AutoPostBack* property is set to *true* and the user changes its text. However, the *TextBox* control does not trigger validation. If user code processes the *TextBox* data in a *Text-Changed* event handler, it might process data that has not been validated. Therefore, we recommend that if you implement a control that supports *AutoPostBack*, you should implement a *CausesValidation* property on that control, even though ASP.NET controls such as the *TextBox* do not offer this property. Unlike buttons that cause action events, controls that cause change events should have their *Causes-Validation* property default set to *false*. When this property is set to *true* by the page developer, your control should trigger validation before raising its change event. It is expected that ASP.NET will follow this recommendation in the future.

Client-Side Validation

In Chapter 13, "Client-Side Behavior," we described how server controls can take advantage of the client-side functionality available in a Web browser to provide an enhanced user experience. We also mentioned that server controls can encapsulate the logic needed to determine the level of client-side functionality that is available and can render accordingly so that they can degrade gracefully rather than cease to function.

The ASP.NET validation framework makes use of this capability to implement a client-side validation framework in addition to the server-side validation framework we have seen. Client-side validation allows the validation that takes place on the server to also take place in the Web browser before the page is submitted to the server. If the page contains invalid user entries, the submission process is interrupted and the user is prompted to fix the errors before continuing. This reduces the number of wasteful or bad requests that a server has to process, validate, and return to the user for corrections. Client-side validation also improves the user experience by immediately alerting the user about errors on the page without requiring the user to wait for the server to process the data and generate a response.

Enabling client-side validation without any additional complexity for the page developer is a valuable feature of Web Forms. Validators automatically check for the JavaScript and DHTML capabilities of the target Web browser before rendering their client script and script file references. The client-side validation framework and the client-side validation logic for the ASP.NET validator controls are implemented in WebUIValidation.js, which is included in the page when client-side behavior of validators is enabled. On typical installations of version 1.0 of the .NET Framework, this script file exists in the c:\inetpub\wwwroot\aspnet_client\system_web\1_0_3705_0 directory.

Validators never disable their server-side validation logic. Server-side validation rules are always executed. This is to ensure the validity of data in all scenarios and provides an additional level of checking. Server-side validation also provides a level of security by ensuring that validation always takes place, even when the request is made from a non–Web browser application that bypasses client-side validation (such as a request handcrafted by a malicious user).

The *ValidationSummary* Control

In addition to the validator controls, ASP.NET includes the *ValidationSummary* control. A page developer can use this control to collect error messages from all validators that have detected invalid user entries and to display the combined set of errors in one location and format. The *ValidationSummary* control simply enumerates the contents of the *Validators* collection of the page and extracts the error messages from each validator in an invalid state. The control can be used either to generate a list of errors in the page or to generate a message box when the user attempts to submit a page with errors. The *Validation-Summary* control works with all validators—meaning that it works with both built-in validators and any custom validators that you might implement.

Validating Text Entry—The *StringValidator* Example

In this section, we will create a new validator named *StringValidator* by deriving from the *BaseValidator* class. *StringValidator* is designed to validate string values entered in a text box. This validator contains the functionality of a *RequiredField-Validator* and ensures that the user enters a string that differs from the text box's initial value. A common requirement of Web applications is to limit the amount of text entered by the user. Therefore, *StringValidator* will also validate that the user's input does not exceed a specified number of characters.

As with the existing validator controls in ASP.NET, *StringValidator* always performs server-side validation. The control performs client-side validation when the browser requesting the page supports JavaScript. Client-side validation allows the *StringValidator* to indicate errors before the page is submitted to the server. This prevents a wasteful round-trip and alerts the user to errors more quickly.

Figure 14-1 illustrates a page containing a *StringValidator* associated with a *TextBox* control in an error state. The page also contains an instance of a *ValidationSummary* control that summarizes the errors on the page.

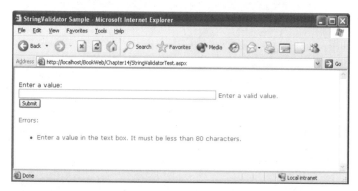

Figure 14-1 The sample page containing the *StringValidator* in its invalid state

Listing 14-1 contains the implementation of the sample page shown in Figure 14-1.

```
<%@ Page language="c#" %>
<%@ Register TagPrefix="msp" Assembly="MSPress.ServerControls"
  Namespace="MSPress.ServerControls" %>
<html>
  <script runat="server">
  protected void Button1_Click(object sender, EventArgs e) {
      if (Page.IsValid) {
          Label1.Text = "You entered: " + TextBox1.Text;
      }
  }
  </script>
  <head>
    <title>StringValidator Sample</title>
  </head>
  <body>
    <form method="post" runat="server">
      <p>
        Enter a value:
        <br />
        <asp:TextBox id="TextBox1" runat="server" Columns="80"/>
        <msp:StringValidator id="StringValidator1" runat="server"
          ControlToValidate="TextBox1"
          MaximumLength="80" IsRequired="true"
          ErrorMessage="Enter a value in the text box. It must be less
than 80 characters."
          Text="Enter a valid value." />
        <br />
        <asp:Button id="Button1" runat="server" Text="Submit"
          OnClick="Button1_Click"/>
        <br />
        <asp:Label id="Label1" runat="server" />
        <br />
        <asp:ValidationSummary runat="server" HeaderText="Errors:"/>
      </p>
    </form>
  </body>
</html>
```

Listing 14-1   StringValidatorTest.aspx

The sample page illustrates the simplicity of incorporating validation into a Web application. The validator control is associated with the *TextBox* by using its *ControlToValidate* property. The code in the page simply checks the *IsValid* property of the *Page* before processing any user input. The validation framework in ASP.NET implements the plumbing needed to allow validators to validate user entries on the client and on the server.

Listing 14-2 shows portions of the HTML that were rendered by the *Text-Box*, the *StringValidator* (distinguished by the boldface font), and the ASP.NET validation framework.

```
<html>
  ...
  <body>
    <form method="post"
      action="StringValidatorTest.aspx" language="javascript"
      onsubmit="ValidatorOnSubmit();">
      ...
    <script language="javascript"
      src="/aspnet_client/system_web/1_0_3705_0/WebUIValidation.js">
    </script>
    <script language="JavaScript" src="/aspnet_client/mspress_servercon
trols/1_0_0_0/StringValidator.js">
    </script>
      ...
      <p>
        Enter a value:
        <br />
        <input name="TextBox1" type="text" size="80" id="TextBox1" />
        <span id="StringValidator1" controltovalidate="TextBox1"
          errormessage="Enter a value in the text box. It must be less
than 80 characters."
            evaluationfunction="StringValidatorEvaluateIsValid"
            initialValue="" isRequired="True" maxLength="80"
            style="color:Red;visibility:hidden;">
            Enter a valid value.
        </span>
        <br />
        <input type="submit" name="Button1" value="Submit"
          onclick="if (typeof(Page_ClientValidate) == 'function')
Page_ClientValidate(); "
          language="javascript" id="Button1" />
        <br />
        <div id="_ctl0" headertext="Errors:"
          style="color:Red;display:none;"></div>
      </p>
      ...
<script language="javascript">
<!--
    var Page_ValidationSummaries =  new Array(document.all["_ctl0"]);
    var Page_Validators =  new Array(document.all["StringValidator1"]);
// -->
</script>
<script language="javascript">
```

Listing 14-2   The HTML generated from StringValidatorTest.aspx   *(continued)*

Listing 14-2   *(continued)*

```
<!--
var Page_ValidationActive = false;
if (typeof(clientInformation) != "undefined" &&
    clientInformation.appName.indexOf("Explorer") != -1) {
    if (typeof(Page_ValidationVer) == "undefined")
        alert("Unable to find script library '/aspnet_client/system_web
/1_0_3705_0/WebUIValidation.js'. Try placing this file manually, or rei
nstall by running 'aspnet_regiis -c'.");
    else if (Page_ValidationVer != "125")
        alert("This page uses an incorrect version of WebUIValidation.j
s. The page expects version 125. The script library is " +
            Page_ValidationVer + ".");
    else
        ValidatorOnLoad();
}

function ValidatorOnSubmit() {
    if (Page_ValidationActive) {
        ValidatorCommonOnSubmit();
    }
}
// -->
</script>
    </form>
  </body>
</html>
```

Listing 14-3 contains the implementation of the *StringValidator* control.

```
using System;
using System.Collections;
using System.ComponentModel;
using System.Configuration;
using System.Globalization;
using System.Reflection;
using System.Web.UI;
using System.Web.UI.WebControls;

namespace MSPress.ServerControls {
    [
    ToolboxData("<{0}:StringValidator runat=\"server\" " +
        "ErrorMessage=\"StringValidator\" " +
        "Text=\"*\"></{0}:StringValidator>")
    ]
    public class StringValidator : BaseValidator {
```

Listing 14-3   StringValidator.cs

```
[
Bindable(true),
Category("Behavior"),
DefaultValue(""),
Description("The initial value from which the new value " +
    "must be different")
]
public string InitialValue {
    get {
        string s = (string)ViewState["InitialValue"];
        return (s == null) ? String.Empty : s;
    }
    set {
        ViewState["InitialValue"] = value;
    }
}


[
Category("Behavior"),
DefaultValue(true),
Description("Whether a value is required.")
]
public virtual bool IsRequired {
    get {
        object b = ViewState["IsRequired"];
        return (b == null) ? true : (bool)b;
    }
    set {
        ViewState["IsRequired"] = value;
    }
}


[
Bindable(true),
Category("Behavior"),
DefaultValue(0),
Description("The maximum length of a valid value")
]
public virtual int MaximumLength {
    get {
        object i = ViewState["MaximumLength"];
        return (i == null) ? 0 : (int)i;
    }
    set {
        ViewState["MaximumLength"] = value;
    }
}
```

(continued)

Listing 14-3   *(continued)*

```
protected override void AddAttributesToRender(
    HtmlTextWriter writer) {
    base.AddAttributesToRender(writer);

    if (RenderUplevel) {
        writer.AddAttribute("evaluationfunction",
            "StringValidatorEvaluateIsValid");

        writer.AddAttribute("initialValue",
            InitialValue.Trim());
        writer.AddAttribute("isRequired",
            IsRequired.ToString(CultureInfo.InvariantCulture));
        writer.AddAttribute("maxLength",
            MaximumLength.ToString(
                CultureInfo.InvariantCulture));
    }
}

private string GetClientIncludes() {
    string clientFilesUrlPrefix = null;

    // Use the config setting to determine where the client
    // files are located. Client files are located in the
    // aspnet_client v-root and then distributed into
    // subfolders by assembly name and assembly version.
    if (Context != null) {
        IDictionary configData =
            (IDictionary)Context.GetConfig(
                "system.web/webControls");
        if (configData != null) {
            clientFilesUrlPrefix =
                (string)configData["clientScriptsLocation"];
        }
    }

    if ((clientFilesUrlPrefix != null) &&
        (clientFilesUrlPrefix.IndexOf("{0}") >= 0)) {
        AssemblyName assemblyName =
            this.GetType().Assembly.GetName();

        string assembly =
            assemblyName.Name.Replace('.', '_').ToLower();
        string version =
            assemblyName.Version.ToString().Replace('.', '_');

        clientFilesUrlPrefix =
            String.Format(clientFilesUrlPrefix, assembly,
```

```
                                  version);
        }

        return String.Format(
            "<script language=\"JavaScript\" src=\"{0}\"></script>",
            clientFilesUrlPrefix + "StringValidator.js");
    }

    protected override bool EvaluateIsValid() {
        // Get the value to be validated.
        string controlValue =
            GetControlValidationValue(ControlToValidate);

        if (controlValue == null) {
            // Implies the validator is not bound to a control.
            return true;
        }

        controlValue = controlValue.Trim();

        if (IsRequired &&
            (controlValue.Equals(InitialValue.Trim()) == true)) {
            return false;
        }

        int maxLength = MaximumLength;
        if ((maxLength != 0) && (controlValue.Length > maxLength)) {
            return false;
        }

        return true;
    }

    protected override void OnPreRender(EventArgs e) {
        base.OnPreRender(e);

        if (RenderUplevel) {
            Page.RegisterClientScriptBlock(
                typeof(StringValidator).FullName,
                GetClientIncludes());
        }
    }
}
}
```

StringValidator derives from the abstract *BaseValidator* class and automatically inherits the functionality needed to participate in the validation framework. *BaseValidator* implements the *IValidator* interface and the logic required to register itself with the *Validators* collection of its *Page*. This ensures that the validator is invoked when the page attempts to determine its valid state. *BaseValidator* is responsible for emitting the reference to the WebUIValidation.js script file and page script (shown in Listing 14-2) that implements the client-side validation framework. *BaseValidator* also implements the *ControlToValidate* property, which allows the page developer to associate validators with corresponding input controls. Finally, *BaseValidator* renders the user interface (UI) of a validator when the validator is in an invalid state. Thus, the *BaseValidator* class performs all the plumbing necessary to fit into the validation framework and allows you to focus on the validation logic that is specific to your validator.

StringValidator implements a number of properties that are specific to its validation functionality. The *IsRequired* property is used to turn on the validation logic that ensures that the user makes an entry in the associated *TextBox*. The *InitialValue* property is used to indicate the initial value of the *TextBox* that must be changed when the *IsRequired* property is set to *true*. The *MaximumLength* property is used to turn on the validation logic that ensures that any entry made by the user in the associated *TextBox* does not exceed the specified length.

StringValidator implements the abstract *EvaluateIsValid* method of *BaseValidator* to implement its own validation logic based on the page developer's choices. This method is called by the server-side validation framework when the page needs to determine its valid state. *StringValidator* returns *true* if and only if all the validity checks are completed successfully. *StringValidator* uses the *GetControlValidationValue* method of *BaseValidator* to retrieve the value that needs to be validated. This helper method encapsulates the logic to find the associated validation target based on the *ControlToValidate* property and to access the value of the property specified via the *ValidationPropertyAttribute* metadata on the associated control class.

The *StringValidator* class is marked with the *ToolboxDataAttribute* metadata attribute. This metadata attribute, which we described in Chapter 5, "Developing a Simple Custom Control," is used to specify the fragment of HTML that is used to instantiate the control when it is first dropped onto the design surface in a design-time environment. The *ToolboxDataAttribute* metadata attribute can be used to specify default values for the *ErrorMessage* and *Text* properties, which are required for any validator to be visible to the user.

StringValidator implements its client-side validation functionality in StringValidator.js. This file is deployed as a client file, which *StringValidator* refers to in the page by generating a *<script src="">* tag. *StringValidator* overrides the *OnPreRender* method of *BaseValidator* to emit the reference to its associated script file. *StringValidator* uses the value of the *RenderUplevel* property of *BaseValidator* to determine whether its client-side validation should be enabled. *BaseValidator* contains all the logic needed to determine when to enable client-side validation. We described in detail how to package client-side behavior into script files and to enable client-side behavior in Chapter 13.

StringValidator.js contains a method that implements the same validation logic as the *EvaluateIsValid* method of the *StringValidator* class. This method is invoked by the client-side validation framework before the page is submitted. If the method returns *false*, the submission process is interrupted. The functionality in StringValidator.js uses the utility functions present in WebUIValidation.js, such as *ValidatorTrim* and *ValidatorGetValue*. WebUIValidation.js implements the ASP.NET client-side validation framework. This client-side validation framework contains a number of other utility functions, including enabling and disabling validators dynamically and converting validation values.

Listing 14-4 shows StringValidator.js.

```
function StringValidatorEvaluateIsValid(val) {
    var valueToValidate =
        ValidatorTrim(ValidatorGetValue(val.controltovalidate));
    if (val.isRequired == 'True') {
        if (valueToValidate == val.initialValue) {
            return false;
        }
    }
    if (val.maxLength != '0') {
        if (valueToValidate.length > parseInt(val.maxLength, 10)) {
            return false;
        }
    }
    return true;
}
```

Listing 14-4   StringValidator.js

Summary

Validation is a core feature of all Web applications. It adds a professional touch to the UI of an application. More important, validation provides a basic layer of input verification before any application logic acts upon the data entered by the user. ASP.NET provides a set of validation controls that are useful across a wide range of scenarios. In addition, ASP.NET offers an extensible framework that allows component developers to create custom validators with new and more specialized validation rules. The validation framework also makes it possible to provide enhanced client-side validation functionality without any effort on the page developer's part.

In this chapter, we looked at the implementation of a custom validator named *StringValidator*, which works the same way as any other built-in validator. In Chapter 17, "Localization, Licensing, and Other Miscellany," we will give another example of a custom validator, *PhoneNumberValidator*, in the context of implementing configurable properties.

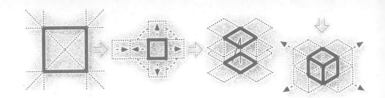

Design-Time Functionality

Design-time functionality refers to the appearance, capabilities, and behavior of a control in a visual designer such as Microsoft Visual Studio .NET. The .NET Framework makes it possible for a custom control to offer the same experience in a designer as the standard ASP.NET controls. To begin with, a control inherits basic design-time functionality from the base *Control* class. Next the .NET Framework allows you to easily customize the default functionality of a control via design-time attributes. Finally, the .NET Framework provides a rich and flexible design-time architecture that enables you to implement advanced design-time features and associate them with your control.

In Chapter 5, "Developing a Simple Custom Control," we described the default design-time functionality available to a control. For example, you saw that without any additional work on your part, a page developer can add your control to the Toolbox of Visual Studio .NET, drag the control from the Toolbox onto the design surface, and select the control on the design surface to cause the property browser to display its properties and events. In Chapter 5 and Chapter 7, "Simple Properties and View State," we showed how you can customize your control's default design-time functionality by applying various design-time metadata attributes.

In this chapter, we will show you how to implement advanced design-time features, such as the special user interface (UI) offered by the *DataList* control for editing its template properties or the color picker UI offered by Web controls for editing their *Color* type properties. We will describe the design-time architecture of the .NET Framework, examine classes that provide advanced design-time functionality (namely type converters, designers, and editors), and show you how to extend those classes and associate them with your control. We'll complete our tour of design-time programming by describing how to debug design-time code.

Implementing design-time features is optional because the base *Control* class provides basic design-time functionality to a server control. However, depending on the functionality of your control, design-time features can greatly enhance the usability of your control in a visual design environment and turn a no-frills control into a professional-looking control that offers a rich design-time experience to the page developer. This difference is especially important if you are developing controls for commercial distribution.

.NET Framework Design-Time Architecture

In the .NET Framework, *designable components* participate in a rich and extensible design-time architecture to create a rapid application development (RAD) experience for the page developer. As we described in Chapter 3, "Component Programming Overview," a designable component is a class that implements the *IComponent* interface or derives directly or indirectly from the *System.ComponentModel.Component* class that implements this interface. For brevity, in this chapter we will use *component* in place of *designable component* when no ambiguity comes of using the shorter term. Because the base *Control* class implements *IComponent*, all server controls are designable components and automatically participate in the design-time architecture of the .NET Framework.

An important aspect of the .NET design-time architecture is that you do not implement design-time capabilities within your control but implement those capabilities in classes outside your control. You then associate those classes with your control via metadata attributes. This separation of the design-time implementation from the run-time implementation makes the design-time architecture flexible and extensible. It also prevents the design-time functionality from impacting your control's run-time behavior.

Four main categories of classes provide advanced design-time functionality:

- **Type converter**   A class that is associated with a type or a property and performs string-to-value conversions as well as conversions between the type it is associated with and other types. The property browser uses type converters to display property values as text strings and to convert user-entered text strings into objects that represent the values of properties. The designer also uses type converters for other tasks, which we will describe in the "Type Converters" section in this chapter. We examined type converters and showed how to implement them for custom types in Chapter 10, "Complex Properties and State Management."

- **Designer**   A class associated with a control that governs the appearance and behavior of the control on the design surface. A designer enables a control to provide a different visual representation at design time than at run time. For example, the *DataList* control uses a designer class to offer WYSIWIG template editing. We'll show you how to implement designers in the "Designers" section of this chapter. Note that, in this context, the term *designer* has a different meaning than the term *visual designer*, which refers to the visual design environment.

- **UI type editor**   A class that is associated with a type or a property and provides a specialized user interface for editing a property. A UI type editor is launched from the property browser and is useful when the simple text entry UI provided by the property browser is not adequate for editing a property. For example, the color picker drop-down list within the property grid that enables a page developer to select a color for the *BackColor* or *ForeColor* property of a Web control in a WYSIWYG fashion is a UI type editor. We'll show you how to implement UI type editors in the "UI Type Editors" section in this chapter.

- **Component editor**   A class associated with a control that provides a UI for editing the properties of a control as a whole. Component editors provide capabilities that are similar to property pages in Microsoft ActiveX controls. A component editor is not a replacement for the property browser but provides a more convenient UI for editing commonly accessed properties of a control. For example, the *DataList* control is associated with a component editor that is launched when a page developer chooses the Property Builder command from the context menu. We'll show you how to implement a component editor in the "Component Editors" section in this chapter.

Figure 15-1 provides an overview of the design-time architecture of the .NET Framework.

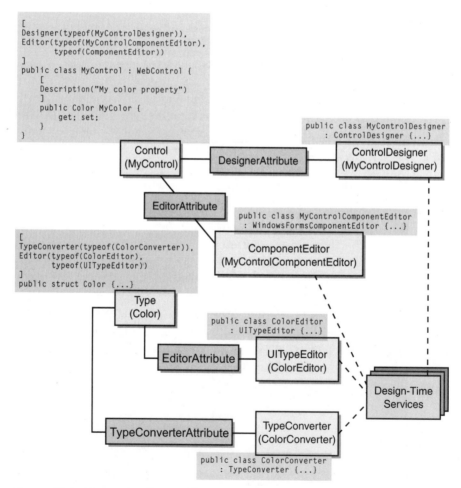

Figure 15-1   The design-time architecture of the .NET Framework

Figure 15-1 uses a hypothetical custom Web control named *MyControl* to demonstrate the relationship between a control and the classes that provide design-time functionality:

- The *System.Drawing.ColorConverter* class is a type converter that enables the property browser to display the value of the *MyColor* property of *MyControl* as a text string. *ColorConverter* derives from the *System.ComponentModel.TypeConverter* class. *ColorConverter* is associated with the *System.Drawing.Color* type of the *MyColor* property via the *System.ComponentModel.TypeConverterAttribute* metadata attribute. Type converters are indirectly associated with a control through the control's property types.

- The *MyControlDesigner* class is a designer that governs the appearance and behavior of the *MyControl* control on the design surface. *MyControlDesigner* derives from *System.Web.UI.Design.ControlDesigner* and is associated with *MyControl* via the *System.ComponentModel.DesignerAttribute* metadata attribute.

- The *System.Drawing.Design.ColorEditor* class is a UI type editor that enables the property browser to offer a special UI in the form of a color picker drop-down list when a page developer clicks the *MyColor* property in the property browser. *ColorEditor* derives from the *System.Drawing.Design.UITypeEditor* class and is associated with the *Color* type via the *System.ComponentModel.EditorAttribute* metadata attribute. UI type editors are indirectly associated with a control through the control's property types.

- The *MyControlComponentEditor* class is a component editor that provides a UI for editing the frequently accessed properties of *MyControl*. *MyControlComponentEditor* derives from *System.Windows.Forms.Design.WindowsFormsComponentEditor* and is associated with *MyControl* via the *EditorAttribute* metadata attribute.

Most of this chapter will be devoted to describing how to implement the classes that provide advanced design-time functionality—designers, UI type editors, and component editors. These classes in turn utilize design-time services that are provided by a visual design environment, such as the Web Forms designer in Visual Studio .NET. We won't describe how to implement design-time services in this book because these are not implemented by control developers but provided by the design-time environment.

Although we described the design-time architecture in terms of controls, the core architecture shown in Figure 15-1 applies to all designable components. In this figure, if you replace *Control* with *IComponent* and replace *ControlDesigner* with *IDesigner*, the resulting illustration will represent the more general design-time architecture of the .NET Framework.

Type Converters

A type converter is a class that derives from *System.ComponentModel.TypeConverter* and performs conversions from a given type to other types and vice versa. Type converters are used both at design time and at run time, as we described in Chapter 10.

At design time, the property browser uses type converters for the following purposes:

■   To convert the values of properties that are not of the *String* type to string representations that can be displayed in the property browser. Conversely, the property browser uses type converters to convert user-entered text strings into objects that represent the appropriate property types. In Chapter 10, we described examples—*MapCircleConverter* and *MapRectangleConverter*—that show how to implement a type converter that performs string-to-value conversions.

■   To provide an expand/collapse UI for subproperties. *System.ComponentModel.ExpandableObjectConverter* provides the base implementation for this functionality. You can extend the *ExpandableObjectConverter* class, as you saw in the *MapShapeConverter* class in Chapter 10.

■   To provide a drop-down list of values for a design-time property in a data-bound control. In Chapter 16, "Data-Bound Controls," we will utilize a type converter that provides this feature.

The control persister, which generates HTML corresponding to controls, uses type converters to persist properties in the form of declarative syntax in an .aspx page. We examined property persistence in Chapter 10 and explained that properties are either persisted on the control's tags or nested within the control's tags.

Because the examples in Chapter 10 and Chapter 16 cover the cases described in the preceding list, we will not provide examples of type converters in this chapter.

TypeConverterAttribute

To associate a type converter with a type, you must apply the *System.ComponentModel.TypeConverterAttribute* metadata attribute to the type, as we described in Chapter 10. You can also apply *TypeConverterAttribute* to a property to associate a type converter with that property. The second technique is useful when the property type does not have an associated type converter or when you want to override the existing type converter associated with the property type.

The constructor of *TypeConverterAttribute* is overloaded. The attribute usage syntax depends on the relative assembly locations of the type and the type converter. The most common usage scenario is where the type converter and the type it is associated with are in the same assembly, or when you are using a built-in type converter from the .NET Framework class library. In those cases, you can pass an early-bound type reference into the constructor, as shown in the following example:

```
[
TypeConverter(typeof(MapCircleConverter))
]
public class MapCircle { ... }
```

When the reference to the type converter can be resolved at compile time, you should use the syntax shown in this example. The scenarios that require a late-bound reference (and the corresponding attribute syntax) are similar to those described in the "DesignerAttribute" section later in this chapter.

Designers

A designer is a class that governs the behavior of a component on the design surface. In the .NET Framework, the *System.ComponentModel.Design.IDesigner* interface specifies core designer functionality. The *System.ComponentModel.Design.ComponentDesigner* class implements this interface and provides base designer functionality to all (designable) components. The core designer architecture is the same in Web Forms and Windows Forms. However, Web Forms and Windows Forms use different rendering engines. The Web Forms designer uses Microsoft Internet Explorer as its rendering engine, while the Windows Forms designer uses GDI+ for rendering. To provide base design-time rendering logic that is relevant to each rendering engine, Web Forms and Windows Forms define their own base designer classes that derive from *ComponentDesigner*. The base class for Web Forms control designers, *System.Web.UI.Design.ControlDesigner*, implements the plumbing to generate HTML for rendering a control at design time. The base class for Windows Forms control designers, *System.Windows.Forms.Design.ControlDesigner*, provides the plumbing for drawing in a native window by using GDI+ at design time.

The *System.Web.UI.Design.ControlDesigner* class is associated with the base *Control* class (via the *DesignerAttribute*) and thus is associated with a server control by default. From here on, we'll simply refer to the base designer class for server controls as *ControlDesigner* because there is no potential for ambiguity. (We do not describe designers for Windows Forms controls in this book.)

To develop a custom control designer, you must implement a class that derives directly or indirectly from *ControlDesigner* and overrides the methods described in the following list. You can then associate the designer class with your control by applying the *DesignerAttribute* metadata attribute, which we'll describe in greater detail at the end of this section.

■   ***GetDesignTimeHtml***   Returns the string that contains the HTML to render at design time. *ControlDesigner* implements this method to return the HTML generated by the control at run time by calling the control's *RenderControl* method. We will describe the implementation pattern for this method shortly.

■   ***GetEmptyDesignTimeHtml***   Returns the HTML to render at design time when the HTML generated by calling *RenderControl* returns an empty string. This can happen when the set of properties required for rendering the control have not been set by the page developer. *ControlDesigner*'s implementation of this method returns a string that indicates the type of the control and its ID, thus enabling identification of the control on the design surface. You can override this method to generate placeholder design-time HTML along with an instructive message for the page developer by using the *CreatePlaceHolderDesignTimeHtml* helper method.

■ **GetErrorDesignTimeHtml**   Returns HTML to render at design time when an error is encountered while generating the design-time HTML. *ControlDesigner* returns an empty string from this method. You can override this method to generate a useful error message in the design-time HTML by invoking the *CreatePlaceHolderDesign-TimeHtml* helper method.

■ **Initialize**   Invoked when the designer is initialized and associated with a component. The base class's implementation of this method checks that the component to which the designer is being attached derives from *Control*. You should override this method to check that the designer is being associated with the control type that you intended it to be used with.

The most important method to implement in a designer is the *GetDesign-TimeHtml* method. The pseudocode in Listing 15-1 shows the implementation pattern for this method.

```
public override string GetDesignTimeHtml() {
    string designTimeHtml = null;
    try {
        // Make changes to the control if needed to ensure a
        // meaningful design-time rendering.
        ⋮
        // Next invoke the base class's method.
        designTimeHtml = base.GetDesignTimeHtml()
    }
    catch (Exception ex) {
        designTimeHtml = GetErrorDesignTimeHtml(ex);
    }
    finally {
        // Undo any changes that you made in the try block.
    }

    if ((designTimeHtml == null) || (designTimeHtml.Length == 0)) {
        designTimeHtml = GetEmptyDesignTimeHtml();
    }

    return designTimeHtml;
}
```

Listing 15-1   Pattern for implementing the *GetDesignTimeHtml* method

> **Note**   If you make changes to a control in *GetDesignTimeHtml* (for example, a *Label* renders the value of its *ID* property as its text at design time when its *Text* property has not been set), you must undo those changes after you have generated the HTML string to render. You should enclose your code in *try/catch/finally* blocks so that you can undo changes (if any) made in the *try* block in the *finally* block.

The base *ControlDesigner* class sets a control's *Visible* property to *true* in the *try* block of its *GetDesignTimeHtml* method so that every control on the page is rendered at design time, even if the control's *Visible* property is set to *false*. *ControlDesigner* sets the value of the *Visible* property back to its actual value in the *finally* block of the *GetDesignTimeHtml* method.

ASP.NET provides two additional base designer classes that derive from *ControlDesigner* and provide designer functionality for common scenarios:

- ***System.Web.UI.Design.TemplatedControlDesigner***   Implements the base functionality to render a design-time UI for editing template properties of templated controls such as *DataList* in a WYSIWIG fashion.

- ***System.Web.UI.Design.ReadWriteControlDesigner***   Implements the base functionality to enable a page developer to select and modify the contents of a container control such as a *Panel* in a WYSIWIG fashion.

We'll now look at examples that illustrate how you can extend the base designer classes to implement designers for common categories of server controls.

Composite Control Designers—The *CompositeControlDesigner* Example

As we described in Chapter 12, "Composite Controls," ASP.NET does not provide a base designer class for composite controls. When you implement a composite control, such as the *CompositeLogin* control we described in Chapter 12, you must implement a designer that ensures that child controls are rendered on the design surface. Listing 15-2 shows the code for a designer that you can use as the base class for composite controls.

```
using System;
using System.ComponentModel;
using System.ComponentModel.Design;
using System.Web.UI;
using System.Web.UI.Design;            — reference system.design

namespace MSPress.ServerControls.Design {

    public class CompositeControlDesigner : ControlDesigner {
        public override string GetDesignTimeHtml() {
            // Retrieve the controls to ensure they are created.
            ControlCollection controls = ((Control)Component).Controls;
            return base.GetDesignTimeHtml();
        }

        public override void Initialize(IComponent component) {
            if (!(component is Control) &&
                !(component is INamingContainer)) {
                throw new ArgumentException(
                    "Component must be a container control.",
                    "component");
            }
            base.Initialize(component);
        }
    }
}
```

Listing 15-2   CompositeControlDesigner.cs

Although this designer ensures that child controls are rendered, it is not a read-write control designer—that is, a page developer cannot select a child control on the design surface to access its object model in the property browser. Later in this section, we'll describe the *ReadWriteControlDesigner* class, which allows page developers to select a control's contents on the design surface. However, a *ReadWriteControlDesigner* renders only those child controls that exist within the control's tags in the declarative syntax of the .aspx page. In short, the design-time architecture currently does not provide any functionality to allow a page developer to access child controls that are programmatically added to your control.

To associate the *CompositeControlDesigner* designer with a composite control, apply the *DesignerAttribute* metadata attribute, as shown in the following example:

```
[
Designer(typeof(CompositeControlDesigner))
]
public class CompositeLogin : WebControl { ... }
```

We'll describe other variations of the *DesignerAttribute* at the end of this section.

Templated Control Designers—The *ContactInfoDesigner* Example

We'll now examine how to implement a designer that provides a UI for editing template properties in a WYSIWYG fashion. To illustrate the concepts, we'll create a *ContactInfoDesigner* designer for the *ContactInfo* templated control we implemented in Chapter 12.

Figure 15-2 shows the *ContactInfo* control with which the *ContactInfoDesigner* class is associated. The Contact Template command appears when the page developer right-clicks the control to access the context menu and selects the Edit Template command.

Figure 15-2 The *ContactInfo* control with which *ContactInfoDesigner* is associated in the Web Forms designer in Visual Studio .NET

Figure 15-3 shows the control after the page developer chooses the Contact Template command shown in Figure 15-2. The control now displays the template editing UI, and the page developer can create the template in a WYSI-WYG fashion by dragging controls from the toolbox onto the template editing surface. To set properties of controls in the template, the page developer selects controls on the template surface and edits their properties in the property browser. To complete editing the template, the page developer right-clicks the control to access the context menu and then chooses the End Template Editing command.

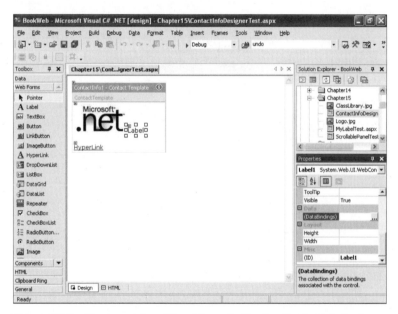

Figure 15-3   The template editing UI created by the *ContactInfoDesigner* class that is associated with the *ContactInfo* control

Before we examine the code for the *ContactInfoDesigner* class, here is a high-level overview of the steps required to implement a designer for a templated control. You must define a class that derives from *System.Web.UI.Design.TemplatedControlDesigner* and implement the following abstract methods of the *TemplatedControlDesigner* base class:

- **GetCachedTemplateEditingVerbs**   Implement this method to return one or more *template editing verbs*. A template editing verb represents a command or action that enables template editing. In Visual Studio .NET a template editing verb creates a command in the context menu that launches the template editing UI. The Contact Template command in Figure 15-2 represents a template editing verb. A template editing verb is a special case of a *designer verb*, which we'll describe in more detail toward the end of this section.

Designer verbs represent commands on the design surface.

- *CreateTemplateEditingFrame*   Implement this method to define the template editing UI. Figure 15-3 shows the template editing UI created by the *ContactInfoDesigner*.

- *GetTemplateContent*   Implement this method to return the text corresponding to the current template definition. The text is the declarative syntax for the template in the .aspx page.

- *SetTemplateContent*   Implement this method to generate a new template instance from the modified contents of the template on the design surface.

A templated control designer also uses an *ITemplateEditingService* service, which is one of the services represented by the Design-Time Services box shown in Figure 15-1.

Listing 15-3 shows the code for the *ContactInfoDesigner* class.

```
using System;
using System.Collections;
using System.ComponentModel;
using System.ComponentModel.Design;
using System.Diagnostics;
using System.Web.UI;
using System.Web.UI.Design;
using System.Web.UI.WebControls;
using MSPress.ServerControls;

namespace MSPress.ServerControls.Design {

    public class ContactInfoDesigner : TemplatedControlDesigner {

        private TemplateEditingVerb[] _templateEditingVerbs;

        #region Design-time HTML
        public override string GetDesignTimeHtml() {
            ContactInfo control = (ContactInfo)Component;

            if (control.ContactTemplate == null) {
                return GetEmptyDesignTimeHtml();
            }
```

Listing 15-3 ContactInfoDesigner.cs

```
        string designTimeHtml = String.Empty;
        try {
            control.DataBind();
            designTimeHtml = base.GetDesignTimeHtml();
        }
        catch (Exception e) {
            designTimeHtml = GetErrorDesignTimeHtml(e);
        }

        return designTimeHtml;
    }

    protected override string GetEmptyDesignTimeHtml() {
        return CreatePlaceHolderDesignTimeHtml("Right-click to " +
            "edit the ContactTemplate property. " +
            "<br>If the ContactTemplate is not specified, a " +
            "default template is used at run time.");
    }

    protected override string GetErrorDesignTimeHtml(Exception e) {
        return CreatePlaceHolderDesignTimeHtml("There was an " +
            "error rendering the ContactInfo control.");
    }
    #endregion Design-time HTML

    #region Template-editing Functionality
    protected override
        TemplateEditingVerb[] GetCachedTemplateEditingVerbs() {
        if (_templateEditingVerbs == null) {
            _templateEditingVerbs = new TemplateEditingVerb[1];
            _templateEditingVerbs[0] =
                new TemplateEditingVerb("Contact Template",
                    0, this);
        }
        return _templateEditingVerbs;
    }

    protected override
        ITemplateEditingFrame CreateTemplateEditingFrame(
            TemplateEditingVerb verb) {
        ITemplateEditingFrame frame = null;

        if ((_templateEditingVerbs != null) &&
            (_templateEditingVerbs[0] == verb)) {
```

(continued)

Listing 15-3   *(continued)*

```
            ITemplateEditingService teService =
                (ITemplateEditingService)GetService(typeof(
                    ITemplateEditingService));

        if (teService != null) {
            Style style =
                ((ContactInfo)Component).ControlStyle;
            frame = teService.CreateFrame(this, verb.Text,
                new string[] { "ContactTemplate" }, style,
                null);
        }
    }

    return frame;
}

private void DisposeTemplateEditingVerbs() {
    if (_templateEditingVerbs != null) {
        _templateEditingVerbs[0].Dispose();
        _templateEditingVerbs = null;
    }
}

public override string GetTemplateContent(
    ITemplateEditingFrame editingFrame, string templateName,
    out bool allowEditing) {
    string content = String.Empty;

    allowEditing = true;

    if ((_templateEditingVerbs != null) &&
        (_templateEditingVerbs[0] == editingFrame.Verb)) {
        ITemplate currentTemplate =
            ((ContactInfo)Component).ContactTemplate;

        if (currentTemplate != null) {
            content = GetTextFromTemplate(currentTemplate);
        }
    }

    return content;
}

public override void SetTemplateContent(
    ITemplateEditingFrame editingFrame, string templateName,
    string templateContent) {
```

```
        if ((_templateEditingVerbs != null) &&
            (_templateEditingVerbs[0] == editingFrame.Verb)) {
            ContactInfo control = (ContactInfo)Component;
            ITemplate newTemplate = null;

            if ((templateContent != null) &&
                (templateContent.Length != 0)) {
                newTemplate = GetTemplateFromText(templateContent);
            }

            control.ContactTemplate = newTemplate;
        }
    }
    #endregion Template-editing Functionality

    public override bool AllowResize {
        get {
            bool templateExists =
                ((ContactInfo)Component).ContactTemplate != null;
            // When templates are not defined, render a read-only
            // fixed-size block. Once templates are defined or
            // are being edited, the control should allow resizing.
            return templateExists || InTemplateMode;
        }
    }

    protected override void Dispose(bool disposing) {
        if (disposing) {
            DisposeTemplateEditingVerbs();
        }
        base.Dispose(disposing);
    }

    public override void Initialize(IComponent component) {
        if (!(component is ContactInfo)) {
            throw new ArgumentException(
                "Component must be a ContactInfo control.",
                "component");
        }
        base.Initialize(component);
    }

    public override void OnComponentChanged(object sender,
        ComponentChangedEventArgs ce) {
        base.OnComponentChanged(sender, ce);
```

(continued)

Listing 15-3 *(continued)*

```
        if (ce.Member != null) {
            string name = ce.Member.Name;

            if (name.Equals("Font") ||
                name.Equals("ForeColor") ||
                name.Equals("BackColor")) {
                DisposeTemplateEditingVerbs();
            }
        }
    }
}
}
```

ContactInfoDesigner demonstrates how to implement the abstract methods of the base *TemplatedControlDesigner* class by performing the following tasks:

■ Implementing the *GetCachedTemplateEditingVerbs* method to create a *TemplateEditingVerb* that appears as a command in the context menu and enables a page developer to launch the UI for editing a template property. A designer for a templated control that has more than one template property can create additional verbs that correspond to other templates or can provide verbs that correspond to template groups. For example, the *DataList* control creates three template editing verbs: Header And Footer Templates, Item Templates, and Separator Template.

■ Implementing the *CreateTemplateEditingFrame* method to create and return the template editing UI corresponding to a given template editing verb. In this method, *ContactInfoDesigner* invokes the *Get-Service* method of the base class to get an *ITemplateEditingService* instance. *ContactInfoDesigner* then invokes the *CreateFrame* method of the *ITemplateEditingService* interface to create an *ITemplateEditingFrame* instance. A template editing frame can contain more than one template. For example, the Item Templates frame created by the designer of the *DataList* control allows a page developer to modify four templates: *ItemTemplate*, *AlternatingItemTemplate*, *SelectedItemTemplate*, and *EditItemTemplate*.

- Implementing the *GetTemplateContent* method to return the text for the current template. To perform this task, *ContactInfo* invokes the *GetTextFromTemplate* helper method of the base class and passes the value of the current template property into it.

- Implementing the *SetTemplateContent* method to generate the template instance from the modified template definition. To perform this task, *ContactInfo* invokes the *GetTemplateFromText* helper method of the base class. *ContactInfo* then assigns the value of the template instance to the *ContactInfo* template property of the control. This assignment subsequently causes the control to render content corresponding to the new template when the *GetDesignTimeHtml* method of the base designer invokes the control's *RenderControl* method.

In addition, *ContactInfoDesigner* overrides the following members it inherits from *ControlDesigner*, which is the base class for *TemplatedControlDesigner*:

- Overrides the *GetDesignTimeHtml* method to invoke *DataBind* on the control in the method's *try* block. As with the page, a designer must invoke *DataBind* on a templated control to ensure that data binding expressions in the template or templates are evaluated.

- Overrides the *GetEmptyDesignTimeHtml* and *GetErrorDesignTime-Html* methods to generate appropriate messages when there is no HTML to render or when there is an error in rendering the control on the design surface.

- Overrides the *AllowResize* property to enable a page developer to resize the control at design time only when the template has content or when the control is in template editing mode.

- Overrides the *Dispose* method to free the cached template editing verbs in a more deterministic manner than waiting for garbage collection.

- Overrides the *OnComponentChanged* method to dispose the cached template editing verbs if the page developer changes the *Font*, *Fore-Color*, or *BackColor* style properties of the control. This action causes the designer to propagate the changes in these properties to the template editing UI when the template editing verbs are re-created.

Read-Write Control Designers—The *ScrollablePanelDesigner* Example

A read-write control designer allows a page developer to add child controls to a container control (such as *Panel*) in a WYSIWIG fashion. A page developer can drag controls from the toolbox onto the region that represents the container control on the design surface and can select the contained controls and edit their properties in the property browser. The *System.Web.UI.Design.ReadWrite-ControlDesigner* implements the base functionality of a read-write control designer.

Before we describe how to extend *ReadWriteControlDesigner*, let's examine what a read-write control designer cannot do:

- Cannot be extended to selectively make some contained controls read-write and others read-only.

- Does not render controls that are programmatically added to the container control. A read-write control designer displays only those controls that are dragged from the toolbox onto the design surface and those that are declaratively added within the control's tags in the .aspx page.

- Does not use the *GetDesignTimeHtml* method to generate or customize its design-time rendering. Instead, a read-write control designer generates an editable region that displays the design-time representation of the contained controls.

The *ReadWriteControlDesigner* is limited in extensibility because its *GetDesignTimeHtml* method is not invoked by the design environment. *ReadWrite-ControlDesigner* renders the styles for the container Web control by adding style attributes to a behavior object associated with the designer. The only features you can add to *ReadWriteControlDesigner* are additional styles that your control might add to *WebControl*'s object model. For example, the *System.Web.UI.Design.WebControls.PanelDesigner* designer derives from *Read-WriteControlDesigner* and adds style attributes corresponding to the *Panel* control's style properties (such as *HorizontalAlign*), which the *Panel* control adds to *WebControl*'s object model.

To show how you can extend the *PanelDesigner* class, we'll implement a designer for the *ScrollablePanel* custom control, which derives from *Panel* and displays scroll bars, as shown in Figure 15-4.

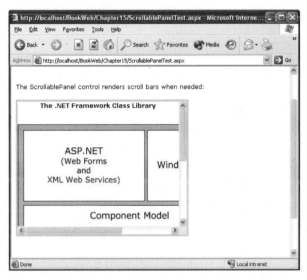

Figure 15-4   The *ScrollablePanel* control viewed in a browser at run time

Figure 15-5 shows the design-time representation of the *ScrollablePanel* control, which has an associated *ScrollablePanelDesigner*.

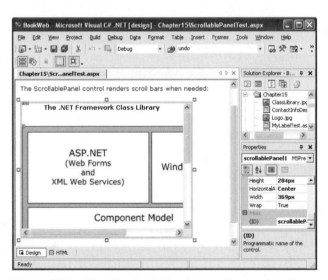

Figure 15-5   The *ScrollablePanel* control in the Web Forms designer

Listing 15-4 contains the code for the *ScrollablePanel* control.

```csharp
using System;
using System.ComponentModel;
using System.ComponentModel.Design;
using System.Web.UI;
using System.Web.UI.WebControls;

namespace MSPress.ServerControls {
    [
    Designer(typeof(
        MSPress.ServerControls.Design.ScrollablePanelDesigner))
    ]
    public class ScrollablePanel : Panel {

        [
        Bindable(true),
        Category("Appearance"),
        DefaultValue(false),
        Description("Specifies whether to render scroll bars."),
        ]
        public virtual bool ScrollBars {
            get {
                object b = ViewState["ScrollBars"];
                return (b == null) ? false : (bool)b;
            }
            set {
                ViewState["ScrollBars"] = value;
            }
        }

        protected override
            void AddAttributesToRender(HtmlTextWriter writer) {
            base.AddAttributesToRender(writer);
            if (ScrollBars == true) {
                if ((Height.IsEmpty == false) ||
                    (Width.IsEmpty == false)) {
                    writer.AddStyleAttribute("overflow", "auto");
                    writer.AddStyleAttribute("overflow-x", "auto");
                    writer.AddStyleAttribute("overflow-y", "auto");
                }
            }
        }
    }
}
```

Listing 15-4 ScrollablePanel.cs

Listing 15-5 contains the code for the *ScrollablePanelDesigner*.

```csharp
using System;
using System.ComponentModel;
using System.ComponentModel.Design;
using System.Diagnostics;
using System.Web.UI.Design;
using System.Web.UI.Design.WebControls;
using System.Web.UI.WebControls;
using MSPress.ServerControls;

namespace MSPress.ServerControls.Design {

    public class ScrollablePanelDesigner : PanelDesigner {

        protected override void MapPropertyToStyle(string propertyName,
            object propertyValue) {
            if ((propertyName == null) || (propertyValue == null)) {
                return;
            }

            try {
                if (propertyName.Equals("ScrollBars")) {
                    ScrollablePanel panel = (ScrollablePanel)Component;
                    bool scrollBars = (bool)propertyValue;
                    if (panel.Height.IsEmpty || panel.Width.IsEmpty) {
                        scrollBars = false;
                    }
                    if (scrollBars == true) {
                        Behavior.SetStyleAttribute("overflow", true,
                            "auto", true);
                        Behavior.SetStyleAttribute("overflowX", true,
                            "auto", true);
                        Behavior.SetStyleAttribute("overflowY", true,
                            "auto", true);
                    }
                    else {
                        Behavior.RemoveStyleAttribute("overflow",
                            true, true);
                        Behavior.RemoveStyleAttribute("overflowX",
                            true, true);
                        Behavior.RemoveStyleAttribute("overflowY",
                            true, true);
                    }
                }
```

Listing 15-5   ScrollablePanelDesigner.cs   *(continued)*

Listing 15-5 *(continued)*

```
            else {
                base.MapPropertyToStyle(propertyName,
                    propertyValue);
            }
        }
        catch {
        }
    }

    protected override void OnBehaviorAttached() {
        base.OnBehaviorAttached();

        ScrollablePanel panel = (ScrollablePanel)Component;
        bool scrollBars = panel.ScrollBars;
        MapPropertyToStyle("ScrollBars", scrollBars);
    }
  }
}
```

ScrollablePanelDesigner shows the tasks to perform when you extend the *ReadWriteControlDesigner* class:

■ Override the *MapPropertyToStyle* method to add style attributes corresponding to style properties of the control to the behavior object that is attached to the designer. In this method, *ScrollablePanelDesigner* adds *overflow* style attributes if the *ScrollBars* property of the *ScrollablePanel* instance is *true* and if the *Height* and *Width* properties of the control are not specified.

■ Override the *OnBehaviorAttached* method to invoke the *MapPropertyToStyle* method, and pass the property name and value into *MapPropertyToStyle*.

In the sample files for this book, we provide the *MyPanelDesigner* class, which shows how to implement a designer that is similar to *PanelDesigner*. *MyPanelDesigner* derives from *ReadWriteControlDesigner* and adds style attributes that correspond to three additional style properties: *HorizontalAlign*, *Wrap*, and *BackImageUrl*. *MyPanelDesigner* is associated with the *MyPanel* control that we implemented in Chapter 11.

Designer Verbs

As mentioned earlier in the chapter, a designer verb represents a command on the design surface. Designer verbs are an integral part of the designer specification. Every designer can offer a collection of designer verbs, as specified in the *System.ComponentModel.Design.IDesigner* interface:

```
DesignerVerbCollection Verbs { get; }
```

Each member of the *Verbs* collection is a *System.Component-Model.Design.DesignerVerb* or a class that derives from it.

In the *ContactInfoDesigner* example presented earlier in this section, we created a template editing verb (*TemplateEditingVerb*) that launches the templated editing UI. *TemplateEditingVerb* derives from *DesignerVerb*.

We'll show you another example of a designer that creates a designer verb in the "Component Editors" section of this chapter

DesignerAttribute

To associate a designer with your control, you must apply the *System.ComponentModel.DesignerAttribute* metadata attribute to the control. The constructor of the *DesignerAttribute* is overloaded. The two–parameter overloads take the type of the designer as their second argument. The default value of the second parameter, the *IDesigner* interface type, is valid for most common scenarios. Therefore, in this chapter, we will describe the one–parameter overloads only.

The attribute usage syntax depends on the assembly location of the designer relative to the assembly location of the control with which it is associated. When the control and its designer are deployed in the same assembly, the constructor of *DesignerAttribute* can take an early-bound type reference to the designer, as shown in the following example:

```
[
Designer(typeof(MSPress.ServerControls.Design.ContactInfoDesigner))
]
public class ContactInfo : WebControl, INamingContainer { ... }
```

If the namespace that contains the designer is referenced with a *using* statement in the control, you can pass in the shorter class name of the designer in the constructor.

You can also use the early-bound syntax when the designer is a built-in class in the .NET Framework. For example, you can associate the *ReadWrite-ControlDesigner* class with a *MyControl* class deployed in a private assembly by using this syntax:

```
using System.Web.UI.Design;
[
Designer(typeof(ReadWriteControlDesigner))
]
public class MyControl : WebControl { ... }
```

If the control and its designer are deployed in different assemblies and the designer is not a built-in class in the .NET Framework, the compiler cannot resolve an early-bound type reference to the designer because the reference creates a circular dependency between the two assemblies. Therefore, you must provide a late-bound reference to the designer—that is, a reference that is resolved at design time. A late-bound type reference is an *assembly qualified type name*, which is represented as a *String* that contains the full type name and the full assembly name. (We'll show examples of assembly qualified type names in a moment.) In this case, you must use the overload of the *Designer-Attribute* constructor that accepts a *String* argument for the type reference.

When the designer is in a private assembly, the full assembly name is merely the name of the assembly, as shown by the second part of the string argument in the following example:

```
[
Designer("MSPress.ServerControls.Design.ContactInfoDesigner, " +
    "MSPress.ServerControls.Design")
]
public class ContactInfo : WebControl, INamingContainer { ... }
```

In this example, we assume that *ContactInfoDesigner* is deployed in the hypothetical *MSPress.ServerControls.Design* private assembly, whereas *ContactInfo* is deployed in the *MSPress.ServerControls* private assembly.

When the designer exists in a shared assembly in the GAC, the full name of the assembly includes the name, version, culture, and public key token of the assembly, as shown by the second part of the string argument in the following example:

```
[
Designer("System.Web.UI.Design.ReadWriteControlDesigner, " +
    "System.Design, Version=1.0.3300.0, Culture=neutral, " +
    "PublicKeyToken=b03f5f7f11d50a3a")
]
public class MyControl : WebControl { ... }
```

Chapter 17 describes shared assemblies and full assembly names in greater detail.

UI Type Editors

A UI type editor is launched from the property browser and provides a custom user interface for editing a property. A UI type editor is useful when the standard UI provided by the property browser—a plain text box—is not adequate for editing a property type. For example, when editing a property of type *System.Drawing.Color*, a drop-down list that visually displays colors and enables a user to make a color selection is much more useful than a text box that accepts color names.

In the .NET Framework, a UI type editor is a class that derives from *System.Drawing.Design.UITypeEditor*. The *System.Drawing.Design.ColorEditor* for editing a color property and the *System.Web.UI.Design.UrlEditor* for editing a URL property are examples of UI type editors.

In this section, we'll show you how to implement your own UI type editor and customize the built-in *System.ComponentModel.Design.CollectionEditor*.

String Editor Example

The *StringEditor* class that we'll implement is a UI type editor that provides a dialog-based UI that makes editing long strings convenient, as shown in Figure 15-6. *StringEditor* can be associated with any property of type *String*.

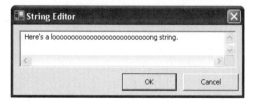

Figure 15-6   The user interface provided by the *StringEditor* class

Listing 15-6 contains the code for the *MyLabel* control that uses *StringEditor*. The *MyLabel* control derives from the standard *Label* control, overrides its *Text* property, and associates *StringEditor* with the property by applying the *EditorAttribute* metadata attribute to the property. We'll describe *EditorAttribute* in more detail at the end of this section. The *MyLabel* control also has a designer and a component editor associated with it. We'll describe those two classes later in the "Component Editors" section.

```csharp
using System;
using System.ComponentModel;
using System.Drawing.Design;
using System.Web.UI;
using System.Web.UI.WebControls;

namespace MSPress.ServerControls {

    [
    Designer(typeof(MSPress.ServerControls.Design.MyLabelDesigner)),
    Editor(typeof(MSPress.ServerControls.Design.MyLabelComponentEditor),
           typeof(ComponentEditor))
    ]
    public class MyLabel : Label {

        [
        Editor(typeof(MSPress.ServerControls.Design.StringEditor),
               typeof(UITypeEditor))
        ]
        public override string Text {
            get {
                return base.Text;
            }
            set {
                base.Text = value;
            }
        }
    }
}
```

Listing 15-6 MyLabel.cs

StringEditor causes the property browser in Visual Studio .NET to display an ellipsis next to the *Text* property of *MyLabel*, as shown in Figure 15-7. The ellipsis indicates that the associated UI type editor creates a modal dialog box for editing the property. Clicking the ellipsis invokes *StringEditor* to edit the property value.

Figure 15-7   Editing style displayed by the property browser for the *Text*
property with which *StringEditor* is associated

Listing 15-7 shows the code for the *StringEditor* class, which launches a
Windows Form and uses input from the form to update the property with
which *StringEditor* is associated.

```
using System;
using System.ComponentModel;
using System.Drawing;
using System.Drawing.Design;
using System.Windows.Forms;
using System.Windows.Forms.Design;

namespace MSPress.ServerControls.Design {

    public class StringEditor : UITypeEditor {

        public override object EditValue(ITypeDescriptorContext context,
            IServiceProvider serviceProvider, object value) {

            if ((context != null) &&
                (serviceProvider != null)) {
                IWindowsFormsEditorService edSvc =
                    (IWindowsFormsEditorService)
                        serviceProvider.GetService(
                            typeof(IWindowsFormsEditorService));
```

Listing 15-7   StringEditor.cs   *(continued)*

Listing 15-7 *(continued)*

```
                    if (edSvc != null) {
                        StringEditorForm form = new StringEditorForm();
                        form.Value = (string)value;

                        DialogResult result = edSvc.ShowDialog(form);
                        if (result == DialogResult.OK) {
                            value = form.Value;
                        }
                    }
                }
            }
            return value;
        }

        public override UITypeEditorEditStyle GetEditStyle(
            ITypeDescriptorContext context) {
            if (context != null) {
                return UITypeEditorEditStyle.Modal;
            }
            return base.GetEditStyle(context);
        }
    }
}
```

StringEditor demonstrates the following steps in implementing a UI type editor:

■   Derives from *System.Drawing.Design.UITypeEditor*

■   Overrides the *EditValue* method to create the user interface, process user input, and assign a value to the property

■   Overrides the *GetEditStyle* method to inform the property browser of the editing style the editor will use, such as a drop-down list or a modal dialog box

Let's examine the *GetEditStyle* and *EditValue* methods in more detail. The return type of the *GetEditStyle* method is the *UITypeEditorEditStyle* enumeration whose values *DropDown*, *Modal*, and *None* indicate the type of UI implemented by the UI type editor. You should return *UITypeEditorEditStyle.Drop-Down* if your UI type editor offers a drop-down UI for property editing. This value causes the property browser to display a drop-down button beside the property, as seen when editing the *BackColor* or *ForeColor* properties of a Web control. You should return *UITypeEditorEditStyle.Modal* if your editor offers a modal dialog box for property editing. This return value causes the property browser to display an ellipsis button beside the property. If you do not override the *GetEditStyle* method, the base class returns the default value *UITypeEditorEditStyle.None*, which tells the property browser that the editor does not offer a user interface for property editing.

The *EditValue* method is where you create and initialize the user interface with the current property value, process user input, and return an updated value for the property. This method has three parameters. The first parameter is the *ITypeDescriptorContext* object, which represents the context where your editor is used. Although more advanced editors use this parameter, the *StringEditor* does not use the first parameter. The second parameter is an *IServiceProvider* object that provides design-time services, as shown in Figure 15-1. The third parameter represents the initial value of the property that the editor is associated with.

To obtain a design-time service, you must invoke the *GetService* method of the *IServiceProvider* object. *StringEditor* requests an *IWindowsFormsEditorService* because it wants to create a Windows Forms–based UI for property editing. The *ShowDialog* method of the *IWindowsFormsEditorService* class launches a dialog-based UI, while the *DropDownControl* method launches a drop-down UI. *StringEditor* invokes the *ShowDialog* method to launch a modal dialog box for property editing, as we describe in the next paragraph.

The remaining task in the *EditValue* method is to create an instance of the form (or control) to pass into the *ShowDialog* (or *DropDownControl*) method and return a value for the property. You must independently implement a Windows Forms *Form* or *Control* that represents the UI that your editor wants to create. *StringEditor* creates an instance of the *StringEditorForm* (shown in a moment) and passes it into the *ShowDialog* method to create a modal dialog box. *StringEditor* returns the user-entered text in the dialog box as the value of the property (of type *String*) with which the editor is associated.

The *StringEditorForm* class that creates the property editing UI offered by *StringEditor* is a *System.Windows.Forms.Form* that contains a multiline text box to enable the user to easily enter arbitrary text. The code for this class appears in the book's sample files. The main features are shown in the class outline in Listing 15-8. We used the Windows Forms designer to create the UI; the designer-generated code that creates the UI is not shown in the listing. *StringEditorForm* defines a *Value* property that delegates to the *Text* property of the *TextBox* it contains. The *Value* property enables *StringEditor* to access the value of the user-entered text in the text box.

```
using System;
using System.Collections;
using System.ComponentModel;
using System.Drawing;
using System.Windows.Forms;

namespace MSPress.ServerControls.Design {

    public class StringEditorForm : System.Windows.Forms.Form {
        private System.Windows.Forms.TextBox textBox1;
        private System.Windows.Forms.Button okButton;
        private System.Windows.Forms.Button cancelButton;

        public StringEditorForm() {
            InitializeComponent();
        }

        public string Value {
            get {
                return textBox1.Text;
            }
            set {
                textBox1.Text = value;
            }
        }

        #region Windows Form Designer generated code
        :
        #endregion
    }
}
```

Listing 15-8   StringEditorForm.cs

Collection Editor Examples

A collection editor enables a page developer to edit a collection property in a WYSIWYG fashion. For example, the *ListBox* control uses a collection editor to provide a UI that enables a page developer to add, remove, or reorder the objects in the *Items* collection.

The *System.ComponentModel.Design.CollectionEditor* is a built-in UI type editor that provides the basic functionality to edit a property of type *System.Collections.IList* in a design-time environment. You can override the methods of *CollectionEditor* to customize it for a specific collection.

CollectionEditor infers the type of the collection items from the *Items* property of the collection. You can override the *CreateCollectionItemType* method in a derived collection editor to return the type of the collection.

If the collection allows more than one type of object, you can override the *CreateNewItemTypes* method to specify the types that are allowed in the collection. Listing 15-9 shows the code for *HotSpotCollectionEditor*, which is associated with the *HotSpotCollection* type that contains two types, *CircleHotSpot* and *RectangleHotSpot*. In Chapter 10, we used the *HotSpotCollection* type and its associated *HotSpotCollectionEditor* in the *ImageMap* example. Figure 10-5 shows the UI created by *HotSpotCollectionEditor*.

```
using System;
using System.ComponentModel;
using System.ComponentModel.Design;
using System.Reflection;


namespace MSPress.ServerControls.Design {

    public class HotSpotCollectionEditor : CollectionEditor {

        public HotSpotCollectionEditor(Type type) : base(type) {
        }

        protected override Type[] CreateNewItemTypes() {
            Type[] types = new Type[] {
                typeof(CircleHotSpot),
                typeof(RectangleHotSpot)
            };
            return types;
        }
    }
}
```

Listing 15-9   HotSpotCollectionEditor.cs

EditorAttribute

To associate an editor with a type, you must apply the *System.Component-Model.EditorAttribute* metadata attribute to the type. You can also apply *Editor-Attribute* to a property to associate an editor with the property. The second technique is useful when the property type does not have an associated editor or when you want to override the existing editor associated with the property type.

The constructor of *EditorAttribute* takes two arguments. The first argument specifies the type of the editor, and the second specifies the base type. The base type is *UITypeEditor*, which we examined earlier in this section, or *System.ComponentModel.ComponentEditor*, which we will describe in the next section.

The common syntax for the *EditorAttribute* uses an early-bound type reference to the editor, as shown in the following example:

```
[
Editor(typeof(MSPress.ServerControls.Design.StringEditor),
    typeof(UITypeEditor))
]
public override string Text { ... }
```

The type reference used in the constructor of *EditorAttribute* depends on the assembly location of the type relative to the assembly location of the editor associated with the type. The scenarios that require a late-bound reference (and their corresponding attribute syntax) are similar to those described in the "DesignerAttribute" section presented earlier in this chapter.

Component Editors

A component editor is a class that provides a custom user interface for editing the properties of a control as a whole. The UI offered by a component editor is analogous to the property pages offered by ActiveX controls. A component editor is not a replacement for the property browser; rather, it offers a more convenient UI for editing the commonly accessed properties of a control. The *DataList* and *DataGrid* controls utilize component editors to offer richer property editing.

In this section, we'll show you how to implement a component editor for the *MyLabel* control we developed earlier in the "UI Type Editors" section.

The *MyLabelComponentEditor* Example

The *MyLabelComponentEditor* that we will now implement provides the UI shown in Figure 15-8 for editing the properties of the *MyLabel* control. The UI that Visual Studio .NET displays for a component editor refers to the editor as a *property builder*. *MyLabelComponentEditor* enables a page developer to edit three properties of *MyLabel*: *BackColor*, *ForeColor*, and *Text*. The editor also provides a UI to launch the color picker dialog box for editing the properties of type *Color*.

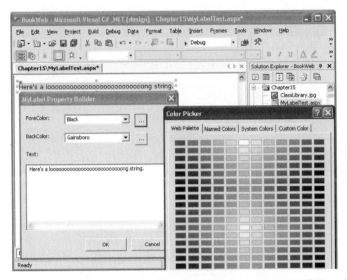

Figure 15-8   The UI created by the *MyLabelComponentEditor* class

We have associated *MyLabelComponentEditor* with *MyLabel* by applying the *EditorAttribute* metadata attribute to the control:

```
[
Editor(typeof(MSPress.ServerControls.Design.MyLabelComponentEditor),
    typeof(ComponentEditor))
]
public class MyLabel : Label { ... }
```

We described *EditorAttribute* in the previous section. Note that the second argument passed into the constructor of the attribute is the type of the *ComponentEditor* class, which is the base class for component editors.

Listing 15-10 contains the code for the *MyLabelComponentEditor* class. *MyLabelComponentEditor* derives from *WindowsFormsComponentEditor*, which in turn derives from *ComponentEditor*. The code demonstrates how to override the *EditComponent* method to create a Windows Forms *Form* for property editing.

```
using System;
using System.Design;
using System.ComponentModel;
using System.ComponentModel.Design;
using System.Windows.Forms;
using System.Windows.Forms.Design;
using MSPress.ServerControls;
```

Listing 15-10   MyLabelComponentEditor.cs   *(continued)*

Listing 15-10   *(continued)*

```
namespace MSPress.ServerControls.Design {

    public class MyLabelComponentEditor : WindowsFormsComponentEditor {

        public override bool EditComponent(
            ITypeDescriptorContext context, object component,
            IWin32Window owner) {
            MyLabel label = component as MyLabel;
            if (label == null) {
                throw new ArgumentException(
                    "Component must be a MyLabel object", "component");
            }

            IServiceProvider site = label.Site;
            IComponentChangeService changeService = null;

            DesignerTransaction transaction = null;
            bool changed = false;

            try {
                if (site != null) {
                    IDesignerHost designerHost = (IDesignerHost)
                        site.GetService(typeof(IDesignerHost));
                    transaction = designerHost.CreateTransaction(
                        "Property Builder");

                    changeService = (IComponentChangeService)
                        site.GetService(typeof(
                            IComponentChangeService));
                    if (changeService != null) {
                        try {
                            changeService.OnComponentChanging(label,
                                null);
                        }
                        catch (CheckoutException ex) {
                            if (ex == CheckoutException.Canceled)
                                return false;
                            throw ex;
                        }
                    }
                }

                try {
                    MyLabelComponentEditorForm form =
                        new MyLabelComponentEditorForm(label);
```

```
                    if (form.ShowDialog(owner) == DialogResult.OK) {
                        changed = true;
                    }
                }
                finally {
                    if (changed && changeService != null) {
                        changeService.OnComponentChanged(label, null,
                            null, null);
                    }
                }
            }
            finally {
                if (transaction != null) {
                    if (changed) {
                        transaction.Commit();
                    }
                    else {
                        transaction.Cancel();
                    }
                }
            }

            return changed;
        }
    }
}
```

Every control has a *Site* property whose type is the *System.Component-Model.ISite* interface. The *ISite* interface derives from the *System.IServicePro-vider* interface whose *GetService* method allows a component to access various design-time services when it is hosted in a design environment. In its implementation of the *EditComponent* method, *MyLabelComponentEditor* retrieves the *IComponentChangeService* and *IDesignerHost* services via the *Site* property associated with the *MyLabel* instance. The *IComponentChangeService* specifies the contract for updating the design surface when components are added, changed, or removed from the design surface. The *IDesignerHost* interface specifies the contract for supporting designer transactions, for managing components and their designers, and for obtaining information on the state of the designer. The .NET Framework does not provide an implementation of these interfaces—they are implemented by a design environment such as the Web Forms designer in Visual Studio .NET. *MyLabelComponentEditor* uses the *IDe-signerHost* instance to start a designer transaction and the *IComponentChange-Service* instance to tell the design environment whether the properties of the *MyLabel* instance are changed by the page developer.

MyLabelComponentEditor creates and launches an instance of the *MyLabelComponentEditorForm* class, which is a Windows Forms *Form* that defines the UI (shown in Figure 15-8) for editing the properties of a *MyLabel* control. The form contains the logic to initialize its own UI with the current property values of the control it is associated with. When the form is committed, it updates the control with the modified values. The code for *MyLabelComponentEditorForm* is shown in Listing 15-11.

```csharp
using System;
using System.Collections;
using System.ComponentModel;
using System.Drawing;
using System.Web.UI.Design;
using System.Windows.Forms;
using MSPress.ServerControls;

namespace MSPress.ServerControls.Design {

    public class MyLabelComponentEditorForm :
        System.Windows.Forms.Form {
        private System.Windows.Forms.Label label1;
        private System.Windows.Forms.ComboBox foreColorCombo;
        private System.Windows.Forms.Button foreColorButton;
        private System.Windows.Forms.Button backColorButton;
        private System.Windows.Forms.ComboBox backColorCombo;
        private System.Windows.Forms.Label label2;
        private System.Windows.Forms.Label textLabel;
        private System.Windows.Forms.TextBox textBox1;
        private System.Windows.Forms.Button okButton;
        private System.Windows.Forms.Button cancelButton;

        private MyLabel _myLabel;

        public MyLabelComponentEditorForm(MyLabel component) {
            InitializeComponent();

            _myLabel = component;

            textBox1.Text = _myLabel.Text;
            foreColorCombo.Text =
                ColorTranslator.ToHtml(_myLabel.ForeColor);
            backColorCombo.Text =
                ColorTranslator.ToHtml(_myLabel.BackColor);
        }
```

Listing 15-11   MyLabelComponentEditorForm.cs

```
#region Windows Form Designer generated code
  ⋮
#endregion

private void okButton_Click(object sender, System.EventArgs e) {
    // We set the properties of the MyLabel instance by using
    // PropertyDescriptors to enable undo functionality
    // after a page developer sets these
    // properties in the designer.
    // If you do not want to provide undo functionality,
    // you can replace the implementation of this method
    // with the simpler code shown in the commented block.
    //
    /*
    try {
        _myLabel.Text = textBox1.Text;
        _myLabel.ForeColor =
            ColorTranslator.FromHtml(
                foreColorCombo.Text.Trim());
        _myLabel.BackColor =
            ColorTranslator.FromHtml(
                backColorCombo.Text.Trim());
    }
    catch {
    }
    */

    PropertyDescriptorCollection props =
        TypeDescriptor.GetProperties(_myLabel);

    try {
        PropertyDescriptor textProperty = props["Text"];
        if (textProperty != null) {
            textProperty.SetValue(_myLabel, textBox1.Text);
        }
    }
    catch {
    }

    try {
        PropertyDescriptor foreColorProperty =
            props["ForeColor"];
        if (foreColorProperty != null) {
            Color foreColor =
                ColorTranslator.FromHtml(
                    foreColorCombo.Text.Trim());
```

(continued)

Listing 15-11 *(continued)*

```
                    foreColorProperty.SetValue(_myLabel, foreColor);
            }
        }
        catch {
        }

        try {
            PropertyDescriptor backColorProperty =
                props["BackColor"];
            if (backColorProperty != null) {
                Color backColor =
                    ColorTranslator.FromHtml(
                        backColorCombo.Text.Trim());
                backColorProperty.SetValue(_myLabel, backColor);
            }
        }
        catch {
        }

        DialogResult = DialogResult.OK;
        Close();
    }

    private void foreColorButton_Click(object sender,
        System.EventArgs e) {
        string color = foreColorCombo.Text.Trim();

        color = ColorBuilder.BuildColor(_myLabel, this, color);
        if (color != null) {
            foreColorCombo.Text = color;
        }
    }

    private void backColorButton_Click(object sender,
        System.EventArgs e) {
        string color = backColorCombo.Text.Trim();

        color = ColorBuilder.BuildColor(_myLabel, this, color);
        if (color != null) {
            backColorCombo.Text = color;
        }
    }
  }
}
```

MyLabelComponentEditorForm derives from *System.Windows.Forms.Form*. The argument of its constructor is a *MyLabel* instance. The constructor uses the initial values of the *BackColor*, *ForeColor*, and *Text* properties of the *MyLabel* instance to initialize the values of the combo boxes and the text box.

The *okButton_Click* event handler is associated with the *okButton Button* instance on the form and updates the *BackColor*, *ForeColor*, and *Text* properties of *MyLabel* with the values in the combo boxes and the text box on the form.

The combo boxes offer a drop-down list of standard color names. In addition, when clicked, the buttons next to the combo boxes launch the color picker dialog box shown in Figure 15-8. The *backColorButton_Click* and *foreColorButton_Click* event handlers associated with the buttons utilize the static *BuildColor* method of the *System.Web.UI.Design.ColorBuilder* class to start the color picker dialog box. The event handlers also update the combo boxes with the color selected by the page developer within the color picker dialog box.

The *ColorBuilder* is a helper class that allows *MyLabelComponentEditor* to easily create a specialized UI for editing a property of type *Color*. In the present version of the .NET Framework, two helper classes provide a custom UI for property editing: *ColorBuilder* and *System.Web.UI.Design.UrlBuilder*. In the future, the .NET Framework might offer additional builder classes for creating a UI geared toward editing specific property types.

Designer Verb That Initiates Component Editing

We'll now show you how to implement a designer verb that launches the component editor. A page developer can launch a component editor in one of three standard ways:

- Click the Property Pages button at the top of the property browser, as shown in Figure 15-9. This button is enabled when a component has an associated component editor. This mechanism does not use a designer verb.

- Click the Property Builder command that appears at the bottom of the property browser, as shown in Figure 15-9. This command represents a designer verb.

- Right-click the component and choose the Property Builder command from the context menu. This command also represents a designer verb.

Figure 15-9 The Property Pages button and the Property Builder designer verb in the property browser of Visual Studio .NET

The first mechanism is available by default when a component has an associated component editor (specified via the *EditorAttribute* metadata attribute). To enable the latter two mechanisms, you have to implement a designer that provides a designer verb that launches the component editor. A designer verb makes the component editor more discoverable by creating commands on the design surface. In Visual Studio .NET, a designer verb creates a command link in the property browser and a menu command in the context menu associated with the control.

Listing 15-12 contains the code for the *MyLabelDesigner* that creates the designer verb shown in Figure 15-9. The designer is associated with *MyLabel* control via the *DesignerAttribute*, as shown in Listing 15-6.

```
using System;
using System.Collections;
using System.ComponentModel;
using System.ComponentModel.Design;
using System.Diagnostics;
using System.Web.UI;
using System.Web.UI.Design;
using System.Web.UI.Design.WebControls;
using System.Web.UI.WebControls;
using MSPress.ServerControls;

namespace MSPress.ServerControls.Design {
```

Listing 15-12   MyLabelDesigner.cs

```
public class MyLabelDesigner : LabelDesigner {

    private DesignerVerbCollection _designerVerbs;

    public override DesignerVerbCollection Verbs {
        get {
            if (_designerVerbs == null) {
                _designerVerbs = new DesignerVerbCollection();
                _designerVerbs.Add(new DesignerVerb(
                    "Property Builder...",
                    new EventHandler(this.OnPropertyBuilder)));
            }

            return _designerVerbs;
        }
    }

    private void OnPropertyBuilder(object sender, EventArgs e) {
        MyLabelComponentEditor compEditor =
            new MyLabelComponentEditor();
        compEditor.EditComponent(Component);
    }

    public override void Initialize(IComponent component) {
        if (!(component is MyLabel)) {
            throw new ArgumentException(
                "Component must be a MyLabel control.",
                "component");
        }
        base.Initialize(component);
    }
}
```

MyLabelDesigner adds a *DesignerVerb* to its *Verbs* collection, which we described earlier in this chapter in the "Designers" section. The constructor of a *DesignerVerb* takes two arguments: a string that specifies a command name, and an event handler that performs some logic in response to the command. *MyLabelDesigner* creates a verb with the text "Property Builder...", which invokes the *OnPropertyBuilder* event handler. In the *OnPropertyBuilder* method, *MyLabelDesigner* creates an instance of *MyLabelComponentEditor* and invokes its *EditComponent* method to launch the component editing UI.

Debugging Design-Time Code

To debug design-time code, you will need two instances of Visual Studio .NET—one for performing design-time actions and the other for performing debugging operations. The following steps describe how to perform design-time debugging:

1.   Start Visual Studio .NET, and open the project that contains the controls and the associated design-time classes that you want to debug.

2.   Bring up the property pages for the project. Under Configuration Properties in the left pane, click Debugging. In the right pane, under Start Action, set Debug Mode to Program and set Start Application to devenv.exe. (If devenv.exe is not included in the path environment variable of your computer, you will have to provide the full path to it.) These two properties will cause the debugger to launch a new instance of Visual Studio .NET when the debugger is started.

3.   Set breakpoints in your code, and start the debugger via the Debug menu or by pressing F5 on the keyboard.

4.   A second instance of Visual Studio .NET will now appear on your screen. In this instance, create a new ASP.NET Web application and add a reference to the debug version of the project that contains the code you want to debug.

5.   In the Web application in the second instance of Visual Studio .NET, drag a control from the Toolbox onto the page. The debugger will pause as soon at it hits the first breakpoint in your code. If you have set a breakpoint in the designer for the control, the debugger will pause as soon as the control is dropped on the design surface.

6.   You can now perform normal debugging operations in the first instance of Visual Studio .NET.

Summary

In this chapter, we examined the design-time architecture of the .NET Framework and showed how to implement classes that provide advanced design-time functionality—designers, UI type editors, and component editors. We also described how to debug design-time code. Design-time features are not required for the functioning of your control in a page but can make the difference between a no-frills control and one that offers rich RAD capabilities in a visual designer. Design-time features are especially important if you are authoring controls for commercial distribution.

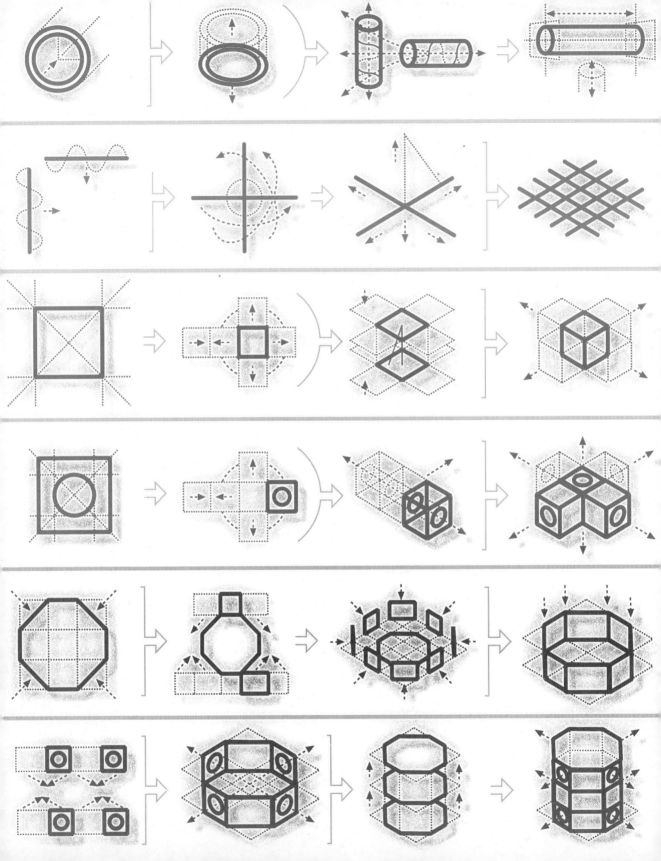

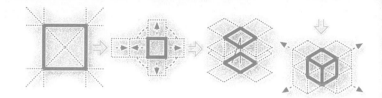

16

Data-Bound Controls

Data binding is the process of associating user interface (UI) elements with a data source to generate a visual representation of data. ASP.NET provides declarative data-binding syntax (<%# %>) that allows a page developer to easily bind data to any read/write property of a server control. When the data source represents a collection of items or records, it is not possible to bind the entire collection to a single property of a control. This scenario requires specialized controls that can enumerate the objects in the collection to generate a visual representation for each enumerated object. Controls that are bound to a collection-based data source are known as *data-bound controls*. In addition to merely displaying data, data-bound controls can offer additional capabilities, such as sorting and editing.

ASP.NET provides a set of versatile data-bound controls (*Repeater*, *DataList*, and *DataGrid*) that cover many common data-binding scenarios. However, when the built-in controls are not adequate, you might need custom data-bound controls. In this chapter, we'll examine the data-binding architecture of the ASP.NET page framework and show you how to implement a custom data-bound server control. In addition, we'll demonstrate how to implement a data-bound control designer, which can greatly enhance the design-time experience offered by a data-bound control.

In this chapter, we will not describe templated data-bound controls, which expose *ITemplate* properties to enable page developers to customize some or all of the control's UI. We'll demonstrate those controls in Chapter 20, "Data-Bound Templated Controls," by combining the implementation of templates (described in Chapter 12, "Composite Controls") with data binding. The *Repeater* and *DataList* controls are examples of templated data-bound controls.

Data Binding Overview

In this section, we'll provide an overview of the data-binding architecture in the page framework. We'll assume that you have used data-binding expressions (<%# %>) in .aspx pages and have used the built-in ASP.NET data-bound controls. We'll first examine how the page supports data-binding expressions and then look at the key concepts of implementing your own data-bound control.

You do not have to perform any additional work in your control to support data-binding expressions. That functionality is implemented in the base *Control* class and is applicable to any read/write property of your control. This is how data-binding expressions work: When the page parser sees a data-binding expression within your control's tags in an .aspx page, the parser generates event handlers that evaluate the data-binding expressions and perform property assignments. The page parser wires up those event handlers to your control's *DataBinding* event, which your control inherits from the *Control* class. In Chapter 2, "Page Programming Model," we described the dynamic compilation model and how the parser generates code from declarative page syntax. In Chapter 9, "Control Life Cycle, Events, and Postback," we described the intrinsic events of the *Control* class, and in Chapter 3, "Component Programming Overview," we defined the .NET Framework event architecture.

As we explained in Chapter 3, each event has a protected *On<Event-Name>* method that raises the event by invoking the event handlers that are associated with it. The *Control* class defines the protected *OnDataBinding* method that raises the *DataBinding* event. *Control* also exposes the public *Data-Bind* method whose default implementation invokes the *OnDataBinding* method. Thus, when a page developer invokes the *DataBind* method of your control, this method in turn raises the *DataBinding* event of your control, which causes the event handlers that are wired to it to be executed. You can see the event handlers that the parser generates and how they are wired to the *Data-Binding* event of your control in the class that the parser generates from the .aspx page by using the technique we described in Chapter 2.

Data binding occurs when the page developer invokes the *DataBind* method of a control. The *DataBind* method of a control recursively invokes the *DataBind* method on each of its child controls in the control tree.

ASP.NET has an explicit data-binding model. Under this model, the page developer invokes data-binding logic only when needed, by calling the *Data-Bind* method. This model offers Web applications a significant gain in performance over the implicit data-binding model in which the data-binding logic is automatically triggered. In a disconnected Web environment, it is not efficient to connect to the data source upon each request because the data binding process might involve creating database connections or other resources and executing time-consuming queries. In general, the page performs data-binding logic on the first request, and controls restore their state on subsequent requests by using the saved view state. If the data changes subsequently, the page developer can rebind either the entire page or a selective group of controls.

Now let's examine the main characteristics of the standard ASP.NET data-bound controls from the perspective of developing a custom data-bound control. The standard data-bound controls expose a *DataSource* property that allows the page developer to specify the data source to bind to. These controls perform data-binding logic when their *DataBind* method is invoked. In addition, these controls restore their state on postback when the page developer does not invoke the *DataBind* method.

Here are the main steps that you must implement to create a data-bound control:

- Expose a *DataSource* property that allows the page developer to specify a source of data to bind to.

- Override the *DataBind* method to implement the logic to enumerate the objects in the assigned data source and to create a child control hierarchy that visually represents the data source. From the *Data-Bind* method, you must first invoke the *OnDataBinding* method of your control to raise the *DataBinding* event. This causes any data-binding expressions that a page developer might have associated with your control to be evaluated, as we explained earlier in this section.

- Override the *CreateChildControls* method to create the child control hierarchy by using the view state saved at the end of the previous request. The *CreateChildControls* method is called on postback if the page does not invoke *DataBind* on your control. As we described in Chapter 12, the default implementation of the *OnPreRender* method invokes *CreateChildControls* unless child controls have been created before the PreRender phase.

We'll look at these steps in greater detail when we implement the *DataBoundTable* control in the next section.

BindableAttribute and the *DataBindings* Property

Microsoft Visual Studio .NET provides a UI (accessed from the property browser) that allows a page developer to easily associate data-binding expressions with a control. The *DataBindings* property in the property browser is a design-time-only property, which is implemented by the *ControlDesigner* base class. This property is associated with a UI type editor that allows page developers to edit data-binding expressions for all the properties of a control marked with *Bindable(true)*. The *Control* and *WebControl* classes use *Bindable(true)* to mark properties that are meaningful to bind data to. You should do the same for any properties to which you want to enable the page developer to bind data.

Later in this chapter, in the "Implementing a Data-Bound Control Designer" section, we'll show you how implement a designer for a data-bound control that provides many design-time features that greatly enhance the control's usability at design time.

Implementing a Data-Bound Control

In this section, we'll develop the *DataBoundTable* control, which demonstrates the key steps in implementing a data-bound control. To keep the example simple, we will not implement support for templates in *DataBoundTable*. (However, we'll demonstrate that feature in the *ListView* control presented in Chapter 20.) *DataBoundTable* displays data in a tabular format, as shown in Figure 16-1.

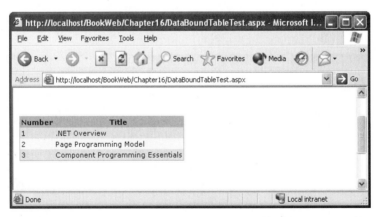

Figure 16-1   The *DataBoundTable* control viewed in a browser

Listing 16-1 contains a page that uses the *DataBoundTable* control.

```
<%@ Page language="c#" %>
<%@ Register TagPrefix="msp" Assembly="MSPress.ServerControls"
  Namespace="MSPress.ServerControls" %>
<html>
  <script runat="server">
  public class TocEntry {
      private int _chapterNumber;
      private string _chapterTitle;

      public TocEntry(int chapterNumber, string chapterTitle) {
          _chapterNumber = chapterNumber;
          _chapterTitle = chapterTitle;
      }

      public int Number {
          get {
              return _chapterNumber;
          }
      }

      public string Title {
          get {
              return _chapterTitle;
          }
      }
  }

  public void Page_Load(object sender, EventArgs e) {
      if (!IsPostBack) {
          ArrayList a = new ArrayList();

          a.Add(new TocEntry(1, ".NET Overview"));
          a.Add(new TocEntry(2, "Page Programming Model"));
          a.Add(new TocEntry(3, "Component Programming Essentials"));

          dataBoundTable1.DataSource = a;
          dataBoundTable1.DataBind();
      }
  }
  </script>
  <body>
    <form method="post" runat="server" ID="Form1">
      <p>
        <msp:DataBoundTable runat="server" id="dataBoundTable1"
          BackColor="LightGoldenrodYellow" ForeColor="Black"
```

Listing 16-1   A page that uses the *DataBoundTable* control   *(continued)*

Listing 16-1   *(continued)*

```
         Font-Name="Verdana" Font-Size="8pt" BorderColor="Tan"
         BorderWidth="1px" GridLines="None" CellPadding="2">
         <HeaderStyle BackColor="Tan" Font-Bold="True" />
         <AlternatingItemStyle BackColor="PaleGoldenrod" />
      </msp:DataBoundTable>
   </p>
 </form>
 </body>
</html>
```

Listing 16-2 shows the code for the *DataBoundTable* control. The control illustrates the following core concepts, which we'll explain after the code listing:

■   Implements a *DataSource* property. *DataBoundTable* allows two different types of objects to be assigned to its *DataSource* property, as we'll describe in a moment in "The *DataSource* Property and Related Members."

■   Creates its child control hierarchy by binding to the data source (in *DataBind*) or by using the saved view state (in *CreateChildControls*). We'll describe details in the "Creating the Control Hierarchy—*DataBind* and *CreateChildControls*" subsection.

■   Implements style-related functionality. *DataBoundTable* shows how to utilize typed styles and optimize performance by applying styles to child controls in the Render phase. We'll explain details in the "Styles and Rendering" subsection. Listing 16-2 does not contain code related to style functionality; you'll see that code later in this section.

```
using System;
using System.Collections;
using System.ComponentModel;
using System.Diagnostics;
using System.Web.UI;
using System.Web.UI.WebControls;


namespace MSPress.ServerControls {

    [
    DefaultProperty("DataSource"),
    Designer(
        typeof(MSPress.ServerControls.Design.DataBoundTableDesigner))
    ]
    public class DataBoundTable : WebControl {
```

Listing 16-2   DataBoundTable.cs

```
    private object _dataSource;

    private TableItemStyle _itemStyle;
    private TableItemStyle _altItemStyle;
    private TableItemStyle _headerStyle;

    #region Data source and related members
    [
    Category("Data"),
    DefaultValue(""),
    Description("The member to bind when the data source is an " +
        "IListSource such as DataSet.")
    ]
    public virtual string DataMember {
        get {
            string s = (string)ViewState["DataMember"];
            return (s == null) ? String.Empty : s;
        }
        set {
            ViewState["DataMember"] = value;
        }
    }

    [
    Bindable(true),
    Category("Data"),
    DefaultValue(null),
    Description("The data source"),
    DesignerSerializationVisibility(
        DesignerSerializationVisibility.Hidden)
    ]
    public virtual object DataSource {
        get {
            return _dataSource;
        }
        set {
            if ((value == null) || (value is IListSource) ||
                (value is IEnumerable)) {
                _dataSource = value;
            }
            else {
                throw new ArgumentException();
            }
        }
    }
}
```

(continued)

Listing 16-2 *(continued)*

```
    protected virtual IEnumerable GetDataSource() {
        if (_dataSource == null) {
            return null;
        }

        IEnumerable resolvedDataSource =
            _dataSource as IEnumerable;
        if (resolvedDataSource != null) {
            return resolvedDataSource;
        }

        IListSource listSource = _dataSource as IListSource;
        if (listSource != null) {
            IList memberList = listSource.GetList();

            if (listSource.ContainsListCollection == false) {
                return (IEnumerable)memberList;
            }

            ITypedList typedMemberList = memberList as ITypedList;
            if (typedMemberList != null) {
                PropertyDescriptorCollection propDescs =
                    typedMemberList.GetItemProperties(
                        new PropertyDescriptor[0]);
                PropertyDescriptor memberProperty = null;

                if ((propDescs != null) && (propDescs.Count != 0)) {
                    string dataMember = DataMember;

                    if (dataMember.Length == 0) {
                        memberProperty = propDescs[0];
                    }
                    else {
                        memberProperty =
                            propDescs.Find(dataMember, true);
                    }

                    if (memberProperty != null) {
                        object listRow = memberList[0];
                        object list =
                            memberProperty.GetValue(listRow);

                        if (list is IEnumerable) {
                            return (IEnumerable)list;
                        }
                    }
                }
```

```
                        throw new Exception("A list corresponding to" +
                            " the selected DataMember was not found.");
                }

                throw new Exception("The selected data source " +
                    "did not contain any data members to bind to.");
            }
        }

        return null;
    }
    #endregion DataSource and related members

    #region Control hierarchy and data binding
    protected override void CreateChildControls() {
        // CreateChildControls re-creates the children (the items)
        // using the saved view state.
        // First clear any existing child controls.
        Controls.Clear();

        // Create the items only if there is view state
        // corresponding to the children.
        if ((ViewState["RowCount"] != null) &&
            (ViewState["ColumnCount"] != null)) {
            CreateControlHierarchy(false);
        }
    }

    protected virtual
        void CreateControlHierarchy(bool useDataSource) {
        IEnumerable dataSource = null;
        int rowCount = 0;
        int columnCount = 0;

        if (useDataSource) {
            dataSource = GetDataSource();
        }
        else {
            dataSource = new object[(int)ViewState["RowCount"]];
        }

        if (dataSource != null) {
            Table table = new Table();
            TableRowCollection rows = table.Rows;
            Controls.Add(table);
```

(continued)

Listing 16-2 *(continued)*

```
PropertyDescriptor[] properties = null;
bool createdHeader = false;

foreach (object dataItem in dataSource) {
    if (createdHeader == false) {
        TableRow headerRow = new TableRow();
        TableCellCollection headerCells =
            headerRow.Cells;

        if (useDataSource) {
            properties =
                GetColumnPropertyDescriptors(dataItem);
            columnCount = properties.Length;
        }
        else {
            columnCount = (int)ViewState["ColumnCount"];
        }

        for (int i = 0; i < columnCount; i++) {
            TableHeaderCell cell =
                new TableHeaderCell();

            if (useDataSource) {
                cell.Text = properties[i].Name;
            }

            headerCells.Add(cell);
        }

        createdHeader = true;
        rows.Add(headerRow);
    }

    TableRow row = new TableRow();
    TableCellCollection cells = row.Cells;

    for (int i = 0; i < columnCount; i++) {
        TableCell cell = new TableCell();

        if (useDataSource) {
            PropertyDescriptor pd = properties[i];

            object cellValue = pd.GetValue(dataItem);
            cell.Text =
                (string)pd.Converter.ConvertTo(
                    cellValue, typeof(string));
        }
```

```
                        cells.Add(cell);
                }

            rows.Add(row);
            rowCount++;
        }
    }

    if (useDataSource) {
        ViewState["RowCount"] = rowCount;
        ViewState["ColumnCount"] = columnCount;
    }
}

public override void DataBind() {
    // Data-bound controls implement custom data-binding logic
    // by overriding this method.

    // The following call raises the DataBinding event,
    // which causes the <%# %> expressions on this control to
    // be evaluated.
    base.OnDataBinding(EventArgs.Empty);

    // Clear the existing control hierarchy.
    Controls.Clear();

    // Clear any existing view state for the children because
    // data binding creates a new hierarchy.
    ClearChildViewState();
    // Start tracking changes made during the data-binding
    // process.
    TrackViewState();

    // Re-create the new control hierarchy using the assigned
    // data source.
    CreateControlHierarchy(true);

    // Set the flag to indicate that child controls have been
    // created so that CreateChildControls does not get called.
    ChildControlsCreated = true;
}

private PropertyDescriptor[] GetColumnPropertyDescriptors(
    object dataItem) {
    ArrayList props = new ArrayList();
```

(continued)

Listing 16-2 *(continued)*

```
            PropertyDescriptorCollection propDescs =
                TypeDescriptor.GetProperties(dataItem);
            foreach (PropertyDescriptor pd in propDescs) {
                Type propType = pd.PropertyType;
                TypeConverter converter =
                    TypeDescriptor.GetConverter(propType);

                if ((converter != null) &&
                    converter.CanConvertTo(typeof(string))) {
                    props.Add(pd);
                }
            }

            props.Sort(new PropertyDescriptorComparer());

            PropertyDescriptor[] columns =
                new PropertyDescriptor[props.Count];
            props.CopyTo(columns, 0);

            return columns;
        }


        private sealed class PropertyDescriptorComparer : IComparer {

            public int Compare(object x, object y) {
                PropertyDescriptor p1 = (PropertyDescriptor)x;
                PropertyDescriptor p2 = (PropertyDescriptor)y;

                return String.Compare(p1.Name, p2.Name);
            }
        }
        #endregion Control hierarchy and data binding

        #region Styles implementation
        ⋮
        #endregion Styles implementation
        #region Methods related to rendering
        ⋮
        #endregion Methods related to rendering
        #region Custom state management for styles
        ⋮
        #endregion Custom state management for styles
    }
}
```

The *DataSource* Property and Related Members

A data-bound control enumerates (iterates over) a collection of data to create and bind UI elements to each enumerated item in the collection. In the .NET Framework, a collection that supports enumeration must implement the *IEnumerable* interface. Therefore, in its core implementation, a data-bound control binds to an *IEnumerable* type.

It might seem obvious that the type of the *DataSource* property should be *IEnumerable*. However, declaring *DataSource* to be of type *IEnumerable* would reduce the versatility of your control, as we will soon show. When *DataSource* is an *IEnumerable* type, the type of object that the page developer assigns to this property must be an *Array*, a *Hashtable*, an *ArrayList*, or any other type that implements *IEnumerable*. However, in many data-binding scenarios, the data source is represented by a *DataSet* (an *IListSource* type), which contains a collection of *DataTable* instances that contain the actual data your control can bind to. To support these scenarios, your control must accept an object implementing *IListSource* as a data source and perform additional work to extract the actual *IEnumerable* object to bind to.

The *DataBoundTable* control illustrates this scenario by showing how to implement a control that accepts two types of data sources—*IEnumerable* and *IListSource*. *DataBoundTable* declares the type of the *DataSource* property as the generic *Object* type and checks that the object passed in into its property setter implements either *IEnumerable* or *IListSource*. When the *DataSource* property is assigned an *IListSource*, *DataBoundTable* needs to determine which list to bind to. For this purpose, *DataBoundTable* defines two additional members—the *DataMember* property and the *GetDataSource* method. The *DataMember* property is a string that represents the name of the list within the *IListSource* collection (such as the name of a *DataTable* in a *DataSet*). When the data source is an *IListSource* (such as a *DataSet*), *GetDataSource* gets the name of the list (the *DataTable*) from the *DataMember* property and returns an *IEnumerable* corresponding to the selected list to bind to. When the data source is an *IEnumerable* instance, *GetDataSource* simply returns the value of the *DataSource* property. The *GetDataSource* method is called from the *CreateChildControls* method, as we'll describe in the next subsection.

The *DataBoundTable* example intentionally demonstrates the more complex case of a data-bound control that allows various types of data sources. If you want to restrict the data source to an *IEnumerable* type, you can declare the type of the *DataSource* property as *IEnumerable* without having to implement the *DataMember* property or the logic in the *GetDataSource* method.

Creating the Control Hierarchy—*DataBind* and *CreateChildControls*

As we described in the "Data Binding Overview" section, a data-bound control uses the data source to create its control hierarchy when the page developer invokes its *DataBind* method. On the other hand, when the page developer does not invoke *DataBind*, the control re-creates its control hierarchy in the *CreateChildControls* method by using its saved view state. *DataBoundTable* illustrates the pattern for implementing these two methods. This is how *DataBoundTable* implements the *DataBind* method:

```
public override void DataBind() {
    base.OnDataBinding(EventArgs.Empty);

    Controls.Clear();
    ClearChildViewState();

    TrackViewState();

    CreateControlHierarchy(true);
    ChildControlsCreated = true;
}
```

The steps performed by *DataBoundTable* in *DataBind* are general, and you should perform them in any data-bound control that you implement:

1. Invoke the *OnDataBinding* method so that the *DataBinding* event is raised and any data-binding expressions associated with your control in the .aspx page are evaluated.

2. Clear any existing child controls because you will re-create the child control hierarchy by using the data source.

3. Clear any view state for child controls because you will bind data to the child controls and not use the saved view state.

4. Start tracking state in your control so that changes made while data binding are persisted in the view state. This call is needed because a page developer might invoke *DataBind* in the Initialize phase, before state tracking has started.

5. Create the child control hierarchy, and bind data to the child controls. *DataBoundTable* implements this logic in the helper *CreateControlHierarchy* method, which we will explain in a moment.

6. Set the *ChildControlsCreated* property to *true*. This indicates that *CreateChildControls* should not be invoked later in your control's life cycle.

The following code shows how *DataBoundTable* overrides the *Create-ChildControls* method:

```
protected override void CreateChildControls() {
    Controls.Clear();
    if ((ViewState["RowCount"] != null) &&
        (ViewState["ColumnCount"] != null)) {
        CreateControlHierarchy(false);
    }
}
```

The implementation of the *CreateChildControls* method demonstrates the steps you must perform in this method:

1. Clear the *Controls* collection because you will re-create the control hierarchy by using the saved view state.

2. Check whether any view state required to re-create the child controls was saved in the previous request. You should create the child control tree only if saved view state exists.

3. Re-create the child controls by using the saved view state. *DataBoundTable* defines the *CreateControlHierarchy* method to create child controls. We'll explain this method next.

Because both the *DataBind* and *CreateChildControls* methods create the child control hierarchy, *DataBoundTable* contains a common code path to perform this task by encapsulating that logic in the helper *CreateControlHierarchy* method. Listing 16-2 shows how *DataBoundTable* implements the *CreateControlHierarchy* method. We recommend that you implement the pattern illustrated by this method in your own controls.

The *CreateControlHierarchy* method defined by *DataBoundTable* takes a Boolean argument that indicates whether to use the data source when creating the child control hierarchy. *DataBind* passes *true* into *CreateControlHierarchy*, while *CreateChildControls* passes *false* into this method.

When the page developer invokes *DataBind* on your control, *DataBind* invokes *CreateControlHierarchy(true)*. Let's examine the logic that is executed in this case. *CreateControlHierarchy* first invokes the *GetDataSource* method (described earlier in this section) to get the data source to bind to. If the data source is not null, *CreateControlHierarchy* creates a *System.Web.UI.WebControls.Table* instance because *DataBoundTable* renders a table. However, you can create a different container more suited to your particular scenario. *Create-ControlHierarchy* adds the *Table* instance to the *Controls* collection. The method then inspects the first data item to infer the number of columns to create and the contents in the header. This method further enumerates over each successive data item to infer the contents of each row. *CreateControlHierarchy* creates *System.Web.UI.WebControls.TableRow* instances and then creates *System.Web.UI.WebControls.TableCell* (or *System.Web.UI.WebControls.TableHeaderCell* for the first row) instances that contain corresponding data from the data item. The method adds the cells to the row and each *TableRow* instance to the *Table* instance. Finally, the method saves the number of rows and columns in the view state.

Now let's examine how *DataBoundTable* creates the control hierarchy on postback when the page does not invoke *DataBind* on the control. In this case, *DataBoundTable* overrides *CreateChildControls* to create the control hierarchy. *CreateChildControls* in turn invokes *CreateControlHierarchy(false)*. In this case, *CreateControlHierarchy* creates a new *Table*—as in the data-binding scenario—and adds the *Table* to the *Controls* collection. However, because a real data source does not exist, the method creates a null array whose length is the number of rows stored in the view state in the previous request. *CreateControlHierarchy* does not use the array to populate table cells but merely as a means for using the same iteration logic with or without a real data source. *CreateControlHierarchy* obtains the number of columns from the value stored in the view state in the previous request. The method successively creates new *TableRows*, adds *TableCells* (or *TableHeaderCells*) to each *TableRow*, and adds each row to the *Table* instance. Because the *Table* instance is already added to the control hierarchy, as soon as a *TableRow* is added to the *Table*, the page framework loads in the view state that was saved during a previous request. This completes the creation of the control hierarchy by using the saved view state. (In Chapter 12, we described how view state is loaded into a child control in the Load View State phase or whenever a child control is added to the control hierarchy after this phase.)

Styles and Rendering

Implementing styles in a data-bound control is not essential. However, styles govern the appearance of data and thus offer significant customization capabilities to the page developer. For example, the *DataBoundTable* shown in Figure 16-1 can display the header differently from the data and mark alternating items by using typed styles. We described typed styles in Chapter 11, "Styles in Controls," and we showed how to create and apply typed styles to child controls in Chapter 12. *DataBoundTable* uses the concepts explained in those two chapters. Listing 16-3 shows how *DataBoundTable* implements styles.

```
public class DataBoundTable : WebControl {
    private TableItemStyle _itemStyle;
    private TableItemStyle _altItemStyle;
    private TableItemStyle _headerStyle;

    #region DataSource, control hierarchy, data binding
    :
    #endregion DataSource, control hierarchy, data binding

    #region Styles implementation
    [
    Category("Appearance"),
    DefaultValue(-1),
    Description("")
    ]
    public virtual int CellPadding {
        get {
            if (ControlStyleCreated == false) {
                return -1;
            }
            return ((TableStyle)ControlStyle).CellPadding;
        }
        set {
            ((TableStyle)ControlStyle).CellPadding = value;
        }
    }


    [
    Category("Appearance"),
    DefaultValue(0),
    Description("")
    ]
    public virtual int CellSpacing {
        get {
            if (ControlStyleCreated == false) {
                return 0;
            }
            return ((TableStyle)ControlStyle).CellSpacing;
        }
        set {
            ((TableStyle)ControlStyle).CellSpacing = value;
        }
    }
}
```

Listing 16-3   Styles implementation in *DataBoundTable*   *(continued)*

Listing 16-3 *(continued)*

```
[
Category("Appearance"),
DefaultValue(GridLines.None),
Description("")
]
public virtual GridLines GridLines {
    get {
        if (ControlStyleCreated == false) {
            return GridLines.None;
        }
        return ((TableStyle)ControlStyle).GridLines;
    }
    set {
        ((TableStyle)ControlStyle).GridLines = value;
    }
}


[
Category("Style"),
Description(""),
DesignerSerializationVisibility(
    DesignerSerializationVisibility.Content),
NotifyParentProperty(true),
PersistenceMode(PersistenceMode.InnerProperty)
]
public TableItemStyle AlternatingItemStyle {
    get {
        if (_altItemStyle == null) {
            _altItemStyle = new TableItemStyle();
            if (IsTrackingViewState) {
                ((IStateManager)_altItemStyle).TrackViewState();
            }
        }
        return _altItemStyle;
    }
}


[
Category("Style"),
Description(""),
DesignerSerializationVisibility(
    DesignerSerializationVisibility.Content),
NotifyParentProperty(true),
PersistenceMode(PersistenceMode.InnerProperty)
]
public TableItemStyle HeaderStyle {
    get {
```

```
            if (_headerStyle == null) {
                _headerStyle = new TableItemStyle();
                if (IsTrackingViewState) {
                    ((IStateManager)_headerStyle).TrackViewState();
                }
            }
            return _headerStyle;
        }
    }


    [
    Category("Style"),
    Description(""),
    DesignerSerializationVisibility(
        DesignerSerializationVisibility.Content),
    NotifyParentProperty(true),
    PersistenceMode(PersistenceMode.InnerProperty)
    ]
    public TableItemStyle ItemStyle {
        get {
            if (_itemStyle == null) {
                _itemStyle = new TableItemStyle();
                if (IsTrackingViewState) {
                    ((IStateManager)_itemStyle).TrackViewState();
                }
            }
            return _itemStyle;
        }
    }


    [
    Bindable(true),
    Category("Appearance"),
    DefaultValue(true),
    Description("")
    ]
    public virtual bool ShowHeader {
        get {
            object b = ViewState["ShowHeader"];
            return (b == null) ? true : (bool)b;
        }
        set {
            ViewState["ShowHeader"] = value;
        }
    }
```

(continued)

Listing 16-3 *(continued)*

```
protected override Style CreateControlStyle() {
    // Because the DataBoundTable renders an HTML table,
    // an instance of a TableStyle is used as the control style.
    TableStyle style = new TableStyle(ViewState);

    // Initialize the style.
    style.CellSpacing = 0;
    style.GridLines = GridLines.Both;

    return style;
}
#endregion Styles implementation

#region Methods related to rendering
protected virtual void PrepareControlHierarchyForRendering() {
    ControlCollection controls = Controls;
    if (controls.Count != 1) {
        return;
    }

    Table table = (Table)controls[0];
    table.CopyBaseAttributes(this);
    if (ControlStyleCreated) {
        table.ApplyStyle(ControlStyle);
    }
    else {
        // Because we haven't created a ControlStyle yet, the
        // default settings for the default style of the control
        // need to be applied to the child table control directly.
        table.CellSpacing = 0;
        table.GridLines = GridLines.Both;
    }

    TableItemStyle altStyle = _itemStyle;
    if (_altItemStyle != null) {
        altStyle = new TableItemStyle();
        altStyle.CopyFrom(_itemStyle);
        altStyle.CopyFrom(_altItemStyle);
    }

    bool expectingHeader = true;
    int rowIndex = 0;

    foreach (TableRow row in table.Rows) {
        if (expectingHeader) {
            expectingHeader = false;

            bool showHeader = ShowHeader;
```

```
                row.Visible = showHeader;
                if (showHeader && (_headerStyle != null)) {
                    row.ApplyStyle(_headerStyle);
                }
            }
            else {
                TableItemStyle style = _itemStyle;

                if (((rowIndex + 1) % 2) == 0) {
                    style = altStyle;
                }

                if (style != null) {
                    row.ApplyStyle(style);
                }
            }

            rowIndex++;
        }
    }


    protected override void Render(HtmlTextWriter writer) {
        // Apply styles to the control hierarchy, and then render
        // the child controls.

        // Styles are applied in the Render phase so that:
        // a) The page developer can change styles after calling
        //     DataBind.
        // b) Changes made to items when applying styles do not
        //     contribute to the view state. This control manages
        //     the state for styles, so having items manage it as
        //     well would be redundant.
        PrepareControlHierarchyForRendering();

        // We don't render a top-level tag for our control because
        // the child Table control provides that tag. Therefore,
        // instead of calling base.Render, we call RenderContents.
        RenderContents(writer);
    }
    #endregion Methods related to rendering

    #region Custom state management for styles
    ⋮
    #endregion Custom state management for styles
}
```

DataBoundTable performs the following style-related tasks:

■ Because *DataBoundTable* renders a table, it overrides the *Create-ControlStyle* method to set the *System.Web.UI.WebControls.TableStyle* typed style as its own *ControlStyle*. We described how to create a new control style in the *MyPanel* example in Chapter 11.

■ Exposes the *CellPadding*, *CellSpacing*, and *GridLines* properties of the *TableStyle* typed style as its own top-level style properties and implements them by delegating to the corresponding properties of its associated *ControlStyle*.

■ Exposes three typed styles to apply to its child controls—*ItemStyle*, *AlternatingItemStyle*, and *HeaderStyle*. We described how to expose typed styles in the *StyledCompositeLogin* example in Chapter 12.

■ Exposes the *ShowHeader* property, which enables the page developer to specify whether to display a header for the table.

■ Implements custom state management to track, save, and load the state of the *ItemStyle*, *AlternatingItemStyle*, and *HeaderStyle* typed styles. The implementation is similar to that shown in the *StyledCompositeLogin* example in Chapter 12. We did not include the code for state management in Listing 16-3; you can see this code in the book's sample files for this chapter.

DataBoundTable applies styles to child controls in the Render phase so that changes caused by applied styles are not persisted in the view state of its child control. As we explained in Chapter 12, this ensures that changes are not persisted twice—in the view state of the parent control and in the view state of the child controls. *DataBoundTable* defines the helper *PrepareControlHierarchyForRendering* method, which applies styles to child controls.

Implementing a Data-Bound Control Designer

If you've used one of the ASP.NET data-bound controls in Visual Studio .NET, you've seen how design-time features greatly enhance the usability of a data-bound control in a visual design environment. In this section, we'll implement the *DataBoundTableDesigner* designer, which demonstrates the key design-time features that a designer can provide to a data-bound control.

Figure 16-2 shows the *DataBoundTable* control used in a Web Forms page in Visual Studio .NET. The designer shadows the *DataSource* and *DataMember* properties. *Shadowing* refers to the process of replacing properties or events with corresponding design-time implementations. The design-time *DataSource* and *DataMember* properties display drop-down lists that respectively contain the data sources and data members that the control can bind to on the design surface. The designer dynamically generates the values in the list. For example, the drop-down list for the *DataSource* property in Figure 16-2 contains *"dataSet1"* and *"dataTable1"*. The string *"dataSet1"* corresponds to the *dataSet1* component in the component tray, and *"dataTable1"* corresponds to the first *DataTable* in *dataSet1*. *DataSet* and *DataTable* implement the *IListSource* interface, which is a type that the *DataBoundTable* allows for its *DataSource* property.

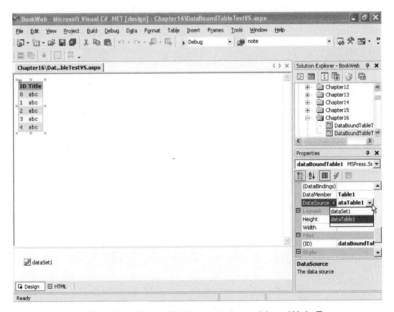

Figure 16-2   The *DataBoundTable* control used in a Web Forms page. The *DataBoundTableDesigner* is associated with the control.

Another feature of the data-bound control designer is that it creates a sample data source at design time, which differs from the run-time data source. If you examine the Web Forms page that generated Figure 16-2, you will see that the data source (*dataTable1*) for the control does not contain any data, yet the control displays data on the design surface. The sample data source is created by the designer and is useful when the real data source is populated with data at run time only. The designer-generated .aspx page and the corresponding code-behind file are included in the sample files for this book.

Listing 16-4 contains the code for the *DataBoundTableDesigner* class. The designer performs the following tasks, which we'll explain after the code listing:

- Defines design-time *DataMember* and *DataSource* properties, which are associated with design-time type converters that will display drop-down lists of values in the property browser.

- Overrides the *PreFilterProperties* method to replace the properties of the *DataBoundTable* control instance with corresponding design-time properties.

- Overrides the *GetDesignTimeHtml* method to create a sample data source to bind to the control and generates HTML for the control by using that data source.

- Implements the *IDataSourceProvider* interface.

```
using System;
using System.Collections;
using System.ComponentModel;
using System.ComponentModel.Design;
using System.Data;
using System.Diagnostics;
using System.Web.UI;
using System.Web.UI.Design;
using System.Web.UI.WebControls;
using MSPress.ServerControls;

using AttributeCollection = System.ComponentModel.AttributeCollection;

namespace MSPress.ServerControls.Design {

    public class DataBoundTableDesigner : ControlDesigner,
        IDataSourceProvider    {

        private DataTable _dummyDataTable;
        private DataTable _designTimeDataTable;

        public string DataMember {
            get {
                return ((DataBoundTable)Component).DataMember;
            }
            set {
                ((DataBoundTable)Component).DataMember = value;
                OnDataSourceChanged();
            }
        }
```

Listing 16-4 DataBoundTableDesigner.cs

```csharp
public string DataSource {
    get {
        DataBinding binding = DataBindings["DataSource"];
        if (binding != null) {
            return binding.Expression;
        }
        return String.Empty;
    }
    set {
        if ((value == null) || (value.Length == 0)) {
            DataBindings.Remove("DataSource");
        }
        else {
            DataBinding binding = DataBindings["DataSource"];

            if (binding == null) {
                binding = new DataBinding("DataSource",
                    typeof(object), value);
            }
            else {
                binding.Expression = value;
            }
            DataBindings.Add(binding);
        }

        OnDataSourceChanged();
        OnBindingsCollectionChanged("DataSource");
    }
}

public override bool DesignTimeHtmlRequiresLoadComplete {
    get {
        // If there is a data source, look it up in the
        // container and require the document to be loaded
        // completely.
        return (DataSource.Length != 0);
    }
}

private IEnumerable GetDesignTimeDataSource(int minimumRows) {
    IEnumerable selectedDataSource =
        ((IDataSourceProvider)
            this).GetResolvedSelectedDataSource();

    DataTable dataTable = _designTimeDataTable;

    // If possible, use the data table corresponding to the
    // selected data source.
```

(continued)

Listing 16-4 *(continued)*

```
        if (dataTable == null) {
            if (selectedDataSource != null) {
                _designTimeDataTable =
                    DesignTimeData.CreateSampleDataTable(
                        selectedDataSource);
                dataTable = _designTimeDataTable;
            }

            if (dataTable == null) {
                // Fall back on a dummy data source if it isn't
                // possible to create a sample data table.
                if (_dummyDataTable == null) {
                    _dummyDataTable =
                        DesignTimeData.CreateDummyDataTable();
                }

                dataTable = _dummyDataTable;
            }
        }

        IEnumerable liveDataSource =
            DesignTimeData.GetDesignTimeDataSource(dataTable,
                minimumRows);
        return liveDataSource;
    }

    public override string GetDesignTimeHtml() {
        DataBoundTable dbt = (DataBoundTable)Component;
        string designTimeHTML = null;

        IEnumerable designTimeDataSource =
            GetDesignTimeDataSource(5);
        try {
            dbt.DataSource = designTimeDataSource;
            dbt.DataBind();

            designTimeHTML = base.GetDesignTimeHtml();
        }
        catch (Exception e) {
            designTimeHTML = GetErrorDesignTimeHtml(e);
        }
        finally {
            dbt.DataSource = null;
        }
        return designTimeHTML;
    }
```

```
protected override string GetErrorDesignTimeHtml(Exception e) {
    return CreatePlaceHolderDesignTimeHtml(
        "There was an error rendering the DataBoundTable.");
}

public override void Initialize(IComponent component) {
    if (!(component is DataBoundTable)) {
        throw new ArgumentException(
            "Component must be a DataBoundTable", "component");
    }
    base.Initialize(component);
}

protected internal virtual void OnDataSourceChanged() {
    _designTimeDataTable = null;
}

protected override
    void PreFilterProperties(IDictionary properties) {
    base.PreFilterProperties(properties);

    PropertyDescriptor prop;

    prop = (PropertyDescriptor)properties["DataSource"];
    Debug.Assert(prop != null);

    // You cannot create the designer DataSource property
    // based on the run-time property because their types do
    // not match. Therefore, you must copy all the attributes
    // from the run-time property.
    AttributeCollection runtimeAttributes = prop.Attributes;
    Attribute[] attrs =
        new Attribute[runtimeAttributes.Count + 1];

    runtimeAttributes.CopyTo(attrs, 0);
    attrs[runtimeAttributes.Count] =
        new TypeConverterAttribute(typeof(DataSourceConverter));
    prop = TypeDescriptor.CreateProperty(this.GetType(),
        "DataSource", typeof(string), attrs);
    properties["DataSource"] = prop;

    prop = (PropertyDescriptor)properties["DataMember"];
    Debug.Assert(prop != null);
    prop = TypeDescriptor.CreateProperty(this.GetType(), prop,
        new Attribute[] {
            new TypeConverterAttribute(
                typeof(DataMemberConverter))
                    });
```

(continued)

Listing 16-4   *(continued)*

```
            properties["DataMember"] = prop;
        }

        #region Implementation of IDataSourceProvider
        object IDataSourceProvider.GetSelectedDataSource() {
            object selectedDataSource = null;

            DataBinding binding = DataBindings["DataSource"];
            if (binding != null) {
                selectedDataSource =
                DesignTimeData.GetSelectedDataSource(Component,
                    binding.Expression);
            }

            return selectedDataSource;
        }

        IEnumerable IDataSourceProvider.GetResolvedSelectedDataSource() {
            IEnumerable selectedDataSource = null;

            DataBinding binding = DataBindings["DataSource"];
            if (binding != null) {
                selectedDataSource =
                    DesignTimeData.GetSelectedDataSource(Component,
                        binding.Expression, DataMember);
            }

            return selectedDataSource;
        }
        #endregion
    }
}
```

Let's look at how *DataBoundTableDesigner* defines the design-time *Data-Member* and *DataSource* properties. The design-time *DataMember* property delegates to the corresponding run-time property. The setter of *DataMember* calls the *OnDataSourceChanged* method to inform the designer that the data source has changed. The design-time *DataSource* property is a *String*; however, the run-time property is an *Object*. This enables the property setter to persist the data source name selected by the page developer, such as *"dataSet1"*, as a data-binding expression. The setter of the design-time *Data-Source* property adds the data-binding expression corresponding to the data source selection to the design-time *DataBindings* property. The setter also invokes the *OnDataSourceChanged* and *OnBindingsCollectionChanged* methods to inform the designer that a data-binding expression has changed. As a result, the code persister generates the data-binding expression of the form *"<%# dataSet1 %>"* as the value of the *DataSource* property in the .aspx page. At run time, when the page is parsed, the data-binding expression causes the page parser to create an event handler (for the control's *DataBinding* event) that assigns the *dataSet1* object to the *DataSource* property. This event handler is invoked when the page developer's code invokes the *DataBind* method of the control.

Now let's examine how *DataBoundTableDesigner* causes the property browser to display a drop-down list of dynamically generated values for the *DataMember* and *DataSource* properties. Any logic to shadow properties must be implemented in the *PreFilterProperties* method. *DataBoundTable-Designer* overrides this method to replace the *DataMember* and *DataSource* run-time properties with the corresponding design-time properties. In the *PreFilterProperties* method, *DataBoundTableDesigner* associates the *System.Web.UI.Design.DataMemberConverter* and *System.Web.UI.Design.Data-SourceConverter* type converters with the design-time *DataMember* and *DataSource* properties. Each of these type converters implements the logic to examine the objects on the design surface and to dynamically generate a list of valid values for the respective property.

DataBoundTableDesigner overrides the *GetDesignTimeHtml* method to use a sample data source to generate HTML for the *DataBoundTable* control at design time. *GetDesignTimeHtml* invokes the helper *GetDesignTimeDataSource* method to perform the task of creating the sample table. The *GetDesignTime-DataSource* method in turn utilizes the methods of the *System.Web.UI.Design.DesignTimeData* helper class, which encapsulates the logic to create a design-time data source that mimics the schema of the selected data source but contains sample data. In its implementation of the *GetDesignTime-Html*, *DataBoundTableDesigner* assigns the sample data source to the *Data-Source* property of the *DataBoundTable* instance and invokes the *DataBind* method on the *DataBoundTable* instance. This causes the control to generate its control hierarchy by using the sample data source the same way as it does at run time by using a real data source. *DataBoundTableDesigner* then generates the HTML to render by invoking the *GetDesignTimeHtml* method of the base class.

A designer for a data-bound control should implement the *System.Web.UI.Design.IDataSourceProvider* interface. *IDataSourceProvider* represents the standard contract for any design-time component to retrieve the data source selected by the page developer for a particular data-bound control. In the *DataBoundTableDesigner* example, the *DataMemberConverter* class dynamically generates a list of values for the *DataMember* property by utilizing a method of the *IDataSourceProvider* interface. The *IDataSourceProvider* interface has two methods—*GetSelectedDataSource* and *GetResolvedSelectedDataSource*. *GetDataSource* uses the string value of the design-time *DataSource* property and returns the object that represents the data source. When the data source is an *IListSource* instance, *GetResolvedSelectedDataSource* returns the actual *IEnumerable* type to bind to. *DataBoundTableDesigner* implements the methods of the *IDataSourceProvider* interface by using the overloaded *GetSelectedDataSource* methods of the *DesignTimeData* helper class.

Summary

In this chapter, we examined the data-binding architecture of the page framework and showed you how to implement a data-bound control. The *DataBoundTable* example illustrates the core data-binding implementation, shows how to support various types of data sources, and uses typed styles for customizing the presentation of data. We also showed how to implement a control designer that shadows the *DataSource* property of the data-bound control at design time. In Chapter 20, we'll implement a more complex data-bound control that uses the core features we described in this chapter as well as offers templates and exposes events for customizing the data-binding process and for handling user actions in the Web browser.

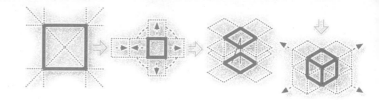

17

Localization, Licensing, and Other Miscellany

Earlier in this part of the book, we provided an in-depth discussion of core control-authoring topics such as rendering, managing state, handling postback data, and adding design-time functionality. In this chapter, we will examine localization and licensing, which will help you add finishing touches to your controls and prepare them for deployment. We will also show you how to incorporate configuration capabilities into your controls to support improved maintainability of pages containing them.

Localization

In an ASP.NET Web application, the page developer is ultimately responsible for localizing the application by appropriately specifying the *culture*, or locale, associated with the pages in the application. As a component developer, you can support the page developer by enabling localization of your controls. To support localization, you should use as few hard-coded strings as possible in the rendering generated by your controls because these strings are impossible to localize. Instead, your controls should expose string properties to which the page developer can assign localized values. If you do use fixed strings in the rendering of your controls, you should package those strings as resources and then provide localized versions of those strings via *satellite assemblies*. Satellite assemblies are resource-only assemblies that contain resource data for a specific culture. We will show how you can create satellite assemblies later in this section. In addition to localizing any strings you use at run time, you should localize strings that are visible to the page developer through the user interface of a design-time tool.

The *System.Globalization.CultureInfo* class is an object that encapsulates preferences specific to a culture, such as the name of the locale (for example, fr-FR, which stands for French that is used in France), the calendar information, and the date and number formatting conventions. Each thread of execution in a managed application has two *CultureInfo* objects associated with it: a *Culture* instance, which affects formatting, sorting, and so on; and a *UICulture* instance, which determines the selection of the satellite assembly whose resources are to be used. These properties default to the locale of the operating system, which might not always be desirable for Web applications because a Web server's culture isn't necessarily significant to the user of the application. These properties can be set in code, as shown here:

```
Thread.CurrentThread.CurrentCulture = new CultureInfo("fr-FR");
Thread.CurrentThread.CurrentUICulure = new CultureInfo("fr-FR");
```

In an .aspx page, the page developer can also specify the culture in a declarative manner within the *Page* directive, as shown here:

```
<%@ Page Culture="fr-FR" UICulture="fr-FR" %>
```

The page automatically sets the *CurrentCulture* and *CurrentUICulture* properties of the thread being used to process the request by using the previous code. As a result, any APIs used by the page developer and by controls on the page that depend on culture-specific information automatically use the culture specified on the page.

Using Resources in Controls

In this section, we will implement a *GreetingLabel* control that mimics a *Label* and incorporates localization to render a localized version of the commonly used "Hello, World" greeting. In addition, *GreetingLabel* demonstrates how you can localize metadata attributes that contain string values that are displayed in the UI of a design-time environment.

Figures 17-1 and 17-2 show the same page requested for the U.S. English (en-US) and France French (fr-FR) cultures. The *GreetingLabel* contained in the page renders text containing the localized greeting.

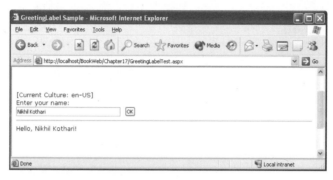

Figure 17-1   U.S. English greeting shown by requesting *http://localhost/BookWeb/Chapter17/GreetingLabelTest.aspx*

Figure 17-2   France French greeting shown by requesting *http://localhost/BookWeb/Chapter17/GreetingLabelTest.aspx?culture=fr-FR*

Notice that the culture to be used is specified as an argument on the query string of the URL in this sample page. In a more realistic application, a page developer might decide to automatically detect it (by using the *HTTP_ACCEPT_LANGUAGE* server variable), or might allow the user to pick a locale, or might use other profile information of the user to determine the culture.

Listing 17-1 contains the page used to demonstrate the *GreetingLabel* control. Notice that this page does not contain any code to localize the control. The code in the page simply sets the culture properties of the current thread.

```
<%@ Page language="c#" %>
<%@ Import Namespace="System.Globalization" %>
<%@ Import Namespace="System.Threading" %>
<%@ Register TagPrefix="msp" Assembly="MSPress.ServerControls"
  Namespace="MSPress.ServerControls" %>
<html>
  <script runat="server">
  public void Page_Init(object sender, EventArgs e) {
      string culture = Request.QueryString["culture"];
      if (culture == null) {
          culture = "en-US";
      }

      CultureInfo newCulture = new CultureInfo(culture);
      Thread.CurrentThread.CurrentCulture = newCulture;
      Thread.CurrentThread.CurrentUICulture = newCulture;

      Literal1.Text = newCulture.Name;
  }

  protected void Button1_Click(object sender, EventArgs e) {
      string text = TextBox1.Text.Trim();
      if (text.Length != 0) {
          GreetingLabel1.UserName = Server.HtmlEncode(text);
          GreetingLabel1.Visible = true;
      }
  }
  </script>
  <head>
    <title>GreetingLabel Sample</title>
  </head>
  <body>
    <form method="post" runat="server" ID="Form1">
      <p>
        [Current Culture: <asp:Literal runat="server" id="Literal1"/>]
        <br />
        Enter your name:
        <br />
        <asp:TextBox id="TextBox1" runat="server" Columns="40"/> 
        <asp:Button id="Button1" runat="server" Text="OK"
          onclick="Button1_Click"/>
        <hr>
        <msp:GreetingLabel id="GreetingLabel1" runat="server"
          Visible="false"/>
      </p>
    </form>
  </body>
</html>
```

Listing 17-1   GreetingLabelTest.aspx

Listing 17-2 contains the code for the *GreetingLabel* control.

```
using System;
using System.ComponentModel;
using System.Web.UI;
using System.Web.UI.WebControls;

namespace MSPress.ServerControls {
    public class GreetingLabel : WebControl {
        [
        Bindable(true),
        DefaultValue(""),
        LocalizedCategory("Greeting"),
        LocalizedDescription("GreetingLabel_UserName")
        ]
        public virtual string UserName {
            get {
                string s = (string)ViewState["UserName"];
                return (s == null) ? String.Empty : s;
            }
            set {
                ViewState["UserName"] = value;
            }
        }

        protected override void RenderContents(HtmlTextWriter writer) {
            string greetingFormat =
                AssemblyResourceManager.GetString(
                    "GreetingLabel_Format");

            if (greetingFormat == null) {
                writer.Write(UserName);
            }
            else {
                writer.Write(greetingFormat, UserName);
            }
        }
    }
}
```

Listing 17-2   GreetingLabel.cs uses localized strings in its rendering and localized metadata.

GreetingLabel demonstrates how a control can use resources that are embedded in the control's assembly or its satellite assemblies. Because *GreetingLabel* uses a fixed formatting string to generate the greeting text, it loads the value of the string from its resources by using the *GetString* method of *AssemblyResourceManager* (shown later in the section). This utility class provides access to resources associated with the control's assembly. Placing the string value into resources allows the control to load localized versions of the greeting format.

GreetingLabel exposes a *UserName* property that is associated with localized versions of the *DescriptionAttribute* and *CategoryAttribute* metadata. Rather than using these attribute types directly, the control uses derived implementations (*LocalizedDescriptionAttribute* and *LocalizedCategoryAttribute*) of these attributes that contain the logic to load their values by using *AssemblyResourceManager*. We will cover their implementation later in this section.

Embedding and Accessing Resources

Resources are defined in .resx files in an XML format. The .resx file is converted into a binary .resources format and embedded into an assembly as part of the compilation process. At run time, the embedded resources can be accessed by using the *System.Resources.ResourceManager* class.

Resources can be classified into two broad categories: *culture-neutral* and *culture-specific*. Culture-neutral resources (typically U.S. English) are embedded into the main assembly and are used when a culture-specific resource is not found as part of a fallback mechanism. Culture-specific resources are embedded into satellite assemblies. Each satellite assembly is associated with one particular culture.

Listings 17-3 and 17-4 show the relevant portions of the .resx files that contain resource strings used by the *GreetingLabel* control.

```
<root>
  ⋮
  <data name="GreetingLabel_UserName">
    <value>The person to whom the greeting is addressed.</value>
  </data>
  <data name="Category_Greeting">
    <value>Greeting</value>
  </data>
  <data name="GreetingLabel_Format">
    <value>Hello,{0}!</value>
  </data>
</root>
```

Listing 17-3   Resources.resx contains the culture-neutral set of resources.

```
<root>
  ⋮
  <data name="GreetingLabel_UserName">
    <value>La personne à qui la salutation est adressée.</value>
  </data>
  <data name="Category_Greeting">
    <value>Salutation</value>
  </data>
  <data name="GreetingLabel_Format">
    <value>Bonjour,{0}!</value>
  </data>
</root>
```

Listing 17-4   Resources.fr-FR.resx contains the France-French versions of the same set of resources.

Microsoft Visual Studio .NET automatically converts these .resx files into .resources during its compilation process. The compiler then embeds the culture-neutral resources into the main assembly and compiles the culture-specific resources into a separate satellite assembly. You can obtain the same results by using the tools provided in the .NET Framework SDK and performing the following steps:

1. Compile the .resx files into .resources files by using the resgen.exe tool:

    ```
    resgen Resources.resx MSPress.ServerControls.Resources.resources

    resgen Resources.fr-FR.resx MSPress.ServerControls.Resources.fr-FR.resources
    ```

2. Compile the main assembly, MSPress.ServerControls.dll, by using csc.exe, and include the culture-neutral resources in MSPress.ServerControls.Resources.resources by using the compiler's */res* option:

    ```
    csc /t:library /out:MSPress.ServerControls.dll
        /r:System.dll /r:System.Web.dll /r:System.Drawing.dll
        /r:System.Design.dll
        /res:MSPress.ServerControls.Resources.resources,
    MSPress.ServerControls.Resources.resources
        *.cs
    ```

3. Generate the satellite assembly for the fr-FR culture, MSPress.ServerControls.resources.dll, by using the al.exe tool:

    ```
    al /t:lib /embed:MSPress.ServerControls.Resources.fr-FR.resources
       /culture:fr-FR /template:MSPress.ServerControls.dll
       /out:MSPress.ServerControls.resources.dll
    ```

To use the satellite assembly in a Web application, you need to place it inside a subfolder of the application's bin directory that has the same name as the culture it corresponds to, such as "fr-FR." For example, if the BookWeb application is rooted at C:\Inetpub\wwwroot\BookWeb and its bin directory is C:\Inetpub\wwwroot\BookWeb\bin, the path containing resources for the France-French culture will be C:\Inetpub\wwwroot\BookWeb\bin\fr-FR.

> **Note** Visual Studio .NET can generate satellite assemblies for a Web control project but does not automatically copy the satellite assemblies into a Web project that depends on the Web control project, even though it does copy the main assembly containing the implementation of the control into the bin directory of the Web application. Therefore, you must create the appropriate directory structure and copy the satellite assembly manually.

The *ResourceManager* class selects the appropriate resources based on the culture specified by the *UICulture* property of the current thread. *ResourceManager* implements a fallback mechanism. For example, when the *UICulture* is "fr-FR" (France-French), it first attempts to load the "fr-FR" version of the resources from a satellite assembly. If it fails to find the correct version, it attempts to locate a less specific "fr" (French) version of the resources. If it fails to find that version as well, it falls back on the culture-neutral version of resources that are embedded in the main assembly. This fallback logic implemented by *ResourceManager* is transparent to an application.

You can use the *ResourceManager* class to access resources directly in your control. However, as shown in Listing 17-2, we used the *AssemblyResourceManager* class instead. The *AssemblyResourceManager* utility class caches an instance of the *ResourceManager* class to provide optimized access to resources associated with the assembly, as Listing 17-5 shows.

```
using System;
using System.Diagnostics;
using System.Globalization;
using System.Reflection;
using System.Resources;
```

Listing 17-5 AssemblyResourceManager.cs

```
namespace MSPress.ServerControls {
    internal sealed class AssemblyResourceManager {
        private static ResourceManager _resources;

        private AssemblyResourceManager() {
        }

        private static void EnsureResources() {
            if (_resources == null) {
                try {
                    _resources =
                        new ResourceManager(
                            "MSPress.ServerControls.Resources",
                            typeof(AssemblyResourceManager).Assembly);
                }
                catch {
                }
            }
        }

        public static object GetObject(string name) {
            return GetObject(null, name);
        }

        public static object GetObject(CultureInfo culture,
                                       string name) {
            EnsureResources();
            if (_resources != null) {
                return _resources.GetObject(name, culture);
            }
            return null;
        }

        public static string GetString(string name) {
            return GetString(null, name);
        }

        public static string GetString(CultureInfo culture,
                                        string name) {
            EnsureResources();
            if (_resources != null) {
                return _resources.GetString(name, culture);
            }
            return null;
        }
    }
}
```

The *AssemblyResourceManager* class has the following key characteristics:

■ Is a thin wrapper around a *ResourceManager* object. *AssemblyResourceManager* instantiates its underlying *ResourceManager* once and caches it in a static variable to optimize the performance associated with resource loading. The implementation loads the resources by their name, "MSPress.ServerControls.Resources." *ResourceManager* contains the logic to load localized resources when needed by loading satellite assemblies with resources with names such as "MSPress.ServerControls.Resources.fr-FR."

■ Is marked as internal—in other words, assembly scoped—because the class is meant for use only by other classes within the same assembly that need to access resources embedded in their common assembly.

■ Provides access to strings and arbitrary objects serialized into resources. Strings are by far the most commonly stored resources and are accessed by using the *GetString* method. However, .resx files and resources files also allow other objects (such as images) to be stored. You can access these objects by using the *GetObject* method.

Although this utility class is optional and *ResourceManager* can be used directly, we strongly recommend that you use this class in your own assembly to benefit from the caching mechanism that it implements.

Localizing Metadata Attributes

Some metadata attributes such as *DescriptionAttribute* and *CategoryAttribute* are used to specify string values that are presented to the user in the UI of a design-time environment. If you want your control to fit in naturally with a localized version of the design-time environment, you need to enable localization of metadata by creating your own assembly-scoped, derived versions of these attribute classes that extract their values from the resources associated with your assembly. The *GreetingLabel* class shown in Listing 17-2 makes use of these derived, localizable metadata attributes for its *UserName* property.

Listing 17-6 shows the implementation of *LocalizedDescriptionAttribute*.

```
using System;
using System.Diagnostics;
using System.ComponentModel;
```

Listing 17-6 LocalizedDescriptionAttribute.cs

```
namespace MSPress.ServerControls {
    [AttributeUsage(AttributeTargets.All)]
    internal sealed class LocalizedDescriptionAttribute :
        DescriptionAttribute {
        private bool _localized;

        public LocalizedDescriptionAttribute(string resourceKey) :
            base(resourceKey) {
        }

        public override string Description {
            get {
                // Localize the description the first time it is
                // accessed by using the current description as the
                // name of the resource and replacing it with the
                // string value retrieved from the resource manager.
                if (_localized == false) {
                    _localized = true;

                    try {
                        string resourceKey = base.Description;
                        string localizedDescription =
                            AssemblyResourceManager.GetString(
                                resourceKey);

                        Debug.Assert(localizedDescription != null,
                            "Resource not found: '" +
                            resourceKey + "'");

                        if (localizedDescription != null) {
                            base.DescriptionValue =
                                localizedDescription;
                        }
                    }
                    catch {
                    }
                }

                return base.Description;
            }
        }
    }
}
```

The implementation of *LocalizedDescriptionAttribute* exhibits the following details:

■ The class derives from *DescriptionAttribute* so that the property browser can use it to retrieve description text for properties and events.

■ *LocalizedDescriptionAttribute* is marked as sealed. Sealed metadata attributes are much more performant.

■ The class is marked as internal, or assembly scoped, because it loads assembly-specific resources and is therefore usable only by classes within the same assembly.

■ The constructor accepts the key to the resource value, rather than the resource value itself. Attribute constructors can take as their parameters only those values that are constant at compile time.

■ When the *Description* property getter is invoked the first time, the attribute implementation loads the resource value. To do so, the implementation uses the *GetString* method of *AssemblyResourceManager* based on the resource key that was specified in the constructor.

Listing 17-7 shows the implementation of *LocalizedCategoryAttribute*.

```csharp
using System;
using System.Diagnostics;
using System.ComponentModel;

namespace MSPress.ServerControls {
    [AttributeUsage(AttributeTargets.All)]
    internal sealed class LocalizedCategoryAttribute :
        CategoryAttribute {

        public LocalizedCategoryAttribute(string resourceKey) :
            base(resourceKey) {
        }

        protected override string GetLocalizedString(string value) {
            string localizedValue = base.GetLocalizedString(value);

            if (localizedValue == null) {
                localizedValue =
                    AssemblyResourceManager.GetString(
                        "Category_" + value);
            }
```

Listing 17-7 LocalizedCategoryAttribute.cs

```
              Debug.Assert(localizedValue != null,
                  "Resource string: 'Category_" + value + "' not found.");
              return "localizedValue;
         }
      }
}
```

The implementation of *LocalizedCategoryAttribute* exhibits the following details:

■ The class derives from *CategoryAttribute* so that the property browser can use it to retrieve category information for properties and events.

■ As with *LocalizedDescriptionAttribute*, the class is marked as both sealed and internal—in other words, assembly scoped.

■ The constructor takes in the nonlocalized name of the category, which is constant at compile time. All attribute constructors are restricted to using constant values for their parameters.

■ *LocalizedCategoryAttribute* overrides the *GetLocalizedString* method to return the localized name of the category. The class first invokes the corresponding method of its base class, *CategoryAttribute*. The base class is responsible for localizing standard category names such as "Appearance" and "Behavior" so that they are consistent across all components. If the base class does not support a particular category name, *LocalizedCategoryAttribute* looks up the localized name of the category in the assembly's resources by using the *AssemblyResource-Manager* class. By convention, the resource key used for a category name is the string *"Category_"* followed by the nonlocalized name.

When you need to localize the controls you develop, you must first define the culture-neutral string resources that you embed into the main assembly. Next you must create your own assembly-specific implementations of *AssemblyResourceManager* and localized metadata attributes based on the code shown in this section. You can then add new satellite assemblies containing localized values of the same string resources for each culture you decide to add support for.

Licensing

A *license* is a policy or agreement between you and the page developer that describes the legal usage of your controls. Licensing enables you to enforce that policy to determine how page developers use your controls and to authorize who can use your controls. Licensing also allows you to enable and disable certain features based on the type of license granted to the developer. Licensing is particularly applicable to commercial control development.

The .NET Framework defines an extensible and common licensing framework for use by all components. The licensing framework isn't designed to be completely tamper-proof. Rather, the licensing framework makes using unlicensed components relatively harder and makes it obvious when a developer is violating the licensing policy. Using the licensing framework, you can incorporate custom and arbitrarily complex licensing schemes for your component, such as the following:

■ A simple scheme that only checks for the existence of valid license data to determine whether to enable your component.

■ A per-usage scheme in which the license expires after a certain date or usage count. This can be helpful in implementing demo versions of your component.

■ A scheme that enables the component only when the request comes from a specific client machine, such as the local machine. This can also be useful in implementing trial versions of your component.

■ A more complex validation scheme that requires page developers to register (and purchase) your component and receive a license that they can include in their applications.

The licensing framework revolves around the *System.Component-Model.LicenseProvider* class, which you must implement to define a licensing scheme. You can then associate this license provider with your component by using the *System.ComponentModel.LicenseProviderAttribute* metadata attribute. Your component should incorporate license validation by invoking the *IsValid* or *Validate* methods of the *LicenseManager* class in its constructor. The *License-Manager* inspects the component's metadata to select the appropriate *LicenseProvider* and to retrieve a validated *License* object from it. *LicenseManager* defines two usage modes: design time and run time. This allows a component to implement different licensing models for design-time usage and run-time usage. The samples in this section will demonstrate how these classes allow you to incorporate licensing into your server controls.

Listing 17-8 contains the implementation of a set of licensed controls associated with various licensing providers.

```
using System;
using System.ComponentModel;
using System.Web.UI.WebControls;

namespace MSPress.ServerControls {
    [LicenseProvider(typeof(ServerLicenseProvider))]
    public class LicensedLabel : Label {
        public LicensedLabel() {
            LicenseManager.Validate(typeof(LicensedLabel));
        }
    }

    [LicenseProvider(typeof(EncryptedLicenseProvider))]
    public class EncryptedLicensedLabel : Label {
        public EncryptedLicensedLabel() {
            LicenseManager.Validate(typeof(EncryptedLicensedLabel));
        }
    }

    [LicenseProvider(typeof(ExpiringLicenseProvider))]
    public class DemoLabel : Label {
        public DemoLabel() {
            LicenseManager.Validate(typeof(DemoLabel));
        }
    }
}
```

Listing 17-8   A set of licensed server controls using varying licensing schemes

The samples in Listing 17-8 demonstrate the two additions you have to make to any control to incorporate licensing. First, you need to add metadata that specifies the type of license provider to use by applying the *LicenseProviderAttribute* attribute. For example, the *DemoLabel* control specifies that the *ExpiringLicenseProvider* class should be used when the control's license is validated. Next you need to invoke the *Validate* method of the *LicenseManager* and pass in your control's type as the argument. All usage of the control will now be subject to your licensing scheme. When a control's license is not found or is invalid, the license provider throws a *System.ComponentModel.LicenseException*.

We will look at the specifics of the license providers used in the samples shown later in this section. Figure 17-3 shows an example of the error page that is generated when an unlicensed control is used on a page.

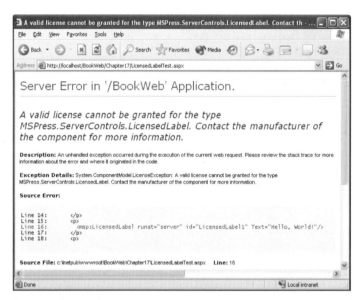

Figure 17-3 An example of the error generated when a page uses an unlicensed control

The licensing model employed by Visual Studio .NET collects license information from components used by a page developer at design time and embeds them as resources into an assembly at compile time, which can then be extracted and inspected for validity at run time. This model does not perfectly fit the needs of server controls and Web applications. When you implement licensing, you should be sure that the licensing scheme satisfies the following critical elements:

■ **Supports a no-compile scenario** ASP.NET Web applications use dynamic compilation and do not necessarily have a precompiled assembly associated with the application. Therefore, the licensing mechanism should not depend on finding licenses embedded as an assembly resource.

■ **Focuses on run-time licensing** Page developers use both visual design-time tools and simple text editors to develop their pages. Therefore, the licensing mechanism should focus on run-time validation rather than on design-time checking.

■ **Supports xcopy deployment** ASP.NET allows page developers to deploy their Web application by copying a folder across computers on their network and to have them continue to work as expected.

Therefore, your licensing scheme should not depend on the registry and other machine-specific resources that do not work with simple xcopy deployment.

■ **Supports a caching mechanism**   License data ideally should be retrieved only once per application, rather than on every page request, because the retrieval logic could involve expensive operations such as opening files and decrypting information. Instead, licenses should be created and cached the first time they are needed. You can still validate cached licenses each time they are used to implement usage-based licenses.

ServerLicenseProvider

In this section, we will use the extensibility of the licensing framework to implement *ServerLicenseProvider*, a custom license provider implementation. *ServerLicenseProvider* offers a framework for implementing licensing schemes optimized for server controls and components. You can expect to see a similar framework built into future versions of ASP.NET, enabling all custom controls to implement their licensing logic by using a shared infrastructure.

The *LicensedLabel* control you saw in Listing 17-8 uses the default licensing scheme built into *ServerLicenseProvider*. The code for this license provider is shown in Listing 17-9.

```
using System;
using System.Collections;
using System.Collections.Specialized;
using System.ComponentModel;
using System.IO;
using System.Diagnostics;
using System.Globalization;
using System.Web;

namespace MSPress.ServerControls {
    public class ServerLicenseProvider : LicenseProvider {
        private static readonly
            ServerLicenseCollector LicenseCollector =
                new ServerLicenseCollector();

        protected virtual ServerLicense CreateLicense(Type type,
            string key) {
            return new ServerLicense(type, key);
        }
```

Listing 17-9   *ServerLicenseProvider* offers a framework for implement-   *(continued)*
ing licensing schemes specific to server controls and components.

Listing 17-9 *(continued)*

```csharp
public override License GetLicense(LicenseContext context,
    Type type, object instance, bool allowExceptions) {
    ServerLicense license = null;
    string errorMessage = null;

    if (context.UsageMode == LicenseUsageMode.Designtime) {
        license = CreateLicense(type, String.Empty);
    }
    else {
        license = LicenseCollector.GetLicense(type);

        if (license == null) {
            string licenseData = GetLicenseData(type);
            if ((licenseData != null) &&
                (licenseData.Length != 0)) {
                if (ValidateLicenseData(type, licenseData)) {
                    ServerLicense newLicense =
                        CreateLicense(type, licenseData);

                    if (ValidateLicense(newLicense,
                        out errorMessage)) {
                        license = newLicense;
                        LicenseCollector.AddLicense(type,
                            license);
                    }
                }
            }
        }
        else {
            if (ValidateLicense(license, out errorMessage) ==
                false) {
                license = null;
            }
        }
    }

    if (allowExceptions && (license == null)) {
        if (errorMessage == null) {
            throw new LicenseException(type);
        }
        else {
            throw new LicenseException(type, instance,
                errorMessage);
        }
    }
```

```
        return license;
}

protected virtual string GetLicenseData(Type type) {
    string licenseData = null;
    Stream licenseStream = null;

    try {
        licenseStream = GetLicenseDataStream(type);
        if (licenseStream != null) {
            StreamReader sr = new StreamReader(licenseStream);
            licenseData = sr.ReadLine();
        }
    }
    finally {
        if (licenseStream != null) {
            licenseStream.Close();
            licenseStream = null;
        }
    }

    return licenseData;
}

protected virtual Stream GetLicenseDataStream(Type type) {
    string assemblyPart = type.Assembly.GetName().Name;
    string versionPart =
        type.Assembly.GetName().Version.ToString();
    string relativePath = "~/licenses/" + assemblyPart + "/" +
        versionPart + "/" + type.FullName + ".lic";

    string licensesFile = null;
    try {
        licensesFile =
            HttpContext.Current.Server.MapPath(relativePath);
        if (File.Exists(licensesFile) == false) {
            licensesFile = null;
        }
    }
    catch {
    }

    if (licensesFile != null) {
        return new FileStream(licensesFile, FileMode.Open,
            FileAccess.Read, FileShare.Read);
    }
    return null;
}
```

(continued)

Listing 17-9 *(continued)*

```
protected virtual bool ValidateLicense(ServerLicense license,
    out string errorMessage) {
    errorMessage = null;
    return true;
}


protected virtual bool ValidateLicenseData(Type type,
    string licenseData) {
    string licenseKey = type.FullName + " is licensed.";
    return String.Compare(licenseKey, licenseData, true,
        CultureInfo.InvariantCulture) == 0;
}



private sealed class ServerLicenseCollector {
    private IDictionary _collectedLicenses;

    public ServerLicenseCollector() {
        _collectedLicenses = new HybridDictionary();
    }

    public void AddLicense(Type objectType,
        ServerLicense license) {
        if (objectType == null) {
            throw new ArgumentNullException("objectType");
        }
        if (license == null) {
            throw new ArgumentNullException("objectType");
        }


        _collectedLicenses[objectType] = license;
    }


    public ServerLicense GetLicense(Type objectType) {
        if (objectType == null) {
            throw new ArgumentNullException("objectType");
        }

        if (_collectedLicenses.Count == 0) {
            return null;
        }

        return (ServerLicense)_collectedLicenses[objectType];
    }
```

```
        public void RemoveLicense(Type objectType) {
            if (objectType == null) {
                throw new ArgumentNullException("objectType");
            }

            _collectedLicenses.Remove(objectType);
        }
    }
}
```

ServerLicenseProvider is associated with a derived license object. The implementation of the *ServerLicense* class is shown in Listing 17-10.

```
using System;
using System.ComponentModel;
using System.Diagnostics;

namespace MSPress.ServerControls {

    public class ServerLicense : License {
        private Type _type;
        private string _key;

        public ServerLicense(Type type, string key) {
            _type = type;
            _key = key;
        }

        public override string LicenseKey {
            get {
                return _key;
            }
        }

        public Type LicensedType {
            get {
                return _type;
            }
        }

        public override void Dispose() {
        }
    }
}
```

Listing 17-10   *ServerLicense* implements the base class of licenses used along with *ServerLicenseProvider*.

The implementation of *ServerLicenseProvider* demonstrates the following key points:

- It derives from *LicenseProvider* so that it can be associated with a component by using the *LicenseProviderAttribute* metadata attribute. *ServerLicenseProvider* overrides the *GetLicense* method of *LicenseProvider* to implement its licensing scheme.

- The class does not implement any design-time licensing. Rather, *ServerLicenseProvider* simply creates a new license. As we mentioned earlier, it is much more important to implement run-time licensing. If you do so, any validation scheme you implement will work, regardless of how the Web application that uses your control was built.

- The default licensing scheme loads license information from .lic text files that are stored within a licenses directory under the root of the Web application. This approach enables the xcopy deployment model. The structure under this directory is based on the name and version of the assembly, and the name of the file is based on the full type name of the component being licensed. For example, the license file associated with the *LicensedLabel* class has the virtual path ~/licenses/MSPress.ServerControls/1.0.0.0/MSPress.ServerControls.LicensedLabel.lic. In this simple, default licensing scheme, the contents of the file simply read "MSPress.ServerControls.LicensedLabel is licensed."

- *ServerLicenseProvider* implements a caching mechanism. Each time a license is created, it is stored in an internal cache managed by the license provider. Each time a license is requested, this cache is first looked up to try to avoid having to load license data from the .lic file. This caching mechanism allows components to incorporate complex licensing schemes without incurring a performance hit from opening the file during each request.

This simplistic model obviously isn't very useful for real licensing purposes. Therefore, *ServerLicenseProvider* also creates a framework for developing custom license providers with more complex validation logic. You can implement custom licensing schemes by deriving your own license provider from *ServerLicenseProvider* and overriding one or more of its virtual methods, which Table 17-1 describes.

Table 17-1   Overridable Methods Defined in *ServerLicenseProvider*

Method	Description
CreateLicense	*protected virtual ServerLicense CreateLicense(Type type, string key)*
	Creates and returns a *ServerLicense* for the specified licensed type and associated validated license data. Allows derived license providers to override this method to return derived license types (for example, *ExpiringLicenseProvider*).
GetLicenseData	*protected virtual string GetLicenseData(Type type)*
	Retrieves license data from a license stream by reading the first line of data in the stream. Derived license providers can override this method to read from other license stores that are not stream based.
GetLicenseDataStream	*protected virtual Stream GetLicenseDataStream(Type type)*
	Opens a stream used to read in license data. This method also contains the logic to form the virtual path to the appropriate .lic file. Derived license providers can override this method to return a custom stream implementation (for example, *EncryptedLicenseProvider*).
ValidateLicense	*protected virtual bool ValidateLicense(ServerLicense license, out string errorMessage)*
	Validates cached licenses. This validation happens each time a license is requested. Derived license providers can override this method to implement per usage–based licensing schemes (such as *ExpiringLicenseProvider*)
ValidateLicenseData	*protected virtual bool ValidateLicenseData(Type type, string licenseData)*
	Validates license data before a license is created and returns *true* if the data is valid. Derived license providers can implement custom validation rules by overriding this method.

ExpiringLicenseProvider

The *DemoLabel* control shown in Listing 17-8 uses *ExpiringLicenseProvider* to implement a licensing scheme with a license that expires after the control has been used a specified number of times. Listings 17-11 and 17-12 contain the implementation of the license provider and its associated license.

```
using System;
using System.Diagnostics;
using System.Globalization;

namespace MSPress.ServerControls {

    public class ExpiringLicenseProvider : ServerLicenseProvider {
        protected override ServerLicense CreateLicense(Type type,
            string key) {
            string[] parts = key.Split(';');
            Debug.Assert(parts.Length == 2);

            return new ExpiringLicense(type, key,
                Int32.Parse(parts[1], CultureInfo.InvariantCulture));
        }

        protected override bool ValidateLicense(ServerLicense license,
            out string errorMessage) {
            errorMessage = null;

            ExpiringLicense testLicense = (ExpiringLicense)license;

            testLicense.IncrementUsageCounter();
            if (testLicense.IsExpired) {
                errorMessage = "The License for " +
                    testLicense.LicensedType.Name + " has expired.";
                return false;
            }
            return true;
        }

        protected override bool ValidateLicenseData(Type type,
            string licenseData) {
            string[] parts = licenseData.Split(';');
            if (parts.Length == 2) {
                return base.ValidateLicenseData(type, parts[0]);
            }
            else {
                return false;
            }
        }
    }
}
```

Listing 17-11 *ExpiringLicenseProvider* implements a usage-based licensing scheme.

```
using System;

namespace MSPress.ServerControls {
    public class ExpiringLicense : ServerLicense {
        private int _usageLimit;
        private int _usageCount;

        public ExpiringLicense(Type type, string key, int usageLimit) :
            base(type, key) {
            _usageLimit = usageLimit;
        }

        public bool IsExpired {
            get {
                return _usageCount > _usageLimit;
            }
        }

        public void IncrementUsageCounter() {
            _usageCount++;
        }
    }
}
```

Listing 17-12   *ExpiringLicense* is used to track usage of the license.

ExpiringLicenseProvider derives from *ServerLicenseProvider* and overrides various methods to implement a usage-based licensing scheme. This class is associated with a derived license object, *ExpiringLicense*, which tracks the usage limit and the usage count. The .lic file associated with *DemoLabel* contains the line "MSPress.ServerControls.DemoLabel is licensed.;5" as its data. The license provider implementation overrides the *ValidateLicense* method to extract the usage limit that is appended to the license data in the .lic file before it is checked for validity and a license object is created. The license provider overrides the *ValidateLicense* method to increment the usage count on the cached license object each time the object is used and to ensure that the license has not expired.

The page developer can modify the textual data in the .lic file. Encrypting license data can help improve the robustness of the licensing scheme.

EncryptedLicenseProvider

The next example shows the implementation of a different license provider. Unlike the samples you've seen so far, *EncryptedLicenseProvider* stores its license data in encrypted form by using the Data Encryption Standard (DES)

cryptography algorithm. A powerful way to use this form of license data is to
encrypt registration information provided by page developers so that only your
license provider can decrypt the information to create a valid license. Listing
17-13 contains the implementation of the license provider.

```
using System;
using System.Diagnostics;
using System.IO;
using System.Security.Cryptography;

namespace MSPress.ServerControls {
    public class EncryptedLicenseProvider : ServerLicenseProvider {
        // This is a 64-bit key generated from the string
        // 5FB281F6.
        private static readonly byte[] encryptionKeyBytes =
            new byte[] {
                0x35, 0x46, 0x42, 0x32, 0x38, 0x31, 0x46, 0x36 };

        protected override Stream GetLicenseDataStream(Type type) {
            Stream baseStream = base.GetLicenseDataStream(type);
            if (baseStream == null) {
                return null;
            }

            DESCryptoServiceProvider des =
                new DESCryptoServiceProvider();
            des.Key = encryptionKeyBytes;
            des.IV = encryptionKeyBytes;

            ICryptoTransform desDecryptor = des.CreateDecryptor();
            return new CryptoStream(baseStream, desDecryptor,
                CryptoStreamMode.Read);
        }
    }
}
```

Listing 17-13 *EncryptedLicenseProvider* works against an encrypted
license file.

EncryptedLicenseProvider derives from *ServerLicenseProvider* and overrides
the *GetLicenseDataStream* method to wrap the underlying *Stream* created by
the base class's corresponding method to read in the license data, with a *CryptoStream* to decrypt license data as it is read in. The *CryptoStream* used in the
sample employs the DES cryptography algorithm with a 64-bit encryption key.

The .lic file associated with the *EncryptedLicensedLabel* control shown in Listing 17-8 is encrypted by using the same key. We have provided the code for the encryption tool, EncLicGen.exe, in EncryptedLicenseGenerator.cs in this book's sample files. The data contained within the .lic file is still "MSPress.ServerControls.EncryptedLicensedLabel is licensed.", but it appears as gibberish because of the encryption. Figure 17-4 shows how this data looks.

Figure 17-4   The encrypted data within MSPress.Server-Controls.EncryptedLicensedLabel.lic

Encryption adds another level of robustness to the licensing scheme. A real licensing scheme you develop for your components might encrypt a combination of your own data and the user's registration information, instead of encrypting a fixed static string as this sample does.

Note that the encryption key is embedded in the code itself in this sample. This is permissible to some degree because the licensing framework is designed to make it harder—not impossible—to break licenses. The Win32 security APIs provide more sophisticated mechanisms for storing encryption keys.

Configurable Properties

Configurable properties of a control are properties whose values can be set in the *<appSettings>* section of the Web application's configuration file, web.config, rather than in every page that uses an instance of the control. These are similar to but not exactly the same as dynamic properties in Visual Studio .NET, which do not apply to server controls. A control can implement configuration support for properties that need to be consistent across the entire application or for properties that might need to be maintained and changed by an administrator once the application has been implemented and deployed. Such properties include database connection strings and names of server resources.

In this section, we will implement a new validator control, *PhoneNumberValidator*, which uses regular expressions to validate phone numbers. This control implements the validation expression as a configurable property so that the pattern for a valid phone number can be defined once across the entire Web application and easily updated. We described how to implement custom validator controls in Chapter 14, "Validator Controls."

Listing 17-14 lists the page used to test the *PhoneNumberValidator* control.

```
<%@ Page language="c#" %>
<%@ Register TagPrefix="msp" Assembly="MSPress.ServerControls"
  Namespace="MSPress.ServerControls" %>
<html>
  <script runat="server">
  protected void Button1_Click(object sender, EventArgs e) {
      if (Page.IsValid) {
          Label1.Text = "You entered: " + TextBox1.Text;
      }
  }
  </script>
  <head>
    <title>PhoneNumberValidator Sample</title>
  </head>
  <body>
    <form method="post" runat="server" ID="Form1">
      <p>
        Enter a phone number:
        <br />
        <asp:TextBox id="TextBox1" runat="server" Columns="25"/>
        <msp:PhoneNumberValidator id="PhoneNumberValidator1"
          runat="server" ControlToValidate="TextBox1"
          ErrorMessage="Enter a valid phone number in the text box. It
must be in (###) ###-#### x#### format. The extension is optional."
          Text="Enter a valid phone number." />
        <br />
        <asp:Button id="Button1" runat="server" Text="Submit"
          OnClick="Button1_Click"/>
        <br />
        <asp:Label id="Label1" runat="server" />
        <br />
        <asp:ValidationSummary runat="server" HeaderText="Errors:"
          id="Validationsummary1"/>
      </p>
    </form>
  </body>
</html>
```

Listing 17-14   PhoneNumberValidatorTest.aspx

Listing 17-15 lists the contents of the web.config file from the Chapter17 folder of the BookWeb Web application. The file defines an *<appSettings>* value that specifies the validation pattern that the *PhoneNumberValidator* control should use. The validation pattern shown matches that of standard U.S. phone numbers with an optional area code and optional extension. Figure 17-5 shows *PhoneNumberValidator* at work on a Web page.

```
<?xml version="1.0" encoding="utf-8" ?>
<configuration>
  <appSettings>
    <add
      key="MSPress.ServerControls.PhoneNumberValidator.Validation
Expression"
      value="((\(\d{3}\) ?)|(\d{3}-))?\d{3}-\d{4}( x\d{1,4})?"/>
  </appSettings>
</configuration>
```

Listing 17-15   The web.config file in the Chapter17 folder that defines the pattern used for phone number validation

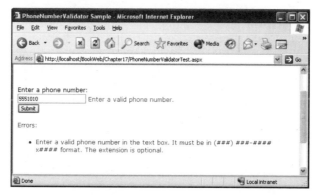

Figure 17-5   The PhoneNumberValidatorTest.aspx page containing the validator in its invalid state

Listing 17-16 contains the code for the *PhoneNumberValidator* control.

```
using System;
using System.Collections;
using System.ComponentModel;
using System.Configuration;
using System.Text.RegularExpressions;
using System.Web.UI;
using System.Web.UI.WebControls;

namespace MSPress.ServerControls {
    [
    ToolboxData("<{0}:PhoneNumberValidator runat=\"server\" " +
        "ErrorMessage=\"PhoneNumberValidator\" " +
        "Text=\"*\"></{0}:PhoneNumberValidator>")
    ]
```

Listing 17-16   PhoneNumberValidator.cs   *(continued)*

Listing 17-16   *(continued)*

```
    public class PhoneNumberValidator : BaseValidator {
        private const string appSettingsKey =
        "MSPress.ServerControls.PhoneNumberValidator.Validation
Expression";
        private const string defaultExpression =
            @"((\(\d{3}\) ?)|(\d{3}-))?\d{3}-\d{4}";

        private bool InDesignMode {
            get {
                if (Site != null) {
                    return Site.DesignMode;
                }
                return false;
            }
        }

        [
        Category("Behavior"),
        DefaultValue(defaultExpression),
        Description(
            "The regular expression used to validate phone numbers")
        ]
        public string ValidationExpression {
            get {
                string s = null;

                s = (string)ViewState["ValidationExpression"];
                if ((s != null) && (s.Length != 0)) {
                    // It's been set on this control instance.
                    return s;
                }

                if (InDesignMode == false) {
                    s = ConfigurationSettings.AppSettings[
                        appSettingsKey];
                    if ((s != null) && (s.Length != 0)) {
                        // Use the value specified in configuration.
                        return s;
                    }
                }

                // Resort to the default, which allows
                // (###) ###-#### or ###-###-#### or ###-####.
                return defaultExpression;
            }
```

```
        set {
            if ((value != null) && (value.Length != 0)) {
                try {
                    // Do a test match to validate the expression.
                    Regex.Match(String.Empty, value);
                }
                catch {
                    throw new ArgumentException(
                        "Invalid regular expression", "value");
                }
            }
            ViewState["ValidationExpression"] = value;
        }
    }

    protected override void AddAttributesToRender(
        HtmlTextWriter writer) {
        base.AddAttributesToRender(writer);

        if (RenderUplevel) {
            // Render the attributes needed for
            // RegularExpressionValidator client-side functionality.
            writer.AddAttribute("evaluationfunction",
                "RegularExpressionValidatorEvaluateIsValid", false);
            writer.AddAttribute("validationexpression",
                ValidationExpression);
        }
    }

    protected override bool EvaluateIsValid() {
        // Get the value to be validated.
        string controlValue =
            GetControlValidationValue(ControlToValidate);

        if (controlValue == null) {
            // Implies that the validator is not bound to a control.
            return true;
        }

        controlValue = controlValue.Trim();

        try {
            Match m =
                Regex.Match(controlValue, ValidationExpression);

            // Must match, and the match must span across the
            // entire value.
```

(continued)

Listing 17-16   *(continued)*

```
            return (m.Success && (m.Index == 0) &&
                (m.Length == controlValue.Length));
        }
        catch {
            return false;
        }
    }
}
}
```

In an ideal world, this validator control would derive from the ASP.NET *RegularExpressionValidator* class. However, the *ValidationExpression* property of that class is nonvirtual and cannot be overridden to add configuration support. Hence, *PhoneNumberValidator* derives directly from the *BaseValidator* class and includes the functionality of *RegularExpressionValidator*. In its implementation of the *EvaluateIsValid* method, *PhoneNumberValidator* uses the regular expression–matching functionality provided by the *System.Text.RegularExpressions.Regex* class. The most interesting aspect of this class is the implementation of the *ValidationExpression* property, which demonstrates the following aspects of configurable properties:

■   A configurable property is implemented as any other property. A configurable property is typically a read/write property—in other words, it has an associated getter and setter. As with any other property, a configurable property should have an appropriate default value and should be associated with the appropriate metadata.

■   The property construct allows you to encapsulate the details of incorporating support for the configuration system. A configurable property's getter accesses the configuration system to retrieve its value if it has not been explicitly set by the page developer. The getter resorts to its default value when the property neither has been set explicitly nor has been set in the configuration file. The setter does not affect the configuration system. The set of name/value pairs in the *<appSettings>* section is exposed for easy access via the *AppSettings* static property of the *ConfigurationSettings* type. A control should define a meaningful and unique name for the value within the *<appSettings>* dictionary. *PhoneNumberValidator* uses its fully qualified type name along with the property name, *MSPress.ServerControls.PhoneNumberValidator.ValidationExpression*, to ensure uniqueness.

■   The configuration value is looked up only at run time. At design time, the control does not have access to the appropriate configuration file. At design time, a configurable property behaves just as any other property. The design-time scenario is determined by checking the *IsDesignMode* property.

Ordinary properties can be turned into configurable properties at any point. The property construct allows you to add this support, without requiring changes in any existing code that uses this property.

Deployment

In this section, we will take a brief look at how you can deploy your server controls and components for use by page developers. ASP.NET Web applications use the same assembly deployment model available to all .NET applications. This model defines two types of assemblies that are based on their deployment mode: *private assemblies* and *shared assemblies*.

Private assemblies are deployed by being placed into the private bin directory of an application. For ASP.NET Web applications, this private bin directory exists directly under the virtual root associated with the Web application. For example, the sample pages in this code are in the BookWeb application or virtual root. If this application is rooted at C:\Inetpub\wwwroot\BookWeb, its associated bin directory is C:\Inetpub\wwwroot\BookWeb\bin. Because the MSPress.ServerControls.dll assembly that contains the samples you have seen in this book is placed in this directory, it is considered a private assembly. A private assembly must be copied into the private bin directory of each application that needs to use it. A private assembly can be referred to by only its name— for example, *MSPress.ServerControls.*

As the name suggests, shared assemblies are shared by multiple applications. Shared assemblies are deployed into the *global assembly cache*, also known as the *GAC*. If you create components that are intended for use by multiple applications, you might consider installation into the GAC. The GAC can also contain multiple versions of your assembly at once. This allows you to deploy a newer version of your component without the risk of inadvertently breaking an existing application that depends on specific behavior of your older implementation. As a result, the GAC must be able to uniquely identify each assembly it contains. This is accomplished by referring to each assembly with its full name, which consists of its name, version, culture, and public key token. For example, the full name of the *System.Web* assembly that contains the implementation of ASP.NET is "System.Web, Version=1.0.3300.0, Culture=neutral, PublicKeyToken=b03f5f7f 11d50a3a."

Assemblies with this four-part name are often referred to as *strongly named assemblies*. The name, version, and culture are specified by using metadata attributes applied to the assembly, and the public key token is derived from the public key of the public/private key pair used to sign the assembly. By convention, assembly-level attributes are specified in an AssemblyInfo.cs file. Listing 17-17 lists relevant portions of the AssemblyInfo.cs file that is compiled into the *MSPress.ServerControls* assembly.

```
using System;
using System.Reflection;

[assembly: AssemblyTitle("MSPress.ServerControls")]
[assembly: AssemblyCulture("")]
[assembly: AssemblyVersion("1.0.0.0")]
```

Listing 17-17   Assembly attributes in AssemblyInfo.cs that contribute to the assembly name

To complete the process of generating a strongly named assembly, you need to sign the assembly with a public/private key pair. A test key pair can be generated by using the sn.exe tool that is included in the .NET Framework SDK by using this command:

```
sn -k MSPress.ServerControls.snk
```

The key pair can be included into the compile process by using the *AssemblyKeyFileAttribute* metadata attribute. *AssemblyKeyFileAttribute* can be added to AssemblyInfo.cs as follows:

```
[assembly: AssemblyKeyFile("MSPress.ServerControls.snk")]
```

Once you have a signed assembly, you can install it into the GAC by using another tool that ships with the .NET Framework SDK, gacutil.exe. To do so, use this command:

```
gacutil /i MSPress.ServerControls.dll
```

The signing process can also be delayed and performed outside your main compile process. Delay signing is described in more detail in the .NET Framework SDK documentation.

Note   When you create a new project in Visual Studio .NET, the project contains an AssemblyInfo.cs file that contains an assembly attribute defining its version as "1.0.*". The asterisk (*) is substituted with a version number that is incremented each time you build your assembly. You should never rely on this auto-increment functionality because it has the side effect of breaking everything else that depends on version numbers. Instead, you should fix all four parts of the version number and choose something along the lines of "1.0.0.0" before continuing with your development.

Summary

In this chapter, we looked at localization and licensing, which are important aspects of developing professional-quality and commercial server controls. We also provided localizable metadata attribute classes and a licensing framework that you can directly incorporate into your own development projects. We discussed how you can add support for configuration into your controls. Finally, we discussed the two deployment models that the .NET Framework provides to allow you to deploy your assemblies for use in applications.

In this part of the book, we have taken an in-depth look at the server control architecture and how you can use it to develop new and powerful controls. In Part V, "Server Control Case Studies," we will implement a set of relatively large and complex controls that illustrate and incorporate various topics covered in this book.

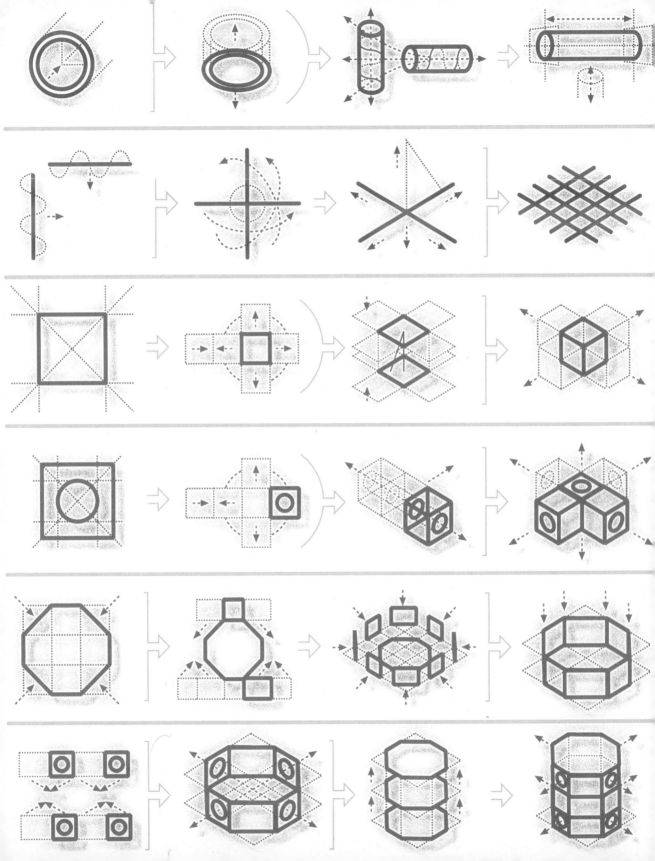

Part IV

Server Components

This part describes XML Web Services and HTTP handlers. It provides a quick overview of creating and deploying Web services and an in-depth explanation of building custom HTTP handlers. This part of the book also shows how to incorporate these technologies into server controls.

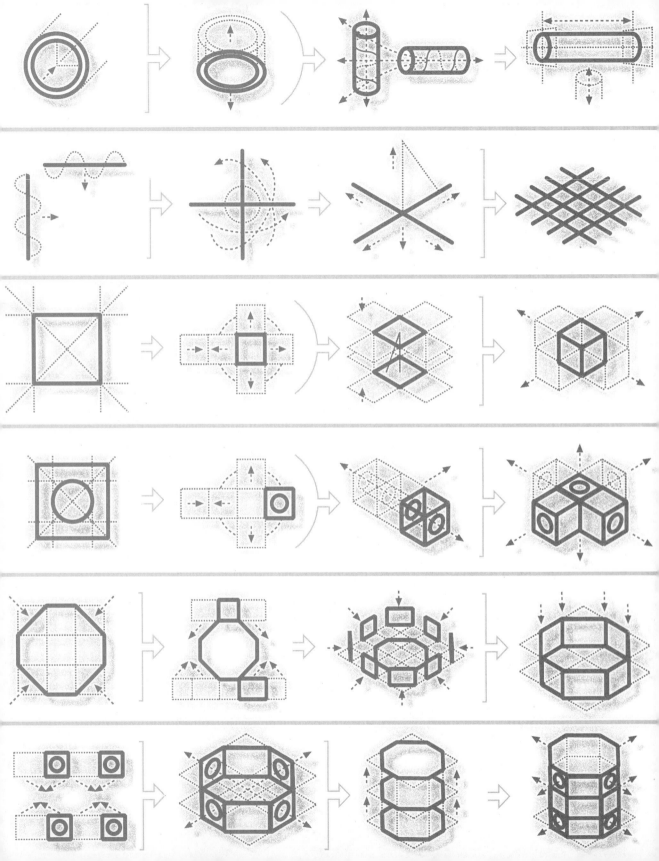

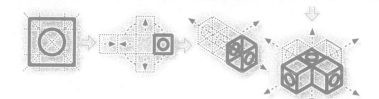

18

XML Web Services

XML Web services represent a new form of Web and distributed application development that allows you to expose functionality and data to a diverse range of client applications on the network. ASP.NET greatly simplifies the development of XML Web services. Furthermore, server controls can simplify the creation of dynamic user interfaces based on information retrieved from Web services by encapsulating the logic to access the Web service.

A detailed discussion of XML Web services is beyond the scope of this book. In this chapter, we will assume that you have some experience developing or using Web services. We will first briefly review the implementation of a simple Web service and then focus on integrating Web service functionality into an associated server control. We also will describe how a control can optimize the performance of the page by caching the results of a Web service instead of accessing it upon every request.

XML Web Services Overview

XML Web services extend component-based programming to the Internet. They provide a mechanism for packaging data and functionality for reuse by a wide variety of client applications distributed across the Internet. Traditional Web applications are geared toward presenting information in a human-readable format. XML Web services allow Web applications to share this same information with other applications. Doing so enables you to reformat and combine this information with other data to provide a more meaningful presentation.

For example, one of the early Web services to be made available publicly was the Microsoft TerraServer .NET Web Service, also referred to as simply Terra-Service and available at *http://terraservice.net*. TerraService provides access to a vast database of aerial and topographical images of locations around the world. Developers can access this Web service in their applications, specify location information such as latitude and longitude, and retrieve images that they can display in their own applications.

Web services are built upon a number of Internet standards. This enables interoperability between servers and clients, even if they are executing on heterogeneous systems. The common substrate of these standards is XML, which is platform independent, easy to use, and widespread in its use. The data transferred between a client application and the Web service is marshaled in the form of SOAP messages. Note that some limited form of data transfer can also take place if you use HTTP GET and POST, but SOAP is the preferred and most capable format for packaging data. The Web service documentation—a description of its API and the format of the SOAP messages used to transfer data between the two endpoints—is provided by using Web Service Description Language (WSDL). Both SOAP messages and WSDL documents are XML documents whose structure can be described by using XML Schema Definition (XSD) files.

Developing an XML Web Service— The *StockWebService* Example

ASP.NET greatly simplifies the development of XML Web services. As you will soon see, you can implement a Web service by defining a class that exposes one or more public methods marked with the *System.Web.Services.WebMethod-Attribute* metadata attribute. You save the class in a file with an .asmx extension and include it in an ASP.NET Web application. ASP.NET handles all the plumbing necessary for exposing these public methods as Web methods that form the API of the Web service that can be invoked from a client application. ASP.NET implements the logic to process incoming requests and invoke the appropriate Web method. The processing logic also handles *marshaling*—the packaging and unpackaging of incoming parameters and the outgoing return value. ASP.NET can automatically generate a WSDL document or contract that describes the API of the Web service. In addition, ASP.NET can generate a set of HTML pages that provide a quick way to test Web methods, as shown in Figure 18-1.

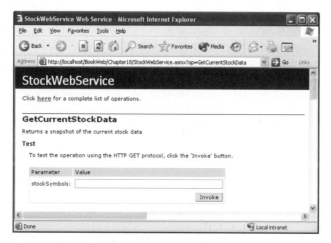

Figure 18-1   The page that ASP.NET automatically generates for testing the *GetCurrentStockData* Web method

Implementing the Web Service

The *StockWebService* that we will implement provides a simple simulation of a stock chart containing a fixed set of stock ticker symbols. This example Web service exposes a method named *GetCurrentStockData*, which provides a snapshot of the stock data that includes the current values, the most recent change in the values, and the time of the last change in the values of the requested stock symbols.

StockWebService is implemented as part of the BookWeb application in StockWebService.asmx, as shown in Listing 18-1.

```
<%@ WebService Language="c#" Class="StockWebService" %>
<%@ Assembly Src="StockServer.cs" %>
using System;
using System.Collections;
using System.Web.Services;
using System.Xml.Serialization;
using BookWeb;

[WebService(Name="StockWebService",
    Namespace="http://localhost/BookWeb/Chapter18/StockWebService",
    Description="A very simple stock tracking simulation")]
public sealed class StockWebService {
    [WebMethod(
        Description="Returns a snapshot of the current stock data")]
```

Listing 18-1   StockWebService.asmx contains the implementation of   *(continued)*
the XML Web service and associated classes.

Listing 18-1 *(continued)*

```
    public StockDataSnapShot GetCurrentStockData(string stockSymbols) {
        if ((stockSymbols == null) || (stockSymbols.Length == 0)) {
            throw new ArgumentNullException("stockSymbols");
        }
        if (StockServer.Instance.IsStarted == false) {
            StockServer.Instance.Start();
        }

        string[] symbols = stockSymbols.Split(';');

        DateTime snapShotTime = StockServer.Instance.LastUpdateTime;
        ArrayList stocks = new ArrayList();

        for (int i = 0; i < symbols.Length; i++) {
            StockServer.StockInfo si =
                StockServer.Instance[symbols[i]];
            if (si != null) {
                stocks.Add(new StockData(si));
            }
        }

        StockDataSnapShot snapShot = new StockDataSnapShot();
        snapShot._snapShotTime = snapShotTime;
        snapShot._stocks =
            (StockData[])stocks.ToArray(typeof(StockData));

        return snapShot;
    }
}

public sealed class StockDataSnapShot {
    [XmlElement("SnapShotTime")] public DateTime _snapShotTime;
    [XmlArray("Stocks")] public StockData[] _stocks;
}

public sealed class StockData {
    [XmlAttribute("Symbol")] public string _symbol;
    [XmlAttribute("Value")] public double _value;
    [XmlAttribute("Change")] public double _change;

    public StockData() { }
    public StockData(StockServer.StockInfo info) {
        _symbol = info.Symbol;
        _value = info.CurrentValue;
        _change = info.Change;
    }
}
```

The file is treated as a Web service by the *WebServiceHandlerFactory*, the HTTP handler associated with .asmx files. The code in the .asmx file is dynamically compiled when the Web service is first requested, by using the same dynamic compilation model that is used for .aspx pages. The Web service implementation just shown illustrates the following concepts:

- The *WebService* directive within an .asmx file is used to indicate the language of the contained code as well as the specific class within the file to be used as the Web service. *StockWebService* is an ordinary class. As an option, when you implement a Web service, you can derive your class from the *System.Web.Services.WebService* base class. This base class provides access to ASP.NET intrinsic objects such as *Session*. *StockWebService* does not require access to these objects.

- The *StockWebService* class contains a public method named *GetCurrentStockData*, which is marked as a Web method by using the *WebMethodAttribute* metadata. The attribute can also provide a more friendly description of the Web service by using the attribute's *Description* property. This description is used by ASP.NET while generating a test page (as shown in Figure 18-1) as well as in generating the WSDL contract.

- The *StockWebService* class uses the optional *WebServiceAttribute* metadata to provide a friendly name and description for the Web service.

- The *GetCurrentStockData* accepts a single parameter containing the stock symbols whose values are being requested. The method returns an instance of *StockDataSnapShot*, which contains an array of *StockData* instances (one for each symbol requested), along with the timestamp of the snapshot.

- ASP.NET handles the incoming request, which is usually a SOAP message, to extract information about the method being called and its parameters. ASP.NET then invokes that method and generates an outgoing response by packaging the return value into a SOAP message. In this example, the *StockDataSnapShot* and *StockData* classes used for the method's return value need to be serialized into an XML format as part of the SOAP message. You can control the structure of the XML content via the *XmlElementAttribute*, *XmlAttributeAttribute*, and other related optional metadata attributes from the *System.Xml.Serialization* namespace that have been applied to the members of these classes.

The Stock Server

As mentioned earlier, *StockWebService* is a simulation of a stock chart. This Web service provides access to stock data that is maintained and updated by the mock stock server running within the same Web application. This stock server is simply an implementation detail that allows the sample to be self-contained.

> **Note**   The Web service implementation shown in Listing 18-1 refers to the *StockServer* implementation in source form using the *Assembly* directive. ASP.NET dynamically compiles the *StockServer* implementation into an assembly when the Web service is first invoked. Alternatively, the *StockServer* implementation could also have been precompiled into an assembly like any other class.

Listing 18-2 shows the implementation of the *StockServer* class.

```
using System;
using System.Collections;
using System.Collections.Specialized;
using System.Configuration;
using System.Globalization;
using System.Timers;

namespace BookWeb {
    public sealed class StockServer {
        public static readonly StockServer Instance =
            new StockServer();

        private Hashtable _stockTable;
        private Timer _timer;
        private DateTime _lastUpdate;

        // All callers must use the single instance of StockServer
        // just shown and not be allowed to create new instances.
        private StockServer() {
            // Initialize the stock table.
            _stockTable = new Hashtable();

            NameValueCollection appSettings =
                ConfigurationSettings.AppSettings;
            int stockCount =
                Int32.Parse(appSettings["StockServer.Count"],
                    CultureInfo.InvariantCulture);
```

Listing 18-2   StockServer.cs implements the mock stock chart simulation.

```
            for (int i = 0; i < stockCount; i++) {
                string symbol =
                    appSettings["StockServer.StockSymbol" + i];
                double initialValue = Double.Parse(
                    appSettings["StockServer.StockValue" + i],
                    CultureInfo.InvariantCulture);
                _stockTable[symbol] =
                    new StockInfo(symbol, initialValue);
            }

            _lastUpdate = DateTime.Now;
        }

        public bool IsStarted {
            get { return (_timer != null); }
        }

        public DateTime LastUpdateTime {
            get { return _lastUpdate; }
        }

        public ICollection Stocks {
            get { return _stockTable.Values; }
        }

        public ICollection Symbols {
            get { return _stockTable.Keys; }
        }

        public StockInfo this[string symbol] {
            get { return (StockInfo)_stockTable[symbol.ToUpper()]; }
        }

        public void Start() {
            lock(typeof(StockServer)) {
                if (_timer == null) {
                    // Two-minute interval
                    _timer = new Timer(2 * 60 * 1000);

                    _timer.Elapsed +=
                        new ElapsedEventHandler(this.Timer_Elapsed);
                    _timer.Enabled = true;
                }
            }
        }
```

(continued)

Listing 18-2   *(continued)*

```csharp
public void Stop() {
    if (_timer != null) {
        lock(typeof(StockServer)) {
            if (_timer != null) {
                _timer.Enabled = false;
                _timer.Elapsed -= new
                    ElapsedEventHandler(this.Timer_Elapsed);
                _timer = null;
            }
        }
    }
}

private void Timer_Elapsed(object sender, ElapsedEventArgs e) {
    lock(typeof(StockServer)) {
        _lastUpdate = DateTime.Now;

        Random r =
            new Random(unchecked((int)_lastUpdate.Ticks));
        foreach (StockInfo s in _stockTable.Values) {
            double randomValue = r.NextDouble();

            // Percentage should be in the range of
            // -0.2 to 0.2.
            double percentChange = (randomValue - 0.5) / 5.0;
            s.UpdateValue(percentChange);
        }
    }
}

// Holds information about a stock.
public sealed class StockInfo {
    private string _symbol;
    private double _value;
    private double _change;

    public StockInfo(string symbol, double initialValue) {
        _symbol = symbol;
        _value = initialValue;
    }

    public double Change {
        get { return _change; }
    }

    public double CurrentValue {
        get { return _value; }
    }
```

```
    public string Symbol {
        get { return _symbol; }
    }

    internal void UpdateValue(double percentChange) {
        double change = _value * percentChange;
        if (_change != 0.0) {
            _change = (change + _change) / 2.0;
        }
        else {
            _change = change;
        }

        _change = (double)Decimal.Round((decimal)_change, 3);
        _value = _value + _change;
    }
  }
 }
}
```

The *StockServer* class loads the list of stock symbols, along with their initial values from the *<appSettings>* section of the Web application's configuration file, and tracks those symbols through its collection of *StockInfo* objects. The implementation uses a *Timer* to periodically update the values of each stock in its collection. The changes are based on percentage fluctuations resulting from random numbers.

Note that there is a single instance of the *StockServer*. This class implements the *singleton* pattern—it implements a private constructor, which restricts the creation of instances. This pattern ensures that all class usage is performed through the single instance it instantiates and makes available through its static *Instance* member. We have used this pattern so that only one copy of stock data in the application is made available to and is shared across all incoming requests. The *StockServer* acquires a lock by synchronizing on the class type before performing any updates to the class's underlying data so that *StockServer* can ensure consistent updates while multiple threads servicing multiple requests safely access the data.

Deploying the Web Service

Once a Web service has been implemented, it needs to be exposed publicly so that it can be discovered and used by client applications. One approach to discovering a Web service implementation is to navigate to the Web service site by using a Web browser. You can configure the site to contain a Web page that describes the set of Web services available on the site, as shown next by using .disco (discovery) files. Another approach to publishing Web services is to register the Web service and its WSDL contract along with your information (used to identify the publisher) with a Universal Description, Discovery, and Integration (UDDI) registry. UDDI is a Web service that allows registration of commercial Web services, acting as a virtual White Pages and Yellow Pages directory.

Microsoft Visual Studio .NET enables Web service discovery by using .disco files and UDDI registries via the Add Web Reference dialog box. This feature can also generate a client proxy (described later in the section). Figure 18-2 shows how the Add Web Reference dialog box looks when a Web service has been discovered.

Figure 18-2   The Add Web Reference dialog box in Visual Studio .NET enables Web service discovery.

A .disco file is used to provide information about the existence of publicly exposed Web services, along with the location of the associated WSDL specification that documents the Web service. Listing 18-3 lists the contents of the Default.disco file, which enables the discovery of *StockWebService* within the BookWeb application.

```xml
<?xml version="1.0" encoding="utf-8" ?>
<discovery xmlns="http://schemas.xmlsoap.org/disco/">
  <contractRef ref="Chapter18/StockWebService.asmx?wsdl"
      docRef="Chapter18/StockWebService.asmx"
      xmlns="http://schemas.xmlsoap.org/disco/scl/" />
```

Listing 18-3   Default.disco enables discovery of the *StockWebService*.

```
  <soap address="Chapter18/StockWebService.asmx"
      xmlns:q1="Chapter18/StockWebService"
      binding="q1:StockWebServiceSoap"
      xmlns="http://schemas.xmlsoap.org/disco/soap/" />
</discovery>
```

> **Note**   A Web application created by Visual Studio .NET contains a .vsdisco file that enables automatic discovery of Web services without requiring the explicit entries needed in the .disco file. However, the .vsdisco file enables the discovery of all Web services in your application, not just the ones you decide to expose. Therefore, we recommend that you delete the automatically created .vsdisco file and instead use a .disco file, as we have done in the BookWeb application.

ASP.NET can automatically provide a .disco file from an .asmx file. The .disco file shown in Listing 18-3 was created by modifying the automatically generated .disco file by navigating to the URL *http://localhost/BookWeb/ Chapter18/StockWebService.asmx?DISCO*. The resulting file is referenced in the Default.aspx page present in the root of the BookWeb application, as shown in Listing 18-4. This allows Visual Studio .NET to list the Web services offered by a Web application by browsing to a page within the application.

```
<html>
<head>
    ⋮
    <link type="text/xml" rel="alternate" href="Default.disco" />
</head>
<body>
⋮
```

Listing 18-4   Fragment of Default.aspx that shows the reference to Default.disco.

Developing Web Service Client Proxies

Client applications call Web services by packaging and transmitting data in the form of SOAP messages. However, implementing this messaging plumbing can be complex and time-consuming. A useful alternative is to employ a *client proxy*. A client proxy is a class that runs within the client application and provides the same public interface as the Web service it represents. A client proxy also contains the logic to package parameters into a SOAP message and send them to the Web service in the form of a Web request, as well as to unpackage the response from the Web service to generate a return value for the proxy's method. By using the proxy, the developer can call the Web service methods just as he or she would call any other class, without having to manually implement the plumbing. Thus, a proxy greatly simplifies Web service usage within client applications.

Visual Studio .NET simplifies the generation of the proxy class. The Add Web Reference dialog box illustrated in Figure 18-2 can automatically create a client proxy when a Web service is referenced. You can also generate the proxy class manually by using the wsdl.exe tool that ships with the .NET Framework SDK. In our example, the proxy class for *StockWebService* has been generated by using wsdl.exe. The specific command used is discussed in the next section.

XML Web Service–Based Server Controls— The *StockGrid* Example

The most common way to use Web services is to reference them and invoke their methods directly. Building dynamic Web pages based on information retrieved from a Web service is also very useful. In these scenarios, you can provide an easier interface to a Web service by developing an associated server control. The server control can encapsulate the tasks of referencing and invoking a Web service by using a built-in client proxy class, and it can hide those details from the page developer. In addition, a control can implement smart logic to decide when to invoke the Web service and when to instead use cached results from a previous call without rendering outdated information. This greatly improves the performance of the Web application by reducing the time it spends making Web requests, especially when using cached results is appropriate. A server control makes it easy to reuse the smart logic across pages and applications.

The sample page shown in Listing 18-5 contains a user interface (UI) based on the stock data retrieved at a regular interval from *StockWebService*. Figure 18-3 shows the *StockGrid* control in customize mode, and Figure 18-4 shows the control in normal mode.

```
<%@ Page language="c#" %>
<%@ Register TagPrefix="mspsc" Assembly="MSPress.ServerComponents"
    Namespace="MSPress.ServerComponents" %>
<html>
  <head>
    <title>StockGrid Sample</title>
    <link href="../Default.css" type="text/css" rel="stylesheet" />
  </head>
  <body>
    <form id="ImageLabelTest" method="post" runat="server">
      <p>
        <mspsc:StockGrid id="StockGrid2" runat="server" Width="210px"
            Font-Size="8pt" Font-Names="Verdana" GridLines="Horizontal"
            BorderStyle="None" StockWebServiceUrl=
              "http://localhost/BookWeb/Chapter18/StockWebService.asmx">
          <AlternateStockRowStyle BackColor="Silver"/>
          <StockHeaderStyle Font-Bold="True" ForeColor="White"
              BackColor="Navy"/>
          <StockRowStyle BackColor="Gainsboro"/>
        </mspsc:StockGrid>
        <hr>
        <asp:LinkButton id="Button1" runat="server" Text="Refresh"/>
      </p>
    </form>
  </body>
</html>
```

Listing 18-5   StockGridTest.aspx is used to demonstrate the *StockGrid*
control.

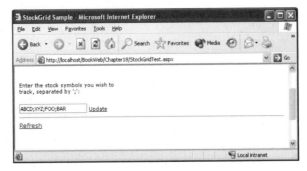

Figure 18-3   The *StockGrid* control in customize mode, allowing the
user to select a sequence of stock symbols

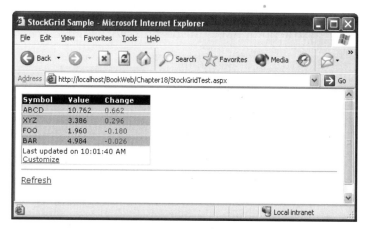

Figure 18-4   The *StockGrid* control in normal mode, showing information about the selected stock symbols

Implementing the Server Control

The *StockGrid* server control renders HTML based on the data retrieved by calling the *GetCurrentStockData* method of *StockWebService*. In particular, this example demonstrates how a server control can be associated with a Web service and how a control can intelligently determine when to access the Web service. The control's implementation is based on several concepts that we first introduced in Part III of this book, "Server Controls—Nuts and Bolts."

Listing 18-6 lists the code of the server control.

```
using System;
using System.Collections;
using System.ComponentModel;
using System.ComponentModel.Design;
using System.Drawing;
using System.Web.UI;
using System.Web.UI.WebControls;
using MSPress.ServerComponents.Proxy;

namespace MSPress.ServerComponents {
    [
    DefaultProperty("StockWebServiceUrl"),
    Designer(typeof(MSPress.ServerComponents.Design.StockGridDesigner),
        typeof(IDesigner))
    ]
```

Listing 18-6   StockGrid.cs contains the implementation of the *StockGrid* control.

```
public class StockGrid : WebControl, INamingContainer {

    private DataGrid _dataGrid;
    private Panel _customizePanel;
    private TextBox _symbolsTextBox;

    private StockDataSnapShot _stockData;
    private bool _updateData;

    [
    Category("Style"),
    Description("Style applied to alternate rows "),
    DesignerSerializationVisibility(
        DesignerSerializationVisibility.Content),
    NotifyParentProperty(true),
    PersistenceMode(PersistenceMode.InnerProperty)
    ]
    public TableItemStyle AlternateStockRowStyle {
        get {
            EnsureChildControls();
            return _dataGrid.AlternatingItemStyle;
        }
    }

    [
    Category("Appearance"),
    DefaultValue(-1),
    Description("Padding inside cells in the stock table")
    ]
    public virtual int CellPadding {
        get {
            if (ControlStyleCreated == false) {
                return -1;
            }
            return ((TableStyle)ControlStyle).CellPadding;
        }
        set {
            ((TableStyle)ControlStyle).CellPadding = value;
        }
    }

    [
    Category("Appearance"),
    DefaultValue(0),
    Description("Spacing between cells in the stock table")
    ]
```

(continued)

Listing 18-6   *(continued)*

```csharp
        public virtual int CellSpacing {
            get {
                if (ControlStyleCreated == false) {
                    return 0;
                }
                return ((TableStyle)ControlStyle).CellSpacing;
            }
            set {
                ((TableStyle)ControlStyle).CellSpacing = value;
            }
        }

        public override ControlCollection Controls {
            get {
                EnsureChildControls();
                return base.Controls;
            }
        }

        [
        Browsable(false),
        DesignerSerializationVisibility(
            DesignerSerializationVisibility.Hidden)
        ]
        public virtual bool CustomizeMode {
            get {
                object b = ViewState["CustomizeMode"];
                return (b == null) ? true : (bool)b;
            }         set {
                ViewState["CustomizeMode"] = value;
            }
        }

        [
        Category("Appearance"),
        DefaultValue(GridLines.Both),
        Description("The style of the grid inside the stock table")
        ]
        public virtual GridLines GridLines {
            get {
                if (ControlStyleCreated == false) {
                    return GridLines.Both;
                }
                return ((TableStyle)ControlStyle).GridLines;
            }
```

```
        set {
            ((TableStyle)ControlStyle).GridLines = value;
        }
    }

    private DateTime LastUpdateTime {
        get {
            object d = ViewState["LastUpdateTime"];
            return (d == null) ? DateTime.Now : (DateTime)d;
        }
        set {
            ViewState["LastUpdateTime"] = value;
        }
    }

    [
    Category("Style"),
    Description("Style applied to the stock table footer"),
    DesignerSerializationVisibility(
        DesignerSerializationVisibility.Content),
    NotifyParentProperty(true),
    PersistenceMode(PersistenceMode.InnerProperty)
    ]
    public TableItemStyle StockFooterStyle {
        get {
            EnsureChildControls();
            return _dataGrid.FooterStyle;
        }
    }

    [
    Category("Style"),
    Description("Style applied to the stock table header"),
    DesignerSerializationVisibility(
        DesignerSerializationVisibility.Content),
    NotifyParentProperty(true),
    PersistenceMode(PersistenceMode.InnerProperty)
    ]
    public TableItemStyle StockHeaderStyle {
        get {
            EnsureChildControls();
            return _dataGrid.HeaderStyle;
        }
    }
```

(continued)

Listing 18-6   *(continued)*

```
[
Category("Style"),
Description(
    "Style applied to rows containing stock information"),
DesignerSerializationVisibility(
    DesignerSerializationVisibility.Content),
NotifyParentProperty(true),
PersistenceMode(PersistenceMode.InnerProperty)
]
public TableItemStyle StockRowStyle {
    get {
        EnsureChildControls();
        return _dataGrid.ItemStyle;
    }
}


[
Bindable(true),
Category("Default"),
DefaultValue(""),
Description("The URL of the Stock Web service to access.")
]
public virtual string StockWebServiceUrl {
    get {
        string s = (string)ViewState["StockWebServiceUrl"];
        return (s == null) ? String.Empty : s;
    }            set {
        if (StockWebServiceUrl.Equals(value) == false) {
            ViewState["StockWebServiceUrl"] = value;
            _updateData = true;
        }
    }
}


[
Browsable(false),
DesignerSerializationVisibility(
    DesignerSerializationVisibility.Hidden)
]
public virtual string Symbols {
    get {
        string s = (string)ViewState["Symbols"];
        return (s == null) ? String.Empty : s;
    }
```

```
        set {
            if (Symbols.Equals(value) == false) {
                ViewState["Symbols"] = value;
                _updateData = true;
            }
        }
    }

    [
    Category("Behavior"),
    DefaultValue(120000),
    Description("The interval (in milliseconds) at which the " +
        "StockWebService is accessed")
    ]
    public virtual int UpdateInterval {
        get {
            object i = ViewState["UpdateInterval"];
            return (i == null) ? 120000 : (int)i;
        }
        set {
            if (value < 0) {
                throw new ArgumentOutOfRangeException("value");
            }
            ViewState["UpdateInterval"] = value;
        }
    }

    protected override void CreateChildControls() {
        Controls.Clear();
        LiteralControl customizeText =
            new LiteralControl("<p>Enter the stock symbols you " +
                "wish to track, separated by ';':</p>");
        LiteralControl separatorText =
            new LiteralControl(" ");

        LinkButton okButton = new LinkButton();
        okButton.Text = "Update";
        okButton.Click += new EventHandler(this.OKButton_Click);

        BoundColumn symbolColumn = new BoundColumn();
        symbolColumn.HeaderText = "Symbol";
        symbolColumn.DataField = "Symbol";

        BoundColumn valueColumn = new BoundColumn();
        valueColumn.HeaderText = "Value";
        valueColumn.DataField = "Value";
        valueColumn.DataFormatString = "{0:0.000}";
```

(continued)

Listing 18-6 *(continued)*

```
            BoundColumn changeColumn = new BoundColumn();
            changeColumn.HeaderText = "Change";
            changeColumn.DataField = "Change";
            changeColumn.DataFormatString = "{0:0.000}";

            _symbolsTextBox = new TextBox();
            _symbolsTextBox.Width = Unit.Percentage(70.0);

            _customizePanel = new Panel();
            _customizePanel.EnableViewState = false;
            _customizePanel.Controls.Add(customizeText);
            _customizePanel.Controls.Add(_symbolsTextBox);
            _customizePanel.Controls.Add(separatorText);
            _customizePanel.Controls.Add(okButton);

            _dataGrid = new DataGrid();
            _dataGrid.ShowFooter = true;
            _dataGrid.AutoGenerateColumns = false;
            _dataGrid.Columns.Add(symbolColumn);
            _dataGrid.Columns.Add(valueColumn);
            _dataGrid.Columns.Add(changeColumn);
            _dataGrid.ItemCreated += new
                DataGridItemEventHandler(this.DataGrid_ItemCreated);
            _dataGrid.ItemDataBound += new
                DataGridItemEventHandler(this.DataGrid_ItemDataBound);

            Controls.Add(_customizePanel);
            Controls.Add(_dataGrid);
        }

        protected override Style CreateControlStyle() {
            TableStyle controlStyle = new TableStyle(ViewState);
            controlStyle.GridLines = GridLines.Both;
            controlStyle.CellSpacing = 0;

            return controlStyle;
        }

        private void CustomizeButton_Click(object sender,
            EventArgs e) {
            CustomizeMode = true;
        }
```

```
private void DataGrid_ItemCreated(object sender,
    DataGridItemEventArgs e) {
    if (e.Item.ItemType == ListItemType.Footer) {
        e.Item.Cells.RemoveAt(2);
        e.Item.Cells.RemoveAt(1);

        TableCell cell = e.Item.Cells[0];
        cell.ColumnSpan = 3;

        Label updateLabel = new Label();

        LinkButton customizeButton = new LinkButton();
        customizeButton.Text = "Customize";
        customizeButton.Click +=
            new EventHandler(this.CustomizeButton_Click);

        cell.Controls.Add(updateLabel);
        cell.Controls.Add(new LiteralControl("<br>"));
        cell.Controls.Add(customizeButton);
    }
}

private void DataGrid_ItemDataBound(object sender,
    DataGridItemEventArgs e) {
    if ((e.Item.ItemType == ListItemType.Item) ||
        (e.Item.ItemType == ListItemType.AlternatingItem)) {
        double change =
            (double)DataBinder.Eval(e.Item.DataItem, "Change");

        if (change != 0.0) {
            TableCell changeCell = e.Item.Cells[2];

            if (change > 0.0) {
                changeCell.ForeColor = Color.Green;
            }
            else {
                changeCell.ForeColor = Color.Red;
            }
        }
    }
    else if (e.Item.ItemType == ListItemType.Footer) {
        Label updateLabel = (Label)e.Item.Cells[0].Controls[0];
        DateTime dt;
```

(continued)

Listing 18-6 *(continued)*

```
            if (_stockData != null) {
                dt = _stockData.SnapShotTime;
            }
            else {
                dt = DateTime.Now;
            }
            updateLabel.Text =
                "Last updated on " + String.Format("{0:T}", dt);
        }
    }

    private void OKButton_Click(object sender, EventArgs e) {
        Symbols = _symbolsTextBox.Text.Trim();
        CustomizeMode = false;
        _updateData = true;
    }

    protected override void OnPreRender(EventArgs e) {
        base.OnPreRender(e);

        if (StockWebServiceUrl.Length == 0) {
            return;
        }

        bool isCustomizeMode =
            CustomizeMode || (Symbols.Length == 0);
        if (isCustomizeMode) {
            return;
        }

        if (ViewState["LastUpdateTime"] == null) {
            // This is the first time around.
            _updateData = true;
        }
        else {
            // If it's been longer than the selected update
            // interval since the last update, it's time to
            // update now.
            DateTime lastUpdateTime = LastUpdateTime;
            DateTime now = DateTime.Now;

            TimeSpan timeSpan =
                new TimeSpan(now.Ticks - lastUpdateTime.Ticks);
            if (timeSpan.Milliseconds > UpdateInterval) {
                _updateData = true;
            }
        }
```

```
    if (_updateData) {
        StockWebService service = new StockWebService();

        // Use the user-selected URL, not the one embedded in
        // the proxy.
        service.Url = StockWebServiceUrl;

        try {
            _stockData = service.GetCurrentStockData(Symbols);

            // Keep track of when the control was last updated.
            LastUpdateTime = DateTime.Now;

            // Create a data source that can be used for data
            // binding. In particular, create BindableStockData
            // objects, which have properties for each field
            // in a StockData object returned by the Web
            // service.
            ArrayList array = new ArrayList();
            for (int i = 0; i < _stockData.Stocks.Length;
                i++) {
                array.Add(new BindableStockData(
                    _stockData.Stocks[i]));
            }

            // Bind the DataGrid with the stock data.
            _dataGrid.DataSource = array;
            _dataGrid.DataBind();
        }
        catch {
        }
    }
}

protected override void Render(HtmlTextWriter writer) {
    if (StockWebServiceUrl.Length == 0) {
        return;
    }

    WebControl visibleControl;

    if (ControlStyleCreated == false) {
        // Force creation of ControlStyle because its default
        // state has nondefault (or nonempty) values.
        Style dummyStyle = ControlStyle;
    }
```

(continued)

Listing 18-6 *(continued)*

```
            string symbols = Symbols;
            bool isCustomizeMode =
                CustomizeMode || (symbols.Length == 0);

            if (isCustomizeMode) {
                visibleControl = _customizePanel;
                _customizePanel.Visible = true;
                _dataGrid.Visible = false;

                _symbolsTextBox.Text = symbols;
            }
            else {
                visibleControl = _dataGrid;
                _customizePanel.Visible = false;
                _dataGrid.Visible = true;
            }

            visibleControl.ApplyStyle(ControlStyle);
            visibleControl.CopyBaseAttributes(this);

            RenderContents(writer);
        }

        private sealed class BindableStockData {
            private StockData _stock;
            public BindableStockData(StockData stock) {
                _stock = stock;
            }

            public double Change {
                get { return _stock.Change; }
            }

            public string Symbol {
                get { return _stock.Symbol; }
            }

            public double Value {
                get { return _stock.Value; }
            }
        }
    }
}
```

The *StockGrid* control is a composite control that implements the composite control pattern described in Chapter 12, "Composite Controls." This includes implementing the *INamingContainer* interface, overriding the *Controls* property to ensure that its contained child controls have been created, and overriding *CreateChildControls* to implement the logic needed to create its child controls on demand. The *StockGrid* control reuses the functionality of the *DataGrid* control to provide style properties such as *StockRowStyle*, *GridLines*, and so on. *StockGrid* also implements event handlers to handle events being raised by the controls it contains, just as a page developer would if these controls were used directly on a page.

The *StockGrid* control implementation illustrates the following concepts:

■ Provides two views—the customize view (shown in Figure 18-3), which allows the user to select the stock symbols to track, and the normal view (shown in Figure 18-4), which lists the selected stocks and their values. The control automatically renders its customize view when it does not have any stock symbols to track. In addition, the control allows the page developer to explicitly activate this view via the *CustomizeMode* property. *StockGrid* contains a *Panel* for its customize view and a *DataGrid* for its normal view. The control toggles the visibility of the *Panel* and *DataGrid* controls by overriding the *Render* method.

■ Fills its *DataGrid* with stock data retrieved from a *StockWebService*. The control offers the *StockWebServiceUrl* property, which the page developer must set to select the appropriate URL of the specific Web service implementation to use. This approach allows the control to be much more flexible than the alternative—having built-in knowledge about the location of one specific Web service. Any Web service can be chosen, as long as it implements the expected *StockWebService* contract.

■ Allows the page developer to programmatically specify the parameter data sent to the Web service's method. In this example, the control offers the *Symbols* property, which allows the page developer to programmatically specify the stocks to track instead of obliging the user to select them through the control's customize view. This also gives the page developer greater flexibility and control over Web service access.

■   The *UpdateInterval* property also adds to the flexibility of the *Stock-Grid* control. A *StockWebService* updates its data at regular intervals. Therefore, it is unnecessary to access the Web service on every request made to the page. Instead, the *StockGrid* control is smart about caching the data. The control accesses the Web service only if a sufficient interval has passed to warrant new stock data. This reduces network traffic, thereby improving the request time for the page. The *UpdateInterval* property allows the page developer to override the control's default settings for the Web service access behavior.

■   Uses a *DataGrid* control as part of its implementation so that it can take advantage of the grid's data-binding model. *StockGrid* calls the *DataBind* method of its *DataGrid* only when it accesses the Web service successfully. The *DataGrid* control is able to re-create itself from view state in the absence of a live data source. This allows *StockGrid* to generate its table of stocks even when it does not access the Web service, without implementing its own caching logic. The control performs the data binding to display updated values in its override of the *OnPreRender* method. This method follows normal user code that might change the properties of the *StockGrid* control (such as the *Symbols* property) earlier in the page life cycle but still enables the control to prepare the contained *DataGrid* for rendering.

StockGrid uses a Web service client proxy generated by using the wsdl.exe tool with the following command:

```
wsdl /language:CS /namespace:MSPress.ServerComponents.Proxy
    /out:StockWebService.cs
    "http://localhost/BookWeb/Chapter18/StockWebService.asmx"
```

The generated proxy is a class that contains the same *GetCurrentStock-Data* method that is exposed as a Web method by the Web service. It is included along with the other sample code for this chapter. In addition, it contains the *StockDataSnapShot* and *StockData* classes used as the return value of the method. The array of *StockData* objects inside the snapshot returned by the Web service provides the data needed to bind the contained *DataGrid* control. However, wsdl.exe generates public fields in these classes. Because the data-binding model in Web Forms works against properties only, *StockGrid* contains a *BindableStockData* class that is a thin wrapper over an actual *StockData* instance. The properties in the wrapper class map to the corresponding fields of the *StockData* instance that it wraps. An *ArrayList* of *BindableStockData* instances is then used as the data source for the *DataGrid* control.

Implementing the Control Designer

The *StockGrid* control is associated with its own control designer, *StockGrid-Designer*. The designer uses dummy data to generate the design-time UI, rather than invoking the Web service at design time. This example also demonstrates how a designer associated with a control that offers multiple views can provide a mechanism to illustrate both views at design time. Figure 18-5 shows *Stock-Grid* in Visual Studio .NET.

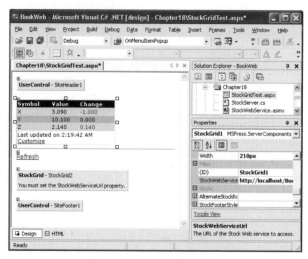

Figure 18-5   The *StockGrid* control selected on the design surface in StockGridTest.aspx

The designer implementation shown in Listing 18-7 is based on the concepts introduced in Chapter 15, "Design-Time Functionality."

```
using System;
using System.ComponentModel;
using System.ComponentModel.Design;
using System.Diagnostics;
using System.Text;
using System.Web.UI.Design;
using System.Web.UI;
using System.Web.UI.WebControls;
using MSPress.ServerComponents;

namespace MSPress.ServerComponents.Design {
    public class StockGridDesigner : ControlDesigner {
```

Listing 18-7   StockGridDesigner.cs shows the implementation of the   *(continued)*
StockGridDesigner.

Listing 18-7   *(continued)*

```csharp
private DesignerVerb _toggleVerb;
private DesignTimeStockObject[] _designTimeData;

public override DesignerVerbCollection Verbs {
    get {
        if (_toggleVerb == null) {
            // Add the custom verb the first time around.
            _toggleVerb = new DesignerVerb("Toggle View",
                new EventHandler(this.OnToggleView));
            DesignerVerbCollection verbs = base.Verbs;
            verbs.Add(_toggleVerb);
        }

        return base.Verbs;
    }
}

public override string GetDesignTimeHtml() {
    StockGrid stockGrid = (StockGrid)Component;

    if (stockGrid.StockWebServiceUrl.Length == 0) {
        return CreatePlaceHolderDesignTimeHtml(
            "You must set the StockWebServiceUrl property.");
    }

    ControlCollection controls = stockGrid.Controls;
    if (stockGrid.CustomizeMode == false) {
        if (_designTimeData == null) {
            _designTimeData =
                new DesignTimeStockObject[] {
                    new DesignTimeStockObject("X", 3.09, -1.0),
                    new DesignTimeStockObject("Y", 10.10, 0.0),
                    new DesignTimeStockObject("Z", 2.14, 0.14)
                };
        }

        DataGrid containedGrid = (DataGrid)stockGrid.Controls[1];
        try {
            containedGrid.DataSource = _designTimeData;
            containedGrid.DataBind();
        }
        catch {
        }
    }
    return base.GetDesignTimeHtml();
}

public override void Initialize(IComponent component) {
```

```
        if (!(component is StockGrid)) {
            throw new ArgumentException(
                "Component must be an StockGrid",
                "component");
        }

        base.Initialize(component);
    }

    private void OnToggleView(object sender, EventArgs e) {
        StockGrid stockGrid = (StockGrid)Component;

        if (stockGrid.CustomizeMode) {
            stockGrid.CustomizeMode = false;
            stockGrid.Symbols = "abc";
        }
        else {
            stockGrid.CustomizeMode = true;
            stockGrid.Symbols = String.Empty;
        }

        UpdateDesignTimeHtml();
    }

    private class DesignTimeStockObject {
        private string _symbol;
        private double _value;
        private double _change;

        public DesignTimeStockObject(string symbol, double value,
            double change) {
            _symbol = symbol;
            _value = value;
            _change = change;
        }

        public double Change {
            get { return _change; }
        }

        public string Symbol {
            get { return _symbol; }
        }
        public double Value {
            get { return _value; }
        }
    }
}
}
```

Like all control designer classes, the *StockGridDesigner* class overrides the *Initialize* method to check that it has been correctly associated as a designer for a *StockGrid*. In addition, *StockGridDesigner* overrides *GetDesignTimeHtml* to customize the design-time display of the *StockGrid* control. This control designer generates a placeholder UI with instructive text indicating that the page developer must first specify a value for the control's *StockWebServiceUrl* property. Once this property has been set, the designer uses the runtime control's rendering functionality to generate design-time HTML. The designer generates dummy data by using an array of *DesignTimeStockObject* objects as the data source for the *DataGrid* contained within *StockGrid*. This allows the control to have a WYSIWYG display without accessing the Web service at design time, which is desirable and essential because a control does not go through its Pre-Render phase when used within a designer. As you might recall, *StockGrid* accesses the Web service it is bound to by overriding *OnPreRender*.

In addition, *StockGridDesigner* provides a Toggle View designer verb (or command), which appears on the control's context menu or as a command link in the property browser to allow the page developer to view both customize and normal views of the *StockGrid* on the design surface.

Summary

XML Web services are one of the most significant and innovative features of the .NET Framework. Furthermore, XML Web services have the potential to fundamentally alter how data is transferred across applications and businesses and how component-based programming can cross traditional application boundaries. ASP.NET simplifies Web service development considerably. The .NET Framework greatly simplifies the consumption of Web services in client applications. As shown in the *StockGrid* control, server controls provide a mechanism for encapsulating intelligent and optimal Web service access that's used to generate dynamic user interfaces in Web applications, while retaining the flexibility of direct Web service access for page developers.

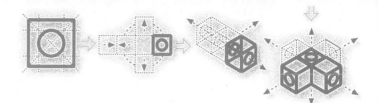

19

HTTP Handlers

In this chapter, we will provide an in-depth look at implementing HTTP handlers. As described in Chapter 1, "ASP.NET Overview," HTTP handlers are a feature of the HTTP runtime architecture in ASP.NET that enables modularization and customization of request processing in a Web application. ASP.NET provides a number of built-in HTTP handlers that are used to process requests for common file types. ASP.NET also enables developers to plug in their own HTTP handler implementations to customize request handling specific to their own application. We will illustrate a couple of real-world HTTP handler implementations and show how you can enhance the usability of your handler by providing an associated server control.

HTTP Handler Overview

In Chapter 1, we provided an overview of the entire request-processing cycle in an ASP.NET Web application and the components involved in that process. An HTTP handler performs the actual work associated with the request. At a high level, the HTTP handler consumes the incoming request data sent to it by the client application and generates an outgoing response containing the results of its request-processing logic.

The HTTP runtime identifies the appropriate HTTP handler to service an incoming request based on the URL of the incoming request. It is typical for the HTTP runtime to create an instance of the HTTP handler directly. However, ASP.NET also allows you to provide an associated HTTP handler factory that can customize the instantiation of your HTTP handler.

ASP.NET provides a number of built-in HTTP handlers and HTTP handler factories in the *System.Web* and *System.Web.UI* namespaces. Table 19-1 lists some of these.

Table 19-1   Common HTTP Handlers and HTTP Handler Factories

File Types	HTTP Handler or HTTP Handler Factory	Description
.aspx files	*PageHandlerFactory*	Creates an instance of a dynamically compiled, derived *Page* class that is used as the HTTP handler
.asmx files	*WebServiceHandlerFactory*	Creates an instance of a dynamically compiled Web service implemented within the file, which is used as the HTTP handler
.ashx files	*SimpleHandlerFactory*	Creates an instance of a dynamically compiled HTTP handler implemented within the file
.ascx, .asax, .config, .cs, and .vb files	*HttpForbiddenHandler*	Prevents access to these files because they are meant for server-side use only
Other extensions	*StaticFileHandler*	Simply outputs the content of the file as its response

You can register your own handler implementations with the HTTP runtime by using configuration entries that map URLs to your handler class within the *<httpHandlers>* section of a Web application's web.config file. The built-in HTTP handlers are registered for all applications in the machine.config file. The following is a fragment from the machine.config file:

```
<configuration>
  <system.web>
    ⋮
    <httpHandlers>
      <add verb="*" path="*.aspx" type="System.Web.UI.PageHandlerFactory"/>
      <add verb="*" path="*.ashx" type="System.Web.UI.SimpleHandlerFactory"/>
      <add verb="*" path="*.ascx" type="System.Web.HttpForbiddenHandler"/>
```

```
        <add verb="*" path="*.config" type="System.Web.HttpForbiddenHandler"/>
        <add verb="GET,HEAD" path="*" type="System.Web.StaticFileHandler"/>
        <add verb="*" path="*" type="System.Web.HttpMethodNotAllowedHandler"/>
        ⋮
    </httpHandlers>
    ⋮
  </system.web>
</configuration>
```

An HTTP handler can process a request in a variety of ways. The page handler handles .aspx files and returns HTML markup text by rendering the page and the controls it contains. The XML Web service handler associated with an .asmx file returns a SOAP response by executing a Web method, or it might generate a Web Services Description Language (WSDL) specification of the service based on the query string of the request. The handler associated with .ascx and .config files simply generates an error page, thereby preventing access to these files because they aren't meant to be viewable. The *XmlHandler* that we will implement later in this chapter generates XML markup. The *Image-LabelHandler* example appearing later in this chapter generates binary JPEG content. In essence, the HTTP runtime does not place arbitrary limitations on the processing that a handler can perform and allows the handler implementation to generate any response supported by the HTTP protocol.

The HTTP handler extensibility feature of ASP.NET is equivalent to the ISAPI filter feature provided by the Microsoft Internet Information Services (IIS) Web server. An *ISAPI filter* is an extensibility mechanism that allows you to implement request-handling logic for specific URLs or file extensions in C or C++. ASP.NET provides a vastly simpler model. In the ASP.NET model, you develop your custom-handling logic by implementing a simple managed class in any .NET programming language, and ASP.NET handles all the plumbing required to interact with IIS.

The *IHttpHandler* Interface

You can create an HTTP handler by implementing the *System.Web.IHttpHandler* interface, which is defined as follows:

```
public interface IHttpHandler {
    public bool IsReusable { get; }
    public void ProcessRequest(HttpContext context);
}
```

This interface contains two members that you must implement:

- The *IsReusable* property determines whether the HTTP runtime can reuse an HTTP handler instance to handle multiple requests.

- The *ProcessRequest* method receives an instance of the *HttpContext* class and implements the logic of the handler. The context object contains information specific to the current request. In particular, this object provides access to the *Request (System.Web.HttpRequest)* object, which includes the request URL and data passed into the handler, and the *Response (System.Web.HttpResponse)* object, which is used by the handler to write out the result it generates.

The *IHttpHandlerFactory* Interface

The HTTP runtime allows you to customize the creation of your HTTP handler implementation by providing an associated *IHttpHandlerFactory* implementation. For example, in ASP.NET, .aspx files are associated with the *PageHandlerFactory*. The *PageHandlerFactory* parses an .aspx file and dynamically creates a class that derives from the *Page* class to represent the contents of the file as described in Chapter 2, "Page Programming Model." This derived page class then serves as the HTTP handler. The *IHttpHandlerFactory* interface is defined as follows:

```
public interface IHttpHandlerFactory {
    public IHttpHandler GetHandler(HttpContext context,
        string requestType, string url, string pathTranslated);
    public void ReleaseHandler(IHttpHandler handler);
}
```

The *GetHandler* method allows you to create your HTTP handler based on the request data. The *ReleaseHandler* method allows you to clean up any resources if applicable, once your handler has been used to process a request. If you do not need to execute any custom logic to create your HTTP handler (that is, your implementation of *GetHandler* simply instantiates an instance of your handler), then you do not need to implement a handler factory.

The "Hello, World" HTTP Handler Example

Our first HTTP handler, *HelloWorldHandler*, demonstrates the basics of implementing a handler. This handler generates HTML markup that displays a "Hello" greeting in the Web browser. Listing 19-1 shows the code for this handler.

```
<%@ WebHandler Language="C#" Class="HelloWorldHandler" %>
using System;
using System.Web;

public class HelloWorldHandler : IHttpHandler {
    public bool IsReusable {
        get { return true; }
    }

    // Handles the request and generates the resulting response.
    public void ProcessRequest(HttpContext context) {
        // The standard request/response objects.
        HttpRequest request = context.Request;
        HttpResponse response = context.Response;

        // Extract the name from the request.
        string name = request.QueryString["name"];

        // Start writing out the response HTML.
        response.ContentType = "text/html";

        response.Write("<html>");
        response.Write("<head>");
        response.Write("<title>Hello World Http Handler</title>");
        response.Write("</head>");
        response.Write("<body>");

        if ((name != null) && (name.Length != 0)) {
            response.Write("<h1>Hello, ");
            response.Write(context.Server.HtmlEncode(name));
            response.Write("!</h1>");
        }
        else {
            response.Write("Usage:<br>");
            response.Write("HelloWorld.ashx?name=&lt;your_name&gt;");
        }

        response.Write("</body>");
        response.Write("</html>");
    }
}
```

Listing 19-1   HelloWorld.ashx

The *HelloWorldHandler* implements *IHttpHandler* and can be used as an HTTP handler in ASP.NET. *HelloWorldHandler* is implemented inside an .ashx file, HelloWorld.ashx. ASP.NET provides .ashx as a generic extension for implementing an HTTP handler without having to add any new configuration entries.

The code in the .ashx file is dynamically compiled upon the first request made to it, by using the same dynamic compilation model that is used for an .aspx file as described in Chapter 2. Every .ashx file must contain a *WebHandler* directive, which is used to specify the class within file that provides the implementation of *IHttpHandler*. All requests to the HelloWorld.ashx file are processed by the handler implemented in this file. Figure 19-1 shows the results of making a request to this file.

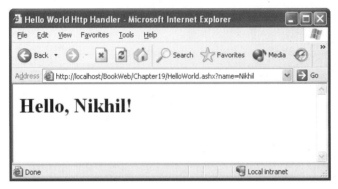

Figure 19-1   The results of making a request to HelloWorld.ashx

The *HelloWorldHandler* class generates HTML markup into the response stream. Therefore, the handler sets the *ContentType* property of the response to *"text/html"*. An HTTP handler should always set the content type of the response it generates, unless the content type can be automatically inferred from the URL. With *HelloWorldHandler*, it is especially important to set the content type of the generated response. This is because the browser making the request cannot infer the content type from the request URL as it can with URLs that have .htm or .html extensions. The handler writes standard HTML markup into the response stream that gets rendered within the browser.

The handler retrieves the *name* parameter from the URL's query string (the text containing name/value pairs following the question mark in the URL) and uses its value as part of the greeting it generates. The *name* value is HTML encoded before it is written into the response stream. This prevents any malicious users from sending script within the *name* value, which is a common case of cross-site scripting. Taking this precaution ensures that the HTTP handler will not suffer from a lapse in security.

When the *name* parameter isn't specified, *HelloWorldHandler* generates HTML that describes its correct usage. Consider following a similar pattern in your HTTP handler implementations by handling missing or invalid parameters gracefully via an informative display that describes the correct usage of the handler when appropriate.

Handling a New Extension—The *XmlHandler* Example

In this section, we'll show you how to create an HTTP handler to handle an extension that isn't handled by ASP.NET in its default configuration. The sample we will implement is named *XmlHandler*. This example handles the .xml extension and enables you to optionally run an XSL transform before the XML data is returned to the browser. Once this handler is implemented and registered within an application, it will be invoked to handle requests to all .xml files within that application.

An .ashx file can handle only requests to itself. On the other hand, the *XmlHandler* needs to handle requests for all .xml files. Therefore, this handler cannot be implemented inside an .ashx file. Instead, *XmlHandler* is implemented in a code file and precompiled into an assembly that is placed into the application's bin directory. The handler class is then associated with the .xml extension in the application's web.config file.

Listing 19-2 shows the code for *XmlHandler*. This code is compiled into the *MSPress.ServerComponents* assembly.

```
using System;
using System.IO;
using System.Web;
using System.Web.Caching;
using System.Xml;
using System.Xml.XPath;
using System.Xml.Xsl;

namespace MSPress.ServerComponents {

    // XmlViewer allows viewing of XML files on the server along with
    // a customized transform using an XSL style sheet.
    public sealed class XmlHandler : IHttpHandler {

        public bool IsReusable {
            get { return true; }
        }

        // Retrieves the contents of a file.
        private string
            GetFileContents(HttpContext context, string filePath) {
            string cacheKey = "XmlHandler." + filePath.ToLower();

            // First look it up in cache.
            string content = (string)context.Cache[cacheKey];
```

Listing 19-2 XmlHandler.cs   *(continued)*

Listing 19-2   *(continued)*

```
        if ((content == null) && File.Exists(filePath)) {
            FileStream stream = null;
            try {
                // Read in the file because it wasn't found in
                // the cache.
                stream = new FileStream(filePath, FileMode.Open,
                    FileAccess.Read, FileShare.Read);

                StreamReader reader = new StreamReader(stream);
                content = reader.ReadToEnd();

                reader.Close();

                // Store it into cache for future use, and
                // associate it with a file dependency so that
                // the cache is freed if the file is changed.
                context.Cache.Insert(cacheKey, content,
                    new CacheDependency(filePath));
            }
            catch {
            }
            finally {
                if (stream != null) {
                    stream.Close();
                    stream = null;
                }
            }
        }
        return content;
    }

    // Handles the request and generates the resulting response.
    public void ProcessRequest(HttpContext context) {
        // The standard request/response objects.
        HttpRequest request = context.Request;
        HttpResponse response = context.Response;

        // Get the path to the .xml file that is being requested
        // and load its content.
        string xmlFile = request.PhysicalPath;
        string xmlContent = GetFileContents(context, xmlFile);
        if (xmlContent == null) {
            throw new HttpException(404, "Not Found");
        }

        // Extract the name of the optional XSL transform to be
        // applied to transform the XML data into HTML.
        string xslFile = request.QueryString["xsl"];
```

```
        if ((xslFile != null) && (xslFile.Length != 0)) {
            // Start writing out the response HTML.
            response.ContentType = "text/html";

            // Load up the .xml and .xsl files, perform the
            // transform, and write out the transformed data.
            xslFile = request.MapPath(xslFile);

            string xslContent = GetFileContents(context, xslFile);
            if (xslContent == null) {
                throw new HttpException(404, "Not Found");
            }

            XslTransform xsl = new XslTransform();
            xsl.Load(new XmlTextReader(
                new StringReader(xslContent)));

            XPathDocument xmlData =
                new XPathDocument(new StringReader(xmlContent));

            xsl.Transform(xmlData, null, response.Output);
        }
        else {
            // Render out the XML directly.
            response.ContentType = "text/xml";
            response.Write(xmlContent);
        }
    }
  }
}
```

The *XmlHandler* can be used in one of two ways. When an .xml file is requested along with an *xsl* argument in the request URL (as shown later in this section), the XML content is transformed by using the specified XSL transform on the server and the resulting HTML content is returned as the response so that it can be displayed in a browser. In this case, the handler specifies the *ContentType* property of the response as *"text/html"*. The handler uses functionality provided by the classes in the *System.Xml.Xsl.XslTransform* and *System.Xml.XPath.XPath-Document* namespaces in the .NET Framework to perform the transformation. When an .xml file is requested by itself, the handler sets the *ContentType* to *"text/xml"* and writes out the contents of the .xml file directly.

This example also demonstrates how an HTTP handler can retrieve the physical path of the file being requested via the *PhysicalPath* property of the *HttpRequest* object retrieved from the *HttpContext* instance that is provided to the handler. The implementation uses the *MapPath* method of the *HttpRequest* object to determine the physical path of the .xsl file passed in as an argument.

It is important to use this method instead of directly using the argument as the full file path. The *MapPath* method ensures that the specified .xsl file is located within the application. This method prevents access to files outside the application (such as system files) by throwing an exception because doing so would create a security hole in the handler.

The *XmlHandler* example also demonstrates using the ASP.NET cache to improve performance. The *GetFileContents* method in Listing 19-2 first attempts to retrieve the cached content. When this content is not found, the implementation reads in the file contents by opening it and stores the contents in the cache, thereby improving performance in a subsequent request. In addition, the cache entry is associated with a file dependency so that the cached file contents are automatically removed from the cache if the file is changed on the disk. In general, an HTTP handler should never perform file access during each request—it should use the caching functionality built into ASP.NET to improve performance when appropriate.

Because this handler is not implemented by using an .ashx file, you need to add the appropriate mapping to the application's web.config file so that the HTTP runtime can locate and route requests for .xml files to this handler. The following fragment from the web.config file shows the relevant portions that create this mapping between all .xml files and the handler implementation:

```
<configuration>
  <system.web>
    <httpHandlers>
      <add verb="*" path="*.xml"
        type="MSPress.ServerComponents.XmlHandler,
MSPress.ServerComponents" />
    </httpHandlers>.
  </system.web>
</configuration>
```

There is one final step you need to perform before you can use the handler. IIS stores information about each application in its metabase. The script map of an application stored in the metabase needs to be updated to include an entry that specifies .xml as another file type handled by ASP.NET. This script map entry is similar to the mapping that exists for .aspx files. You can perform this update manually by using the IIS administration tool, as shown in the Figure 19-2.

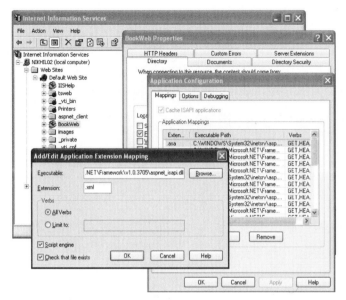

Figure 19-2   IIS administration user interface for adding a script map entry

You can also make the same settings programmatically. Consider providing a setup script with your HTTP handler if you plan to deploy it widely. The VBScript code in Listing 19-3 uses IIS Active Directory objects to add mapping for the .xml extension by copying the entry for .aspx files in the BookWeb application.

```
Dim iisObject
Set iisObject = GetObject("IIS://localhost/w3svc/1/root/BookWeb")
AddXmlMapping()

Sub AddXmlMapping()
    Dim scriptMapsObject
    Dim xmlMapping
    Dim newMappings
    Dim mappingCount
    Dim i

    mappingCount = 0
    scriptMapsObject = iisObject.Get("ScriptMaps")
    For Each mapping In scriptMapsObject
        mappingCount = mappingCount + 1
```

Listing 19-3   AddXmlMapping.vbs   *(continued)*

Listing 19-3 *(continued)*

```
        If (Left(mapping, 5) = ".aspx") Then
            xmlMapping = ".xml" + Right(mapping, Len(mapping) - 5)
            mappingCount = mappingCount + 1
        End If
    Next

    ReDim newMappings(mappingCount - 1)

    i = 0
    For Each mapping In scriptMapsObject
        newMappings(i) = mapping
        i = i + 1
    Next
    newMappings(mappingCount - 1) = xmlMapping

    iisObject.Put "ScriptMaps", newMappings
    iisObject.SetInfo

    WScript.Echo ".xml added to script map"
End Sub
```

Listings 19-4 and 19-5 show the .xml and .xsl files used as sample files. Figure 19-3 shows the HTML resulting from the XSL transformation.

```
<?xml version="1.0" encoding="utf-8" ?>
<marketData date="11/03/2001">
  <index name="Dow">
    <value>9323.54</value>
    <change>59.64</change>
  </index>
  <index name="NASDAQ">
    <value>1745.73</value>
    <change>-0.57</change>
  </index>
  <index name="S&amp;P">
    <value>1087.22</value>
    <change>3.12</change>
  </index>
</marketData>
```

Listing 19-4 MarketData.xml

```xml
<?xml version="1.0" encoding="utf-8" ?>
<xsl:stylesheet version="1.0"
  xmlns:xsl="http://www.w3.org/1999/XSL/Transform">
<xsl:template match="/">
  <html>
    <body>
      <xsl:apply-templates/>
    </body>
  </html>
</xsl:template>
<xsl:template match="marketData">
  <table style="font-family: verdana; font-size: 8pt">
    <tr>
      <td colspan="3">Market Data for <xsl:value-of select="@date"/></td>
    </tr>
    <tr style="font-weight:bold">
      <td>Index</td>
      <td>Value</td>
      <td>Change</td>
    </tr>
    <xsl:apply-templates/>
  </table>
</xsl:template>
<xsl:template match="marketData/index">
  <tr>
    <td><xsl:value-of select="@name"/></td>
    <td><xsl:value-of select="value"/></td>
    <td>
      <xsl:if test="change &lt; 0">
        <xsl:attribute name="style">
          <xsl:text>color:red</xsl:text>
        </xsl:attribute>
      </xsl:if>
      <xsl:if test="change &gt; 0">
        <xsl:attribute name="style">
          <xsl:text>color:green</xsl:text>
        </xsl:attribute>
      </xsl:if>
      <xsl:value-of select="change"/>
    </td>
  </tr>
</xsl:template>
</xsl:stylesheet>
```

Listing 19-5   MarketData.xsl

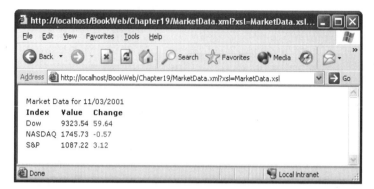

Figure 19-3 HTML resulting from the XSL transformation by making a request to MarketData.xml

Dynamic Images—The *ImageLabelHandler* Example

In this section, we will show you how to use an HTTP handler to generate binary data in the form of a dynamic image generated by parameters passed in via a query string. The traditional approach of generating dynamic images involves temporary files, which need to be periodically deleted. HTTP handlers provide a clean way to serve these dynamic images without requiring on-disk persistence. A variety of Web application scenarios involve dynamic images— stock charts, e-card previews, image watermarking, renderings of product catalog images that are stored in a database, and so on.

The *ImageLabelHandler* is a simple example of dynamic image generation. This handler generates a JPEG image containing the specified text rendered in the specified formatting by using GDI+ functionality present in the .NET Framework. You could use such a component in a font gallery application that allows a user to experiment with fonts and make selections before downloading them onto his or her machine. In addition to the HTTP handler, this example implements an associated custom control that enhances the developer experience of using the handler from an .aspx page. Figure 19-4 illustrates the handler and its associated control in a test page.

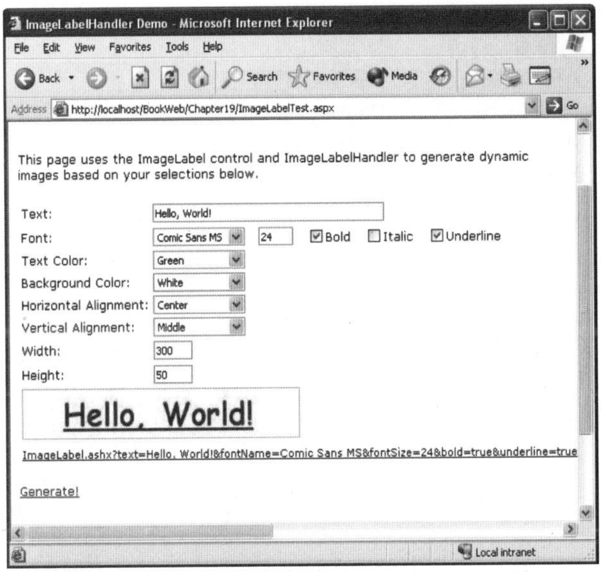

Figure 19-4   *ImageLabelHandler* being used within ImageLabel-
Test.aspx

This sample demonstrates a third mechanism for implementing HTTP handlers. Here the code for the handler is compiled into an assembly that is placed in the application's bin directory, and the .ashx file simply contains a reference to the class in the assembly. This is particularly useful when you need to deploy your HTTP handler in a compiled assembly without distributing the source code.

Here is the .ashx file used to reference the implementation of the HTTP handler:

```
<%@ WebHandler Language="C#"
   Class="MSPress.ServerComponents.ImageLabelHandler" %>
```

Listing 19-6 shows the code for the *ImageLabelHandler*, which is compiled into the *MSPress.ServerComponents* assembly.

```
using System;
using System.ComponentModel;
using System.Collections;
using System.Drawing;
using System.Drawing.Drawing2D;
using System.Drawing.Imaging;
using System.Web;
```

Listing 19-6   ImageLabelHandler.cs   *(continued)*

Listing 19-6 *(continued)*

```
// ImageLabelHandler generates an image with text based on
// arguments passed in to it.
public class ImageLabelHandler : IHttpHandler {
    private int _width;
    private int _height;
    private int _fontSize;
    private bool _bold;
    private bool _italic;
    private bool _underline;
    private string _fontName;
    private Color _foreColor;
    private Color _backColor;
    private StringAlignment _horizontalAlign;
    private StringAlignment _verticalAlign;
    private string _text;

    // Initialize the rendering information.
    public ImageLabelHandler() {
        _width = 100;
        _height = 100;
        _fontName = "Verdana";
        _fontSize = 10;
        _foreColor = Color.Black;
        _backColor = Color.White;
        _horizontalAlign = StringAlignment.Near;
        _verticalAlign = StringAlignment.Near;
        _text = String.Empty;
    }

    public bool IsReusable {
        get {
            // The handler contains member data specific to a single
            // request; the same instance can't be used to handle
            // multiple requests.
            return false;
        }
    }

    // Initializes the parameters used to render the label from
    // arguments specified in the request query string or from
    // post data.
    private void InitializeParameters(HttpRequest request) {
        string s;

        // Text parameter
        s = request["text"];
```

```
if ((s != null) && (s.Length != 0)) {
    _text = s;
}

// Similarly initialize fontName.
⋮

s = request["fontSize"];
if ((s != null) && (s.Length != 0)) {
    _fontSize = Int32.Parse(s);
}

// Similarly initialize width, height.
⋮

s = request["bold"];
if ((s != null) && (s.Length != 0)) {
    _bold = Boolean.Parse(s);
}

// Similarly initialize italic, underline.
⋮

// Color information (optional)
s = request["foreColor"];
if ((s != null) && (s.Length != 0)) {
    _foreColor = (Color)TypeDescriptor.GetConverter(
        typeof(Color)).ConvertFromInvariantString(s);
}

// Similarly initialize backColor.
⋮

// Alignment information
s = request["horizAlign"];
if ((s != null) && (s.Length != 0)) {
    if (String.Compare(s, "left", true) == 0) {
        _horizontalAlign = StringAlignment.Near;
    }
    else if (String.Compare(s, "center", true) == 0) {
        _horizontalAlign = StringAlignment.Center;
    }
    else if (String.Compare(s, "right", true) == 0) {
        _horizontalAlign = StringAlignment.Far;
    }
```

(continued)

Listing 19-6 *(continued)*

```
            else {
                throw new ArgumentOutOfRangeException("horizAlign",
                    "Unsupported horizontal alignment");
            }
        }

        // Similarly initialize verticalAlign.
        ⋮
        }
    }

    // Handles the request and generates the resulting response.
    public void ProcessRequest(HttpContext context) {
        // The standard request/response objects
        HttpRequest request = context.Request;
        HttpResponse response = context.Response;

        Image image = null;
        Graphics g = null;

        StringFormat textFormat = null;
        Font textFont = null;
        Brush textBrush = null;
        Brush backBrush = null;

        try {
            // Extract the request parameters.
            InitializeParameters(request);

            // Create the image and the rendering surface.
            image = new
                Bitmap(_width, _height, PixelFormat.Format32bppArgb);
            g = Graphics.FromImage(image);

            // Fill the rendering surface.
            backBrush = new SolidBrush(_backColor);
            g.FillRectangle(backBrush, 0, 0, _width, _height);

            if (_text.Length != 0) {
                // Create the associated rendering objects.
                textFormat =
                    new StringFormat(StringFormatFlags.NoWrap);
                textFormat.Alignment = horizontalAlign;
                textFormat.LineAlignment = verticalAlign;
```

```
                    FontStyle style = FontStyle.Regular;
                    if (_bold) {
                        style |= FontStyle.Bold;
                    }
                    if (_italic) {
                        style |= FontStyle.Italic;
                    }
                    if (_underline) {
                        style |= FontStyle.Underline;
                    }
                    textFont =
                        new Font(_fontName, (float)_fontSize, style);
                    textBrush = new SolidBrush(_foreColor);

                    // Render the text based on all the input parameters.
                    g.DrawString(_text, textFont, textBrush,
                        new RectangleF(0, 0, _width, _height),
                        textFormat);
                }

                // Write out the image to the output stream.
                response.ContentType = "image/jpeg";
                image.Save(response.OutputStream, ImageFormat.Jpeg);
            }
            catch (Exception) {
            }
            finally {
                if (backBrush != null)
                    backBrush.Dispose();
                if (textBrush != null)
                    textBrush.Dispose();
                if (textFormat != null)
                    textFormat.Dispose();
                if (textFont != null)
                    textFont.Dispose();
                if (image != null)
                    image.Dispose();
                if (g != null)
                    g.Dispose();
            }
        }
    }
}
```

The *ImageLabelHandler* returns *false* for its implementation of the *IsReusable* property. The handler implementation maintains the request parameters as instance data. Therefore, an existing instance of the handler cannot be reused to handle subsequent requests.

The *ImageLabelHandler* supports a number of parameters in the request URL, such as the text to be shown and its font characteristics, colors, and alignment. *ImageLabelHandler* also provides default values for all these parameters, so that the user can specify them only if needed. The constructor of the handler initializes all the parameters to their default values. As a result, the *Initialize-Parameters* helper method is used to extract the parameters that were specified by using the *QueryString* name/value pairs available on the request object to override specific default values. A well-designed HTTP handler should be able to handle incoming requests with missing parameters as appropriate, typically by falling back on a predictable default behavior.

Like all handlers, *ImageLabelHandler* implements its primary functionality in its *ProcessRequest* method. The implementation can be divided into four parts: initialization based on request parameters, rendering of the text, writing or saving the in-memory rendered image into the response stream, and disposing resources and objects. The *ImageLabelHandler* uses the rich drawing functionality provided by GDI+ in the *System.Drawing* namespace and its sub-namespaces. GDI+ provides a number of objects representing fonts, colors, brushes, and string formatting, making it simple to render the specified text in a rich manner. Note that these objects must be disposed of at the end of each request so that they can free their underlying resources as soon as possible. If these objects are not disposed of, they can cause scalability problems. The *ImageLabelHandler* always ensures disposal of these objects by using a *try/catch/finally* construct.

Once the image is rendered, GDI+ provides the functionality to save the objects into an arbitrary stream in a specified format. In this example, the handler saves the rendered image in JPEG format. Because GDI+ can write to any stream, the image is saved directly into the response's output stream, thereby eliminating the need to copy bytes of data from one location to another. Note that the *ImageLabelHandler* sets the *ContentType* of the response appropriately to *"image/jpeg"*.

The *ImageLabel* Control and Designer

It is typical for HTTP handlers such as *ImageLabelHandler* to accept a number of request parameters to enable customization of their output. By default, the programming model associated with an HTTP handler is simply a string URL that must be generated by the page developer. A server control can enhance the developer experience associated with an HTTP handler by encapsulating the logic of generating the URL with the correct parameters based on the control's property values. The control allows the developer to access the HTTP handler without having full knowledge of the correct URL syntax needed to invoke the handler.

Listing 19-7 contains the code for the *ImageLabel* control, which simplifies the use of the *ImageLabelHandler* shown in Listing 19-6.

```csharp
using System;
using System.ComponentModel;
using System.ComponentModel.Design;
using System.Drawing;
using System.Drawing.Design;
using System.Text;
using System.Web.UI;
using System.Web.UI.Design;
using System.Web.UI.WebControls;
using Image = System.Web.UI.WebControls.Image;

namespace MSPress.ServerComponents {

    [
    DefaultProperty("Text"),
    Designer(typeof(MSPress.ServerControls.Design.ImageLabelDesigner),
        typeof(IDesigner))
    ]
    public class ImageLabel : Image {

        public override Unit Height {
            get {
                return base.Height;
            }
            set {
                if (value.IsEmpty || (value.Type == UnitType.Pixel)) {
                    base.Height = value;
                }
                else {
                    throw new ArgumentException("Only pixel units " +
                        "are supported for Height", "value");
                }
            }
        }

        [
        Category("Appearance"),
        DefaultValue(HorizontalAlign.NotSet),
        Description(
            "The horizontal alignment of the text within the image")
        ]
```

Listing 19-7   ImageLabel.cs   *(continued)*

Listing 19-7   *(continued)*

```
    public HorizontalAlign HorizontalAlign {
        get {
            object o = ViewState["HorizontalAlign"];
            if (o == null) {
                return HorizontalAlign.NotSet;
            }
            return (HorizontalAlign)o;
        }
        set {
            if ((value < HorizontalAlign.NotSet) ||
                (value > HorizontalAlign.Right)) {
                throw new ArgumentOutOfRangeException("value");
            }
            ViewState["HorizontalAlign"] = value;
        }
    }

    [
    Category("Behavior"),
    DefaultValue(""),
    Description("The URL to ImageLabelHandler.ashx"),
    Editor(typeof(UrlEditor),
        typeof(UITypeEditor))
    ]
    public string ImageLabelHandlerUrl {
        get {
            object o = ViewState["ImageLabelHandlerUrl"];
            if (o == null) {
                return String.Empty;
            }
            return (string)o;
        }
        set {
            ViewState["ImageLabelHandlerUrl"] = value;
        }
    }

    [
    Bindable(false),
    Browsable(false),
    DesignerSerializationVisibility(
        DesignerSerializationVisibility.Hidden),
    EditorBrowsable(EditorBrowsableState.Never)
    ]
    public override string ImageUrl {
        get {
            return CreateImageLabelUrl();
        }
```

```
        set {
            throw new NotSupportedException("You should set the " +
                "properties of the control instead.");
        }
    }


    [
    Category("Appearance"),
    DefaultValue(""),
    Description("The text to be shown in the control")
    ]
    public string Text {
        get {
            object o = ViewState["Text"];
            if (o == null) {
                return String.Empty;
            }
            return (string)o;
        }
        set {
            ViewState["Text"] = value;
        }
    }


    [
    Category("Appearance"),
    DefaultValue(VerticalAlign.NotSet),
    Description("The vertical alignment of the text within " +
        "the image")
    ]
    public VerticalAlign VerticalAlign {
        get {
            object o = ViewState["VerticalAlign"];
            if (o == null) {
                return VerticalAlign.NotSet;
            }
            return (VerticalAlign)o;
        }
        set {
            if ((value < VerticalAlign.NotSet) ||
                (value > VerticalAlign.Bottom)) {
                throw new ArgumentOutOfRangeException("value");
            }
            ViewState["VerticalAlign"] = value;
        }
    }
}
```

(continued)

Listing 19-7 *(continued)*

```
public override Unit Width {
    get {
        return base.Width;
    }
    set {
        if (value.IsEmpty || (value.Type == UnitType.Pixel)) {
            base.Width = value;
        }
        else {
            throw new ArgumentException("Only pixel units " +
                "are supported for Width", "value");
        }
    }
}


private string CreateImageLabelUrl() {
    string handlerUrl = ImageLabelHandlerUrl;
    if (handlerUrl.Length == 0) {
        throw new ApplicationException("ImageHandlerUrl has " +
            "not been set to a valid value.");
    }

    StringBuilder url = new StringBuilder(1024);
    bool argAppended = false;

    url.Append(handlerUrl);
    url.Append('?');

    string text = Text;
    if (text.Length != 0) {
        url.Append("text=");
        url.Append(text);
        argAppended = true;
    }

    string fontName = Font.Name;
    if (fontName.Length != 0) {
        if (argAppended)
            url.Append('&');
        url.Append("fontName=");
        url.Append(fontName);
        argAppended = true;
    }
```

```
FontUnit fontSize = Font.Size;
if ((fontSize.IsEmpty == false) &&
    (fontSize.Type == FontSize.AsUnit) &&
    (fontSize.Unit.Type == UnitType.Point)) {
    if (argAppended)
        url.Append('&');
    url.Append("fontSize=");
    url.Append((((int)fontSize.Unit.Value).ToString());
    argAppended = true;
}

if (Font.Bold) {
    if (argAppended)
        url.Append('&');
    url.Append("bold=true");
    argAppended = true;
}

if (Font.Italic) {
    if (argAppended)
        url.Append('&');
    url.Append("italic=true");
    argAppended = true;
}

if (Font.Underline) {
    if (argAppended)
        url.Append('&');
    url.Append("underline=true");
    argAppended = true;
}

Color foreColor = ForeColor;
if (foreColor.IsEmpty == false) {
    if (argAppended)
        url.Append('&');
    url.Append("foreColor=");
    url.Append(TypeDescriptor.GetConverter(
        typeof(Color)).ConvertToInvariantString(foreColor));
    argAppended = true;
}

Color backColor = BackColor;
if (backColor.IsEmpty == false) {
    if (argAppended)
        url.Append('&');
```

(continued)

Listing 19-7 *(continued)*

```
        url.Append("backColor=");
        url.Append(TypeDescriptor.GetConverter(
            typeof(Color)).ConvertToInvariantString(backColor));
        argAppended = true;
    }

    Unit width = Width;
    if (width.IsEmpty == false) {
        if (argAppended)
            url.Append('&');
        url.Append("width=");
        url.Append(((int)width.Value).ToString());
        argAppended = true;
    }

    Unit height = Height;
    if (height.IsEmpty == false) {
        if (argAppended)
            url.Append('&');
        url.Append("height=");
        url.Append(((int)height.Value).ToString());
        argAppended = true;
    }

    HorizontalAlign horizAlign = HorizontalAlign;
    if (horizAlign != HorizontalAlign.NotSet) {
        if (argAppended)
            url.Append('&');
        url.Append("horizAlign=");
        url.Append(horizAlign.ToString());
        argAppended = true;
    }

    VerticalAlign vertAlign = VerticalAlign;
    if (vertAlign != VerticalAlign.NotSet) {
        if (argAppended)
            url.Append('&');
        url.Append("vertAlign=");
        url.Append(vertAlign.ToString());
        argAppended = true;
    }

    return url.ToString();
    }
    }
}
```

The *ImageLabel* control uses several server control authoring concepts that we covered in Part III of this book, "Server Controls—Nuts and Bolts."

ImageLabel derives from *Image* (and not *Label*) because all the standard *Image* properties (such as *AlternateText*) apply to dynamically generated images as well. This control adds a *Text* property, which is used to set the text rendered in the dynamic image. The control overrides the *Width* and *Height* properties to restrict their range to pixel units because the handler implementation can work only by using pixel dimensions.

The *ImageLabel* control generates the URL to the *ImageLabelHandler* with the appropriate request string by using its current property values. Because the control is associated with an HTTP handler, it offers the *ImageLabelHandlerUrl* property, which allows the developer to specify the location of the handler itself. This is the property that ties the control to its associated handler. Because the control is responsible for automatically computing the source URL of the image, it overrides the *ImageUrl* property so that it cannot be set by the page developer.

As specified in the metadata for the *ImageLabel* class, the control is associated with its own designer, *ImageLabelDesigner*. Chapter 15, "Design-Time Functionality," covered the basics of implementing control designers. All controls that are associated with an HTTP handler should provide a custom designer that approximates a reasonable design-time appearance without having to invoke the handler at design time. This is primarily because the designer updates design-time appearance on every property change and because invoking a remote URL often can result in a sluggish user experience while generating spurious requests that the server will need to handle.

Listing 19-8 contains the code for the *ImageLabelDesigner* class.

```
using System;
using System.ComponentModel;
using System.ComponentModel.Design;
using System.Diagnostics;
using System.IO;
using System.Text;
using System.Web.UI;
using System.Web.UI.Design;
using System.Web.UI.WebControls;
using MSPress.ServerComponents;

namespace MSPress.ServerComponents.Design {
```

Listing 19-8   ImageLabelDesigner.cs

(continued)

Listing 19-8 *(continued)*

```
public class ImageLabelDesigner : ControlDesigner {
    public override string GetDesignTimeHtml() {
        ImageLabel imageLabel = (ImageLabel)Component;

        Table designerTable = new Table();
        TableRow row = new TableRow();
        TableCell cell = new TableCell();

        designerTable.Rows.Add(row);
        row.Cells.Add(cell);

        cell.Text = imageLabel.Text;
        if (cell.Text.Length == 0) {
            cell.Text = "[" + imageLabel.ID + "]";
        }

        cell.ApplyStyle(imageLabel.ControlStyle);
        cell.HorizontalAlign = imageLabel.HorizontalAlign;
        cell.VerticalAlign = imageLabel.VerticalAlign;

        StringBuilder sb = new StringBuilder(512);
        HtmlTextWriter writer =
            new HtmlTextWriter(new StringWriter(sb));

        designerTable.RenderControl(writer);
        return sb.ToString();
    }

    public override void Initialize(IComponent component) {
        if (!(component is ImageLabel)) {
            throw new ArgumentException(
                "Component must be an ImageLabel",
                "component");
        }
        base.Initialize(component);
    }
}
```

The designer overrides the *GetDesignTimeHtml* method, which is called by the designer framework to create a design-time representation of the control. In its implementation, the *ImageLabelDesigner* creates instances of the *Table*, *TableRow*, and *TableCell* controls to approximate the runtime image characteristics. The designer then copies over the text and relevant style properties (such as colors and fonts) from its associated *ImageLabel* control onto the table controls. The designer then renders the table and uses the resulting HTML as its design-time representation. Thus, the designer provides a reasonable approximation of the rendering that will be generated by the HTTP handler at runtime.

Listing 19-9 shows the *ImageLabel* control being used declaratively and programmatically in the ImageLabelTest.aspx sample page.

```
<%@ Page Language="c#" %>
<%@ Register TagPrefix="mspsc" Namespace="MSPress.ServerComponents"
  Assembly="MSPress.ServerComponents" %>
<%@ Import Namespace="System.Drawing" %>
<script runat="server">
private void Page_Load(object sender, EventArgs e) {
    imageLabel1.Text = textTextBox.Text;
    imageLabel1.Font.Name = fontNameDropDown.SelectedItem.Text;
    imageLabel1.Font.Size = new FontUnit(fontSizeTextBox.Text.Trim());
    imageLabel1.Font.Bold = boldCheckBox.Checked;
    imageLabel1.Font.Italic = italicCheckBox.Checked;
    imageLabel1.Font.Underline = underLineCheckBox.Checked;
    imageLabel1.Width =
        Unit.Pixel(Int32.Parse(widthTextBox.Text.Trim()));
    imageLabel1.Height =
        Unit.Pixel(Int32.Parse(heightTextBox.Text.Trim()));
    imageLabel1.ForeColor =
        Color.FromName(foreColorDropDown.SelectedItem.Text);
    imageLabel1.BackColor =
        Color.FromName(backColorDropDown.SelectedItem.Text);
    imageLabel1.HorizontalAlign =
        (HorizontalAlign)Int32.Parse(
            horizAlignDropDown.SelectedItem.Value);
    imageLabel1.VerticalAlign =
        (VerticalAlign)Int32.Parse(
            vertAlignDropDown.SelectedItem.Value);

    string s = imageLabel1.ImageUrl;
    imageHyperLink.Text = s;
    imageHyperLink.NavigateUrl = s;
}
</script>

<html>
  <body>
    <form id="ImageLabelTest" method="post" runat="server">
      <p>
        This page uses the ImageLabel control and ImageLabelHandler to
        generate dynamic images based on your selections below.
```

Listing 19-9   ImageLabelTest.aspx   *(continued)*

Listing 19-9 *(continued)*

```
        </p>
        <table width="100%" border="0">
          <!-- HTML and server controls used to generate UI to customize the
               ImageLabel are not shown here-->
          <tr>
            <td nowrap colspan="2">
              <mspsc:ImageLabel id="imageLabel1" runat="server"
                EnableViewState="False" BorderStyle="Solid"
                BorderWidth="1px" BorderColor="LightSkyBlue"
                ImageLabelHandlerUrl="ImageLabel.ashx" />
            </td>
          </tr>
        </table>
        <asp:LinkButton id="generateButton" runat="server"
          Text="Generate!" />
      </form>
    </body>
</html>
```

HTTP Handlers and Session State

Some HTTP handlers might require access to objects stored in ASP.NET session state. For example, a page requires session state because script within the page could use the *Session* object to store data across requests. By default, an HTTP handler does not have access to session data.

An HTTP handler can indicate its need for session state by implementing one of two interfaces. If the handler requires read-only access to the objects stored in session state, it can implement *System.Web.SessionState.IReadOnlySessionState*. If the handler requires read-write access, it needs to implement *System.Web.SessionState.IRequiresSessionState*. Both of these interfaces are marker interfaces—in other words, they do not contain any methods. They simply help the HTTP runtime identify which handlers require session state. Listing 19-10 shows an implementation of a handler that requires access to session state.

```
<%@ WebHandler Language="C#" Class="StatefulHandler" %>
using System;
using System.Web;
using System.Web.SessionState;
```

Listing 19-10 Outline of an HTTP handler that requires access to session state

```
public class StatefulHandler : IHttpHandler, IRequiresSessionState {
    public bool IsReusable {
        get {...}
    }
    public void ProcessRequest(HttpContext context) {
        HttpSessionState session = context.Session;
        :
    }
}
```

Summary

HTTP handlers provide a simple but powerful model that allows you to customize the request-handling functionality built into ASP.NET. This model also allows you to provide logic to handle new extensions without having to learn the details of implementing an ISAPI for IIS. Furthermore, HTTP handlers allow you to cleanly implement processing logic that does not generate HTML markup. Finally, you can associate HTTP handlers with a type-safe programming model and a rich design-time experience by providing an associated server control that encapsulates the logic of generating the URL used to access the HTTP handler.

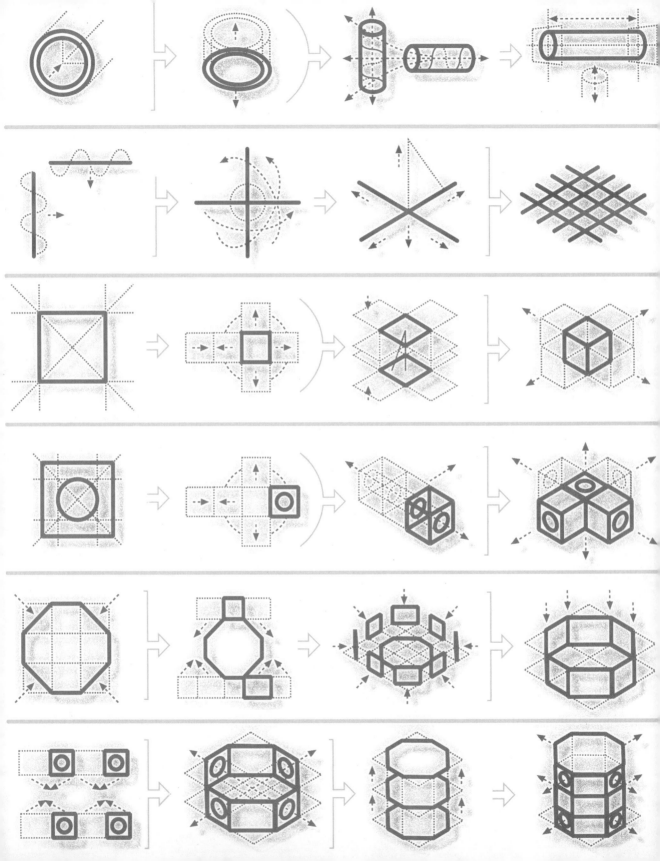

Part V

Server Control Case Studies

This part contains examples of real-world controls that are similar to the standard set of ASP.NET server controls that ship with the .NET Framework. The sample controls in this part of the book bring together the concepts described in earlier chapters and provide an implementation of a set of professional-quality controls.

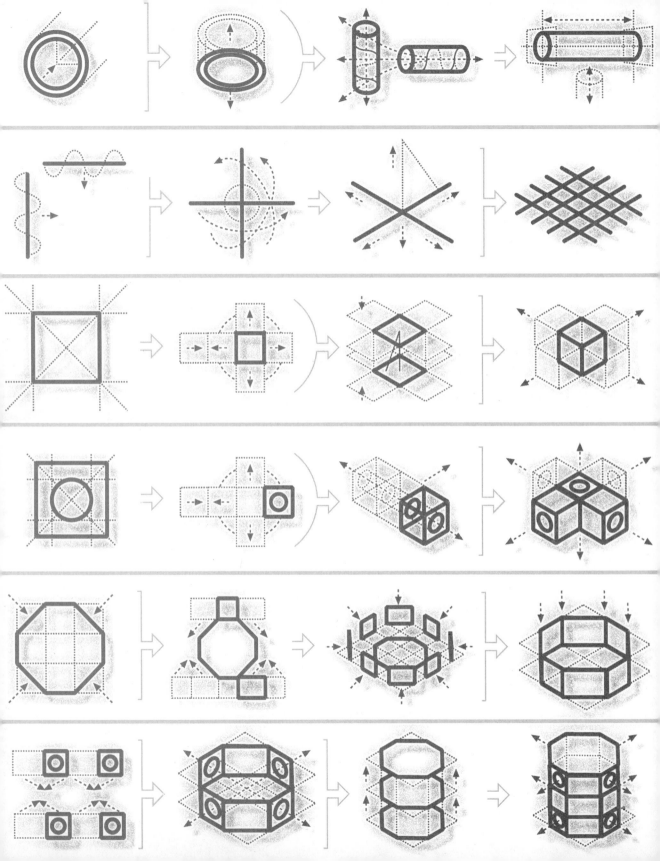

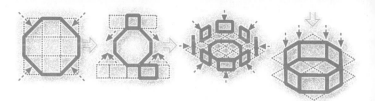

20

Data-Bound Templated Controls

The majority of Web applications built by page developers are data driven and contain dynamic content. Web applications contain pages to present data as well as to collect data from users. A number of common Web application scenarios such as stock quote reports, product catalogs, and search engines are primarily focused on data access and data presentation. ASP.NET, the Web Forms programming model, and server controls all dramatically simplify the development of high-performance, data-driven Web applications and pages, both at run time and design time. Web applications offer a wide variety of data presentations, ranging from simple tables to more complex, visually pleasing renderings that blend seamlessly into the design and structure of the overall application.

In Chapter 16, "Data-Bound Controls," we implemented the *DataBound-Table* control, which illustrates basic data-binding functionality and features such as style-based customization. In this chapter, we will develop a *ListView* control that implements those features in addition to raising events and supporting template-based customization. *ListView* is a data-bound templated control that provides the ability to generate a customizable, interactive, columnar representation of data in a data source.

The *ListView* Control

The *ListView* control is a data-bound control. This control exposes a *Data-Source* property that can be associated with a collection of objects or data records by the page developer. *ListView* is responsible for generating a scrollable user interface (UI) that contains a rendering for each object in the associated data source. To allow the page developer to define the visual characteristics and the layout of the rendering for each object, the *ListView* control exposes various style and template properties for customization.

Figure 20-1 demonstrates the *ListView* control in a sample page that generates a scrollable view of information about a set of book titles.

Figure 20-1   The *ListView* control being used to generate a scrollable, columnar rendering

Listing 20-1 shows the sample page used in Figure 20-1.

```
<%@ Page language="c#" %>
<%@ Import Namespace="System.IO" %>
<%@ Import Namespace="System.Data" %>
<%@ Register TagPrefix="mspwc" Namespace="MSPress.WebControls"
  Assembly="MSPress.WebControls" %>
<html>
  <script runat="server">
  private DataSet GetDataSource() {
      FileStream fs = null;
      DataSet ds = null;
```

Listing 20-1   ListViewTest.aspx

```
    try {
        fs = new FileStream(Server.MapPath("TitlesDB.xml"),
            FileMode.Open, FileAccess.Read);
        ds = new DataSet();
        ds.ReadXml(fs);
    }
    finally {
        if (fs != null) {
            fs.Close();
            fs = null;
        }
    }

    return ds;
}

private string GetAuthor(string authorID) {
    DataSet ds = (DataSet)listView1.DataSource;
    DataView dv = new DataView(ds.Tables["Author"]);

    dv.RowFilter = "au_id = '" + authorID + "'";
    return (string)dv[0]["au_name"];
}

private void listView1_OnSelectedIndexChanged(object sender,
    EventArgs e) {
    label1.Text = "Selected title: '" +
        listView1.DataKeys[listView1.SelectedIndex] + ".'";
}

public void Page_Load(object sender, EventArgs e) {
    if (!IsPostBack) {
        listView1.DataSource = GetDataSource();
        listView1.DataBind();
    }
}
</script>
<head>
  <title>ListView Sample</title>
</head>
<body>
  <form method="post" runat="server" ID="Form1">
    <mspwc:ListView runat="server" id="listView1"
      ShowScrollBars="true" Columns="2" BorderStyle="Solid"
      BorderColor="Gainsboro" BorderWidth="1px"
      Enableclickselect="true"
```

(continued)

Listing 20-1   *(continued)*

```
      OnSelectedIndexChanged="listView1_OnSelectedIndexChanged"
      DataKeyField="title" DataMember="Title">
      <ItemTemplate>
        <asp:Table runat="server" Font-Names="Verdana"
          Font-Size="8pt">
          <asp:TableRow>
            <asp:TableCell>
              <asp:Image runat="server"
                ImageUrl='<%# DataBinder.Eval(Container.DataItem,
"title_id", "images\\Title-{0}.gif") %>'/>
            </asp:TableCell>
            <asp:TableCell valign="top">
              <asp:Label runat="server"
                text='<%# DataBinder.Eval(Container.DataItem,
"title") %>'/>
              <br />
              <asp:Label runat="server"
                text='<%# GetAuthor((string)DataBinder.Eval(
Container.DataItem, "au_id")) %>'/>
              <br />
              <asp:Label runat="server"
                text='<%# DataBinder.Eval(Container.DataItem, "price",
"{0:c}") %>'/>
              <br />
              <br />
              <asp:LinkButton runat="server" CommandName="Select"
                Text="Select"/>
            </asp:TableCell>
          </asp:TableRow>
        </asp:Table>
      </ItemTemplate>
      <HeaderTemplate>
        Book Titles
      </HeaderTemplate>
      <SelectedItemStyle BackColor="Gainsboro" BorderStyle="Solid"
        BorderColor="Gray" BorderWidth="1px"/>
      <HeaderStyle BackColor="Navy" ForeColor="White"
        Font-Bold="true"/>
      <ViewStyle height="275px" Width="600px"/>
    </mspwc:ListView>
    <br />
    <asp:Label runat="server" id="label1" Text="Select a title:"/>
  </form>
 </body>
</html>
```

The sample page uses an instance of a *System.Data.DataSet* class as the data source. The *DataSet* is loaded from data that is persisted into an .xml file named TitlesDB.xml. The .xml file contains data based on the pubs database that is available as a sample database with Microsoft SQL Server. We use an XML file for persisting data (instead of using a database) because we want to keep the sample simple and self-contained rather than demonstrate complex data access logic. A representative portion of the .xml file used in the sample is shown in Listing 20-2.

```xml
<?xml version="1.0" encoding="utf-8" ?>
<TitlesDB>
  <xsd:schema id="TitlesDB" xmlns=""
    xmlns:xsd="http://www.w3.org/2001/XMLSchema"
    xmlns:msdata="urn:schemas-microsoft-com:xml-msdata">
    ⋮
  </xsd:schema>
  <Author>
    <au_id>213-46-8915</au_id>
    <au_name>Marjorie Green</au_name>
    <phone>415 986-7020</phone>
    <address>309 63rd St. #411</address>
    <city>Oakland</city>
    <state>CA</state>
    <zip>94618</zip>
  </Author>
  ⋮
  <Title>
    <title_id>BU1032</title_id>
    <au_id>213-46-8915</au_id>
    <title>The Busy Executive's Database Guide</title>
    <price>19.99</price>
    <pubdate>1991-06-12T07:00:00</pubdate>
  </Title>
  ⋮
</TitlesDB>
```

Listing 20-2   TitlesDB.xml

ListView Specification

The *ListView* control exposes a *DataSource* property, which is a characteristic of all data-bound controls. The *DataSource* property is typed as an *Object* and accepts any object whose type implements either the *System.Collections.IEnumerable* or *System.ComponentModel.IListSource* interface as a valid data source.

This requirement allows the page developer to use various types of objects as valid data sources. These types include *ArrayList*, *DataView*, *DataSet*, *Data-Reader* and arbitrary arrays and collections. The *ListView* control enumerates the objects in the data source that it is bound to and creates a child control hierarchy for each enumerated object that is rendered, thus generating a visual representation of the data.

The *ListView* control implements the same explicit data-binding model used by the standard ASP.NET data-bound controls. This implies that the *List-View* control uses only its assigned data source to enumerate data when the page developer calls the *DataBind* method. The explicit data-binding model allows Web applications to optimize data access logic. This model allows the page developer to determine whether and when the *ListView* control should access its data source and build its control hierarchy. The *ListView* control also stores information in view state, which allows the control to re-create the control hierarchy during postbacks without requiring an actual instance of the data source. This further reduces the amount of data access that a Web application needs to perform, which in turn improves performance.

The *ListView* control allows the page developer to customize the rendering it creates through style and template properties. The page developer can use templates to define the structure and layout as well as the content and controls used to generate the rendering of each object in the data source. These templates are repeated for each object that is enumerated in the data source. The page developer can also use one or more of the style properties exposed by the *ListView* control to customize the visual appearance and formatting of the rendering. Together, these properties allow the page developer to incorporate the *ListView* control and blend it seamlessly into the rest of the Web application's UI.

Finally, the *ListView* control is associated with a custom designer, *List-ViewDesigner*, which allows the control to offer a rich experience in a design-time environment such as Microsoft Visual Studio .NET. The designer allows you to select data sources and modify the content of the template properties at design time. In addition, the designer generates a WYSIWYG representation of the control by using a sample data source.

ListView Implementation

The *ListView* implementation is based on several of the core control-authoring concepts that we described in Part III of the book, "Server Controls—Nuts and Bolts." The following sections illustrate those concepts by using fragments from the source code for the *ListView* control and its related classes. The complete implementation is provided in the WebControls directory along with the code samples from the book, which you'll find on its companion Web site.

> **Note** You also can compile the control without using the Visual Studio .NET project. Navigate to the directory that contains the contents of the sample code (for example, c:\BookCode\CSharp) and run the batch file, BuildWebControls.bat, which simply calls the C# compiler with the right set of command-line arguments.

Data-Bound Controls

The *ListView* control illustrates the basic characteristics and implementation patterns that apply to all data-bound controls, as discussed in Chapter 16.

Listing 20-3 illustrates these core aspects of data-bound controls.

```
public class ListView : WebControl, INamingContainer,
                        IPostBackEventHandler {
    private object _dataSource;
    private DataKeyCollection _dataKeys;

    public virtual object DataSource {
        get {
            return _dataSource;
        }
        set {
            if ((value == null) || (value is IListSource) ||
                (value is IEnumerable)) {
                _dataSource = value;
            }
            else {
                throw new ArgumentException();
            }
        }
    }

    public virtual string DataMember {
        get { ... }
        set { ... }
    }
```

Listing 20-3 Implementing the essentials of a data-bound control   *(continued)*

Listing 20-3 *(continued)*

```
public virtual string DataKeyField {
    get { ... }
    set { ... }
}

public DataKeyCollection DataKeys {
    get {
        if (_dataKeys == null) {
            _dataKeys = new DataKeyCollection(this.DataKeysArray);
        }
        return _dataKeys;
    }
}

private ArrayList DataKeysArray {
    get {
        object o = ViewState["DataKeys"];
        if (o == null) {
            o = new ArrayList();
            ViewState["DataKeys"] = o;
        }
        return (ArrayList)o;
    }
}

public override void DataBind() {
    // Data-bound controls implement custom data-binding logic by
    // overriding this method.

    // We still want the DataBinding event to fire, so any
    // <%# %> expressions on this control get evaluated first.
    base.OnDataBinding(EventArgs.Empty);

    // Now re-create the new control hierarchy using the assigned
    // data source.
    Controls.Clear();

    // We also want to throw out any view state for children if it
    // exists because we're creating a new hierarchy. And then
    // start tracking changes made during the data-binding process.
    ClearChildViewState();
    TrackViewState();

    CreateControlHierarchy(true);
```

```
        // Mark the flag indicating child controls have been created
        // so that CreateChildControls does not get called.
        ChildControlsCreated = true;
    }

    protected override void CreateChildControls() {
        // If this gets called, we are re-creating children (the items)
        // from view state.
        Controls.Clear();

        // We can create the items if we have view state, so we check
        // for the number of items we created during a previous request
        // via a call to the DataBind method.
        if (ViewState["Items"] != null) {
            CreateControlHierarchy(false);
        }
    }

    protected virtual void CreateControlHierarchy(bool useDataSource) {
        IEnumerable dataSource = null;
        int itemCount = 0;

        _items = null;

        ArrayList dataKeysArray = DataKeysArray;
        string dataKeyField = null;

        if (useDataSource) {
            dataSource = GetDataSource();

            dataKeysArray.Clear();
            dataKeyField = DataKeyField;
        }
        else {
            dataSource = new object[(int)ViewState["Items"]];
        }

        if (dataSource != null) {
            Table outerTable = new Table();
            Controls.Add(outerTable);

            ListViewItem headerItem = null;
            ListViewItem footerItem = null;

            if (_headerTemplate != null) {
                TableRow headerRow = new TableRow();
```

(continued)

Listing 20-3 *(continued)*

```
            outerTable.Rows.Add(headerRow);
            headerItem =
                CreateListViewItem(headerRow, -1,
                    ListViewItemType.Header, null, useDataSource);
        }

        TableRow bodyRow = new TableRow();
        outerTable.Rows.Add(bodyRow);

        TableCell bodyCell = new TableCell();
        bodyRow.Cells.Add(bodyCell);

        ListViewPanel viewPanel = new ListViewPanel();
        bodyCell.Controls.Add(viewPanel);

        ListViewTable innerTable = CreateListViewTable();
        viewPanel.Controls.Add(innerTable);

        TableRow itemsRow = new TableRow();
        innerTable.Rows.Add(itemsRow);

        int editIndex = EditIndex;
        int selectedIndex = SelectedIndex;

        int itemIndex = 0;
        foreach (object dataItem in dataSource) {
            ListViewItemType itemType = ListViewItemType.Item;

            if (itemIndex == editIndex) {
                itemType |= ListViewItemType.EditItem;
            }
            if (itemIndex == selectedIndex) {
                itemType |= ListViewItemType.SelectedItem;
            }

            CreateListViewItem(itemsRow, itemIndex, itemType,
                dataItem, useDataSource);
            itemIndex++;
            itemCount++;

            if (useDataSource && (dataKeyField.Length != 0)) {
                dataKeysArray.Add(
                    DataBinder.GetPropertyValue(dataItem,
                        dataKeyField));
            }
        }
    }
```

```
            if (_footerTemplate != null) {
                TableRow footerRow = new TableRow();
                outerTable.Rows.Add(footerRow);
                CreateListViewItem(footerRow, -1,
                    ListViewItemType.Footer, null, useDataSource);
            }

            _items = CreateListViewItemCollection(itemsRow.Cells,
                headerItem, footerItem);
        }

        if (useDataSource) {
            ViewState["Items"] = itemCount;
        }
    }

    protected virtual ListViewItem CreateListViewItem(int itemIndex,
        ListViewItemType itemType) {
        return new ListViewItem(itemIndex, itemType);
    }

    private ListViewItem CreateListViewItem(TableRow rowContainer,
        int itemIndex, ListViewItemType itemType, object dataItem,
        bool dataBind) {
        ListViewItem item = CreateListViewItem(itemIndex, itemType);
        ListViewItemEventArgs e = new ListViewItemEventArgs(item);

        ITemplate template = GetTemplateForItem(item);
        if (template != null) {
            template.InstantiateIn(item);
        }

        OnItemCreated(e);
        rowContainer.Cells.Add(item);

        if (dataBind) {
            item.DataItem = dataItem;
            item.DataBind();

            OnItemDataBound(e);
        }

        return item;
    }
```

(continued)

Listing 20-3 *(continued)*

```
protected virtual ListViewItemCollection
    CreateListViewItemCollection(TableCellCollection cells,
        ListViewItem headerItem, ListViewItem footerItem) {
    return new ListViewItemCollection(cells, headerItem,
        footerItem);
}

protected virtual ListViewTable CreateListViewTable() {
    return new ListViewTable();
}

protected virtual IEnumerable GetDataSource() {
    if (_dataSource == null) {
        return null;
    }

    IEnumerable resolvedDataSource = _dataSource as IEnumerable;
    if (resolvedDataSource != null) {
        return resolvedDataSource;
    }

    IListSource listSource = _dataSource as IListSource;
    if (listSource != null) {
        IList memberList = listSource.GetList();

        if (listSource.ContainsListCollection == false) {
            return (IEnumerable)memberList;
        }

        ITypedList typedMemberList = memberList as ITypedList;
        if (typedMemberList != null) {
            PropertyDescriptorCollection propDescs =
                typedMemberList.GetItemProperties(
                    new PropertyDescriptor[0]);
            PropertyDescriptor memberProperty = null;

            if ((propDescs != null) && (propDescs.Count != 0)) {
                string dataMember = DataMember;

                if (dataMember.Length == 0) {
                    memberProperty = propDescs[0];
                }
                else {
                    memberProperty =
                        propDescs.Find(dataMember, true);
                }
```

```
                     if (memberProperty != null) {
                         object listRow = memberList[0];
                         object list = memberProperty.GetValue(listRow);

                         if (list is IEnumerable) {
                             return (IEnumerable)list;
                         }
                     }
                     throw new Exception("A list corresponding to " +
                         "the selected DataMember was not found.");
                 }

                 throw new Exception("The selected data source did " +
                     "not contain any data members to bind to.");
             }
         }

         return null;
     }

     protected virtual void OnItemCreated(ListViewItemEventArgs e) {
         ListViewItemEventHandler handler =
             (ListViewItemEventHandler)Events[EventItemCreated];
         if (handler != null) {
             handler(this, null);
         }
     }

     protected virtual void OnItemDataBound(ListViewItemEventArgs e) {
         ListViewItemEventHandler handler =
             (ListViewItemEventHandler)Events[EventItemDataBound];
         if (handler != null) {
             handler(this, null);
         }
     }
 }
```

The primary characteristic of a data-bound control is its *DataSource* property. *ListView* exposes a *DataSource* property of type *Object*. A control should allow the page developer to use a variety of objects as valid data sources when appropriate. *ListView* accepts objects that implement either the *IEnumerable* or the *IListSource* interfaces as valid data sources. Objects that implement these interfaces include arbitrary arrays, all collections such as *ArrayList*, and other data-centric objects, such as *DataReader*, *DataSet*, and *DataView*. Note that the assigned data source is held in a member variable, instead of in the *ViewState* dictionary. This is because a data source is a reference to another object that is valid only during a single request and should not be serialized into a textual format.

A data-bound control enumerates the data contained in its associated data source. Therefore, the most basic interface that an object must implement to be used as a data source is *IEnumerable*. When the object implements *IListSource* instead, which has the semantics of a collection of lists of data, *ListView* uses the value of its *DataMember* property to identify the specific list to use as the actual data source object that is enumerated. For example, the *DataSet* class implements the *IListSource* interface and contains a collection of *DataView* objects, each representing a specific *DataTable* contained in the *DataSet*. *ListView* encapsulates the logic of extracting the appropriate list of data to enumerate from the assigned *IListSource* object in its *GetDataSource* helper method. The *GetDataSource* method was described in detail in Chapter 16, along with the implementation of the *DataBoundTable* control.

The other characteristic shared by all data-bound controls is the implementation of data-binding logic in an override of the *DataBind* method. *ListView* first calls the *OnDataBinding* method to raise the *DataBinding* event. This event triggers the evaluation of any data-binding expressions that the user might have specified for properties of the *ListView* control. Once these expressions have been evaluated, the *ListView* control proceeds to enumerate the data contained within its assigned data source. The *DataBind* method is the only method in which a data-bound control should access its data source. The *ListView* control clears its current controls collection and any view state associated with its child controls because it creates a new control hierarchy in its data-binding implementation. *ListView* encapsulates the logic of creating the control hierarchy in a method named *CreateControlHierarchy*, which is described next. Once *ListView* has created its control hierarchy, it sets the *ChildControlsCreated* property to *true* so that its *CreateChildControls* method will not be called.

ListView also calls the same *CreateControlHierarchy* method from its override of the *CreateChildControls* method. *CreateChildControls* is called when the *ListView* control is required to create its control hierarchy because the page developer has not explicitly invoked the data-binding process via a call to the *DataBind* method. In this scenario, the *ListView* control is required to re-create the same hierarchy from information that it stored in view state during the data-binding process.

The *CreateControlHierarchy* method encapsulates the logic of creating the control hierarchy for both scenarios—when the control hierarchy is created as part of the data-binding process and when the control hierarchy is re-created from view state. This encapsulation forces a single implementation to create the control hierarchy and ensures that the resulting hierarchy is the same in both scenarios. This process is important because view state for controls gets reloaded into controls based on their relative positions within the control tree. In this method, the control enumerates the data source, creates the appropriate controls to represent each enumerated object, and adds those controls to the control hierarchy. The resulting control hierarchy is recursively data-bound if the *ListView* control is itself in the process of being data bound. To use the same code path and enumeration logic, the implementation of *CreateControlHierarchy* creates an array of null values as a dummy data source and enumerates that array when the control hierarchy is being re-created from view state. In this case, the actual values are restored from view state. Finally, when *CreateControlHierarchy* is called during the data-binding process, it stores the number of objects enumerated in the control's view state. This number is retrieved to determine the number of values to create in the dummy data source.

In *ListView*, the implementation of *CreateControlHierarchy* creates a *Table* as a child control, which contains a header, footer, and table body. The table body contains a *Panel*, which in turn contains a nested table. This nested table contains a number of *ListViewItem* objects that are derived from the *TableCell* class. Each *ListViewItem* corresponds to a single enumerated object in the data source. Because it contains these child controls, the *ListView* control is a composite control. In addition, *ListView* contains child controls that might have associated postback data or might require events routed to them. Therefore, *ListView* implements the *INamingContainer* interface. Composite controls were described in Chapter 12, "Composite Controls."

The *ListView* control raises the *ItemCreated* and *ItemDataBound* events to allow a page developer to programmatically customize the creation and data binding of controls used to render the contents of the data source. The *ItemCreated* event is raised when a *ListViewItem* is created and has been initialized to its default state. The page developer can handle this event to customize the layout and controls contained within the *ListViewItem* before that control is added to the control hierarchy. The *ItemDataBound* event is raised when a *ListViewItem* has been data-bound. The page developer can handle this event to perform additional data-binding logic or customize the controls contained within the *ListViewItem* based on the data they are bound to. This event does not occur when the *ListView* control re-creates its control hierarchy from its saved view state.

Templates

The *ListView* control offers various template properties (such as *ItemTemplate*, *HeaderTemplate*, and *FooterTemplate*) that enable the page developer to customize the layout and content of the rendered UI. Templates were discussed in Chapter 12.

Listing 20-4 illustrates the implementation of template properties in *ListView*.

```
public class ListView : WebControl, INamingContainer,
                        IPostBackEventHandler {
    private ITemplate _itemTemplate;

    public ITemplate EditItemTemplate {
        get { ... }
        set { ... }
    }

    public ITemplate FooterTemplate {
        get { ... }
        set { ... }
    }

    public ITemplate HeaderTemplate {
        get { ... }
        set { ... }
    }

    [
    TemplateContainer(typeof(ListViewItem))
    ]
    public ITemplate ItemTemplate {
        get {
            return _itemTemplate;
        }
        set {
            _itemTemplate = value;
        }
    }

    private ListViewItem CreateListViewItem(TableRow rowContainer,
        int itemIndex, ListViewItemType itemType, object dataItem,
        bool dataBind) {
        ListViewItem item = CreateListViewItem(itemIndex, itemType);
        ListViewItemEventArgs e = new ListViewItemEventArgs(item);
```

Listing 20-4   Implementing a templated control

```
            ITemplate template = GetTemplateForItem(item);
            if (template != null) {
                template.InstantiateIn(item);
            }

            OnItemCreated(e);
            rowContainer.Cells.Add(item);

            if (dataBind) {
                item.DataItem = dataItem;
                item.DataBind();

                OnItemDataBound(e);
            }

            return item;
        }

        protected virtual ITemplate GetTemplateForItem(ListViewItem item) {
            ITemplate template = null;
            switch (item.ItemType) {
                case ListViewItemType.Header:
                    template = _headerTemplate;
                    break;
                case ListViewItemType.Footer:
                    template = _footerTemplate;
                    break;
                default:
                    template = _itemTemplate;
                    if ((item.ItemType & ListViewItemType.EditItem) != 0) {
                        if (_editItemTemplate != null) {
                            template = _editItemTemplate;
                        }
                    }
                    break;
            }
            return template;
        }
    }
```

The *ListView* control creates an instance of the *ListViewItem* template container for each object it enumerates in the data source. Listing 20-5 contains the implementation of the *ListViewItem* class.

```
public class ListViewItem : TableCell, INamingContainer {
    private int _itemIndex;
    private object _dataItem;
    private ListViewItemType _itemType;

    public ListViewItem(int itemIndex, ListViewItemType itemType) {
        _itemIndex = itemIndex;
        _itemType = itemType;
    }

    public virtual object DataItem {
        get {
            return _dataItem;
        }
        set {
            _dataItem = value;
        }
    }

    public int ItemIndex {
        get {
            return _itemIndex;
        }
    }

    public virtual ListViewItemType ItemType {
        get {
            return _itemType;
        }
    }
    :
}
```

Listing 20-5   The *ListViewItem* implementation, which contains the
instantiated template

The *ListView* control contains several template properties (such as
ItemTemplate) that are typed as *System.Web.UI.ITemplate*. The implementation
of a template property is straightforward. The property getter and setter simply
provide access to a template field. The ASP.NET page parser does the work of
parsing template content and assigning the control an *ITemplate* instance as its
property value, as we described in Chapter 12.

The *ListView* control uses its templates by calling the *InstantiateIn* method
of *ITemplate* as it creates and adds *ListViewItem* controls to its control hierarchy
in the *CreateListViewItem* method. Each *ListViewItem* is a naming container.
This preserves the uniqueness of IDs across individual *ListViewItem* instances,
even though the same template can be instantiated more than once. When the

ListView control creates its control hierarchy during the data-binding process, it calls the *DataBind* method of each *ListViewItem* it creates, which recursively calls the *DataBind* method on each control created from the template. This ensures that any data-binding expressions within the template are evaluated as the *ListView* control enumerates data in its data source.

Data-binding expressions that contain the text "Container.DataItem" are common. In this context, *Container* represents the naming container of the template's contents. In the *ListView* control, each *ListViewItem* is the naming container for the contents of the template instantiated within it. The page parser requires knowledge of the type of the container so that it can correctly declare a variable named *Container* in the code it generates and so that the compiler can successfully resolve the expression *Container.DataItem*. To retrieve this information, the page parser examines a template property for the *Template-ContainerAttribute* metadata attribute. You can use this attribute to specify the actual type of the naming container for a specific template. The *ListView* control uses this metadata attribute to indicate that the container for its templates is a *ListViewItem*.

Styles and State Management

The *ListView* control offers various style properties (such as *ItemStyle* and *SelectedItemStyle*) that enable the page developer to customize the visual characteristics of the rendered UI. We discussed styles and state management related to styles in Chapter 11, "Styles in Controls." We discussed how to utilize typed styles for child controls in the *StyledCompositeLogin* example in Chapter 12.

Listing 20-6 illustrates the implementation of style properties in *ListView*.

```
public class ListView : WebControl, INamingContainer,
                        IPostBackEventHandler {
    private TableItemStyle _itemStyle;

    public TableItemStyle ItemStyle {
        get {
            if (_itemStyle == null) {
                _itemStyle = new TableItemStyle();
                if (IsTrackingViewState) {
                    ((IStateManager)_itemStyle).TrackViewState();
                }
            }
            return _itemStyle;
        }
    }
}
```

Listing 20-6   Implementing style properties and managing their view state   *(continued)*

Listing 20-6 *(continued)*

```
public TableItemStyle EditItemStyle {
    get { ... }
}

public TableItemStyle FooterStyle {
    get { ... }
}

public virtual GridLines GridLines {
    get {
        if (ControlStyleCreated == false) {
            return GridLines.None;
        }
        return ((TableStyle)ControlStyle).GridLines;
    }
    set {
        ((TableStyle)ControlStyle).GridLines = value;
    }
}

public TableItemStyle HeaderStyle {
    get { ... }
}

public TableItemStyle SelectedItemStyle {
    get { ... }
}

protected override Style CreateControlStyle() {
    // Because the ListView renders an HTML table, a
    // an instance of a TableStyle is used as the control style.
    TableStyle style = new TableStyle(ViewState);

    // This is also the right spot to initialize the style.
    style.CellSpacing = 0;

    return style;
}

protected override void LoadViewState(object savedState) {
    object baseState = null;
    object[] myState = null;

    if (savedState != null) {
        myState = (object[])savedState;
        Debug.Assert(myState.Length == 6);
```

```
            baseState = myState[0];
        }

        // Always call the base class, even if the state is null, so
        // that the base class gets a chance to fully implement its
        // LoadViewState functionality.
        base.LoadViewState(baseState);

        if (myState == null) {
            return;
        }

        // For performance reasons, the styles are created only if
        // state exists for them.

        if (myState[1] != null)
            ((IStateManager)ItemStyle).LoadViewState(myState[1]);
        ⋮
}

protected override object SaveViewState() {
        object[] myState = new object[6];

        // Again, the styles are saved only if they have
        // been created.

        myState[0] = base.SaveViewState();
        myState[1] = (_itemStyle != null) ?
            ((IStateManager)_itemStyle).SaveViewState() : null;
        ⋮

        // We don't check for all nulls because the control is
        // almost certain to have some view state, because like
        // most data-bound controls, it saves information to
        // re-create itself without a live data source on
        // round-trips.
        return myState;
}

protected override void TrackViewState() {
        base.TrackViewState();

        // Again, the tracking is propagated only to those
        // styles that have been created. New styles created
        // thereafter will be marked as tracking view state when
        // they are demand-created.
```

(continued)

Listing 20-6 *(continued)*

```
        if (_itemStyle != null)
            ((IStateManager)_itemStyle).TrackViewState();
        ⋮
    }
}
```

ListView implements each of its style properties, such as *ItemStyle* as read-only properties. In the property getter, *ListView* creates an instance of *Table-ItemStyle* on demand. It is important that styles are created only when they are required because they can impact performance by affecting the size of view state and by increasing the complexity of the rendering process. Style properties are always implemented as read-only properties. This allows the control to assume full responsibility for the style's state management.

Styles contain the ability to manage their properties in view state. However, it is the responsibility of the control that is using a style to include the style instance in its own implementation of state management. This is described briefly here. Chapter 12 gives a more detailed explanation.

ListView overrides the *SaveViewState* method to return an object that includes the view state corresponding to each of its style properties. The control creates an object array that contains the view state of its base class and the view state of each of its style properties. *ListView* implements the corresponding logic of restoring view state to its style properties by overriding the *LoadViewState* method. The state object handed to the control is cast into an object array. The *LoadViewState* override then calls the corresponding method of its base class. The implementation then loads any non-null view state into the corresponding style properties. Finally, *ListView* allows its style properties to manage their properties in view state by overriding the *TrackViewState* method and calling *TrackViewState* on each non-null style instance. The page framework calls the *TrackViewState* method to mark the end of the Initialize phase, after which property value changes are tracked in view state. *ListView* calls the same method to mark the end of the Initialize phase of any styles that have been created. The style property getter also calls *TrackViewState* on any style created subsequently.

The *ListView* control overrides its *CreateControlStyle* method to create a *TableStyle*. *ListView* applies this control style to the *Table* control it contains. The control style is the control's primary style and is used to implement a control's top-level style properties, such as *ForeColor*, *BackColor*, and *Font*. *TableStyle* contains additional table-specific style properties, such as *GridLines* and *CellSpacing*. These properties are exposed as top-level style properties by *ListView* and are implemented by delegating to the corresponding properties of the underlying control style instance.

Rendering

The *ListView* control renders a multicolumn list of *ListViewItem* controls in which each *ListViewItem* represents a single object in the data source that the *ListView* is associated with. We described the rendering process and related rendering methods in Chapter 8, "Rendering."

Listing 20-7 illustrates how *ListView* overrides the appropriate rendering methods to generate its HTML representation. It defines the *PrepareControlHierarchyForRendering* helper method, which performs the task of applying styles to child controls before they are rendered.

```
public class ListView : WebControl, INamingContainer,
                        IPostBackEventHandler {

    protected virtual void PrepareControlHierarchyForRendering() {
        ControlCollection controls = Controls;
        if (controls.Count != 1) {
            return;
        }

        Table outerTable = (Table)controls[0];
        outerTable.CopyBaseAttributes(this);
        if (ControlStyleCreated) {
            outerTable.ApplyStyle(ControlStyle);
        }
        else {
            // Because we didn't create a ControlStyle yet, the
            // settings for the default style of the control need to
            // be applied to the child table control directly.
            outerTable.CellSpacing = 0;
        }

        TableRowCollection rows = outerTable.Rows;
        TableCell bodyCell = null;

        if (_headerTemplate != null) {
            TableRow headerRow = rows[0];
            if (ShowHeader) {
                if (_headerStyle != null) {
                    headerRow.Cells[0].MergeStyle(_headerStyle);
                }
            }
            else {
                headerRow.Visible = false;
            }
```

Listing 20-7   Customizing the rendering process   *(continued)*

Listing 20-7 *(continued)*

```
        bodyCell = rows[1].Cells[0];
    }
    if (_footerTemplate != null) {
        TableRow footerRow = rows[rows.Count - 1];
        if (ShowFooter) {
            if (_footerStyle != null) {
                footerRow.Cells[0].MergeStyle(_footerStyle);
            }
        }
        else {
            footerRow.Visible = false;
        }
    }

    if (bodyCell == null) {
        bodyCell = rows[0].Cells[0];
    }

    ListViewPanel viewPanel = (ListViewPanel)bodyCell.Controls[0];
    if (_viewStyle != null) {
        viewPanel.ApplyStyle(_viewStyle);

        if (ShowScrollBars) {
            viewPanel.Style["overflow"] = "scroll";
            viewPanel.Style["overflow-x"] = "auto";
            viewPanel.Style["overflow-y"] = "auto";
        }
    }

    ListViewTable bodyTable = (ListViewTable)viewPanel.Controls[0];
    bodyTable.Columns = Columns;

    foreach (ListViewItem item in _items) {
        TableItemStyle style = _itemStyle;
        TableItemStyle compositeStyle = null;
        ListViewItemType itemType = item.ItemType;

        if (((itemType & ListViewItemType.EditItem) != 0) &&
            (_editItemStyle != null)) {
            if (style != null) {
                compositeStyle = new TableItemStyle();
                compositeStyle.CopyFrom(style);
                compositeStyle.CopyFrom(_editItemStyle);
            }
```

```
            else {
                style = _editItemStyle;
            }
        }
        if (((itemType & ListViewItemType.SelectedItem) != 0) &&
            (_selectedItemStyle != null)) {
            if (compositeStyle != null) {
                compositeStyle.CopyFrom(_selectedItemStyle);
            }
            else if (style != null) {
                compositeStyle = new TableItemStyle();
                compositeStyle.CopyFrom(style);
                compositeStyle.CopyFrom(_selectedItemStyle);
            }
            else {
                style = _selectedItemStyle;
            }
        }

        if (compositeStyle != null) {
            item.MergeStyle(compositeStyle);
        }
        else if (style != null) {
            item.MergeStyle(style);
        }

        if (_renderClickSelectScript) {
            if ((itemType & ListViewItemType.SelectedItem) == 0) {
                item.Attributes["onclick"] =
                    Page.GetPostBackEventReference(this,
                        "S" + item.ItemIndex);
                item.Style["cursor"] = "hand";
            }
        }
    }
}


protected override void Render(HtmlTextWriter writer) {
    // Styles are applied as late as the render time.
    // a) User can change styles after calling DataBind.
    // b) Changes made to items during style application do
    //    not contribute to the view state. This control
    //    manages the state for styles, so having items
    //    manage it as well would be redundant.
    PrepareControlHierarchyForRendering();
```

(continued)

Listing 20-7   *(continued)*

```
        // We don't render out tags corresponding to ListView
        // itself. We need to render its contents only.
        // Therefore, instead of calling base.Render, we call
        // RenderContents.
        RenderContents(writer);
    }
}
```

Each server control typically renders a single top-level tag. *ListView* renders an HTML *<table>* as its top-level tag. The *ListView* control itself does not generate any tag of its own. *ListView* generates the entire *<table>* tag by rendering the *Table* control that it contains in its *Controls* collection. Therefore, the *ListView* control overrides its *Render* method to skip the rendering logic in its base class and instead calls *RenderContents*, which renders the contents of its *Controls* collection.

Before calling *RenderContents*, the *Render* method override in *ListView* calls the *PrepareControlHierarchyForRendering* method. This method is responsible for applying style attributes to the contained items, setting the visibility of the items, and so on. These operations are performed during the Render phase for two primary reasons. First, delaying the application process allows the page developer to change style properties and toggle the visibility of various parts of the *ListView* control at any point in the page life cycle before the Render phase. Second, the application of styles does not result in any additional view state when done during the Render phase. This is because any state that needs to be managed is collected during the Save View State phase, which precedes the Render phase.

Listing 20-8 contains the implementation of the *ListViewTable* helper class used by the *ListView* control. *ListViewTable* holds a collection of *ListViewItem* controls as the cells of its first row and renders them into a multicolumn list. The *ListViewTable* instance is created by the *CreateControlHierarchy* method of *ListView*.

```
public class ListViewTable : Table {
    private int _columns;

    public ListViewTable() {
        _columns = 1;
        CellSpacing = 4;
        CellPadding = 0;
        GridLines = GridLines.None;
        BorderWidth = 0;
```

Listing 20-8   Implementation of *ListViewTable*, which renders its cells   *(continued)*
into a multicolumn list

```
        Width = Unit.Percentage(100);
        Height = Unit.Percentage(100);
    }

    public int Columns {
        get {
            return _columns;
        }
        set {
            if (value < 1) {
                throw new ArgumentOutOfRangeException("value");
            }
            _columns = value;
        }
    }

    protected override void RenderContents(HtmlTextWriter writer) {
        if (Rows.Count != 1) {
            return;
        }
        TableCellCollection cells = Rows[0].Cells;
        int cellsRendered = 0;
        bool endTagRequired = false;

        foreach (TableCell cell in cells) {
            if (cellsRendered == 0) {
                writer.RenderBeginTag(HtmlTextWriterTag.Tr);
                endTagRequired = true;
            }

            if (cell.Visible) {
                cell.RenderControl(writer);
                cellsRendered++;
            }

            if (cellsRendered == _columns) {
                writer.RenderEndTag();
                endTagRequired = false;
                cellsRendered = 0;
            }
        }

        if (endTagRequired) {
            writer.RenderEndTag();
        }
    }
}
```

The *ListViewTable* class derives from the *Table* control. Like all other tables, *ListViewTable* can contain rows and its rows can contain cells. The *ListView* control creates instances of *ListViewItem* classes and adds them to the *Cells* collection of the first row of *ListViewTable*. *ListViewTable* overrides the default rendering of a *Table* by overriding the *RenderContents* method. Instead of rendering its rows, *ListViewTable* renders *ListViewItems* directly by rendering the cells contained in its first row. In addition, *ListViewTable* renders markup to create *<tr>* tags between the cells so that the result is a rendering of cells distributed across one or more columns. The number of columns is exposed as a property on the *ListViewTable* class, which is initialized by the *ListView* control.

Events

A data-bound control typically exposes its own set of events based on events raised by the controls in its control hierarchy. This provides a more intuitive programming model because it does not require the page developer to wire up event handler delegates to individual controls created by *ListView*. The *ListView* control raises the *SelectedIndexChanged* and the *ItemCommand* events, which allow the page developer to write server-side code to handle the user's interactions with the control's rendering in a Web browser. Raising server-side events for user actions was discussed in Chapter 9, "Control Life Cycle, Events, and Postback."

The event-raising functionality of *ListView* is shown in Listing 20-9.

```
public class ListView : WebControl, INamingContainer,
                        IPostBackEventHandler {
    private static readonly object EventSelectedIndexChanged =
        new object();
    private static readonly object EventItemCommand = new object();
    public const string SelectCommandName = "Select";

    public event ListViewCommandEventHandler ItemCommand {
        add {
            Events.AddHandler(EventItemCommand, value);
        }
        remove {
            Events.RemoveHandler(EventItemCommand, value);
        }
    }


    [
    Category("Action"),
    Description("Raised when the selection changes")
    ]
```

Listing 20-9   Handling and raising client events and bubbled server events

```
public event EventHandler SelectedIndexChanged {
    add {
        Events.AddHandler(EventSelectedIndexChanged, value);
    }
    remove {
        Events.RemoveHandler(EventSelectedIndexChanged, value);
    }
}

protected override bool OnBubbleEvent(object sender, EventArgs e) {
    ListViewCommandEventArgs lce = e as ListViewCommandEventArgs;

    if (lce != null) {
        OnItemCommand(lce);

        if (lce.CommandType == ListViewCommandType.Select) {
            int oldSelectedIndex = SelectedIndex;
            if (oldSelectedIndex != lce.Item.ItemIndex) {
                SelectedIndex = lce.Item.ItemIndex;
                OnSelectedIndexChanged(EventArgs.Empty);
            }
        }
        return true;
    }
    return false;
}

protected virtual void OnItemCommand(ListViewCommandEventArgs e) {
    ListViewCommandEventHandler handler =
        (ListViewCommandEventHandler)Events[EventItemCommand];
    if (handler != null) {
        handler(this, null);
    }
}

protected virtual void OnSelectedIndexChanged(EventArgs e) {
    EventHandler handler =
        (EventHandler)Events[EventSelectedIndexChanged];
    if (handler != null) {
        handler(this, null);
    }
}

protected virtual void PrepareControlHierarchyForRendering() {
    ⋮

    foreach (ListViewItem item in _items) {
        ⋮
```

(continued)

Listing 20-9 *(continued)*

```
            if (_renderClickSelectScript) {
                if ((itemType & ListViewItemType.SelectedItem) == 0) {
                    item.Attributes["onclick"] =
                        Page.GetPostBackEventReference(this,
                            "S" + item.ItemIndex);
                    item.Style["cursor"] = "hand";
                }
            }
        }
    }

    #region Implementation of IPostBackEventHandler
    void IPostBackEventHandler.RaisePostBackEvent(
        string eventArgument) {
        if ((eventArgument.Length > 1) && (eventArgument[0] == 'S')) {
            SelectedIndex = Int32.Parse(eventArgument.Substring(1));
            OnSelectedIndexChanged(EventArgs.Empty);
        }
    }
    #endregion
}
```

ListViewItem derives from *TableCell* and contains an instantiated template within the *ListView* control hierarchy. *ListViewItem* participates in the event-bubbling mechanism, as shown in Listing 20-10.

```
public class ListViewItem : TableCell, INamingContainer {
    ⋮
    protected override bool OnBubbleEvent(object sender, EventArgs e) {
        CommandEventArgs ce = e as CommandEventArgs;

        if (ce != null) {
            ListViewCommandEventArgs lce =
                new ListViewCommandEventArgs(this, sender, ce);
            RaiseBubbleEvent(this, lce);

            return true;
        }
        return false;
    }
}
```

Listing 20-10 Event bubbling in the *ListViewItem* class

ListViewItem handles a bubbled *Command* event and in turn bubbles a *ListViewCommand* event. Listing 20-11 shows the implementation of the *List-ViewCommandEventArgs* class and the associated *ListViewCommand-EventHandler* delegate.

```csharp
public class ListViewCommandEventArgs : CommandEventArgs {

    private ListViewItem _item;
    private object _commandSource;
    private ListViewCommandType _commandType;

    public ListViewCommandEventArgs(ListViewItem item,
        object commandSource, CommandEventArgs originalArgs) :
        base(originalArgs) {
        _item = item;
        _commandSource = commandSource;

        string cmdName = originalArgs.CommandName;
        if (String.Compare(cmdName, ListView.SelectCommandName, true,
                           CultureInfo.InvariantCulture) == 0) {
            _commandType = ListViewCommandType.Select;
        }
        else if (String.Compare(cmdName, ListView.EditCommandName,
            true, CultureInfo.InvariantCulture) == 0) {
            _commandType = ListViewCommandType.Edit;
        }
        else if (String.Compare(cmdName, ListView.UpdateCommandName,
            true, CultureInfo.InvariantCulture) == 0) {
            _commandType = ListViewCommandType.Update;
        }
        else if (String.Compare(cmdName, ListView.CancelEditCommandName,
            true, CultureInfo.InvariantCulture) == 0) {
            _commandType = ListViewCommandType.CancelEdit;
        }
        else if (String.Compare(cmdName, ListView.DeleteCommandName,
            true, CultureInfo.InvariantCulture) == 0) {
            _commandType = ListViewCommandType.Delete;
        }
        else {
            _commandType = ListViewCommandType.Custom;
        }
    }

    public object CommandSource {
        get {
            return _commandSource;
        }
    }

    public ListViewCommandType CommandType {
```

Listing 20-11   Implementation of *ListViewCommandEventArgs* and definition of *ListViewCommandEventHandler*   *(continued)*

Listing 20-11   *(continued)*

```
        get {
            return _commandType;
        }
    }

    public ListViewItem Item {
        get {
            return _item;
        }
    }
}

public delegate void ListViewCommandEventHandler(object sender,
    ListViewCommandEventArgs e);
```

The *ListView* control defines two events that signal user action, *ItemCommand* and *SelectedIndexChanged*. As per the standard event implementation described in Chapter 3, "Component Programming Overview," the *ListView* control contains two public event properties with add and remove accessors as well as the associated protected virtual methods that raise the event by invoking any event-handler delegates that have been wired up to the event.

The *ListView* control raises the *ItemCommand* event when any control (such as a *Button* or *LinkButton*) within the *ListView* control hierarchy raises the *Command* event. A template that contains a *Button* control results in multiple instances of the *Button* within the control hierarchy. The *ItemCommand* event allows the page developer to handle an event on a single control rather than handling events on each *Button* instance. The *ListView* and *ListViewItem* classes work together by using event bubbling to implement the event. Event bubbling was described in Chapter 12. *Button* controls bubble their *Command* event up their parent hierarchy. The *ListViewItem* control overrides *OnBubbleEvent* and handles *Command* events. The control stops the bubbling of the original event and instead bubbles an *ItemCommand* event. The *ItemCommand* event is associated with an instance of *ListViewCommandEventArgs* and contains a reference to the *ListViewItem* that contained the *Button* that the user clicked. This reference adds context to the original *Command* event, which allows the page developer to take the appropriate action based on the *ListViewItem* associated with the event. The *ListView* control also overrides *OnBubbleEvent* to handle bubbled *ItemCommand* events, and it invokes any event-handler delegates that have been wired up to this event.

The *ListView* control also raises the *SelectedIndexChanged* event. This event occurs in one of two ways. If a page developer places a *Button* with its

CommandName property set to "Select," the *ListView* control raises the *Selected-IndexChanged* event from its override of the *OnBubbleEvent* method. The second way this event can occur is by the script generated by the *ListView* control that allows the user to select a *ListViewItem* by clicking anywhere on an item's rendering in the Web browser. The click causes the page to be submitted back to the server. The *ListView* control implements the *IPostBackEventHandler* interface to map client-side events into equivalent server-side events, as described in Chapter 9. In its implementation of the *RaisePostBackEvent* method, the *ListView* control selects the appropriate *ListViewItem*, as identified by the argument passed into the method, and then raises the *SelectedIndex-Changed* event.

Client Script Functionality

The *ListView* control uses JavaScript in the Web browser client to enable a more intuitive selection behavior. The enhanced selection model provided by the control allows the user to click anywhere on the region representing an item to select it. A page developer can also place a Select button within the *ItemTemplate* of the *ListView* to enable selection in Web browsers that do not support the required client-side functionality. We described the basics of using script-based functionality in Chapter 13, "Client-Side Behavior."

Listing 20-12 illustrates various parts of the *ListView* implementation that are responsible for creating this client-side experience.

```
public class ListView : WebControl, INamingContainer,
                        IPostBackEventHandler {
    private bool _renderClickSelectScript;

    public bool EnableClickSelect {
        get {
            object b = ViewState["EnableClickSelect"];
            return (b == null) ? false : true;
        }
        set {
            ViewState["EnableClickSelect"] = value;
        }
    }

    private void DetermineRenderClickSelectScript() {
        // Determine whether to render client script-based
        // functionality.
        _renderClickSelectScript = false;
```

Listing 20-12   Implementing client-side behavior to enable an enhanced   *(continued)*
selection model

Listing 20-12 *(continued)*

```
        if ((Page != null) && (Page.Request != null)) {
            // The page developer can decide to turn off the feature
            // completely.
            if (EnableClickSelect) {
                // The next set of checks involve looking at the
                // capabilities of the browser making the request.
                HttpBrowserCapabilities browserCaps =
                    Page.Request.Browser;
                bool hasEcmaScript =
                    (browserCaps.EcmaScriptVersion.CompareTo(
                        new Version(1, 2)) >= 0);
                bool hasDOM = (browserCaps.MSDomVersion.Major >= 4);

                _renderClickSelectScript = hasEcmaScript && hasDOM;
            }
        }
    }

    protected override void OnPreRender(EventArgs e) {
        base.OnPreRender(e);

        DetermineRenderClickSelectScript();
        if (_renderClickSelectScript) {
            // Page.GetPostBackEventReference automatically
            // registers the page's postback script. However, if
            // this is done during Render, the script will be
            // rendered at the end of the page. We want the
            // script up at the start, so the browser has already
            // seen the script while it's still loading the
            // rest of the page. Thus, clicking items works
            // while the page is loading as well.
            string dummyValue =
                Page.GetPostBackEventReference(this, String.Empty);
        }
    }

    protected virtual void PrepareControlHierarchyForRendering() {
        ⋮
        foreach (ListViewItem item in _items) {
            ⋮

            if (_renderClickSelectScript) {
                if ((itemType & ListViewItemType.SelectedItem) == 0) {
                    item.Attributes["onclick"] =
                        Page.GetPostBackEventReference(this,
```

```
                            "S" + item.ItemIndex);
                    item.Style["cursor"] = "hand";
                }
            }
        }
    }
}
```

ListView overrides the *OnPreRender* method to determine the level of its client-script functionality and prepare itself for rendering the HTML needed to implement its client-side behavior. The control encapsulates the logic of determining the level of its client-side behavior into a method named *Determine-RenderClickSelectScript*. By default, this method inspects the properties of an *HttpBrowserCapabilities* object, which it retrieves by using the *Browser* property of the containing page's *Request* object. This *HttpBrowserCapabilities* object includes information about the capabilities of the Web browser making the current request. In particular, the implementation checks for the availability of JavaScript 1.2 and later and the DHTML Document Object Model. In addition, this method first checks the value of the control's *EnableClickSelect* property, which allows page developers to turn off the enhanced selection behavior and the automatic detection logic. This property defaults to *true*, which enables the automatic detection logic based on the Web browser's capabilities.

To implement its client-side behavior, the *ListView* control renders Java-Script to handle the *onclick* DHTML event on each *<td>* tag corresponding to a *ListViewItem*. The control retrieves the script required to programmatically initiate a postback by using the *GetPostBackEventReference* method of its containing page. This method accepts an event target and an event argument. The control is passed in as the event target, and the index of the *ListViewItem* is passed in as the event argument. The script is added as the value of the *onclick* attribute to each *ListViewItem*. As a result, in the Render phase of the page, each *ListViewItem* renders itself and its *onclick* attribute. Note that the control adds these attributes during the Render phase, which follows the Save View State phase—according to the control life cycle described in Chapter 9. Thus, the changes made to the *Attributes* collection do not result in additional view state.

Design-Time Attributes

The *ListView* implementation uses various design-time attributes to specify metadata for its type, properties, and events and to enhance its design-time experience on a visual design surface. We discussed some of these designer attributes in Chapter 15, "Design-Time Functionality," and describe them in Appendix A, "Metadata Attributes."

Listing 20-13 provides a representative sampling of design-time attributes used in the *ListView* implementation.

```
[
DefaultEvent("SelectedIndexChanged"),
DefaultProperty("DataSource"),
Designer(typeof(MSPress.WebControls.Design.ListViewDesigner),
    typeof(IDesigner))
]
public class ListView : WebControl, INamingContainer,
                         IPostBackEventHandler {

    [
    Browsable(false),
    DesignerSerializationVisibility(
        DesignerSerializationVisibility.Hidden),
    ]
    public DataKeyCollection DataKeys {
        get { ... }
    }


    [
    Bindable(true),
    Category("Data"),
    DefaultValue(null),
    Description("The data source containing data to be rendered"),
    DesignerSerializationVisibility(
        DesignerSerializationVisibility.Hidden)
    ]
    public virtual object DataSource {
        get { ... }
        set { ... }
    }


    [
    Category("Behavior"),
    DefaultValue(false),
    Description("Whether to enable the click-select behavior")
    ]
    public bool EnableClickSelect {
```

Listing 20-13   Various design-time metadata attributes on the class and on its properties and events

```
        get { ... }
        set { ... }
    }


    [
    Category("Style"),
    Description("The style applied to all items"),
    DesignerSerializationVisibility(
        DesignerSerializationVisibility.Content),
    NotifyParentProperty(true),
    PersistenceMode(PersistenceMode.InnerProperty)
    ]
    public TableItemStyle ItemStyle {
        get { ... }
    }


    [
    Browsable(false),
    DefaultValue(null),
    PersistenceMode(PersistenceMode.InnerProperty),
    TemplateContainer(typeof(ListViewItem))
    ]
    public ITemplate ItemTemplate {
        get { ... }
    }


    [
    Category("Action"),
    Description("Raised when a button in an Item is clicked")
    ]
    public event ListViewCommandEventHandler ItemCommand {
        add { ... }
        remove { ... }
    }
}
```

Let's examine the metadata attributes presented in Listing 20-13:

■ ***DefaultEventAttribute*** Applied to the class. Allows the designer to create and wire up an event handler when the control is double-clicked on the design surface.

■ ***DefaultPropertyAttribute*** Applied to the class. Specifies the property that should be highlighted in the designer's property browser when the control is selected.

- ***DesignerAttribute***   Applied to the class. Associates a designer with the control. We will describe the designer implementation in a moment.

- ***CategoryAttribute***   Applied to properties and events. Allows the property browser to categorize properties and events into logical groupings.

- ***DescriptionAttribute***   Applied to properties and events. Allows the property browser to provide short help text for each property and event.

- ***DesignerSerializationVisibilityAttribute*** **and** ***PersistenceMode-Attribute***   Applied to properties. Specify whether a property's value should be serialized into the .aspx file and the persistence mode used for serialization.

- ***DefaultValueAttribute***   Applied to properties. Indicates the default value of the property, which allows the property browser to emphasize those properties that have been changed from their default state. This attribute also allows the control persister to determine which property values have changed and need to be persisted into the .aspx file.

- ***BrowsableAttribute***   Applied to properties. Indicates whether a property should be made visible in the property browser.

- ***BindableAttribute***   Applied to properties. Indicates whether a property should appear in the data-binding UI of the design surface.

Designer Implementation

The *ListView* control is associated with a custom designer by using the *DesignerAttribute* metadata attribute, as shown in Listing 20-13. This designer allows the *ListView* control to provide a rich design-time experience, including design-time data binding and template editing. We discussed implementing design-time functionality in Chapter 15. In that chapter, we showed how to implement a designer for a templated control, and in Chapter 16, we described how to implement a designer for data-bound control. The *ListViewDesigner* that we will now implement combines template editing with design-time data binding.

Data-Bound Control Designer

As a designer associated with a data-bound control, the *ListViewDesigner* enables selection of data sources in a designer and generates HTML for rendering at design time by binding the *ListView* control with a sample data source. We discussed the basic functionality of data-bound control designers in Chapter 16. Figure 20-2 shows the *ListView* control on the design surface with a WYSI-WYG rendering that uses sample data.

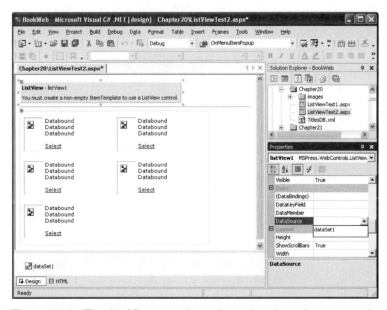

Figure 20-2   The *ListView* control creating a data-bound representation in the designer

Listing 20-14 illustrates the core aspects of all data-bound control designers in the context of a *ListView* control.

```
public class ListViewDesigner : TemplatedControlDesigner,
    IDataSourceProvider {
    private DataTable _dummyDataTable;
    private DataTable _designTimeDataTable;

    public string DataKeyField {
        get {
            return ((ListView)Component).DataKeyField;
        }
```

Listing 20-14   Enabling data source selection and design-time data binding in *ListViewDesigner*   *(continued)*

Listing 20-14 *(continued)*

```
        set {
            ((ListView)Component).DataKeyField = value;
        }
    }

    public string DataMember {
        get {
            return ((ListView)Component).DataMember;
        }
        set {
            ((ListView)Component).DataMember = value;
            OnDataSourceChanged();
        }
    }

    public string DataSource {
        get {
            DataBinding binding = DataBindings["DataSource"];

            if (binding != null) {
                return binding.Expression;
            }
            return String.Empty;
        }
        set {
            if ((value == null) || (value.Length == 0)) {
                DataBindings.Remove("DataSource");
            }
            else {
                DataBinding binding = DataBindings["DataSource"];

                if (binding == null) {
                    binding = new DataBinding("DataSource",
                        typeof(object), value);
                }
                else {
                    binding.Expression = value;
                }
                DataBindings.Add(binding);
            }

            OnDataSourceChanged();
            OnBindingsCollectionChanged("DataSource");
        }
    }
}
```

```
public override bool DesignTimeHtmlRequiresLoadComplete {
    get {
        // If we have a data source, we're going to look it up in
        // the container and require the document to be loaded
        // completely.
        return (DataSource.Length != 0);
    }
}

private IEnumerable GetDesignTimeDataSource(int minimumRows) {
    IEnumerable selectedDataSource =
        ((IDataSourceProvider)this).GetResolvedSelectedDataSource();
    DataTable dataTable = _designTimeDataTable;

    // Use the data table corresponding to the selected data source
    // if possible.
    if (dataTable == null) {
        if (selectedDataSource != null) {
            _designTimeDataTable =
                DesignTimeData.CreateSampleDataTable(
                    selectedDataSource);
            dataTable = _designTimeDataTable;
        }

        if (dataTable == null) {
            // Fall back on a dummy data source if we can't create
            // a sample data table.
            if (_dummyDataTable == null) {
                _dummyDataTable =
                    DesignTimeData.CreateDummyDataTable();
            }

            dataTable = _dummyDataTable;
        }
    }

    IEnumerable liveDataSource =
        DesignTimeData.GetDesignTimeDataSource(dataTable,
            minimumRows);
    return liveDataSource;
}

public override string GetDesignTimeHtml() {
    ListView lv = (ListView)Component;
```

(continued)

Listing 20-14 *(continued)*

```
        if (lv.ItemTemplate == null) {
            return GetEmptyDesignTimeHtml();
        }

        string designTimeHTML = null;

        IEnumerable designTimeDataSource = GetDesignTimeDataSource(5);

        bool dataKeyFieldChanged = false;
        string oldDataKeyField = null;

        try {
            lv.DataSource = designTimeDataSource;

            oldDataKeyField = lv.DataKeyField;
            if (oldDataKeyField.Length != 0) {
                dataKeyFieldChanged = true;
                lv.DataKeyField = String.Empty;
            }
            lv.DataBind();

            designTimeHTML = base.GetDesignTimeHtml();
        }
        catch (Exception e) {
            designTimeHTML = GetErrorDesignTimeHtml(e);
        }
        finally {
            lv.DataSource = null;
            if (dataKeyFieldChanged) {
                lv.DataKeyField = oldDataKeyField;
            }
        }
        return designTimeHTML;
    }

    protected internal virtual void OnDataSourceChanged() {
        _designTimeDataTable = null;
    }

    protected override void PreFilterProperties(
        IDictionary properties) {
        base.PreFilterProperties(properties);

        PropertyDescriptor prop;

        prop = (PropertyDescriptor)properties["DataSource"];
        Debug.Assert(prop != null);
```

```
    // We can't create the designer DataSource property based on
    // the run-time property because these types do not match.
    // Therefore, we have to copy over all the attributes from the
    // runtime and use them that way.
    AttributeCollection runtimeAttributes = prop.Attributes;
    Attribute[] attrs = new Attribute[runtimeAttributes.Count + 1];

    runtimeAttributes.CopyTo(attrs, 0);
    attrs[runtimeAttributes.Count] =
        new TypeConverterAttribute(typeof(DataSourceConverter));
    prop = TypeDescriptor.CreateProperty(this.GetType(),
        "DataSource", typeof(string), attrs);
    properties["DataSource"] = prop;

    prop = (PropertyDescriptor)properties["DataMember"];
    Debug.Assert(prop != null);
    prop = TypeDescriptor.CreateProperty(
        this.GetType(), prop,
        new Attribute[] {
            new TypeConverterAttribute(typeof(DataMemberConverter))
        });
    properties["DataMember"] = prop;

    prop = (PropertyDescriptor)properties["DataKeyField"];
    Debug.Assert(prop != null);
    prop = TypeDescriptor.CreateProperty(
        this.GetType(), prop,
        new Attribute[] {
            new TypeConverterAttribute(typeof(DataFieldConverter))
        });
    properties["DataKeyField"] = prop;
}

#region Implementation of IDataSourceProvider
object IDataSourceProvider.GetSelectedDataSource() {
    object selectedDataSource = null;

    DataBinding binding = DataBindings["DataSource"];
    if (binding != null) {
        selectedDataSource =
            DesignTimeData.GetSelectedDataSource(Component,
                binding.Expression);
    }

    return selectedDataSource;
}
```

(continued)

Listing 20-14   *(continued)*

```
IEnumerable IDataSourceProvider.GetResolvedSelectedDataSource() {
    IEnumerable selectedDataSource = null;

    DataBinding binding = DataBindings["DataSource"];
    if (binding != null) {
        selectedDataSource =
            DesignTimeData.GetSelectedDataSource(Component,
                binding.Expression, DataMember);
    }

    return selectedDataSource;
}
#endregion
}
```

The *ListViewDesigner* contains an implementation of the *DataMember*, *DataKeyField*, and *DataSource* properties. These properties are used to *shadow*, or replace, the corresponding properties of the runtime by overriding the *PreFilterProperties* method. The implementation of *PreFilterProperties* creates new *PropertyDescriptor* objects with the appropriate metadata attributes. The result of this shadowing is that the *DataMember* and *DataSource* properties that appear in the designer's property browser window are implemented by the designer, not by the selected *ListView* control. The *DataMember* and *DataKeyField* properties are replaced with design-time properties that are associated with custom type converters: *DataMemberConverter* and *DataFieldConverter*. These type converters are meant for design-time usage only and are therefore not directly associated with the properties on the *ListView* class. The *DataSource* property is replaced for a couple of reasons. First, the design-time property is associated with the *DataSourceConverter* type converter, which is also meant for design-time use only. This converter enumerates all objects on the page that can be used as a data source and presents them as choices for the page developer. In addition, the designer's *DataSource* property operates on the *ListView* control's collection of data bindings and persists the page developer's data source selection in the form of a data binding.

The *ListViewDesigner* also overrides the *GetDesignTimeHtml* method to data-bind the *ListView* control to a sample data source before rendering it to generate the design-time representation. *ListViewDesigner* encapsulates the logic to create a data source that matches the schema of the selected data source in the *GetDesignTimeDataSource* method. The implementation of this method uses the helper methods available in the *System.Web.UI.Design.DesignTimeData* class.

Template Editing

ListViewDesigner uses the template editing functionality of the design surface to allow WYSIWYG editing of its template properties. We discussed the main concepts behind template editing in Chapter 15. Figure 20-3 shows an instance of the *ListView* control in template editing mode.

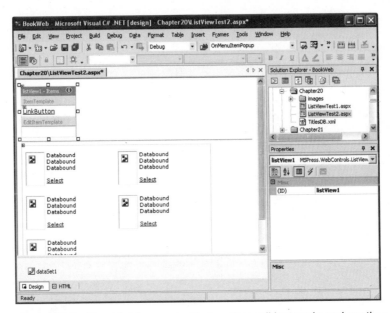

Figure 20-3   The *ListView* control in template editing mode and another control with a template defined

Listing 20-15 contains the code from the *ListViewDesigner* class that implements the template editing feature of the control.

```csharp
public class ListViewDesigner : TemplatedControlDesigner,
                                IDataSourceProvider {
    private const int HeaderFooterTemplates = 0;
    private const int ItemTemplates = 1;


    private static string[] HeaderFooterTemplateNames =
        new string[] { "HeaderTemplate", "FooterTemplate" };
    private const int HeaderTemplate = 0;
    private const int FooterTemplate = 1;


    private static string[] ItemTemplateNames =
        new string[] { "ItemTemplate", "EditItemTemplate" };
```

Listing 20-15   Template editing in *ListViewDesigner*   *(continued)*

Listing 20-15   *(continued)*

```
private const int ItemTemplate = 0;
private const int EditItemTemplate = 1;

private TemplateEditingVerb[] _templateEditingVerbs;

public override bool AllowResize {
    get {
        return InTemplateMode ||
            (((ListView)Component).ItemTemplate != null);
    }
}

protected override ITemplateEditingFrame CreateTemplateEditingFrame(
    TemplateEditingVerb verb) {
    ITemplateEditingFrame frame = null;

    if ((_templateEditingVerbs != null) &&
        ((IList)_templateEditingVerbs).Contains(verb)) {
        ITemplateEditingService teService = (ITemplateEditingService)
            GetService(typeof(ITemplateEditingService));

        if (teService != null) {
            ListView lv = (ListView)Component;
            string[] templateNames = null;
            Style[] templateStyles = null;

            switch (verb.Index) {
                case HeaderFooterTemplates:
                    templateNames = HeaderFooterTemplateNames;
                    templateStyles =
                        new Style[] {
                            lv.HeaderStyle, lv.FooterStyle
                        };
                    break;
                case ItemTemplates:
                    templateNames = ItemTemplateNames;
                    templateStyles =
                        new Style[] {
                            lv.ItemStyle, lv.EditItemStyle
                        };
                    break;
            }
            frame = teService.CreateFrame(this, verb.Text,
                templateNames, lv.ControlStyle, templateStyles);
```

```
            }
        }
        return frame;
    }


    protected override void Dispose(bool disposing) {
        if (disposing) {
            DisposeTemplateEditingVerbs();
        }
        base.Dispose(disposing);
    }

    private void DisposeTemplateEditingVerbs() {
        if (_templateEditingVerbs != null) {
            for (int i = 0; i < _templateEditingVerbs.Length; i++) {
                _templateEditingVerbs[i].Dispose();
            }
            _templateEditingVerbs = null;
        }
    }


    protected override
        TemplateEditingVerb[] GetCachedTemplateEditingVerbs() {
        if (_templateEditingVerbs == null) {
            _templateEditingVerbs = new TemplateEditingVerb[2];

            _templateEditingVerbs[0] =
                new TemplateEditingVerb("Header and Footer",
                    HeaderFooterTemplates, this);
            _templateEditingVerbs[1] =
                new TemplateEditingVerb("Items", ItemTemplates, this);
        }
        return _templateEditingVerbs;
    }

    public override string GetTemplateContainerDataItemProperty(
        string templateName) {
        return "DataItem";
    }


    public override IEnumerable GetTemplateContainerDataSource(
        string templateName) {
        return
            ((IDataSourceProvider)this).GetResolvedSelectedDataSource();
    }
```

(continued)

Listing 20-15   *(continued)*

```
public override string GetTemplateContent(
    ITemplateEditingFrame editingFrame, string templateName,
    out bool allowEditing) {
    allowEditing = true;

    if ((_templateEditingVerbs != null) &&
        ((IList)_templateEditingVerbs).Contains(
            editingFrame.Verb)) {
        ListView lv = (ListView)Component;
        ITemplate template = null;

        switch (editingFrame.Verb.Index) {
            case HeaderFooterTemplates:
                if (templateName.Equals(
                    HeaderFooterTemplateNames[HeaderTemplate])) {
                    template = lv.HeaderTemplate;
                }
                else if (templateName.Equals(
                    HeaderFooterTemplateNames[FooterTemplate])) {
                    template = lv.FooterTemplate;
                }
                break;
            case ItemTemplates:
                if (templateName.Equals(
                    ItemTemplateNames[ItemTemplate])) {
                    template = lv.ItemTemplate;
                }
                else if (templateName.Equals(
                    ItemTemplateNames[EditItemTemplate])) {
                    template = lv.EditItemTemplate;
                }
                break;
        }

        string templateContent = String.Empty;
        if (template != null) {
            templateContent = GetTextFromTemplate(template);
        }

        return templateContent;
    }
    return String.Empty;
}

public override void OnComponentChanged(object sender,
    ComponentChangedEventArgs e) {
```

```csharp
        if (e.Member != null) {
            string memberName = e.Member.Name;
            if (memberName.Equals("Font") ||
                memberName.Equals("ForeColor") ||
                memberName.Equals("BackColor") ||
                memberName.Equals("ItemStyle") ||
                memberName.Equals("HeaderStyle") ||
                memberName.Equals("FooterStyle") ||
                memberName.Equals("EditItemStyle")) {
                DisposeTemplateEditingVerbs();
            }
        }

        base.OnComponentChanged(sender, e);
}

public override void SetTemplateContent(
    ITemplateEditingFrame editingFrame, string templateName,
    string templateContent) {
    if ((_templateEditingVerbs != null) &&
        ((IList)_templateEditingVerbs).Contains(
            editingFrame.Verb)) {
        ListView lv = (ListView)Component;
        ITemplate newTemplate = null;

        try {
            newTemplate = GetTemplateFromText(templateContent);
        }
        catch {
            return;
        }

        switch (editingFrame.Verb.Index) {
            case HeaderFooterTemplates:
                if (templateName.Equals(
                    HeaderFooterTemplateNames[HeaderTemplate])) {
                    lv.HeaderTemplate = newTemplate;
                }
                else if (templateName.Equals(
                    HeaderFooterTemplateNames[FooterTemplate])) {
                    lv.FooterTemplate = newTemplate;
                }
                break;
            case ItemTemplates:
                if (templateName.Equals(
                    ItemTemplateNames[ItemTemplate])) {
```

(continued)

Listing 20-15 *(continued)*

```
                    lv.ItemTemplate = newTemplate;
                }
                else if (templateName.Equals(
                    ItemTemplateNames[EditItemTemplate])) {
                    lv.EditItemTemplate = newTemplate;
                }
                break;
            }
        }
    }
}
```

ListViewDesigner enables template editing by deriving from *Templated-ControlDesigner* and implementing its abstract methods. These methods were described in detail in Chapter 15. *ListViewDesigner* overrides the *Get-CachedTemplateEditingVerbs* to create a list of *TemplateEditingVerb* instances. Each verb corresponds to a logical group of templates and is used to create entries in the context menu of the designer. *ListViewDesigner* overrides the *CreateTemplateEditingFrame* to create the UI associated with editing the selected *TemplateEditingVerb*. Finally, the *ListViewDesigner* overrides the *GetTemplate-Content* and *SetTemplateContent* methods to provide access to the control's template text and to update the control's templates with modified template text.

Summary

The *ListView* control and its associated designer, the *ListViewDesigner* class that we implemented in this chapter, represent the reference implementation of a data-bound templated control and control designer. The implementation provided in this example is based on the same techniques and patterns used in the implementation of the standard ASP.NET data-bound templated controls, such as the *DataList* control.

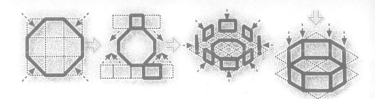

21

DHTML-Based Server Controls

DHTML capabilities of modern Web browsers such as Microsoft Internet Explorer 4 and later enable page developers and designers to create visually appealing, interactive, and intuitive user interfaces (UIs) in their Web applications. At the same time, most Web applications need to target the widest possible audience, which implies that they should be able to support Web browsers with little or no DHTML capabilities. Server controls allow you to address this scenario by encapsulating the logic to target multiple Web browsers into reusable components. Page developers can easily reuse these controls to create Web applications that optimize user experience based on the capabilities offered by the user's Web browser. The validation controls in ASP.NET are an example of server controls that use DHTML and client-side JavaScript for client-side validation. These controls gracefully degrade to server-side validation if a Web browser does not provide the necessary client-side capabilities.

In this chapter, we will describe a *DatePicker* control that is DHTML-enabled and encapsulates logic for targeting multiple Web browsers.

The *DatePicker* Control

The *DatePicker* control offers an intuitive mechanism for date entry in a Web application. In addition to providing a text box for manual entry, the control contains a pop-up calendar for visually selecting a date and navigating across different months. This combination is a popular mechanism for selecting dates and can be found on various commercial Web sites, such as Expedia.com (*http://www.expedia.com*).

Figures 21-1 through 21-4 demonstrate the *DatePicker* control being used in an .aspx page.

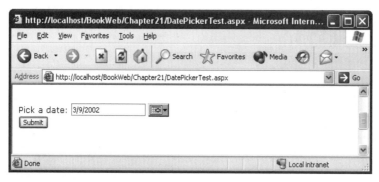

Figure 21-1   The *DatePicker* UI in its default state

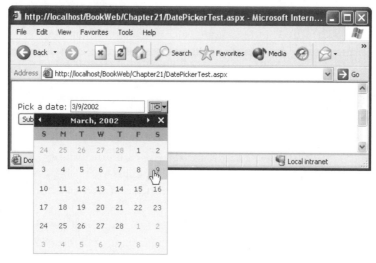

Figure 21-2   The *DatePicker* and its pop-up calendar UI

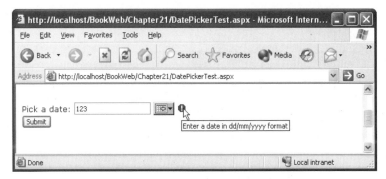

Figure 21-3   The *DatePicker* in an error state as the result of an invalid date entry

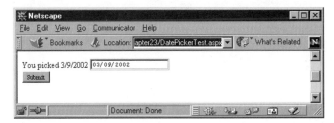

Figure 21-4   The *DatePicker* used in a Web browser (Netscape 4.71) that does not support DHTML

Listing 21-1 shows the DatePickerTest.aspx page that was used in Figures 21-1 through 21-4.

```
<%@ Page language="C#" %>
<%@ Register TagPrefix="mspwc" Namespace="MSPress.WebControls"
  Assembly="MSPress.WebControls" %>
<html>
  <head>
    <script runat="server">
      public void datePicker1_OnDateChanged(object sender,
          EventArgs e) {
          label1.Text = "You picked " +
              datePicker1.SelectedDate.ToShortDateString();
      }
    </script>
  </head>
  <body>
    <form runat="server">
```

Listing 21-1   DatePickerTest.aspx   *(continued)*

Listing 21-1   *(continued)*

```
     <p>
        <asp:Label runat="server" id="label1" text="Pick a date:" />
        <mspwc:DatePicker runat="server" id="datePicker1"
          onDateChanged="datePicker1_OnDateChanged"
          ValidationMessage="Enter a date in dd/mm/yyyy format">
          <CalendarStyle Font-Name="Verdana" Font-Size="8pt"
            ForeColor="DarkSlateBlue" BackColor="beige"
            BorderStyle="Solid" BorderWidth="1px" BorderColor="Tan"
            Width="220px" Height="220px"/>
          <DayHeaderStyle Font-Bold="true" BackColor="Tan"/>
          <TitleStyle Font-Bold="true" BackColor="DarkRed"
            ForeColor="Beige"/>
          <SelectedDayStyle BackColor="#ccccff"/>
          <OtherMonthDayStyle ForeColor="#cc9966"/>
          <TodayDayStyle BackColor="PaleGoldenRod"/>
        </mspwc:DatePicker>
        <asp:RequiredFieldValidator runat="server"
          ControlToValidate="datePicker1"
          ErrorMessage="(A date is required)" />
        <br>
        <asp:Button runat="server" Text="Submit" />
     </p>
   </form>
  </body>
</html>
```

Here is the fragment of HTML rendered by the *DatePicker* control in the sample page in Listing 21-1.

```
<span id="datePicker1"
    dp_htcURL="/aspnet_client/mspress_webcontrols/1_0_0_0/Calendar.htc"
    dp_width="220px" dp_height="220px"
    dp_calendarStyle="color:DarkSlateBlue;background-color:Beige;font-
family:'Verdana';font-size:8pt;border:1px Tan Solid;"
    dp_titleStyle="color:Beige;background-color:DarkRed;font-weight:
bold;"
    dp_dayHeaderStyle="background-color:Tan;font-weight:bold;"
    dp_otherMonthDayStyle="color:#CC9966;"
    dp_todayDayStyle="background-color:PaleGoldenrod;"
    dp_selectedDayStyle="background-color:#CCCCFF;">
  <input name="datePicker1:dateTextBox" type="text" maxlength="10"
      id="datePicker1_dateTextBox" />
  <img hspace="4" onclick="dp_showDatePickerPopup(this,
document.all['datePicker1_dateTextBox'], document.all['datePicker1'])"
      src="/aspnet_client/mspress_webcontrols/1_0_0_0/Picker.gif"
      align="AbsMiddle" border="0" style="height:21px;width:34px;" />
  <span title="Enter a date in dd/mm/yyyy format"
      id="datePicker1__ctl1"
```

```
      controltovalidate="datePicker1_dateTextBox"
      errormessage="Enter a date in dd/mm/yyyy format"
      display="Dynamic"
      evaluationfunction="RegularExpressionValidatorEvaluateIsValid"
      validationexpression="^\s*(\d{1,2})([-./])(\d{1,2})\2((\d{4})|(\d
{2}))\s*$"
      style="color:Red;display:none;">
    <img src="/aspnet_client/mspress_webcontrols/1_0_0_0/Error.gif"
        align="AbsMiddle" border="0" style="height:16px;width:16px;" />
  </span>
</span>
```

DatePicker Specification

Most complex server controls are implemented as composite controls that reuse the functionality of other existing server controls. *DatePicker* is implemented as a composite control that contains other standard ASP.NET server controls as part of its *Controls* collection—a *TextBox*, an *Image*, and a *RegularExpression-Validator*. Besides reusing their rendering functionality, the *DatePicker* control uses the *TextBox* control to implement its text-entry UI and its postback capabilities and uses the validator control to validate the format of the date and ensure valid entries.

When the Web browser client supports DHTML and JavaScript, *DatePicker* uses those capabilities to offer an interactive date-selection UI, which includes a drop-down calendar and month navigation. The *DatePicker* control packages its client functionality into a set of script files, which are included in the page during the rendering process. When the page is rendered to a Web browser that does not support DHTML, the *DatePicker* control provides an alternative UI—a plain text box—but preserves its core functionality to allow the user to enter a date.

Like all server controls, the *DatePicker* control has an object model that allows page developers to program against it from server-side code. The *DatePicker* control's object model mimics that of the standard ASP.NET *TextBox* control and includes properties such as *AutoPostBack* and *Columns*. However, rather than providing a *Text* property of type *String* and a *TextChanged* event as the standard *TextBox* control does, the *DatePicker* control offers a *SelectedDate* property of type *DateTime* as well as a *DateChanged* event. In addition, *DatePicker* allows the page developer to customize the appearance of the pop-up calendar by using style properties that are similar to the standard ASP.NET *Calendar* control.

As with all well-designed server controls, the *DatePicker* control includes an associated designer that enhances its appearance on a visual design surface to provide a WYSIWYG view of the control.

DatePicker and *DatePickerDesigner* Implementation

The *DatePicker* implementation is based on several of the control authoring concepts that we described in Part III of the book, "Server Controls—Nuts and Bolts." This section illustrates those concepts by using fragments from the source code for the *DatePicker* control. You'll find the complete implementation in the book's DatePicker.cs and DatePickerDesigner.cs sample files inside the WebControls project.

> **Note**   You can compile the control without using the Microsoft Visual Studio .NET project. Navigate to the directory that contains the sample file (for example, c:\BookCode\CSharp), and run the BuildWebControls.bat batch file, which simply makes a call to the C# compiler with the right set of command-line arguments.

Composite Control

As we mentioned earlier, *DatePicker* is a composite control that contains three child controls within its *Controls* collection: a *TextBox*, an *Image*, and a *RegularExpressionValidator*. Composite controls were described in detail in Chapter 12, "Composite Controls."

Listing 21-2 illustrates general concepts that apply to all composite controls.

```
public class DatePicker : WebControl, INamingContainer {
    private TextBox _dateTextBox;
    private Image _pickerImage;
    private Image _errorImage;
    private RegularExpressionValidator _dateValidator;
    ⋮
    public override ControlCollection Controls {
        get {
            // Always override the Controls property and
            // ensure that its Controls collection is valid.
            EnsureChildControls();
            return base.Controls;
        }
    }
}
```

Listing 21-2   The essence of implementing a composite control

```
protected override void CreateChildControls() {
    _dateTextBox = new TextBox();
    _pickerImage = new Image();
    _errorImage = new Image();
    _dateValidator = new RegularExpressionValidator();

    // EnableViewState is true for the TextBox and false for all
    // other child controls.
    // The TextBox needs view state in its TextChanged event
    // implementation. However, all the other controls are set up
    // here or customized during Render. Therefore, they do not
    // contribute to view state. Additionally, setting their
    // EnableViewState to false tells the page framework to
    // skip them completely, which makes for a small performance
    // improvement.

    _dateTextBox.ID = "dateTextBox";
    _dateTextBox.MaxLength = 10;
    _dateTextBox.TextChanged +=
        new EventHandler(this.dateTextBox_TextChanged);

    _pickerImage.EnableViewState = false;
    _pickerImage.ImageUrl = GetClientFileUrl("Picker.gif");
    _pickerImage.ImageAlign = ImageAlign.AbsMiddle;
    _pickerImage.Attributes["hspace"] = "4";
    _pickerImage.Width = new Unit(34);
    _pickerImage.Height = new Unit(21);

    _errorImage.EnableViewState = false;
    _errorImage.ImageUrl = GetClientFileUrl("Error.gif");
    _errorImage.ImageAlign = ImageAlign.AbsMiddle;
    _errorImage.Width = new Unit(16);
    _errorImage.Height = new Unit(16);

    _dateValidator.EnableViewState = false;
    _dateValidator.ControlToValidate = "dateTextBox";
    _dateValidator.ValidationExpression =
        "^\\s*(\\d{1,2})([-./])(\\d{1,2})\\2" +
        "((\\d{4})|(\\d{2}))\\s*$";
    _dateValidator.Display = ValidatorDisplay.Dynamic;
    _dateValidator.Controls.Add(_errorImage);

    // All the controls are fully initialized with their
    // property values before they are added to the control tree.
    // This way, the property values become part of the controls'
    // initial state and do not contribute to view state.
```

(continued)

Listing 21-2   *(continued)*

```
        Controls.Add(_dateTextBox);
        Controls.Add(_pickerImage);
        Controls.Add(_dateValidator);
    }
    ⋮
}
```

Like all composite controls, the *DatePicker* implements the *INaming-Container* interface. This interface is a marker interface, which causes the page framework to create a new scope for names or IDs of controls contained inside the control. This allows the *DatePicker* to assign its contained *TextBox* control an ID of "dateTextBox" without worrying about multiple controls with the same ID (should the page developer place more than a single *DatePicker* control on the same page). A new naming scope under the control also allows the page framework to uniquely identify the *TextBox* so that it can correctly load post-back data containing the user's input to update its text.

DatePicker implements all the logic for creating its contained controls by overriding the *CreateChildControls* method. The *DatePicker* control overrides this method to create and initialize its contained *TextBox*, *Image*, and *Regular-ExpressionValidator* controls. *DatePicker* then adds these other controls into its *Controls* collection in the order in which they should be rendered. Note that the *DatePicker* optimizes its view state usage by initializing the controls before adding them into its *Controls* collection and by setting the *EnableViewState* property of some of its controls to *false*.

DatePicker, like all composite controls, overrides its inherited *Controls* property to ensure that its *Controls* collection is valid by calling the *Ensure-ChildControls* method. This guarantees that any other code accessing the *DatePicker* control's contained controls is handed the right set of controls. If the control collection needs to be updated, *DatePicker* should set its *ChildControls-Created* property to *false*. This will cause the control's *CreateChildControls* implementation to be called the next time a call is made to *EnsureChildControls*.

Delegated Properties

Delegated properties are properties exposed by a composite control that rely on properties implemented by contained (child) controls. Delegated properties allow the users of a composite control to indirectly access properties of its child controls without directly referencing the children. The *DatePicker* implementation gives general guidelines for implementing properties of this nature.

Listing 21-3 illustrates properties that the *DatePicker* control delegates to its contained *TextBox* and *RegularExpressionValidator* controls.

```
[
DefaultValue(false)
]
public virtual bool ReadOnly {
    get {
        EnsureChildControls();
        return _dateTextBox.ReadOnly;
    }
    set {
        EnsureChildControls();
        _dateTextBox.ReadOnly = value;
    }
}

public virtual string ValidationMessage {
    get {
        string s = (string)ViewState["ValidationMessage"];
        return (s == null) ? String.Empty : s;
    }
    set {
        ViewState["ValidationMessage"] = value;
    }
}

protected override void RenderContents(HtmlTextWriter writer) {
    ⋮
    // First prepare the text box for rendering by applying this
    // control's style and any attributes to it.
    if (ControlStyleCreated) {
        _dateTextBox.ApplyStyle(ControlStyle);
    }
    _dateTextBox.CopyBaseAttributes(this);
    _dateTextBox.RenderControl(writer);
    ⋮
    if (_dateValidator.Visible) {
        // Delegate the ValidationMessage property of the control
        // to the validator, before it gets rendered.
        _dateValidator.ErrorMessage = ValidationMessage;
        _dateValidator.RenderControl(writer);
    }
}
```

Listing 21-3   Defining and implementing delegated properties

DatePicker illustrates two kinds of property delegation: *immediate delegation* and *delayed delegation*. We'll discuss both these delegation types now.

Immediate Delegation

The *DatePicker* implements its *ReadOnly* property by delegating immediately to the *ReadOnly* property of the contained *TextBox* control in its property accessors. Because this property is immediately delegated, both the getter and setter first call *EnsureChildControls* to ensure that the current *Controls* collection is valid. Furthermore, the *DatePicker* chooses the same default value for its property as the *TextBox* so that the semantics of its property are the same as those of the property implementation to which it delegates. In this case, the *TextBox* is responsible for managing the value of the *ReadOnly* property in its own view state.

Delayed Delegation

The *ValidationMessage* property is an example of a property that is not immediately delegated to the contained *RegularExpressionValidator*. Instead, the *DatePicker* delegates this property value to its contained validator control right before it is rendered. This delayed delegation is necessary because the *EnableViewState* property of the contained validator is set to *false* to minimize the resulting view state, as shown in Listing 21-2. As a result, the *DatePicker* control (the container) is responsible for managing the *ValidationMessage* property value in its own view state. Because view state is collected prior to rendering, any changes made during the Render phase do not increase the view state size.

Another example of delegation that is not immediately obvious is the delegation of the *DatePicker* control's style properties and attributes collection. These are applied to the contained *TextBox* control just before the control is rendered. At its core, a *DatePicker* is a variation of a *TextBox* and therefore delegates its entire visual appearance to its contained *TextBox* while managing those properties in its own view state.

Styles and State Management

The *DatePicker* contains various style properties that enable the page developer to customize its rendered UI—for example, *CalendarStyle*, *DayStyle*, and *TodayDayStyle*. We discussed styles in Chapter 11, "Styles in Controls," and we discussed state management concepts in Chapter 7, "Simple Properties and View State" and Chapter 10, "Complex Properties and State Management." As with delegated properties, styles allow a page developer to customize the contents of a composite control without having to understand the structure of the composite control's control tree and index into its *Controls* collection.

Styles have the ability to manage their properties in view state. However, it is the responsibility of the control using a style to include the style instance in its own implementation of view state management, as shown in Listing 21-4.

```
private TableStyle _calendarStyle;
public virtual TableStyle CalendarStyle {
    get {
        if (_calendarStyle == null) {
            _calendarStyle = new TableStyle();
            if (IsTrackingViewState) {
                ((IStateManager)_calendarStyle).TrackViewState();
            }
        }
        return _calendarStyle;
    }
}

protected override void LoadViewState(object savedState) {
    object baseState = null;
    object[] myState = null;

    if (savedState != null) {
        myState = (object[])savedState;
        if (myState.Length != 8) {
            throw new ArgumentException("Invalid view state");
        }
        baseState = myState[0];
    }

    // Always call the base class, even if the state is null, so
    // that the base class gets a chance to fully implement its
    // LoadViewState functionality.
    base.LoadViewState(baseState);

    if (myState == null) {
        return;
    }

    // For performance reasons, the styles are created only if state
    // exists for them. It is especially important to optimize
    // their creation in complex controls because styles are
    // relatively complex objects and have an
    // impact on the rendering logic.
    if (myState[1] != null)
        ((IStateManager)CalendarStyle).LoadViewState(myState[1]);
    ⋮
}

protected override object SaveViewState() {
    object[] myState = new object[8];
```

Listing 21-4   Implementing style properties and managing their view state   *(continued)*

Listing 21-4   *(continued)*

```
        // Again, note that the styles are saved only if they have
        // been created.
        myState[0] = base.SaveViewState();
        myState[1] = (_calendarStyle != null) ?
            ((IStateManager)_calendarStyle).SaveViewState() : null;
        ⋮


        for (int i = 0; i < 8; i++) {
            if (myState[i] != null) {
                return myState;
            }
        }


        // Another performance optimization. If no modifications were made
        // to any properties from their persisted state, the view state
        // for this control is null. Returning null rather than an array
        // of null values helps minimize the view state significantly.
        return null;
    }

    protected override void TrackViewState() {
        base.TrackViewState();

        // Again, note that the tracking is propagated only to those styles
        // that have been created. New styles created thereafter will be
        // marked as tracking view state when they are created on demand.

        if (_calendarStyle != null)
            ((IStateManager)_calendarStyle).TrackViewState();
        ⋮
    }
```

DatePicker implements a read-only property for each of its style properties, such as *CalendarStyle*. In the property getter, *DatePicker* creates an instance of a *TableStyle* on demand. It is important to create styles only when required because they can impact performance by affecting the size of view state and can impact the complexity of the rendering process. Style properties are always implemented as read-only properties. This allows the control to assume complete responsibility for the style's state management. The control could not make this assumption if the property was read-write and the control could be handed a reference to an external style object, causing the style to be managed in view state twice—once by the real owner of the style and another time by the control that was handed a reference.

DatePicker overrides the *SaveViewState* method to return an object array that contains the view state of its base class and the view state for each of its style properties. The view state for the base class stored in the first array entry contains various properties, including *ForeColor*, *Font*, *Height*, and *Width*. The other array entries contain view state for any style objects that have been instantiated. This array is returned as the view state for the *DatePicker* if any one of its array entries contains a non-null value. If the array does not contain any view state, the control returns null for its own view state. This is done to optimize the size of the view state.

DatePicker implements the corresponding logic of restoring view state to its style properties by overriding the *LoadViewState* method. The state object handed to the control is cast to an object array. The *LoadViewState* override should always call its base class's implementation of *LoadViewState*. *DatePicker* hands the value in the first entry of the array to its base class. For each of the other array entries, the implementation loads any non-null view state into the corresponding style properties. Because the implementation uses the style properties, any necessary style objects are created on demand.

Finally, *DatePicker* allows its style properties to manage their values in view state by overriding the *TrackViewState* method. The page framework calls the *TrackViewState* method to mark the end of the Initialize phase, after which property value changes are tracked in view state. *DatePicker* overrides this method to mark the end of the Initialize phase of any style objects that have already been created. Because styles are created on demand, the style property getters also call the style's *TrackViewState* method if the style is being created after the control's *TrackViewState* method has been called, as indicated by the control's *IsTrackingViewState* property.

Client Script Functionality

The *DatePicker* uses DHTML and JavaScript to implement a pop-up calendar UI and provide month navigation on the client. The basics of using script-based functionality were described in Chapter 13, "Client-Side Behavior."

Listing 21-5 illustrates various parts of the *DatePicker* implementation that are responsible for providing a rich client experience.

```
private bool _renderClientScript;
private bool _renderPopupScript;
[
DefaultValue(true)
]
public bool EnableClientScript {
    get {
        object b = ViewState["EnableClientScript"];
```

Listing 21-5 Adding client script functionality to use the DHTML capabilities of a Web browser   *(continued)*

Listing 21-5 *(continued)*

```
            return (b == null) ? true : (bool)b;
        }
        set {
            ViewState["EnableClientScript"] = value;
        }
    }
}

protected override void OnPreRender(EventArgs e) {
    base.OnPreRender(e);
    DetermineClientScriptLevel();
    if (_renderClientScript) {
        Page.RegisterClientScriptBlock(typeof(DatePicker).FullName,
            GetClientScriptInclude("DatePicker.js"));
    }

    // Propagate the setting into the validator as well, because it
    // is logically part of this control now.
    _dateValidator.EnableClientScript = EnableClientScript;
}

private void DetermineClientScriptLevel() {
    // In a client script enabled control, always determine whether to
    // render the client script functionality.
    // The decision should be based on both browser capabilities and
    // the page developer's choice.

    _renderClientScript = false;
    _renderPopupScript = false;
    if ((Page != null) && (Page.Request != null)) {
        // The page developer can decide to turn off script completely.
        if (EnableClientScript) {
            // The next set of checks involves looking at the
            // capabilities of the browser making the request.
            // The DatePicker needs to verify whether the browser has
            // EcmaScript (JavaScript) version 1.2+ and whether the
            // browser supports DHTML and, optionally, DHTML behaviors.

            HttpBrowserCapabilities browserCaps = Page.Request.Browser;
            bool hasEcmaScript =
                (browserCaps.EcmaScriptVersion.CompareTo(
                    new Version(1, 2)) >= 0);
            bool hasDOM = (browserCaps.MSDomVersion.Major >= 4);
            bool hasBehaviors =
                (browserCaps.MajorVersion > 5) ||
                ((browserCaps.MajorVersion == 5) &&
                (browserCaps.MinorVersion >= .5));
```

```
                    _renderClientScript = hasEcmaScript && hasDOM;
                    _renderPopupScript = _renderClientScript && hasBehaviors;
            }
        }
}


private string GetClientFileUrl(string fileName) {
    if (ClientFilesUrlPrefix == null) {
        // Use the config setting to determine where the client files
        // are located. Client files are located in the aspnet_client
        // v-root and then distributed into subfolders by assembly name
        // and assembly version.
        string location = null;
        if (Context != null) {
            IDictionary configData =
                (IDictionary)Context.GetConfig("system.web/webControls");
            if (configData != null) {
                location = (string)configData["clientScriptsLocation"];
            }
        }

        if (location == null) {
            location = String.Empty;
        }
        else if (location.IndexOf("{0}") >= 0) {
            AssemblyName assemblyName = GetType().Assembly.GetName();

            string assembly =
                assemblyName.Name.Replace('.', '_').ToLower();
            string version =
                assemblyName.Version.ToString().Replace('.', '_');

            location = String.Format(location, assembly, version);
        }

        ClientFilesUrlPrefix = location;
    }
    return ClientFilesUrlPrefix + fileName;
}


private string GetClientScriptInclude(string scriptFile) {
    return "<script language=\"JavaScript\" src=\"" +
        GetClientFileUrl(scriptFile) + "\"></script>";
}


private string GetCssFromStyle(Style style) {
    ⋮
}
```

(continued)

Listing 21-5 *(continued)*

```
protected override void AddAttributesToRender(HtmlTextWriter writer) {
    ⋮
    if (_renderClientScript) {
        if (_renderPopupScript) {
            writer.AddAttribute("dp_htcURL",
                GetClientFileUrl("Calendar.htc"), false);
        }
        if (AutoPostBack) {
            writer.AddAttribute("dp_autoPostBack", "true", false);
        }
        if (_calendarStyle != null) {
            ⋮
            string s = GetCssFromStyle(_calendarStyle);
            if (s.Length != 0) {
                writer.AddAttribute("dp_calendarStyle", s, false);
            }
        }
        ⋮
    }
}

protected override void RenderContents(HtmlTextWriter writer) {
    ⋮
    bool showPicker = _renderClientScript;
    ⋮
    if (showPicker) {
        string pickerAction;
        if (_renderPopupScript) {
            pickerAction =
                "dp_showDatePickerPopup(this, document.all['" +
                _dateTextBox.ClientID + "'], document.all['" +
                ClientID + "'])";
        }
        else {
            pickerAction =
                "dp_showDatePickerFrame(this, document.all['" +
                _dateTextBox.ClientID + "'], document.all['" +
                ClientID + "'], document.all['" + ClientID +
                "_frame'], document)";
        }
        _pickerImage.Attributes["onclick"] = pickerAction;
        _pickerImage.RenderControl(writer);

        if (_renderPopupScript == false) {
            // Use an IFRAME instead of a DHTML pop-up.
            writer.AddAttribute(HtmlTextWriterAttribute.Id,
                ClientID + "_frame");
```

```
        writer.AddAttribute(HtmlTextWriterAttribute.Src,
            GetClientFileUrl("CalendarFrame.htm"));
        ⋮

        writer.RenderBeginTag(HtmlTextWriterTag.Iframe);
        writer.RenderEndTag();
    }
}
⋮
}
```

In Internet Explorer 4, *DatePicker* uses a floating *<iframe>* to implement the drop-down calendar and month navigation. In Internet Explorer 5.0 and later, the control uses new functionality offered by the browser—DHTML behaviors and DHTML pop-up windows—to implement the same features. On other Web browsers (often referred to as downlevel Web browsers), the control simply provides a text box. *DatePicker* packages its client functionality in a separate script file.

DatePicker overrides the *OnPreRender* method to determine the level of its client script functionality and prepare itself for rendering the HTML needed to implement its client functionality without any additional support from the page developer. When the control's client functionality is enabled, it includes a reference to its associated script file within the page by calling the *RegisterClient-ScriptBlock* method of the *Page* class. The client script is generated only once by the page, even with multiple *DatePicker* controls on the page. Finally, the *DatePicker* delegates its choice for enabling script-based functionality to its contained *RegularExpressionValidator* so that the validator control can perform similar actions in its own *OnPreRender* implementation.

The *DatePicker* examines the capabilities of the requesting Web browser described by the properties of an *HttpBrowserCapabilities* object retrieved from *Page.Request.Browser*. The *DatePicker* checks for the availability of Java-Script 1.2 and DHTML. In addition, *DatePicker* checks for the availability of DHTML behaviors and DHTML pop-up windows by verifying the version of the Web browser.

DatePicker implements an *EnableClientScript* property whose default value is *true*. This allows the page developer to completely turn off the client-side functionality for a specific control instance by disabling the logic it contains to automatically detect the capabilities of the Web browser client.

The *DatePicker* has a number of associated client files—the script include (DatePicker.js), the DHTML behavior (Calendar.htc), the *<iframe>* source (Calendar.htm), and the picker image (Picker.gif). The *GetClientFileUrl* method contains the logic to create URLs of the form */aspnet_client/ mspress_webcontrols/1_0_0_0/DatePicker.js*, which allow access to the client files installed into a shared location (c:\inetpub\wwwroot\aspnet_client) used by ASP.NET server controls.

The final piece of implementation that enables client script functionality is the rendering logic itself. The *DatePicker* renders various expando (or custom) attributes—such as *dp_htcURL*, *dp_autoPostBack*, and *dp_calendarStyle*—that are used by the included client script by overriding the *AddAttributesToRender* method. In its *Render* method override, *DatePicker* renders the image used to implement the picker when its client script functionality is enabled. In addition, the control hooks up DHTML events such as *onclick* to JavaScript functions implemented in the script include, such as *dp_showDatePickerPopup* and *dp_showDatePickerFrame*. Finally, the *DatePicker* uses its *ClientID* property value in calls to the JavaScript functions so that the script functionality can uniquely identify the HTML elements associated with all *DatePicker* controls on the page.

Rendering

We described the rendering process and related methods in Chapter 8, "Rendering." Listing 21-6 illustrates how the *DatePicker* overrides various rendering methods to customize its HTML representation.

```
protected override void AddAttributesToRender(HtmlTextWriter writer) {
    // We do not call the base class AddAttributesToRender
    // because, in the DatePicker, the attributes and styles applied
    // to the control affect the contained TextBox. The DatePicker
    // itself renders out as a <span>, which contains only the ID
    // attribute and any attributes needed for the pop-up calendar and
    // client script.
    writer.AddAttribute(HtmlTextWriterAttribute.Id, ClientID);

    if (_renderClientScript) {
        if (_renderPopupScript) {
            writer.AddAttribute("dp_htcURL",
                GetClientFileUrl("Calendar.htc"), false);
        }
        ⋮
    }
}

protected override void Render(HtmlTextWriter writer) {
    // Ensure that this control is inside a <form runat="server">.
```

Listing 21-6   Overriding the appropriate rendering methods to customize rendering

```
        if (Page != null) {
            Page.VerifyRenderingInServerForm(this);
        }
        base.Render(writer);
    }


    protected override void RenderContents(HtmlTextWriter writer) {
        // Now render the actual text box and picker UI.

        Debug.Assert(_dateTextBox != null);
        Debug.Assert(_pickerImage != null);
        Debug.Assert(_dateValidator != null);

        // First, prepare the text box for rendering by applying this
        // control's style and any attributes onto it.
        // This is done as part of Render, so any changes made to the text
        // box are not persisted in view state. The values are already
        // being held as part of this control's view state, so having the
        // text box also store them would be redundant.
        if (ControlStyleCreated) {
            _dateTextBox.ApplyStyle(ControlStyle);
        }
        _dateTextBox.CopyBaseAttributes(this);
        _dateTextBox.RenderControl(writer);

        bool showPicker = _renderClientScript;
        ⋮
        if (showPicker) {
            ⋮
            _pickerImage.RenderControl(writer);
        }


        ⋮
        if (_dateValidator.Visible) {
            _dateValidator.ErrorMessage = ValidationMessage;
            _dateValidator.RenderControl(writer);
        }
    }
```

Usually each server control renders one top-level HTML tag. For example, the *DatePicker* renders a top-level *<span>* tag, which then contains all rendering associated with the contained controls. The *DatePicker* overrides the *Add-AttributesToRender* method to specify the attributes that are rendered on its top-level tag. At a minimum, each control should render its *ClientID* property value as the *id* attribute of the top-level tag. In addition, the *DatePicker* renders a number of expando attributes (such as *dp_htcURL*) that are used by its associated client script.

The *Render* method that *DatePicker* inherits from *WebControl* is responsible for rendering the begin tag, the contents, and the end tag. *DatePicker* simply reuses that logic. However, *DatePicker* overrides the *Render* method to verify whether the control has been correctly placed within a *<form runat="server">* tag by the page developer. The *DatePicker* depends on form postback and enforces this requirement by making a call to the *VerifyRenderingInServerForm* method of the *Page* class.

Finally, the *DatePicker* overrides the default implementation of *Render-Contents*, which simply renders all the contained children. *DatePicker* overrides this logic to delegate various properties to the appropriate child controls before they are rendered, as well as to optionally render the HTML corresponding to the control's client script functionality.

Events

The *DatePicker* control raises the *DateChanged* event so that the page developer can write server-side code to handle the user's date selection. Raising server-side events that correspond to user actions in the Web browser was discussed in greater detail in Chapter 9, "Control Life Cycle, Events, and Postback." The *DatePicker* control's event implementation is shown in Listing 21-7.

```
private static readonly object EventDateChanged = new object();
public event EventHandler DateChanged {
    add {
        Events.AddHandler(EventDateChanged, value);
    }
    remove {
        Events.RemoveHandler(EventDateChanged, value);
    }
}

protected override void CreateChildControls() {
    _dateTextBox = new TextBox();
    ⋮
    _dateTextBox.TextChanged +=
        new EventHandler(this.dateTextBox_TextChanged);
    ⋮
}

protected virtual void OnDateChanged(EventArgs e) {
    EventHandler handler = (EventHandler)Events[EventDateChanged];
```

Listing 21-7   Handling and raising events

```
        if (handler != null) {
            handler(this, e);
        }
    }


    private void dateTextBox_TextChanged(object sender, EventArgs e) {
        // Handles the TextChanged event of the contained TextBox.

        try {
            string text = _dateTextBox.Text.Trim();
            DateTime date =
                DateTime.Parse(text, CultureInfo.InvariantCulture);

            // Determines whether the selected date has changed.
            if ((IsDateSelected == false) || !(date.Equals(SelectedDate))) {
                SelectedDate = date;
                OnDateChanged(EventArgs.Empty);
            }
        }
        catch {
            // A bad date was entered - remove it from the ViewState, which
            // effectively sets SelectedDate back to the current date
            // and IsDateSelected to false.
            ViewState.Remove("SelectedDate");
        }
    }
```

DatePicker defines the *DateChanged* event that signals that the date entered in the text box has changed. However, *DatePicker* does not implement its event from scratch by implementing *IPostBackDataHandler* or by performing any postback processing. Rather, this control bases its event implementation on the *TextChanged* event of its contained *TextBox*. In its *CreateChildControls* implementation, the *DatePicker* control wires up its *dateTextBox_TextChanged* method as the event handler for the *TextChanged* event of its contained *TextBox*. Thus, the *DatePicker* implementation reuses the existing server-side event functionality provided by an existing control. In its event handler implementation, the *DatePicker* creates an instance of a *DateTime* object by parsing the *TextBox* control's text, detects whether the selected date has changed, and then proceeds to raise its own *DateChanged* event by calling the *OnDateChanged* method.

Validation

The *DatePicker* control performs validation by containing a *RegularExpression-Validator* and, in addition, supports the ASP.NET validation framework by providing a validation property. Validation was discussed in Chapter 14, "Validator Controls." Listing 21-8 demonstrates using and supporting validation.

```
[
ValidationProperty("SelectedDateText")
]
public class DatePicker : WebControl, INamingContainer {

    [
    Browsable(false),
    DesignerSerializationVisibility(
        DesignerSerializationVisibility.Hidden),
    EditorBrowsable(EditorBrowsableState.Never)
    ]
    public string SelectedDateText {
        get {
            if (IsDateSelected) {
                return String.Format(CultureInfo.InvariantCulture,
                    "{0:d}", new object[] { SelectedDate });
            }
            return String.Empty;
        }
    }


    protected override void CreateChildControls() {
        _dateTextBox = new TextBox();
        _dateValidator = new RegularExpressionValidator();

        _dateTextBox.ID = "dateTextBox";
        ⋮

        _dateValidator.ControlToValidate = "dateTextBox";
        _dateValidator.ValidationExpression =
            "^\\s*(\\d{1,2})([-./]" +
            ")(\\d{1,2})\\2(((\\d{4})|(\\d{2}))\\s*$";
        _dateValidator.Display = ValidatorDisplay.Dynamic;
    }
}
```

Listing 21-8   Using and supporting validation

As mentioned, the *DatePicker* control contains an instance of the *Regular-ExpressionValidator* control. *DatePicker* associates this control with the contained

TextBox instance to enforce that date entries made by the user appear in either the dd/mm/yyyy or the dd/mm/yy format.

The *DatePicker* participates in the ASP.NET server-side validation framework by providing the *SelectedDateText* property for validation by using the *ValidationProperty* attribute on the class. The control also participates in the client-side validation framework. A validator control that is hooked up to the *DatePicker* control is essentially hooked up to the *<span>* tag rendered by the control. The client-side validation framework automatically detects and hooks up all the *<input>* elements within a *<span>* tag, and thus the contents of the *<input type="text">* element rendered by the contained *TextBox* control are automatically validated.

Design-Time Attributes

The *DatePicker* implementation uses various design-time attributes to offer metadata for its class, properties, and events to enhance the design-time experience of the control on a visual design surface. We present these designer attributes in Appendix A, "Metadata Attributes."

Listing 21-9 shows a sampling of design-time attributes used in the *DatePicker* implementation and in ASP.NET server controls.

```
[
DefaultEvent("DateChanged"),
DefaultProperty("SelectedDate"),
Designer(typeof(MSPress.WebControls.Design.DatePickerDesigner),
    typeof(IDesigner))
]
public class DatePicker : WebControl, INamingContainer {

    [
    Category("Style"),
    Description("The style used to customize the popup calendar."),
    DesignerSerializationVisibility(
        DesignerSerializationVisibility.Content),
    NotifyParentProperty(true),
    PersistenceMode(PersistenceMode.InnerProperty)
    ]
    public virtual TableStyle CalendarStyle {
        ⋮
    }
```

Listing 21-9   Designer attributes on the class, properties, and events   *(continued)*

Listing 21-9 *(continued)*

```
    [
    Category("Behavior"),
    DefaultValue(true),
    Description(
        "Whether to enable the client script based functionality."),
    ]
    public bool EnableClientScript {
        ⋮
    }


    [
    Browsable(false),
    DesignerSerializationVisibility(
        DesignerSerializationVisibility.Hidden)
    ]
    public virtual bool IsDateSelected {
        ⋮
    }


    [
    Category("Change"),
    Description("Raised when the user selects a new date.")
    ]
    public event EventHandler DateChanged {
        ⋮
    }
}
```

The following list describes the effects of the metadata attributes used by *DatePicker*:

■   The *DefaultEvent* attribute on the class allows the designer to create and wire up an event handler when the control is double-clicked on the design surface.

■   The *DefaultProperty* attribute specifies the property that should be highlighted in the designer's property browser when the control is selected.

■   The *Designer* attribute associates a designer class specific to the control, as described in the following section.

■   The *Category* attribute on properties and events allows the property browser to categorize properties and events into logical groupings.

■   The *Description* attribute on properties and events allows the property browser to provide short help text for each property and event.

- The *DesignerSerializationVisibility* and *PersistenceMode* attributes are used to specify whether and how a property is persisted into the .aspx file.

- The *DefaultValue* attribute allows the property browser to emphasize properties that have been changed from their default state and enables the control persister to determine which properties need to be persisted into the .aspx file.

- The *Browsable* attribute is used to specify whether a property is made visible in the designer's property browser.

Designer Implementation

The *DatePicker* control has an associated designer that allows the control to cleanly separate design time–specific functionality from the runtime control implementation and provide this functionality through a different class used only at design time. We discussed control designers in Chapter 15.

Listing 21-10 illustrates the implementation of a simple control designer for the *DatePicker* control.

```
namespace MSPress.WebControls.Design {
    ⋮
    public class DatePickerDesigner : ControlDesigner {
        private static string ClientFilePathPrefix;
        ⋮

        public override string GetDesignTimeHtml() {
            // The designer can assume knowledge of the runtime control
            // because they go hand in hand. Therefore, the DatePicker
            // designer can index into the Controls collection.

            ControlCollection childControls =
                (DatePicker)Component).Controls;
            Debug.Assert(childControls.Count == 3);
            Debug.Assert(childControls[1] is Image);
            Debug.Assert(childControls[2] is
                RegularExpressionValidator);

            // Changing the URL of the picker image to the file
            // location is specific to the designer; thus, it is
            // done here.
```

Listing 21-10 Implementation of the designer   *(continued)*

Listing 21-10 *(continued)*

```
            Image pickerImage = (Image)childControls[1];
            pickerImage.ImageUrl =
                "file:///" + GetClientFilePath("Picker.gif");

            // The validator should not show up in design view; thus,
            // for design-time scenarios, its visibility is set to
            // false.
            RegularExpressionValidator validator =
                (RegularExpressionValidator)childControls[2];
            validator.Visible = false;

            return base.GetDesignTimeHtml();
        }


        public override void Initialize(IComponent component) {
            // Check correct usage of the designer - in other words,
            // that it has been associated with the right type of
            // runtime control - so that all the assumptions a designer
            // makes will hold.
            if (!(component is DatePicker)) {
                throw new ArgumentException(
                    "Component must be a DatePicker", "component");
            }
            base.Initialize(component);
        }
    }
}
```

The *DatePickerDesigner* follows the general guidelines related to designers and is implemented in a *Design* subnamespace of the *MSPress.WebControls* namespace that contains the control. Furthermore, the designer class is named by appending the word *Designer* to the control's class name.

The *DatePickerDesigner* overrides the *Initialize* method from the *Control-Designer* class to verify that the component it is being associated with is an instance of a *DatePicker*. This check allows the designer implementation to safely make assumptions about the runtime control it is associated with.

The *DatePickerDesigner* overrides the *GetDesignTimeHtml* method from the *ControlDesigner* class to customize the runtime control before it is rendered to produce HTML that is shown on a visual design surface. In particular, the designer hides the *RegularExpressionValidator* contained inside the *DatePicker*. The designer also resets the *ImageUrl* property of the *Image* control contained inside the *DatePicker* with a *file:///*-based URL. The designer makes this setting so that the image can be successfully loaded by the design surface and the control provides a WYSIWYG experience.

The *DatePickerDesigner* also retrieves the *Controls* collection of its associated runtime control. All designers associated with composite controls should do this. As shown in Listing 21-2, the *DatePicker* overrides its *Controls* property to ensure a valid *Controls* collection. The designer calls this property, which ensures a valid collection of controls that is then rendered to produce a non-empty design-time appearance. Figure 21-5 shows the *DatePicker* control used in the Web Forms designer.

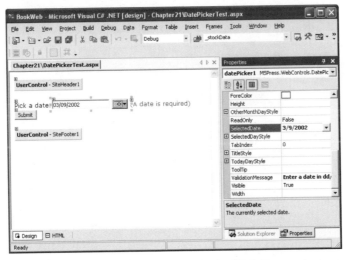

Figure 21-5   The *DatePicker* used in the Web Forms designer inside Visual Studio .NET

Summary

The *DatePicker* control provides an intuitive date-entry UI and programming model that automatically utilizes the capabilities of the Web browser client, without requiring its users to understand its client script functionality. *DatePicker* is an example of a real-world server control that might be a useful addition to the server controls toolbox of a page developer or page designer. You can enhance the *DatePicker* implementation shown in this chapter by adding support for localized calendars if a particular Web application has a globalization requirement.

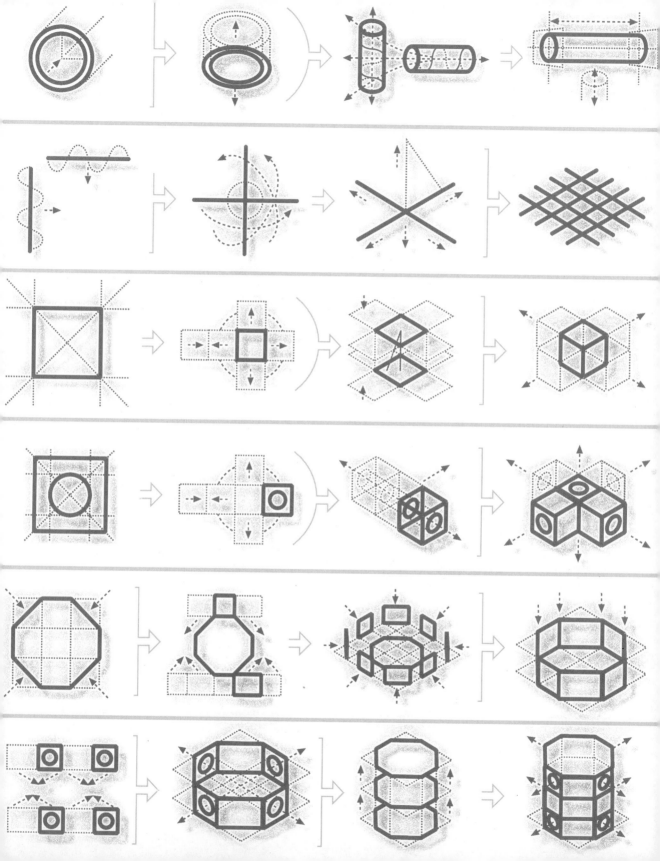

Part VI

Appendixes

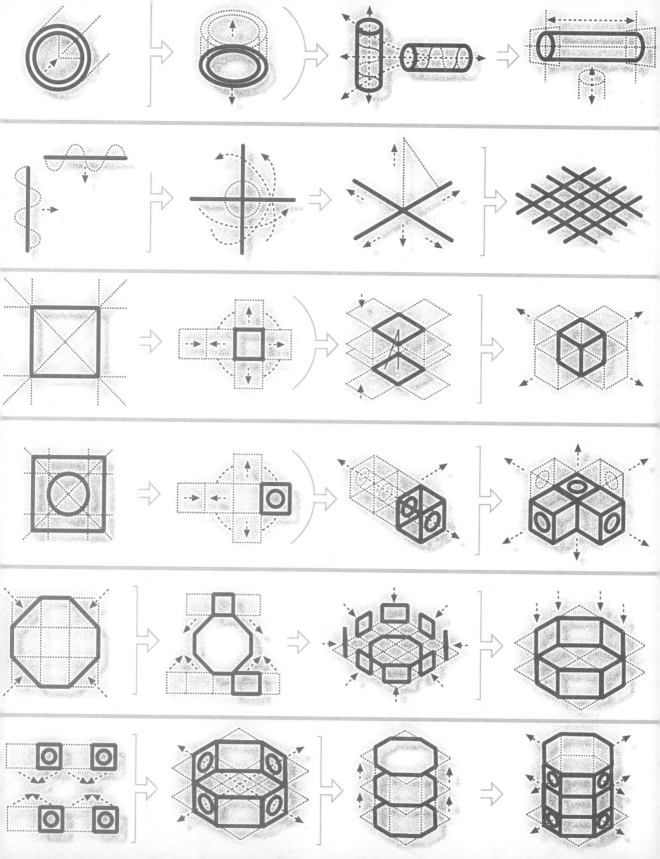

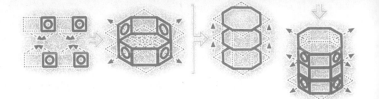

Appendix A

Metadata Attributes

This appendix describes the set of metadata attributes that are commonly applied to server controls. The attributes are listed under two broad categories:

■ Design-time attributes

■ Parse-time attributes

Design-Time Attributes

Your control does not require design-time attributes to function in a page. However, design-time attributes are essential for your control to function properly in a visual designer. The designer, the property browser, and other design-time elements use the metadata supplied by design-time attributes for the following purposes:

■ To display properties and events

■ To perform design-time serialization

■ To associate classes that implement design-time functionality with a control or with a property type

In the following subsections, we'll group design-time attributes according to their functionality.

Attributes for Displaying Properties and Events

The following attributes are used to display properties and events at design time.

Table A-1   *System.ComponentModel.BindableAttribute*

Summary	Tells the property browser whether it is meaningful to bind data to the property. Properties marked with *Bindable(true)* are displayed in the DataBinding dialog box that can be launched from the property browser and used by the page developer to associate data-binding expressions with properties.
Applied to	Properties only
Sample usage	*[Bindable(true)]*
Parameter type	*Boolean*
Default value	*false*
Example	The *ContactInfo* control in Listing 12-7
Remarks	If a property is not marked with *Bindable(true)*, a page developer can still associate a data-binding expression with the property by manually entering the expression in the .aspx page.

Table A-2   *System.ComponentModel.BrowsableAttribute*

Summary	Tells the property browser whether to display the property or event in the property browser.
Applied to	Properties and events
Sample usage	*[Browsable(false)]*
Parameter type	*Boolean*
Default value	*true*
Example	The *PageTracker* control in Listing 7-4
Remarks	The property browser displays all public properties and events by default. Apply this attribute only if you want to override the default behavior.

Table A-3   *System.ComponentModel.CategoryAttribute*

Summary	Provides a category name under which to display the property or event. This attribute enables the property browser to display properties and events in logical groupings.
Applied to	Properties and events
Sample usage	*[Category("Behavior")]*
Parameter type	*String*
Default value	"Default"

Table A-3   *System.ComponentModel.CategoryAttribute*   *(continued)*

Example	The *PageTracker* control in Listing 7-4
Remarks	This attribute can be localized, as described in Chapter 17, "Localization, Licensing, and Other Miscellany."

Table A-4   *System.ComponentModel.DefaultEventAttribute*

Summary	Tells the property browser which control event is its default event. This allows the page developer to write event-handling code for the default event by double-clicking the control on the design surface.
Applied to	Events only
Sample usage	*[DefaultEvent("Click")]*
Parameter type	*String*
Default value	None
Example	The *SimpleButton* control in Listing 9-3

Table A-5   *System.ComponentModel.DefaultPropertyAttribute*

Summary	Tells the property browser which control property is its default property. When the page developer selects the control on the design surface, the property browser highlights that property.
Applied to	Properties only
Sample usage	*[DefaultProperty("TrackingMode")]*
Parameter type	*String*
Default value	None
Example	The *PageTracker* control in Listing 7-4

Table A-6   *System.ComponentModel.DescriptionAttribute*

Summary	Provides a brief description, which the property browser displays when the user selects the property or event.
Applied to	Properties and events
Sample usage	*[Description("The type of tracking to perform")]*
Parameter type	*String*
Default value	None
Example	The *PageTracker* control in Listing 7-4
Remarks	This attribute can be localized, as described in Chapter 17.

Table A-7   *System.ComponentModel.EditorBrowsableAttribute*

Summary	Tells the code editor whether to display IntelliSense support for a property, method, or event.
Applied to	Properties, methods, and events
Sample usage	*[EditorBrowsable(EditorBrowsableState.Never)]*
Parameter type	An *EditorBrowsableState* enumeration that has the following values:
	Advanced Browsable only when the developer wants to view advanced members. This setting is used by the Microsoft Visual Basic .NET code editor.
	Always Always browsable in the code editor.
	Never Never browsable in the code editor.
Default value	*EditorBrowsableState.Always*
Example	The *HitTracker* control in Listing 9-13
Remarks	The code editor displays IntelliSense support by default. Apply this attribute only if you want to override the default behavior.

Attributes for Design-Time Serialization

These attributes tell the designer how to serialize the control and its properties. Serialization is the process of generating HTML in the page corresponding to the changes in the Design view.

Table A-8   *System.ComponentModel.DefaultValueAttribute*

Summary	Provides a default value for the property.
Applied to	Properties
Sample usage	*[DefaultValue(BorderStyle.NotSet)]*
Parameter type	Any primitive type, enumeration, or string literal. See this attribute's remarks to provide a default value for a complex property.
Default value	None
Example	The *LoginUI* control in Listing 8-6
Remarks	You can provide a default value for a complex property if the property type has an associated type converter. In that case, you must use the two-parameter form of the attribute, in which the first parameter specifies the type of the property and the second specifies a string representation of the value—for example,
	[DefaultValue(typeof(Color), "Black")].

Table A-9   *System.ComponentModel.DesignerSerializationVisibilityAttribute*

Summary	Tells the designer whether to serialize the property or the contents of the property. A complex property has contents—that is, subproperties or collection items.
Applied to	Properties
Sample usage	*[DesignerSerializationVisibility(DesignerSerializationVisibility.Content)]*
Parameter type	The *DesignerSerializationVisibility* enumeration that has the following values: *Content* Causes the contents of the property (such as its subproperties or collection items) to be serialized. *Hidden* Hides the property from the serialization mechanism. *Visible* Serializes the value of the property.
Default value	*DesignerSerializationVisibility.Visible*
Example	The *MapDemo* control in Listing 10-6
Remarks	By default, the code generator serializes the value of the property. This attribute allows you either to override the default behavior and exclude a property from the serialization mechanism, or to serialize the contents of the property (such as its subproperties or collection items) instead of the property itself.

Table A-10   *System.ComponentModel.NotifyParentPropertyAttribute*

Summary	Tells the property browser to bubble change notifications from a subproperty to the parent property or to the control.
Applied to	Complex properties and their subproperties
Sample usage	*[NotifyParentProperty(true)]*
Parameter type	*Boolean*
Default value	*false*
Example	The *MapDemo* control in Listing 10-6

Table A-11   *System.Web.UI.PersistChildrenAttribute*

Summary	Tells the designer whether the nested content within the control's tags corresponds to child controls or to properties.
Applied to	Controls
Sample usage	*[PersistChildren(false)]*

(continued)

Table A-11   *System.Web.UI.PersistChildrenAttribute*   *(continued)*

Parameter type	*Boolean*
Default value	A value of *true* implies that the nested content corresponds to children.
Remarks	*WebControl* is marked with *PersistChildren(false)*. If your control derives from *WebControl*, you need to reapply this attribute only if you are implementing a control whose nested content corresponds to child controls.

Table A-12   *System.Web.UI.PersistenceModeAttribute*

Summary	Tells the designer whether to persist a property on the control's tag or as a nested property.
Applied to	Properties
Sample usage	*[PersistenceMode(PersistenceMode.InnerProperty)]*
Parameter type	The *PersistenceMode* enumeration that has the following values:
	Attribute Causes the property to be persisted as an attribute on the control's tag.
	EncodedInnerDefaultProperty Causes the property to be persisted as the only content within the control's tags. The content is HTML encoded.
	InnerDefaultProperty Causes the property to be persisted as the only content within the control's tags.
	InnerProperty Causes the property to be persisted, along with any other properties of the control, as nested content within the control's tags.
Default value	*PersistenceMode.Attribute*
Example	The *MapDemo* control in Listing 10-6

Table A-13   *System.Web.UI.TagPrefixAttribute*

Summary	Tells the designer to generate a *Register* directive that maps a tag prefix to a namespace and an assembly. The directive is generated in the .aspx page when the page developer drags the control from the toolbox onto the design surface.
Applied to	Assemblies that contain server controls
Sample usage	*[assembly:TagPrefix("MSPress.ServerControls", "msp")]*
Parameters	The first parameter specifies the namespace name, and the second parameter allows y0ou to specify a tag prefix (analogous to *asp*) for the controls in your assembly.

Table A-13 *System.Web.UI.TagPrefixAttribute*   *(continued)*

Example	The "Applying *TagPrefixAttribute*" section in Chapter 5, "Developing a Simple Custom Control."
Remarks	The *Register* directive is generated only if the page developer drags the control from the toolbox onto the design surface. The directive is not generated if the page developer manually adds the HTML for the control to the page.

Attributes for Associating Classes That Provide Advanced Design-Time Functionality

These attributes enable you to associate classes that provide advanced design-time functionality with your control.

Table A-14 *System.ComponentModel.DesignerAttribute*

Summary	Associates a designer with a control.
Applied to	Controls
Sample usage	*[Designer(typeof(ScrollablePanelDesigner)]*
Example	The *ScrollablePanel* control in Listing 15-4
Remarks	The example shows an early-bound type reference to the designer. Chapter 15, "Design-Time Functionality," describes the syntax for a late-bound type reference, which is needed when the designer and the control reside in different assemblies.

Table A-15 *System.ComponentModel.EditorAttribute*

Summary	Associates a UI type editor with a type or a property. Also associates a component editor with a control.
Applied to	Classes or properties
Sample usage	*[Editor(typeof(MSPress.ServerControls.Design.StringEditor), typeof(UITypeEditor))]* or *[Editor(typeof(MSPress.ServerControls.Design.MyLabelComponent-Editor), typeof(ComponentEditor))]*
Example	The *MyLabel* control in Listing 15-6
Remarks	The first argument is the type of the editor, and the second is the base type of the editor. The example shows an early-bound type reference to an editor. Chapter 15 describes the syntax for a late-bound type reference, which is needed when the editor and the type (or control) reside in different assemblies.

Table A-16   *System.ComponentModel.TypeConverterAttribute*

Summary	Associates a type converter with a type or a property.
Applied to	Classes and properties
Sample usage	*[TypeConverter(typeof(MapCircleConverter))]*
Example	The *MapCircle* type in Listing 10-5
Remarks	The example shows an early-bound type reference to a type converter. Chapter 15 describes the syntax for a late-bound type reference, which is needed when the type converter and the type (or control) reside in different assemblies.

Parse-Time Attributes

These attributes are used by the page parser to parse the syntax of an .aspx page and generate code for the class that corresponds to the page.

Table A-17   *System.Web.UI.ControlBuilderAttribute*

Summary	Associates a custom control builder with a control.
Applied to	Controls
Sample usage	*[ControlBuilder(typeof(InnerTextLabelControlBuilder))]*
Example	The *InnerTextLabel* control in Listing 12-10
Remarks	The *ControlBuilder* class is associated with the base *Control* class and thus with every server control. Apply *ControlBuilderAttribute* only if you want to associate a custom control builder with your control.

Table A-18   *System.Web.UI.ParseChildrenAttribute*

Summary	Informs the parser whether to interpret the nested content within a control's tag as properties or as child controls.
Applied to	Controls
Sample usage	*[ParseChildren(true)]*
	or
	[ParseChildren(true, "HotSpots")]

Table A-18 *System.Web.UI.ParseChildrenAttribute* *(continued)*

Example	The *ImageMap* control in Listing 10-13
Remarks	The constructor takes in a Boolean value that indicates whether the parser should parse nested content as properties. *Control* is not marked with this attribute, which implies that the parser treats nested content as child controls. *WebControl* is marked with *Parse-Children(true)*. Therefore, the parser treats nested content as properties. You can override the parsing logic associated with the base class by reapplying this attribute to your control.
	The two-parameter form of this attribute takes in a property name as its second argument. When the two-parameter form is used, the nested content within the control's tags must correspond to the property specified in the second argument.

Table A-19 *System.Web.UI.TemplateContainerAttribute*

Summary	Informs the parser of the type of the container control of an *ITemplate* property. The parser uses this type as the exact type of the *Container* in data-binding expressions.
Applied to	Properties of type *ITemplate*
Sample usage	*[TemplateContainer(typeof(ContactPanel)]*
Example	The *ContactInfo* control in Listing 12-7

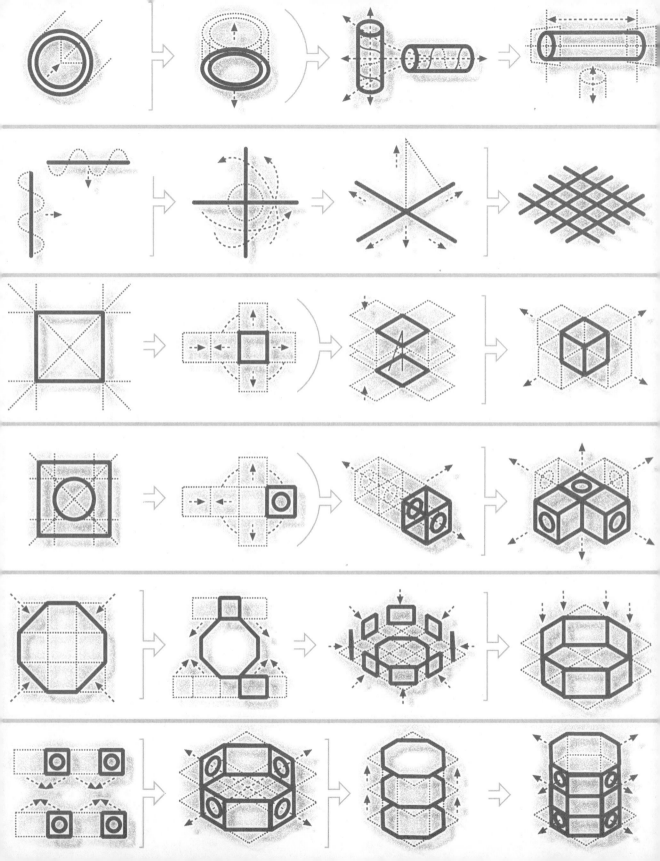

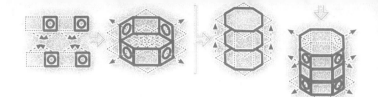

Appendix B

Object Model for Common Classes

This appendix lists the public and protected members of the core classes related to control authoring.

```
System.Web.UI.Control
public class Control : IComponent, IParserAccessor {
    public Control();

    // Reference to parent controls in the control tree
    public virtual Page Page { get; set; }
    public virtual Control Parent { get; }
    public Control BindingContainer { get; }
    public virtual Control NamingContainer { get; }

    // Identification within the control tree
    public virtual string ClientID { get; }
    public virtual string ID { get; set; }
    public virtual string UniqueID { get; }

    // References to child controls in the control tree
    protected bool ChildControlsCreated { get; set; }
    public virtual ControlCollection Controls { get; }
    protected virtual void CreateChildControls();
    protected virtual ControlCollection CreateControlCollection();
    protected virtual void EnsureChildControls();
    public virtual bool HasControls();
    public virtual Control FindControl(string id);
    protected virtual void AddParsedSubObject(object obj);

    // State management
    public virtual bool EnableViewState { get; set; }
    protected bool HasChildViewState { get; }
    protected bool IsTrackingViewState { get; }
```

(continued)

System.Web.UI.Control   *(continued)*

```
       protected virtual StateBag ViewState { get; }
       protected void ClearChildViewState();
       protected virtual void LoadViewState(object savedState);
       protected virtual object SaveViewState();
       protected virtual void TrackViewState();

       // Visibility and rendering
       public virtual bool Visible { get; set; }
       protected virtual void Render(HtmlTextWriter writer);
       protected virtual void RenderChildren(HtmlTextWriter writer);
       public void RenderControl(HtmlTextWriter writer);

       // Data-binding support
       public virtual void DataBind();

       // IComponent related
       public ISite Site { get; set; }
       public virtual void Dispose();

       // Utility API
       protected virtual HttpContext Context { get; }
       protected string MapPathSecure(string virtualPath);
       public virtual string TemplateSourceDirectory { get; }
       public string ResolveUrl(string relativeUrl);

       // Events
       public event EventHandler DataBinding;
       public event EventHandler Disposed;
       public event EventHandler Init;
       public event EventHandler Load;
       public event EventHandler PreRender;
       public event EventHandler Unload;

       protected virtual void OnDataBinding(EventArgs e);
       protected virtual void OnInit(EventArgs e);
       protected virtual void OnLoad(EventArgs e);
       protected virtual void OnPreRender(EventArgs e);
       protected virtual void OnUnload(EventArgs e);

       protected EventHandlerList Events { get; }

       protected virtual bool OnBubbleEvent(object source, EventArgs args);
       protected void RaiseBubbleEvent(object source, EventArgs args);
}
```

System.Web.UI.WebControls.WebControl

```
public class WebControl : Control, IAttributeAccessor {
    protected WebControl();
    public WebControl(HtmlTextWriterTag tag);
    protected WebControl(string tag);

    // Style properties and methods
    public virtual Color ForeColor { get; set; }
    public virtual Color BackColor { get; set; }
    public virtual FontInfo Font { get; }
    public virtual BorderStyle BorderStyle { get; set; }
    public virtual Color BorderColor { get; set; }
    public virtual Unit BorderWidth { get; set; }
    public virtual Unit Width { get; set; }
    public virtual Unit Height { get; set; }
    public virtual string CssClass { get; set; }
    public bool ControlStyleCreated { get; }
    public Style ControlStyle { get; }
    public CssStyleCollection Style { get; }
    protected virtual Style CreateControlStyle();
    public void ApplyStyle(Style s);
    public void MergeStyle(Style s);

    // Non-style related properties
    public AttributeCollection Attributes { get; }
    public virtual string AccessKey { get; set; }
    public virtual bool Enabled { get; set; }
    public virtual short TabIndex { get; set; }
    public virtual string ToolTip { get; set; }
    public void CopyBaseAttributes(WebControl controlSrc);

    // Rendering
    protected virtual HtmlTextWriterTag TagKey { get; }
    protected virtual string TagName { get; }
    protected virtual void RenderContents(HtmlTextWriter writer);
    public virtual void RenderBeginTag(HtmlTextWriter writer);
    public virtual void RenderEndTag(HtmlTextWriter writer);
    protected virtual void AddAttributesToRender(HtmlTextWriter writer);
}
```

System.Web.UI.WebControls.Style

```
public class Style : Component, IStateManager {
    public Style();
    public Style(StateBag bag);

    // Basic style properties
    public Color ForeColor { get; set; }
    public Color BackColor { get; set; }
    public FontInfo Font { get; }
    public BorderStyle BorderStyle { get; set; }
    public Color BorderColor { get; set; }
    public Unit BorderWidth { get; set; }
    public Unit Width { get; set; }
    public Unit Height { get; set; }
    public string CssClass { get; set; }

    // Style operations
    public virtual void CopyFrom(Style s);
    public virtual void MergeWith(Style s);
    public virtual void Reset();

    // State management
    protected bool IsTrackingViewState { get; }

    // Rendering related
    public void AddAttributesToRender(HtmlTextWriter writer);
    public virtual void AddAttributesToRender(HtmlTextWriter writer,
        WebControl owner);
}
```

System.Web.UI.WebControls.FontInfo

```
public sealed class FontInfo {
    // Basic properties
    public string Name { get; set; }
    public string[] Names { get; set; }
    public FontUnit Size { get; set; }
    public bool Bold { get; set; }
    public bool Italic { get; set; }
    public bool Underline { get; set; }
    public bool Strikeout { get; set; }
    public bool Overline { get; set; }

    // Style operations related
    public void CopyFrom(FontInfo f);
    public void MergeWith(FontInfo f);
}
```

System.Web.UI.IStateManager

```
public interface IStateManager {
    public bool IsTrackingViewState { get; }
    public void LoadViewState(object state);
    public object SaveViewState();
    public void TrackViewState();
}
```

System.Web.UI.IPostBackDataHandler

```
public interface IPostBackDataHandler {
    public bool LoadPostData(string postDataKey,
        NameValueCollection postCollection);
    public void RaisePostDataChangedEvent();
}
```

System.Web.UI.IPostBackEventHandler

```
public interface IPostBackEventHandler {
    public void RaisePostBackEvent(string eventArgument);
}
```

System.Web.UI.Page

```
public abstract class TemplateControl : Control, INamingContainer {
    protected TemplateControl();

    public Control LoadControl(string virtualPath);
    public ITemplate LoadTemplate(string virtualPath);
    public Control ParseControl(string content);
}

public class Page : TemplateControl, IHttpHandler {
    public Page();

    // Postback related
    public bool IsPostBack { get; }
    public bool SmartNavigation { get; set; }
    protected virtual NameValueCollection DeterminePostBackMode();
    protected virtual void RaisePostBackEvent(
        IPostBackEventHandler sourceControl,
        string eventArgument);
    public void RegisterRequiresPostBack(Control control);
    public virtual void VerifyRenderingInServerForm(Control control);

    // Rendering related
    public string ClientTarget { get; set; }
```

(continued)

System.Web.UI.Page   *(continued)*

```
protected string ContentType { set; }
protected virtual HtmlTextWriter CreateHtmlTextWriter(
    TextWriter tw);

// Client-script related
public string GetPostBackClientEvent(Control control,
    string argument);
public string GetPostBackClientHyperlink(Control control,
    string argument);
public string GetPostBackEventReference(Control control);
public string GetPostBackEventReference(Control control,
    string argument);
public bool IsClientScriptBlockRegistered(string key);
public bool IsStartupScriptRegistered(string key);
public void RegisterArrayDeclaration(string arrayName,
    string arrayValue);
public virtual void RegisterClientScriptBlock(string key,
    string script);
public virtual void RegisterHiddenField(string hiddenFieldName,
    string hiddenFieldInitialValue);

// State management
protected bool EnableViewStateMac { get; set; }
protected virtual object LoadPageStateFromPersistenceMedium();
protected virtual void SavePageStateToPersistenceMedium(
    object viewState);

public void RegisterOnSubmitStatement(string key, string script);
public virtual void RegisterRequiresRaiseEvent(
    IPostBackEventHandler control);
public virtual void RegisterStartupScript(string key,
    string script);

// Globalization
protected int CodePage { set; }
protected string Culture { set; }
protected string UICulture { set; }
protected int LCID { set; }

// Validation
public bool IsValid { get; }
public ValidatorCollection Validators { get; }
public virtual void Validate();

// IHttpHandler implementation
public bool IsReusable { get; }
public void ProcessRequest(HttpContext context);
```

```
    // Page-intrinsic objects
    public HttpApplicationState Application { get; }
    public Cache Cache { get; }
    public HttpRequest Request { get; }
    public HttpResponse Response { get; }
    protected string ResponseEncoding { set; }
    public HttpServerUtility Server { get; }
    public virtual HttpSessionState Session { get; }

    // Tracing
    public TraceContext Trace { get; }
    protected bool TraceEnabled { set; }
    protected TraceMode TraceModeValue { set; }

    // Miscellaneous
    public string MapPath(string virtualPath);
    protected int TransactionMode { set; }
    public IPrincipal User { get; }
    public string ErrorPage { get; set; }
}
```

System.Web.UI.Design.ControlDesigner

```
public class HtmlControlDesigner : ComponentDesigner {
    public HtmlControlDesigner();

    public IHtmlControlDesignerBehavior Behavior { get; set; }

    public DataBindingCollection DataBindings { get; }
    protected virtual void OnBindingsCollectionChanged(string propName);
}

public class ControlDesigner : HtmlControlDesigner {
    public ControlDesigner();

    // Design-time HTML related
    public virtual bool DesignTimeHtmlRequiresLoadComplete { get; }
    public virtual string GetDesignTimeHtml();
    protected virtual string GetEmptyDesignTimeHtml();
    protected virtual string GetErrorDesignTimeHtml(Exception e);
    protected string CreatePlaceHolderDesignTimeHtml();
    protected string CreatePlaceHolderDesignTimeHtml(
        string instruction);
    public virtual void UpdateDesignTimeHtml();

    // Persistence related
    public virtual string GetPersistInnerHtml();
```

(continued)

System.Web.UI.Design.ControlDesigner *(continued)*

```
    public virtual void OnComponentChanged(object sender,
        ComponentChangedEventArgs ce);

    public virtual bool AllowResize { get; }
    protected object DesignTimeElementView { get; }
}
```

Using C# Documentation Comments

C# supports documentation comments for classes and class members. The comments use an XML syntax that allows you to generate reference documentation for your classes. The C# Programmer's Reference in MSDN contains a detailed listing of the documentation tags. The following code fragment provides an example of this feature.

```
/// <summary>
/// A data-bound templated control that generates a columnar, scrollable
/// scrollable representation of the data in a data source.
/// </summary>
public class ListView : WebControl {
    /// <summary>
    /// Gets or sets the value containing the list of values to be
    /// rendered.
    /// </summary>
    public object DataSource { get; set; }

    /// <summary>
    /// Creates the control tree used to generate the visual
    /// representation of data in the control's data source.
    /// </summary>
    /// <param name="useDataSource">
    /// Whether the hierarchy should be created from the data source
    /// or if it should be recreated using view state.
    /// </param>
    protected virtual void CreateControlHierarchy(bool useDataSource)
        { ... }
}
```

You can use the */doc* option of the C# compiler to generate an XML file that consists of all the documentation comments you have added for any types in your assembly. For example, the command used to build an assembly and its associated documentation is

```
csc /t:library /out:MyControls.dll
    /r:System.dll /r:System.Web.dll /r:System.Drawing.dll
    /r:System.Design.dll
    /doc:MyControls.xml *.cs
```

The XML documentation can be used to generate help content in HTML format using an .xsl file that transforms the XML documentation comments syntax into HTML markup. An example .xsl file is included in this book's sample files to demonstrate this.

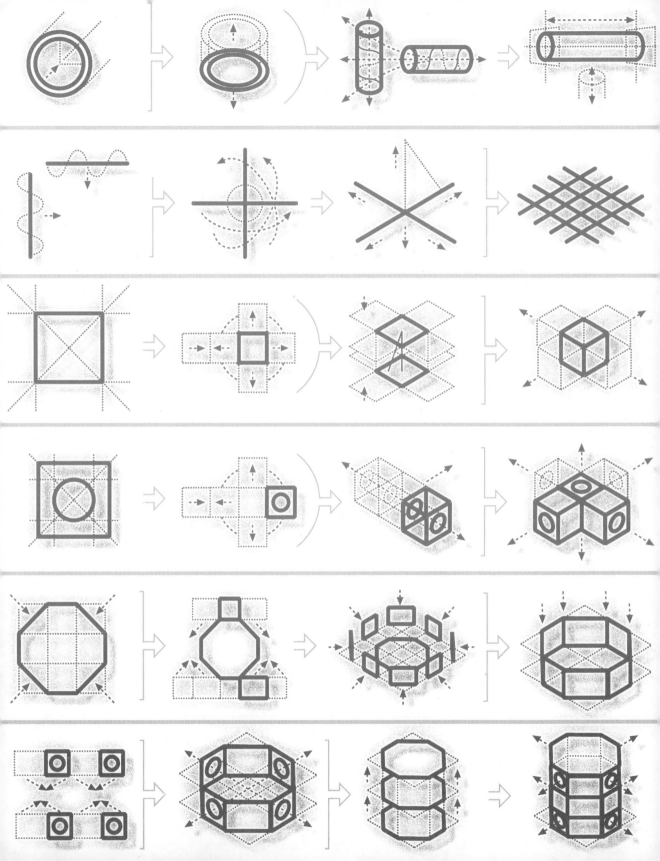

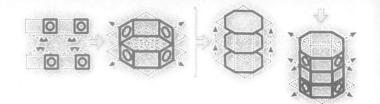

Appendix C

Microsoft ASP.NET Web Matrix

ASP.NET Web Matrix is a simple, lightweight development environment for building ASP.NET Web applications quickly and easily. Web Matrix was developed by a small group of people on the ASP.NET team at Microsoft in an attempt to reach out to the Web development community and experiment with new ideas and thoughts in the realm of Web development tools. Web Matrix is completely implemented in managed code by using C# and various technologies available in the .NET Framework.

Web Matrix contains a number of features that provide a rich design experience for creating Web Forms pages, user controls, and XML Web services. These features are described in the "Web Matrix Features" section of this appendix. Figure C-1 shows the Web Matrix development environment in Design view, and Figure C-2 shows this development environment in Code view when you work on an .aspx file.

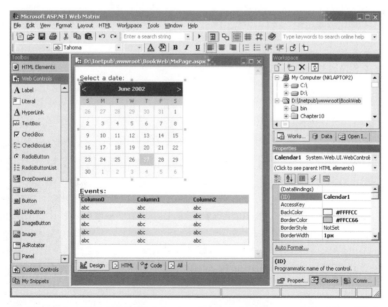

Figure C-1 The Web Matrix development environment with a Web Forms page in Design view

653

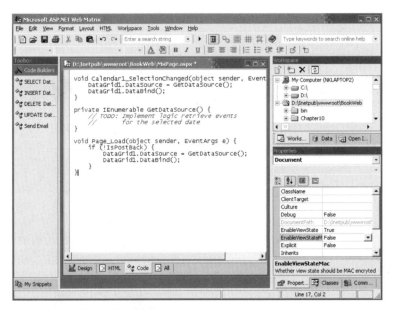

Figure C-2   The Web Matrix development environment with a Web Forms page in Code view

As of this writing, the Technology Preview release of Web Matrix (version 0.5) is available as a small (just over 1 MB), free download from *http://www.asp.net/webmatrix*. You'll find additional information about the product and information about future updates at the same URL.

Web Matrix Features

Web Matrix is an easy-to-use tool that provides a simple approach to building ASP.NET Web applications. Its core features include the following:

■ **Page designer**   Allows you to rapidly create ASP.NET pages and user controls within a WYSIWYG design surface or within a syntax-highlighting source editor. The designer allows you to drag and drop server controls onto the design surface, customize their properties, and associate event handlers. Web Matrix supports the single-file model in which server-side code is embedded within the .aspx file. The page designer offers multiple logical views of the same file to separate code and content during development. The page designer can be seen in Figures C-1 and C-2.

■ **Development Web server**   Web Matrix provides a development Web server that allows you to run and test your application without requiring Microsoft Internet Information Services (IIS) to be installed on your development machine. Web Matrix also supports running your application within the context of an IIS virtual root.

■ **Online component gallery**   The toolbox in Web Matrix can be customized with additional components that you develop. In addition, Web Matrix is directly tied to an online component gallery that contains a repository of custom controls that can be browsed or searched. Figure C-6 illustrates toolbox customization using the online component gallery.

■ **File-based workspace**   Web Matrix allows you to work on individual files without imposing the concept of a project. In addition, Web Matrix allows you to work directly against an FTP connection.

■ **SQL and Microsoft Data Engine database management**   Web Matrix contains a simple data administration feature that allows you to create or connect to an existing SQL or MSDE database and create and modify tables and stored procedures. Web Matrix also contains wizards that can generate code to access and modify these database objects programmatically from within your application. Figure C-3 shows the data administration functionality.

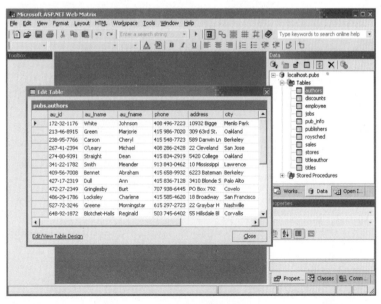

Figure C-3   The SQL and MSDE database management features of Web Matrix

■ **XML Web services support** Web Matrix allows you to create .asmx files and add methods that contain the implementation of the XML Web service. In addition, Web Matrix contains an add-in that you can use to create a client proxy class for a specified Web service. You can use the proxy class from your application to access the Web service.

■ **Class browsing** Web Matrix allows you to browse and search classes from any assembly to inspect their object model (properties, methods, and events) along with associated metadata. The class browsing functionality also allows you to navigate to associated help topics in the MSDN .NET Framework reference documentation. Figure C-4 depicts the class browsing feature.

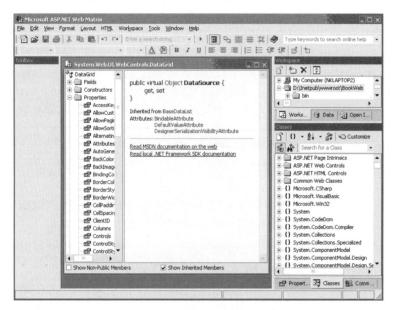

Figure C-4 Class browsing within Web Matrix

■ **Community** Web Matrix contains a gateway to the ASP.NET community that includes links to ASP.NET discussion forums and newsgroups as well as other independent ASP.NET Web sites. The community feature also integrates with Microsoft Windows Messenger to provide access to your Messenger contacts within the tool. Figure C-5 contains various views provided by the community tool window.

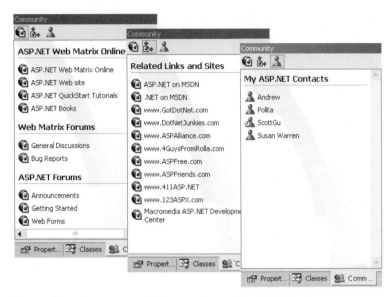

Figure C-5   The community integration within Web Matrix

Web Matrix for Component Developers

Web Matrix does not currently support the creation of components and controls by itself. Furthermore, this development environment does not allow the creation or compilation of class library projects that are a feature of Microsoft Visual Studio .NET. However, Web Matrix still offers useful functionality if you are a component developer authoring ASP.NET server controls—especially if you are developing these components by using the .NET Framework SDK alone.

Web Matrix is built upon the common .NET designer framework described in Chapter 15, "Design-Time Functionality." Web Matrix contains an implementation of various design surface interfaces and services that are used by control designers and other design-time classes. It enables the same property browser functionality, UI type editors, type converters, and other design-time features that are characteristic of the designer experience associated with your control in Visual Studio .NET. Web Matrix contains a design surface that interacts with server controls and their associated designers in the same way as Visual Studio .NET. As a result, Web Matrix can be used to quickly and easily test your server controls and their design-time features in a designer. Although it is possible to develop server controls by using any code editor along with the tools provided in the .NET Framework SDK, you cannot test the design-time features of your control without a development tool that provides a rich design surface. Web Matrix makes this kind of design surface available to control developers, in addition to the one provided by Visual Studio .NET.

> **Note**   Web Matrix grew out of on an internal tool used by developers on the ASP.NET team at Microsoft. This internal tool was used to quickly and easily exercise and test the design-time functionality of the standard ASP.NET server controls without creating Web application projects inside Visual Studio .NET.

As a control developer, you should ensure that your controls work within Web Matrix so that they can be used in applications developed in both Web Matrix and Visual Studio .NET.

Web Matrix's integration with an online component gallery should be particularly interesting to component developers. As mentioned, this feature allows page developers to browse, search, and learn about server controls stored in an online repository of components. In addition, Web Matrix enables page developers to download selected components from this gallery and have them installed into their toolbox automatically. Figure C-6 contains the Web Matrix UI that interacts with the component gallery.

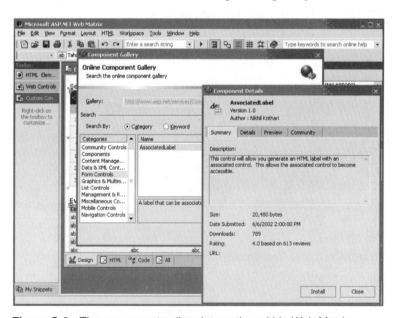

Figure C-6   The component gallery integration within Web Matrix

As a component developer, you will no doubt be interested in publishing your controls to the component gallery so that they can be downloaded by any Web Matrix user. The documentation associated with Web Matrix provides more details on packaging your component and describes how to publish to the gallery.

Summary

The Web Matrix site (*http://www.asp.net/webmatrix*) contains a walkthrough of using the tool to create a Web application and provides a more detailed look at the tool's features. As of this writing, the first Technology Preview of ASP.NET Web Matrix has been announced, and the ASP.NET team hopes to work with members of the Web development community to gather feedback and suggestions for future work on this tool.

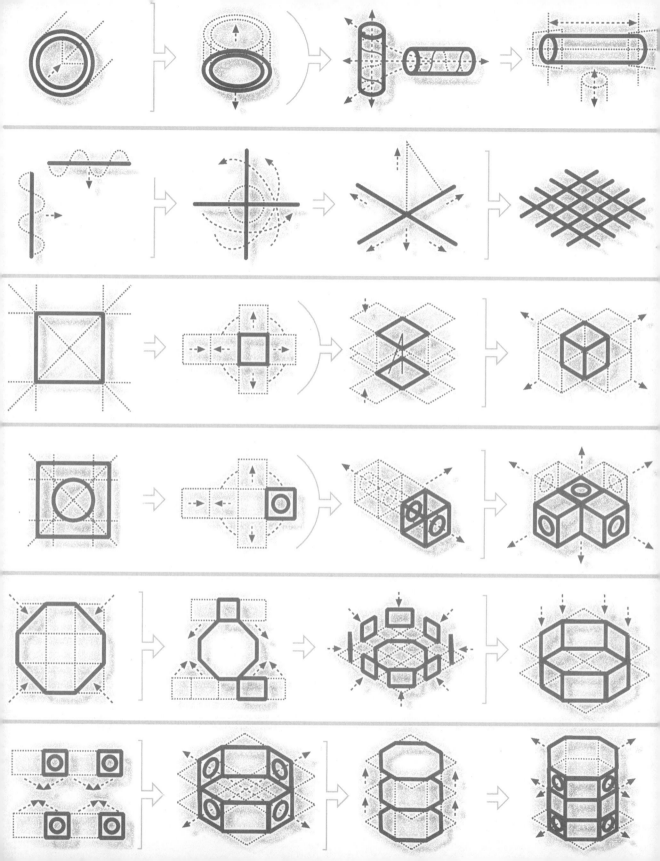

Index

Send feedback about this index to *mspindex@microsoft.com*

Symbols

<% %> (data binding syntax), 422
~ (tilde), 66

A

accessor methods, 93
AddAttributesToRender method, 278–79, 286, 291
ADO.NET
  class library, 5–6
  data tables. *See* DataSets
Application objects
  PageTracker example, 132–40
  view state with, 124–25
application-specific user controls, 73–76
.ascx extension
  HTTP handlers for, 520–21
  user control model, 59
.ashx files, 520, 524
.asmx extension, 490, 520
ASP (Active Server Pages)
  .NET. *See* ASP.NET
  Response.Write, 142
  server-side includes, 60
ASP.NET
  defined, 3
  extensibility of, 10–11
  namespaces, table of, 7
  request processing, 8–10
  Web Matrix. *See* Web Matrix
  XML Web services. *See* Web services
.aspx files
  example, simple, 14
  HTTP handlers, 520–21
  parsing of, 21–22
assemblies
  AssemblyInfo.cs file, 484–85
  attributes, 92
  custom controls, 90–92
  full names, 483–84
  GAC. *See* GAC (Global Assembly Cache)
  key pairs for, 484
  locations of, 91

private, 91–92, 483
satellite. *See* satellite assemblies
shared. *See* shared assemblies
signing, 484
stingily named, 484
user control model, 60, 67–68
assembly qualified type names, 400
AssemblyResourceManager example, 458–60
attributes, metadata
  AddAttributesToRender method, 278–79, 286, 291
  applying, 52–53
  association of functionality, 639–40
  BindableAttribute, 634
  BrowsableAttribute, 51–52, 130, 132, 137–38, 590, 634
  CategoryAttribute, 131, 634–35
  class-level, 52–53
  complex properties with, 218–22
  ControlBuilderAttribute, 640
  custom controls, adding to, 100–102
  DatePicker control example, 625–27
  declarations, 51–52
  declarative specification by users, 271–73
  DefaultEventAttribute, 635
  DefaultPropertyAttribute, 100, 635
  DefaultValueAttribute, 131, 636
  DescriptionAttribute, 635
  design time, 52
  DesignerAttribute, 639
  DesignerSerializationVisibilityAttribute, 131, 137, 637
  design-time, 130–31, 633–40
  EditorAttribute, 639
  EditorBrowsableAttribute, 636
  event-level, 53
  expando attributes, 271–73
  localization of attributes, 460–63
  LocalizedDescriptionAttribute example, 460–62
  meanings of, 131
  metadata, 51–52

M

Nikhil Kothari

Nikhil Kothari is a Software Design Engineer Lead at Microsoft in the .NET Framework and ASP.NET teams, where he is responsible for the design and development of the Web Forms feature area. He is also the architect of the new ASP.NET development tool named ASP.NET Web Matrix. Nikhil has written MSDN articles and has spoken at conferences such as the PDC. He can be reached at nikhilko@microsoft.com.

Nikhil worked as a developer in the Visual InterDev and Visual Basic teams before joining the .NET Frameworks group. Prior to joining Microsoft, he completed his bachelor's degree in Information and Computer Science at the University of California, Irvine. On a beautiful sunny day, you might find Nikhil out on his bike or on a road-trip with his camera exploring the Northwest.

Vandana Datye

Vandana Datye is a freelance programmer/writer who has been programming with the .NET Framework and ASP.NET since the early, pre-beta days of the .NET Framework. She has written documentation and coded samples for MSDN about authoring server controls and other areas relevant to component programming.

Vandana holds a Ph.D. in physics from Carnegie-Mellon University. Before making a transition to the world of commercial software, she did research involving scientific computation and mathematical modeling at several major universities. She has research publications in pure and applied physics and in environmental science. Vandana lives in Redmond, WA with her husband and daughter. In her spare time, she enjoys day hiking and traveling with her family.

Folding Ruler

Rulers come in all sizes and types—from the 6-inch one that you might have on your desk to the autocrat that lords it over a vast domain. With regular markings in feet, inches and inch fractions, the **folding ruler** is a handy measuring device that folds and opens smoothly and is easy to read and use in concrete work, surveying, and excavation. Carpenters use it to measure short distances for placing studs. Masons use it to space brick courses accurately. Compact when folded—needing no more room than the average ruler—folding rulers have traditionally been made of wood or metal but increasingly are made of fiberglass to withstand water and rough use on the construction site.

At Microsoft Press, we use tools to illustrate our books for software developers and IT professionals. Tools very simply and powerfully symbolize human inventiveness. They're a metaphor for people extending their capabilities, precision, and reach. From simple calipers and pliers to digital micrometers and lasers, these stylized illustrations give each book a visual identity, and a personality to the series. With tools and knowledge, there's no limit to creativity and innovation. Our tagline says it all: *the tools you need to put technology to work.*

The manuscript for this book was prepared and galleyed using Microsoft Word. Pages were composed by Microsoft Press using Adobe FrameMaker+SGML for Windows, with text in Garamond and display type in Helvetica Condensed. Composed pages were delivered to the printer as electronic prepress files.

Cover Designer:	Methodologie, Inc.
Interior Graphic Designer:	James D. Kramer
Principal Compositor:	Paula Gorelick
Interior Artist:	Joel Panchot
Copy Editor:	Michelle Goodman
Indexer:	Bill Meyers

The road to .NET
starts with the
core MCAD
self-paced training kits!

Get the training you need to build the broadest range of applications quickly—and get industry recognition, access to inside technical information, discounts on products, invitations to special events, and more—with the new Microsoft Certified Application Developer (MCAD) credential. MCAD candidates must pass two core exams and one elective exam. The best way to prepare is with the core set of MCAD/MCSD TRAINING KITS. Each features a comprehensive training manual, lab exercises, reusable source code, and sample exam questions. Work through the system of self-paced lessons and hands-on labs to gain practical experience with essential development tasks. By the end of each course, you're ready to take the corresponding exams for MCAD or MCSD certification for Microsoft .NET.

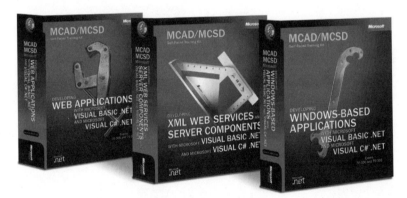

MCAD/MCSD Self-Paced Training Kit: Developing Windows®-Based Applications with Microsoft® Visual Basic® .NET and Microsoft Visual C#™ .NET
Preparation for exams 70-306 and 70-316
U.S.A. $69.99
Canada $99.99
ISBN: 0-7356-1533-0

MCAD/MCSD Self-Paced Training Kit: Developing Web Applications with Microsoft Visual Basic .NET and Microsoft Visual C# .NET
Preparation for exams 70-305 and 70-315
U.S.A. $69.99
Canada $99.99
ISBN: 0-7356-1584-5

MCAD/MCSD Self-Paced Training Kit: Developing XML Web Services and Server Components with Microsoft Visual Basic .NET and Microsoft Visual C# .NET
Preparation for exams 70-310 and 70-320
U.S.A. $69.99
Canada $99.99
ISBN: 0-7356-1586-1

Microsoft Press® products are available worldwide wherever quality computer books are sold. For more information, contact your book or computer retailer, software reseller, or local Microsoft® Sales Office, or visit our Web site at microsoft.com/mspress. To locate your nearest source for Microsoft Press products, or to order directly, call 1-800-MSPRESS in the United States (in Canada, call 1-800-268-2222).

Prices and availability dates are subject to change.

Microsoft®
microsoft.com/mspress

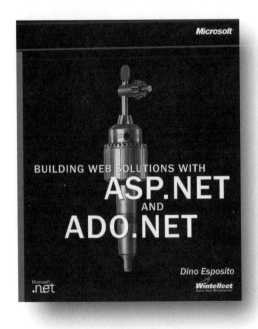

The definitive
one-stop resource
for developing on the revolutionary
.NET platform

This core reference for Microsoft® .NET provides everything you need to know to build robust, Web-extensible applications for the revolutionary Microsoft development platform. Leading Windows® programming authority Jeff Prosise masterfully distills this new Web-enabled programming paradigm and its Framework Class Library—easily one of the most complex collections ever assembled—into a conversational, easy-to-follow programming reference you can repeatedly visit to resolve specific .NET development questions. Prosise clearly explains all the critical elements of application development in the .NET environment, including Windows Forms, Web Forms, and XML Web services—illustrating key concepts with inline code examples and many complete sample programs. All the book's sample code and programs—most of them written in C#—appear on the companion CD-ROM so you can study and adapt them for your own Web-based business applications.

Microsoft®
microsoft.com/mspress